Random House
Italian
Dictionary

Second Edition

ITALIAN · ENGLISH
ENGLISH · ITALIAN
ITALIANO · INGLESE
INGLESE · ITALIANO

Edited by
Robert A. Hall, Jr.
CORNELL UNIVERSITY
Revised by
Vieri Samek-Lodovici, Ph.D.

RANDOM HOUSE
NEW YORK

Abbreviations

abbr.	abbreviation	*math.*	mathematics
adj.	adjective	*med.*	medicine
adv.	adverb	*mil.*	military
Amer.	American	*n.*	noun
Brit.	British	*naut.*	nautical
coll.	colloquial	*num.*	number
comm.	commercial	*pl.*	plural
conj.	conjunction	*pred.*	predicate
dem.	demonstrative	*prep.*	preposition
eccles.	ecclesiastical	*pron.*	pronoun;
econ.	economics		pronunciation
f.	feminine	*refl.*	reflexive
fam.	familiar	*sg.*	singular
fig.	figuratively	*tr.*	transitive (used only
geom.	geometry		with verbs which also
gram.	grammar; grammatical		have reflexive use to
interj.	interjection		indicate intransitive
intr.	intransitive		meaning)
lit.	literally	*typogr.*	typography
m.	masculine	*vb.*	verb

Months and Days of the Week

January	gennàio	*Monday*	lunedì
February	febbràio	*Tuesday*	martedì
March	marzo	*Wednesday*	mercoledì
April	aprile	*Thursday*	giovedì
May	màggio	*Friday*	venerdì
June	giugno	*Saturday*	sàbato
July	lùglio	*Sunday*	doménica
August	agosto		
September	settèmbre		
October	ottobre		
November	novèmbre		
December	dicèmbre		

Concise Pronunciation Guide

Italian

Letter   **Pronunciation**

a   Like English *a* in *father*.

b   As in English.

c   Before *e* or *i*, and sometimes at the end of words, like English *ch*.
Elsewhere, like English *k*.

ch   Before *e* or *i*, like English *k*.

ci   Before *a, o,* or *u*, like English *ch*.

d   As in English.

é   ("closed *e*") Like English *ay* in *day*, but with no final *y*-like glide.

è   ("open *e*") Like English *e* in *bet*.

e   Like English *e* in *bet*.

f   As in English.

g   Before *e* or *i*, like English *g* in *gem*.
Elsewhere, like English *g* in *go*.

gh   Before *e* or *i*, like English *g* in *go*.

gi   Before *a, o,* or *u*, like English *g* in *gem*.

gl   Before *i*, normally like English *lli* in *million*.

gli   Before *a, e, o,* or *u*, like English *lli* in *million*.

gn   Like English *ny* in *canyon*.

h   After *c* and *g*, indicates "hard" pronunciation of preceding consonant letter.
Elsewhere, silent.

i   After *c, g,* and (normally) *sc*, before *a, o,* or *u*, indicates "soft" pronunciation of preceding consonant letter or letters.
Elsewhere:
When unstressed and before or after another vowel, like English *y*.
Otherwise, like English *i* in *machine*, but with no final *y*-like glide.

j   At the end of words, when replacing *ii* in some noun plurals, like Italian *i*.
Otherwise, like English *y*.

k   As in English.

Italian Letter	Pronunciation
l	Like English *l* in *like*, but with the tongue behind the upper front teeth.
m	As in English.
n	As in English.
ó	("closed *o*") Like English *o* in *go*, but with no final *w*-like glide.
ò	("open *o*") Like English *o* in *bought*.
o	Like English *o* in *bought*.
p	As in English.
qu	Like English *qu* in *quick*.
r	Not at all like American English *r;* a quick flap of the tip of the tongue on the gumridge.
s	Between vowels, like English *s* in *lease* (in southern Italy); like *s* in *please* (in northern Italy); sometimes like *s* in *lease* and sometimes like *s* in *please* (in central Italy). Before *b, d, g, l, m, n, r, v,* like English *z.* Elsewhere, like English *s* in *same, stick.*
sc	Before *e* or *i,* and occasionally at the end of words, like English *sh.* Elsewhere, like English *sk.*
sch	Before *e* or *i,* like English *sk.*
sci	Before *a, o,* or *u,* like English *sh.*
t	As in English.
u	When unstressed and before or after another vowel, like English *w.* Otherwise, like English *oo* in *boot,* but without final *w*-like glide.
v	As in English.
w	Rare; like English *v.*
x	Rare; like English *x.*
z	Like English *ts* in *cats* or like English *dz* in *adze.*

Consonant Length

All Italian consonants occur both single (short) and double (long); in the latter instance, the time of their pronunciation lasts from one-and-a-half to two times that of the single consonants.

Italian Accentuation

In most conventional writing and printing, spoken stress is marked by a grave accent (`), but only when it falls on the last syllable of a word: *città, vendè, lunedì, cantò, tribù.* An accent is placed over the vowel letter of some words to distinguish them from others having the same spelling and pronunciation but differing in meaning: *è* "is" versus *e* "and." In other instances, stress is usually left unmarked, although it may fall on any syllable up to the sixth from the end.

However, Italians are very sensitive to misplaced stress, even though accent marks are not customarily used in Italian spelling. In this dictionary, therefore, as in most Italian dictionaries, the occurrence of stress is indicated with an accent mark whenever it does not fall on the next-to-the-last syllable, and also in all words ending in *-ia, -io.* In addition, the presence of the open varieties of *e* and *o*, to which Italians are also sensitive, is marked by a grave accent (`) in all its occurrences, even in the next-to-the-last syllable.

Noun and Adjective Plurals

Virtually all Italian nouns form their plurals by changing the final vowel. The following are the principal patterns of noun plural formation:

Final Vowel		Examples	
Singular	Plural	Singular	Plural
-a *(f.)*	-e	ròsa	ròse
-a *(m.)*	-i	dramma	drammi
-o *(m.)*	-i	libro	libri
-o *(m.)*	-a *(f.)*	bràccio	bràccia
-e *(m., f.)*	-i *(m., f.)*	fiume	fiumi
		parte	parti

Nouns ending in unstressed *-i*, in stressed vowels, or in consonants; family names; and abbreviations are normally unchanged in the plural: *crisi, città, tram; Scaglione; auto, radio.*

Adjectives ending in *-o* follow the pattern of *libro* for the masculine and that of *rosa* for the feminine; those ending in *-e* follow the pattern of *fiume, parte* for both masculine and feminine.

Regular Verbs

Infinitive	Present	Future	Preterite	Past Part.
cantare	canto	canterò	cantai	cantato
dormire	dormo	dormirò	dormii	dormito
finire	finisco	finirò	finii	finito
temere	temo	temerò	temèi	temuto
véndere	vendo	venderò	vendèi	venduto

Irregular Verbs

Infinitive	Present	Future	Preterite	Past Part.
accèndere	accendo	accenderò	accesi	acceso
andare	vado	andrò	andai	andato
aprire	apro	aprirò	apèrsi	apèrto
avere	ho	avrò	èbbi	avuto
bere	bevo	berrò	bevvi	bevuto
cadere	cado	cadrò	caddi	caduto
cìngere	cingo	cingerò	cinsi	cinto
còcogliere	colgo	coglierò	colsi	colto
concèdere	concedo	concederò	concèssi	concèsso
condurre	conduco	condurrò	condussi	condotto
dare	do	darò	diedi	dato
difèndere	difendo	difenderò	difesi	difeso
dire	dico	dirò	dissi	detto
dovere	devo	dovrò	dovèi	dovuto
èssere	sono	sarò	fui	stato
fare	fàccio	farò	feci	fatto
fóndere	fondo	fonderò	fusi	fuso
giacere	giàccio	giacerò	giacqui	giaciuto
morire	muòio	morirò	morii	mòrto
nàscere	nasco	nascerò	nacqui	nato
parere	paio	parrò	parsi	parso
porre	pongo	porrò	posi	posto
potere	pòsso	potrò	potèi	potuto
rèndere	rèndo	renderò	resi	reso
salire	salgo	salirò	salii	salito
sapere	sò	saprò	seppi	saputo
scégliere	scelgo	sceglierò	scelsi	scelto
stare	sto	starò	stetti	stato
tenere	tengo	terrò	tenni	tenuto
trarre	traggo	trarrò	trassi	tratto
uscire	esco	uscirò	uscii	uscito
valere	valgo	varrò	valsi	valso
vedere	vedo	vedrò	vidi	visto *or* veduto
venire	vengo	verrò	venni	venuto
vìvere	vivo	vivrò	vissi	vissuto
volere	vòglio	vorrò	vòlli	voluto

Numerals

Cardinal

1	uno, una		32	trentadue
2	due		38	trentòtto
3	tre		40	quaranta
4	quattro		50	cinquanta
5	cinque		60	sessanta
6	sèi		70	settanta
7	sètte		80	ottanta
8	òtto		90	novanta
9	nòve		100	cènto
10	dièci		101	centuno
11	ùndici		102	centodue
12	dódici		200	duecènto
13	trédici		300	trecènto
14	quattòrdici		400	quattrocènto
15	quindici		500	cinquecènto
16	sédici		600	seicènto
17	diciassètte		700	settecènto
18	diciòtto		800	ottocènto
19	diciannòve		900	novecènto
20	venti		1,000	mille
21	ventuno, ventuna		2,000	duemila
22	ventidue		3,000	tremila
28	ventòtto		100,000	centomila
30	trenta		1,000,000	un milione
31	trentuno, trentuna		2,000,000	due milioni

Ordinal

1st	primo		15th	decimoquinto
2nd	secondo			or quindicésimo
3rd	tèrzo		16th	decimosèsto
4th	quarto			or sedicésimo
5th	quinto		17th	decimosèttimo
6th	sèsto			or diciassettésimo
7th	sèttimo		18th	decimottavo
8th	ottavo			or diciottésimo
9th	nòno		19th	decimonòno
10th	dècimo			or diciannovésimo
11th	decimoprimo		20th	ventésimo
	or undicésimo		21st	ventésimoprimo
12th	decimosecondo		30th	trentésimo
	or dodicésimo		40th	quarantésimo
13th	decimotèrzo		100th	centésimo
	or tredicésimo		1000th	millésimo
14th	decimoquarto			
	or quattordicésimo			

A

a, *prep.* at; in; to; by.
àbaco, *n.m.* abacus.
abate, *n.m.* abbot.
abbàcchio, *n.m.* lamb.
abbagliante, *adj.* dazzling.
abbagliare, *vb.* dazzle.
abbàglio, *n.m.* mistake.
abbaiamento, *n.m.* bark; barking.
abbaiare, *vb.* bark, bay.
abbaìno, *n.m.* dormer.
abbandonare, *vb.* abandon, forsake, relinquish, vacate.
abbandonato, *adj.* abandoned.
abbandono, *n.m.* abandon, abandonment.
abbassamento, *n.m.* lowering, abasement.
abbassare, *vb.* lower, abase; debase; (*refl.*) stoop; subside.
abbassato, *adj.* lowered; downcast.
abbasso, *interj.* down with!
abbastanza, *adv.* enough.
abbàttere, *vb.* knock down, fell; dishearten; (*refl.*) droop.
abbattimento, *n.m.* disheartenment, dismay, dejection.
abbattuto, *adj.* despondent.
abbazìa, *n.f.* abbey.
abbecedàrio, *n.m.* speller, primer; ABCs.
abbellimento, *n.m.* embellishment.
abbellire, *vb.* beautify, embellish.
abbeverare, *vb.* water (animals).
abbiente, *adj.* well-to-do, upper-middle-class.
abbigliare, *vb.* dress up, accouter.
abbigliamento maschile, *n.m.* menswear.
abbigliatura, *n.f.* accouterments.
abbonacciare, *vb.* becalm.
abbonamento, *n.m.* subscription.
bigliètto d'a., season ticket.
abbonarsi, *vb.* subscribe.
abbonato, *n.m.* subscriber.
abbondante, *adj.* abundant, plentiful.
abbondantemente, *adv.* abundantly.

abbondanza, *n.f.* abundance, plenty.
abbondare, *vb.* abound.
abbordàbile, *adj.* accessible.
abbordare, *vb.* accost.
abborracciare, *vb.* bungle.
abbozzare, *vb.* sketch.
abbòzzo, *n.m.* sketch, draft.
abbracciare, *vb.* embrace, clasp, hug.
abbràccio, *n.m.* embrace, clasp, hug.
abbreviamento, *n.m.* abridgement.
abbreviare, *vb.* abbreviate, abridge, shorten.
abbreviatura, *n.f.* abbreviation.
abbronzare, *vb.* tan.
abbronzato, *adj.* sunburnt.
abbronzatura, *n.f.* sunburn, tan.
abbrustolire, *vb.* toast.
abbrutire, *vb.* brutalize, degrade.
abbuono, *n.m.* allowance.
abdicare, *vb.* abdicate.
abdicazione, *n.f.* abdication.
aberrante, *adj.* aberrant.
aberrare, *vb.* be aberrant.
aberrazione, *n.f.* aberration.
abete, *n.m.* fir.
abiètto, *adj.* abject.
àbile, *adj.* skillful, clever, able, adroit, capable, cunning, deft.
abilità, *n.f.* ability, skill, cleverness, adeptness, cunning.
abilitazione, *n.f.* qualification; license.
abilmente, *adv.* skillfully, ably, adeptly, capably.
Abissinia, *n.f.* Abyssinia.
abissino, *n. and adj.* Abyssinian.
abisso, *n.m.* abyss, chasm.
abitàbile, *adj.* habitable, livable.
abitante, *n.m.* inhabitant, dweller, resident.
abitare, *vb.* live, dwell, reside, inhabit.
abitazione, *n.f.* dwelling, habitation, residence.
àbito, *n.m.* dress, suit, habit.
abituale, *adj.* habitual, usual, accustomed.
abituare, *vb.* accustom, habituate.

abituarsi a, *vb.* get accustomed to.

abitùdine, *n.f.* habit.

abiura, *n.f.* abjuration.

abiurare, *vb.* abjure.

ablativo, *n.m. and adj.* ablative.

abluzione, *n.f.* ablution.

abnegare, *vb.* abnegate.

abnegazione, *n.f.* abnegation.

abnorme, *adj.* abnormal.

abolire, *vb.* abolish.

abolizione, *n.f.* abolition.

abominare, *vb.* abominate, loathe.

abominazione, *n.f.* abomination.

abominévole, *adj.* abominable, loathsome.

aborìgeno, 1. *n.m.* aborigine. **2.** *adj.* aboriginal, native.

aborrimento, *n.m.* abhorrence.

aborrire, *vb.* abhor.

abortire, *vb.* abort; be abortive.

abortivo, *adj.* abortive.

aborto, *n.m.* abortion.

abrasione, *n.f.* abrasion.

abrasivo, *n.m. and adj.* abrasive.

abrogare, *vb.* abrogate.

abrogazione, *n.f.* abrogation.

àbside, *n.f.* apse.

a buòn mercato, *adv.* cheap; cheaply.

abusare di, *vb.* abuse, misuse.

abusivamente, *adv.* abusively.

abusivo, *adj.* abusive.

abuso, *n.m.* abuse.

acàcia, *n.f.* acacia.

acanto, *n.m.* acanthus.

àcaro, *n.m.* acarus, mite.

a cavalcioni, *adv.* astride.

accadèmia, *n.f.* academy.

accadèmico, *adj.* academic.

accadere, *vb.* happen, befall, occur, take place.

accalcare, *vb.* crowd.

accaldato, *adj.* hot.

accampamento, *n.m.* camp, encampment.

accampare, *vb.* camp, encamp.

accanire, *vb.* persist.

accanimento, *n.m.* animosity.

accanto, *adv.* beside, alongside.

accanto a, *prep.* beside, next to, alongside.

accantonamento, *n.m.* cantonment.

accaparrare, *vb.* corner.

accarezzare, *vb.* caress, fondle, stroke.

accattone, *n.m.* beggar.

accavallare, *vb.* cross one's legs; overlap.

accecare, *vb.* blind.

accelerare, *vb.* accelerate, speed up.

accelerato, *n.m.* local (train).

acceleratore, *n.m.* accelerator.

accelerazione, *n.f.* acceleration.

accèndere, *vb.* light, switch on, ignite, kindle.

accendisìgaro, *n.m.* cigar-lighter, cigarette-lighter.

accennare, *vb.* hint.

accensione, *n.f.* ignition.

accentare, *vb.* accent, stress.

accènto, *n.m.* accent, stress.

accentuare, *vb.* accent.

accerchiare, *vb.* encircle, ring around.

accertarsi, *vb.* ascertain.

accessìbile, *adj.* accessible.

accèsso, *n.m.* access, approach; fit.

accessòrio, 1. *n.m.* accessory; attachment. **2.** *adj.* accessory; adjunct.

accetta, *n.f.* hatchet.

accettàbile, *adj.* acceptable.

accettabilità, *n.f.* acceptability.

accettabilmente, *adv.* acceptably.

accettare, *vb.* accept.

accettazione, *n.f.* acceptance.

accètto, *adj.* acceptable.

acciàio, *n.m.* steel.

accidentale, *adj.* accidental.

accidentalmente, *adv.* accidentally.

accigliato, *adj.* frowning, glum.

acciuga, *n.f.* anchovy.

acclamare, *vb.* acclaim.

acclamazione, *n.f.* acclamation.

acclimare, *vb.* acclimate.

acclimatare, *vb.* acclimate.

acclività, *n.f.* acclivity.

acclùdere, *vb.* enclose.

accogliènza, *n.f.* reception.

accògliere, *vb.* receive, entertain.

accòlito, *n.m.* acolyte.

accollata, *n.f.* accolade.

accomodante, *adj.* accommodating.

accomodare, *vb.* accommodate; mend; *(refl.)* make oneself comfortable; compromise.

accomodazione, *n.f.* accommodation.

accompagnamento, *n.m.* accompaniment.

accompagnare, *vb.* accompany.

accompagnatore, *n.m.* accompanist.

acconciare, *vb.* fix.

acconciatura, *n.f.* hair-do.

accondiscendénza, *n.f.* condescension.

accondiscéndere, *vb.* condescend.

acconsentire, *vb.* consent.

accontentare, *vb.* content.

accoppiare, *vb.* couple; mate.

accorciare, *vb.* shorten, curtail.

accordare, *vb.* tune.

accòrdo, *n.m.* agreement, accord; compact; concord; chord. **d'a.,** in agreement.

accosciarsi, *vb.* squat.

accostare, *vb.* bring near, approach, come alongside *(naut.);* leave ajar (door).

accovacciare, *vb.* crouch.

accreditare, *vb.* accredit.

accréscere, *vb.* accrue, increase, boost, enhance, heighten.

accrescimento, *n.m.* increase, accretion, accrual, boost.

accucciarsi, *vb.* crouch.

accudire, *vb.* look after, attend.

accumulàbile, *adj.* cumulative.

accumulare, *vb.* accumulate.

accumulatore, *n.m.* battery, accumulator.

accumulazione, *n.f.* accumulation.

accuratamente, *adv.* accurately, carefully.

accuratezza, *n.f.* accuracy, carefulness.

accurato, *adj.* accurate, careful.

accusa, *n.f.* accusation, indictment.

accusare, *vb.* accuse, arraign, indict. **a. ricevuta di,** acknowledge receipt of.

accusativo, *n.m. and adj.* accusative.

accusato, *n.m.* accused.

accusatore, *n.m.* accuser.

acerbamente, *adv.* prematurely, bitterly, sharply.

acerbità, *n.f.* acerbity.

acèrbo, *adj.* sour, unripe.

àcero, *n.m.* maple.

acetato, *n.m.* acetate.

acètico, *adj.* acetic.

acetilène, *n.m.* acetylene.

aceto, *n.m.* vinegar.

acidificare, *vb.* acidify.

acidità, *n.f.* acidity.

àcido, *n.m. and adj.* acid, sour.

acidòsi, *n.f.* acidosis.

acìdulo, *adj.* acidulous.

àcino, *n.m.* berry, grape.

acme, *n.f.* acme.

acne, *n.f.* acne.

acqua, *n.f.* water.

acquafòrte, *n.f.* etching.

acquàio, *n.m.* sink.

acquarèllo, *n.m.* watercolor.

acquàrio, *n.m.* aquarium.

acquàtico, *adj.* aquatic.

acquavite, *n.f.* brandy.

acquazzone, *n.m.* heavy shower, cloudburst.

acquedotto, *n.m.* aqueduct.

àcqueo, *adj.* aqueous.

acquiescenza, *n.f.* acquiescence.

acquietarsi, *vb.* calm down, acquiesce.

acquisitivo, *adj.* acquisitive.

acquistare, *vb.* acquire.

acquisto, *n.m.* acquisition.

acre, *adj.* acrid, acrimonious; tart.

acrèdine, *n.f.* acrimony.

acrimònia, *n.f.* acrimony.

acro, *n.m.* acre.

acròbata, *n.m.* acrobat.

acròstico, *n.m.* acrostic.

acume, *n.m.* acumen.

acùstica, *n.f.* acoustics.

acutamente, *adv.* acutely, sharply.

acutezza, *n.f.* acuteness, sharpness.

acuto, *adj.* acute, sharp, keen, pointed, shrewd.

ad, *prep.* at; in; to; by.

adàgio, **1.** *n.m.* adage. **2.** *adv.* slowly; gently.

adamantino, *adj.* adamant.
Adamo, *n.m.* Adam.
adattàbile, *adj.* adaptable.
adattabilità, *n.f.* adaptability.
adattamento, *n.* adaptation; fitting.
adattare, *vb.* adapt.
adattévole, *adj.* adaptive.
adatto, *adj.* suitable, right for, fitting.
addèbito, *n.m.* debit, charge.
addensare, *vb.* densify, thicken.
addentrarsi, *vb.* enter into, penetrate.
addestramento, *n.m.* training, preparation, instruction.
addestrare, *vb.* train, prepare, instruct.
addetto, 1. *n.m.* attachè. 2. *adj.* assigned, employed.
addìo, *interj.* hello; good-bye, adieu, farewell.
addirittura, *adv.* altogether, all in all, positively.
additare, *vb.* point out.
addizionale, *adj.* additional.
addizionare, *vb.* add.
addizione, *n.f.* addition.
addobbare, *vb.* adorn, decorate.
addobbo, *n.m.* ornament.
addolorare, *vb.* grieve, *tr.,; (refl.)* sorrow.
addolorato, *adj.* sorrowful.
addòme, *n.m.* abdomen.
addomesticare, *vb.* tame.
addomesticato, *adj.* tame.
addominale, *adj.* abdominal.
addormentarsi, *vb.* *(refl.)* fall asleep.
addottrinare, *vb.* indoctrinate.
addurre, *vb.* lead up, bring up, adduce.
adenòide, *adj.* adenoid.
adeguato, *adj.* adequate, satisfactory.
aderènte, *n.m.* adherent, member (of association, etc.).
aderènza, *n.f.* adherence, support; relation.
aderire, *vb.* adhere, cling, stick, support, join.
adescare, *vb.* allure, entice, lure.
adescatore, *adj.* alluring.
adesione, *n.f.* adhesion; adherence; assent. **dar a.**, join, support.

adesività, *n.f.* adhesiveness, adherence.
adesivo, *n.m. and adj.* adhesive.
adèsso, *adv.* now.
adiacènte, *adj.* adjacent, adjoining.
adibire, *vb.* designate, assign; use as.
adirarsi, *vb.* get angry.
adirato, *adj.* angry, cross.
adocchiare, *vb.* spot, glance at.
adolescènte, *n. and adj.* adolescent.
adolescènza, *n.f.* adolescence.
adoperare, *vb.* use.
adoràbile, *adj.* adorable.
adorare, *vb.* adore, worship.
adorazione, *n.f.* adoration, worship.
adornamento, *n.m.* adornment.
adorno, *adj.* adorned.
adottare, *vb.* adopt.
adozione, *n.f.* adoption.
adrenalina, *n.f.* adrenalin.
adulare, *vb.* adulate, flatter, fawn upon.
adulatore, *n.m.* flatterer.
adulazione, *n.f.* adulation, flattery.
adùltera, *n.f.* adulteress.
adulterante, *n. and adj.* adulterant.
adulterare, *vb.* adulterate.
adultèrio, *n.m.* adultery.
adùltero, *n.m.* adulterer.
adulto, *n. (m.) and adj.* adult, grown-up.
adunata, *n.f.* gathering, meeting.
adunco, *adj.* hooked.
aerare, *vb.* aerate, air.
aerazione, *n.f.* aeration.
aèreo, 1. *n.m.* aircraft, airplane. 2. *adj.* aerial.
aerodinàmico, *adj.* streamlined.
aereolinea, *n.f.* airline.
aeronàutica, *n.f.* aeronautics.
aeroplano, *n.m.* airplane.
aeropòrto, *n.m.* airport.
aeroscalo, *n.m.* airport.
afa, *n.f.* sultriness; mugginess.
affàbile, *adj.* affable.
affabilità, *n.f.* affability.
affabilmente, *adv.* affably.
affaccendato, *adj.* busy.
affamato, *adj.* famished, ravenous.

affare, *n.m.* affair, concern; bargain, deal; (*pl.*) business.

affascinante, *adj.* fascinating, glamorous.

affascinare, *vb.* fascinate, allure, captivate, charm.

affaticare, *vb.* fatigue.

afferènte, *adj.* afferent.

affermare, *vb.* affirm, state.

affermativamente, *adv.* affirmatively.

affermativo, *adj.* affirmative.

affermazione, *n.f.* affirmation, statement.

afferrare, *vb.* grasp, grip, seize, catch, snatch.

affettare, *vb.* affect; slice.

affettato, *adj.* affected; finicky, prim.

affettazione, *n.f.* affectation; frill.

affettuosamente, *adv.* affectionately.

affettuoso, *adj.* affectionate.

affezione, *n.f.* affection, attachment.

affibbiare, *vb.* buckle.

affidare, *vb.* entrust.

affiggere, *vb.* post.

affiliare, *vb.* affiliate.

affiliazione, *n.f.* affiliation.

affine, *adj.* related, akin, allied.

affinità, *n.f.* affinity.

affissare, *vb.* affix.

affisso, *n.m.* affix.

affittare, *vb.* lease, let, rent.

affitto, *n.m.* lease, rent.

affliggere, *vb.* afflict, distress.

afflizione, *n.f.* affliction, distress.

affluènte, *n.m.* tributary.

affluire, *vb.* rush.

afflusso, *n.m.* rush.

affollare, *vb.* crowd.

affollarsi, *vb.* come together in crowds, flock.

affondare, *vb.* sink.

affrancare, *vb.* enfranchise.

affrancatura, *n.f.* postage.

affresco, *n.m.* fresco.

affrettare, *vb.* hasten, haste, hurry, quicken, speed.

affrettatamente, *adv.* hastily.

affrettato, *adj.* hasty.

affrontare, *vb.* face, go to meet; affront, insult.

affronto, *n.m.* affront, insult.

affumicare, *vb.* smoke; blacken.

affumicato, *adj.* smoked.

aforisma, *n.m.* aphorism.

afoso, *adj.* sultry; muggy.

Àfrica, *n.f.* Africa.

africano, *n.* and *adj.* African.

afrodisiaco, *adj.* aphrodisiac.

afta, *n.f.* aphtha, mouth sore.

àgata, *n.f.* agate.

àgave, *n.f.* century plant.

agènda, *n.f.* note-book.

agènte, *n.m.* agent, representative, intermediary; (chemical) agent.

agenta di borsa, *n.m.* stockbroker.

agente di polizia, *n.m.* or *f.* police officer.

agenzia, *n.f.* agency.

agevolare, *vb.* facilitate, ease.

agèvole, *adj.* easy, comfortable.

agganciare, *vb.* clasp.

aggancio, *n.m.* docking; fastener, clasp.

aggettivo, *n.m.* adjective.

agghiacciare, *vb.* freeze; horrify, petrify.

aggiogare, *vb.* yoke; subjugate.

aggiornamento, *n.m.* adjournment.

aggiornare, *vb.* adjourn; bring up to date.

aggiùngere, *vb.* add.

aggiunto, 1. *n.* and *adj.* adjunct. **2.** *adj.* added, extra.

aggiustamento, *n.m.* adjustment.

aggiustare, *vb.* adjust.

aggiustatore, *n.m.* adjuster.

aggiustatura, *n.f.* adjustment.

agglutinare, *vb.* agglutinate.

agglutinazione, *n.f.* agglutination.

aggravamento, *n.m.* aggravation.

aggravare, *vb.* aggravate.

aggregare, *vb.* aggregate.

aggregato, *n.m.* aggregate.

aggregazione, *n.f.* aggregation.

aggressione, *n.f.* aggression.

aggressivamente, *adv.* aggressively.

aggressività, *n.f.* aggressiveness.

aggressivo, *adj.* aggressive.

aggressore, *n.m.* aggressor.
aggrottare, *vb.* wrinkle. **a. le ciglia,** frown, scowl.
aggrovigliare, *vb.* snarl, tangle.
àgile, *n.f.* agile, nimble.
agilità, *n.f.* agility.
àgio, *n.m.* ease, leisure.
agire, *vb.* act.
agitare, *vb.* agitate; wave, flourish; stir; *(refl.)* fidget, toss.
agitatore, *n.m.* agitator.
agitazione, *n.f.* agitation.
àglio, *n.m.* garlic.
agnèllo, *n.m.* lamb.
agnòstico, *n. and adj.* agnostic.
ago, *n.f.* needle. **a. da rammendo,** darning-needle.
agonia, *n.f.* agony.
agonizzante, *adj.* agonized.
agonizzare, *vb.* be in agony.
agopuntura, *n.f.* acupuncture.
agosto, *n.m.* August.
agràrio, *adj.* agrarian.
agricoltore, *n.m.* farmer.
agricultura, *n.f.* agriculture, farming.
agrifòglio, *n.m.* holly.
agrimensore, *n.m.* surveyor.
agro, *adj.* sour, tart, acidic.
agrodolce, *adj.* sweet and sour; (fig.) bittersweet.
agrumi, *n.m.pl.* citrus fruits.
aguzzare, *vb.* sharpen.
ahi, *interj.* ouch!
Aia, *n.f.* l'A., The Hague.
airone, *n.m.* heron.
aiutante, *n.m.* assistant, helper, adjutant, aide.
aiutare, *vb.* help, aid, assist, befriend.
aiuto, *n.m.* help, aid, assistance.
ala, *n.f.* wing.
alacre, *adj.* active, brisk, eager.
alacrità, *n.f.* alacrity.
alambicco, *n.m.* still.
alba, *n.f.* dawn, daybreak.
albèrgo, *n.m.* hotel, hostelry.
àlbero, *n.m.* tree; mast, shaft, spar.
albicòcca, *n.f.* apricot.
albino, *n.m. and adj.* albino.
album, *n.m.* album.
albume, *n.m.* albumen.
àlcali, *n.m.* alkali.
alcalino, *adj.* alkaline.

alce, *n.m.* elk.
àlcole, *n.m.* alcohol.
àlcool, *n.m.* alcohol.
alc(o)òlico, *adj.* alcoholic.
alcòva, *n.f.* alcove.
alcuni, *adj. and n.m.* some.
alfabètico, *adj.* alphabetical.
alfabèto, *n.m.* alphabet.
alfalfa, *n.f.* alfalfa.
alfiere, *n.m.* ensign.
àlgebra, *n.f.* algebra.
àlias, *adv.* alias.
aliante, *n.m.* glider.
àlibi, *n.m.* alibi.
alienare, *vb.* alienate, estrange.
alièno, *adj.* alien, foreign, strange.
alimentare, 1. *vb.* feed, nourish. **2.** *adj.* pertaining to food, alimentary.
alimentàrio, *adj.* alimentary.
alimento, *n.m.* food, nourishment.
aliscafo, *n.m.* hovercraft.
allacciare, *vb.* enlace.
allargare, *vb.* broaden, widen.
allarmare, *vb.* alarm, startle.
allarme, *n.m.* alarm, alert.
allarme d'incendio, *n.m.* fire alarm.
allarmista, *n.m.* alarmist.
alleanza, *n.f.* alliance.
alleare, *vb.* ally.
alleato, 1. *n.m.* ally. **2.** *adj.* allied.
allegare, *vb.* allege.
alleggerire, *vb.* lighten.
allegoria, *n.f.* allegory.
allegria, *n.f.* merriment, cheerfulness, mirth.
allegro, *adj.* lively, merry, cheerful, frisky, jolly.
allenamento, *n.m.* training; practice, preparation.
allenare, *vb.* train, coach.
allenatore, *n.m.* trainer, coach.
allentamento, *n.m.* letdown.
allentare, *vb.* loosen, relax.
allergia, *n.f.* allergy.
allevamento, *n.m.* breeding; ranch, farm.
allevare, *vb.* train, breed, foster, nurture, raise, rear.
allevatore, *n.m.* trainer, breeder.
alleviare, *vb.* alleviate, allay, relieve.
allietare, *vb.* gladden.

alligatore, *n.m.* alligator.

allineamento, *n.m.* alignment, laying out.

allineare, *vb.* align, line up.

allòdola, *n.f.* lark.

alloggiare, *vb.* lodge, put up, accommodate, billet.

allòggio, *n.m.* lodging, accommodation, billet.

allontanarsi, *vb.* go away, stray.

allora, *adv.* then.

allòro, *n.m.* laurel.

allucinare, *vb.* hallucinate.

allucinazione, *n.f.* hallucination.

allùdere, *vb.* allude.

allume, *n.m.* alum.

alluminio, *n.m.* aluminum.

allunaggio, *n.m.* moon landing.

allungare, *vb.* lengthen, extend, elongate, reach out.

allusione, *n.f.* allusion, reference.

allusivo, *adj.* allusive.

alluvione, *n.f.* flood, inundation.

almanacco, *n.m.* almanac.

almeno, *adv.* at least.

alpaca, *n.m.* alpaca.

Alpi, *n.f. (pl.)* Alps.

alpino, *adj.* Alpine.

alt, *interj.* halt!

alta fedeltà, *n.f.* high fidelity.

altalena, *n.f.* seesaw; swing.

altamente, *adv.* highly.

altare, *n.m.* altar.

alterare, *vb.* alter.

alterazione, *n.f.* alteration.

alternare, *vb.* alternate.

alternativa, *n.f.* alternative.

alternativo, *adj.* alternative, alternate.

altezza, *n.f.* height; Highness.

altitùdine, *n.f.* altitude.

alto, *adj.* high, lofty, tall; loud. **in a.,** *adv.* on high, aloft.

altoparlante, *n.m.* loudspeaker.

altopiano, *n.m.* plateau.

altrimenti, *adv.* otherwise, else.

altro, *adj.* other, else.

altrove, *adv.* elsewhere.

altruismo, *n.m.* altruism.

altura, *n.f.* height.

alunno, *n.m.* pupil.

alveare, *n.m.* beehive.

alzaia, *n.f.* hawser.

alzare, *vb.* raise.

alzarsi, *vb.* get up, rise.

amàbile, *adj.* amiable, likable, lovable.

amaca, *n.f.* hammock.

amàlgama, *n.m.* amalgam.

amalgamare, *vb.* amalgamate.

amante, 1. *n.m.* lover; *f.* mistress. **2.** *adj.* fond.

amaramente, *adv.* bitterly.

amare, *vb.* love.

amareggiare, *vb.* embitter.

amarezza, *n.f.* bitterness.

amaro, *adj.* bitter.

ambasciata, *n.f.* embassy; message.

ambasciatore, *n.m.* ambassador.

ambedue, *adj. and pron.* both.

ambidèstro, *adj.* ambidextrous.

ambientale, *adj.* environmental, ecological.

ambiènte, *n.m.* environment, habitat.

ambiguità, *n.f.* ambiguity.

ambiguo, *adj.* ambiguous.

ambire, *vb.* aim at; aspire to.

ambivalente, *adj.* ambivalent.

ambizione, *n.f.* ambition.

ambizioso, *adj.* ambitious.

ambra, *n.f.* amber.

ambulanza, *n.f.* ambulance.

ambulatòrio, *n. and adj.* ambulatory.

Amburgo, *n.m.* Hamburg.

amèba, *n.f.* amoeba.

amenità, *n.f.* amenity.

Amèrica, *n.f.* America.

americano, *n. and adj.* American.

ametista, *n.f.* amethyst.

amica, *n.f.* friend.

amicarsi, *vb.* befriend; gain favor.

amichévole, *adj.* friendly, amicable.

amichevolezza, *n.f.* friendliness.

amicizia, *n.f.* friendship, amity.

amico, 1. *n.m.* friend. **2.** *adj.* friendly.

àmido, *n.m.* starch.

ammaccare, *vb.* bruise.

ammaccatura, *n.f.* bruise.

ammalato, *adj.* sick.

ammaliare, *vb.* bewitch.

ammassare, *vb.* amass, hoard; lump.

ammasso, *n.m.* hoard, pile.

ammènda, *n.f.* fine.

ammèttere, *vb.* admit.

ammezzato, *n.m.* entresol, mezzanine.

ammiccare, *vb.* wink.

amministrare, *vb.* administer, manage.

amministrativo, *adj.* administrative.

amministratore, *n.m.* administrator, executive, manager.

amministrazione, *n.f.* administration, management.

ammiràbile, *adj.* admirable.

ammirabilmente, *adv.* admirably.

ammiràglia, *adj.* nave a., flagship.

ammiragliato, *n.m.* admiralty.

ammiràglio, *n.m.* admiral.

ammirare, *vb.* admire.

ammiratore, *n.m.* admirer.

ammirazione, *n.f.* admiration.

ammirévole, *adj.* admirable.

ammissìbile, *adj.* admissible.

ammissione, *n.f.* admission, admittance.

ammobiliare, *vb.* furnish.

ammollire, *vb.* soften, mollify.

ammonìaca, *n.f.* ammonia.

ammonimento, *n.m.* warning.

ammonire, *vb.* admonish, warn, caution.

ammonizione, *n.f.* admonition.

ammontare, *vb.* amount.

ammonticchiare, *vb.* collect; pile up.

ammorbidire, *vb.* soften; baste.

ammortare, *vb.* pay off, redeem.

ammortire, *vb.* deaden.

ammortizzare, *vb.* amortize.

ammucchiare, *vb.* heap, pile, stack.

ammuffito, *adj.* musty.

ammutinamento, *n.m.* mutiny.

ammutolire, *vb.* be struck dumb; strike dumb, dumbfound; silence.

amnesia, *n.f.* amnesia.

amniocentèsi, *n.f.* amniocentesis.

amnistia, *n.f.* amnesty.

amo, *n.m.* hook, bait; deceit.

amorale, *adj.* amoral.

amorazzo, *n.m.* love affair; intrigue.

amore, *n.m.* love.

amorfo, *adj.* amorphous.

amoroso, *adj.* amorous, of love.

ampère, *n.m.* ampere.

ampiamente, *adv.* extensively, diffusely.

ampiezza, *n.f.* breadth.

àmpio, *adj.* ample; extensive; broad, wide.

amplèsso, *n.m.* (sexual) embrace.

ampliamento, *n.m.* widening.

ampliare, *vb.* amplify.

amplificare, *vb.* amplify.

ampollina, *n.f.* cruet.

ampolloso, *adj.* stilted.

amputare, *vb.* amputate.

amputato, **1.** *n.m.* amputee. **2.** *adj.* amputated.

amuleto, *n.m.* amulet, talisman.

anabbagliante, *n.m.* dimmed headlight.

anacronismo, *n.m.* anachronism.

anàgrafe, *n.f.* registrar's office.

analfabèta, *n.* and *adj.* illiterate.

analfabetismo, *n.m.* illiteracy.

analgèsico, *n.m.* analgesic.

anàlisi, *n.f.* analysis, test.

analista, *n.m.* analyst.

analìtico, *adj.* analytic.

analizzare, *vb.* analyze.

analogìa, *n.f.* analogy.

anàlogo, *adj.* analogous.

ànanas, *n.m.* pineapple.

anarchìa, *n.f.* anarchy.

anatomìa, *n.f.* anatomy.

anca, *n.f.* haunch, hip.

ancella, *n.f.* handmaid.

anche, *adv.* also, too; even.

anchilòstoma, *n.m.* hookworm.

ància, *n.f.* reed.

ancora, *adv.* still, yet.

àncora, *n.f.* anchor.

ancorare, *vb.* anchor.

ancorraggio, *n.m.* anchorage.

andare, *vb.* go; fare; be (health). **a. bene,** a, fit; become. **a. a zonzo,** loaf, loiter, lounge; saunter.

andàrsene, *vb.* go away.

andatura, *n.f.* gait.

andazzo, *n.m.* the way things are going.

anèddoto, *n.m.* anecdote.

anelare, *vb.* pant.

anèllo, *n.m.* ring, link.

anemìa, *n.f.* anemia.

anestesìa, *n.f.* anesthesia.

anestètico, *n.m.* and *adj.* anesthetic.

anestetista, n.m. anesthetist.
anèto, n.m. dill.
anfibio, 1. n.m. amphibian. **2.** adj. amphibious.
anfiteatro, n.m. amphitheater.
àngelo, n.m. angel.
angolare, adj. angular.
àngolo, n.m. angle, corner.
angòscia, n.f. anguish, heartache.
anguilla, n.f. eel.
ànice, n.m. anise.
anile, n.m. anil, bluing.
anilina, n.f. aniline.
ànima, n.f. soul.
animale, n.m. and adj. animal.
animare, vb. animate.
animazione, n.f. animation.
ànimo, n.m. spirit, animus, mind.
animosità, n.f. animosity.
ànitra, n.f. duck.
annali, n.m. (pl.) annals.
annegare, vb. drown.
annegato, n.m. drowned man.
annerire, vb. blacken.
annessione, n.f. annexation.
annèsso, n.m. annex.
annèttere, vb. annex.
annichilire, vb. annihilate.
annidarsi, vb. nestle.
annientamento, n.m. annihilation.
annientare, vb. annihilate, destroy.
anniversàrio, n.m. anniversary.
anno, n.m. year.
annodare, vb. tie.
annoiare, vb. annoy, bore, harass.
annotare, vb. annotate.
annotazione, n.f. annotation.
annuale, n.m. and adj. annual, yearly.
annualità, n.f. annuity.
annullamento, n.m. annulment, cancellation, nullification.
annullare, vb. annul, cancel, nullify, void.
annunciare, vb. announce.
annunciatore, n.m. announcer.
annunciatrice, n.f. announcer.
annunziare, vb. announce.
annunzio, n.m. announcement, advertisement.
ànnuo, adj. annual.
ànodo, n.m. anode.
anomalia, n.f. anomaly.

anòmalo, adj. anomalous.
anònimo, adj. anonymous.
anormale, adj. abnormal.
anormalità, n.f. abnormality.
anormalmente, adv. abnormally.
ansa, n.f. loop.
ansando, adj. panting, breathless.
ansante, adj. panting, out of breath.
ansia, n.f. anxiety.
ansietà, n.f. anxiety, concern, worry.
ansimare, vb. pant, be out of breath.
ansioso, adj. anxious.
antagonismo, n.m. antagonism.
antagonista, n.m. antagonist, opponent, villain.
antàrtico, n.m. and adj. antarctic.
Antàrtide, n.f. Antarctica.
antebellico, adj. prewar.
antecedente, adj. antecedent.
antenato, n.m. ancestor, forebear, forefather.
antenna, n.f. antenna; (radio) aerial.
anteprima, n.f. preview.
anteriore, adj. anterior, previous, fore.
antiàcido, adj. antacid.
antiaèreo, adj. antiaircraft.
anticamente, adv. in ancient times, formerly.
anticàmera, n.f. anteroom.
anticipare, vb. anticipate; advance (payment).
anticipato, adj. anticipated, foregone.
anticipazione, n.f. anticipation.
anticipo, n.m. advance payment; down payment. **in a.,** beforehand.
anticlericale, adj. anticlerical.
antico, adj. ancient, antique.
anticoncezionale, adj. and n.m. contraceptive, birth control.
anticonformista, n.m. nonconformist.
anticòrpo, n.m. antibody.
antidoto, n.m. antidote.
antìfona, n.f. anthem.
antìlope, n.f. antelope.
antimònio, n.m. antimony.
antinucleare, n.f. antinuclear.
antipasto, n.m. hors d'oeuvres, appetizer.

antipatìa, *n.f.* antipathy, dislike.
antipàtico, *adj.* disagreeable, nasty.
antiquato, *adj.* antiquated.
antiquità, *n.f.* antiquity.
antisèttico, *n.m. and adj.* antiseptic.
antisociale, *adj.* antisocial.
antitossina, *n.f.* antitoxin.
antologìa, *n.f.* anthology.
antrace, *n.m.* anthrax.
antracite, *n.f.* anthracite.
antropologìa, *n.f.* anthropology.
antropològico, *adj.* anthropological.
anzi, *conj.* on the contrary.
anziano, *n.m.* senior citizen, elder; *adj.* senior, aged.
apatìa, *n.f.* apathy.
apàtico, *adj.* apathetic.
ape, *n.f.* bee.
apèrto, *adj.* open, overt.
apertura, *n.f.* opening, aperture, gap.
apiàrio, *n.m.* apiary.
àpice, *n.m.* apex.
apogèo, *n.m.* apogee, high point, heyday.
apologìa, *n.f.* apology.
apoplessìa, *n.f.* apoplexy.
apoplèttico, *adj.* apoplectic.
apòstata, *n.m.* apostate.
apostòlico, *adj.* apostolic.
apòstolo, *n.m.* apostle.
appaciamento, *n.m.* appeasement.
appannare, *vb.* tarnish.
appannatura, *n.f.* tarnish.
apparato, *n.m.* apparatus.
apparecchiare, *vb.* set the table; dress.
apparècchio, *n.m.* apparatus.
apparènte, *adj.* apparent.
apparènza, *n.f.* appearance, guise.
apparire, *vb.* appear.
appariscente, *adj.* showy, gaudy, ostentatious.
apparizione, *n.f.* apparition.
appartamento, *n.m.* apartment, flat.
appartato, *adj.* secluded; lonely.
appartenènza, *n.f.* belonging, appurtenance.
appartenere, *vb.* belong, pertain.

appassionato, *adj.* passionate.
appassire, *vb.* fade, wilt.
appellante, *n.m.* appellant.
appellare, *vb.* appeal.
appèllo, *n.m.* appeal, call, roll-call.
appena, *adv.* hardly, scarcely, just, barely.
appendectomìa, *n.f.* appendectomy.
appendere, *vb.* hang.
appendiabiti, *n.m.* hook, peg.
appendice, *n.f.* appendix, appendage.
appendicite, *n.f.* appendicitis.
Appennini, *n.m.pl.* the Apennines.
appesantire, *vb.* weigh down; grow heavy.
appetito, *n.m.* appetite.
appezzamento, *n.m.* lot, plot.
appiattire, *vb.* flatten.
appiccicare, *vb.* stick.
applaudire, *vb.* applaud, cheer, clap.
applàuso, *n.m.* applause, cheer, plaudit.
applicàbile, *adj.* applicable.
applicare, *vb.* apply.
applicazione, *n.f.* application.
appoggiare, *vb.* support, back (up), lean.
appòggio, *n.m.* support, backing; foothold, footing; furtherance.
appollaiarsi, *vb.* roost, perch.
apportare, *vb.* bring, fetch.
apposito, *adj.* appropriate.
apposizione, *n.f.* apposition.
appòsta, *adv.* on purpose, advisedly, deliberately.
apprendere, *vb.* learn.
apprendista, *n.m.* apprentice.
apprezzàbile, *adj.* appreciable.
apprezzamento, *n.m.* appreciation.
apprezzare, *vb.* appreciate, value, prize.
approfittare, *vb.* profit.
approfondire, *vb.* deepen.
appropriato, *adj.* appropriate.
appropriarsi, *vb.* appropriate.
approssimare, *vb.* approximate.
approssimativamente, *adv.* approximately.
approssimativo, *adj.* approximate.

approssimazione, *n.f.* approximation.

approvare, *vb.* approve.

approvazione, *n.f.* approval, approbation.

appuntamento, *n.m.* appointment, date, engagement, rendezvous, tryst.

aprile, *n.m.* April.

aprire, *vb.* open, unlock.

apriscàtole, *n.m.* can-opener.

àquila, *n.f.* eagle.

aquilino, *adj.* aquiline.

aquilone, *n.m.* kite.

aquilòtto, *n.m.* eaglet.

aràbile, *adj.* arable.

àrabo, 1. *n.* Arab. **2.** *adj.* Arabic.

aràchide, *n.f.* peanut.

aragosta, *n.f.* lobster.

aràldica, *n.f.* heraldry.

aràldico, *adj.* heraldic.

araldo, *n.m.* herald.

arància, *n.f.* orange.

aranciata, *n.f.* orangeade; *adj.* orange.

arància, *n.m.* orange tree.

arare, *vb.* plow.

aratro, *n.m.* plow.

arbitrare, *vb.* arbitrate.

arbitràrio, *adj.* arbitrary, highhanded.

arbitrato, *n.m.* arbitration.

àrbitro, *n.m.* arbiter, arbitrator, judge, referee, umpire.

arbòreo, *adj.* arboreal.

arboscello, *n.m.* shrub.

arbusto, *n.m.* shrub.

arca, *n.f.* ark.

arcàico, *adj.* archaic.

arcangelo, *n.m.* archaugel.

arcano, *adj.* arcane; supernatural; secret.

archeologìa, *n.f.* archaeology.

archetto, *n.m.* little bow. **gambe ad a.,** bow legs.

architetto, *n.m.* architect.

architettònico, *adj.* architectural.

architettura, *n.f.* architecture.

archiviare, *vb.* file.

archìvio, *n.m.* archives, file.

arcidiòcesi, *n.f.* archdiocese.

arciduca, *n.m.* archduke.

arcière, *n.m.* archer.

arcipèlago, *n.m.* archipelago.

arcivéscovo, *n.m.* archbishop.

arco, *n.m.* arc, arch; bow. **tiro con l'a.,** archery.

arcobaleno, *n.m.* rainbow.

ardènte, *adj.* ardent, burning.

àrdere, *vb.* burn.

ardèsia, *n.f.* slate.

ardimento, *n.m.* boldness.

ardire, *vb.* be bold, dare.

arditamente, *adv.* boldly.

ardito, *adj.* bold.

ardore, *n.m.* ardor.

àrduo, *adj.* arduous, difficult.

àrea, *n.f.* area.

àrem, *n.m.* harem.

arena, *n.f.* sand, arena.

arenària, *n.f.* sandstone.

arenarsi, *vb.* get stranded.

arenile, *n.m.* sandy beach, strand; sand pit.

argano, *n.m.* winch.

argènteo, *adj.* silver.

argenterìa, *n.f.* silverware.

Argentina, *n.f.* Argentine.

argentino, *adj.* silvery; Argentine.

argènto, *n.m.* silver.

argilla, *n.f.* clay.

argilloso, *adj.* clayey.

arginare, *vb.* embank, dam, stem.

àrgine, *n.m.* embankment.

argomento, *n.m.* argument, topic.

arguire, *vb.* argue; deduce, conclude.

arìa, *n.f.* air, (music) aria.

àrido, *adj.* arid.

aringa, *n.f.* herring.

arioso, *adj.* airy.

aristòcrate, *n.m.* aristocrat.

aristocràtico, *adj.* aristocratic.

aristocrazìa, *n.f.* aristocracy.

aritmètica, *n.f.* arithmetic.

Arlecchino, *n.m.* Harlequin.

arma, *n.f.* arm (weapon). **a. da fuòco,** firearm.

armàdio, *n.m.* clothes-closet.

armamento, *n.m.* armament.

arma nucleare, *n.f.* nuclear weapon.

armare, *vb.* arm.

armatore, *n.m.* shipowner.

armatura, *n.f.* armor.

armerìa, *n.f.* armory.

armistizio, *n.m.* armistice.

armonìa, *n.f.* harmony.

armònica, *n.f.* harmonica.

armònico, *adj.* harmonic.
armonioso, *adj.* harmonious, dulcet.
armonizzare, *vb.* harmonize.
arnese, *n.m.* tool, implement, instrument.
àrnica, *n.f.* arnica.
aròma, *n.m.* aroma.
aromàtico, *adj.* aromatic.
arpa, *n.f.* harp.
arpìa, *n.f.* harpy.
arpione, *n.f.* harpoon.
arrabbiarsi, *vb.* get angry.
arrabbiato, *adj.* angry.
arraffare, *vb.* grab.
arrampicarsi, *vb.* climb, creep, clamber up, scramble up.
arrampicatore, *n.m.* climber.
arrangiare, *vb.* arrange, settle.
arrecare, *vb.* cause; bring.
arredamento, *n.m.* furnishing; interior decoration.
arredare, *vb.* furnish; decorate, arrange.
arrèndersi, *vb.* surrender.
arrestare, *vb.* arrest, apprehend; *(refl.)* stall.
arrèsto, *n.m.* arrest.
arretrato, *adj.* out-of-date.
arricchire, *vb.* enrich.
arricciare, *vb.* curl.
arringa, *n.f.* harangue.
arringare, *vb.* harangue.
arrischiare, *vb.* risk.
arrivare, *vb.* arrive.
arrivista, *n.m. or f.* social climber.
arrivo, *n.m.* arrival.
arrogante, *adj.* arrogant.
arroganza, *n.f.* arrogance.
arrogarsi, *vb.* arrogate, assume.
arrossire, *vb.* blush.
arrostire, *vb.* roast.
arròsto, *n.m.* roast.
arrotolare, *vb.* roll up, coil.
arruffare, *vb.* ruffle, bristle.
arrugginire, *vb.* rust.
arrugginito, *adj.* rusty.
arruolare, *vb.* enroll; levy.
arsenale, *n.m.* arsenal; dockyard, navy yard.
arsènico, *n.m.* arsenic.
arte, *n.f.* art, trade, craft, craftsmanship, guild.
artèria, *n.f.* artery.
arteriale, *adj.* arterial.

arterioscleròsi, *n.f.* arteriosclerosis.
artesiano, *adj.* artesian.
àrtico, *adj.* Arctic.
articolare, *vb.* articulate.
articolato, *adj.* articulate.
articolazione, *n.f.* articulation; joint.
artìcolo, *n.m.* article, item. **a. di fondo,** editorial.
artificiale, *adj.* artificial.
artificialità, *n.f.* artificiality.
artifìcio, *n.m.* artifice.
artigiano, *n.m.* artisan, craftsman.
artiglière, *n.m.* gunner.
artiglierìa, *n.f.* artillery.
artìglio, *n.m.* talon, claw.
artista, *n.m. or f.* artist.
artìstico, *adj.* artistic.
arto, *n.m.* limb.
artrite, *n.f.* arthritis.
artrosi, *n.f.* osteoarthritis.
arzigogolare, *vb.* daydream, fancy.
arzillo, *adj.* spry.
asbèsto, *n.m.* asbestos.
ascèlla, *n.f.* armpit.
ascendente, *n.m.* ascendancy (over); rising; influence.
ascensionale, *adj.* upward, ascensional.
Ascensione, *n.f. (eccles.)* Ascension, Assumption.
ascensore, *n.m.* elevator, lift.
ascèsso, *n.m.* abscess.
ascètico, *n.m. and adj.* ascetic.
àscia, *n.f.* axe.
asciugamani, *n.m.* handtowel.
asciugapiatti, *n.m.* dishtowel.
asciugare, *vb.* dry, blot, wipe.
asciutto, *adj.* dry.
ascoltare, *vb.* listen to, hearken to, hark.
ascrivere, *vb.* ascribe.
asfalto, *n.m.* asphalt.
asfissìa, *n.f.* asphyxia.
asfissiare, *vb.* asphyxiate, smother.
Asia, *n.f.* Asia.
asiàtico, *adj.* Asian.
asimmetrìa, *n.f.* asymmetry.
àsino, *n.m.* ass, donkey.
asma, *n.m.* asthma. **a. del fièno,** hay fever.

asmàtico, *adj.* asthmatic.

aspàrago, *n.m.* asparagus.

asperità, *n.f.* asperity.

aspettare, *vb.* await, wait (for); *(refl.)* expect.

aspettativa, *n.f.* expectation, expectancy.

aspètto, *n.m.* aspect, appearance, look; meaning.

aspirante, *n.m.* aspirant.

aspirare, *vb.* aspire, aspirate.

aspiratore, *n.m.* aspirator.

aspirazione, *n.f.* aspiration, suction.

aspirina, *n.f.* aspirin.

asportare, *vb.* remove.

asprezza, *n.f.* harshness.

aspro, *adj.* harsh.

assaggiare, *vb.* test, try, assay, sample.

assaggio, *n.m.* taste, sample, small quantity.

assai, *adv.* a lot, much.

assalire, *vb.* assail, attack, beset.

assalitore, *n.m.* assailant, attacker.

assaltare, *vb.* assault.

assalto, *n.m.* assault, bout, round.

assaporare, *vb.* savor, enjoy.

assassinare, *vb.* assassinate.

assassìnio, *n.m.* assassination, murder.

assassino, *n.m.* assassin, murderer.

asse, 1. *n.m.* axis, axle. **2.** *n.f.* board, plank.

asse a rotelle, *n.m.* skateboard.

assecondare, *vb.* go along with; agree with, favor.

assediante, *n.m.* besieger.

assediare, *vb.* besiege, beset.

assèdio, *n.m.* siege.

assegnàbile, *adj.* assignable.

assegnamento, *n.m.* assignment.

assegnare, *vb.* assign, allot, allocate.

assegnazione, *n.f.* assignment, allotment.

assegno, *n.m.* check; allowance.

assegno (per) viaggiatori, *n.m.* traveler's check.

assemblaggio, *n.m.* assembly.

assemblèa, *n.f.* assembly, gathering, meeting.

assembramento, *n.m.* gathering, crowd.

assennato, *adj.* sensible.

assènso, *n.m.* assent.

assente, 1. *n.* absentee. **2.** *adj.* absent.

assenteismo, *n.m.* absenteeism; indifference.

assentire, *vb.* assent.

assenza, *n.f.* absence.

assènzio, *n.m.* absinthe.

asserire, *vb.* assert.

asservire, *vb.* enslave.

asserzione, *n.f.* assertion.

assessore, *n.m.* assessor.

assetato, *adj.* thirsty; eager.

assetto, *n.m.* good order; trim.

asseverare, *vb.* asseverate.

asseverazione, *n.f.* asseveration.

assicurare, *vb.* assure, insure.

assicurazione, *n.f.* assurance, insurance.

assiduamente, *adv.* assiduously.

assìduo, *adj.* assiduous.

assimilare, *vb.* assimilate.

assimilativo, *adj.* assimilative.

assimilazione, *n.f.* assimilation.

assìoma, *n.m.* axiom.

assistènte, *n. and adj.* assistant.

assistente mèdico, *n.m.* paramedic.

assistènza, *n.f.* attendance, assistance, relief. **a. sociale,** social work.

assistere, *vb.* be present.

asso, *n.m.* ace.

associare, *vb.* associate, affiliate.

associazione, *n.f.* association, affiliation.

assoggettare, *vb.* subject.

assolo, *n.m.* solo.

assolutamente, *adv.* absolutely.

assolutezza, *n.f.* absoluteness.

assolutismo, *n.m.* absolutism.

assoluto, *adj.* absolute, complete, total.

assoluzione, *n.f.* absolution, acquittal.

assòlvere, *vb.* absolve, acquit.

assomiglianza, *n.f.* likeness.

assomigliare, *vb.* resemble, look like.

assonanza, *n.f.* assonance.

assonnato, *adj.* sleepy, drowsy.

assopirsi, *vb.* drowse.

assorbènte, 1. *n.m.* absorbent. **2.** *adj.* absorbent, absorbing.
assorbimento, *n.m.* absorption.
assorbire, *vb.* absorb.
assorbito, *adj.* absorbed.
assordare, *vb.* deafen.
assortimento, *n.m.* assortment.
assortire, *vb.* assort, sort.
assortito, *adj.* assorted.
assorto, *adj.* absorbed.
assottigliare, *vb.* reduce, make thin.
assuefare, *vb.* get used to, addict; inure.
assuefazione, *n.f.* addiction.
assùmere, *vb.* assume, take on.
assunzione, *n.f.* employment; assumption.
assurdamente, *adv.* absurdly.
assurdità, *n.f.* absurdity, nonsense.
assurdo, 1. *n.m.* absurdity. **2.** *adj.* absurd, preposterous.
astèmio, *adj.* abstemious.
astenersi, *vb.* abstain, refrain.
asterisco, *n.m.* asterisk.
asteròide, *n.m.* asteroid.
astigmatismo, *n.m.* astigmatism.
astinènza, *n.f.* abstinence.
àstio, *n.m.* grudge.
astrale, *adj.* astral, of the stars.
astrarre, *vb.* abstract.
astratto, *adj.* abstract, abstracted.
astrazione, *n.f.* abstraction.
astringènte, *adj.* astringent.
astro, *n.m.* star, aster.
astrofisica, *n.f.* astrophysics.
astrologia, *n.f.* astrology.
astronauta, *n.m.* astronaut.
astronave, *n.f.* spaceship.
astronomia, *n.f.* astronomy.
astruso, *adj.* abstruse.
astuccio, *n.m.* case.
astuto, *adj.* astute, artful, clever, canny, cunning, designing.
astùzia, *n.f.* guile.
atassìa, *n.f.* ataxia.
atelier, *n.m.* workshop, studio; fashion house.
ateneo, *n.m.* university.
àteo, 1. *n.m.* atheist. **2.** *adj.* atheistic, godless.
atìpico, *adj.* atypical.
atlante, *n.m.* atlas.
atlàntico, *adj.* Atlantic.

atlèta, *n.m.* athlete.
atlètico, *adj.* athletic.
atletismo, *n.m.* athletics.
atmosfèra, *n.f.* atmosphere.
atmosfèrico, *adj.* atmospheric.
atòllo, *n.m.* atoll.
atòmico, *adj.* atomic.
àtomo, *n.m.* atom.
atonale, *adj.* atonal.
atroce, *adj.* atrocious, heinous.
atrocemente, *adj.* atrociously, dreadfully.
atrocità, *n.f.* atrocity.
atrofìa, *n.f.* atrophy.
atropina, *n.f.* atropine.
attaccàbile, *adj.* assailable.
attaccamento, *n.m.* attachment.
attaccapanni, *n.m.* coathanger.
attaccare, *vb.* attach, fasten, hitch, tack, stick; attack, assail.
attaccatìccio, *adj.* sticky.
attacco, *n.m.* attack, onslaught.
atteggiamento, *n.m.* attitude.
atteggiarsi, *vb.* take an attitude.
attentamente, *adv.* attentively, carefully.
attènto, *adj.* attentive, careful, thoughtful.
attenuare, *vb.* attenuate.
attenzione, *n.f.* attention, carefulness, notice.
atterràggio, *n.m.* landing. **pista d'a.,** landing strip, runway.
atterrare, *vb.* land.
atterrire, *vb.* terrify.
attesa, *n.f.* wait. **in a. di,** while waiting for, pending.
attestare, *vb.* attest, vouch for.
àttimo, *n.m.* instant.
attinio, *n.m.* actinium.
attirare, *vb.* attract, entice, lure, decoy.
attitùdine, *n.f.* aptitude.
attivamente, *adv.* actively, busily.
attivare, *vb.* activate.
attivatore, *n.m.* activator.
attivazione, *n.f.* activation.
attivismo, *n.m.* activism.
attività, *n.f.* activity.
attivo, 1. *n.m.* asset. **2.** *adj.* active, busy.
attizzare, *vb.* stir, poke.
atto, 1. *n.m.* act, deed. **2.** *adj.* apt, fitted.
attore, *n.m.* actor; plaintiff.

attorno, *adv.* about, around.

attraènte, *adj.* attractive, engaging, fetching.

attrarre, *vb.* attract.

attraversare, *vb.* cross, go through, pass through.

attravèrso, *adv. and prep.* across, through.

attrazione, *n.f.* attraction.

attrezzare, *vb.* rig.

attrezzatura, *n.f.* rig.

attrezzista, *n.m.* gymnast.

attrezzo, *n.m.* tool, implement.

attribuìbile, *adj.* attributable.

attribuire, *vb.* attribute.

attribuzione, *n.f.* attribution.

attrice, *n.f.* actress.

attrizione, *n.f.* attrition.

attualità, *n.f.* reality, current significance; *(pl.)* newsreel.

attuare, *vb.* actuate.

attuàrio, *n.m.* actuary.

attutire, *vb.* silence.

audace, *adj.* audacious, bold, daring.

audàcia, *n.f.* audacity, boldness, daring.

audiovisivo, *adj.* audiovisual.

auditòrio, *n.m.* auditorium.

audizione, *n.f.* audition.

augurare, *vb.* augur; wish.

augùrio, *n.m.* greeting.

àula, *n.f.* hall; classroom.

aumentare, *vb.* augment, increase, raise, enhance; escalate.

aumènto, *n.m.* increase, raise, rise.

àureo, *n.m.* golden.

aurèola, *n.f.* halo.

auricolare, *adj.* auricular.

aurìfero, *adj.* gold-bearing.

auriga, *n.m.* charioteer.

aurora, *n.f.* dawn.

ausiliare, *n.m. and adj.* auxiliary.

auspicio, *n.m.* auspice.

austerità, *n.f.* austerity.

austèro, *adj.* austere, severe; unadorned.

Austria, *n.f.* Austria.

austrìaco, *adj.* Austrian.

aut-aut, *conj.* yes or no; *n.m.* dilemma.

autenticare, *vb.* authenticate.

autenticità, *n.f.* authenticity.

autèntico, *adj.* authentic.

autista, *n.m.* chauffeur, (auto) driver.

àuto, *n.f.* auto.

autobiografìa, *n.f.* autobiography.

àutobus, *n.m.* bus.

autocarro, *n.m.* truck, lorry.

autoclave, *n.f.* sterilizer.

autòcrate, *n.m.* autocrat.

autocrazìa, *n.f.* autocracy.

autògrafo, *n.m.* autograph.

autolìnea, *n.f.* bus line.

autòma, *n.m.* automaton, robot.

automaticamente, *adv.* automatically.

automàtico, *adj.* automatic.

automòbile, *n.f.* automobile.

automobilista, *n.m.* motorist.

automobilìstico, *adj.* pertaining to automobiles, automotive.

automotrice, *n.f.* railcar.

autonoleggio, *n.m.* car rental.

autonomìa, *n.f.* autonomy.

autònomo, *adj.* autonomous.

autoparcheggio, *n.m.* parking area.

autopsìa, *n.f.* autopsy.

autoradio, *n.f.* car radio.

autore, *n.m.* author.

autorévole, *adj.* authoritative.

autorevolmente, *adv.* authoritatively.

autorimessa, *n.f.* garage.

autorità, *n.f.* authority.

autoritàrio, *adj.* authoritarian.

autoritratto, *n.m.* self-portrait.

autorizzare, *vb.* authorize, empower, entitle.

autorizzazione, *n.f.* authorization.

autosalone, *n.m.* car showroom, car dealer.

autostop, *n.m.* hitchhiking.

autotreno, *n.m.* trailer truck.

autunno, *n.m.* autumn, fall.

avambràccio, *n.m.* forearm.

avamposto, *n.m.* outpost.

avana, *adj.* brown, beige.

avanguàrdia, *n.f.* vanguard.

avanti, 1. *adv.* in front, ahead, onward, forward, before; (clock) fast. **2.** *prep.* before, in front of. **3.** *interj.* come in!

avanzamento, *n.m.* advancement.

avanzare, *vb.* advance; be left over.

avanzato, *adj.* advanced.

avanzo, *n.m.* relic, left-over, surplus.

avaria, *n.f.* damage.

avariare, *vb.* damage.

avarizia, *n.f.* avarice.

avaro, 1. *n.m.* miser. 2. *adj.* avaricious, miserly, grasping, stingy.

avemmaria, *n.f.* Hail Mary.

avena, *n.f.* oats.

avere, *vb.* have.

avianiello, *n.m.* aviary.

aviatore, *n.m.* aviator, flier.

aviatrice, *n.f.* aviatrix.

aviazione, *n.f.* aviation.

àvido, *adj.* avid, greedy.

aviogetto, *n.m.* jet plane.

aviolinea, *n.f.* airline.

aviorimessa, *n.f.* hangar.

aviotrasportato, *adj.* airborne.

avòrio, *n.m.* ivory.

avornìello, *n.m.* laburnum.

avvelenare, *vb.* poison.

avvenimento, *n.m.* event, happening, occurrence.

avvenire, *n.m.* future, futurity.

avventato, *adj.* reckless.

avventìzio, *adj.* adventitious.

avvènto, *n.m.* advent.

avventore, *n.m.* regular customer.

avventura, *n.f.* adventure.

avventurare, *vb.* adventure; risk.

avventurière, *n.m.* adventurer.

avventurosamente, *adv.* adventurously.

avventuroso, *adj.* adventurous, enterprising, venturesome.

avverare, *vb.* realize, fulfil; verify; become true.

avverbiale, *adj.* adverbial.

avvèrbio, *n.m.* adverb.

avversare, *vb.* oppose.

avversàrio, *n.* adversary.

avversione, *n.f.* aversion.

avversità, *n.f.* adversity, hardship.

avvèrso, *adj.* adverse; averse.

avvertenza, *n.f.* warning.

avvertire, *vb.* warn, alert, advert.

avviare, *vb.* start, begin.

avvicinarsi a, *vb.* approach.

avvilimento, *n.m.* abasement.

avvilire, *vb.* abase, debase.

avviluppare, *vb.* envelop.

avvincente, *adj.* charming, engaging.

avvìo, *n.m.* start, beginning.

avvisare, *vb.* inform, advise.

avviso, *n.m.* advice; news, information, notice, notification; warning.

avvitare, *vb.* screw.

avvizzire, *vb.* wither.

avvocato, *n.m. or f.* advocate, lawyer.

avvòlgere, *vb.* wrap up, enfold, wind.

ayatolla(h), *n.m.* ayatollah.

aziènda, *n.f.* firm, concern.

azione, *n.f.* action; share (of stock).

azionista, *n.m.* stockholder.

azzittire, *vb.* shut someone up.

azzuffarsi, *vb.* get into a scrap.

azzurro, *adj.* blue, azure.

B

babau, *n.m.* ogre, bogeyman.

babbeo, *n.m.* fool, idiot.

babbo, *n.m.* dad, daddy, pop, pa.

babbuino, *n.m.* baboon.

bacca, *n.f.* berry.

baccano, *n.m.* uproar, racket, row.

baccèllo, *n.m.* pod, shell.

bacchetta, *n.f.* wand, (conductor's) baton.

baciare, *vb.* kiss.

bacillo, *n.m.* bacillus.

bacino, *n.m.* basin, dock. **b. di carenaggio,** dry dock.

bàcio, *n.m.* kiss.

baco, *n.m.* worm. **b. da seta,** silkworm.

bada, *n.* **a b.,** at bay.

badare, *vb.* heed, look out, mind.

badessa, *n.f.* abbess.

badìa, *n.f.* abbey.

badile, *n.m.* shovel.

baffo, *n.m.* mustache.

bagagliaio, *n.m.* trunk.

bagàglio, n.m. baggage, luggage.
bagarinaggio, n.m. scalping.
bagliore, n.m. glare.
bagnante, n.m. or f. bather.
bagnare, vb. bathe, soak.
bagnino, n.m. bath attendant, life-guard.
bagno, n.m. bath.
bàia, n.f. bay.
baio, adj. bay (color).
baionetta, n.f. bayonet.
balaùstra, n.f. balustrade.
balaustrata, n.f. balustrade.
balbettare, vb. babble, stammer.
balbettìo, n.m. babble.
balbuziènte, n.m. stammerer, stutterer, babbler.
balcone, n.m. balcony.
baldacchino, n.m. canopy.
baldòria, n.f. carousing, revelry, spree.
balena, n.f. whale.
balenare, vb. flash.
baleno, n.m. flash.
bàlia, n.f. nurse.
balìstica, n.f. ballistics.
balla, n.f. bale.
ballàbile, n.m. dance tune.
ballare, vb. dance.
ballata, n.f. ballad, ballade.
ballatòio, n. catwalk.
ballerina, n.f. dancer, ballerina.
ballerino, n.m. dancer.
ballo, n.m. dance, dancing; ballet; ball.
balneare, adj. pertaining to baths or bathing.
balsàmico, adj. balmy, balsamous.
bàlsamo, n.m. balsam, balm.
baluardo, n.m. bulwark.
balzare, vb. bound, leap, dart.
balzo, n.m. bound, leap, dart.
bambina, n.f. child, little girl.
bambinaia, n.f. nurse.
bambinesco, adj. childish, babyish.
bambino, n.m. child, little boy.
bàmbola, n.f. doll.
bambù, n.m. bamboo.
banale, adj. banal, commonplace, hackneyed.
banalità, n.f. banality, platitude.
banana, n.f. banana.
banca, n.f. bank.

bancàrio, adj. pertaining to banks.
bancarotta, n.f. bankruptcy.
banchetto, n.m. banquet, feast.
banchière, n.m. banker.
banchina, n.f. pier.
banchisa, n.f. ice pack.
banco, n.m. bench; counter; desk; stall; bank.
banconota, n.f. bank note.
banda, n.f. band, gang; fillet.
bandièra, n.f. banner, flag, ensign.
bandire, vb. banish, exile.
bandista, n.m. bandsman.
bandito, n.m. bandit, outlaw.
banditore, n.m. crier, auctioneer.
bando, n.m. banishment, exile.
bar, n.m. bar, coffee shop, cafe.
bara, n.f. coffin.
baracca, n.f. hut; barrack.
baraonda, n.f. chaos.
barare, vb. cheat.
baratro, n.m. abyss.
barattare, vb. barter, swap.
baratto, n.m. barter, swap.
barba, n.f. beard.
barbabiètola, n.f. beet.
barbàrie, n.f. barbarism.
barbarismo, n.m. barbarism.
bàrbaro, 1. n.m. barbarian. **2.** adj. barbarous.
barbetta, n.f. little beard, goatee.
barbière, n.m. barber.
barbitùrico, n.m. barbiturate.
barbuto, adj. bearded.
barca, n.f. boat. **b. a remi,** rowboat.
barcollare, vb. stagger, totter.
bardare, vb. caparison, harness.
bardatura, n.f. caparison; harness.
barèlla, n.f. litter, stretcher.
barile, n.m. barrel, cask.
bariletto, n.m. keg.
bàrio, n.m. barium.
barista, n.m. bartender.
baritono, n.m. baritone.
barlume, n.m. glimmer, gleam.
baro, n.m. cardsharp.
baròcco, adj. baroque.
barometrico, adj. barometric.
baròmetro, n.m. barometer.
baronale, adj. baronial.
barone, n.m. baron.
baronessa, n.f. baroness.

barricare, *vb.* barricade.
barricata, *n.f.* barricade.
barrièra, *n.f.* barrier.
barzelletta, *n.f.* joke.
basare, *vb.* base, ground.
base, *n.f.* base, basis, footing, ground.
basetta, *n.f.* whisker.
basilare, *adj.* fundamental; basilar.
Basilèa, *n.f.* Basel.
basilico, *n.m.* basil.
bassezza, *n.f.* baseness.
basso, 1. *n.m.* bass. 2. *adj.* low, vile, base; bass.
bassofondo, *n.m.* slum.
bastardo, *n.m. and adj.* bastard, mongrel.
bastare, *vb.* suffict, be enough.
bastione, *n.m.* rampart.
bastonare, *vb.* club.
bastone, *n.m.* baton, stick, club, staff, rod, bat, cane.
battàglia, *n.f.* battle.
battaglièro, *adj.* bellicose, war-like, combative.
battàglio, *n.m.* clapper.
battaglione, *n.m.* battalion.
battèllo, *n.m.* boat.
battente, *n.m.* shutter.
bàttere, *vb.* beat, batter, hit, shoot?
batterìa, *n.f.* battery.
battèrio, *n.m.* bacterium. **battèri,** *pl.* bacteria.
batteriologìa, *n.f.* bacteriology.
batteriòlogo, *n.m.* bacteriologist.
battesimale, *adj.* baptismal.
battésimo, *n.m.* baptism, christening.
battezzare, *vb.* baptize, christen.
battibecco, *n.m.* squabble.
battipalo, *n.m.* ram.
battista, *n.m.* Baptist.
battistèro, *n.m.* baptistery.
bàttito, *n.m.* beat.
battuto, *adj.* beaten.
batùffolo, *n.m.* wad.
baùle, *n.m.* trunk.
bauxite, *n.f.* bauxite.
bauva, *n.f.* drivel.
bazzicare, *vb.* hang around.
bavaglino, *n.m.* bib.
bavaglio, *n.m.* gag.
bazàr, *n.m.* bazaar.

bazzècola, *n.f.* trifle.
beatamente, *adv.* blissfully.
beatificare, *vb.* beatify.
beatitùdine, *n.f.* bliss, beatitude.
beato, *adj.* blissful, blessed.
beccare, *vb.* peck.
becco, *n.m.* beak, bill; burner; spout.
Befana, *n.f.* old woman who brings presents on Twelfth Night.
bèffa, *n.f.* gibe.
beffarsi di, *vb.* gibe at, jeer at, mock.
bèlga, *adj.* Belgian.
Bèlgio, *n.m.* Belgium.
bella, *n.f.* beauty; sweetheart; final draft; (sports) final game.
belletto, *n.m.* make-up.
bellezza, *n.f.* beauty. **salone di b.,** beauty parlor.
bèllico, *adj.* military, relating to war.
bellicosamente, *adv.* belligerently.
bellicoso, *adj.* bellicose, belligerent.
belligerante, *adj.* belligerent.
belligeranza, *n.f.* belligerence.
bellimbusto, *n.m.* dandy.
bellino, *adj.* cunning, cute, pretty, good-looking.
bèllo, *adj.* beautiful, fine, fair, handsome, lovely.
bellumore, *n.m.* way, wit.
belva, *n.f.* wild beast; (fig.) brute.
belvedere, *n.m.* observation post, lookout.
benchè, *conj.* although.
benda, *n.f.* bandage; blindfold; headband.
bendare, *vb.* blindfold.
bène, 1. *n.m.* good, asset. **b. mobile,** chattel. 2. *adv.* well.
benedettino, *n.m. and adj.,* Benedictine.
benedetto, *adj.* blessed.
benedire, *vb.* bless.
benedizione, *n.f.* benediction, blessing.
benefattore, *n.m.* benefactor.
benefattrice, *n.f.* benefactress.
beneficare, *vb.* benefit.
beneficenza, *n.f.* charity.
beneficiàrio, *n.m.* beneficiary.

beneficio, *n.m.* benefit, advantage, profit.

benèfico, *adj.* beneficent.

benèssere, *n.m.* welfare.

benevolènza, *n.f.* benevolence.

benevolmente, *adv.* benevolently.

benèvolo, *adj.* benevolent, kindly.

bèni, *n.m.pl.* goods, estate.

benignità, *n.f.* benignity.

benigno, *adj.* benign.

benvenuto, *adj.* welcome.

benzina, *n.f.* benzine, gasoline.

bere, *vb.* drink.

beri-bèri, *n.m.* beriberi.

Berna, *n.f.* Bern.

berretto, *n.m.* cap.

bersàglio, *n.m.* target.

bestémmia, *n.f.* blasphemy, curse-word, expletive, oath.

bestemmiare, *vb.* blaspheme, curse, swear.

bestemmiatore, *n.m.* blasphemer.

bèstia, *n.f.* beast.

bestiale, *adj.* bestial, beastly.

bestiame, *n.m.* cattle; animals, livestock.

bèttola, *n.f.* (low-class) wineshop.

betulla, *n.f.* birch.

bevanda, *n.f.* beverage, drink.

bevìbile, *adj.* drinkable.

bevitore, *n.m.* drinker.

biada, *n.f.* fodder, forage.

biancheria, *n.f.* linen, laundry.

bianco, *n.m.* white, blank.

biancospino, *n.m.* hawthorn.

biascicare, *vb.* mumble, utter indistinctly; ramble.

biasimare, *vb.* blame.

biàsimo, *n.f.* blame.

Bìbbia, *n.f.* Bible.

biberon, *n.m.* baby bottle.

bìbita, *n.f.* drink.

bìblico, *adj.* Biblical.

bibliografìa, *n.f.* bibliography.

bibliotèca, *n.f.* library.

bibliotecàrio, *n.m.* librarian.

bicarbonato, *n.m.* bicarbonate.

bicchière, *n.m.* glass.

bicentennale, *adj.* bicentennial.

bicicletta, *n.f.* bicycle.

bicìpite, *n.m.* biceps.

bidèllo, *n.m.* janitor.

bidone, *n.m.* large can.

biennale, *adj.* biennial; biannual.

biènnio, *n.m.* two-year period.

bietta, *n.f.* wedge, cleat.

bifocale, *adj.* bifocal.

biforcazione, *n.f.* crotch; junction.

bigamìa, *n.f.* bigamy.

bìgamo, 1. *n.* bigamist. 2. *adj.* bigamous.

bighellone, *n.m.* gadabout, loafer.

bigliettàrio, *n.m.* ticket agent; (tram, bus) conductor.

biglietto, *n.m.* note; (money) bill; card; ticket. **b. di visita,** calling card.

bigotterìa, *n.f.* bigotry.

bigottismo, *n.m.* bigotry.

bigòtto, 1. *n.* bigot. 2. *adj.* bigoted.

bilància, *n.f.* balance, scales.

bilanciare, *vb.* balance.

bilaterale, *adj.* bilateral.

bile, *n.f.* bile.

biliardo, *n.m.* billiards.

biliare, *adj.* bilious.

bilingue, *adj.* bilingual.

bilioso, *adj.* bilious.

bimbo, *n.m.* child, baby.

bimensile, *adj.* bimonthly (twice a month).

bimestrale, *adj.* bimonthly (every two months).

bimèstre, *n.m.* two months' period.

bimetàllico, *adj.* bimetallic.

binàrio, 1. *n.m.* track. 2. *adj.* binary.

binda, *n.f.* jack.

binòcolo, *n.m.* binoculars, spy-glasses. **b. da teatro,** opera-glasses.

binoculare, *adj.* binocular.

binòmio, *n.m.* binomial.

biochìmica, *n.f.* biochemistry.

biodegradàbile, *adj.* biodegradable.

biografìa, *n.f.* biography.

biogràfico, *adj.* biographical.

biògrafo, *n.m.* biographer.

biologìa, *n.f.* biology.

biologicamente, *adv.* biologically.

biològico, *adj.* biological.

biondo, *adj.* blond(e), fair.

biopsìa, *n.f.* biopsy.
biòssido, *n.m.* dioxide.
bipartitismo, *n.m.* two-party system.
bipede, *n.m. and adj.* biped.
biplano, *n.m.* biplane.
bipolare, *adj.* bipolar.
biposto, *n.m.* two-seater.
birba, *n.f.* rascal, scoundrel.
birbone, *n.m.* naughty boy, trickster.
birichinata, *n.f.* prank.
birichino, *adj.* naughty.
birra, *n.f.* ale, beer.
birraio, *n.m.* brewer.
bisbigliare, *vb.* whisper.
bisbiglio, *n.m.* whisper.
biscòtto, *n.m.* cracker, biscuit, cookie.
bisecare, *vb.* bisect.
bisestile, *adj.* **anno b.,** leap year.
bisettimanale, *adj.* twice weekly, biweekly.
bismuto, *n.m.* bismuth.
bisnònno, *n.m.* great-grandfather.
bisognare, *vb.* be necessary.
bisogno, *n.m.* need, want.
bisognoso, *adj.* needy.
bisonte, *n.m.* bison.
bistecca, *n.f.* beefsteak, steak.
bisticciarsi, *vb.* quarrel, argue, bicker.
bistìccio, *n.m.* quarrel, argument; pun.
bistrattare, *vb.* mistreat.
bivacco, *n.m.* bivouac.
bivio, *n.m.* (road) fork, junction.
bizzèffe, *n.f.pl.* **a b.,** galore.
blandire, *vb.* blandish, coax.
blando, *adj.* bland; suave.
blatta, *n.f.* cockroach.
bleso, *adj.* lisping.
blindato, *adj.* armored. **carro b.,** tank.
bloccare, *vb.* block.
blòcco, *n.m.* bloc; block; blockade.
blu, *adj.* blue.
blue jeans, *n.m.pl.* blue jeans.
bluff, *n.m.* bluff (at cards, etc.).
bluffare, *vb.* bluff (at cards, etc.).
bluffatore, *n.m.* bluffer.
blusa, *n.f.* blouse.
bòa, *n.f.* buoy.

bobina, *n.f.* bobbin, reel, spool; coil.
bocca, *n.f.* mouth. **a b. aperta,** open-mouthed, agape.
boccapòrto, *n.m.* hatch, hatchway.
boccheggiamento, *n.m.* gasp.
boccheggiare, *vb.* gasp.
bòccia, *n.f.* bowl.
bocciare, *vb.* fail, flunk.
boccone, *n.m.* morsel, swallow.
boemo, *n.m. and adj.* Bohemian.
boia, *n.m.* executioner.
boicottàggio, *n.m.* boycott.
boicottare, *vb.* boycott.
boliviano, *adj.* Bolivian.
bolla, *n.f.* bubble.
bollare, *vb.* stamp.
bollettino, *n.m.* bulletin.
bollire, *vb.* boil.
bollo, *n.m.* stamp.
bòlo, *n.m.* cud.
bomba, *n.f.* bomb; bombshell. **b. atòmica,** atom bomb. **b. al neutrone,** neutron bomb.
bombardamento, *n.m.* bombardment.
bombardare, *vb.* bombard, shell.
bombardière, *n.m.* bomber, bombardier.
bomboletta nebulizzante, *n.f.* aerosol bomb.
bonìfica, *n.f.* reclamation.
bonificare, *vb.* reclaim.
bontà, *n.f.* goodness.
borbottamento, *n.m.* mumbling, gibberish.
borbottare, *vb.* mutter.
bordata, *n.f.* broadside.
bordèllo, *n.m.* brothel.
bordo, *n.m.* board (side of ship); edge, brink, rim. **a b. di,** *prep.* aboard, on board (of).
borghese, *adj.* bourgeois, middle-class.
borghesìa, *n.f.* bourgeoisie, middle class.
borgo, *n.m.* village, burg, borough.
bòrico, *adj.* boric.
borsa, *n.f.* bag, brief-case, pouch, purse; fellowship; stock exchange. **b. di stùdio,** scholarship.
borsaiòlo, *n.m.* pickpocket.

borsetta, *n.f.* little bag, purse, handbag.
borsista, *n.m.* scholarship holder.
borsistico, *adj.* stock exchange.
borsite, *n.f.* bursitis.
boscàglia, *n.f.* underbrush, thicket.
boschetto, *n.m.* grove.
bosco, *n.m.* wood.
boscoso, *adj.* wooded.
bòsso, *n.m.* boxwood.
bòssolo, *n.m.* cartridge-case.
botànica, *n.f.* botany.
botànico, *adj.* botanical.
bòtola, *n.f.* trap door, hatch.
bottaio, *n.m.* cooper.
bòtte, *n.f.* cask, hogshead.
bottega, *n.f.* shop.
botteghino, *n.m.* box-office.
bottìglia, *n.f.* bottle, jar.
bottino, *n.m.* booty, plunder, loot.
bottone, *n.m.* button.
bovaro, *n.m.* cattleman.
bovino, *adj.* bovine.
bòzze, *n.f.pl.* proof. **b. in colonna,** galley-proof. **b. impaginate,** page-proof.
bòzzolo, *n.m.* cocoon.
braccialetto, *n.m.* bracelet.
bracciata, *n.f.* armful.
braccio, *n.m.* arm; fathom.
brace, *n.f.* embers.
brache, *n.f.pl.* breeches, pants.
brama, *n.f.* ardent desire, craving, eagerness, longing.
bramare, *vb.* desire ardently, covet, crave, long for, yearn for.
bramino, *n.m.* Brahman.
bramosamente, *adv.* desirously, covetously, eagerly.
bramosìa, *n.f.* greed; avidity.
bramoso, *adj.* desirous, covetous, eager.
brànchia, *n.f.* gill.
brandire, *vb.* brandish.
brano, *n.m.* passage, excerpt.
Brasile, *n.m.* Brazil.
brasiliano, *adj.* Brazilian.
bravata, *n.f.* bravado.
bravo, 1. *n.* henchman. **2.** *adj.* fine.
brèccia, *n.f.* breach.
brefotròfio, *n.m.* foundling hospital.
Brètone, *n.m.* Briton.

brève, *adj.* brief, short.
brevemente, *adv.* briefly.
brevettare, *vb.* patent.
brevetto, *n.m.* patent.
brevità, *n.f.* brevity, briefness.
brezza, *n.f.* breeze.
briccone, *n.m.* rascal, rogue.
bricconesco, *adj.* roguish.
briciola, *n.f.* crumb.
brigantino, *n.m.* brig.
brigata, *n.f.* brigade.
briglia, *n.f.* bridle.
brillante, *adj.* brilliant.
brillare, *vb.* shine.
brillo, *adj.* tipsy.
brina, *n.f.* frost.
brindare, *vb.* toast.
brindisi, *n.m.* toast, health.
brio, *n.m.* vim, verve.
brioso, *adj.* lively, sprightly.
briscola, *n.f.* trump (card).
britànnico, *adj.* British.
brìvido, *n.m.* shudder, shiver, chill.
brizzolato, *adj.* grizzled.
bròcca, *n.f.* jug, pitcher.
broccato, *n.m.* brocade.
bròcco, *n.m.* nag.
bròdo, *n.m.* broth, bouillon. **b. ristretto,** consommé.
bròglio, *n.m.* scheme, plot, intrigue.
bronchiale, *adj.* bronchial.
bronchite, *n.f.* bronchitis.
brontolamento, *n.m.* grumble.
brontolare, *vb.* grumble, growl; rumble.
brontolìo, *n.m.* rumble.
bronzo, *n.m.* bronze.
brucare, *vb.* browse.
bruciare, *vb.* burn, scorch.
bruciatura, *n.f.* burn.
bruciore di stòmaco, *n.m.* heartburn.
bruco, *n.m.* caterpillar, cankerworm.
brughièra, *n.f.* heath, moor.
bruna, *n.f.* brunette.
brunire, *vb.* burnish.
bruno, *n.m.* brown.
bruscamente, *adv.* brusquely.
brusco, *adj.* brusque.
brùscolo, *n.m.* cinder.
brutale, *adj.* brutal.
brutalità, *n.f.* brutality.

bruto, *n.m. and adj.* brute.
bruttezza, *n.f.* ugliness.
brutto, *adj.* ugly, homely.
buca, *n.f.* pit, pot-hole.
bucato, *n.m.* laundry.
buccia, *n.f.* hull, husk, peel, rind, skin.
buccina, *n.f.* bugle.
buco, *n.m.* hole.
budello, *n.m.* bowel, intestine, gut.
budino, *n.m.* pudding.
bue, *n.m.* ox; beef.
bùfalo, *n.m.* buffalo.
buffonata, *n.f.* antic.
buffone, *n.m.* buffoon, jester.
bugìa, *n.f.* lie, fabrication, falsehood.
bugiardo, 1. *n.m.* liar. **2.** *adj.* lying.
bugigàttolo, *n.m.* cubbyhole.
bùio, 1. *n.m.* darkness. **2.** *adj.* dark.
bulbo, *n.m.* bulb.
búlgaro, *adj.* Bulgarian.
bulletta, *n.f.* tack.
bullone, *n.m.* bolt.

bungalò, *n.m.* bungalow.
buoncostume, *n.f.* morals.
buongustaio, *n.m.* gourmet.
buòn mercato, *n.m.* cheapness.
buòno, 1. *n.m.* bond. **2.** *adj.* good.
buonsenso, *n.m.* common sense.
buontempone, *n.m.* merry fellow.
buonumore, *n.m.* good mood.
burattino, *n.m.* puppet.
bùrbero, *adj.* gruff.
burla, *n.f.* trick, practical joke, prank.
burlone, *n.m.* joker.
burro, *n.m.* butter.
burrone, *n.m.* ravine, canyon, gulch, gully.
bussare, *vb.* knock.
bussata, *n.f.* knock.
bùssola, *n.f.* compass.
busta, *n.f.* envelope.
busto, *n.m.* bust; bodice, corset.
buttafuòri, *n.m.* bouncer (nightclub).
buttare, *vb.* throw, toss.

C

C (on water faucets) — **caldo,** *adj.* hot.
càbala, *n.f.* cabala.
cabina, *n.f.* cabin, stateroom.
cablogramma, *n.m.* cablegram.
cacao, *n.m.* cocoa.
càccia, *n.m.* fighter plane.
càccia, *n.f.* hunt, hunting, chase.
cacciare, *vb.* hunt, chase; stick; shove.
cacciatore, *n.m.* hunter, chaser.
cacciatorpedinière, *n.m.* destroyer.
cacciatrice, *n.f.* huntress.
cacciavite, *n.m.* screw-driver.
cachi, *n.m.* khaki.
càcio, *n.m.* cheese.
cacofonìa, *n.f.* cacophony.
cadauno, 1. *adj.* each; apiece. **2.** *pron.* each one.
cadàvere, *n.m.* cadaver, corpse.
cadavèrico, *adj.* cadaverous.
cadènza, *n.f.* cadence, cadenza.
cadere, *vb.* fall. **lasciar c.,** drop.
cadetto, *n.m.* cadet.

càdmio, *n.m.* cadmium.
caduta, *n.f.* fall.
caffè, *n.m.* coffee; café; buffet.
caffeina, *n.f.* caffeine.
cagionare, *vb.* occasion, cause.
cagionévole, *adj.* sickly, weak.
cagna, *n.f.* bitch.
caimano, *n.m.* cayman.
calabrese, *n.m. or f. and adj.* Calabrian.
calabrone, *n.m.* bumblebee, hornet.
calafatare, *vb.* calk.
calafato, *n.m.* calker.
calamità, *n.f.* calamity, woe.
calamitoso, *adj.* calamitous.
calapranzi, *n.m.* dumbwaiter.
calare, *vb.* lower.
calcagno, *n.m.* heel.
calcare, *adj.* calcareous. **pietra c.,** limestone.
calce, *n.f.* lime.
calcestruzzo, *n.m.* concrete.
calciatore, *n.m.* soccer player.
calcificare, *vb.* calcify.

calcina, *n.f.* mortar.
càlcio, *n.m.* calcium; kick; soccer; butt (of gun).
calcolàbile, *adj.* calculable.
calcolare, *vb.* calculate.
calcolatore, 1. *adj.* calculating. 2. *n.m.* computer.
calcolatrice elettrònica, *n.f.* computer.
càlcolo, *n.m.* calculus; calculation. **c. biliare,** gallstone.
caldaia, *n.f.* boiler, caldron, furnace.
caldarròsta, *n.f.* roasted chestnut.
caldo, 1. *n.m.* heat. **2.** *adj.* hot, warm.
caleidoscòpio, *n.m.* kaleidoscope.
calendàrio, *n.m.* calendar.
caletta, *n.f.* joggle.
càlibro, *n.m.* caliber; calipers.
càlice, *n.m.* chalice; calyx.
calicò, *n.m.* calico.
callifugo, *n.m.* corn-plaster.
calligrafia, *n.f.* calligraphy, handwriting.
callista, *n.m.* chiropodist.
callo, *n.m.* callus, corn.
callosità, *n.f.* callousness.
calloso, *adj.* callous, horny.
calma, *n.f.* calm, composure; stillness.
calmante, *n.m.* tranquilizer.
calmare, *vb.* calm, soothe; still.
calmo, *adj.* calm, composed; still.
calore, *n.m.* heat, warmth.
caloria, *n.f.* calorie.
calòrico, *adj.* caloric.
calorìfero, *n.m.* heater.
calorìmetro, *n.m.* calorimeter.
caloroso, *adj.* warm.
calpestare, *vb.* tread on.
calùnnia, *n.f.* calumny, slander.
calunniare, *vb.* calumniate, slander, slur.
Calvàrio, *n.m.* Calvary.
calvìzie, *n.f.sg.* baldness.
calvo, *adj.* bald.
calza, *n.f.* stocking, *(pl.)* hose.
calzamàglia, *n.f.* tights, leggings, leotards.
calzare, *vb.* shoe.
calzascarpe, *n.m.* shoe horn.
calzatura, *n.f.* footwear.

calzetteria, *n.f.* hosiery.
calzettone, *n.m.* thick sock.
calzino, *n.m.* sock.
calzolaio, *n.m.* shoemaker, cobbler.
calzoncini, *n.m.pl.* shorts.
calzoni, *n.m.pl.* trousers.
camaleonte, *n.m.* chameleon.
cambiale, *n.f.* promissory note, IOU.
cambiamento, *n.m.* change, shift.
cambiare, *vb.* change, shift.
cambiavalute, *n.m.* moneychanger.
cambio, *n.m.* change; relief. **c. di velocità,** *n.f.* gearshift.
cambrì, *n.m.* cambric.
camèlia, *n.f.* camelia.
càmera, *n.f.* room, chamber; (legislative) house.
camerata, *n.m.* comrade, buddy, pal.
cameratismo, *n.m.* camaraderie, comradeship.
camerièra, *n.f.* chambermaid, waitress; stewardess, flight attendant.
camerière, *n.m.* manservant; waiter; bellboy; steward, flight attendant; valet.
camerino, *n.m.* dressing room.
càmice, *n.m.* smock.
camìcia, *n.f.* shirt.
camicìòla, *n.f.* undershirt.
camiciòtto, *n.m.* smock.
camino, *n.m.* chimney.
camion, *n.m.* truck.
camioncino, *n.m.* light truck; utility.
cammèllo, *n.m.* camel.
cammèo, *n.m.* cameo.
camminare, *vb.* walk, step.
cammino, *n.m.* road.
camòscio, *n.m.* chamois.
campagna, *n.f.* country, countryside; campaign.
campana, *n.f.* bell.
campanèllo, *n.m.* (little) bell.
campanette, *n.f.pl.* glockenspiel.
campanile, *n.m.* bell-tower, belfry, steeple.
campeggiare, *vb.* camp.
campeggiatore, *n.m.* camper.
campeggio, *n.m.* camping.

campionàrio, 1. *adj.* pertaining to samples. 2. *n.m.* sample.

campionato, *n.m.* championship.

campione, *n.m.* champion; sample.

campo, *n.m.* field.

camposanto, *n.m.* cemetery, churchyard, graveyard.

camuffamento, *n.m.* disguise, camouflage.

camuffare, *vb.* disguise, camouflage.

Canadà, *n.m.* Canada.

canadese, *adj.* Canadian.

canàglia, *n.f.* rascal, scoundrel; rabble.

canagliata, *n.f.* roguery, knavery, mean trick.

canale, *n.m.* canal, channel, duct, inlet.

canalizzare, *vb.* canalize.

canalone, *n.m.* ravine.

cànapa, *n.f.* hemp.

canapè, *n.m.* couch, sofa.

Canàrie, *n.f.pl.* Canary Islands.

canarino, *n.m.* canary.

cancan, *n.m.* clamor, uproar.

cancellare, *vb.* cancel, erase, delete, efface, obliterate.

cancellatura, *n.f.* erasure.

cancelleria, *n.f.* chancellery. **oggetti di c.,** stationery.

cancellière, *n.m.* chancellor.

cancèllo, *n.m.* gate.

cancrena, *n.f.* gangrene.

cancrenoso, *adj.* gangrenous.

cancro, *n.m.* cancer, canker.

candeggina, *n.f.* bleach.

candela, *n.f.* candle. **c. d'accensione,** spark-plug.

candelabro, *n.m.* candelabrum.

candelière, *n.m.* candlestick.

candidamente, *adv.* candidly.

candidato, *n.m.* candidate, nominee.

candidatura, *n.f.* candidacy.

càndido, *adj.* candid.

candire, *vb.* caramelize.

candito, *adj.* candied.

candore, *n.m.* candor.

cane, *n.m.* dog, hound, cock (of gun). **c. poliziotto,** police dog, bloodhound.

cànfora, *n.f.* camphor.

canguro, *n.m.* kangaroo.

canile, *n.m.* doghouse, kennel.

canino, *adj.* canine.

canna, *n.f.* reed, cane.

cannèlla, *n.f.* cinnamon.

cannibale, *n.m.* cannibal.

cannone, *n.m.* cannon.

cannoneggiamento, *n.m.* cannonade.

cannonièra, *n.f.* gunboat.

cannonière, *n.m.* cannoneer.

cannùccia di paglia, *n.f.* straw (for drinking).

canòa, *n.f.* canoe.

cànone, *n.m.* canon; rent.

canònico, 1. *n.m.* canon. 2. *adj.* canonical.

canonizzare, *vb.* canonize.

canottàggio, *n.m.* rowing, boating.

canottièra, *n.f.* undershirt, tank top.

canovaccio, *n.m.* canvas.

cantare, *vb.* sing, chant; (hen, goose) cackle; (rooster) crow.

cantautore, *n.m.* singer.

canticchiare, *vb.* hum, croon.

cantina, *n.f.* basement; canteen.

canto, *n.m.* corner; song, singing, chant.

cantuccio, *n.m.* nook.

canuto, *adj.* grey-haired, white-haired.

canzonare, *vb.* mock, ridicule; banter.

canzone, *n.f.* song.

càos, *n.m.* chaos.

caòtico, *adj.* chaotic.

capace, *adj.* capable, able.

capacità, *n.f.* capacity, ability.

capanna, *n.f.* cabin, hut, shack.

capannèllo, *n.m.* small crowd.

capannone, *n.m.* large shed, depot.

capàrbio, *adj.* wilful.

capatina, *n.f.* brief visit.

capello, *n.m.* hair.

capestro, *n.m.* halter.

capezzale, *n.m.* **al c. di,** at the bedside of.

capézzolo, *n.m.* nipple.

capillare, *adj.* capillary.

capire, *vb.* understand.

capitale, 1. *n.f.* capital (city). 2. *n.m.* capital (money). 3. *adj.* capital.

capitalismo, *n.m.* capitalism.
capitalista, *n.m.* capitalist.
capitalistico, *adj.* capitalistic.
capitalizzare, *vb.* capitalize.
capitalizzazione, *n.f.* capitalization.
capitano, *n.m.* captain.
capitare, *vb.* happen, befall.
capitolare, *vb.* capitulate.
capitolo, *n.m.* chapter.
capitombolare, *vb.* tumble.
capitómbolo, *n.m.* tumble.
capo, *n.m.* head, chief, chieftain, head-man, leader, principal.
capobanda, *n.m.* bandmaster; gang leader.
capofitto, *adv.* a c., headlong.
capolavoro, *n.m.* masterpiece.
capolìnea, *n.m.* terminus.
caporale, *n.m.* corporal.
capotreno, *n.m.* conductor (of train).
capovòlgere, *vb.* overturn, upset, capsize.
cappa, *n.f.* cape.
cappèlla, *n.f.* chapel.
cappellano, *n.m.* chaplain.
cappellièra, *n.f.* hatbox, bandbox.
cappèllo, *n.m.* hat, bonnet.
càpperi, *interj.* Wow!
càppero, *n.m.* caper.
càppio, *n.m.* loop.
cappone, *n.m.* capon.
cappòtto, *n.m.* heavy coat.
cappùccio, *n.m.* hood.
capra, *n.f.* goat.
capraio, *n.m.* goat-herd.
capretto, *n.m.* kid.
capriccio, *n.m.* caprice, whim.
capricciosamente, *adv.* capriciously.
capricciosità, *n.f.* capriciousness.
capriccioso, *adj.* capricious, fanciful, flighty, temperamental.
caprifòglio, *n.m.* honeysuckle.
capriòla, *n.f.* caper, somersault.
capriòlo, *n.m.* roe deer.
càpsula, *n.f.* capsule.
captare, *vb.* intercept; pick up.
capzioso, *adj.* captious.
carabina, *n.f.* carbine.
carabinière, *n.m.* Italian military policeman.
caraffa, *n.f.* carafe, decanter.

caramèlla, *n.f.* caramel.
caramente, *adv.* dearly.
carato, *n.m.* carat.
caràttere, *n.m.* character.
caratterìstica, *n.f.* characteristic.
caratteristicamente, *adv.* characteristically.
caratterìstico, *adj.* characteristic.
caratterizzare, *vb.* characterize.
caratterizzazione, *n.f.* characterization.
carbónchio, *n.m.* carbuncle.
carbone, *n.m.* charcoal; coal.
carbonèlla, *n.f.* charcoal.
carbònio, *n.m.* carbon.
carbonizzare, *vb.* char.
carburante, *n.m.* fuel.
carburatore, *n.m.* carburetor.
carburo, *n.m.* carbide.
carcassa, *n.f.* carcass; hulk.
càrcere, *n.m.* jail.
carcerière, *n.m.* jailer.
carcinogènico, *adj.* carcinogenic.
carciòfo, *n.m.* artichoke.
cardellino, *n.m.* goldfinch.
cardìaco, *adj.* cardiac.
cardinale, *n.m. and adj.* cardinal.
càrdine, *n.m.* hinge.
carenare, *vb.* careen.
carestia, *n.f.* famine.
carezza, *n.f.* caress; endearment.
carezzévole, *adj.* caressing.
cariarsi, *vb.* decay.
càrica, *n.f.* charge.
caricare, *vb.* load, charge; (watch) wind.
caricatore, *n.m.* loader; charger; cartridge.
caricatura, *n.f.* caricature.
càrico, 1. *n.m.* load, cargo, charge, freight. **2.** *adj.* loaded, fraught.
càrie, *n.f.* caries, decay.
carino, *adj.* cute, pretty, nice.
carisma, *n.m.* charisma.
carità, *n.f.* charity, charitableness.
caritatévole, *adj.* charitable, benevolent.
caritatevolmente, *adv.* charitably, benevolently.
carlinga, *n.f.* cockpit.
carnagione, *n.f.* complexion.
carnale, *adj.* carnal.
carne, *n.f.* meat; flesh.

carnéfice, *n.m.* executioner.

carneficina, *n.f.* carnage, slaughter.

carnevale, *n.m.* carnival.

carnivoro, *adj.* carnivorous.

carnoso, *adj.* fleshy.

caro, 1. *adv.* dear(ly). **2.** *adj.* dear, expensive.

carosèllo, *n.m.* carousel, merry-go-round.

caròta, *n.f.* carrot.

carovana, *n.f.* caravan, trailer.

carovita, *n.m.* high cost of living.

carpa, *n.f.* carp.

carpire, *vb.* seize, grab.

carponi, *adv.* **a c.** on all fours.

carretta per bagagli, *n.f.* baggage cart.

carrettata, *n.f.* carload.

carrettière, *n.m.* carter, drayman.

carrièra, *n.f.* career.

carro, *n.m.* car; cart, wagon; chariot; dray, van. **c. armato,** tank. **c. fùnebre,** hearse. **c. di scorta,** tender.

carròzza, *n.f.* carriage, coach, (railroad) car. **c. lètti,** sleeper. **c. ristorante,** diner.

carrozzèlla, *n.f.* baby-carriage, perambulator.

carrozzino, *n.m.* side-car.

carta, *n.f.* paper; card; chart; map; charter. **c. a carbone,** carbon paper. **c. assorbente,** blotter, blotting paper. **c. di crèdito,** credit card. **c. da léttere,** notepaper. **c. velina,** tissue-paper; onionskin. **c. da parati,** wallpaper. **c. intestata,** letterhead.

cartéggio, *n.m.* correspondence (mail).

cartèlla, *n.f.* portfolio; folder.

cartèllo, *n.m.* cartel; placard; poster, sign. **c. pubblicitàrio,** billboard.

cartièra, *n.f.* paper mill.

cartilàgine, *n.f.* cartilage, gristle.

cartina, *n.f.* map.

cartolaio, *n.m.* stationer.

cartolerìa, *n.f.* stationery store.

cartolina, *n.f.* postcard.

cartomante, *n.m.* or *f.* fortuneteller.

cartoncino, *n.m.* thin cardboard.

cartone, *n.m.* cardboard, pasteboard; cartoon (picture).

cartuccia, *n.f.* cartridge.

casa, *n.f.* house, home. **in c.,** indoors. **c. colònica,** farmhouse.

casacca, *n.f.* coat; shirt.

casàccio, *n.m.* **a c.,** haphazard, helter-skelter; at random.

casalingo, *adj.* home; homelike.

casamatta, *n.m.* bunker.

cascata, *n.f.* cascade, waterfall.

casèlla, *n.f.* pigeonhole; P.O. box.

casèrma, *n.f.* barracks.

casetta, *n.f.* cottage.

casimiro, *n.m.* cashmere.

casino, *n.m.* casino.

caso, *n.m.* case; happening; chance. **per c.,** by accident.

cassa, *n.f.* case; chest; box; cashier's office or desk. **c. da mòrto,** coffin. **c. di rispàrmio,** savings bank.

cassafòrte, *n.f.* strongbox; safe.

cassare, *vb.* overrule.

casseruòla, *n.f.* casserole.

cassetta, *n.f.* box; cassette.

cassettina, *n.f.* casket.

cassetto, *n.m.* drawer; till.

cassière, *n.m.* cashier; teller.

cassone, *n.m.* caisson.

casta, *n.f.* caste.

castagna, *n.f.* chestnut.

castagno, 1. *n.m.* chestnut tree. **2.** *adj.* tan.

castèllo, *n.m.* castle, château. **c. di prua,** forecastle.

castigare, *vb.* castigate, chastise, chasten.

castigo, *n.m.* chastisement.

castità, *n.f.* chastity.

casto, *adj.* chaste.

castòro, *n.m.* beaver.

castrare, *vb.* castrate, emasculate; geld.

castrone, *n.m.* gelding, wether.

casuale, *adj.* casual; perfunctory.

casualmente, *adv.* casually.

casùpola, *n.f.* hut.

cataclisma, *n.m.* cataclysm.

catacomba, *n.f.* catacomb.

catàlogo, *n.m.* catalogue.

catapulta, *n.f.* catapult.

catarro, *n.m.* catarrh; cold.

catarsi, *n.f.* catharsis.

catasta, *n.f.* heap, pile, stack.

catastale, *adj.* land office.

catasto, *n.m.* land office, real estate register.

catàstrofe, *n.f.* catastrophe.

catechismo, *n.m.* catechism.

catechizzare, *vb.* catechize.

categoria, *n.f.* category.

categòrico, *adj.* categorical.

catena, *n.f.* chain; range.

catenaccio, *n.m.* bolt.

cateratta, *n.f.* cataract; floodgate.

catetère, *n.m.* catheter.

catino, *n.m.* basin.

càtodo, *n.m.* cathode.

catòrcio, *n.m.* piece of junk.

catrame, *n.m.* tar.

càttedra, *n.f.* teacher's desk; professorship.

cattedrale, *n.f.* cathedral.

cattivèria, *n.f.* badness, mischief.

cattivo, *adj.* bad, evil; mischievous.

cattolicismo, *n.m.* Catholicism.

cattòlico, *adj.* Catholic.

cattura, *n.f.* capture.

catturare, *vb.* capture.

catturatore, *n.m.* capturer, captor.

caucciú, *n.m.* rubber.

càusa, *n.f.* cause; lawsuit; case. **a c. di,** because of.

causalità, *n.f.* causality, causation.

causare, *vb.* cause, bring about; encompass.

càustico, *adj.* caustic.

cautèla, *n.f.* caution.

cautèrio, *n.m.* cautery.

cauterizzare, *vb.* cauterize.

càuto, *adj.* cautious; gingerly.

cauzione, *n.f.* bail; security.

cava, *n.f.* quarry.

cavalcare, *vb.* ride (horseback).

cavalcata, *n.f.* cavalcade.

cavalcavìa, *n.m.* overpass.

cavalcioni, *adv.* **a c.** astride.

cavalière, *n.m.* knight, cavalier, horseman, rider.

cavalla, *n.f.* mare.

cavalleresco, *adj.* chivalric.

cavallerìa, *n.f.* cavalry; chivalry.

cavalletta, *n.f.* grasshopper.

cavalletto, *n.m.* easel.

cavallo, *n.m.* horse; (chess) knight. **c. a dòndolo,** rocking-horse; hobby-horse. **c. da guerra,** warhorse, charger. **c.-vapore,** horsepower.

cavatappi, *n.m.sg.* corkscrew.

cavèrna, *n.f.* cavern, cave.

cavezza, *n.f.* halter.

caviale, *n.m.* caviar.

cavìglia, *n.f.* ankle.

cavità, *n.f.* cavity; hole.

cavo, 1. *n.m.* hollow; cable. 2. *adj.* hollow.

cavolfiore, *n.m.* cauliflower.

càvolo, *n.m.* cabbage; kale.

cazzòtto, *n.m.* punch, sock.

cazzuòla, *n.f.* trowel.

cecchino, *n.m.* sniper.

cece, *n.m.* chickpea.

cecità, *n.f.* blindness.

cédere, *vb.* yield, cede, surrender, give in; back down; subside.

cèdola, *n.f.* coupon.

cèdro, *n.m.* cedar.

C.E., *acronym f.* (Comunità Europea), E.C.

cèffo, *n.m.* thug, snout. **brutto c.,** ugly mug.

ceffone, *n.m.* slap in the face.

celare, *vb.* conceal.

celebrante, *n.m.* celebrant.

celebrare, *vb.* celebrate.

celebrazione, *n.f.* celebration.

cèlebre, *adj.* celebrated, famous.

celebrità, *n.f.* celebrity.

celerità, *n.f.* speed, quickness, celerity.

celèste, *adj.* celestial.

cèlia, *n.f.* joke, banter, chaff.

celiare, *vb.* joke, banter, chaff.

celibato, *n.m.* celibacy.

cèlibe, *adj.* celibate; single, unmarried.

cèlla, *n.f.* cell.

cellòfane, *n.m.* cellophane.

cèllula, *n.f.* cell.

cellulare, *adj.* cellular.

cellulòide, *n.f.* celluloid.

cellulosa, *n.f.* cellulose.

cèltico, *adj.* Celtic.

cementare, *vb.* cement.

cemento, *n.m.* cement, concrete.

cena, *n.f.* supper.

cenàcolo, *n.m.* coterie; Last Supper.

céncio, *n.m.* rag.

cencioso, *adj.* ragged.
cénere, *n.f.* ashes.
cenno, *n.m.* sign, hint.
censimento, *n.m.* census.
censore, *n.m.* censor.
censòrio, *adj.* censorious.
censura, *n.f.* censure; censorship.
censurare, *vb.* censor.
centenàrio, *n.m. and adj.* centenary.
centennale, *n.m. and adj.* centennial.
centésimo, 1. *n.m.* cent; 100th part. **2.** *adj.* hundredth.
centigrado, *adj.* centigrade.
centinaio, *n.m.* group of 100.
cènto, *num.* hundred.
centrale, *adj.* central.
centralino, *n.m.* switchboard.
centralizzare, *vb.* centralize.
cèntro, *n.m.* center. **c. da tàvola,** centerpiece.
centrocampo, *n.m.* (soccer) midfield.
ceppi, *n.m.pl.* fetters.
ceppo, *n.m.* log, stump.
cera, *n.f.* wax; beeswax; mien.
ceralacca, *n.f.* sealing-wax.
ceràmica, *n.f.* ceramics.
ceràmico, *adj.* ceramic.
cercare, *vb.* seek, look for, hunt for.
cérchia, *n.f.* circle (of friends).
cérchio, *n.m.* circle; hoop; ring.
cereale, *n.m. and adj.* cereal.
cerebrale, *adj.* cerebral.
cèreo, *adj.* waxen; pale.
cerimònia, *n.f.* ceremony.
cerimoniale, *n.m.* ceremonial.
cerimonioso, *adj.* ceremonious.
cerino, *n.m.* wax match.
cernièra, *n.f.* hinge; clasp; zipper.
cèrnita, *n.f.* selection, choice; sorting.
cero, *n.m.* church candle.
certamente, *adv.* certainly.
certezza, *n.f.* certainty, certitude.
certificare, *vb.* certify.
certificato, *n.m.* certificate.
certificazione, *n.f.* certification.
cèrto, *adj.* certain, sure.
cèrva, *n.f.* doe; hind; roe.
cervèllo, *n.m.* brain.
cervellòtico, *adj.* preposterous, absurd; extravagant.

cervicale, *adj.* cervical.
cervice, *n.f.* cervix.
cèrvo, *n.m.* stag; deer.
cesellare, *vb.* chisel.
cesèllo, *n.m.* chisel.
cesòie, *n.f.pl.* shears.
cespùglio, *n.m.* bush.
cespuglioso, *adj.* bushy.
cessare, *vb.* cease, stop, quit.
cessazione, *n.f.* cessation.
cessione, *n.f.* cession.
cesta, *n.f.* basket; hamper.
cèto, *n.m.* class.
cetriòlo, *n.m.* cucumber.
che, 1. *pron.* who; which; what. **2.** *prep.* than. **3.** *conj.* that.
chè, *conj.* for, because; so that.
chemioterapìa, *n.f.* chemotherapy.
cherubino, *n.m.* cherub.
chi, *pron.* who; whom.
chiàcchiera, *n.f.* chatter, chat.
chiacchierare, *vb.* chatter, chat, gab.
chiacchierone, *n.m.* chatterbox.
chiamare, *vb.* call, summon.
chiamata, *n.f.* call, summons.
chiaramente, *adv.* clearly.
chiarezza, *n.f.* clarity, clearness.
chiarificare, *vb.* clarify.
chiarificazione, *n.f.* clarification.
chiarimento, *n.m.* enlightenment.
chiarina, *n.f.* clarion.
chiarire, *vb.* clear, clear up.
chiaro, *adj.* clear, bright, lucid, plain. **c. di luna,** mooonlight.
chiarore, *n.m.* brightness.
chiaroveggènte, *n. and adj.* clairvoyant; fortune-teller.
chiaroveggènza, *n.f.* clairvoyance.
chiasso, *n.m.* uproar, fuss, hullabaloo.
chiassoso, *adj.* uproarious; obstreperous.
chiatta, *n.f.* barge.
chiave, *n.f.* key; clef. **c. inglese,** wrench.
chiàvica, *n.f.* sewer.
chiavistèllo, *n.m.* bolt, lock.
chiazza, *n.f.* spot, blotch, mottle.
chicca, *n.f.* sweet, candy; (coll.) gossip.
chicchessìa, *pron. indef.* anybody, anyone.

chicco, *n.m.* grain; seed.
chièdere, *vb.* ask for, request, beg.
chièsa, *n.f.* church.
chìglia, *n.f.* keel.
chilociclo, *n.m.* kilocycle.
chilogramma, *n.m.* kilogram.
chilometràggio, *n.m.* distance in kilometers.
chilòmetro, *n.m.* kilometer.
chilowatt, *n.m.* kilowatt.
chìmica, *n.f.* chemistry.
chimicamente, *adv.* chemically.
chìmico, 1. *n.* chemist. **2.** *adj.* chemical.
chimono, *n.m.* kimono.
chinino, *n.m.* quinine.
chiocciare, *vb.* cluck.
chiòdo, *n.m.* nail; spike; clove.
chiòsa, *n.f.* gloss.
chiosare, *vb.* gloss.
chiòsco, *n.m.* kiosk.
chiòstro, *n.m.* cloister.
chirurgìa, *n.f.* surgery.
chirurgo, *n.m.* surgeon.
chitarra, *n.f.* guitar.
chiùdere, *vb.* close, shut. **c. a chiave,** lock.
chiunque, *pron.* whoever; whomever.
chiusa, *n.f.* lock.
chiusura, *n.f.* closure; fastening. **c. lampo,** zipper.
ci, *pron.* us; to us.
ci, *pro-phrase* (replaces phrases introduced by prepositions of place) here, there; to it; at it.
ciabattino, *n.m.* cobbler.
ciambellano, *n.m.* chamberlain.
cianfrusàglia, *n.f.* gimcrack; trash.
ciao, *interj.* hi!; so long!
ciarlare, *vb.* chatter, jabber, prattle.
ciarlatanismo, *n.m.* charlatanism.
ciarlatano, *n.m.* charlatan, mountebank.
ciarpame, *n.m.* junk.
ciascuno, *pron.* each one.
cibare, *vb. intr.* feed, nourish.
cibàrie, *n.f.pl.* food, groceries.
cibo, *n.m.* food.
cicala, *n.f.* cicada.
cicatrice, *n.f.* scar.

cicatrizzare, *vb.* scar.
cicca, *n.f.* butt.
cicchetto, *n.m.* nip, shot (of liquor); lecture.
cìccia, *n.f.* flesh, fat.
cicisbèo, *n.m.* gigolo.
ciclamato, *n.m.* cyclamate.
ciclista, *n.m. or f.* bicyclist.
ciclo, *n.m.* cycle.
ciclomotore, *n.m.* moped.
ciclone, *n.m.* cyclone.
ciclotrone, *n.m.* cyclotron.
cicogna, *n.f.* stork.
cicòria, *n.f.* chicory.
cicuta, *n.f.* hemlock.
ciecamente, *adv.* blindly.
cièco, *adj.* blind.
cièlo, *n.m.* heaven; sky.
cifra, *n.f.* cipher; figure.
cifràrio, *n.m.* code.
cìglio, *n.m.* eyelash, cilia.
cigno, *n.m.* swan.
cigolare, *vb.* creak, squeak.
cigolìo, *n.m.* squeak.
ciliare, *adj.* ciliary.
ciliègia, *n.f.* cherry.
ciliègio, *n.m.* cherry-tree.
cilìndrico, *adj.* cylindrical.
cilindro, *n.m.* cylinder.
cima, *n.f.* peak.
cimare, *vb.* clip, trim.
cìmbalo, *n.m.* gong.
cimèlio, *n.m.* relic, souvenir.
cìmice, *n.f.* bedbug.
ciminièra, *n.f.* smoke-stack; funnel.
cimitèro, *n.m.* cemetery; churchyard.
Cina, *n.f.* China.
cincona, *n.f.* cinchona.
cinèllo, *n.m.* cymbal.
cìnema, *n.m.* cinema, movies; (movie) theater.
cinematogràfico, *adj.* cinematic, of the movies.
cinematògrafo, *n.m.* cinema, movies; (movie) theater.
cinese, *adj.* Chinese.
cinètico, *adj.* kinetic.
cìngere, *vb.* gird.
cìnghia, *n.f.* strap.
cinguettare, *vb.* chirp.
cinguettìo, *n.m.* chirping.
cìnico, 1. cynic. **2.** *adj.* cynical.

ciniglia, *n.f.* chenille.
cinismo, *n.m.* cynicism.
cinofilo, *n.m.* dog lover.
cinquanta, *num.* fifty.
cinque, *num.* five.
cinta, *n.f.* fence, wall.
cintura, *n.f.* belt, girdle, sash; waist.
ciò, *pron.* this; that; it.
ciòcco, *n.m.* log.
cioccolato, *n.m.* chocolate.
cioè, *conj.* that is; namely.
ciòttolo, *n.m.* pebble, stone; cobblestone.
cipolla, *n.f.* onion; chive.
ciprèsso, *n.m.* cypress.
cipria, *n.f.* face-powder.
circo, *n.m.* circus.
circolare, 1. *n.m. and adj.* circular. **2.** *vb.* circulate.
circolatòrio, *adj.* circulatory.
circolazione, *n.f.* circulation; currency.
circolo, *n.m.* circle, club.
circoncìdere, *vb.* circumcise.
circoncisione, *n.f.* circumcision.
circondare, *vb.* surround, encompass.
circondàrio, *n.m.* district, surroundings, neighborhood.
circonferènza, *n.f.* circumference, girth.
circonlocuzione, *n.f.* circumlocution.
circoscrìvere, *vb.* circumscribe.
circonvenire, *vb.* circumvent.
circonvenzione, *n.f.* circumvention.
circospètto, *adj.* circumspect.
circostante, *adj.* surrounding, neighboring.
circostanza, *n.f.* circumstance.
circostanziale, *adj.* circumstantial.
circostanziatamente, *adv.* circumstantially.
circùito, *n.m.* circuit.
cirrìpede, *n.m.* barnacle.
cirròsi, *n.f.* cirrhosis.
ciste, *n.f.* cyst.
cistèrna, *n.f.* cistern.
citare, *vb.* cite; quote; summon.
citazione, *n.f.* citation; quotation; summons.
cìtrico, *adj.* citric.

citrullo, *n.m.* fool.
città, *n.f.* city, town. **c. universitària,** campus.
cittadella, *n.f.* citadel.
cittadina, *n.f.* woman citizen; small city.
cittadinanza, *n.f.* citizenship; citizenry.
cittadino, *n.m.* citizen.
ciucco, *n.m.* drunk.
ciuco, *n.m.* donkey.
ciuffo, *n.m.* tuft.
ciuffolòtto, *n.m.* bullfinch.
ciurma, *n.f.* crew; gang; mob.
civetta, *n.f.* owl; coquette, flirt.
civettare, *vb.* coquet, flirt.
civetteria, *n.f.* coquetry.
cìvico, *adj.* civic.
civile, 1. *n. and adj.* civilian. **2.** *adj.* civil; civilized.
civilizzare, *vb.* civilize.
civiltà, *n.f.* civilization; civility.
clàcson, *n.m.* klaxon; horn.
clamore, *n.m.* clamor.
clamoroso, *adj.* noisy, blatant, clamorous, obstreperous.
clan, *n.m.* clan, tribe.
clandestinamente, *adv.* clandestinely.
clandestino, *n.m. and adj.* clandestine, secret.
clangore, *n.m.* clangor.
claretto, *n.m.* claret.
clarinettista, *n.m.* clarinetist.
clarinetto, *n.m.* clarinet.
classe, *n.f.* class.
classicismo, *n.m.* classicism.
clàssico, *adj.* classic; classical.
classificàbile, *adj.* classifiable.
classificare, *vb.* classify, class; grade.
classificazione, *n.f.* classification.
claudicante, *n.m. and adj.* limping, lame.
clàusola, *n.f.* clause.
claustrofobìa, *n.f.* claustrophobia.
clausura, *n.f.* seclusion.
clava, *n.f.* cudgel, nightstick.
clavicémbalo, *n.m.* harpsichord.
clavìcola, *n.f.* collarbone.
clemènte, *adj.* lenient.
clemènza, *n.f.* clemency.
cleptòmane, *n.m.* kleptomaniac.

cleptomanìa, *n.f.* kleptomania.

clericale, *adj.* clerical.

clericalismo, *n.m.* clericalism.

clèro, *n.m.* clergy.

clessìdra, *n.f.* sandglass; water clock.

cliènte, *n.m.* client, customer; guest.

clientèla, *n.f.* clientele.

clima, *n.m.* climate.

climàtico, *adj.* climatic.

clìnica, *n.f.* clinic.

clinicamente, *adv.* clinically.

clìnico, *adj.* clinical.

clistère, *n.m.* enema.

cloaca, *n.f.* sewer.

clorìdrico, *adj.* hydrochloric.

clòro, *n.m.* chlorine.

clorofìlla, *n.f.* chlorophyll.

cloroformìo, *n.m.* chloroform.

cloruro, *n.m.* chloride.

coabitare, *vb.* live together.

coagulare, *vb.* coagulate.

coagulazione, *n.f.* coagulation.

coalizione, *n.f.* coalition.

coalizzarsi, *vb.* coalesce.

cobalto, *n.m.* cobalt.

còbra, *n.m.* cobra.

cocaìna, *n.f.* cocaine.

cocainòmane, *n.m.* cocaine addict.

coccarda, *n.f.* cockade; bow.

cocchière, *n.m.* coachman.

còcchio, *n.m.* coach.

coccinèlla, *n.f.* ladybug.

còcco, *n.m.* coconut tree.

coccodrìllo, *n.m.* crocodile.

coda, *n.f.* tail.

codardìa, *n.f.* cowardice.

codardo, 1. *n.m.* coward. **2.** *adj.* cowardly, craven.

codeìna, *n.f.* codeine.

còdice, *n.m.* codex; code. **c. (di avviamento) postale,** zip code.

codificare, *vb.* codify.

coeguale, *adj.* coequal.

coercitìvo, *adj.* coercive, compulsive.

coercizione, *n.f.* coercion, duress.

coerènte, *adj.* coherent, consistent.

coesione, *n.f.* cohesion.

coesistenza, *n.f.* coexistence.

coesìstere, *vb.* coexist.

coesìvo, *adj.* cohesive.

còfano, *n.m.* coffer; (auto) hood; (*Brit.*) bonnet.

còffa, *n.f.* crow's-nest.

cogitare, *vb.* cogitate.

cògliere, *vb.* pick, pluck, gather, cull.

cognata, *n.f.* sister-in-law.

cognato, *n.m.* brother-in-law.

cognizione, *n.f.* cognition, knowledge.

cognome, *n.m.* family name, surname.

coibènte, *adj.* nonconducting.

coincidènte, *adj.* coincident; co-incidental.

coincidènza, *n.f.* coincidence; (transport) connection.

coincìdere, *vb.* coincide; connect.

coinquilino, *n.m.* co-tenant, one who lives in the same building.

coinvòlgere, *vb.* involve.

colare, *vb.* strain.

colatòio, *n.m.* colander.

colazione, *n.f.* light meal; lunch. **prima c.,** breakfast.

colèi, *pron. dem. f. sg.* that one; that woman, she.

colèra, *n.f.* cholera.

colino, *n.m.* strainer.

còlla, *n.f.* glue, paste.

collaborare, *vb.* collaborate.

collaboratore, *n.m.* collaborator.

collaborazione, *n.f.* collaboration.

collaborazionista, *n.f.* collaborationist.

collana, *n.f.* necklace.

collant, *n.m.* panty hose.

collante, *n.m.* adhesive.

collare, 1. *n.m.* collar. **2.** *vb.* glue.

collasso, *n.m.* collapse.

collaterale, *n.m. and adj.* collateral.

collaudare, *vb.* test.

collaudatore, *n.m.* tester, inspector.

collàudo, *n.m.* test.

collazionare, *vb.* collate.

collèga, *n.m.* colleague.

collegamento, *n.m.* connection, liaison.

collegare, *vb.* connect, link.

còlle, *n.m.* hill.

Còlle, il C., *n.m.* the residence of the President.

còllera, *n.f.* choler, anger, wrath.
collèrico, *adj.* choleric.
collettivamente, *adv.* collectively, jointly.
collettivo, *adj.* collective, joint.
colletto, *n.m.* collar.
collezione, *n.f.* collection.
collezionista, *n.m.* collector.
collina, *n.f.* hill.
còllo, *n.m.* neck; package.
collocare, *vb.* locate; place.
colloquiale, *adj.* colloquial.
colloquialismo, *n.m.* colloquialism.
colloquialmente, *adv.* colloquially.
collòquio, *n.m.* colloquy; interview.
collusione, *n.f.* collusion.
colmare, *vb.* fill.
colombo, *n.m.* dove.
colònia, *n.f.* colony, settlement.
Colònia, *n.f.* Cologne.
coloniale, *adj.* colonial.
colonizzare, *vb.* colonize.
colonizzazione, *n.f.* colonization.
colonna, *n.f.* column; *(typogr.)* galley.
colonnato, *n.m.* colonnade.
colonnèllo, *n.m.* colonel.
colòno, *n.m.* colonist, settler; farmer.
colorare, *vb.* stain.
colorazione, *n.f.* coloration.
colore, *n.m.* color, hue; paint; stain; suit. **di c.,** colored.
colorificio, *n.m.* paint factory, dye factory.
colorire, *vb.* color.
colorito, *n.m.* coloring, complexion.
coloritura, *n.f.* coloring.
coloro, *pron. dem. m. f. pl.* those, those men, those women, they.
colossale, *adj.* colossal.
Colossèo, *n.m.* Coliseum.
colpa, *n.f.* fault, guilt.
colpetto, *n.m.* little blow, tap.
colpévole, 1. *n.m.* culprit. **2.** *adj.* guilty, culpable.
colpevolmente, *adv.* guiltily.
colpire, *vb.* hit, strike, rap, smite.
colpito, *adj.* stricken.
colpo, *n.m.* blow; stroke; clout, hit, rap; shot.

colposo, *adj.* unpremeditated.
coltèllo, *n.m.* knife. **c. a serramànico,** jack-knife.
coltivare, *vb.* cultivate, till; grow, raise.
coltivatore, *n.m.* cultivator.
coltivazione, *n.f.* cultivation.
colto, *adj.* cultured, cultivated, educated.
coltre, *n.f.* blanket, layer.
coltrone, *n.m.* quilt.
coltura, *n.f.* cultivation.
còma, *n.m.* coma.
colui, *pron. dem. m. sg.* that one, that man, he.
comandamento, *n.m.* commandment.
comandante, *n.m.* commander.
comandare, *vb.* command, order, bid.
comando, *n.m.* command.
comare, *n.f.* godmother.
combaciare, *vb.* match, fit closely together, coincide.
combattènte, *n.m.* combatant, fighter.
combàttere, *vb.* combat, fight, battle.
combattimento, *n.m.* combat, fight, fray.
combinare, *vb.* combine.
combinazione, *n.f.* combination; union suit.
combrìccola, *n.f.* coterie.
combustìbile, 1. *n.m.* fuel. **2.** *adj.* combustible.
combustione, *n.f.* combustion.
come, 1. *adv.* how. **2.** *prep. and conj.* like; as.
cometa, *n.f.* comet.
còmico, 1. *n.m.* comedian. **2.** *adj.* comic, comical, funny.
comìgnolo, *n.m.* chimney pot.
cominciamento, *n.m.* beginning; commencement.
cominciare, *vb.* begin, commence, start.
comitato, *n.m.* committee, board, commission.
commèdia, *n.f.* comedy.
commemorare, *vb.* commemorate.
commemorativo, *adj.* commemorative, memorial.

commemorazione, *n.f.* commemoration.

commentare, *vb.* comment.

commento, *n.m.* comment; commentary.

commerciale, *adj.* commercial.

commercialismo, *n.m.* commercialism.

commercializzare, *vb.* commercialize.

commercialmente, *adv.* commercially.

commerciante, *n.m.* business man, merchant, trader.

commerciare, *vb.* trade.

commèrcio, *n.m.* commerce, trade.

commesso, *n.m.* salesman. **c. viaggiatore,** travelling salesman.

commestìbile, *adj.* edible.

comméttere, *vb.* commit.

commiato, *n.m.* leave.

commilitone, *n.m.* comrade in arms.

comminare, *vb.* fix (a penalty).

commiserare, *vb.* commiserate.

commisurato, *adj.* commensurate.

commissariato, *n.m.* commissary.

commissàrio, *n.m.* commissioner.

commissione, *n.f.* commission; committee; errand.

committente, *n.m. and f.* buyer, purchaser.

commòsso, *adj.* moved; deeply felt.

commovènte, *adj.* moving; affecting; touching.

commozione, *n.f.* commotion, stir.

commuòvere, *vb.* move; affect; touch (emotionally).

commutare, *vb.* switch, commute.

commutazione, *n.f.* commutation.

comodamente, *adv.* comfortably.

comodino, *n.m.* night table.

còmodo, 1. *n.m.* ease; leisure. **2.** *adj.* comfortable; leisurely; snug.

compaesano, *n.m.* compatriot.

compàgine, *n.f.* structure; strict union, connection.

compagna, *n.f.* companion.

compagnìa, *n.f.* company, companionship.

compagno, *n.m.* companion; mate; partner.

companàtico, *n.m.* food (generic); food to eat with bread.

comparàbile, *adj.* comparable.

comparare, *vb.* compare.

comparativamente, *adv.* comparatively.

comparativo, *adj.* comparative.

compare, *n.m.* godfather; crony.

comparire, *vb.* appear.

compassione, *n.f.* compassion.

compassionévole, *adj.* compassionate.

compassionevolmente, *adv.* compassionately.

compasso, *n.m.* compass.

compatìbile, *adj.* compatible.

compatriòta, *n.m.* compatriot, fellow-countryman.

compattezza, *n.f.* compactness.

compatto, *adj.* compact.

compensare, *vb.* compensate.

compensativo, *adj.* compensatory.

compensazione, *n.f.* compensation. **stanza di c.,** clearing-house.

compènso, *n.m.* compensation.

comperare, *vb.* buy, purchase.

competènte, *adj.* competent, (law) cognizant.

competentemente, *adv.* competently.

competènza, *n.f.* competence, fitness, (legal) cognizance.

compètere, *vb.* compete; be within the province of.

competitivo, *adj.* competitive.

competizione, *n.f.* competition.

compiacènza, *n.f.* complaisance, kindness.

compilare, *vb.* compile.

compilatore, *n.m.* compiler.

compimento, *n.m.* completion, achievement, accomplishment.

compire, *vb.* complete, finish, accomplish, achieve.

compito, *adj.* accomplished.

cómpito, *n.m.* task, assignment.

compleanno, *n.m.* birthday.

complemento, *n.m.* complement.

complessità, *n.f.* complexity.

complesso, *n.m.* and *adj.* complex, complicated.

completamente, *adv.* completely; altogether; outright; wholly; quite; throughout; utterly.

completamento, *n.m.* completion.

completare, *vb.* complete.

completezza, *n.f.* completeness.

complèto, *adj.* complete; thorough; utter.

complicare, *vb.* complicate.

complicato, *adj.* complicated, involved, intricate.

complicazione, *n.f.* complication; intricacy.

còmplice, *n.m.* and *f.* accomplice.

complicità, *n.f.* complicity.

complimentare, *vb.* compliment.

complimento, *n.m.* compliment.

complòtto, *n.m.* plot.

componènte, *n.m.* and *adj.* component.

comporre, *vb.* compose.

comportamento, *n.m.* behavior.

comportare, *vb.* entail, involve; *(refl.)* behave, act.

compòsito, *adj.* composite, compound.

compositore, *n.m.* composer.

composizione, *n.f.* composition.

compostezza, *n.f.* composure.

composto, 1. *n.m.* compound. 2. *adj.* composed; compound; composite.

compra, *n.f.* purchase.

comprare, *vb.* buy; purchase.

compratore, *n.m.* buyer, purchaser.

compravéndita, *n.f.* transaction.

compréndere, *vb.* comprehend; comprise.

comprensìbile, *adj.* comprehensible.

comprensione, *n.f.* comprehension, understanding.

comprensivo, *adj.* comprehensive.

compreso, *adj.* comprised; including.

comprèssa, *n.f.* compress; (med.) tablet.

compressione, *n.f.* compression.

comprèsso, *adj.* compressed.

compressore, *n.m.* compressor.

comprimàrio, *n.m.* associate chief of staff.

comprìmere, *vb.* compress.

compromesso, *n.m.* compromise.

comprométtere, *vb.* compromise, endanger.

compropriètà, *n.f.* joint ownership.

comprovare, *vb.* prove.

compunto, *adj.* contrite, remorseful, repentant.

compunzione, *n.f.* compunction.

computare, *vb.* compute.

computazione, *n.f.* computation.

comunale, *adj.* communal.

comune, *adj.* common.

comunella, *n.f.* master-key.

comunemente, *adv.* commonly.

comunicàbile, *adj.* communicable.

comunicante, *n.m.* communicant.

comunicare, *vb.* communicate; *(refl.)* take communion.

comunicativo, *adj.* communicative.

comunicato, *n.m.* communiqué.

comunicazione, *n.f.* communication.

comunione, *n.f.* communion.

comunismo, *n.m.* communism.

comunista, *adj.* and *n.m.* or *f.* communist.

comunità, *n.f.* community.

comunque, *adv.* however; howsoever.

con, *prep.* with.

conca, *n.f.* washbowl, basin, tub.

concavo, *adj.* concave.

concèdere, *vb.* grant, concede, allow.

concentramento, *n.m.* gathering.

concentrare, *vb.* concentrate.

concentrato, 1. *adj.* concentrated. 2. *n.m.* tomato paste.

concentrazione, *n.f.* concentration.

concepìbile, *adj.* conceivable.

concepibilmente, *adv.* conceivably.

concepire, vb. conceive.
concèrnere, vb. concern.
concertare, vb. concert.
concertista, n.m. and f. concert performer.
concèrto, n.m. concert; concerto.
concessionàrio, n.m. agent, dealer.
concessione, n.f. concession; grant, bestowal.
concètto, n.m. concept.
concettuale, adj. conceptual.
concezione, n.f. conception, idea.
conchìglia, n.f. conch-shell.
conciare, vb. tan.
conciliàbolo, n.m. secret meeting.
conciliare, vb. conciliate.
conciliativo, adj. conciliatory.
conciliatore, n.m. conciliator.
conciliazione, n.f. conciliation.
concimare, vb. manure.
concime, n.m. compost, manure.
concisamente, adv. concisely.
concisione, n.f. concision, conciseness.
conciso, adj. concise.
concitare, vb. excite, rouse.
conclave, n.m. conclave.
conclùdere, vb. conclude.
conclusione, n.f. conclusion.
conclusivamente, adv. conclusively.
conclusivo, adj. conclusive.
concomitante, adj. concomitant.
concordare, vb. agree.
concordato, n.m. concordat.
concòrde, adj. concordant, agreeing.
concorrènte, n.m. or f. competitor; (sports) entrant.
concorrènza, n.f. concurrence; competition.
concórrere, vb. compete; concur.
concorso, n.m. competition; tournament; contribution; concurrence; rush (of people).
concozione, n.f. concoction.
concretamente, adv. concretely.
concretezza, n.f. concreteness.
concrèto, adj. concrete.
concubina, n.f. concubine.
concuòcere, vb. concoct.
concupire, vb. covet.
concupiscènte, adj. lustful.
concupiscènza, n.f. lust.

concussione, n.f. concussion.
condanna, n.f. condemnation; doom; conviction; sentence.
condannàbile, adj. condemnable.
condannare, vb. condemn, doom; sentence.
condannato, n.m. convict.
condensare, vb. condense; thicken.
condensatore, n.m. condenser.
condensazione, n.f. condensation.
condimento, n.m. condiment, seasoning; dressing; relish.
condire, vb. season, use condiments.
condividere, vb. share.
condizionale, adj. conditional.
condizionalmente, adv. conditionally.
condizionare, vb. condition.
condizione, n.f. condition; status.
condoglianza, n.f. condolence.
condolere, vb. condole.
condomìnio, n.m. condominium.
condonare, vb. condone.
condotta, n.f. conduct, behavior; bearing; deportment.
condotto, n.m. conduct.
conducènte, n.m. driver.
condurre, vb. conduct, lead, guide; drive (a car); (refl.) behave.
conduttività, n.f. conductivity.
conduttivo, adj. conductive.
conduttore, n.m. conductor.
conduttura, n.f. flue.
confederarsi, vb. confederate.
confederato, n.m. confederate.
confederazione, n.f. confederation, confederacy.
conferènza, n.f. conference; lecture.
conferenzière, n.m. lecturer.
conferire, vb. confer, bestow.
conferma, n.f. confirmation.
confermare, vb. confirm.
confessare, vb. confess, admit; avow.
confessionale, n.m. and adj. confessional.
confessione, n.f. confession, admission, avowal.
confessore, n.m. confessor.

confetterìa, *n.f.* confectionery, confectioner's shop.

confettière, *n.m.* confectioner.

confètto, *n.m.* candy; confection.

confettura, *n.f.* candy; confection.

confezione, *n.f.* ready-to-wear dress.

confidare, *vb.* confide, entrust; rely.

confidènte, 1. *n.m. or f.* confidant. **2.** *adj.* confident.

confidentemente, *adv.* confidently.

confidènza, *n.f.* confidence.

confidenziale, *adj.* confidential.

confinare, *vb.* abut; border; confine; verge.

confine, *n.m.* boundary, border.

confisca, *n.f.* confiscation.

confiscare, *vb.* confiscate.

conflagrazione, *n.f.* conflagration.

conflitto, *n.m.* conflict, strife.

confóndere, *vb.* confuse, confound, addle, bewilder, befuddle.

conformarsi, *vb.* conform.

conformazione, *n.f.* conformation.

conforme, *adj.* in accordance, in conformity.

conformemente, *adv.* accordingly, in conformity.

conformista, *n.m.* conformer, conformist.

conformità, *n.f.* conformity, accordance.

confortare, *vb.* comfort; encourage.

confortatore, *n.m.* comforter.

confòrto, *n.m.* comfort; encouragement.

confrontare, *vb.* compare; confront.

confronto, *n.m.* comparison; collation.

confusione, *n.f.* confusion, blur, mix-up, turmoil.

confuso, *adj.* confused, addled, bewildered.

confutare, *vb.* disprove, refute.

confutazione, *n.f.* disproof, refutation; rebuttal.

congedare, *vb.* dismiss.

congedo, *n.m.* dismissal; leave.

congegno, *n.m.* contrivance, device, contraption, gadget; gearing.

congelamento, *n.m.* congealment; freezing; frostbite.

congelare, *vb.* congeal, freeze.

congelatore, *n.m.* freezer.

congenitamente, *adv.* congenitally.

congènito, *adj.* congenital.

congestione, *n.f.* congestion.

congettura, *n.f.* conjecture, surmise.

congetturare, *vb.* conjecture, surmise.

congiùngere, *vb.* join, splice.

congiuntamente, *adv.* conjointly.

congiuntivite, *n.f.* conjunctivitis.

congiuntivo, 1. *n.m.* (*gram.*) subjunctive. **2.** *adj.* (verbs) subjunctive; (pronouns) conjunctive.

congiunto, *adj.* joint.

congiunzione, *n.f.* conjunction; join.

congiura, *n.f.* conspiracy.

congiurare, *vb.* conspire.

congiurato, *n.m.* conspirator.

conglomerare, *vb.* conglomerate.

conglomerato, *n.m. and adj.* conglomerate.

conglomerazione, *n.f.* conglomeration.

congratularsi con, *vb.* congratulate.

congratulatòrio, *adj.* congratulatory.

congregarsi, *vb.* congregate.

congregazione, *n.f.* congregation.

congrèsso, *n.m.* congress; convention.

coniare, *vb.* coin, mint.

cònico, *adj.* conic.

coniglièra, *n.f.* hutch.

coniglietto, *n.m.* little rabbit, bunny.

coniglio, *n.m.* rabbit.

cònio, *n.m.* coinage.

coniugale, *adj.* conjugal.

coniugare, *vb.* conjugate.

coniugazione, *n.f.* conjugation.

connessione, *n.f.* connection.

connèsso, *adj.* related.

connèttere, *vb.* connect.

connivènte, *adj.* conniving.

connivènza, *n.f.* connivance.
connotare, *vb.* connote.
connotazione, *n.f.* connotation.
connubiale, *adj.* connubial.
còno, *n.m.* cone.
conoscènza, *n.f.* acquaintance, knowledge, cognizance.
conóscere, *vb.* know, be acquainted with.
conoscitore, *n.m.* connoisseur.
conosciuto, *adj.* known, acquainted.
conquista, *n.f.* conquest.
conquistàbile, *adj.* conquerable.
conquistare, *vb.* conquer.
conquistatore, *n.m.* conqueror.
consacrare, *vb.* consecrate.
consacrazione, *n.f.* consecration.
consapévole, *adj.* conscious, aware.
consciamente, *adv.* consciously.
cònscio, *adj.* conscious, aware.
consecutivamente, *adv.* consecutively.
consecutivo, *adv.* consecutive.
consegna, *n.f.* consignment, delivery.
consegnare, *vb.* consign, deliver.
consènso, *n.m.* concurrence, agreement, assent, consent; consensus.
consentire, *vb.* consent, accede.
conseguènte, *adj.* consequent.
conseguentemente, *adv.* consequently.
conseguènza, *n.f.* consequence.
conseguenziale, *adj.* consequential.
consèrva, *n.f.* jam, preserves; compote.
conservare, *vb.* conserve, keep, preserve, retain, store.
conservativo, *adj.* preservative.
conservatore, *n.m. and adj.* conservative.
conservatòrio, *n.m.* conservatory.
conservazione, *n.f.* conservation, preservation.
consideràbile, *adj.* considerable.
considerabilmente, *adv.* considerably.
considerare, *vb.* consider.
considerazione, *n.f.* consideration.

considerévole, *adj.* considerable.
consigliare, *vb.* advise, counsel.
consigliatamente, *adv.* advisedly.
consigliatore, *n.m.* adviser.
consiglière, *n.m.* councilor, counselor.
consiglio, *n.m.* advice, counsel; council; board.
consistènza, *n.f.* consistency.
consistere, *vb.* consist.
consolare, *adj.* consular.
consolare, *vb.* console, comfort, solace.
consolato, *n.m.* consulate; consulship.
consolatore, *n.m.* consoler, comforter.
consolazione, *n.f.* consolation, solace.
cònsole, *n.m.* consul.
consolidare, *vb.* consolidate.
cònsolida reale, *n.f.* larkspur.
consonante, *n.f. and adj.* consonant.
consòrte, *n.m. and f.* consort, mate.
consòrzio, *n.m.* syndicate; trust.
consòrzio automobilìstico, *n.m.* car pool.
constare, *vb.* consist of, be composed of.
constatare, *vb.* verify; observe; remark.
consuèto, *adj.* customary.
consuetùdine, *n.f.* custom.
consulènte, *n.m. and f.* adviser, expert.
consulènza, *n.f.* expert advice.
consultare, *vb.* consult.
consultatore, *n.m.* consultant.
consultazione, *n.f.* consultation.
consulto, *n.m.* consultation.
consumare, *vb.* consume; expend, wear out.
consumato, *adj.* worn out; experienced; consummate.
consumatore, *n.m.* consumer.
consumazione, *n.f.* consummation.
consumismo, *n.m.* consumerism.
consumo, *n.m.* consumption; wear.

consuntivo, 1. *adj.* final, end-of-year (*e.g.*, report). **2.** *n.m.* balance sheet.

contàbile, *n.m.* bookkeeper.

contabilità, *n.f.* accounting, bookkeeping.

contachilòmetri, *n.m.* odometer, speedometer.

contadino, 1. *n.m.* peasant; countryman; farmer. **2.** *adj.* peasant; rustic.

contàgio, *n.m.* contagion.

contagioso, *adj.* contagious.

contagocce, *n.m.* dropper.

contaminare, *vb.* contaminate; pollute.

contaminazione, *n.f.* contamination; infection.

contanti, *n.m.pl.* cash.

contare, *vb.* count; **c. su** count on, rely on.

contatore, *n.m.* meter.

contattare, *vb.* contact.

contatto, *n.m.* contact.

conte, *n.m.* count, earl.

contèa, *n.f.* county.

contegno, *n.m.* reserved attitude, reserved behavior.

contemplare, *vb.* contemplate.

contemplativo, *adj.* contemplative.

contemplazione, *n.f.* contemplation.

contemporàneo, *adj.* contemporary.

contendènte, *n.m.* contender.

contèndere, *vb.* contend, quarrel.

contenere, *vb.* contain.

contentezza, *n.f.* contentment, gladness.

contènto, *adj.* glad, happy, content.

contenzione, *n.f.* contention.

contesa, *n.f.* contest.

contessa, *n.f.* countess.

contestàbile, *adj.* contestable.

contestare, *vb.* contest.

contestazione, *n.f.* dispute, disagreement; notification.

contesto, *n.m.* context.

contìguo, *adj.* contiguous.

continentale, *adj.* continental.

continènte, 1. *n.m.* continent. **2.** *adj.* continent, chaste.

continènza, *n.f.* continence.

contingènte, *adj.* contingent.

contingènza, *n.f.* contingency.

continuamente, *adv.* continually.

continuare, *vb.* continue.

continuazione, *n.f.* continuation.

continuità, *n.f.* continuity.

contìnuo, *adj.* continual, continuous. **corrènte contìnua,** direct current.

conto, *n.m.* account; bill; check; count. **rèndere c. di,** account for. **rèndersi c. di,** realize.

contòrcere, *vb.* contort; (*refl.*) writhe.

contorno, *n.m.* contour; side-dish.

contorsione, *n.f.* contortion.

contorsionista, *n.m.* contortionist.

contorto, *adj.* contorted, twisted.

contrabbandare, *vb.* smuggle.

contrabbandière, *n.m.* smuggler.

contrabbando, *n.m.* contraband, smuggling.

contrabbasso, *n.m.* contrabass.

contraccolpo, *n.m.* rebound; repercussion; recoil.

contraddicìbile, *adj.* contradictable.

contraddire, *vb.* contradict, gainsay.

contraddistìnguere, *vb.* qualify, characterize, earmark.

contraddittòrio, *adj.* contradictory.

contraddizione, *n.f.* contradiction.

contraffare, *vb.* counterfeit; forge; imitate; impersonate.

contraffattore, *n.m.* forger; impersonator.

contraffazione, *n.f.* forgery; impersonation.

contraffòrte, *n.m.* buttress.

contralto, *n.m.* contralto; alto.

contrappeso, *n.m.* counterbalance.

contrariare, *vb.* spite.

contràrio, *adj.* contrary; reverse.

contrarre, *vb.* contract; (*refl.*) shrink.

contrastare, *vb.* contrast.

contrasto, *n.m.* contrast.

contrattacco, *n.m.* counter-attack.

contrattatore, *n.m.* contractor.

contratto, *n.m.* contract.

contravvenire, *vb.* infringe upon, transgress.

contravventore, *n.m.* violator.

contravvenzione, *n.f.* misdemeanor, violation, summons.

contrazione, *n.f.* contraction.

contribuènte, *n.m.* taxpayer.

contribuire, *vb.* contribute.

contributivo, *adj.* contributive.

contributo, *n.m.* contribution.

contributore, *n.m.* contributor.

contributòrio, *adj.* contributory.

contribuzione, *n.f.* contribution.

contrito, *adj.* contrite.

contrizione, *n.f.* contrition.

contro, *prep.* against, versus. c. assegno, C.O.D.

controazione, *n.f.* counteraction.

controbàttere, *vb.* counterattack; rebut, dispute.

controcorrènte, *adv.* upstream.

controcurva, *n.f.* reverse curve.

controffensiva, *n.f.* counteroffensive.

controfigura, *n.f.* stuntman, stand-in.

controllàbile, *adj.* controllable.

controllare, *vb.* check; inspect; audit.

controllo, *n.m.* check; restraint; inspection; audit.

controllo delle nàscite, *n.m.* birth control, contraception.

controllore, *n.m.* controller; inspector; auditor; ticket-collector.

controluce, 1. *adv.* against the light. 2. *n.f.* back lighting.

contromandare, *vb.* countermand.

contromano, *adv.* against traffic.

contromarca, *n.f.* check.

controparte, *n.f.* opponent.

contropartita, *n.f.* counterpart.

contropelo, *adv.* against the grain; close (shave).

Controriforma, *n.f.* Counter-Reformation.

controspionàggio, *n.m.* counterespionage.

controvèrsia, *n.f.* controversy.

controvèrso, *adj.* controversial.

contumace, *adj.* defaulting.

contumàcia, *n.f.* default.

contusione, *n.f.* contusion.

convalescènte, *adj.* convalescent.

convalescènza, *n.f.* convalescence.

conveniènte, *adj.* convenient; advisable; suitable, fitting.

convenientemente, *adv.* conveniently.

conveniènza, *n.f.* convenience; advisability; suitability; propriety.

convenire, *vb.* come together, convene; be suitable; become; befit.

convènto, *n.m.* convent; monastery.

convenzionale, *adj.* conventional.

convenzionalmente, *adv.* conventionally.

convenzione, *n.f.* convention; covenant.

convergènte, *adj.* convergent.

convergènza, *n.f.* convergence.

convèrgere, *vb.* converge.

conversare, *vb.* converse.

conversatore, *n.m.* conversationalist.

convèrso, *adj.* converse.

convertìbile, *adj.* convertible.

convertire, *vb.* convey.

convertitore, *n.m.* converter.

convertitore, *n.m.* converter.

convertitrice, *n.f.* converter.

convèsso, *adj.* convex.

convincènte, *adj.* convincing, cogent.

convìncere, *vb.* convince.

convincimento, *n.m.* persuasion, belief.

convinzione, *n.f.* conviction.

convitato, *adj. and n.m.* invited guest.

convivènte, *n.m. and f.* roommate.

conviviale, *adj.* convivial.

convocare, *vb.* convoke.

convocazione, *n.f.* convocation.

convogliare, *vb.* convoy.

convòglio, *n.m.* convoy, train, procession.

convulsione, *n.f.* convulsion.

convulsivo, *adj.* convulsive.

cooperare, vb. cooperate.
cooperativa, n.f. cooperative.
cooperativamente, adv. cooperatively.
cooperativo, adj. cooperative.
cooperazione, n.f. cooperation.
coordinare, vb. coordinate.
coordinatore, n.m. coordinator.
coordinazione, n.f. coordination.
coòrte, n.m. cohort.
copèrchio, n.m. lid.
copèrta, n.f. cover, blanket.
copertina, n.f. cover (of book).
copertone, n.m. tire casing; tarpaulin.
copertura, n.f. cover, covering.
còpia, n.f. copy; copiousness.
copiare, vb. copy.
copiativo, adj. copying; indelible.
copiatore, n.m. copier.
copiosamente, adv. copiously.
copiosità, n.f. copiousness.
copioso, adj. copious.
copista, n.m. copyist.
coppa, n.f. cup, mug, flagon, goblet.
cóppia, n.f. couple.
coprifuòco, n.m. curfew.
coprire, vb. cover.
coraggio, n.m. courage, bravery; gameness; gallantry; mettle.
coraggiosamente, adv. courageously, gamely, gallantly.
coraggioso, adj. brave, courageous; game; gallant.
corale, adj. choral.
corallino, adj. coral.
corallo, n.m. coral.
Corano, n.m. Koran.
corazza, n.f. armorplate, breastplate; shell.
còrda, n.f. string, rope, cord; chord.
cordiale, n.m. and adj. cordial, hearty.
cordialità, n.f. cordiality.
cordialmente, adv. cordially.
cordiglièra, n.f. ladder; run.
cordòglio, n.m. affliction, sorrow, grief.
cordone, n.m. cordon.
cordovano, n.m. cordovan.
Corèa, n.m. Korea.
coreggiato, n.m. flail.
coreografia, n.f. choreography.

coreògrafo, n.m. choreographer.
coriàceo, adj. coriaceous, tough.
coriàndoli, n.m.pl. confetti.
coricare, vb. lay down, bed down.
corista, n.m. chorister.
cormorano, n.m. cormorant.
cornamusa, n.f. bagpipe.
còrnea, n.f. cornea.
cornetta, n.f. cornet.
cornettista, n.m. cornetist.
cornice, n.m. frame, mantel.
cornicione, n.m. cornice.
còrno, n.m. horn.
cornucòpia, n.m. or f. cornucopia.
còro, n.m. chorus, choir; chancel.
corollàrio, n.m. corollary.
corona, n.f. crown. **c. nobiliare,** coronet.
coronàrio, adj. coronary.
còrpo, n.m. body; corps.
corporale, adj. corporal.
corporato, adj. corporate.
corporazione, n.f. corporation; guild.
corpòreo, adj. corporeal, bodily.
corpulènto, adj. corpulent, burly, portly.
corpùscolo, n.m. corpuscle.
corredare, vb. equip, outfit; provide.
corredino, n.m. layette, baby's outfits.
corrèdo, n.m. equipment, outfit.
corrèggere, vb. correct, amend, right.
correità, n.f. complicity.
correlare, vb. correlate.
correlazione, n.f. correlation.
corrènte, 1. n.f. current; stream. **c. alternata,** alternating current. **c. continua,** direct current. **c. d'ària,** draft. **2.** adj. current: (in dates) instant.
correntemente, adv. currently.
correntista, n.m. depositor.
córrere, vb. run; race.
corresponsàbile, 1. adj. jointly responsible. **2.** n.m. accomplice, co-respondent.
correttamente, adv. correctly.
correttezza, n.f. correctness.
correttivo, adj. corrective.
corrètto, adj. correct, right.
correzione, n.f. correction.

còrricòrri, *n.m.* rush.

corridoio, *n.m.* corridor, hallway; lobby.

corridore, *n.m.* runner.

corriera, *n.f.* bus.

corrière, *n.m.* courier.

corrispondènte, 1. *n.* correspondent. 2. *adj.* corresponding; correspondent.

corrispondènza, *n.f.* correspondence.

corrispóndere, *vb.* correspond.

corroborante, *adj.* corroborating.

corroborare, *vb.* corroborate.

corroborativo, *adj.* corroborative.

corroborazione, *n.f.* corroboration.

corródere, *vb.* corrode.

corrómpere, *vb.* corrupt; bribe.

corrosione, *n.f.* corrosion.

corrosivo, *adj.* corrosive.

corroso, *adj.* corroded.

corrotto, *adj.* corrupted.

corrugare, *vb.* corrugate, wrinkle.

corruttibile, *adj.* corruptible.

corruttivo, *adj.* corruptive.

corruttore, *n.m.* corrupter; briber.

corruzione, *n.f.* corruption; bribery.

corsa, *n.f.* race; ride; trip.

corso, *n.m.* course.

còrso, *adj.* Corsican.

corte, *n.f.* court.

cortéccia, *n.f.* bark.

corteggiamento, *n.m.* courting, courtship.

corteggiare, *vb.* court, woo.

corteggiatore, *n.m.* wooer, beau, suitor.

cortèo, *n.m.* cortege, procession; pageant.

cortese, *adj.* courteous, accommodating, polite.

cortesìa, *n.f.* courtesy, politeness.

cortigiana, *n.f.* courtesan, prostitute.

cortigiano, *n.m.* courtier.

cortile, *n.m.* courtyard, patio.

cortina, *n.f.* curtain.

corto, *adj.* short; stupid; (of sea) choppy.

corvetta, *n.f.* corvette.

corvino, *adj.* raven.

còrvo, *n.m.* crow; raven.

còsa, *n.f.* thing.

còscia, *n.f.* thigh.

cosciènza, *n.f.* consciousness; conscience.

coscienziosamente, *adv.* conscientiously.

coscienzioso, *adj.* conscientious, painstaking.

cosciòtto, *n.m.* leg of lamb.

coscritto, *n.m. and adj.* conscript.

coscrizione, *n.f.* conscription.

così, *adv.* so, thus.

cosiddetto, *adj.* so-called.

cosmètico, *n.m. and adj.* cosmetic.

còsmico, *adj.* cosmic.

còsmo, *n.m.* cosmos.

cosmologìa, *n.f.* cosmology.

cosmonàuta, *n.m. and f.* astronaut.

cosmopolita, *adj.* cosmopolitan.

còso, *n.m.* thingumajig.

cospàrgere, *vb.* scatter, intersperse, sprinkle, strew.

cospètto, *n.m.* presence.

cospicuamente, *adv.* conspicuously.

cospicuità, *n.f.* conspicuousness.

cospìcuo, *adj.* conspicuous.

còsta, *n.f.* coast.

costante, *adj.* constant, fixed, firm.

costantemente, *adv.* constantly.

costanza, *n.f.* constancy.

costare, *vb.* cost.

costata, *n.f.* rib roast, rack.

costeggiare, *vb.* flank, coast, sail alongside.

costei, *pron.dem.f.sg.* this one, this woman, she.

costellazione, *n.f.* constellation.

costernare, *vb.* dismay.

costernazione, *n.f.* consternation, dismay.

costì, *adv.* there.

costièro, *adj.* coastal.

costipazione, *n.f.* constipation.

costituènte, *adj.* constituent.

costituire, *vb.* constitute.

costituzionale, *adj.* constitutional.

costituzione, *n.f.* constitution.

còsto, *n.m.* cost, expense.

còstola, *n.f.* rib.
costoletta, *n.f.* chop, rib.
costosamente, *adv.* expensively.
costoro, *pron. dem.* *m.f.pl.* these, these men, these women, they.
costoso, *adj.* costly, dear, expensive, valuable.
costringere, *vb.* force, coerce, compel, constrict, constrain.
costruire, *vb.* construct, build, erect.
costruttivamente, *adv.* constructively.
costruttivo, *adj.* constructive.
costruttore, *n.m.* builder, constructor.
costruzione, *n.f.* construction, erection.
costui, *pron. dem.* *m.sg.* this one, this man, he.
costume, *n.m.* costume, garb; custom; *(pl.)* mores.
còte, *n.f.* hone.
cotenna, *n.f.* pigskin, scalp.
cotiglione, *n.m.* cotillion.
cotognata, *n.f.* quince jam.
cotoletta, *n.f.* cutlet.
cotone, *n.m.* cotton.
cotonificio, *n.m.* cotton mill.
cotonina, *n.f.* cotton cloth, cretonne.
còtto, *adj.* cooked; done.
covare, *vb.* brood, hatch; smolder.
covata, *n.f.* brood.
covo, *n.m.* den, lair.
covone, *n.m.* sheaf.
crampo, *n.m.* cramp.
crànio, *n.m.* cranium, skull.
cratère, *n.m.* crater.
cravatta, *n.f.* necktie.
creare, *vb.* create.
creativo, *adj.* creative.
creatore, *n.m.* creator.
creatura, *n.f.* creature.
creazione, *n.f.* creation.
credente, *n.m.* believer.
credenza, *n.f.* belief; credence; cupboard; dresser.
credenziali, *f.pl.* credentials.
crédere, *vb.* believe, think.
credìbile, *adj.* credible, believable.
credibilità, *n.f.* credibility.
crèdito, *n.m.* credit.
creditore, *n.m.* creditor.

credo, *n.m.* credo, creed.
credulità, *n.f.* credulity.
crèdulo, *adj.* credulous, gullible.
credulone, *n.m.* dupe.
crèma, *n.f.* cream.
crema caramella, *n.f.* custard.
cremaglièra, *n.f.* rack.
cremare, *vb.* cremate.
crematòrio, *adj.* crematory.
cremazione, *n.f.* cremation.
cremerìa, *n.f.* creamery.
crèmisi, *adj.* crimson.
creosòto, *n.m.* creosote.
crèpa, *n.f.* crack, chink.
crepàccio, *n.m.* crevasse.
crepacuòre, *n.m.* heartbreak.
crepùscolo, *n.m.* twilight, dusk.
créscere, *vb.* grow.
créscita, *n.f.* growth.
crespo, 1. *n.m.* crepe. 2. *adj.* wavy; crisp.
cresta, *n.f.* crest, ridge; (rooster's) comb.
crèta, *n.f.* clay.
cricca, *n.f.* clique, clan.
cricco, *n.m.* jack.
criminale, *adj.* criminal.
criminologìa, *n.f.* criminology.
criminòlogo, *n.m.* criminologist.
criminoso, *adj.* criminal; incriminating.
crinale, *n.m.* edge, ridge.
crine, *n.f.* hair.
crinièra, *n.f.* mane.
criochirurgìa, *n.f.* cryosurgery.
cripta, *n.f.* crypt.
crisàlide, *n.f.* chrysalis.
crisàntemo, *n.m.* chrysanthemum.
crisi, *n.f.* crisis.
cristallerìe, *n.f.pl.* glassware.
cristallino, *adj.* crystalline.
cristallizzare, *vb.* crystallize.
cristallo, *n.m.* crystal; cut glass.
cristianésimo, *n.m.* Christianity.
cristianità, *n.f.* Christendom.
cristiano, *n.* and *adj.* Christian.
Cristo, *n.m.* Christ.
critèrio, *n.m.* criterion.
crìtica, *n.f.* criticism, critique, fault finding.
criticare, *vb.* criticize.
crìtico, 1. *n.* critic. 2. *adj.* critical.
crittografìa, *n.f.* cryptography.
crittogramma, *n.m.* cryptogram.

crivellare, *vb.* sift; screen.
crivèllo, *n.m.* sieve; screen.
croato, *n.m. and adj.* Croatian.
Croàzia, *n.f.* Croatia.
croccante, *adj.* crisp.
crocchetta, *n.f.* croquette.
croce, *n.f.* cross.
crocefissione, *n.f.* crucifixion.
crocefisso, *n.m.* crucifix.
crocevìa, *n.f.* crossroads.
crociata, *n.f.* crusade.
crociato, *n.m.* crusader.
crocicchio, *n.m.* crossroads.
crocièra, *n.f.* crusade.
crocifìggere, *vb.* crucify.
cròco, *n.m.* crocus.
crogiolo, *n.m.* crucible.
crollare, *vb.* collapse, crash.
cròllo, *n.m.* collapse, crash.
cromàtico, *adj.* chromatic.
cròmo, *n.m.* chrome, chromium.
cromosòma, *n.m.* chromosome.
crònaca, *n.f.* chronicle.
cronicamente, *adv.* chronically.
crònico, *adj.* chronic.
cronista, *n.m.* chronicler; (newspaper) columnist; (radio) commentator.
cronologìa, *n.f.* chronology.
cronològico, *adj.* chronological.
cronometrare, *vb.* time.
cronòmetro, *n.m.* chronometer, stopwatch.
crosta, *n.f.* crust; scab.
crostàceo, *n.m. and adj.* crustacean.
crostata, *n.f.* tart.
crostino, *n.m.* crouton; canapé.
crostoso, *adj.* crusty.
crucciato, *adj.* worried, upset.
crùccio, *n.m.* chagrin.
cruciale, *adj.* crucial.
crucivèrba, *n.m.* cross-word puzzle.
crudèle, *adj.* cruel.
crudeltà, *n.f.* cruelty.
crudezza, *n.f.* crudeness.
crudità, *n.f.* crudity.
crudo, *adj.* crude, raw.
crumiro, *n.m.* scab, strikebreaker.
cruna, *n.f.* eye (of a needle).
crusca, *n.f.* bran.
cruscòtto, *n.m.* dashboard.
Cuba, *n.f.* Cuba
cubano, *adj.* Cuban.

cubatura, *n.f.* volume.
cùbico, *adj.* cubic.
cubìcolo, *n.m.* cubicle.
cubismo, *n.m.* cubism.
cubo, *n.m.* cube.
cubo per flash, *n.m.* flashcube.
cuccetta, *n.f.* berth, bunk.
cucchiaiata, *n.f.* spoonful.
cucchiaino, *n.m.* teaspoon.
cùccia, *n.f.* dog's bed.
cùcciolo, *n.m.* puppy.
cucchiàio, *s.m.* spoon, tablespoon; tablespoonful.
cucina, *n.f.* kitchen, cuisine; cooking. **c. econòmica,** range. **libro di c.,** cookbook.
cucinare, *vb.* cook.
cucire, *vb.* sew.
cucitura, *n.f.* sewing; seam.
cuculo, *n.m.* cuckoo.
cuffia, *n.f.* cap; hood; earphone.
cugina, *n.f.* cousin.
cugino, *n.m.* cousin.
cùi, *pron.* which; to which; whom; to whom; of which; whose.
cùlice, *n.m.* gnat.
culinàrio, *adj.* culinary.
culla, *n.f.* cradle.
cullare, *vb.* cradle, lull.
culminante, *adj.* culminating, climactic.
culminare, *vb.* culminate.
cùlmine, *n.m.* top, summit; climax.
culo, *n.m.* posterior.
culto, *n.m.* cult; worship.
cultore, *n.m.* enthusiast (of arts); expert.
cultura, *n.f.* culture.
culturale, *adj.* cultural.
cumulativo, *adj.* cumulative.
cùneo, *n.m.* wedge.
cunetta, *n.f.* gutter.
cuòco, *n.m.* cook, chef.
cuòio, *n.m.* leather.
cuòre, *n.m.* heart.
cupè, *n.m.* coupé.
cupidìgia, *n.f.* greed, cupidity.
cupo, *adj.* sullen.
cùpola, *n.f.* cupola, dome.
cura, *n.f.* care; cure; worry.
curare, *vb.* care for, take care of, nurse, nurture, tend; (*refl.*) care.
curativo, *adj.* healing, curative.
curato, *n.m.* curate.

curatore, *n.m.* curator.
curia, *n.f.* curia.
curiosare, *vb.* browse; pry, snoop.
curiosità, *n.f.* curiosity, curio.
curioso, *adj.* curious.
curricolo, *n.m.* curriculum.
curva, *n.f.* curve.
curvare, *vb.* curve, bend, warp; hunch; *(refl.)* stoop.
curvatura, *n.f.* curvature; crook.
curvo, *adj.* curved, bent; stooped.
cuscinetto, *n.m.* pad; stamp pad;

(machinery) bearing. **stato c.,** buffer state. **c. a rotolamento,** roller bearing. **c. a sfere,** ball bearing.
cuscino, *n.m.* cushion.
custòde, *n.m.* custodian, guardian, keeper.
custòdia, *n.f.* custody, charge.
custodire, *vb.* guard.
cutàneo, *adj.* cutaneous.
cute, *n.f.* skin.
cutìcola, *n.f.* cuticle.

D

da, *prep.* from; by; for; fit for, suitable for; characteristic of; at . . .'s (house, shop, etc.).
dabbasso, *adv.* downstairs.
dabbène, *adj.* honest, upright.
dado, *n.m.* die (*pl.* dice).
daga, *n.f.* dagger.
dàina, *n.f.* hind.
dàino, *n.m.* buck.
dàlia, *n.f.* dahlia.
daltònico, *adj.* color blind.
dama, *n.f.* lady; checkers.
damasco, *n.m.* damask.
damerino, *n.m.* dandy, fop.
damigèlla, *n.f.* damsel. **d. d'onore,** maid of honor, bridesmaid.
damigiana, *n.f.* demijohn.
danese, *adj.* Danish.
Danimarca, *n.f.* Denmark.
dannare, *vb.* damn.
dannazione, *n.f.* damnation.
danneggiare, *vb.* harm, damage, injure; mar.
danno, *n.m.* harm, damage, detriment, hurt, injury.
dannoso, *adj.* harmful, baneful, detrimental, hurtful, injurious.
danza, *n.f.* dance.
danzare, *vb.* dance.
dappertutto, *adv.* everywhere; throughout.
dardo, *n.m.* dart.
dare, *vb.* give.
dàrsena, *n.f.* marina, dock, basin.
data, *n.f.* date.
datare, *vb.* date (administrative).
dati, *n.m.pl.* data.
datore, *n.m.* giver. **d. di lavoro,** employer.

dàttero, *n.m.* date.
dattilògrafa, *vb.* typist.
dattilografare, *vb.* type.
dattiloscritto, *n.m.* typed.
davanti, 1. *n.m.* front. **2.** *adv.* before. **d. a,** *prep.* before.
davanzale, *n.m.* sill.
davvero, *adv.* indeed, really.
dàzio, *n.m.* excise.
dèa, *n.f.* goddess.
debilitare, *vb.* debilitate.
debitamente, *adv.* duly.
debito, 1. *n.m.* debt, debit. **2.** *adj.* due.
debitore, *n.m.* debtor.
débole, *adj.* weak, feeble, faint, frail, puny.
debolezza, *n.f.* weakness, feebleness, failing, frailty.
debolmente, *adv.* weakly, faintly.
debordare, *vb.* overflow.
debuttante, *n.* debutant(e).
debutto, *n.m.* debut.
dècade, *n.f.* decade.
decadènza, *n.f.* decline, decay, decadence.
decalcomania, *n.f.* decalcomania.
decadènte, *adj.* decadent.
decadènza, *n.f.* decay, decadence, decline.
decadere, *vb.* decay, decline, lapse.
decaffeinizzato, *adj.* decaffeinated.
decano, *n.m.* dean.
decapitare, *vb.* behead, decapitate.
deceduto, *adj.* deceased.

decelerare, vb. decelerate.
decènnio, n.m. decade.
decènte, adj. decent.
decentralizzare, vb. decentralize.
decentramento, n.m. decentralization.
decentrare, vb. decentralize.
decènza, n.f. decency.
dècibel, n.m. decibel.
decidere, vb. decide; (refl.) decide, make up one's mind, resolve.
deciduo, adj. deciduous.
decifrare, vb. decipher, decode.
decimale, adj. decimal.
decimare, vb. decimate.
dècimo, adj. tenth.
decimonòno, adj. nineteenth.
decimosèsto, adj. sixteenth.
decimotèrzo, adj. thirteenth.
decimottavo, adj. eighteenth.
decisione, n.f. decision, resolve.
decisivo, adj. decisive.
declamare, vb. delaim.
declamazione, n.f. declamation.
declinare, vb. decline.
declinazione, n.f. declension.
declino, n.m. decline, decrease.
declivio, n.m. slope.
decollare, vb. take off.
decomporre, vb. decompose, decay.
decomposizione, n.f. decomposition, decay.
decongestionante, adj. decongestant.
decontaminare, vb. decontaminate.
decorare, vb. decorate.
decorativo, adj. decorative.
decoratore, n.m. decorator.
decorazione, n.f. decoration.
decòro, n.m. decorum.
decoroso, adj. decorous.
decorrènza, n.f. beginning; effective date.
decrèpito, adj. decrepit.
decréscere, vb. diminish, decrease.
decretare, vb. decree; enact.
decreto, n.m. decree; enactment.
decuplicare, vb. multiply tenfold.
dèdica, n.f. dedication.
dedicare, vb. dedicate, devote; (refl.) become addicted.
dedurre, vb. deduce, deduct.

deduttivo, adj. deductive.
deduzione, n.f. deduction.
deferènte, adj. deferent.
deferènza, n.f. deference.
defezione, n.f. defection.
deficiènte, adj. deficient.
deficiènza, n.f. deficiency.
dèficit, n.m. deficit.
definibile, adj. definable.
definire, vb. define, determine.
definitivamente, adj. definitely.
definitivo, adj. definitive, final.
definito, adj. definite; finite.
definizione, n.f. definition.
deflagrare, vb. explode, burst.
deflagrazione, n.f. burst, explosion.
deflazionare, vb. deflate.
deflazione, n.f. deflation.
deflèttere, vb. deflect.
deformare, vb. deform.
deforme, adj. deformed.
deformità, n.f. deformity.
defraudare, vb. defraud.
defunto, adj. defunct, deceased.
degenerare, vb. degenerate.
degenerato, n.m. and adj. degenerate.
degenerazione, n.f. degeneration.
degènte, adj. bedridden.
degènza, n.f. hospitalization.
degnarsi, vb. deign.
degno, adj. worthy.
degradare, vb. degrade, demote.
degradazione, n.f. degradation.
degustare, vb. taste.
deificare, vb. deify.
deità, n.f. deity.
delatore, n.m. informer, spy.
delegare, vb. delegate.
delegato, n.m. delegate.
delegazione, n.f. delegation.
deletèrio, adj. deleterious, harmful.
delfino, n.m. dolphin.
deliberare, vb. deliberate.
deliberatamente, adv. deliberately.
deliberativo, adj. deliberative.
deliberato, adj. deliberate.
deliberazione, n.f. advisement; deliberation.
delicatezza, n.f. delicacy.
delicato, adj. delicate, dainty.

delimitare, *vb.* delimit, define.

delineare, *vb.* delineate.

delinquènte, *adj.* delinquent.

delinquènza, *n.f.* delinquency.

delirante, *adj.* delirious.

delirare, *vb.* be delirious, rave.

delìrio, *n.m.* delirium.

delitto, *n.m.* crime.

delìzia, *n.f.* delight.

delizioso, *adj.* delicious.

delucidare, *vb.* explain.

delùdere, *vb.* delude; disappoint.

delusione, *n.f.* delusion; disappointment.

demagògo, *n.m.* demagogue.

demarcazione, *n.f.* demarcation.

demènte, *adj.* demented.

demeritare, *vb.* forfeit.

demèrito, *n.m.* demerit.

democràtico, 1. *n.m.* democrat. **2.** *adj.* democratic.

democrazìa, *n.f.* democracy.

demolire, *vb.* demolish.

demolizione, *n.f.* demolition.

demonìaco, *adj.* demoniacal, fiendish.

demònio, *n.m.* demon, fiend.

demoralizzare, *vb.* demoralize.

denaro, *n.m.* money.

denaturare, *vb.* denature.

denigrare, *vb.* denigrate, blacken, slander, cast aspersions on, belittle.

denigrazione, *n.f.* slander, aspersion.

denominatore, *n.m.* denominator.

denominazione, *n.f.* denomination.

densità, *n.f.* density.

dènso, *adj.* dense, thick.

dentale, *adj.* dental.

dènte, *n.m.* tooth; cog.

dentellare, *vb.* indent.

dentellatura, *n.f.* indentation.

dentièra, *n.f.* denture; gearing. **ferrovia a d.,** cog railway.

dentifrìcio, *n.m.* dentifrice.

dentista, *n.m.* dentist.

dentro, *adv. and prep.* inside, within.

denuclearizzare, *vb.* denuclearize.

denudare, *vb.* denude.

denùncia, *n.f.* denunciation.

denunciare, *vb.* denounce; report.

denutrito, *adj.* undernourished, starving.

denutrizione, *n.f.* undernourishment, starvation.

deodorante, *n.m.* deodorant.

deodorare, *vb.* deodorize.

depennare, *vb.* cross out, strike out, expunge.

deperìbile, *adj.* perishable.

deplorare, *vb.* deplore.

deplorévole, *adj.* deplorable.

deporre, *vb.* depose; put down, set down; lay.

deportare, *vb.* deport.

deportazione, *n.f.* deportation.

depositante, *n.m.* depositor.

depositare, *vb.* deposit.

depòsito, *n.m.* deposit; depot. **d. bagagli,** checkroom.

deposizione, *n.f.* deposition, statement.

depravare, *vb.* deprave.

depravazione, *n.f.* depravity.

deprecare, *vb.* deprecate, decry.

depredamento, *n.m.* depredation.

depressione, *n.f.* depression.

deprezzamento, *n.m.* depreciation.

deprezzare, *vb.* depreciate, cheapen.

deprìmere, *vb.* depress.

deputato, *n.m.* deputy, representative.

deragliare, *vb.* derail.

derelitto, *adj.* derelict.

deretano, *n.m.* buttocks, behind.

derìdere, *vb.* deride, mock, laugh at, ridicule.

derisione, *n.f.* derision, mockery.

derisivo, *adj.* derisive.

deriva, *n.f.* drift. **alla d.,** adrift.

derivare, *vb.* derive.

derivativo, *adj.* derivative.

derivato, 1. *adj.* derived. **2.** *n.m.* byproduct, derivative.

derivazione, *n.f.* derivation.

dermatologìa, *n.f.* dermatology.

dermatòlogo, *n.m.* dermatologist.

dèroga, *n.f.* derogation; exception.

derogatòrio, *adj.* derogatory.

derubare, *vb.* rob.

descrittivo, *adj.* descriptive.
descrizione, *n.f.* description.
desensibilizzare, *vb.* desensitize.
desèrto, *n.m.* desert; wilderness.
desideràbile, *adj.* desirable.
desiderabilità, *n.f.* desirability.
desiderare, *vb.* desire, want, wish.
desidèrio, *n.m.* desire, wish.
desideroso, *adj.* desirous.
designare, *vb.* designate, nominate.
designato, *n.m.* nominee.
designazione, *n.f.* designation.
desinènza, *n.f.* ending.
desìstere, *vb.* desist.
desolante, *adj.* desolating, distressing.
desolare, *vb.* desolate.
desolato, *adj.* desolate, afflicted, sorry..
desolazione, *n.f.* desolation, sorrow.
dèspota, *n.m.* despot.
dessèrt, *n.m.* dessert.
destare, *vb.* awaken.
destinare, *vb.* destine.
destinatàrio, *n.m.* addressee.
destinazione, *n.f.* destination.
destino, *n.m.* destiny, doom.
destituire, *vb.* dismiss, remove.
destituito, *adj.* destitute.
destituzione, *n.f.* destitution.
desto, *adj.* awake.
dèstra, *n.f.* right.
destramente, *adv.* skillfully, dexterously.
destreggiarsi, *vb.* manage shrewdly.
destrezza, *n.f.* adroitness, adeptness, dexterity, skill.
destrièro, *n.m.* steed.
dèstro, *adj.* adroit, adept, deft, skillful, dexterous, handy; right.
destròrso, *adj. and adv.* clockwise.
destròsio, *n.m.* destrose.
desùmere, *vb.* gather; infer.
detenere, *vb.* detain.
detenzione, *n.f.* detention.
detergènte, *n.m. and adj.* detergent.
deteriorare, *vb.* deteriorate.
deterioramento, *n.m.* deterioration.
determinare, *vb.* determine.

determinazione, *n.f.* determination.
determinismo, *n.m.* determinism.
detestare, *vb.* detest, abhor.
detestazione, *n.f.* detestation, abhorrence.
detonare, *vb.* detonate.
detonazione, *n.f.* detonation, report.
detrarre, *vb.* detract.
detrimento, *n.m.* detriment.
detriti, *n.m.pl.* debris.
detronizzare, *vb.* dethrone.
dettagliare, *vb.* detail.
dettàglio, *n.m.* detail. **al d.,** at retail.
dettare, *vb.* dictate.
dettatura, *n.f.* dictation.
devastare, *vb.* devastate, ravage.
devastazione, *n.f.* devastation, havoc, ravage.
deviante, *adj.* negative; misleading.
deviare, *vb.* deviate.
deviazione, *n.f.* deviation, detour.
dèvio, *adj.* devious.
devitalizzare, *vb.* devitalize.
dev.mo, (for **devotissimo,** *adj.*): **Vostro d.,** yours truly.
devoluzione, *n.f.* transfer; charity.
devòto, *adj.* devout, devoted, godly.
devozione, *n.f.* devotion.
di, *prep.* of; than.
dì, *n.m.* day.
diabète, *n.m.* diabetes.
diabòlico, *adj.* diabolic, devilish.
diàcono, *n.m.* deacon.
diadèma, *n.m.* diadem, coronet.
diaframma, *n.m.* diaphragm; midriff.
diàgnosi, *n.f.* diagnosis.
diagnosticare, *vb.* diagnose.
diagnòstico, *adj.* diagnostic.
diagonale, *adj.* diagonal.
diagonalmente, *adv.* diagonally.
diagramma, *n.m.* diagram.
dialètto, *n.m.* dialect.
diàlogo, *n.m.* dialogue.
diamante, *n.m.* diamond.
diametrale, *adj.* diametrical.
diàmetro, *n.m.* diameter.
diàmine!, *interj.* the dickens!

diàpason, *n.m.* tuning fork.

diapositiva, *n.f.* slide.

diàrio, *n.m.* diary.

diarrèa, *n.f.* diarrhea.

diatermìa, *n.f.* diathermy.

diatriba, *n.f.* diatribe.

diavolerìa, *n.f.* deviltry, evil plot, trick.

diàvolo, *n.m.* devil.

dibàttere, *vb.* debate; (*refl.*) flounder.

dibattimento, *n.m.* debate.

dibàttito, *n.m.* debate, discussion.

di buon' ora, *adv.* early.

dicastèro, *n.m.* department, ministry.

dicèmbre, *n.m.* December.

dicerìa, *n.f.* gossip, rumor.

dichiarare, *vb.* declare, explain. **d. ricevuta di**, acknowledge receipt of.

dichiarativo, *adj.* declarative.

dichiarazione, *n.f.* declaration: explanation.

diciannòve, *num.* nineteen.

diciannovésimo, *adj.* nineteenth.

diciassètte, *num.* seventeen.

diciassettésimo, *adj.* seventeenth.

diciottésimo, *adj.* eighteenth.

diciòtto, *num.* eighteen.

dicitura, *n.f.* caption, legend.

didàttico, *adj.* didactic.

didiètro, *n.m.* behind.

dièci, *num.* ten.

diecimila, *adj., n.m., num.* ten thousand.

dièsis, *n.f.* sharp (music).

dièta, *n.f.* diet.

dietètica, *n.f.* dietetics.

dietètico, *adj.* dietetic, dietary.

dietista, *n.m.* dietitian.

diètro a, *prep.* behind.

dietrofrònt, *n.m.* about face.

difatti, *adv.* indeed.

difèndere, *vb.* defend, advocate.

difensìbile, *adj.* defensible.

difensivo, *adj.* defensive.

difensore, *n.m.* defender, advocate.

difesa, *n.f.* defense, advocacy.

difettare, *vb.* be lacking.

difètto, *n.m.* defect, fault, flaw.

difettoso, *adj.* defective, faulty.

diffamare, *vb.* defame, libel, malign.

diffamatòrio, *adj.* defamatory, libelous.

diffamazione, *n.f.* defamation.

differènte, *adj.* different.

differènza, *n.f.* difference.

differenziàle, *adj.* differential.

differenziare, *vb.* differentiate.

differire, *vb.* defer, put off; differ.

difficile, *adj.* difficult.

difficoltà, *n.f.* difficulty.

difficoltoso, *adj.* fussy.

diffida, *n.f.* warning; intimation.

diffidare di, *vb.* mistrust.

diffidènte, *adj.* distrustful.

diffóndere, *vb.* diffuse, spread; (*refl.*) expatiate, dwell upon.

difforme, *adj.* different; divergent.

diffrazione, *n.f.* diffraction.

diffusione, *n.f.* diffusion.

diffuso, *adj.* diffuse, widespread.

difterite, *n.f.* diphtheria.

diga, *n.f.* dike, dam, levee.

digerìbile, *adj.* digestible.

digerire, *vb.* digest.

digestione, *n.f.* digestion.

digestivo, *adj.* digestive.

digitale, **1.** *n.f.* digitalis, foxglove. **2.** *adj.* digital.

digiunare, *vb.* fast.

digiuno, *n.m.* fast.

dignificare, *vb.* dignify.

dignità, *n.f.* dignity, respect.

dignitàrio, *n.m.* dignitary.

dignitoso, *adj.* dignified.

digradante, *adj.* sloping, dimming.

digredire, *vb.* digress.

digressione, *n.f.* digression.

digressivo, *adj.* discursive.

digrignare, *vb.* gnash.

dilapidato, *adj.* dilapidated.

dilapidazione, *n.f.* dilapidation, disrepair.

dilatare, *vb.* dilate.

dilatòrio, *adj.* dilatory.

dilèmma, *n.m.* dilemma.

dilettante, *n.m.* amateur.

dilettévole, *adj.* delightful, delectable.

dilètto, **1.** *n.m.* delight. **2.** *adj.* beloved, darling.

diligènte, *adj.* diligent.

diligènza, n.f. diligence.

diluire, vb. dilute.

dilungare, vb. stretch; dwell.

diluviare, vb. rain cats and dogs.

dilùvio, n.m. deluge.

diluzione, n.f. dilution.

dimagrante, adj. reducing.

dimagrire, vb. lose weight, slim down.

dimenare, vb. wag; (refl.) toss about; flounce.

dimensione, n.f. dimension.

dimenticare, vb. forget.

diméntico, adj. forgetful.

dimésso, adj. humble; shabby; dismissed, discharged.

dimestichezza, n.f. familiarity.

diméttere, vb. dismiss; (refl.) resign, quit.

dimezzare, vb. halve, cut in half.

diminuire, vb. diminish, lessen, abate, decrease, dwindle, let up, subside.

diminutivo, n.m. and adj. diminutive.

diminuzione, n.f. diminution, lessening, abatement, decrease.

dimissione, n.f. resignation.

dimora, n.f. abode, dwelling.

dimostràbile, adj. demonstrable.

dimostrare, vb. demonstrate.

dimostrativo, adj. demonstrative.

dimostratore, n.m. demonstrator.

dimostrazione, n.f. demonstration.

dinàmica, n.f. dynamics.

dinàmico, adj. dynamic.

dinamite, n.f. dynamite.

dìnamo, n.f. dynamo.

dinanzi, adv. and adj. before; in front.

dinastìa, n.f. dynasty.

diniègo, n.m. denial.

dinosàuro, n.m. dinosaur.

dintorni, n.m.pl. environs, surroundings.

dìo, n.m. god.

diòcesi, n.f. diocese, bishopric.

diottrìa, n.f. diopter.

dipanare, vb. reel off, unwind.

dipartimentale, adj. departmental.

dipartimento, n.m. department.

dipartita, n.f. departure; demise, death.

dipendènte, n.m. and adj. dependent.

dipendènza, n.f. dependence.

dipèndere, vb. depend.

dipìngere, vb. paint, depict.

dipìnto, n.m. painting.

diplòma, n.m. diploma.

diplomàtico, 1. n.m. diplomat. **2.** adj. diplomatic.

diplomazia, n.f. diplomacy.

dipòrto, n.m. sport.

diradare, vb. thin out, diminish; become less frequent.

diramazione, n.f. junction.

dire, vb. say.

direttamente, adv. directly.

direttìssimo, n.m. express train.

direttivo, adj. directive, directional.

dirètto, adj. direct; directed; bound; lineal; right; through.

direttorato, n.m. directorate.

direttore, n.m. director; conductor; editor; manager; principal.

direzione, n.f. direction, management.

dirìgere, vb. direct; manage; aim; conduct; steer; edit.

dirigìbile, n.m. and adj. dirigible.

dirimpètto, adv. **a,** prep. opposite; facing.

diritti, n.m.pl. civil rights. **d. d'autore,** copyright.

diritto, 1. n.m. right; law. **2.** adj., adv. straight; upright.

diroccare, vb. knock down, demolish.

diroccato, adj. dilapidated, crumbling.

dirottare, n.m. hijacker.

dirotto, adv. **a d.** excessively.

dirupo, n.m. cliff, ravine.

disaccòrdo, n.m. discord, variance.

disadatto, n.m. unfit.

disadorno, adj. unadorned, bare, plain.

disagio, n.m. discomfort.

disapprovare, vb. disapprove.

disapprovazione, n.f. disapproval.

disarmare, vb. disarm.

disarmo, n.m. disarmament.

disastro, *n.m.* disaster, debacle.
disastroso, *adj.* disastrous.
discendènte, *n.m. and f.* descendant.
discépolo, *n.m.* disciple.
discèrnere, *vb.* discern.
discesa, *n.f.* descent.
discettare, *vb.* dispute, debate.
disciplina, *n.f.* discipline.
disciplinare, 1. *adj.* disciplinary. **2.** *vb.* discipline.
disco, 1. *n.m.* disc, record. **2.** *adj.* disco (music).
dìscolo, *n.m.* undisciplined child, urchin.
disconóscere, *vb.* disavow, disclaim, disown.
disconoscimento, *n.m.* disavowal, disclaimer.
discordante, *adj.* discordant.
discordare, *vb.* disagree, be discordant.
discòrdia, *n.f.* discord.
discórrere, *vb.* discourse.
discorso, *n.m.* speech, discourse, talk, address.
discotèca, *n.f.* record library; discotheque.
discrèdito, *n.m.* discredit.
discrepante, *adj.* discrepant.
discrepanza, *n.f.* discrepancy.
discreto, *adj.* discreet; moderate; fair.
discrezione, *n.f.* discretion.
discriminare, *vb.* discriminate.
discriminazione, *n.f.* discrimination.
discussione, *n.f.* discussion.
discusso, *adj.* moot.
discùtere, *vb.* discuss.
discutìbile, *adj.* debatable.
disdegnare, *vb.* disdain, spurn.
disdegno, *n.m.* disdain, scorn.
disdegnoso, *adj.* disdainful, scornful.
disdétta, *n.f.* cancellation; misfortune.
disdicévole, *adj.* unbecoming.
disdire, *vb.* cancel, terminate (contract), retract.
disegnare, *vb.* design; draw.
disegnatore, *n.m.* designer; draftsman.
disegno, *n.m.* picture; cartoon; design; drawing.

diserbante, *n.m.* weed killer.
diseredare, *vb.* disinherit.
disertare, *vb.* desert.
disertore, *n.m.* deserter.
diserzione, *n.f.* desertion.
disfare, *vb.* undo.
disfatta, *n.f.* defeat.
disfattismo, *n.m.* defeatism.
disfida, *n.f.* challenge.
disfigurare, *vb.* disfigure.
disfunzione, *n.f.* malfunction, disorder.
disgèlo, *n.m.* thaw.
disgràzia, *n.f.* misfortune, mishap, accident; disgrace.
disgraziato, *adj.* unfortunate, unlucky.
disgustare, *vb.* disgust.
disgusto, *n.m.* disgust, distaste.
disgustoso, *adj.* disgusting, distasteful, nasty.
disidratare, *vb.* dehydrate.
disillùdere, *vb.* disillusion.
disillusione, *n.f.* disillusion.
disimballare, *vb.* unpack.
disimpegnare, *vb.* disengage.
disincanto, *n.m.* disenchantment.
disinfettante, *n.m.* disinfectant.
disinfettare, *vb.* disinfect.
disingannare, *vb.* undeceive, disabuse.
disintegrare, *vb.* disintegrate.
disinteressato, *adj.* disinterested, unselfish, impartial.
disinterèsse, *n.m.* indifference.
dislessia, *n.f.* dyslexia.
dislocamento, *n.m.* displacement.
disobbediènte, *adj.* disobedient.
disoccupato, *adj.* unemployed.
disonestà, *n.f.* dishonesty.
disonèsto, *adj.* dishonest; foul.
disonorante, *adj.* disgraceful.
disonorare, *vb.* dishonor, disgrace.
disonore, *n.m.* dishonor, disgrace.
disonorévole, *adj.* dishonorable, discreditable, disreputable.
disordinare, *vb.* disorder.
disordinato, *adj.* disorderly.
disòrdine, *n.m.* disorder, litter.
disorganizzare, *vb.* disorganize.
disorientamento, *n.m.* confusion, disorientation.

disorientato, *adj.* confused, puzzled.

disossare, *vb.* bone.

disotto, *adv.* underneath, below; downstairs.

dispàccio, *n.m.* dispatch.

disparato, *adj.* disparate.

dìspari, *adj.* odd.

disparità, *n.f.* disparity.

disparte: in d., *adv.* apart, aloof.

dispènsa, *n.f.* pantry.

dispensàbile, *adj.* dispensable.

dispensare, *vb.* dispense.

dispensàrio, *n.m.* dispensary.

dispensazione, *n.f.* dispensation.

dispepsìa, *n.f.* dyspepsia.

dispèptico, *adj.* dyspeptic.

disperare, *vb.* despair.

disperato, 1. *n.m.* desperado. **2.** *adj.* desperate; forlorn, hopeless.

disperazione, *n.f.* desperation, despair, hopelessness.

dispèrdere, *vb.* disperse, waste.

dispersione, *n.f.* dispersal.

dispersivo, *adj.* dispersive.

disperso, 1. *n.m.* missing in action. **2.** *adj.* missing, lost; scattered.

dispètto, *n.m.* spite.

dispiacènte, *adj.* sorry; displeasing.

dispiacere, 1. *n.m.* displeasure. **2.** *vb.* displease.

disponìbile, *adj.* available.

disporre, *vb.* dispose, arrange; range.

dispositivo, *n.m.* device.

disposizione, *n.f.* disposition; disposal; instruction; arrangement.

dispòtico, *adj.* despotic.

dispotismo, *n.m.* despotism.

dispregiativo, *adj.* derogatory, pejorative.

disprezzare, *vb.* despise, disparage, scorn, slight.

disprèzzo, *n.m.* contempt, scorn, slight.

dìsputa, *n.f.* dispute, controversy.

disputàbile, *adj.* disputable.

disputare, *vb.* dispute.

disquisizione, *n.f.* disquisition.

dissacrare, *vb.* desecrate.

dissecare, *vb.* dissect.

disseminare, *vb.* disseminate.

dissènso, *n.m.* dissent, disagreement, dissension.

dissenterìa, *n.f.* dysentery.

dissentire, *vb.* dissent, disagree.

disserrare, *vb.* unlock.

dissertazione, *n.f.* dissertation.

disservìzio, *n.m.* disservice, bad service.

dissetare, *vb.* quench (one's) thirst.

dissezione, *n.f.* dissection.

dissidènte, *adj.* and *n.m.* dissident.

dissìdio, *n.m.* dispute, discord.

dissìmile, *adj.* dissimilar, unlike.

dissimulare, *vb.* dissimulate, dissemble.

dissipare, *vb.* dissipate, dispel.

dissipazione, *n.f.* dissipation.

dissociare, *vb.* dissociate.

dissolutezza, *n.f.* dissoluteness, dissipation.

dissoluto, *adj.* dissolute, dissipated.

dissoluzione, *n.f.* dissolution.

dissolvènza, *n.f.* fading, fade-out, dissolve.

dissòlvere, *vb.* dissolve.

dissonante, *adj.* dissonant.

dissonanza, *n.f.* dissonance.

dissotterrare, *vb.* unearth.

dissuadere, *vb.* dissuade.

distaccamento, *n.m.* detachment *(mil.)*.

distaccare, *vb.* detach.

distacco, *n.m.* detachment.

distante, *adj.* distant.

distanza, *n.f.* distance.

distare, *vb.* be distant.

distèndere, *vb.* distend.

distensione, *n.f.* détente.

distesa, *n.f.* expanse; extent; spread.

disteso, *adj.* spread.

distillare, *vb.* distill.

distillatore, *n.m.* distiller.

distillatòrio, *n.m.* distillery.

distillazione, *n.f.* distillation.

distìnguere, *vb.* distinguish.

distinta, *n.f.* list, note.

distintamente, *adv.* distinctly.

distintivo, 1. *n.m.* badge. **2.** *adj.* distinctive.

distinto, *adj.* distinct.

distinzione, *n.f.* distinction.

distògliere, *vb.* deter.
distòrcere, *vb.* distort.
distrarre, *vb.* distract.
distratto, *adj.* absentminded.
distrazione, *n.f.* distraction.
distretto, *n.m.* district.
distribuire, *vb.* distribute, apportion, deal out, dole out.
distributore, *n.m.* distributor.
distribuzione, *n.f.* distribution; deal.
districare, *vb.* disentangle, extricate, unravel.
distrofia, *n.f.* dystrophy.
distrùggere, *vb.* destroy.
distruttìbile, *adj.* destructible.
distruttivo, *adj.* destructive.
distruzione, *n.f.* destruction.
disturbare, *vb.* disturb, trouble.
disturbo, *n.m.* disturbance, trouble.
disubbidiènza, *n.f.* disobedience.
disubbidire, *vb.* disobey.
disuguale, *adj.* uneven.
disumano, *adj.* inhumane, cruel.
disunire, *vb.* disunite.
disuso, *n.m.* disuse.
ditale, *n.m.* thimble.
dito, *n.m.* finger. **d. del piède**, toe.
ditta, *n.f.* firm.
dittàfono, *n.m.* dictaphone.
dittatore, *n.m.* dictator.
dittatoriale, *adj.* dictatorial.
dittatura, *n.f.* dictatorship.
dittòngo, *n.m.* dipthong.
diurètico, *adj.* diuretic.
diurno, *adj.* daytime.
diva, *n.f.* famous singer, diva.
divagare, *vb.* ramble, get off the subject.
divampare, *vb.* burst into flames.
divano, *n.m.* divan, davenport, lounge.
divàrio, *n.m.* difference.
divenire, *vb.* become; get.
diventare, *vb.* become; get.
divèrbio, *n.m.* altercation, argument.
divergènte, *adj.* divergent.
divergènza, *n.f.* divergence.
divèrgere, *vb.* diverge.
diversione, *n.f.* diversion.
diversità, *n.f.* diversity.
diversivo, *n.m.* distraction.
divèrso, *adj.* diverse, different.

divertènte, *adj.* amusing.
divertimento, *n.m.* amusement, hobby, recreation, entertainment, fun.
divertire, *vb.* amuse, divert, entertain; *(refl.)* have a good time.
dividendo, *n.m.* dividend.
divìdere, *vb.* divide, split.
divièto, *n.m.* prohibition.
divinare, *vb.* divine.
divincolare, *vb.* wriggle.
divinità, *n.f.* divinity.
divinizzare, *vb.* deify; predict.
divino, *adj.* divine, godlike.
divisa, *n.f.* uniform.
divisìbile, *adj.* divisible.
divisione, *n.f.* division.
divismo, *n.m.* star system.
divisòrio, *adj.* dividing.
divorare, *vb.* devour.
divorziare, *vb.* divorce.
divòrzio, *n.m.* divorce.
divulgare, *vb.* divulge.
dizionàrio, *n.m.* dictionary.
dizione, *n.f.* diction.
dóccia, *n.f.* shower.
dòcile, *adj.* docile, tame, submissive, amenable.
documentare, *vb.* document.
documentàrio, *adj.* documentary.
documentazione, *n.f.* documentation.
documento, *n.m.* document.
dodicésimo, *adj.* twelfth.
dódici, *num.* twelve.
dogana, *n.f.* customs, customshouse.
doganière, *n.m.* customs officer.
dòglia, *n.f.* sharp pain.
dòglie, *n.f.pl.* labor pains.
dògma, *n.m.* dogma.
dogmaticità, *n.f.* assertiveness.
dogmàtico, *adj.* dogmatic, assertive.
dogmatismo, *n.m.* dogmatism.
dolce, **1.** *n.m.* candy, bonbon. **2.** *adj.* sweet.
dolcemente, *adv.* sweetly, soothingly.
dolcezza, *n.f.* sweetness.
dolciastro, *adj.* sweetish; mellifluous.
dolciume, *n.m.* sweet.
dolènte, *adj.* sore.

dolere, vb. hurt, pain; (refl.) complain.

dòllaro, n.m. dollar.

dòlo, n.m. fraud, guile.

dolore, n.m. sorrow, pain, ache, grief.

doloroso, adj. dolorous, sorrowful, mournful, painful, grievous.

doloso, adj. fradulent, malicious.

domanda, n.f. question; request; application; demand; query.

domandare, vb. ask; demand; request; query; (refl.) wonder.

domani, n.m. and adv. tomorrow.

domare, vb. tame.

domattina, adv. tomorrow morning.

doménica, n.f. Sunday.

domèstica, n.f. housemaid.

domesticare, vb. domesticate.

domèstico, 1. n. servant. 2. adj. domestic.

domicìlio, n.m. domicile.

dominante, adj. dominant.

dominare, vb. dominate, sway.

dominazione, n.f. domination.

domìnio, n.m. domain, dominion.

dòmino, n.m. domino.

donare, vb. donate.

donatore, vb. giver.

donazione, n.f. donation.

donchisciottesco, adj. quixotic.

donde, adv. whence.

dondolare, vb. rock, swing.

dònna, n.f. woman.

donnaiòlo, n.m. playboy.

dònnola, n.f. weasel.

dono, m. gift, grant, present.

dopo, 1. adv. afterwards. 2. prep. after. **d. che,** conj. after.

dopobarba, n.m. aftershave (lotion).

dopodomani, adv. the day after tomorrow.

dopoguerra, n.m. postwar era.

doppiamente, adv. doubly.

doppiare, vb. double.

doppiétta, n.f. double-barreled shotgun.

dóppio, adj. double; duplex.

dorare, vb. gild.

dorato, adj. gilt.

doratura, n.f. gilt.

dormiglione, n.m sleepyhead.

dormire, vb. sleep.

dormitòrio, n.m. dormitory.

dormivéglia, n.m. drowsiness, doze

dorsale, adj. dorsal, pertaining to the back.

dòrso, n.m. back.

dosare, vb. dose.

dosatura, n.f. dosage.

dòse, n.f. dose.

dòsso, n.m. back.

dotare, vb. endow.

dotato, adj. gifted.

dotazione, n.f. endowment.

dòte, n.f. dowry.

dòtto, 1. n. scholar. 2. adj. learned.

dottorato, n.m. doctorate.

dottore, n.m. doctor.

dottrina, n.f. doctrine; learning.

dottrinàrio, adj. doctrinaire.

dove, adv. where.

dovere, 1. n.m. duty. 2. vb. owe; be supposed to; have to; ought; must.

dovunque, adv. wherever.

dovuto, adj. due, owing.

dozzina, n.f. dozen.

dozzinale, adj. cheap second rate, ordinary.

draga, n.f. dredge.

dragamine, n.m. minesweeper.

dragare, vb. dredge.

dragone, n.m. dragon.

dramma, n.m. dram; drama, play.

drammàtica, n.f. dramatics.

drammàtico, adj. dramatic.

drammatizzare, vb. dramatize.

drammaturgìa, n.f. dramaturgy, play-writing.

drammaturgo, n.m. dramatist, playwright.

drappeggiare, vb. drape.

drappeggio, n.m. drapery, drapes.

drappèllo, n.m. platoon.

dràstico, adj. drastic.

drenàggio, n.m. drainage.

drizza, n.f. halyard.

drizzare, vb. straighten.

dròga, n.f. drug.

dromedàrio, n.m. dromedary.

duale, adj. and adv. dual.

dualismo, n.m. dualism.

dùbbio, 1. n.m. doubt. 2. adj. doubtful, dubious.

dubbioso, adj. doubtful.

dubitare, *vb.* doubt.
duca, *n.m.* duke.
ducato, *n.m.* duchy, dukedom.
duce, *n.m.* (Fascist) leader.
duchessa, *n.f.* duchess.
due, *num.* two.
duecento, *num.* two hundred; **il D.** the thirteenth century.
duellante, *n.m.* duellist.
duellare, *vb.* duel.
duèllo, *n.m.* duel.
duetto, *n.m.* duet.
duna, *n.f.* dune.
dunque, *adv.* therefore; so; then.
duòmo, *n.m.* cathedral.
duplicare, *vb.* duplicate.

duplicato, *n.m.* duplicate.
duplicazione, *n.f.* duplication.
duplicità, *n.f.* duplicity, double-dealing.
duràbile, *adj.* durable, enduring.
durabilità, *n.f.* durability.
duramente, *adv.* hard.
durante, *prep.* during.
durare, *vb.* endure, last.
durata, *n.f.* duration.
duraturo, *adj.* lasting, enduring.
durévole, *adj.* lasting.
durezza, *n.f.* hardness.
duro, *adj.* hard.
durone, *n.m.* callosity.
dùttile, *adj.* ductile.

E

e, *conj.* and.
èbano, *n.m.* ebony.
ebbène, *interj.* well!
ebbrezza, *n.f.* intoxication.
ebràico, *n. and adj.* Hebrew, Hebraic; Jewish.
ebrèo, *n. and adj.* Hebrew; Jew(ish).
ebùrneo, *adj.* of ivory.
ecatombe, *n.f.* massacre, carnage.
eccèdere, *vb.* exceed.
eccellènte, *adj.* excellent.
eccellènza, *n.f.* excellence.
Eccellènza, *n.f.* Excellency.
eccèllere, *vb.* excel.
eccentricità, *n.f.* eccentricity.
eccèntrico, *adj.* eccentric.
eccessivo, *adj.* excessive.
eccèsso, *n.m.* excess.
eccètto, *prep.* except; but.
eccettuare, *vb.* except.
eccezionale, *adj.* exceptional.
eccezione, *n.f.* exception.
eccitàbile, *adj.* excitable, high-strung, hot-headed.
eccitamento, *n.m.* excitement.
eccitare, *vb.* excite.
eccitazione, *n.f.* excitement.
ecclesiàstico, 1. *n.* ecclesiastic, cleric, clergyman. **2.** *adj.* ecclesiastical.
ècco, *vb.* here is; there is; lo; behold.
echeggiare, *vb.* echo.
eclissare, *vb.* eclipse.

eclissi, *n.f.* eclipse.
eco, *n.m.* echo.
ecologìa, *n.f.* ecology.
ecològico, *adj.* ecological.
economìa, *n.f.* economy, thrift. **e. politica,** economics.
economicamente, *adv.* economically, cheaply.
econòmico, *adj.* economic, economical, cheap.
economista, *n.m.* economist.
economizzare, *vb.* economize, save.
ecosistèma, *n.m* ecosystem.
ecumènico, *adj.* ecumenical.
eczèma, *n.m.* eczema.
ed, *conj.* and.
édera, *n.f.* ivy.
edìcola, *n.f.* newsstand.
edificare, *vb.* edify, build.
edifìcio, *n.m.* edifice, building.
edìle, *adj.* building, construction.
edilìzia, *n.f.* building trade.
editore, *n.m.* publisher.
editorìa, *n.f.* publishing industry.
editoriale, *adj.* editorial.
editto, *n.m.* edict.
edizione, *n.f.* edition, publication.
edonismo, *n.m.* hedonism.
edòtto, *adj.* aware, informed.
educare, *vb.* educate, train.
educativo, *adj.* educational.
educatore, *n.m.* educator.
educazione, *n.f.* education, breeding, manners.

effeminato, *adj.* effeminate.
effervescènza, *n.f.* effervescence.
effettivamente, *adv.* effectively; in effect.
effettivo, *adj.* effective.
effètto, *n.m.* effect.
effettuare, *vb.* effect, bring about, contrive.
efficace, *adj.* efficacious, effectual.
efficàcia, *n.f.* efficacy.
efficiènte, *adj.* efficient.
efficientemente, *adv.* efficiently.
efficiènza, *n.f.* efficiency.
effigie, *n.f.* effigy.
effìmero, *adj.* ephemeral.
egemonìa, *n.f.* hegemony.
ègida, *n.f.* aegis, auspices, protection.
Egitto, *n.m.* Egypt.
egiziano, *adj.* Egyptian.
egli, *pron.* he.
egoìsmo, *n.m.* egoism, selfishness.
egoìstico, *adj.* selfish.
egotìsmo, *n.m.* egotism.
egotìsta, *n.m.* egotist.
egrègio, *adj.* eminent.
eguaglianza, *n.f.* equality.
éhi, *interj.* hey!
eiaculare, *vb.* ejaculate.
eiezione, *n.f.* ejection.
elaborare, *vb.* elaborate.
elaborato, *adj.* elaborate, complicated.
elaborazione, *n.f.* data processing.
elasticità, *n.f.* elasticity.
elàstico, *n.m. and adj.* elastic.
elefante, *n.m.* elephant.
elefantesco, *adj.* elephantine.
elegante, *adj.* elegant, smart.
eleganza, *n.f.* elegance.
elèggere, *vb.* elect.
eleggìbile, *adj.* eligible.
eleggibilità, *n.f.* eligibility.
elegìa, *n.f.* elegy.
elegìaco, *adj.* elegiac.
elementare, *adj.* elemental, elementary.
elemento, *n.m.* element.
elemòsina, *n.f.* charity, alms, dole.
elencare, *vb.* list, itemize.
elènco, *n.m.* list. **e. telefònico,** telephone directory.

elettivo, *adj.* elective.
elettricista, *n.m.* electrician.
elettricità, *n.f.* electricity.
elèttrico, *adj.* electric, electrical.
elettrocardiogramma, *n.m.* electrocardiogram.
elettrocuzione, *n.f.* electrocution.
elèttrodo, *n.m.* electrode.
elettrodomèstici, *n.m.pl.* electric household appliances.
elettrògeno, *adj.* generating (unit).
elettròlisi, *n.f.* electrolysis.
elettromotrice, *n.f.* electric railcar.
elettrone, *n.m.* electron.
elettrònica, *n.f.* electronics.
elettrònico, *adj.* electronic.
elettrotreno, *n.m.* express train of electric railcars.
elevare, *vb.* elevate.
elevazione, *n.f.* elevation.
elezione, *n.f.* election.
èlfo, *n.m.* elf.
èlica, *n.f.* propeller.
elicòttero, *n.m.* helicopter.
elìdere, *vb.* elide, suppress, annul.
eliminare, *vb.* eliminate.
eliminazione, *n.f.* elimination.
èlio, *n.m.* helium.
eliocèntrico, *adj.* heliocentric.
eliògrafo, *n.m.* heliograph.
eliotipìa, *n.f.* blueprint.
eliotròpio, *n.m.* heliotrope.
elisìr, *n.m.* elixir.
ella, *pron.f.* she; (very formal) you.
ellènico, *adj.* Hellenic.
ellenìsmo, *n.m.* Hellenism.
ellisse, *n.m.* ellipse.
èlmo, *n.m.* helmet.
elocuzione, *n.f.* elocution.
elogiare, *vb.* eulogize.
elògio, *n.m.* eulogy.
eloquènte, *adj.* eloquent.
eloquentemente, *adv.* eloquently.
eloquènza, *n.f.* eloquence.
èlsa, *n.f.* hilt.
elucidare, *vb.* elucidate.
elùdere, *vb.* elude, dodge, evade.
elusivo, *adj.* elusive.
emaciato, *adj.* emaciated.
emanare, *vb.* emanate.
emancipare, *vb.* emancipate.

emancipatore, *n.m.* emancipator.
emancipazione, *n.f.* emancipation.
emarginare, *vb.* neglect; put aside.
emarginato, *n.m. and adj.* misfit, outcast.
ematite, *n.f.* hematite.
embargo, *n.m.* embargo.
emblèma, *n.m.* emblem, badge.
emblemàtico, *adj.* emblematic.
embolìa, *n.f.* embolism.
embriologìa, *n.f.* embryology.
embrionale, *adj.* embryonic.
embrione, *n.m.* embryo.
emendamento, *n.m.* amendment.
emendare, *vb.* amend, emend.
emergènte, *adj.* emergent.
emergènza, *n.f.* emergency.
emèrgere, *vb.* emerge.
emèrito, *adj.* emeritus.
emersione, *n.f.* emersion.
emètico, *adj.* emetic.
eméttere, *vb.* emit; send forth; issue; utter.
emiciclo, *n.m.* hemicycle; legislative chamber.
emicrània, *n.f.* migraine.
emigrante, *n.m. and adj.* emigrant.
emigrare, *vb.* emigrate.
emigrazione, *n.f.* emigration.
eminènte, *adj.* eminent.
eminènza, *n.f.* eminence.
emisfèro, *n.m.* hemisphere.
emissàrio, *n.m.* emissary.
emissione, *n.f.* issue.
emittènte, 1. *adj.* issuing; transmitting; broadcasting. 2 *n.f.* issuer; transmitter; broadcast station.
emofilìa, *n.f.* hemophilia.
emoglobina, *n.f.* hemoglobin.
emolliènte, *n.m. and adj.* emollient.
emolumento, *n.m.* emolument.
emorragìa, *n.f.* hemorrhage.
emorròide, *n.f.* hemorrhoid, pile.
emotivo, *adj.* emotional.
emozionàbile, *adj.* emotional.
emozione, *n.f.* emotion.
empiastro, *n.m.* plaster.
émpio, *adj.* impious, blasphemous, godless.
empìreo, *adj.* empyreal, sublime.

empìrico, *adj.* empirical. **rimèdio e.,** nostrum.
empòrio, *n.m.* mart, emporium.
emulare, *vb.* emulate.
emulsione, *n.f.* emulsion.
encefalite, *n.f.* encephalitis.
encèfalo, *n.m.* encephalon.
enclìclica, *n.f.* encyclical.
enciclopedìa, *n.f.* encyclopaedia.
endèmico, *adj.* endemic.
endòcrino, *adj.* endocrine.
endovenoso, *adj.* intravenous.
energìa, *n.f.* energy.
enèrgico, *adj.* energetic.
energùmeno, *n.m.* possessed person, madman; bully.
ènfasi, *n.f.* emphasis.
enfàtico, *adj.* emphatic.
enfisèma, *n.m.* emphysema.
enigma, *n.m.* enigma, riddle.
enigmàtico, *adj.* enigmatic.
ennè, *n.m.* henna.
enòlogo, *n.m.* oenologist.
enòrme, *adj.* enormous.
enormità, *n.f.* enormity.
enteroclisma, *n.m.* enema, colonic irrigation.
entità, *n.f.* entity.
entrare, *vb.* enter.
entrata, *n.f.* entrance, entry; admission; revenue; input.
entro, *prep.* in; within.
entrotèrra, *n.m.* inland.
entusiasmo, *n.m.* enthusiasm.
entusiasta, *n.m. or f.* enthusiast, devotee.
entusiàstico, *adj.* enthusiastic.
enumerare, *vb.* enumerate.
enumerazione, *n.f.* enumeration.
enunciare, *vb.* enunciate.
enunciazione, *n.f.* enunciation.
epàtica, *n.f.* hepatica.
epàtico, *adj.* hepatic.
eperlano, *n.m.* smelt.
èpico, *adj.* epic.
epicurèo, *n.m.* epicure.
epidemìa, *n.f.* epidemic.
epidèmico, *adj.* epidemic.
epidèrmide, *n.f.* epidermis.
Epifanìa, *n.f.* Epiphany.
epigramma, *n.m.* epigram.
epilessìa, *n.f.* epilepsy.
epìlogo, *n.m.* epilogue.
episcopato, *n.m.* bishopric.
episòdio, *n.m.* episode.

epìstola, n.f. epistle.
epitàffio, n.m. epitaph.
epìteto, n.m. epithet.
epitomare, vb. epitomize.
epìtome, n.f. epitome.
època, n.f. epoch.
epopéa, n.f. epic.
epurare, vb. purify, cleanse, purge.
equanimità, n.f. equanimity.
equatore, n.m. equator.
equatoriale, adj. equatorial.
equazione, n.f. equation.
equèstre, adj. equestrian.
equidistante, adj. equidistant.
equilàtero, adj. equilateral.
equilibrare, vb. balance, equilibrate.
equilibrato, adj. balanced; level.
equilìbrio, n.m. balance, equilibrium; poise.
equino, adj. equine.
equinòzio, n.m. equinox.
equipaggiare, vb. rig.
equipàggio, n.m. crew; equipment; rig.
equipe, n.f. team.
equità, n.f. equity.
equitazione, n.f. equitation, horsemanship.
equivalènte, adj. equivalent.
equivalere, vb. be equivalent.
equìvoco, 1. n.m. mistake. **2.** adj. equivocal.
èquo, adj. equable, equitable, fair, just.
èra, n.f. era.
eràrio, n.m. treasury.
èrba, n.f. grass; herb.
erbàccia, n.f. weed.
erbàceo, n.m. herbaceous.
erbàrio, n.m. herbarium.
erbicida, n.m. weed killer.
erbìvoro, adj. herbivorous.
erboso, adj. grassy.
ercùleo, adj. Herculean.
erède, n.m. heir.
eredità, n.f. heredity; heritage; inheritance.
ereditare, vb. inherit.
ereditàrio, adj. hereditary.
ereditièra, n.f. heiress.
eremita, n.m. hermit.
eremitàggio, n.m. hermitage.

èremo, n.m. hermitage, monastery.
eresìa, n.f. heresy.
erètico, 1. n. heretic. **2.** adj. heretical.
erètto, adj. erect, upright.
erezione, n.f. erection.
èrgere, vb. raise.
ergo, adv. thus, therefore.
èrica, n.f. heather.
erìgere, vb. erect, raise.
ermellino, n.m. ermine.
ermètico, adj. hermetic.
èrnia, n.f. hernia.
eròdere, vb. erode.
eròe, n.m. hero.
eroicamente, adv. heroically.
eròico, adj. heroic.
eroìna, n.f. heroine; heroin.
eroìsmo, n.m. heroism.
erosione, n.f. erosion.
erosivo, adj. erosive.
eròtico, adj. erotic.
erotismo, n.m. eroticism.
èrpete, n.f. herpes, shingles.
erpicare, vb. harrow.
èrpice, n.m. harrow.
errabondo, adj. vagrant, roaming.
errante, adj. errant.
errare, vb. err, make a mistake, be wrong; wander; rove.
erràtico, adj. erratic.
errato, adj. wrong, mistaken.
erròneo, adj. erroneous, mistaken.
errore, n.m. error, mistake, blunder, slip.
èrto, adj. steep.
erudito, 1. n. scholar. **2.** adj. erudite.
erudizione, n.f. erudition, scholarship.
eruttare, vb. erupt.
eruzione, n.f. eruption; rash.
esacerbare, vb. embitter, exasperate.
esagerare, vb. exaggerate.
esagerazione, n.f. exaggeration.
esàgono, n.m. hexagon.
esalare, vb. exhale.
esalazione, n.f. fume.
esaltare, vb. exalt, elate.
esaltato, adj. exalted, elated.

esaltazione, *n.f.* exaltation, elation.

esame, *n.m.* examination; canvass; survey.

esaminando, *n.m.* examinee.

esaminare, *vb.* examine; canvass; survey.

esangue, *adj.* bloodless.

esànime, *adj.* exanimate, inanimate.

esasperante, *adj.* irritating.

esasperare, *vb.* exasperate.

esasperazione, *n.f.* exasperation.

esattamente, *adv.* exactly.

esatto, *adj.* exact.

esattòre, *n.m.* tax collector.

esaudire, *vb.* grant, fulfil.

esauriènte, *adj.* exhaustive; indepth.

esaurimento, *n.m.* exhaustion.

esaurire, *vb.* exhaust, deplete.

esca, *n.f.* bait; tinder.

eschimese, *n.m.* Eskimo pie.

esclamare, *vb.* exclaim.

esclamazione, *n.f.* exclamation.

esclùdere, *vb.* exclude.

esclusione, *n.f.* exclusion.

esclusivo, *adj.* exclusive.

escogitare, *vb.* excogitate, devise.

escoriare, *vb.* excoriate.

escremento, *n.m.* excrement.

escursione, *n.f.* excursion, jaunt, junket, outing.

esecràbile, *adj.* execrable.

esecutivo, *adj.* executive.

esecutore, *n.m.* executor.

esecuzione, *n.f.* execution, enforcement; performance, rendition.

esegèsi, *n.f.* exegesis.

eseguire, *vb.* execute, enforce; perform.

esèmpio, *n.m.* example.

esemplare, 1. *n.m.* copy. **2.** *adj.* exemplary.

esemplificare, *vb.* exemplify.

esentare, *vb.* exempt; dispense.

esènte, *adj.* exempt; immune. e. da dogana, duty-free.

esenzione, *n.f.* exemption.

esèquie, *n.f.pl.* funeral rites.

esercènte, *n.m.* store owner, dealer, merchant.

esercitare, *vb.* exercise; exert; drill, practice.

esercitazione, *n.f.* practice, drill.

esèrcito, *n.m.* army.

esercìzio, *n.m.* exercise.

esibire, *vb.* exhibit, display.

esibizione, *n.f.* exhibition, display.

esibizionismo, *n.m.* exhibitionism.

esigènza, *n.f.* exigency; requirement.

esìgere, *vb.* exact, require, demand.

esiguo, *adj.* thin, scanty, meager.

esilarante, *adj.* exhilarating, cheering.

esilarare, *vb.* exhilarate.

èsile, *adj.* weak, slender, thin.

esiliare, *vb.* exile, banish.

esilio, *n.m.* exile, banishment.

esìmio, *adj.* eminent.

esistènte, *adj.* existent, extant.

esistènza, *n.f.* existence, being.

esistere, *vb.* exist.

esitante, *adj.* hesitant.

esitare, *vb.* hesitate, falter, waver.

esitazione, *n.f.* hesitation.

èsodo, *n.m.* exodus.

esòfago, *n.m.* esophagus.

esonerare, *vb.* exonerate.

esorbitante, *adj.* exorbitant.

esorcizzare, *vb.* exorcise.

esortare, *vb.* exhort; plead with.

esortativo, *adj.* exhortatory.

esortazione, *n.f.* exhortation.

esotèrico, *adj.* esoteric.

esòtico, *adj.* exotic.

espàndere, *vb.* expand.

espansione, *n.f.* expansion.

espansivo, *adj.* expansive, effusive.

espanso, 1. *adj.* expanded, flared. **2.** *n.m.* styrofoam.

espatriato, *adj.* expatriate.

espediente, *n.m. and adj.* expedient; makeshift.

espèllere, *vb.* expel, drive out, eject, evict, oust.

esperiènza, *n.f.* experience.

esperimentare, *n.m.* experiment; experience.

esperimento, *n.m.* experiment.

espèrto, *n.m. and adj.* expert; experienced, practiced, proficient.

espettorare, *vb.* expectorate.

espiare, *vb.* expiate, atone for.

espiazione, *n.f.* expiation, atonement.

espirare, *vb.* expire.

espirazione, *n.f.* expiration.

espletivo, *adj.* expletive.

esplicare, *vb.* explicate; carry out; practice.

esplicativo, *adj.* explanatory.

esplicito, *adj.* explicit.

esplòdere, *vb.* explode.

esplorare, *vb.* explore.

esplorativo, *adj.* exploratory.

esploratore, *n.m.* explorer; scout.

esplorazione, *n.f.* exploration.

esplosione, *n.f.* explosion, blast.

esplosivo, *n.m. and adj.* explosive.

esponente, *n.m.* exponent.

esporre, *vb.* expose.

esportare, *vb.* export.

esportazione, *n.f.* export, exportation.

espositivo, *adj.* expository.

esposizione, *n.f.* exposition; exposé; exposure; show.

esposto, *n.m.* exposé.

espressamente, *adv.* expressly.

espressione, *n.f.* expression.

espressivo, *adj.* expressive.

esprèsso, *n.m. and adj.* express; special delivery; coffee 'espresso.'

esprimere, *vb.* express.

espropriare, *vb.* expropriate.

espugnare, *vb.* conquer.

espulsione, *n.f.* expulsion, ejection, eviction, ouster.

espùngere, *vb.* expunge.

espurgare, *vb.* expurgate.

essa, *pron.f.sg.* she; it.

esse, *pron.f.pl.* they.

essènza, *n.f.* essence.

essenziale, *adj.* essential.

essenzialmente, *adv.* essentially.

èssere, 1. *n.* being. 2. *vb.* be.

essi, *pron.m.pl.* they.

essiccatòio, *n.m.* drier.

esso, *pron.m.sg.* he; it.

essudare, *vb.* exude.

essudato, *n.m.* exudation.

èst, *n.m.* east.

èstasi, *n.f.* ecstasy, rapture.

estasiare, *vb.* send into ecstasies, enrapture.

estate, *n.f.* summer.

estemporàneo, *adj.* extemporaneous.

estèndere, *vb.* extend, enlarge, broaden.

estensione, *n.f.* extent; extension; range.

estenuante, *adj.* enervating, exhausting.

estenuare, *vb.* extenuate.

esteriore, *adj.* exterior, outer, outward.

esteriormente, *adv.* outwardly.

esternare, *vb.* manifest, express.

estèrno, *adj.* external, outside.

èstero, 1. *n.m.* foreign parts. 2. *adj.* foreign; external.

estesamente, *adv.* extensively.

esteso, *adj.* extensive; far-flung.

estètica, *n.f.* aesthetics.

estètico, *adj.* aesthetic.

estetista, *n.m. and f.* beautician.

èstimo, *n.m.* evaluation, appraisal, quotation.

estìnguere, *vb.* extinguish, quench.

estinto, *adj.* extinct.

estintore, *n.m.* fire extinguisher.

estinzione, *n.f.* extinction.

estirpare, *vb.* extirpate.

estivo, *adj.* of summer.

estòllere, *vb.* extol.

estòrcere, *vb.* extort.

estorsione, *n.f.* extortion.

estra-, *prefix.* extra-.

estradare, *vb.* extradite.

estradizione, *n.f.* extradition.

estràneo, *adj.* extraneous.

estrapolare, *vb.* extrapolate.

estrarre, *vb.* extract.

estratto, *n.m.* extract.

estrazione, *n.f.* extraction.

estremamente, *adv.* extremely, exceedingly.

estremista, *n.m. and f.* extremist.

estremità, *n.f.* extremity; end; butt.

estrèmo, 1. *n.* fullback. 2. *adj.* extreme, utmost.

èstro, *n.m.* whim, inspiration; fancy; imagination.

estroverso, *adj.* extrovert.

estuàrio, *n.m.* estuary.

esuberante, *adj.* exuberant; ebullient.

èsule, *n.m. and f.* exile.

esultante, *adj.* exultant.

esultare, *vb.* exult.
esumare, *vb.* exhume; resurrect.
esumazione, *n.f.* exhumation.
età, *n.f.* age.
ètere, *n.m.* ether.
etèreo, *adj.* ethereal.
eternamente, *adv.* eternally, for-evermore.
eternità, *n.f.* eternity; eon.
etèrno, *adj.* eternal.
eterodossia, *n.f.* heterodoxy.
eterodòsso, *adj.* heterodox.
eterogèneo, *adj.* heterogeneous, motley.
eterosessuale, *adj.* heterosexual.
ètica, *n.f.* ethics.
etichetta, *n.f.* label; docket; sticker; tag.
ètico, *adj.* ethical; hectic.
etìlico, *adj.* ethyl.
etimologìa, *n.f.* etymology.
ètnico, *adj.* ethnic.
etnografìa, *n.f.* ethnography.
etnologìa, *n.f.* ethnology.
èttaro, *n.m.* hectare.
ètto, *n.m.* hectogram.
ettogramma, *n.m.* hectogram.
eucalipto, *n.m.* eucalyptus.
eucaristìa, *n.f.* Eucharist.
eufemismo, *n.m.* euphemism.
eufònico, *adj.* euphonious.
euforìa, *n.f.* euphoria, elation.
eugenètica, *n.f.* eugenics.
eugènico, *adj.* eugenic.
eunuco, *n.m.* eunuch.
Europa, *n.f.* Europe.
europèo, *adj. and n.* European.
eurovisione, *n.f.* European televi-sion chain.
eutanasìa, *n.f.* euthanasia.
evacuare, *vb.* evacuate.
evanescènte, *adj.* evanescent.
evangelista, *n.m.* evangelist.
evaporare, *vb.* evaporate.
evaporazione, *n.f.* evaporation.
evasione, *n.f.* evasion; escape.
evasivo, *adj.* evasive.
evenènza, *n.f.* eventuality, chance, circumstance.
evènto, *n.m.* outcome.
eversivo, *adj.* destructive.
evidènte, *adj.* evident.
evidentemente, *adv.* evidently.
evidènza, *n.f.* evidence.
evirare, *vb.* emasculate.
evitàbile, *adj.* avoidable.
evitare, *vb.* avoid, evade, eschew, obviate.
èvo, *n.m.* times, age, era.
evocare, *vb.* evoke.
evoluzione, *n.f.* evolution.
evoluzionista, *n.m.* evolutionist.
evòlvere, *vb.* evolve.
evviva, *interj.* hurrah (for).
extra, *adj.* extra.
ex voto, *n.m.* votive offering.

F

F (on water faucets) — **freddo,** *adj.* cold.
fa, *adv.* ago.
fàbbrica, *n.f.* factory, mill; (archi-tecture) fabric.
fabbricante, *n.m.* manufacturer.
fabbricare, *vb.* build; manufac-ture, fabricate.
fabbricazione, *n.f.* manufacture; fabrication.
fabbro, *n.m.* smith. **f. ferraio,** blacksmith.
faccendière, *n.m.* busybody.
faccetta, *n.f.* facet.
facchino, *n.m.* porter.
faccia, *n.f.* face.
facciata, *n.f.* facade.
facèto, *adj.* facetious, witty, hu-morous.
facchino, *n.m.* porter.
facciale, *adj.* facial.
fàcile, *adj.* easy, facile.
facilità, *n.f.* facility, ease, easiness.
facilitare, *vb.* facilitate.
facilmente, *adv.* easily.
facinoroso, *adj.* violent, riotous; bullying.
facoltà, *n.f.* faculty, knack, power.
facoltativo, *adv.* optional.
facsimile, *n.m.* facsimile.
factotum, *n.m.* handy-man; jack-of-all-trades.
fàggio, *n.m.* beech.
fagiano, *n.m.* pheasant.

fagiòlo, *n.m.* string bean.
faglia, *n.f.* faille.
fagòtto, *n.m.* bassoon.
fàida, *n.f.* feud; vengeance.
falcata, *n.f.* stride.
falce, *n.f.* scythe.
falciare, *vb.* mow.
falco, *n.m.* hawk.
falcone, *n.m.* falcon.
falconerìa, *n.f.* falconry.
falegname, *n.m.* carpenter.
falla, *n.f.* leak.
fallace, *adj.* fallacious.
fallàcia, *n.f.* fallacy.
fallìbile, *adj.* fallible.
fallimento, *n.m.* bankruptcy; failure.
fallire, *vb.* fail; go bankrupt.
fallito, *adj.* bankrupt.
fallòcrate, *adj.* macho.
falò, *n.m.* bonfire.
falsetto, *n.m.* falsetto.
falsificare, *vb.* falsify, fake, counterfeit.
falsificatore, *n.f.* faker.
falsificazione, *n.f.* falsification.
falsità, *n.f.* falsity.
falso, 1. *n.m.* counterfeit, fake. **2.** *adj.* false, counterfeit.
fama, *n.f.* fame.
fame, *n.f.* hunger; starvation. **aver f.,** be hungry.
famigerato, *adj.* notorious.
famiglia, *n.f.* family; household.
familiare, *adj.* familiar, well-known; acquainted.
familiarità, *n.f.* familiarity.
familiarizzare, *vb.* familiarize.
famoso, *adj.* famous, famed.
fanale, *n.m.* lamp; light. **f. anteriore,** headlight.
fanàtico, *n.m. and adj.* fanatic, fanatical.
fanatismo, *n.m.* fanaticism.
fanciulla, *n.f.* maiden; girl.
fanciullescamente, *adv.* childishly; boyishly.
fanciullesco, *adj.* childish; boyish.
fanciullezza, *n.f.* childhood; boyhood; girlhood.
fanciullo, *n.m.* child; boy.
fandònia, *n.f.* fib; story, tale; *(pl.)* nonsense.
fanfara, *n.f.* fanfare.

fanfarone, *n.m.* boaster, braggart.
fanghìglia, *n.f.* slush.
fango, *n.m.* mud, mire.
fangoso, *adj.* muddy.
fannullone, *n.m.* idler, slacker; bum.
fantascienza, *n.f.* science fiction.
fantasìa, *n.f.* fantasy, imagination. **di f.,** fancy.
fantasma, *n.m.* phantom.
fantasticherìa, *n.f.* reverie, daydream.
fantàstico, *adj.* fantastic.
fante, *n.m.* infantryman.
fanterìa, *n.f.* infantry.
fantino, *n.m.* jockey.
fantoccio, *n.m.* puppet, dummy.
farabutto, *n.m.* scoundrel, rascal.
faraona, *n.f.* guinea fowl.
faraone, *n.m.* Pharaoh.
farcire, *vb.* stuff.
fardèllo, *n.m.* burden.
fare, *vb.* do; make. **f. a meno di,** go without. **f. finta di,** pretend to.
farètra, *n.f.* quiver (arrowcase).
farfalla, *n.f.* butterfly.
farfugliare, *vb.* mutter, mumble.
farina, *n.f.* flour; farina; meal.
faringe, *n.f.* pharynx.
farmacìa, *n.f.* drug store, pharmacy.
farmacista, *n.m.* druggist, pharmacist.
faro, *n.m.* beacon, lighthouse.
farsa, *n.f.* farce.
farsesco, *adj.* farcical.
fàscia, *n.f.* band; bandage.
fàscino, *n.m.* fascination; charm; glamor.
fàscio, *n.m.* bundle; sheaf; Fascist group.
fascismo, *n.m.* fascism.
fascista, *n. and adj.* fascist.
fase, *n.f.* phase, stage.
fastìdio, *n.m.* annoyance, bother, trouble, unpleasantness, nuisance.
fastidioso, *adj.* fastidious; bothersome, troublesome.
fasto, *n.m.* pomp.
fastoso, *adj.* pompous.
fata, *n.f.* fairy.
fatale, *adj.* fatal; fateful.
fatalità, *n.f.* fatality.

fatalmente, vb. fatally.
fatica, n.f. fatigue; toil, hard work.
faticare, vb. toil.
fato, n.m. fate.
fattìbile, adj. feasible.
fattispècie, n.f. **nella f.** in this particular case.
fatto, n.m. fact; deed, feat.
fattore, n.m. maker; factor; steward; granger.
fattorìa, n.f. farm; grange; homestead; ranch; station.
fattorino, n.m. messenger, delivery boy.
fattura, n.f. invoice.
fatturare, vb. invoice.
fàuci, n.f.pl. jaws.
fàuna, n.f. fauna.
fàuno, n.m. faun.
fàusto, adj. prosperous; propitious, lucky.
fava, n.f. bean.
favo, n.m. honeycomb.
fàvola, n.f. fable.
favoloso, adj. fabulous.
favore, n.m. favor; behalf. **a f. di,** in behalf of. **per f.,** please.
favorévole, adj. favorable, auspicious.
favorire, vb. favor.
favoritismo, n.m. favoritism.
favorito, n.m. and adj. favorite.
fazione, n.f. faction.
fazzoletti detergenti, n.m.pl. facial tissues.
fazzoletto, n.m. handkerchief.
febbraio, n.m. February.
fèbbre, n.f. fever.
febbrile, adj. feverish.
febbrilmente, adv. feverishly.
fèccia, n.f. dregs; lees; (pl.) faeces.
fèci, n.f.pl. feces.
fecondo, adj. fecund.
fede, n.f. faith, creed.
fededegno, adj. trustworthy, reliable.
fedele, adj. faithful, true.
fedeltà, n.f. faithfulness, allegiance, fidelity.
fèdera, n.f. pillowcase.
federale, adj. federal.
federazione, n.f. federation.

fedìfrago, adj. unfaithful.
fedina, n.f. police record. **avere la f. sporca,** to have a bad record.
fégato, n.m. liver; pluck; guts.
felce, n.f. fern.
felice, adj. happy, felicitous.
felicemente, adv. happily.
felicità, n.f. felicity, happiness.
felicitare, vb. congratulate; felicitate; compliment.
felicitazione, n.f. congratulation; felicitation.
felino, adj. feline.
fellone, n.m. felon.
feltro, n.m. felt.
fémmina, n.f. female.
femminile, adj. female, feminine.
femminilità, n.f. femininity.
femminismo, n.m. feminism.
fèmore, n.m. femur, thighbone.
fèndere, vb. split, cleave, crack.
fenditura, n.f. split, cleft, crack.
fenomenale, adj. phenomenal.
fenòmeno, n.m. phenomenon.
fèretro, n.m. coffin.
feriale, adj. weekday.
fèrie, n.f.pl. holiday, vacation.
ferire, vb. wound, injure.
ferita, n.f. wound, injury.
ferito, n.m. wounded person, casualty.
feritòia, n.f. loophole.
ferma biancherìa, n.m. clothespin.
fermamente, adv. firmly, fast.
fermare, vb. stop, halt, stay.
fermata, n.f. stop, halt. **f. intermèdia,** stop-over.
fermatura, n.f. fastening.
fermentare, vb. ferment.
fermentazione, n.f. fermentation.
fermento, n.m. ferment.
fermezza, n.f. firmness.
fermo, adj. firm, fixed, fast, steady. **f. pòsta,** general delivery. **mettere il f. su,** garnishee.
feroce, adj. ferocious, fierce.
ferocemente, adv. ferociously.
feròcia, n.f. ferocity.
ferragosto, n.m. Assumpion; mid-August holiday.
ferramenta, n.f.pl. hardware.
ferrare, vb. shoe.
fèrreo, adj. iron.

ferrièra, *n.f.* ironworks.
fèrro, *n.m.* iron. **f. da stirare,** flat-iron. **f. di cavallo,** horseshoe.
ferrovia, *n.f.* railroad.
ferroviàrio, *adj.* railroad.
fèrtile, *adj.* fertile.
fertilità, *n.f.* fertility.
fertilizzante, *n.m.* fertilizer.
fertilizzare, *vb.* fertilize.
fertilizzazione, *n.f.* fertilization.
fervènte, *adj.* fervent.
ferventemente, *adv.* fervently.
fèrvido, *adj.* fervid.
fervore, *n.m.* fervor, fervency.
fesseria, *n.f.* nonsense, blunder, trifle.
fesso, *adj.* cracked; crazy.
fessura, *n.f.* split, cleavage, cranny, fissure; slit; slot.
fèsta, *n.f.* feast, festival, fête, holiday, vacation.
festeggiare, *vb.* celebrate.
festività, *n.f.* festivity.
festivo, *adj.* festive. **giorno f.,** holiday.
festone, *n.m.* festoon.
fetale, *adj.* fetal.
feticcio, *n.m.* fetish.
fètido, *adj.* fetid.
fèto, *n.m.* fetus.
fetore, *n.m.* stench.
fetta, *n.f.* slice, fillet.
feudale, *adj.* feudal.
feudalismo, *n.m.* feudalism.
fèudo, *n.m.* fief, feud.
fiaba, *n.f.* fairy tale.
fiacco, *adj.* limp.
fiàccola, *n.f.* torch.
fiala, *n.f.* vial.
fiamma, *n.f.* flame, blaze.
fiammante, *adj.* flaming, **nuovo f.,** brand new.
fiammeggiare, *vb.* flame, blaze; flare.
fiammìfero, *n.m.* match.
fiammingo, 1. *n.* Fleming; fla-mingo. **2.** *adj.* Flemish.
fiancheggiare, *vb.* flank.
fianco, *n.m.* flank; hip; side. **di f. a,** beside, abreast of.
fiasco, *n.m.* flask; fiasco; flop.
fiato, *n.m.* breath.
fibbia, *n.f.* buckle.
fibra, *n.f.* fiber.
fibroso, *adj.* fibrous.

ficcanaso, *n.m.* nosy person, busybody.
ficcare, *vb.* put; thrust, stick, shove.
fico, *n.m.* fig.
fidanzamento, *n.m.* betrothal, engagement.
fidanzare, *vb.* betroth, affiance; *(refl.)* get engaged.
fidanzata, *n.f.* fiancée.
fidanzato, *n.m.* fiancé.
fidatezza, *n.f.* dependability.
fidènte, *adj.* reliant.
fido, *adj.* dependable.
fidùcia, *n.f.* trust.
fiduciàrio, *adj.* fiduciary.
fiducioso, *adj.* trustful, confident.
fièle, *n.m.* gall. **vescica del f.,** gall-bladder.
fienile, *n.m.* hayloft.
fièno, *n.m.* hay.
fièra, *n.f.* fair. **f. campionària,** sample fair.
fifone, *n.m.* (coll.) scaredy-cat, coward.
figlia, *n.f.* daughter.
figliare, *vb.* have a litter.
figliastra, *n.f.* stepdaughter.
figliastro, *n.m.* stepson, stepchild.
figliata, *n.f.* litter.
figlio, *n.m.* son.
figliòccio, *n.m.* godchild.
figliòla, *n.f.* daughter; girl.
figliòlo, *n.m.* son; boy.
figura, *n.f.* figure.
figurare, *vb.* figure.
figurarsi, *vb.* imagine, fancy, en-visage.
figuratamente, *adv.* figuratively.
figurato, *adj.* figurative.
figurina, *n.f.* figurine.
fila, *n.f.* file; line; row; rank; tier.
filàccia inglese, *n.f.* lint.
filamento, *n.m.* filament.
filantropia, *n.f.* philanthropy.
filare, *vb.* spin.
filastròcca, *n.f.* rhyme; children's song.
filatèlica, *n.f.* philately.
filato, *n.m.* yarn.
filetto, *n.m.* fillet.
filiale, *adj.* filial.
filigrana, *n.f.sg.* filigree.
film, *n.m.* movie.
filo, *n.m.* thread; string; clew; wire.

filobus, *n.m.* trolley-bus.
filogovernativo, *adj.* on the government side.
filone, *n.m.* vein, lode.
filosofia, *n.f.* philosophy.
filosòfico, *adj.* philosophical.
filòsofo, *n.m.* philosopher.
filovia, *n.f.* trolley-bus line.
filtrare, *vb.* filter.
filtro, *n.m.* filter.
filza, *n.f.* string; collection; file.
finale, 1. *n.m.* finale. **2.** *adj.* final, eventual.
finalista, *n.m.* finalist.
finalità, *n.f.* finality; purpose.
finalmente, *adv.* finally.
finanza, *n.f.* finance.
finanziàrio, *adj.* financial.
finanzière, *n.m.* financier.
finchè, *conj.* till, until.
fine, *n.m.* purpose; *f.* end, finish.
finesettimana, *n.m.* weekend.
finèstra, *n.f.* window.
finezza, *n.f.* finesse.
fingere, *vb.* pretend, feign, assume, make believe.
finimondo, *n.m.* disaster, fracas.
finire, *vb.* end, finish.
fino, *adj.* fine; pure.
fino a., *prep.* as far as; until, till. **f. dove?** how far? **f. a quando?** how long?
finòcchio, *n.m.* fennel; *(slang)* pederast.
finora, *adv.* up to now, so far, hereto, hitherto.
finta, *n.f.* pretense, make-believe.
finto, *adj.* pretended, fictional, mock, make-believe.
finzione, *n.f.* fiction; figment.
fiòcco, *n.m.* flake; (boat) jib. **f. da cipria,** powder-puff.
fiòcina, *n.f.* harpoon.
fiocinare, *vb.* harpoon.
fiòco, *adj.* hoarse.
fionda, *n.f.* sling.
fioraio, *n.m.* florist.
fiòrdo, *n.m.* fjord, inlet.
fiore, *n.m.* flower, bloom, blossom.
fiorentino, *adj.* Florentine.
fioretto, *n.m.* foil.
fiori, *n.m.pl.* clubs (cards).
fiorire, *vb.* flower, bloom, blossom; flourish.

fiorista, *n.m.* florist.
fiorito, *adj.* flowery.
fiòtto, *n.m.* stream.
Firènze, *n.f.* Florence.
firma, *n.f.* signature.
firmare, *vb.* sign; endorse.
firmatàrio, *n.m.* signer, responsible party.
fisarmònica, *n.f.* accordion.
fiscale, *adj.* fiscal.
fischiare, *vb.* whistle.
fischietto, *n.m.* whistle *(instrument)*.
fischio, *n.m.* whistle *(sound)*.
Fisco, *n.m.* *(coll.)* Internal Revenue Service.
fisica, *n.f.* physics.
fisico, 1. *n.m.* physicist; physique. **2.** *adj.* physical.
fisima, *n.f.* caprice, whim, fancy; nonsense.
fisiologia, *n.f.* physiology.
fisioterapia, *n.f.* physiotherapy.
fissare, *vb.* fix; set; appoint; assess (a fine); fasten.
fissazione, *n.f.* fixation.
fissione, *n.f.* fission.
fisso, *adj.* fixed; set.
fistola, *n.f.* fistula *(pathology)*.
fittiziamente, *adv.* fictitiously.
fittìzio, *adj.* fictitious.
fitto, *adj.* thick.
fiume, *n.m.* river.
fiumicino, *n.m.* stream, creek.
fiutare, *vb.* smell.
fiuto, *n.m.* scent; smell; flair.
flàccido, *adj.* flaccid.
flacone, *n.m.* flacon.
flagellante, *n.m.* flagellant.
flagellare, *vb.* flagellate.
flagrante, *adj.* flagrant.
flagrantemente, *adv.* flagrantly.
flan, *n.m.* custard.
flanèlla, *n.f.* flannel.
flautista, *n.m.* flautist.
flàuto, *n.m.* flute.
flèbile, *adj.* feeble, weak.
flebite, *n.f.* phlebitis.
flèmma, *n.m.* phlegm.
flemmàtico, *adj.* phlegmatic.
flessìbile, *adj.* flexible; limp.
flessibilità, *n.f.* flexibility.
flessione, *n.f.* inflection.
flessuoso, *adj.* lithe.
flèttere, *vb.* flex.

flirt, *n.m.* flirtation.

flirtare, *vb.* flirt.

floreale, *adj.* floral.

flòscio, *adj.* soft; flabby.

flòtta, *n.f.* fleet.

fluènte, *adj.* glib.

fluidità, *n.f.* fluidity.

flùido, *n.m. and adj.* fluid.

fluorescènte, *adj.* fluorescent.

fluoroscòpio, *n.m.* fluoroscope.

flusso, *n.m.* flux.

fluttuare, *vb.* fluctuate.

fluttuazione, *n.f.* fluctuation.

fluviale, *adj.* fluvial, river.

fòbia, *n.f.* phobia.

fòca, *n.f.* seal.

focàccia, *n.f.* cake.

focale, *adj.* focal.

foce, *n.f.* mouth (of river); outfall.

focolare, *n.m.* fireplace, hearth.

focolàio, *n.m.* focus *(pathology)*; hotbed.

focoso, *adj.* fiery.

fòdera, *n.f.* lining.

fòdero, *n.m.* sheath.

foga, *n.f.* enthusiasm, ardor.

fòggia, *n.f.* shape, guise.

foggiare, *vb.* make; forge; shape.

fòglia, *n.f.* leaf; blade (of grass); foil.

fogliame, *n.m.* foliage.

fòglio, *n.m.* sheet.

fogliolina, *n.f.* leaflet.

fogliuto, *adj.* leafy.

fogna, *n.f.* drain; sewer.

folata, *n.f.* gust.

folclore, *n.m.* folklore.

folgorante, *adj.* striking.

folgorare, *vb.* strike *(lightning)*.

folgore, *n.f.* thunderbolt.

fòlio, *n.m.* folio.

fòlla, *n.f.* crowd; crush; mob.

folle, *adj.* crazy; mad.

folletto, *n.m.* elf, hobgoblin.

follìa, *n.f.* folly.

follìcolo, *n.m.* follicle.

folto, *adj.* thick; bushy.

fomentare, *vb.* foment.

fonda, *n.f.* anchorage; **alla f.** at anchor.

fondale, *n.m.* backdrop; ocean floor.

fondamentale, *adj.* fundamental, basic.

fondamento, *n.m.* foundation.

fondare, *vb.* found.

fondatore, *n.m.* founder.

fondazione, *n.f.* foundation.

fondènte, *n.m.* fondant.

fóndere, *vb.* melt; (metal) cast; fuse; (ore) smelt.

fonderìa, *n.f.* foundry.

fondina, *n.f.* holster.

fonditore, *n.m.* melter; smelter; caster.

fondo, *n.m.* bottom; fund.

fonètico, *adj.* phonetic.

fontana, *n.f.* fountain.

fonte, *n.f.* spring; source.

foràggio, *n.m.* forage; fodder.

forare, *vb.* bore, pierce, puncture.

foratura, *n.f.* puncture.

fòrbici, *n.f.pl.* scissors.

forca, *n.f.* pitchfork; gallows.

forchetta, *n.f.* fork.

forcina, *n.f.* hairpin, bobby pin.

fòrcipe, *n.m.* forceps.

forènse, *adj.* forensic.

forèsta, *n.f.* forest, wood.

forestièro, 1. *n.* foreigner. 2. *adj.* foreign.

fórfora, *n.f.* dandruff.

forgiare, *vb.* forge, shape.

forma, *n.f.* form, mold, shape; (shoe) last.

formàggio, *n.m.* cheese.

formaldèide, *n.f.* formaldehyde.

formale, *adj.* formal.

formalità, *n.f.* formality.

formalmente, *adv.* formally.

formare, *vb.* form, mold, shape; (telephone) dial (a number).

formativo, *adj.* formative.

formato, *n.m.* format.

formazione, *n.f.* formation.

formica, *n.f.* ant.

formicàio, *n.m.* anthill.

formicolare, *vb.* swarm.

formidàbile, *adj.* formidable.

formoso, *adj.* buxom, shapely.

fòrmula, *n.f.* formula.

formulare, *vb.* formulate.

formulazione, *n.f.* formulation.

fornace, *n.f.* furnace; kiln.

fornaio, *n.m.* baker.

fornèllo, *n.m.* stove.

fornire, *vb.* furnish, equip, supply.

fornitura, *n.f.* supply.

forno, *n.m.* oven; bakery.

foro, *n.m.* hole, bore, vent.

fòro, *n.m.* forum.

forse, *adv.* perhaps, maybe, possibly.

forsennato, *n.m.* frantic, mad.

forsìzia, *n.f.* forsythia.

fòrte, 1. *n.m.* forte. **2.** *adj.* strong; loud. **3.** *adv.* loud.

fortemente, *adv.* strongly; hard.

fortezza, *n.f.* fort, fortress; fortitude.

fortificare, *vb.* fortify.

fortificazione, *n.f.* fortification.

fortino, *n.m.* blockhouse, redoubt.

fortùito, *adj.* fortuitous, chance.

fortuna, *n.f.* fortune, luck.

fortunale, *n.m.* tempest, storm.

fortunato, *adj.* fortunate, lucky.

forùncolo, *n.m.* boil; pimple.

forviante, *adj.* misleading.

forviare, *vb.* mislead.

fòrza, *n.f.* force, strength.

forzare, *vb.* force.

forzato, *adj.* forced; forcible.

foschìa, *n.f.* fog.

fosco, *adj.* dark, dreary, dusky, grim, somber.

fòsforo, *n.m.* phosphorus.

fòssa, *n.f.* moat.

fossato, *n.m.* ditch.

fossetta, *n.f.* dimple.

fòssile, *n.m. and adj.* fossil.

fossilizzare, *vb.* fossilize.

fosso, *n.m.* ditch.

fotocopia, *n.f.* photocopy.

fotocopiatore, *n.m.* photocopier.

fotoelèttrico, *adj.* photoelectric.

fotogènico, *adj.* photogenic.

fotografare, *vb.* photograph.

fotografìa, *n.f.* photograph; photography.

fotògrafo, *n.m.* photographer.

fotogramma, *n.m.* frame.

fotomontaggio, *n.m.* photomontage.

fra, *prep.* between, among, amid.
f. pòco, soon, by-and-by, presently.

frac, *n.m.* tails (coat).

fracassare, *vb.* smash.

fracasso, *n.m.* uproar, fuss, ado, fracas.

fràdicio, *adj.* soaked; rotten.

fràgile, *adj.* fragile, brittle, frail.

fràgola, *n.f.* strawberry.

fragore, *n.m.* clang, crash.

fragrante, *adj.* fragrant.

fragranza, *n.f.* fragrance.

fraintèndere, *vb.* misunderstand, misconstrue.

frammentare, *vb.* fragment.

frammentàrio, *adj.* fragmentary.

frammento, *n.m.* fragment.

frana, *n.f.* landslide.

franare, *vb.* crumble; slide; collapse.

francamente, *adv.* frankly, candidly.

francese, 1. *n.m.* Frenchman; *f.* Frenchwoman. **2.** *adj.* French.

franchezza, *n.f.* frankness, candidness, directness.

franchìgia, *n.f.* immunity, franchise, exemption.

Frància, *n.f.* France.

franco, *adj.* frank, candid, straightforward.

francobollo, *n.m.* postage stamp.

frangènte, *n.m.* breaker; *(pl.)* surf.

fràngere, *vb.* break, crush.

frangia, *n.f.* fringe; (hair-do) bang.

frangi-ònde, *n.m.* breakwater.

frantumare, *vb.* shatter, smash.

frappé, *n.m.* shake, frappé.

frapporre, *vb.* interpose, insert.

frase, *n.f.* phrase; sentence.

fràssino, *n.m.* ash-tree.

frastagliare, *vb.* indent.

frastuòno, *n.m.* uproar, racket.

frate, *n.m.* friar.

fratellanza, *n.f.* brotherhood.

fratellastro, *n.m.* half-brother; step-brother.

fratèllo, *n.m.* brother.

fraternamente, *adv.* fraternally.

fraternità, *n.f.* fraternity.

fraternizzare, *vb.* fraternize.

fratèrno, *adj.* brotherly, fraternal.

fratricida, *n.m.* fratricide (person).

fratricìdio, *n.m.* fratricide (act).

fratta, *n.f.* thicket.

frattèmpo, *n.m.* meantime, meanwhile, interim.

frattura, *n.f.* fracture.

fratturare, *vb.* fracture.

fraudolentemente, *adv.* fraudulently.

fraudolento, *adj.* fraudulent.
frazione, *n.f.* fraction.
fréccia, *n.f.* arrow; directional signal.
freddamente, *adv.* coldly.
freddare, *vb.* chill; kill.
freddezza, *n.f.* coldness.
freddo, 1. *n.m.* cold; chill. **2.** *adj.* cold, chilly. **aver f.,** feel cold. **far f.,** be cold.
freddura, *n.f.* pun.
fregare, *vb.* rub.
fregata, *n.f.* rub; frigate.
fregatura, *n.f.* swindle, fraud.
fregiare, *vb.* decorate; fret.
frèmito, *n.m.* thrill.
frenare, *vb.* brake; check.
frenesia, *n.f.* frenzy.
frenètico, *adj.* frantic, frenzied.
freno, *n.m.* brake; check.
frenologia, *n.f.* phrenology.
frequentare, *vb.* frequent, attend, haunt.
frequentatore, *n.m.* habitué.
frequènte, *adj.* frequent.
frequentemente, *adv.* frequently.
frequènza, *n.* frequency.
freschezza, *n.f.* freshness.
fresco, 1. *n.m.* coolness. **2.** *adj.* cool; fresh.
fretta, *n.f.* haste, hurry, hustle, rush.
frettolosamente, *adv.* hastily.
frettoloso, *adj.* hasty, cursory.
fricassèa, *n.f.* fricassee.
friggere, *vb.* fry.
frigido, *adj.* frigid.
frigorifero, *n.m.* refrigerator; freezer.
frittata, *n.f.* omelet.
frittèlla, *n.f.* fritter, pancake.
frivolezza, *n.f.* frivolousness.
frivolità, *n.f.* frivolity.
frìvolo, *adj.* frivolous.
frizione, *n.f.* friction; rubbing; (auto) clutch.
fròde, *n.f.* fraud.
frontale, *adj.* frontal; head on.
fronte, *n.m.* forehead, brow; front.
fronteggiare, *vb.* face.
frontièra, *n.f.* frontier, border.
fròttola, *n.f.* fib, canard; *(pl.)* nonsense.

frugale, *adj.* frugal.
frugalità, *n.f.* frugality.
fruizione, *n.f.* fruition.
frumento, *n.m.* wheat.
frusciare, *vb.* rustle.
fruscio, *n.m.* rustle.
frusta, *n.f.* lash, whip.
frustare, *vb.* lash, whip.
frustino, *n.m.* horsewhip.
frusto, *adj.* worn, threadbare.
frustrare, *vb.* frustrate, foil, thwart.
frustrazione, *n.f.* frustration.
frutta, *n.f.* fruit.
fruttare, *vb.* yield, produce.
frutteto, *n.m.* orchard.
fruttificare, *vb.* fructify.
fruttivéndolo, *n.m.* greengrocer, fruit merchant.
frutto, *n.m.* fruit.
fruttuoso, *adj.* fruitful.
fucilare, *vb.* shoot.
fucile, *n.m.* gun, rifle.
fucileria, *n.f.* fusillade.
fucina, *n.f.* forge, smithy.
fuco, *n.m.* drone.
fùcsia, *n.f.* fuchsia.
fuga, *n.f.* flight, escape, getaway; fugue.
fugace, *adj.* fleeting.
fugare, *vb.* dispel; put to flight.
fuggènte, *adj.* transitory, passing, fleeting.
fuggiasco, *n.m.* fugitive.
fuggifuggi, *n.m.* stampede.
fuggire, *vb.* flee; elope; run away.
fuggitivo, *n.m. and adj.* fugitive.
fulcro, *n.m.* fulcrum.
fulgore, *n.m.* radiance.
fuliggine, *n.f.* soot.
fulminare, *vb.* fulminate.
fulminazione, *n.f.* fulmination.
fùlmine, *n.m.* (bolt of) lightning; thunderbolt.
fulvo, *adj.* tawny.
fumaiòlo, *n.m.* smokestack.
fumare, *vb.* smoke.
fumetto, *n.m.* comic strip. **giornalino a fumetti,** comic book.
fumigare, *vb.* fumigate.
fumigatore, *n.m.* fumigator.
fumo, *n.m.* smoke.
fune, *n.f.* rope.
fùnebre, *adj.* funeral.

funerale, n.m. funeral.
funèreo, adj. funereal.
funèsto, adj. mournful, sad.
fungicida, n.m. fungicide.
fungo, n.m. fungus; mushroom.
funivìa, n.f. cableway.
funzionale, adj. functional.
funzionare, vb. function; work; run.
funzionàrio, n.m. functionary, official.
funzione, n.f. function.
fuòchi d'artifìcio, m.pl. fireworks.
fuochista, n.m. fireman.
fuòco, n.m. fire, blaze; focus.
fuòri, adv. out; outside; forth. **f. di,** outside.
fuorilegge, n.m. and f. outlaw.
fuoristrada, 1. n.m. four-wheel drive vehicle. **2.** adj. off-road.
fuoriuscito, n.m. exile.
furbo, adj. crafty, tricky, sly, shrewd.

furènte, adj. furious.
furfante, n.m. blackguard, scoundrel, villain.
furgone, n.m. van.
fùria, n.f. fury.
furibondo, adj. wild, furious.
furioso, adj. furious; wild.
furore, n.m. furor, fury.
furtivamente, adv. stealthily.
furtivo, adj. furtive, stealthy.
furto, n.m. theft, burglary, larceny, robbery.
fusa, n.f.pl. **fare le f.,** to purr.
fusìbile, 1. n.m. fuse. **2.** adj. easily melted.
fusione, n.f. fusion, merger; (nuclear) meltdown.
fuso, adj. molten.
fusolièra, n.f. fuselage.
fustigare, vb. flog.
fùtile, adj. futile.
futilità, n.f. futility.
futuro, n.m. and adj. future.
futurologìa, n.f. futurology.

G

gabardina, n.f. gabardine.
gàbbia, n.f. cage.
gabbiano, n.m. gull.
gabinetto, n.m. cabinet; toilet; closet; office.
gagliardo, adj. sturdy.
gaiamente, adv. gaily.
gaiezza, n.f. gaiety.
gaio, adj. gay, cheerful, jolly, blithe, debonair.
gala, n.f. frill; gala.
galante, adj. gallant.
galàssia, n.f. galaxy.
galatèo, n.m. etiquette, good manners.
galèa, n.f. galley.
galeone, n.m. galleon.
galla, n.f. **a g.,** afloat.
galleggiare, vb. float.
gallerìa, n.f. gallery; tunnel; arcade.
gàllico, adj. Gallic.
gallina, n.f. hen.
gallismo, n.m. machismo.
gallo, n.m. rooster, cock.
gallone, n.m. stripe; chevron; gallon.

galoppare, vb. gallop.
galòppo, n.m. gallop.
galòscia, n.f. galosh.
galvanizzare, vb. galvanize.
galvanoplàstica, n.f. electroplating.
gamba, n.f. leg.
gamberetto, n.m. shrimp.
gambo, n.m. stalk.
gamma, n.f. scale; gamut.
ganàscia, n.f. jaw; brake shoe.
gancio, n.m. clip; clasp; hook.
gànghero, n.m. hinge.
gara, n.f. competition.
garage, n.m. garage.
garante, n.m. and f. guarantor.
garantire, vb. guarantee.
garanzìa, n.f. guarantee; guaranty; bail.
garbùglio, n.m. tangle.
gardènia, n.f. gardenia.
gareggiare, vb. vie, compete.
gargarismo, n.m. gargle.
gargarizzare, vb. gargle.
garòfano, n.m. carnation.
garrota, n.f. garrote.
gàrrulo, adj. garrulous.

garza, *n.f.* gauze; cheesecloth.
garzone, *n.m.* helper, shop-boy.
gas, *n.m.* gas.
gasdotto, *n.m.* gas pipeline.
gasòlio, *n.m.* diesel oil.
gassoso, *adj.* gassy, gaseous.
gàstrico, *adj.* gastric.
gastrite, *n.f.* gastritis.
gastronomìa, *n.f.* gastronomy.
gastronòmico, *adj.* gastronomic.
gatta, *n.f.* cat.
gattino, *n.m.* kitten.
gatto, *n.m.* cat, tomcat.
gavòtta, *n.f.* gavotte.
gazzèlla, *n.f.* gazelle.
gazzetta, *n.f.* gazette.
gelare, *vb.* freeze.
gelatàio, *n.m.* ice-cream dealer.
gelatina, *n.f.* gelatine; jelly.
gelatinoso, *adj.* gelatinous.
gelato, *n.m.* ice cream.
gèlido, *adj.* chilly, frosty.
gelone, *n.m.* chilblain.
gelosìa, *n.f.* jealousy.
geloso, *adj.* jealous.
gelso, *n.m.* mulberry.
gelsomino, *n.m.* jasmine.
gemèllo, *n.m.* twin.
gèmere, *vb.* groan, moan.
gèmito, *n.m.* moan, groan.
gèmma, *n.f.* gem; bud.
gemmare, *vb.* bud.
gendarme, *n.m.* policeman.
gène, *n.m.* gene.
genealogìa, *n.f.* genealogy, pedigree.
genealògico, *adj.* genealogical.
generale, *n.m. and adj.* general.
generalità, *n.f.* generality.
generalizzare, *vb.* generalize.
generalizzazione, *n.f.* generalization.
generalmente, *adv.* generally.
generare, *vb.* generate, beget, breed, engender.
generatore, *n.m.* generator.
generazione, *n.f.* generation.
gènere, *n.m.* kind, gender, genre, genus. **g. alimentari,** foodstuffs.
genèrico, *adj.* generic.
gènero, *n.m.* son-in-law.
generosamente, *adv.* generously.
generosità, *n.f.* generosity.
generoso, *adj.* generous.
gènesi, *n.f.* genesis.

genètica, *n.f.* genetics.
genètico, *adj.* genetic.
gengiva, *n.f.* gum.
geniale, *adj.* ingenious, clever.
gènio, *n.m.* genius; engineering.
genitale, *adj.* genital.
genitali, *n.m.pl.* genitals.
genitivo, *n.m. and adj.* genitive.
genitore, *n.m.* parent.
gennaio, *n.m.* January.
genocidio, *n.m.* genocide.
Gènova, *n.f.* Genoa.
genovese, *adj.* Genoese.
gentàglia, *n.f.* disreputable people, rabble.
gènte, *n.f.* people, folks.
gentile, *adj.* gentile; nice, kind.
gentilezza, *n.f.* kindness.
gentilìzio, *adj.* of noble family.
gentiluòmo, *n.m.* gentleman.
genuflèttersi, *vb.* genuflect.
genuinamente, *adv.* genuinely.
genuinità, *n.f.* genuineness.
genuino, *adj.* genuine.
genziana, *n.f.* gentian.
geografìa, *n.f.* geography.
geogràfico, *adj.* geographical.
geògrafo, *n.m.* geographer.
geometrìa, *n.f.* geometry.
geomètrico, *adj.* geometric.
geopolìtica, *n.f.* geopolitics.
gerànio, *n.m.* geranium.
gerarchìa, *n.f.* hierarchy.
geràrchico, *adj.* hierarchical.
gerente, *n.m.* manager.
gèrgo, *n.m.* jargon, slang.
geriatrìa, *n.f.* geriatrics.
Germània, *n.f.* Germany.
germànico, *adj.* Germanic.
gèrme, *n.m.* germ.
germicida, *n.m.* germicide.
germinale, *adj.* germinal.
germinare, *vb.* germinate.
germogliare, *vb.* sprout.
germóglio, *n.m.* sprout; shoot.
geroglìfico, *adj.* hieroglyphic.
Gerusalèmme, *n.f.* Jerusalem.
gesso, *n.m.* chalk; gypsum.
gessoso, *adj.* chalky.
gestante, *adj.* pregnant.
gestazione, *n.f.* gestation.
gesticolare, *vb.* gesticulate.
gesticolazione, *n.f.* gesticulation.
gèsto, *n.m.* gesture.

gestore, *n.m.* manager.
Gesù, *prop.m.* Jesus.
gesuita, *n.m.* Jesuit.
gettare, *vb.* throw; hurl; cast; dash; flip.
gèttito, *n.m.* yield.
gètto, *n.m.* throw; cast; jet.
gettone, *n.m.* token.
gherìglio, *n.m.* kernel.
ghermire, *vb.* snatch.
gherone, *n.m.* gusset.
ghette, *f.pl.* panty hose.
ghiacciaia, *n.f.* ice-box.
ghiacciaio, *n.m.* glacier.
ghiàccio, *n.m.* ice.
ghiaia, *n.f.* gravel.
ghianda, *n.f.* acorn.
ghiandaia, *n.f.* jay.
ghiàndola, *n.f.* gland.
ghigliottina, *n.f.* guillotine.
ghignare, *vb.* grin; sneer.
ghingano, *n.m.* gingham.
ghiotto, *adj.* gluttonous.
ghiottone, 1. *n.m.* gutton, gourmand. **2.** *adj.* greedy.
ghiottoneria, *n.f.* greediness.
ghirigoro, *n.m.* curlycue, doodle.
ghirlanda, *n.f.* garland, wreath.
ghiro, *n.m.* dormouse.
ghisa, *n.f.* cast iron.
già, 1. *adj.* former; sometime. **2.** *adv.* already, formerly.
giacca, *n.f.* coat, jacket.
giacchè, *conj.* since.
giacchetta, *n.f.* jacket.
giàcchio, *n.m.* dragnet.
giacere, *vb.* lie.
giaciglio, *n.m.* cot.
giacimento, *n.m.* field.
giacinto, *n.m.* hyacinth.
giada, *n.f.* jade.
giaguaro, *n.m.* jaguar.
giallo, *adj.* yellow.
giàmbico, *adj.* iambic.
giammai, *adv.* never.
Giappone, *n.m.* Japan.
giapponese, *adj.* Japanese.
giara, *n.f.* jar.
giardinetta, *n.f.* station wagon.
giardinière, *n.m.* gardener.
giardino, *n.m.* garden. **g. d'infànzia,** kindergarten.
giarrettièra, *n.f.* garter.
giavellòtto, *n.m.* javelin.
gibbone, *n.m.* gibbon.

giga, *n.f.* jig.
gigante, *n.m.* giant.
gigantesco, *adj.* gigantic; giant.
giglio, *n.m.* lily.
gilè, *n.m.* vest; waistcoat.
gimnòto, *n.m.* electric eel.
ginecologia, *n.f.* gynaecology.
ginepro, *n.m.* juniper.
Ginèvra, *n.f.* Geneva.
ginevrino, *adj.* Genevan.
ginnàsio, *n.m.* high school.
ginnasta, *n.m.* gymnast.
ginnàstica, *n.f.* gymnastics.
ginnàstico, *adj.* gymnastic.
ginócchio, *n.m.* knee.
giocare, *vb.* play. **g. d'azzardo,** gamble.
giocatore, *n.m.* player. **g. d'azzardo,** gambler.
giocàttolo, *n.m.* toy.
giòco, *n.m.* game. **g. d'azzardo,** game of chance; gambling.
giocondo, *adj.* jocund.
giogo, *n.m.* yoke.
giòia, *n.f.* joy, glee.
gioiellerìa, *n.f.* jewelry.
gioiellière, *n.m.* jeweler.
gioièllo, *n.m.* jewel.
gioire, *vb.* rejoice; gloat.
gioioso, *adj.* joyful, happy, blithe, gleeful.
giornalaio, *n.m.* news-vendor.
giornale, *n.m.* newspaper; journal; daily.
giornalièro, *adj.* daily.
giornalismo, *n.m.* journalism.
giornalista, *n.m.* journalist.
giornata, *n.f.* day.
giorno, *n.m.* day. **g. feriale,** weekday; workday. **g. festivo,** holiday.
gióvane, *adj.* young.
giovanile, *adj.* youthful; juvenile.
giovedì, *n.m.* Thursday.
giovènca, *n.f.* heifer.
gioviale, *adj.* jovial.
giovinezza, *n.f.* youth.
giradischi, *n.m.* record player.
giraffa, *n.f.* giraffe.
giramondo, *n.m.* globetrotter.
girare, *vb.* turn, revolve, spin, whirl; crank; endorse.
girasole, *n.m.* sunflower.
girata, *n.f.* endorsement.
giretto, *n.m.* spin.
girino, *n.m.* tadpole.

giro, *n.m.* turn; revolution; round.
prèndere in g., make fun of; kid.
giroscòpio, *n.m.* gyroscope.
girotondo, *n.m.* ring-around-a-rosy.
girovago, *adj.* itinerant.
gita, *n.f.* outing; picnic.
gittata, *n.f.* range (of gun).
giù, *adv.* down.
giubbotto, *n.m.* jacket.
giubilante, *adj.* jubilant.
giubilèo, *n.m.* jubilee.
giudaismo, *n.m.* Judaism.
giudèo, *n.m.* Jew.
giudicare, *vb.* judge; deem.
giùdice, *n.m.* judge.
giudiziàrio, *adj.* judiciary; judicial.
giudìzio, *n.m.* judgment, discernment.
giudizioso, *adj.* judicious.
giugno, *n.m.* June.
giugulare, *adj.* jugular.
giulivo, *adj.* happy, joyful.
giullare, *n.m.* joker.
giuncata, *n.f.* junket.
giunchìglia, *n.f.* jonquil.
giunco, *n.m.* rush.
giùngere, *vb.* join; arrive.
giungla, *n.f.* jungle.
giuntura, *n.f.* juncture, joint.
giuramento, *n.m.* oath.
giurare, *vb.* swear.
giurato, *n.m.* juror.
giurìa, *n.f.* jury.
giurisdizione, *n.f.* jurisdiction.
giurisprudènza, *n.f.* jurisprudence.
giurista, *n.m.* jurist.
giustacuòre, *n.m.* jerkin.
giustamente, *adv.* justly, fairly.
giustezza, *n.f.* fairness.
giustificàbile, *adj.* justifiable.
giustificare, *vb.* justify.
giustificazione, *n.f.* justification.
giustìzia, *n.f.* justice; righteousness.
giustiziare, *vb.* execute.
giusto, *adj.* just, fair; even, right; righteous; sound.
glabro, *adj.* smooth, hairless.
glaciale, *adj.* glacial. **zona g.,** frigid zone.
gladiatore, *n.m.* gladiator.
gladìolo, *n.m.* gladiolus.

glassa, *n.f.* icing.
glaucòma, *n.m.* glaucoma.
gli, 1. *def. art.* m.pl. the. **2.** *pron. 3. sg.m.* dative. to him.
glicerina, *n.f.* glycerine.
glicine, *n.m.* wisteria.
globale, *adj.* global.
glòbo, *n.m.* globe. **g. dell'òcchio,** eyeball.
globulare, *adj.* globular.
glòbulo, *n.m.* globule.
glòria, *n.f.* glory.
gloriarsi, *vb.* glory.
glorificare, *vb.* glorify.
glorificazione, *n.f.* glorification.
glorioso, *adj.* glorious.
glossàrio, *n.m.* glossary.
glucòsio, *n.m.* glucose.
glutinoso, *adj.* glutinous.
gnòcco, *n.m.* dumpling.
gobba, *n.f.* hunchback (woman); hump; hunch.
gobbo, *n.m.* humpback, hunchback.
gòccia, *n.f.* drop.
gocciamento, *n.m.* dripping.
gocciolare, *vb.* drip.
godere, *vb.* enjoy; (*refl.*) bask in.
godìbile, *adj.* enjoyable.
godimento, *n.m.* enjoyment.
goffàggine, *n.f.* clumsiness.
gòffo, *adj.* awkward, clumsy, gawky, uncouth.
gola, *n.f.* throat; gorge; gullet.
golf, *n.m.* golf; sweater.
golfo, *n.m.* gulf.
goliardo, *n.m.* university student; goliard.
golosità, *n.f.* gluttony.
goloso, *adj.* gluttonous.
gòmena, *n.f.* hawser.
gomitata, *n.f.* hit with the elbow, nudge.
gómito, *n.m.* elbow.
gomma, *n.f.* gum; rubber. **g. lacca,** shellac.
gommista, *n.m.* tire dealer.
gommoso, *adj.* gummy.
góndola, *n.f.* gondola.
gondolière, *n.m.* gondolier.
gonfiamento, *n.m.* inflation; swelling up.
gonfiare, *vb.* inflate; swell; bloat; (*refl.*) bulge.

gonfio, *adj.* inflated; swollen; baggy.
gonfiore, *n.m.* swelling.
gong, *n.m.* gong.
gònna, *n.f.* skirt.
gonnèlla, *n.f.* gown; petticoat.
gonorrèa, *n.f.* gonorrhea.
gonzo, *n.m.* fool, blockhead.
gorgo, *n.m.* whirlpool.
gorgogliare, *vb.* gurgle.
gorgoglio, *n.m.* gurgle.
gorilla, *n.m.* gorilla.
gota, *n.f.* cheek.
gòtico, *adj.* Gothic.
gotta, *n.f.* gout (medical).
governante, *n.f.* governess.
governare, *vb.* govern.
governativo, *adj.* governmental.
governatorato, *n.m.* governorship.
governatore, *n.m.* governor.
governatoriale, *adj.* gubernatorial.
govèrno, *n.m.* government.
gozzo, *n.m.* goiter.
gozzovìglia, *n.f.* revel.
gozzovigliare, *vb.* revel.
gracchiare, *vb.* caw.
gràcchio, *n.m.* grackle.
gracidare, *vb.* croak.
gradale, *n.m.* grail.
gradatamente, *adv.* by degrees.
gradévole, *adj.* pleasing; acceptable; agreeable.
gradevolmente, *adv.* pleasingly; agreeably; acceptably.
gradino, *n.m.* step.
gradire, *vb.* like; appreciate.
grado, *n.m.* degree; grade; rank.
graduale, *adj.* gradual.
gradualmente, *adv.* gradually.
graduare, *vb.* graduate.
graduatòria, *n.f.* ranking.
graduazione, *n.f.* foreclosure.
graffa, *n.f.* clamp; bracket.
graffiare, *vb.* scratch.
graffiatura, *n.f.* scratch.
gràffio, *n.m.* scratch.
grafia, *n.f.* writing.
gràfico, 1. *n.m.* graph. 2. *adj.* graphic.
grafite, *n.f.* graphite.
grafologia, *n.f.* graphology.
grammàtica, *n.f.* grammar.
grammaticale, *adj.* grammatical.

grammàtico, *n.m.* grammarian.
grammo, *n.m.* gram.
grammòfono, *n.m.* gramophone, phonograph.
gramo, *adj.* miserable, sad, poor.
granaio, *n.m.* granary; barn.
granata, *n.f.* grenade.
granatina, *n.f.* grenadine.
granato, *n.m.* garnet.
Gran Bretagna, *n.f.* Great Britain.
grancassa, *n.f.* bass drum.
grànchio, *n.m.* crab.
grandangolare, *n.m* wide-angle lens.
grande, *adj.* big; large; great; grand.
grandezza, *n.f.* greatness, grandeur; size; magnitude.
grandinare, *vb.* hail.
grandinata, *n.f.* hailstorm.
gràndine, *n.f.* hail.
grandiosamente, *adv.* grandiosely, grandly.
grandioso, *adj.* grandiose.
granello, *n.m.* grain, seed.
granito, *n.m.* granite.
grano, *n.m.* grain; bead. **g. saraceno,** buckwheat.
granturco, *n.m.* corn; maize.
granulare, 1. *adj.* granular. 2. *vb.* granulate.
granulazione, *n.f.* granulation.
granèllo, *n.m.* granule.
grappa, *n.f.* clamp.
gràppolo, *n.m.* bunch, cluster.
grassatore, *n.m.* highway robber.
grassazione, *n.f.* hold-up.
grassetto, *adj.* chubby; boldface.
grasso, 1. *n.m.* fat; grease. 2. *adj.* fat; stout; fatty; greasy.
grassòccio, *adj.* plump, buxom.
grata, *n.f.* lattice.
graticola, *n.f.* grate; grill; grid; gridiron; griddle; broiler.
gratifica, *n.f.* bonus.
gratificare, *vb.* gratify.
gratificazione, *n.f.* gratification; bonus.
gratis, *adv.* free, without charge.
gratitùdine, *n.f.* gratitude.
grato, *adj.* grateful, thankful; pleasing.
grattacapo, *n.m.* concern, worry.
grattacièlo, *n.m.* skyscraper.

grattare, vb. scratch.
grattùgia, n.f. grater.
grattugiare, vb. grate.
gratuitamente, adv. gratis.
gratùito, adj. free, gratis, complimentary, gratuitous.
gravare, vb. burden.
grave, adj. grave; grievous.
gravemente, adj. gravely.
gràvida, adj.f. pregnant, big with child.
gravidanza, n.f. pregnancy.
gravità, n.f. gravity.
gravitare, vb. gravitate.
gravitazione, n.f. gravitation.
gravoso, adj. burdensome, oppressive.
gràzia, n.f. grace.
gràzie, interj. thanks!
graziosamente, adv. graciously.
grazioso, adj. gracious; pretty; becoming; comely.
Grècia, n.f. Greece.
grèco, adj. Greek.
gregàrio, adj. gregarious.
gregge, n.m. flock, herd.
greggio, 1. n.m. crude oil. **2.** adj. unrefined.
grembiule, n.m. apron.
grèmbo, n.m. lap.
gretto, adj. mean; shabby.
grezzo, adj. raw.
gridare, vb. cry; shout, yell.
grido, n.m. cry; shout, yell.
grigiastro, adj. grayish.
grìgio, adj. gray; drab.
grilletto, n.m. trigger.
grillo, n.m. cricket.
grisou, n.m. firedamp.
gròg, n.m. grog.
gronda, n.f. eaves.
grondaia, n.f. gutter.
grossagrana, n.f. grosgrain.
gròsso, adj. big; large; fat.
grossolanamente, adv. grossly.
grossolanità, n.f. coarseness; grossness.
grossolano, adj. coarse; gross.
grotta, n.f. grotto.
grottesco, adj. grotesque.
grovìglio, n.m. ravel, tangle, snarl.
gru, n.f. crane; derrick.
grùccia, n.f. crutch.
grugnire, vb. grunt.

grugnito, n.m. grunt.
grumo, n.m. clot.
gruppo, n.m. group, clump, cluster; gang.
gruzzolo, n.m. hoard, savings, stock.
guadagnare, vb. earn; gain.
guadagno, n.m. gain, profit; (pl.) earnings.
guadare, vb. wade, ford, cross.
guado, n.m. ford.
guaìna, n.f. sheath.
guaio, n.m. trouble, woe.
guaire, vb. yelp; whimper.
guància, n.f. cheek; jowl.
guanciale, n.m. pillow.
guanto, n.m. glove; gauntlet.
guardaboschi, n.m. park ranger.
guardacòste, adj. coast guard.
guardare, vb. look at; guard; gaze; regard; watch; (refl.) beware.
guardaròba, n.m. cloakroom; wardrobe.
guardaspalle, n.m. bodyguard.
guàrdia, n.f. guard; watch.
guardiano, n.m. guardian; caretaker; watchman.
guardina, n.f. guard-house.
guardingo, adj. wary.
guardone, n.m. voyeur, Peeping Tom.
guarìbile, adj. curable.
guarigione, n.f. cure, recovery.
guarire, vb. cure, heal.
guarnigione, n.f. garrison.
guarnire, vb. garnish.
guarnizione, n.f. garnishment; gasket.
guastafeste, n.m. spoilsport.
guastare, vb. spoil, mar.
guazzabùglio, n.m. mess; hash.
guèrra, n.f. war.
guerresco, adj. warlike.
guerrièro, n.m. warrior.
guerrìglia, n.f. guerrilla.
guerrigliero, n.m. guerrilla fighter.
gufo, n.m. owl.
gùglia, n.f. spire.
guida, n.f. guide; guidance; leadership; guidebook; directory.
guidare, vb. guide; drive (auto).
guinzàglio, n.m. leash.

guisa, *n.f.* manner, way. **a g. di** under the guise of.
guizzare, *vb.* wriggle; flash.
guru, *n.m.* guru.
gùscio, *n.m.* shell.
gustare, *vb.* taste.

gustativo, *adj.* gustatory, involving taste.
gusto, *n.m.* taste; gusto; relish.
gustoso, *adj.* tasty, appetizing, palatable.
gutturale, *adj.* guttural.

H,I

hascisc, *n.m.* hashish.
hennè, *n.m.pl.* henna.
hertz, *n.m.* hertz.
holliwoodiano, *adj.* Hollywood-like.
hurrá, *interj.* Hurrah!
i, *def. art. m.pl.* the.
iarda, *n.f.* yard.
iato, *n.m.* hiatus.
iattura, *n.f.* misfortune.
ibernazione, *n.f.* hibernation.
ibisco, *n.m.* hibiscus.
ibridazione, *n.f.* cross-fertilization.
ìbrido, *adj.* hybrid.
icòne, *n.f.* icon.
iddìo, *n.m.* god.
idèa, *n.f.* idea.
ideale, *adj.* ideal.
idealismo, *n.m.* idealism.
idealista, *n.m.* idealist.
idealìstico, *adj.* idealistic.
idealizzare, *vb.* idealize.
idealmente, *adj.* ideally.
idèntico, *adj.* identical.
identificàbile, *adj.* identifiable.
identificare, *vb.* identify.
identificazione, *n.f.* identification.
identità, *n.f.* identity.
ideologìa, *n.f.* ideology.
idìlliaco, *adj.* idyllic.
idìllio, *n.m.* idyll.
idiòma, *n.m.* idiom.
idiòta, 1. *n.m.* idiot. 2. *adj.* idiotic.
idiozìa, *n.f.* idiocy.
idolatra, *n.m. or f.* idolater.
idolatrare, *vb.* idolize.
idolatrìa, *n.* idolatry.
ìdolo, *n.m.* idol.
idoneità, *n.f.* fitness.
idòneo, *adj.* fit; qualified.
idrante, *n.m.* hydrant.
idrato di carbone, *n.m.* carbohydrate.

idràulico, 1. *n.m.* plumber. 2. *adj.* hydraulic.
idroclòrico, *adj.* hydrochloric.
idroelèttrico, *adj.* hydroelectric.
idrofobìa, *n.f.* hydrophobia.
idrògeno, *n.m.* hydrogen.
idropisìa, *n.f.* dropsy.
idroscalo, *n.m.* seaplane airport.
idroterapèutica, *n.f.* hydrotherapy.
idrovolante, *n.m.* seaplane; hydroplane.
ièna, *n.f.* hyena.
ièri, *n.m. and adv.* yesterday.
igiène, *n.f.* hygiene; sanitation.
igiènico, *adj.* hygienic; sanitary.
ignaro, *adj.* ignorant.
ignòbile, *adj.* ignoble.
ignominioso, *adj.* ignominious.
ignorante, *adj.* ignorant.
ignorantone, *n.m.* ignoramus.
ignoranza, *n.f.* ignorance.
ignòto, *adj.* unknown.
ignudo, *adj.* naked.
il, *def. art. m.sg.* the.
ilare, *adj.* hilarious.
ilarità, *n.f.* hilarity.
illanguidire, *vb.* languish, get weak.
illècito, *adj.* illicit.
illegale, *adj.* illegal.
illeggìbile, *adj.* illegible.
illeggibilmente, *adv.* illegibly.
illegittimità, *n.f.* illegitimacy.
illegìttimo, *adj.* illegitimate.
illeso, *adj.* unhurt.
illibato, *adj.* pure, untouched.
illimitatamente, *adv.* boundlessly.
illimitato, *adj.* unlimited; boundless; limitless.
illògico, *adj.* illogical.
illuminare, *vb.* illuminate; light up; brighten; enlighten.
illuminazione, *n.f.* illumination.

illuminismo, *n.m.* Age of Enlightenment.
illusione, *n.f.* illusion.
illusòrio, *adj.* illusory; illusive.
illustrare, *vb.* illustrate.
illustrativo, *adj.* illustrative.
illustrazione, *n.f.* illustration.
illustre, *adj.* illustrious.
imam, *n.m.* imam.
imbacuccare, *vb.* wrap up.
imbaldanzire, *vb.* embolden; animate.
imballàggio, *n.m.* packing.
imballare, *vb.* pack.
imbalsamare, *vb.* embalm.
imbambolato, *adj.* stunned; gazing; sleepy.
imbandire, *vb.* set the table; prepare lavishly.
imbarazzare, *vb.* embarrass.
imbarazzo, *n.m.* embarrassment.
imbarcare, *vb.* embark.
imbastire, *vb.* baste.
imbattìbile, *adj.* unbeatable.
imbavagliare, *vb.* gag.
imbecille, *n.m. and adj.* imbecile; half-wit; moron.
imbèrbe, *adj.* beardless.
imbiancare, *vb.* whiten; bleach.
imboccare, *vb.* feed by mouth.
imboccatura, *n.f.* mouthpiece; nozzle.
imboscata, *n.f.* ambush. **tendere un' i.,** to ambush.
imbottire, *vb.* pad; stuff.
imbottita, *n.f.* quilt.
imbottitura, *n.f.* wadding; padding; batting.
imbrattare, *vb.* soil; stain; daub.
imbrattatura, *n.f.* daub.
imbrogliare, *vb.* embroil; entangle.
imbròglio, *n.m.* trick, cheat, fraud.
imbronciato, *adj.* sulky, surly.
imbucare, *vb.* mail.
imbuto, *n.m.* funnel.
imitare, *vb.* imitate; mimic.
imitativo, *adj.* imitative.
imitatore, *n.m.* mimic; imitator.
imitazione, *n.f.* imitation.
immacolato, *adj.* immaculate.
immagazzinare, *vb.* store.
immaginàbile, *adj.* imaginable.
immaginare, *vb.* imagine; fancy.

immaginàrio, *adj.* imaginary.
immaginativo, *adj.* imaginative.
immaginazione, *n.f.* fancy, imagination.
immàgine, *n.f.* image.
immaginoso, *adj.* fanciful.
immane, *adj.* huge.
immanènte, *adj.* immanent.
immateriale, *adj.* immaterial.
immaturo, *adj.* immature.
immediatamente, *adv.* immediately, instantly; directly; forthwith; presently.
immediato, *adj.* immediate, instant.
immènso, *adj.* immense.
immèrgere, *vb.* immerse, dip.
immeritato, *adj.* undeserved.
immigrante, *n. and adj.* immigrant.
immigrare, *vb.* immigrate.
imminènte, *adj.* imminent.
immischiarsi, *vb.* interfere, meddle, tamper.
immiserire, *vb.* impoverish.
immissione, *n.m.* letting in, introduction.
immòbile, *adj.* immobile, motionless, immovable.
immobilizzare, *vb.* immobilize.
immoderato, *adj.* immoderate.
immodèstia, *n.f.* immodesty.
immodèsto, *adj.* immodest.
immorale, *adj.* immoral.
immoralità, *n.f.* immorality.
immoralmente, *adv.* immorally.
immortalare, *vb.* immortalize.
immortale, *adj.* immortal, deathless.
immortalità, *n.f.* immortality.
immune, *adj.* immune.
immunità, *n.f.* immunity.
immunizzare, *vb.* immunize.
immutàbile, *adj.* immutable.
impaginare, *vb.* arrange in pages.
impalare, *vb.* impale.
impalcatura, *n.f.* scaffolding.
impallidire, *vb.* pale; blanch; fade.
impantanarsi, *vb.* bog down.
imparare, *vb.* learn.
imparentato, *adj.* related, kindred.
impartire, *vb.* impart.
imparziale, *adj.* impartial.

impastare, *vb.* knead.
impaziènte, *adj.* impatient, eager.
impazientemente, *adv.* impatiently, eagerly.
impaziènza, *n.f.* impatience, eagerness.
impazzire, *vb.* go crazy.
impazzito, *adj.* gone crazy, deranged.
impeccàbile, *adj.* impeccable.
impedimento, *n.m.* impediment, hindrance.
impedire, *vb.* impede, hinder, hamper, avert, balk, forestall, prevent.
impegnare, *vb.* pledge; pawn.
impegno, *n.m.* undertaking, commitment.
impegolare, *vb.* entangle, get mixed up with.
impèllere, *vb.* impel.
impenetràbile, *adj.* impenetrable.
impenitènte, *adj.* impenitent.
impennarsi, *vb.* rear.
impensàbile, *adj.* unthinkable.
imperante, *adj.* prevailing.
imperativo, *n.m. and adj.* imperative.
imperatore, *n.m.* emperor.
imperatrice, *n.f.* empress.
impercettìbile, *adj.* imperceptible.
imperfètto, *adj.* imperfect.
imperfezione, *n.f.* imperfection.
imperiale, *adj.* imperial.
imperialismo, *n.m.* imperialism.
imperioso, *adj.* imperious.
imperituro, *adj.* imperishable; immortal.
impermeàbile, **1.** *n.m.* raincoat. **2.** *adj.* water-proof.
imperniare, *vb.* pivot.
impèro, *n.m.* empire.
imperscrutàbile, *adj.* inscrutable.
impersonale, *adj.* impersonal.
impersonare, *vb.* impersonate.
impersonatore, *n.m.* impersonator.
impertèrrito, *adj.* impassible; undaunted.
impertinènte, *adj.* impertinent.
impertinènza, *n.f.* impertinence.
impèrvio, *adj.* impervious.

impeto, *n.m.* impetus.
impettito, *adj.* puffed up with pride.
impetuosamente, *adv.* impetuously; boisterously.
impetuoso, *adj.* impetuous; boisterous; dashing; heady.
impiallacciare, *vb.* veneer.
impiantare, *vb.* implant.
impianto, *n.m.* installation; plant.
impiccagione, *n.f.* hanging.
impiccare, *vb.* hang.
impiccatore, *n.m.* hangman.
impiccio, *n.m.* jam, fix, pickle, predicament, scrape.
impiccione, *n.m.* busybody, meddler.
impiegare, *vb.* employ; use.
impiegata, *n.f.* employee.
impiegato, *n.m.* employee, clerk.
impiègo, *n.m.* employment, job.
impietrire, *vb.* petrify.
impigliare, *vb.* entangle.
impigrire, *vb.* get lazy.
impinzare, *vb.* stuff, fill.
implacàbile, *adj.* implacable.
implicare, *vb.* implicate; imply; involve.
implicazione, *n.f.* implication.
implìcito, *adj.* implicit, implied.
implorare, *vb.* implore, beg, plead with.
implume, *adj.* featherless.
impollinare, *vb.* pollinate.
imponderàbile, *adj.* imponderable.
imporre, *vb.* impose; levy.
importante, *adj.* important, momentous.
importanza, *n.f.* importance.
importare, *vb.* import; be important, matter.
importazione, *n.f.* import, importation.
importunare, *vb.* importune.
importuno, *adj.* importunate.
imposizione, *n.f.* imposition.
impossìbile, *adj.* impossible.
impossibilità, *n.f.* impossibility.
imposta, *n.f.* tax, duty, levy. **i. sul valore aggiunto**, value-added tax.
impostare, *vb.* mail, post.
impostura, *n.f.* imposture, humbug.

impotènte, *adj.* impotent, powerless, helpless.

impotènza, *n.f.* impotence.

impoverire, *vb.* impoverish.

impregnare, *vb.* impregnate.

imprenditore, *n.m.* contractor; entrepreneur. **i. di pompe fùnebri**, undertaker.

impresa, *n.f.* enterprise, undertaking; feat.

impresàrio, *n.m.* impresario, theatrical manager.

impressionante, *adj.* impressive.

impressionare, *vb.* impress.

impressione, *n.f.* impression.

imprigionare, *vb.* imprison.

imprìmere, *vb.* impress.

improbàbile, *adj.* improbable, unlikely.

impronta, *n.f.* mark; print. **i. digitale**, fingerprint.

impròprio, *adj.* improper.

improvvisare, *vb.* improvise.

improvviso, 1. *n.m.* impromptu. 2. *adj.* unforeseen; sudden, abrupt.

impudènte, *adj.* impudent, cocky.

impudicìzia, *n.f.* immodesty, shamelessness.

impùdico, *adj.* immodest, shameless; lewd.

impugnare, *vb.* impugn.

impulsivo, *adj.* impulsive.

impulso, *n.m.* impulse.

impunità, *n.f.* impunity.

impurità, *n.f.* impurity.

impuro, *adj.* impure.

imputare, *vb.* impute; accuse; impeach.

imputato, *n.m.* defendant.

imputridire, *vb.* rot; *(refl.)* go rotten; (egg) addle.

in, *prep.* in; into.

inàbile, *adj.* ineligible; unfitted.

inabissare, *vb.* sink.

inabitàbile, *adj.* uninhabitable.

inaccessìbile, *adj.* inaccessible.

inaccettàbile, *adj.* unacceptable.

inadempiente, *adj.* defaulting.

inalare, *vb.* inhale.

inalienàbile, *adj.* inalienable.

inamidare, *vb.* starch.

inano, *adj.* inane.

inarcare, *vb.* arch, bend, curve.

inaridire, *vb.* parch.

inaspettatamente, *adv.* unexpectedly.

inaspettato, *adj.* unexpected.

inattivo, *adj.* inactive, dormant.

inaugurale, *adj.* inaugural.

inaugurare, *vb.* inaugurate.

inaugurazione, *n.f.* inauguration.

inavvertenza, *n.f.* oversight.

inavvertitamente, *adv.* inadvertently.

incandescènte, *adj.* incandescent, glowing.

incandescènza, *n.f.* incandescence, glow.

incantamento, *n.m.* incantation.

incantare, *vb.* enchant, charm.

incantatore, *n.m.* enchanter, charmer.

incantatrice, *n.f.* enchantress, charmer.

incantésimo, *n.m.* spell.

incantèvole, *adj.* enchanting.

incanto, *n.m.* enchantment, charm.

incanutire, *vb.* turn gray (hair).

incapace, *adj.* unable.

incapacità, *n.f.* incapacity; disability.

incaparbire, *vb.* turn obstinate.

incappare, *vb.* meet, run into.

incarcerare, *vb.* incarcerate.

incaricare, *vb.* charge, entrust, commission.

incàrico, *n.m.* charge; commission, task, assignment.

incarnato, *adj.* incarnate.

incarnazione, *n.f.* incarnation.

incartamento, *n.m.* dossier.

incassare, *vb.* box up; cash.

incatenare, *vb.* chain.

incatramare, *vb.* tar.

incavo, *n.m.* dent.

incendiàrio, *n.m. and adj.* incendiary.

incèndio, *n.m.* fire. **i. doloso**, arson.

incenerire, *vb.* reduce to ashes.

incènso, *n.m.* incense, frankincense.

incentivo, *n.m.* incentive.

incerare, *vb.* wax.

incertezza, *n.f.* uncertainty, suspense.

incèrto, *adj.* uncertain.

incespicare, *vb.* stumble, falter.

incessante, adj. incessant, ceaseless.

incèsto, n.m. incest.

inchièsta, n.f. inquiry; inquest.

inchinarsi, vb. bow.

inchino, n.m. bow.

inchiodare, vb. nail.

inchiòstro, n.m. ink.

inciampare, vb. stumble.

incidentale, adj. incidental.

incidentalmente, adv. incidentally.

incidènte, n.m. accident; incident.

incidènza, n.f. incidence.

incìdere, vb. incise, engrave; record.

incinta, adj.f. pregnant.

incipiènte, adj. incipient.

incipriare, vb. powder.

incirca, adv. about, approximately. **all'i.,** more or less.

incisione, n.f. incision; engraving; gravure; recording.

incisivo, adj. incisive. **dènte i.,** incisor.

inciso, 1. n.m. parenthetical clause. **per i.,** incidentally. **2.** adj. engraved.

incisore, n.m. engraver.

incitare, vb. incite.

incivile, adj. uncivilized.

inclinare, vb. incline; list; slant; tilt; tip.

inclinazione, n.f. inclination; tilt; list; penchant.

inclùdere, vb. include.

inclusivo, adj. inclusive.

incoerente, adj. incoherent.

incògnito, adj. incognito.

incollare, vb. glue, paste.

incollatura, n.f. sizing.

incolpare, vb. blame, accuse.

incolpato, n.m. accused, blamed.

incolpatore, n.m. blamer, accuser.

incombènte, adj. incumbent.

incombustibile, adj. fireproof, incombustible.

incominciare, vb. begin.

incomodare, vb. inconvenience.

incòmodo, adj. inconvenient.

incomparàbile, adj. incomparable.

incompatìbile, adj. incompatible.

incompetènte, adj. unqualified.

incompleto, adj. incomplete.

incomprensìbile, adj. incomprehensible.

inconcepìbile, adj. inconceivable.

incondizionato, adj. unqualified.

incònscio, adj. unconscious.

inconsiderato, adj. rash.

inconsulto, adj. rash, unadvised.

incontrare, vb. meet, encounter.

incontro, 1. n.m. meeting, encounter; match. **2.** prep. towards; opposite.

incoraggiamento, n.m. encouragement, urging, abetment.

incoraggiare, vb. encourage, urge, abet.

incoraggiatore, n.m. encourager, urger, abettor.

incornare, vb. gore.

incorniciare, vb. frame.

incoronare, vb. crown.

incoronazione, n.f. coronation.

incorporare, vb. incorporate; embody.

incorpòreo, adj. incorporeal; disembodied.

incorreggìbile, adj. incorrigible.

incórrere, vb. incur.

incostante, adj. inconstant, fickle.

incostanza, n.f. inconstancy, fickleness.

incredìbile, adj. incredible.

incredulità, n.f. incredulity.

incrèdulo, adj. incredulous.

incremento, n.m. increment.

increspare, vb. ruffle.

increspatura, n.f. ruffle; ripple.

incriminare, vb. incriminate.

incriminazione, n.f. incrimination.

incrociare, vb. cross; intersect; cruise.

incrociato, adj. crossed; crisscross.

incrociatore, n.m. cruiser.

incrocio, n.m. crossing; cross; intersection.

incrostare, vb. incrust.

incubatrice, n.f. incubator.

ìncubo, n.m. nightmare.

incùdine, n.f. anvil.

inculcare, vb. inculcate.

incuneare, vb. wedge.

incuràbile, adj. incurable.

incurante, *adj.* not caring, nonchalant.

incùria, *n.f.* negligence, carelessness.

incursione, *n.f.* inroad, raid.

indebitato, *adj.* indebted.

indebolire, *vb.* weaken; sap.

indefinitamente, *adv.* indefinitely.

indefinito, *adj.* indefinite.

indegnità, *n.f.* indignity; unworthiness.

indegno, *adj.* unworthy.

indelèbile, *adj.* indelible.

indenne, *adj.* unharmed, undamaged, unscathed.

indennità, *n.f.* indemnity.

indennizzare, *vb.* indemnify.

inderogàbile, *adj.* inescapable, intransgressible.

indi, *adv.* thence.

India, *n.f.* India.

indiana, *n.f.* chintz.

indiano, *adj.* Indian.

indicare, *vb.* indicate, point to.

indicativo, *n.m. and adj.* indicative.

indicatore, *n.m.* indicator.

indicazione, *n.f.* indication.

indice, *n.m.* index; forefinger.

indietreggiare, *vb.* back (up); go backwards; recoil.

indiètro, *adv.* backwards; aft; behind; slow.

indifeso, *adj.* defenseless, unprotected.

indifferente, *adj.* indifferent, casual, nonchalant.

indifferentemente, *adv.* indifferently, casually.

indifferenza, *n.f.* indifference, casualness, disregard.

indìgeno, 1. *n.m.* aborigine, native. **2.** *adj.* indigenous, aboriginal, native.

indigènte, *adj.* indigent.

indigestione, *n.f.* indigestion.

indignato, *adj.* indignant.

indignazione, *n.f.* indignation.

indimenticàbile, *adj.* unforgettable.

indipendènte, *adj.* independent.

indipendènza, *n.f.* independence.

indire, *vb.* announce; notify.

indiretto, *adj.* indirect.

indirizzare, *vb.* address.

indirizzàrio, *n.m.* mailing list.

indirizzo, *n.m.* address; direction.

indisciplina, *n.f.* lack of discipline, unruliness.

indiscreto, *adj.* indiscreet.

indiscrezione, *n.f.* indiscretion.

indiscusso, *adj.* unquestioned.

indiscutìbile, *adj.* indisputable.

indispensàbile, *adj.* indispensable.

indisposizione, *n.f.* indisposition; distemper.

indisposto, *adj.* indisposed, unwell.

indistinto, *adj.* indistinct, blurred.

individuale, *adj.* individual.

individualità, *n.f.* individuality.

individualmente, *adv.* individually.

individuo, *n.m.* individual; fellow.

indivisìbile, *adj.* indivisible.

indiziare, *vb.* cast suspicion on.

indìzio, *n.m.* indication, clue; symptom.

ìndole, *n.f.* nature, disposition, temperament.

indolènte, *adj.* indolent.

Indonèsia, *n.f.* Indonesia.

indorare, *vb.* gild.

indossare, *vb.* put on, don.

indovinare, *vb.* guess.

indovinèllo, *n.m.* riddle, conundrum, puzzle.

indùbbio, *adj.* certain, undisputed, sure.

indugiare, *vb.* delay, loiter, dally, dawdle, lag, linger.

indùgio, *n.m.* delay.

indulgènte, *adj.* indulgent.

indulgènza, *n.f.* indulgence.

indùlgere, *vb.* indulge.

indurire, *vb.* harden, steel.

indurre, *vb.* induce.

indùstria, *n.f.* industry.

industriale, 1. *n.* industrialist. **2.** *adj.* industrial, manufacturing.

industrioso, *adj.* industrious.

induttivo, *adj.* inductive.

induzione, *n.f.* induction.

inebriante, *adj.* intoxicating, heady.

inebriare, *vb.* inebriate, intoxicate.

ineguale, *adj.* unequal.
ineleggìbile, *adj.* ineligible.
inerènte, *adj.* inherent.
inèrte, *adj.* inert.
inèrzia, *n.f.* inertia.
inesattèzza, *n.f.* inaccuracy, mistake.
inesorabile, *adj.* inexorable.
inespèrto, *adj.* inexperienced, callow.
inesplicabile, *adj.* inexplicable.
inespugnàbile, *adj.* impregnable.
inestimàbile, *adj.* priceless.
inètto, *adj.* inept.
inevaso, *adj.* outstanding, unfinished.
inevitàbile, *adj.* inevitable.
infallibile, *adj.* infallible.
infame, *adj.* infamous.
infàmia, *n.f.* infamy.
infante, *n.m.* infant.
infantile, *adj.* infantile, childish, childlike, babyish.
infantilità, *n.f.* childishness.
infànzia, *n.f.* infancy, childhood.
infarcire, *vb.* stuff, cram.
infastidire, *vb.* annoy, bother, irk, be troublesome.
infaticàbile, *adj.* indefatigable.
infatuare, *vb.* infatuate.
infàusto, *adj.* ill-omened, ominous.
infedele, *n. and adj.* unfaithful, infidel.
infedeltà, *n.f.* infidelity.
infelice, *adj.* unhappy; unlucky.
inferènza, *n.f.* inference.
inferiore, *adj.* inferior, lower; under.
inferiorità, *n.f.* inferiority.
inferire, *vb.* infer.
infermerìa, *n.f.* infirmary.
infermièra, *n.f.* nurse.
infermità, *n.f.* infirmity.
infermo, *adj.* infirm.
infernale, *adj.* infernal, hellish.
infèrno, *n.m.* hell.
inferriata, *n.f.* grating.
infervorare, *vb.* excite, animate.
infestare, *vb.* infest.
infettare, *vb.* infect.
infettivo, *adj.* infectious.
infètto, *adj.* infected.
infezione, *n.f.* infection.

infiacchire, *vb.* enfeeble, weaken, enervate.
infiammàbile, *adj.* inflammable.
infiammare, *vb.* inflame.
infiammatòrio, *adj.* inflammatory.
infiammazione, *n.f.* inflammation.
infido, *adj.* untrustworthy, false.
infìggere, *vb.* fix, stick.
infilare, *vb.* string, thread.
infiltrare, *vb.* infiltrate.
infiltrazione, *n.f.* infiltration; leakage.
ìnfimo, *adj.* lowest, bottom; mean.
infine, *adv.* finally.
infinità, *n.f.* infinity.
infinitesimale, *adj.* infinitesimal.
infinito, 1. *n.m.* infinite; infinitive.
2. *adj.* infinite.
infisso, *n.m.* fixture.
inflazione, *n.f.* inflation.
inflessione, *n.f.* inflection.
inflìggere, *vb.* inflict.
inflizione, *n.f.* infliction.
influènte, *adj.* influential.
influènza, *n.f.* influence; influenza; grippe.
influsso, *n.m.* influence.
infoltire, *vb.* thicken.
infondato, *adj.* groundless.
infòndere, *vb.* inspire, infuse, instill.
inforcatura, *n.f.* crotch.
informare, *vb.* inform; acquaint, appraise; *(refl.)* inquire.
informàtica, *n.f.* computer science.
informatizzare, *vb.* computerize.
informazione, *n.f.* piece of information; *(pl.)* information.
informe, *adj.* formless.
infornare, *vb.* bake, broil, cook in the oven.
infornata, *n.f.* batch.
infossato, *adj.* sunken.
inframmettènte, *adj.* meddlesome, officious.
inframméttere, *vb.* interject; *(refl.)* meddle.
inframmezzare, *vb.* intersperse, interpose.
infràngere, *vb.* infringe.
infrangìbile, *adj.* unbreakable.

infranto, *adj.* crushed, smashed.

infrarosso, *n.m.* infrared.

infrazione, *n.m.* infraction, violation.

infruttuoso, *adj.* fruitless, unsuccessful.

infuòri, *adv.* all' i. di, except for, outside of.

infuriare, *vb.* become infuriated, rage.

ingabbiare, *vb.* cage.

ingannare, *vb.* deceive, trick, fool, beguile, cheat, bluff, double-cross, hoax, hoodwink, mislead.

ingannatore, **1.** *n.m.* deceiver, cheater. **2.** *adj.* deceitful.

ingannévole, *adj.* deceptive, treacherous.

inganno, *n.m.* deceit, deception, trickery, bluff, hocus-pocus.

ingarbugliare, *vb.* tangle; garble.

ingegnère, *n.m.* engineer.

ingegneria, *n.f.* engineering.

ingegnosamente, *adv.* cleverly, ingeniously.

ingegnosità, *n.f.* cleverness, ingeniousness.

ingegnoso, *adj.* clever, ingenious.

ingelosire, *vb.* make jealous.

ingente, *adj.* enormous, huge, vast.

ingènuo, *adj.* naïve; artless.

ingerènza, *n.f.* interference.

ingerire, *v.b.* ingest, swallow; interfere.

Inghilterra, *n.f.* England.

inghiottire, *vb.* swallow; gulp.

inginocchiarsi, *vb.* kneel.

ingiùngere, *vb.* enjoin.

ingiunzione, *n.f.* injunction.

ingiùria, *n.f.* insult, abuse.

ingiuriare, *vb.* insult, abuse.

ingiuriosamente, *adv.* insultingly.

ingiurioso, *adj.* insulting, abusive.

ingiustificato, *adj.* unwarranted.

ingiustìzia, *n.f.* injustice.

ingiusto, *adj.* unjust, unfair.

inglese, **1.** *n.m. or f.* Englishman; Englishwoman. **2.** *adj.* English.

ingollare, *vb.* gobble, gulp down.

ingombrante, *adj.* cumbersome.

ingombrare, *vb.* encumber, clog, clutter.

ingozzare, *vb.* guzzle.

ingranàggio, *n.m.* gear, gearing.

ingranare, *vb.* mesh.

ingrandimento, *n.m.* enlargement, aggrandizement.

ingrandire, *vb.* enlarge, aggrandize, magnify.

ingranditore, *n.m.* enlarger.

ingrassare, *vb.* fatten.

ingravidare, *vb.* render pregnant, impregnate.

ingrediènte, *n.m.* ingredient.

ingrèsso, *n.m.* entrance, entry.

ingròsso, *n.m.* all'i., wholesale.

inguine, *n.m.* groin.

inibire, *vb.* inhibit.

inibizione, *n.f.* inhibition.

iniettare, *vb.* inject.

iniezione, *n.f.* injection.

inimicìzia, *n.f.* enmity; feud.

inimitàbile, *adj.* inimitable.

ininterrotto, *adj.* continuous, uninterrupted.

iniquità, *n.f.* iniquity.

iniquo, *adj.* unrighteous.

iniziale, *n.f. and adj.* initial.

iniziare, *vb.* initiate, begin, start.

iniziativa, *n.f.* initiative.

iniziazione, *n.f.* initiation.

inizio, *n.m.* beginning, inception, start.

innaffiare, *vb.* water.

innalzare, *vb.* raise, hoist.

innamorare, *vb.* enamor.

innamorarsi, *vb.* fall in love.

innamorata, *n.f.* sweetheart.

innamorato, *n.m.* sweetheart.

innanzi, **1.** *adv.* forward, further. **2.** *prep.* before.

innàrio, *n.m.* hymnal.

innegàbile, *adj.* undeniable.

innervosire, *vb.* make nervous, get on one's nerves.

innescare, *vb.* prime.

innestare, *vb.* graft.

innèsto, *n.m.* graft.

inno, *n.m.* hymn. **i. nazionale,** national anthem.

innocènte, *adj.* innocent; harmless; blameless.

innocènza, *n.f.* innocence.

innòcuo, *adj.* innocuous, harmless.

innovare, *vb.* innovate, change, reform.

innovazione, *n.f.* innovation.

innumerévole, *adj.* innumerable, countless, myriad.

inoculare, *vb.* inoculate.

inoculazione, *n.f.* inoculation.

inodoro, *adj.* odorless.

inoffensivo, *adj.* harmless, inoffensive.

inoltre, *adv.* besides, furthermore.

inondare, *vb.* inundate, flood, swamp.

inondazione, *n.f.* inundation, flood.

inorridire, *vb.* be horrified.

inossidàbile, *adj.* rust-proof.

inquietare, *vb.* worry; *(refl.)* be concerned.

inquièto, *adj.* uneasy.

inquilino, *n.m.* occupant, tenant.

inquinamento, *n.m.,* pollution.

inquinare, *vb.* pollute.

inquirente, *adj.* investigating.

inquisizione, *n.f.* inquisition.

insabbiare, *vb.* cover with sand; shelve.

insaccare, *vb.* put in a bag.

insalata, *n.f.* salad.

insalubre, *adj.* unhealthy.

insanguinato, *adj.* gory.

insània, *n.f.* insanity.

insano, *adj.* insane.

insaporire, *vb.* flavor.

insaputa, *n.f.* **all'i. di,** without the knowledge of.

insediamento, *n.m.* installation.

insediare, *vb.* install.

insegna, *n.f.* standard; signboard; coat of arms; ensign; *(pl.)* insignia.

insegnante, *n.m. or f.* teacher.

insegnare, *vb.* teach.

inseguimento, *n.m.* pursuit.

inseguire, *vb.* follow, pursue.

insenatura, *n.f.* bay, inlet, cove.

insensìbile, *adj.* insensible, insensitive, unfeeling.

insensibilità, *n.f.* insensitivity, callousness.

inseparàbile, *adj.* inseparable.

inserire, *vb.* insert, put in.

inserto, *n.m.* insert; article, file.

inservìbile, *adj.* unusable.

inserzione, *n.f.* insertion; advertisement.

inserzionista, *n.m.* advertiser.

insetticida, *adj.* **pólvere i.,** insecticide.

insètto, *n.m.* insect, bug.

insidioso, *adj.* insidious.

insième, 1. *n.m.* ensemble. **2.** *adv.* together.

insigne, *adj.* remarkable; famous; notable.

insignificante, *adj.* insignificant.

insignificanza, *n.f.* insignificance.

insinuare, *vb.* insinuate.

insinuazione, *n.f.* insinuation, innuendo.

insìpido, *adj.* insipid, tasteless.

insistènte, *adj.* insistent.

insistènza, *n.f.* insistence.

insìstere, *vb.* insist.

insito, *adj.* innate, inborn, inbred.

insoddisfazione, *n.f.* dissatisfaction.

insolazione, *n.f.* sunstroke.

insolènte, *adj.* insolent, insulting, abusive.

insolentemente, *adv.* insolently.

insolènza, *n.f.* insolence.

insòlito, *adj.* unusual.

insomma, *adv.* in conclusion.

insònnia, *n.f.* insomnia.

insopportàbile, *adj.* unbearable.

instàbile, *adj.* unsteady.

installare, *vb.* install.

installazione, *n.f.* installation.

insù, *adv.* **all'i.,** uphill; upwards.

insuccesso, *n.m.* failure.

insufficiènte, *adj.* insufficient.

insulare, *adj.* insular.

insulina, *n.f.* insulin.

insulso, *adj.* dull, insipid.

insultare, *vb.* insult, abuse.

insulto, *n.m.* insult, abuse.

insuperàbile, *adj.* insuperable.

insurrezione, *n.f.* insurrection.

intaccare, *vb.* notch, nick.

intangìbile, *adj.* intangible.

intanto, *adv.* meanwhile.

intàrsio, *n.m.* inlay; inlaid work.

intascare, *vb.* pocket.

intatto, *adj.* intact.

intavolare, *vb.* start; launch.

integèrrimo, *adj.* incorruptible.

integrale, *adj.* integral.

integrare, *vb.* integrate.

integrità, *n.f.* integrity.

intellètto, n.m. intellect; understanding.

intellettuale, adj. intellectual.

intelligènte, adj. intelligent, smart.

intelligènza, n.f. intelligence; wit.

intelligènzia, n.f. intelligentsia.

intelligìbile, adj. intelligible.

intensificare, vb. intensify.

intensivo, adj. intensive.

intènso, adj. intense.

intènto, n.m. and adj. intent.

intenzionale, adj. intentional.

intenzionalmente, adv. intentionally, designedly.

intenzione, n.f. intention.

interamente, adv. entirely, wholly.

intercapedine, n.f. interstice.

intercèdere, vb. intercede.

intercettare, vb. intercept.

interdetto, 1. n.m. interdict. 2. adj. speechless.

interdire, vb. interdict.

interessante, adj. interesting.

interessare, vb. interest, concern; affect; (refl.) concern oneself.

interèsse, n.m. interest, concern.

interfaccia, n.f. interface.

interferènza, n.f. interference.

interiezione, n.f. interjection.

interiora, n.f.pl. entrails.

interiore, adj. interior, inner, inside.

interlùdio, n.m. interlude.

intermediàrio, 1. n.m. intermediary, mediator, go-between. 2. adj. intermediary.

intermèdio, adj. intermediate.

intermissione, n.f. intermission.

intermittènte, adj. intermittent.

internare, vb. intern.

internazionale, adj. international.

internazionalismo, n.m. internationalism.

internista, n.m. and f. internist.

intèrno, 1. n.m. inside. 2. adj. internal; inner, inside; inland.

intero, adj. entire, whole.

interpellare, vb. consult, ask.

interporre, vb. interpose.

interpretare, vb. interpret, construe.

interpretazione, n.f. interpretation.

intèrprete, n.m. interpreter.

interramento, n.m. burial.

interrare, vb. bury.

interrogare, vb. interrogate, question.

interrogatòrio, n.m. cross-examination.

interrogativo, adj. interrogative.

interrogazione, n.f. interrogation.

interrómpere, vb. interrupt; discontinue.

interruttore, n.m. switch.

interruzione, n.f. interruption, break.

interscàmbio, n.m. interchange.

intersecare, vb. intersect.

intersezione, n.f. intersection.

interstìzio, n.m. interstice.

intervallo, n.m. interval; headway.

intervenire, vb. intervene.

intervènto, n.m. intervention.

intervista, n.f. interview.

intervistare, vb. interview.

intesa, n.f. agreement.

inteso, adj. understood.

intestino, 1. n.m. intestine, bowel, gut. 2. adj. intestine.

intimamente, adv. intimately; inwardly.

intimare, vb. intimate; command.

intimidazione, n.f. intimidation.

intimidire, vb. intimidate, daunt.

intimità, n.f. intimacy; privacy.

intimo, adj. intimate; inward. più l., innermost.

intìngere, vb. dip; soak.

intingolo, n.m. sauce, dip.

intirizzire, vb. benumb; stiffen.

intitolare, vb. entitle.

intollerante, adj. intolerant.

intonacare, vb. plaster.

intònaco, n.m. plaster.

intonare, vb. intone.

intonazione, n.f. intonation.

intonso, adj. untrimmed, uncut.

intontire, vb. daze.

intontito, adj. groggy.

intoppo, n.m. impediment, obstacle, hindrance.

intorbidire, vb. confuse, cloud.

intorno, adv. around; about;

round. **i. a,** *prep.* around; about; round.
intossicare, *vb.* intoxicate.
intossicazione, *n.f.* intoxication.
intralciare, *vb.* hinder.
intràlcio, *n.m.* hindrance.
intrallazzo, *n.m.* plot, swindle.
intrappolare, *vb.* trap.
intraprèndere, *vb.* undertake, start.
intravedere, *vb.* glimpse.
intrecciare, *vb.* braid.
intréccio, *n.m.* plot.
intrepidamente, *adv.* dauntlessly, fearlessly.
intrepidezza, *n.f.* intrepidity, fearlessness.
intrèpido, *adj.* intrepid, dauntless, fearless.
intricato, *adj.* intricate.
intrigante, 1. *n.m.* schemer. **2.** *adj.* intriguing.
intrìdere, *vb.* soak.
intrigare, *vb.* intrigue.
intrigo, *n.m.* intrigue.
intrìnseco, *adj.* intrinsic.
introdotto, *adj.* introduced; wellconnected.
introdurre, *vb.* introduce.
introduttivo, *adj.* introductory.
introduzione, *n.f.* introduction.
introspezione, *n.f.* introspection.
introvertito, *adj.* introvert.
intrùdere, *vb.* intrude, obtrude.
intruso, *n.m.* intruder.
intuire, *vb.* sense.
intuitivo, *adj.* intuitive.
intuizione, *n.f.* intuition.
inumano, *adj.* inhuman.
inumidire, *vb.* dampen, humidify, moisten, wet.
inùtile, *adj.* useless, needless.
invadente, *adj.* intrusive.
invàdere, *vb.* invade, overrun.
invàlido, 1. *n.* invalid. **2.** *adj.* disabled; invalid.
invano, *adv.* in vain.
invariàbile, *adj.* invariable.
invasione, *n.f.* invasion.
invasore, *n.m.* invader.
invecchiare, *vb.* grow old, age.
invece, *adv.* instead.
inventare, *vb.* invent.
inventàrio, *n.m.* inventory.

inventivo, *adj.* inventive.
inventore, *n.m.* inventor.
invenzione, *n.f.* invention.
invernale, *adj.* of winter, wintry.
invèrno, *n.m.* winter.
invèrso, *adj.* inverse.
invertebrato, *n.m. and adj.* invertebrate.
investigare, *vb.* investigate.
investigazione, *n.f.* investigation; inquiry.
investimento, *n.m.* investment.
investire, *vb.* invest; run into.
inveterato, *adj.* inveterate.
invettiva, *n.f.* invective.
inviare, *vb.* send.
inviato, *n.m.* envoy, messenger; (journalism) correspondent.
invìdia, *n.f.* envy.
invidiàbile, *adj.* enviable.
invidiare, *vb.* envy, begrudge.
invidioso, *adj.* envious.
invigorire, *vb.* invigorate.
inviluppare, *vb.* enmesh.
invincìbile, *adj.* invincible.
invio, *n.m.* mailing, shipment, dispatch.
invisìbile, *adj.* invisible.
invitante, *adj.* appealing, inviting.
invitare, *vb.* invite, ask.
invito, *n.m.* invitation; bid.
invitto, *adj.* undefeated.
invocare, *vb.* invoke.
invocazione, *n.f.* invocation.
involontàrio, *adj.* involuntary.
involto, *n.m.* wrapper; bundle.
invòlucro, *n.m.* wrapping.
invulneràbile, *adj.* invulnerable.
inzuppare, *vb.* drench; soak, dunk.
Io, 1. *pron.* I. **2.** *n.* ego.
iòdio, *n.m.* iodine.
iòsa, *adv.* **a i.** in abundance.
iperacidità, *n.f.* hyperacidity.
ipèrbole, *n.f.* hyperbole.
ipercrìtico, *adj.* hypercritical.
ipersensitivo, *adj.* hypersensitive.
ipertensione, *n.f.* hypertension.
ipnòsi, *n.f.* hypnosis.
ipnòtico, *adj.* hypnotic.
ipnotismo, *n.m.* hypnotism.
ipnotizzare, *vb.* hypnotize.
ipocondrìa, *n.f.* hypochondria.
ipocondrìaco, *n.m. and adj.* hypochondriac.

ipocrisìa, *n.f.* hypocrisy, cant.
ipòcrita, *n.m.* hypocrite.
ipòcrito, *adj.* hypocritical.
ipodèrmico, *adj.* hypodermic.
ipotèca, *n.f.* mortgage.
ipotecare, *vb.* mortgage.
ipotenusa, *n.f.* hypotenuse.
ipòtesi, *n.f.* hypothesis.
ipotètico, *adj.* hypothetical.
ìppico, *adj.* horse; horse-racing.
ippòdromo, *n.m.* hippodrome;
race-track.
ippopòtamo, *n.m.* hippopotamus.
ira, *n.f.* anger, ire, wrath.
Iràk, *n.m.* Iraq.
irato, *adj.* irate, wrathful.
ìride, *n.f.* iris.
irìdio, *n.m.* iridium.
ìris, *n.f.* iris.
Irlanda, *n.f.* Ireland.
irlandese, *adj.* Irish.
ironìa, *n.f.* irony.
irònico, *adj.* ironical.
irradiare, *vb.* beam, shine, radiate.
irradiazione, *n.f.* radiation.
irraggiungìbile, *adj.* unreacha-
ble, unobtainable.
irragionévole, *adj.* irrational, absurd.
irrazionale, *adj.* irrational.
irreale, *adj.* unreal.
irrecuperàbile, *adj.* irrecovera-
ble.
irrefutàbile, *adj.* irrefutable.
irregolare, *adj.* irregular; fitful.
irregolarità, *n.f.* irregularity.
irremissìbile, *adj.* unpardonable.
irreprensìbile, *adj.* irreprehensible, faultless.
irreprensibilmente, *adv.* irreprehensibly, faultlessly.
irrequièto, *adj.* restless.
irresistìbile, *adj.* irresistible.
irresponsàbile, *adj.* irresponsible.
irretire, *vb.* snare, entrap, entice.
irrevocàbile, *adj.* irrevocable.
irriconoscìbile, *adj.* unrecognizable.
irrìdere, *vb.* deride, mock.
irriducìbile, *adj.* stubborn, in-
domitable.
irrigare, *vb.* irrigate.

irrigazione, *n.f.* irrigation.
irrigidire, *vb.* stiffen.
irrilevante, *adj.* irrelevant.
irrispettoso, *adj.* disrespectful.
irritàbile, *adj.* irritable, on edge,
edgy, fretful.
irritabilità, *n.f.* irritability, fretfulness.
irritabilmente, *adv.* irritably,
fretfully.
irritante, *adj.* irritant.
irritare, *vb. tr.* irritate, fret, gall,
vex.
irritato, *adj.* irritated, cross.
irritazione, *n.f.* irritation.
irriverènte, *adj.* irreverent.
irrompere, *vb.* burst.
irrorare, *vb.* sprinkle; wet.
irsuto, *adj.* hirsute.
iscrìvere, *vb.* inscribe; enroll, register.
iscrizione, *n.f.* inscription; enrollment, registration.
isola, *n.f.* island.
isolamento, *n.m.* isolation; insulation.
isolare, *vb.* isolate; insulate.
isolatore, *n.m.* insulator.
isolazione, *n.f.* isolation.
isolazionista, *n.m.* isolationist.
isolotto salvagènte, *n.m.* safety
island.
isòscele, *adj.* isosceles.
ispànico, *adj.* Hispanic.
ispettore, *n.m.* inspector.
ispezionare, *vb.* inspect.
ispezione, *n.f.* inspection.
ìspido, *adj.* shaggy.
ispirare, *vb.* inspire.
ispirazione, *n.f.* inspiration.
Israèle, *n.m.* Israel.
israeliano, *adj.* Israeli.
israelita, *n.m.* Israelite.
israelìtico, *adj.* Israelite.
issare, *vb.* hoist.
istallare, *vb.* install, set up; settle.
istantànea, *n.f.* snapshot.
istantàneo, *adj.* instantaneous.
istante, *n.m.* instant.
istanza, *n.f.* request, instance.
isterectomìa, *n.f.* hysterectomy.
istèrico, *adj.* hysterical.
isterismo, *n.m.* hysteria, hysterics.
istigare, *vb.* instigate.

istillare, vb. instill.
istintivo, adj. instinctive.
istinto, n.m. instinct.
istituto, n.m. institute.
istituzione, n.f. institution.
istmo, n.m. isthmus.
ìstrice, n.f. hedgehog.
istriònica, n.f. histrionics.
istriònico, adj. histrionic.
istruire, vb. instruct.
istruttivo, adj. instruction.
istruttore, n.m. instructor.

istruttrice, n.f. instructress.
istruzione, n.f. education, culture.
istupidito, adj. dulled, dazed.
Itàlia, n.f. Italy.
italiano, n.m. and adj. Italian.
itàlico, adj. Italic.
itineràrio, n.m. itinerary.
itterìzia, n.f. jaundice.
ittiologìa, n.f. ichthyology.
iuta, n.f. jute.
ivi, adv. there.

J,K

jeans, m.pl. jeans.
Jugoslàvia, n.f. Yugoslavia.
jugoslavo, adj. Yugoslav.
kapút, adj. finished; damaged.
karakiri, n.m. harakiri.
karate, n.m. karate.

kg., abbr. kilogram.
kilohertz, n.m. kilohertz.
km., abbr. kilometer.
kohl, n.m. mascara.
kw., abbr. kilowatt.

L

l', 1. def. art. the. 2. pron. 3. sg. him; her.
la, 1. pron. her; it; you. 2. def. art. f. the.
là, adv. there.
labbro, n.m. lip. **l. leporino**, hair-lip.
labiale, adj. labial.
làbile, adj. weak.
labirinto, n.m. labyrinth, maze.
laboratòrio, n.m. laboratory.
laborioso, adj. laborious, industrious.
lacca, n.f. lacquer.
laccare, vb. lacquer.
lacchè, n.m. lackey, flunkey.
làccio, n.m. string; trap; noose; lariat, lasso; loop.
lacerare, vb. lacerate.
lacerazione, n.f. laceration.
lacònico, adj. laconic.
làcrima, n.f. tear.
laddove, conj. while, whereas.
ladro, n.m. thief, burglar.
ladrone, n.m. robber.
laggiù, adv. down there.
lagnanza, n.f. complaint, grievance.
lagnarsi, vb. complain.

lago, n.m. lake.
laguna, n.f. lagoon.
laicato, n.m. laity.
làico, 1. n. layman. 2. adj. lay.
lama, n.f. blade.
lambiccato, adj. overelaborate.
lambire, vb. lap.
lamentare, vb. lament, bewail.
lamentazione, n.f. lamentation.
lamentela, n.f. complaint.
lamentévole, adj. lamentable.
lamento, n.m. lament.
lametta, n.f. razor blade.
laminare, vb. laminate.
làmpada, n.f. lamp.
lampadàrio, n.m. chandelier.
lampadina, n.f. light bulb. **l. tascàbile**, flashlight.
lampante, adj. evident, manifest; shining.
lampeggiare, vb. lighten.
lampeggiatore, n.m. blinker.
lampo, n.m. (flash of) lightning.
lampone, n.m. raspberry.
lana, n.f. wool. **l. di acciaio** n.f. steel wool.
lancetta, n.f. pointer, hand.
lància, n.f. lance, spear; launch.

lanciafiamme, n.m. flamethrower.
lanciarazzi, n.m. rocket launcher.
lanciare, vb. hurl, cast, chuck, fling, launch, pitch, sling, throw.
lanciatore, n.m. pitcher.
lancinante, adj. excruciating.
landa, n.f., moor; wasteland.
lànguido, adj. languid; lackadaisical.
languire, vb. languish, pine.
languore, n.m. languor.
lanificio, n.m. wool mill.
lanolina, n.f. lanolin.
lantèrna, n.f. lantern.
lanùgine, n.f. down, fuzz.
lanuginoso, adj. fluffy, downy; fuzzy.
lapalissiano, adj. obvious, evident.
lapidare, vb. stone.
làpis, n.m. pencil.
lardo, n.m. lard.
largamente, adv. broadly, widely.
largheggiare, vb. be lavish.
larghezza, n.f. breadth; width.
largire, vb. to give liberally.
largo, adj. broad, wide; (music) largo.
làrice, n.m. larch.
laringe, n.f. larynx.
laringite, n.f. laryngitis.
larva, n.f. larva; grub; ghost.
lasciare, vb. let; leave; quit. **l. stare,** let alone.
làscito, n.m. legacy.
lascivo, adj. lascivious, lecherous.
làser, n.m. laser.
lassativo, n.m. and adj. laxative.
lassismo, n.m. laxity.
lasso, n.m. period (of time).
lassù, adv. up there.
lastra, n.f. plate; sheet; slab.
latènte, adj. latent.
laterale, adj. lateral.
latifondo, n.m. large estate.
latino, n.m. and adj. Latin.
latitanza, n.f. hiding (used of criminals).
latitùdine, n.f. latitude.
lato, 1. n.m. side, standpoint. 2. adj. wide.
latore, n.m. bearer.
latrare, vb. howl, bay.

latrato, n.m. howl, bay.
latrina, n.f. latrine, lavatory, toilet, privy.
latta, n.f. tin.
lattaia, n.f. milkmaid, dairymaid.
lattaio, n.m. milkman, dairyman.
lattante, 1. n.m. baby. 2. adj. unweaned.
latte, n.m. milk.
làtteo, adj. milky.
lattería, n.f. dairy; milk-bar.
làttico, adj. lactic.
lattòsio, n.m. lactose.
lattuga, n.f. lettuce.
làudano, n.m. laudanum.
làurea, n.f. degree.
laurearsi, vb. graduate.
laureato, adj. laureate.
làuro, n.m. laurel; bay.
làuto, adj. magnificent, sumptuous, abundant.
lava, n.f. lava.
lavabiancheria, n.m. washing machine.
lavabo, n.m. wash-basin.
lavagna, n.f. blackboard; slate.
lavàggio, n.m. washing.
lavanda, n.f. lavender.
lavandaia, n.f. laundress.
lavandaio, n.m. laundryman.
lavandería, n.f. laundry.
lavandino, n.m. sink.
lavapiatti, n.f. dishwater.
lavare, vb. wash, launder.
lavata, n.f. washing. **l. di capo,** scolding.
lavativo, adj. lazy; tiresome (person).
lavatòio, n.m. washroom.
lavorare, vb. work.
lavoratore, n.m. worker.
lavorìo, n.m. bustle, activity.
lavoro, n.m. work.
laziale, adj. of Latium.
Làzio, n.m. Latium.
le, 1. def. art. f.pl. the. 2. pron. 3. sg. dative to her; 3. pl.f them.
leale, adj. loyal.
lealista, n.m. loyalist.
lealtà, n.f. loyalty.
lebbra, n.f. leprosy.
lebbroso, 1. n. leper. 2. adj. leprous.
lécca-lécca, n.m. lollypop.

leccapièdi, n.m. bootlicker.
leccare, vb. lick.
leccato, adj. affected; polished.
lega, n.f. league; alloy.
legale, adj. legal, lawful.
legalità, n.f. legality.
legalizzare, vb. legalize.
legame, n.m. tie, bond, link.
legamento, n.m. ligament.
legare, vb. bequeath, leave (in will); bind, tie.
legato, n.m. bequest, legacy.
legatore, n.m. bookbinder.
legatoria, n.f. bindery, bookbindery.
legatura, n.f. ligature; (music) slur.
legazione, n.f. legation.
legge, n.f. law.
leggènda, n.f. legend.
leggendàrio, adj. legendary.
lèggere, vb. read.
leggerezza, n.f. lightness; levity.
leggermente, adv. lightly.
leggero, adj. light.
leggiadro, adj. lovely.
leggìbile, adj. legible.
legione, n.f. legion.
legislatore, n.m. legislator.
legislazione, n.f. legislation.
legittimità, n.f. legitimacy.
legìttimo, adj. legitimate, lawful.
legna, n.f. firewood.
legnata, n.f. clubbing, thrashing.
legname, n.m. lumber, timber.
legume, n.m. vegetable, legume.
lèi, pron. she; her; you.
lembo, n.m. hem; flap.
lena, n.f. energy; enthusiasm.
lentamente, adv. slowly.
lènte, n.f. lens; eyeglass.
lentezza, n.f. slowness.
lentìcchia, n.f. lentil.
lentìggine, n.f. freckle.
lentigginoso, adj. freckled.
lento, adj. slow, slack, sluggish.
lenzuòla, n.f.pl. sheets, bedclothes.
lenzuòlo, n.m. sheet.
leone, n.m. lion.
leopardo, n.m. leopard.
lèpre, n.f. hare.
lèsbica, n.f. lesbian.
lèsbico, adj. lesbian.

lesione, n.f. lesion.
lèssico, n.m. lexicon.
lesto, adj. quick, nimble.
letale, adj. lethal.
letame, n.m. dung, manure, muck.
letargìa, n.f. lethargy.
letàrgico, n.m. lethargic.
letargo, n.m. lethargy.
letìzia, n.f. happiness, joy.
lèttera, n.f. letter.
letterale, adj. literal.
letteràrio, adj. literary.
letterato, adj. literate.
letteratura, n.f. literature.
lettièra, n.f. bedstead; litter; (animal's) bed.
lettiga, n.f. stretcher.
lettino, n.m. cot.
lètto, n.m. bed; couch. **l. ad acqua,** waterbed. **l. del mare,** seabed.
lettore, n.m. reader.
lettura, n.f. reading.
leucèmia, n.f. leukemia.
lèva, n.f. lever; levy.
levante, 1. n.m. east; levant. **2.** adj. rising.
levare, vb. raise; (refl.) get up, arise.
levatrice, n.f. midwife.
levigare, vb. smooth.
levigato, adj. smooth.
levrière, n.m. greyhound.
lezione, n.f. lesson.
leziosaggìre, n.f. affectation, simpering.
lezioso, adj. mincing, mannered.
lézzo, n.m. stench; filth.
li, pron. 3. pl.m. them.
lì, adv. there.
libagione, n.f. libation.
libbra, n.f. pound.
libéccio, n.m. southwest wind.
liberale, adj. liberal, generous, bounteous.
liberalismo, n.m. liberalism.
liberalità, n.f. liberality, generosity, bounty.
liberare, vb. liberate, deliver, free, relieve, release, rescue.
liberazione, n.f. liberation, deliverance, relief, release, rescue.
liberismo, n.m. free trade.

fibero, *adj.* free.
libertà, *n.f.* liberty, freedom.
libertino, *n.m. and adj.* libertine.
libidinoso, *adj.* libidinous.
libraio, *n.m.* bookseller.
librerìa, *n.f.* bookstore.
libretto, *n.m.* booklet; (opera) libretto.
libro, *n.m.* book. **l. in brossura,** paperback.
liceale, *adj.* high school.
licènza, *n.f.* license; furlough; leave.
licenziamento, *n.m.* discharge.
licenziare, *vb.* discharge, fire, sack.
licenzioso, *adj.* licentious.
licèo, *n.m.* high school.
lichene, *n.m.* lichen.
lido, *n.m.* beach, shore, seashore.
lietamente, *adv.* gladly.
lièto, *adj.* glad, pleased.
lieve, *adj.* light; slight.
lièvito, *n.m.* leaven.
ligio, *adj.* devoted.
lignàggio, *n.m.* lineage, ancestry.
lignite, *n.f.* lignite.
ligure, *adj.* Ligurian.
ligustro, *n.m.* privet.
lillà, *n.m.* lilac.
lima, *n.f.* file.
limaccioso, *adj.* miry, muddy.
limare, *vb.* file.
limatura, *n.f.* filings.
limbo, *n.m.* limbo.
limitare, *vb.* limit.
limitazione, *n.f.* limitation.
limite, *n.m.* limit, bound.
limo, *n.m.* mud, mire.
limonare, *vb.* spoon.
limonata, *n.f.* lemonade.
limone, *n.m.* lemon.
limoso, *adj.* slimy.
limpido, *adj.* limpid.
lince, *n.f.* lynx. **l. persiana,** caracul.
linciàggio, *n.m.* lynching.
linciare, *vb.* lynch.
lindo, *adj.* neat.
linea, *n.f.* line; figure.
lineare, *adj.* linear.
linfa, *n.f.* lymph; sap.
lingua, *n.f.* tongue, language.
linguaggio, *n.m.* language.

linguista, *n.m.* linguist.
linguìstica, *n.f.* linguistics.
linguìstico, *adj.* linguistic.
linimento, *n.m.* liniment.
lino, *n.m.* linen.
liquefare, *vb.* liquefy.
liquidare, *vb.* liquidate.
liquidazione, *n.f.* liquidation.
fliquido, *n.m. and adj.* liquid.
liquirìzia, *n.f.* licorice.
liquore, *n.m.* liquor; liqueur.
lira, *n.f.* lira; lyre.
liricismo, *n.m.* lyricism.
lìrico, *adj.* lyric; operatic.
lisciare, *vb.* smooth.
liscio, *adj.* smooth, sleek.
lista, *n.f.* list; menu, bill of fare; stripe.
listèllo, *n.m.* lath.
litanìa, *n.f.* litany.
lite, *n.f.* fight, quarrel, struggle, affray, brawl, row.
litigante, *n.m.* litigant.
litigare, *vb.* quarrel, bicker, row.
litigioso, *adj.* quarrelsome, argumentative, rowdy.
litografare, *vb.* lithograph.
litografìa, *n.f.* lithography, lithograph.
litro, *n.m.* liter.
liturgìa, *n.f.* liturgy.
litùrgico, *adj.* liturgical.
liuto, *n.m.* lute.
livellare, *vb.* level.
livellatrice, *n.f.* bulldozer.
livèllo, *n.m.* level.
lìvido, *adj.* livid.
livore, *n.m.* hatred; envy.
Livorno, *n.m.* Leghorn.
livrèa, *n.f.* livery.
lizza, *n.f.* **essere in l.** be in competition.
lo, 1. *pron.* him; it; you. **2.** *def. art.* the.
lòbo, *n.m.* lobe.
locale, *adj.* local.
località, *n.f.* locality, locale.
localizzare, *vb.* localize.
locanda, *n.f.* inn.
locandina, *n.f.* playbill; flyer.
locomotiva, *n.f.* locomotive, engine.
locomotore, *n.m.* locomotive.

locomozione, *n.f.* locomotion.

locusta, *n.f.* locust.

locuzione, *n.f.* expression.

lodare, *vb.* praise, commend, laud.

lòde, *n.f.* praise, commendation.

lodévole, *adj.* praiseworthy, commendable, laudable.

lodevolmente, *adv.* praiseworthily, commendably.

logaritmo, *n.m.* logarithm.

lòggia, *n.f.* loge.

loggione, *n.m.* top gallery.

lògica, *n.f.* logic.

lògico, *adj.* logical.

logorare, *vb.* wear out.

logorìo, *n.m.* wear and tear.

lògoro, *adj.* worn-out, shabby.

lombàggine, *n.f.* lumbago.

Lombardìa, *n.f.* Lombardy.

lombardo, *adj.* Lombard.

lombata, *n.f.* loin.

lombo, *n.m.* loin; sirloin.

lombrico, *n.m.* earthworm.

londinese, *adj.* of London.

Londra, *n.f.* London.

longevità, *n.f.* longevity.

longèvo, *adj.* long-lived.

longitudinale, *adj.* longitudinal.

longitùdine, *n.f.* longitude.

lontananza, *n.f.* distance.

lontano, 1. *adj.* distant, far. **2.** *adv.* far away, far off, afar.

lóntra, *n.f.* otter.

lonza, *n.f.* pork loin.

lòppa, *n.f.* chaff.

loquace, *adj.* loquacious, talkative.

lordo, *adj.* soiled; (weight) gross.

lordume, *n.m.* filth.

loro, *pron.* they; their; theirs; them; to them; you; your; yours; to you.

losanga, *n.f.* lozenge.

losco, *adj.* sly; questionable, suspicious.

lòto, *n.m.* lotus; mud, mire.

lotta, *n.f.* struggle, fight.

lottare, *vb.* struggle, wrestle.

lotterìa, *n.f.* lottery, raffle.

lotto, *n.m.* lot.

lozione, *n.f.* lotion.

lùbrico, *adj.* lewd.

lubrificante, *n.m. and adj.* lubricant.

lubrificare, *vb.* lubricate, grease, oil.

lucchetto, *n.m.* padlock.

luccicare, *vb.* glitter.

lùccio, *n.m.* pike.

lùcciola, *n.f.* firefly; glowworm.

luce, *n.f.* light.

lucernàrio, *n.m.* skylight.

lucèrtola, *n.f.* lizard.

lucidare, *vb.* polish, shine.

lucidatura, *n.f.* polish.

luci di città, *n.f.pl.* parking lights.

luciditá, *n.f.* shininess, gloss.

lùcido, 1. *n.m.* polish. **2.** *adj.* shiny, glossy.

lucrare, *vb.* profit; earn.

lucrativo, *adj.* lucrative.

lucro, *n.m.* profit, gain, earning.

lucrosamente, *adv.* gainfully.

lucroso, *adj.* gainful.

lùglio, *n.m.* July.

lùi, *pron.* he; him.

lumaca, *n.f.* snail.

luminoso, *adj.* luminous, bright, light, shining.

lunare, *adj.* lunar.

lunàtico, *n.m. and adj.* lunatic.

lunedì, *n.m.* Monday.

lunga, *adj.* **di gran l.,** by far.

lungamente, *adv.* long.

lunghezza, *n.f.* length.

lungo, 1. *adj.* long. **2.** *prep.* along.

luogo, *n.m.* place. **l. comune,** cliché. **aver l.,** take place.

lupa, *n.f.* she-wolf.

lupo, *n.m.* wolf.

lùppolo, *n.m.* hop.

lusingare, *vb.* flatter, cajole.

lusingatore, *n.m.* flatterer.

lusinghe, *n.f.pl.* flattery.

lusinghièro, *adj.* flattering.

lusso, *n.m.* luxury. **di l.,** de luxe.

lussuoso, *adj.* luxurious.

lussureggiante, *adj.* luxuriant, lush.

lustrascarpe, *n.m.* bootblack.

lustro, *n.m.* luster.

luterano, *adj.* Lutheran.

lutto, *n.m.* mourning.

M

ma, *conj.* but.

màcabro, *adj.* macabre.

maccheroni, *n.m.pl.* macaroni.

màcchia, *n.f.* spot, blemish, stain, blot; underbrush, brushwood.

macchiare, *vb.* spot, blot.

macchietta, *n.f.* flock.

macchiettato, *adj.* spotted, dappled.

màcchina, *n.f.* machine; engine. **m. da scrivere,** typewriter.

macchinare, *vb.* scheme.

macchinàrio, *n.m.* machinery.

macchinista, *n.m.* engineer; machinist.

macchinoso, *adj.* complicated.

macedònia, *n.f.* fruit salad.

macellaio, *n.m.* butcher.

macellare, *vb.* butcher, slaughter.

macèllo, *n.m.* butchery, slaughter.

macerare, *vb.* soak.

macèrie, *n.f.pl.* rubble, debris.

macigno, *n.m.* boulder.

màcina, *n.f.* grindstone.

macinacaffè, *n.m.* coffee grinder.

macinare, *vb.* grind, mill.

madornale, *adv.* gross.

madre, *n.f.* mother; (cheque) stub.

madrigale, *n.m.* madrigal.

madrina, *n.f.* godmother.

maestà, *n.f.* majesty.

maestoso, *adj.* majestic.

maestra, *n.f.* teacher.

maestrìa, *n.f.* ability, skill.

maestro, *n.m.* master, teacher.

mafia, *f.* mafia.

magari, *adv.* perhaps even.

magazzinàggio, *n.m.* storage.

magazzino, *n.m.* storehouse; (arms) depot, armory.

maggese, *n.m.* fallow field. **a m.,** fallow.

màggio, *n.m.* May.

maggioranza, *n.f.* majority.

maggiorazione, *n.f.* increase, appreciation.

maggiordòmo, *n.m.* butler.

maggiore, 1. *n.* major; elder; senior. **2.** *adj.* greater; elder; greatest; eldest.

maggiorenne, 1. *adj.* over 18 years old, of age. **2.** *n.m.* adult.

maggiormente, *adv.* mostly.

Magi, *n.m.pl.* Magi, Wise Men.

magia, *n.f.* magic.

màgico, *adj.* magic.

magione, *n.f.* mansion; dwelling.

magistrale, *adj.* masterly, magistral.

magistrato, *n.m.* magistrate.

magistratura, *n.f.* judiciary.

màglia, *n.f.* jersey; stitch.

maglietta, *n.f.* T-shirt.

màglio, *n.m.* mallet.

magnànimo, *adj.* magnanimous, high-minded.

magnate, *n.m.* magnate.

magnèsio, *n.m.* magnesium.

magnète, *n.m.* magnet.

magnètico, *adj.* magnetic.

magnetizzare, *vb.* magnetize.

magnetòfono, *n.m.* tape recorder.

magnificare, *vb.* extol, praise; magnify.

magnificènza, *n.f.* magnificence.

magnìfico, *adj.* magnificent.

magniloquènte, *adj.* grandiloquent.

mago, *n.m.* magician.

magro, *adj.* lean, gaunt, meager, spare, thin.

mai, *adv.* ever; never.

maiale, *n.m.* pig; pork.

maionese, *n.m.* mayonnaise.

malamente, *adv.* badly.

malària, *n.f.* malaria.

malato, *adj.* sick, ill, ailing.

malattia, *n.f.* sickness, malady, illness, ailment, disease.

malaugùrio, *n.m.* ill omen, jinx.

malavita, *n.f.* underworld.

maldicènza, *n.f.* scandal.

male, 1. *n.m.* evil; pain, ache, hurt. **m. di mare,** seasickness. **2.** *adv.* badly.

maledetto, *adj.* accursed.

maledire, *vb.* curse.

maledizione, *n.f.* curse.

malevolènza, *n.f.* malice.

malèvolo, *adj.* malevolent.

malfattore, *n.m.* ruffian.

malgrado, *prep.* despite.

maligno, *adj.* malignant.

malinconìa, *n.f.* melancholy.
malincònico, *adj.* melancholy.
malìzia, *n.f.* malice.
malizioso, *adj.* mischievous.
malleàbile, *adj.* malleable.
mallevadore, *n.m.* guarantor; sponsor.
malore, *n.m.* illness.
malsano, *adj.* unhealthy.
malsicuro, *adj.* uncertain; unsafe.
malto, *n.m.* malt.
maltrattare, *vb.* maltreat, mistreat.
malvàgio, *adj.* wicked, fell.
malvagità, *n.f.* wickedness.
malvaròsa, *n.f.* hollyhock.
malvisto, *adj.* unpopular.
mamma, *n.f.* mother.
mammèlla, *n.f.* breast; udder.
mammìfero, *n.m.* mammal.
manata, *n.f.* handful.
mancanza, *n.f.* lack; failure; shortage. **in m. di,** failing; lacking.
mancare, *vb.* be missing, be lacking; fail.
mància, *n.f.* tip, gratuity.
mancorrente, *n.m.* hand-rail.
mandare, *vb.* send.
mandato, *n.m.* mandate; warrant.
mandìbola, *n.f.* jaw.
mandolino, *n.m.* mandolin.
màndorla, *n.f.* almond.
màndorlo, *n.m.* almond-tree.
mandria, *n.f.* herd, drove.
mandrillo, *n.m.* mandrill.
maneggiare, *vb.* handle.
manette, *n.f.pl.* handcuffs.
manganello, *n.m.* bludgeon, cudgel.
manganese, *n.m.* manganese.
mangiàbile, *adj.* edible, eatable.
mangiapane, *n.m.* loafer, idler.
mangiare, *vb.* eat.
mangiatòia, *n.f.* manger.
mangime, *n.m.* fodder.
manìa, *n.f.* mania, craze, fad.
manìaco, *n.m. and adj.* maniac.
mànica, *n.f.* sleeve.
mànico, *n.m.* handle, haft.
manicòmio, *n.m.* madhouse, (insane) asylum.
manicotto, *n.m.* muff.
manicure, *n.f.* manicure.

manièra, *n.f.* manner, way, fashion.
manierismo, *n.m.* mannerism.
manifestare, *vb.* manifest, evince.
manifestazione, *n.f.* demonstration.
manifèsto, 1. *n.m.* manifesto. **2.** *adj.* manifest.
manìglia, *n.f.* handle.
manipolare, *vb.* manipulate.
manna, *n.f.* manna, godsend.
mannaia, *n.f.* axe, chopper, cleaver.
mano, *n.f.* hand.
manodòpera, *n.f.* labor.
manomettere, *vb.* tamper with.
manòpola, *n.f.* knob; mitten.
manoscritto, *n.m. and adj.* manuscript.
manovale, *n.m.* laborer, helper.
manovèlla, *n.f.* handle, crank.
manòvra, *n.f.* maneuver.
manovrare, *vb.* maneuver.
mansuèto, *adj.* tame.
mantèllo, *n.m.* cloak, mantle, wrap.
mantenere, *vb.* maintain, keep.
mantenimento, *n.m.* maintenance.
màntice, *n.m.* bellows.
Màntova, *n.f.* Mantua.
mantovano, *adj.* Mantuan.
manuale, 1. *n.m.* manual, handbook. **2.** *adj.* manual.
manùbrio, *n.m.* handle-bar.
manufatto, *n.m.* manufactured article.
manzo, *n.m.* steer; beef.
mappa, *n.f.* map.
marasma, *n.m.* chaos, confusion.
marca, *n.f.* brand.
marcare, *vb.* mark.
marchese, *n.m.* marquis.
marchigiano, *adj.* of the Marche.
màrchio, *n.m.* stamp, hallmark.
màrcia, *n.f.* march.
marciapiède, *n.m.* sidewalk.
marciare, *vb.* march.
màrcio, *adj.* rotten, decayed; (egg) addled.
marcire, *vb.* rot, decay.
marciume, *n.m.* rottenness.
mare, *n.m.* sea.
marèa, *n.f.* tide.
maremoto, *n.m.* seaquake.

maresciallo, *n.m.* marshal.

margarina, *n.f.* margarine.

margherita, *n.f.* daisy.

marginale, *adj.* marginal, borderline.

màrgine, *n.m.* margin, edge.

marijuana, *n.f.* marijuana.

marina, *n.f.* navy; marine.

marinaio, *n.m.* mariner, sailor.

marinare, *vb.* marinate. **m. la scuola**, cut school.

marino, *adj.* marine.

marionetta, *n.f.* marionette.

maritale, *adj.* marital.

maritare, *vb.* marry.

marito, *n.m.* husband.

marìttimo, *adj.* maritime; marine.

marmàglia, *n.f.* riffraff, rabble.

marmellata, *n.f.* marmalade; jam.

marmitta, *n.f.* muffler.

marmo, *n.m.* marble.

marmòcchio, *n.m.* brat.

marmotta, *n.f.* ground hog.

maroso, *n.m.* billow.

marrone, *n.m.* maroon; chestnut.

marrùbio, *n.f.* horehound.

Marsiglia, *n.f.* Marseilles.

martedì, *n.m.* Tuesday.

martellare, *vb.* hammer.

martèllo, *n.m.* hammer.

martinèllo, *n.m.* jack.

màrtire, *n.m.* martyr.

martìrio, *n.m.* martyrdom.

marziale, *adj.* martial.

marzo, *n.m.* March.

mascalzone, *n.m.* scoundrel, blackguard; crook.

mascèlla, *n.f.* jaw.

màschera, *n.f.* mask; usher. **m. antigas**, gas mask.

mascherare, *vb.* mask.

mascherata, *n.f.* masquerade.

maschile, *adj.* masculine.

maschio, **1.** *n.* male; cock; buck. **2.** *adj.* masculine; male.

massa, *n.f.* mass; bulk; lump.

massacrare, *vb.* massacre, slaughter.

massacro, *n.m.* massacre, slaughter.

massaggiare, *vb.* massage.

massaggiatore, *n.m.* masseur.

massàggio, *n.m.* massage.

massaia, *n.f.* housekeeper; housewife.

massìccio, *adj.* massive; solid.

màssima, *n.f.* maxim.

màssimo, *n.m. and adj.* maximum.

masso, *n.m.* rock, boulder.

massone, *n.m.* Mason.

massonerìa, *n.f.* Masonry.

masticare, *vb.* chew, masticate.

masticatore, *n.m.* chewer.

mastice, *n.m.* mastic; putty.

mastro, *n.m.* master. **libro m.**, ledger.

matassa, *n.f.* skein, hank.

matemàtica, *n.f.* mathematics.

matemàtico, *adj.* mathematical.

materasso, *n.m.* mattress.

matèria, *n.f.* matter; subject.

materiale, *n.m. and adj.* material.

materialismo, *n.m.* materialism.

materializzare, *vb.* materialize.

maternità, *n.f.* maternity.

matèrno, *adj.* maternal.

matita, *n.f.* pencil; crayon.

matriarcato, *n.m.* matriarchy.

matrice, *n.f.* matrix; stub.

matrìcola, *n.f.* freshman.

matrigna, *n.f.* stepmother.

matrimònio, *n.m.* matrimony; marriage; match.

matrona, *n.f.* matron.

mattacchione, *n.m.* jester, joker.

mattarello, *n.m.* rolling pin.

mattatòio, *n.m.* stockyards.

mattina, *n.f.* morning.

mattinata, *n.f.* morning; matinée.

mattino, *n.m.* morning.

mattone, *n.m.* brick.

mattutino, *adj.* morning.

maturare, *vb.* ripen; mature.

maturato, *adj.* ripened; mellow.

maturità, *n.f.* maturity.

maturo, *adj.* mature; ripe; grown.

mausolèo, *n.m.* mausoleum.

mazza, *n.f.* bludgeon, cudgel.

mazzo, *n.m.* bunch; (cards) pack.

me, *pron.* me.

meandro, *n.m.* meander(ing), winding; labyrinth.

meccànico, **1.** *n.m.* mechanic. **2.** *adj.* mechanical.

meccanismo, *n.m.* mechanism, machinery.

meccanizzare, *vb.* mechanize.

mecenate, *n.m.* patron.

medàglia, *n.f.* medal.

medaglione, *n.m.* medallion; locket.

mèdia, *n.f.* average; mean.

mediano, *adj.* median.

mediante, *prep.* through, by means of.

mediatore, *n.m.* ombudsman.

medicare, *vb.* medicate.

medicina, *n.f.* medicine.

mèdico, 1. *n.* doctor, physician. **2.** *adj.* medical.

mèdio, *adj.* middle; average; medium; mean; mid-.

mediòcre, *adj.* mediocre.

mediocrità, *n.f.* mediocrity.

medioevale, *adj.* mediaeval.

medioèvo, *n.m.* Middle Ages.

Medio Oriente, *n.m.* Middle East.

meditare, *vb.* meditate, muse.

meditazione, *n.f.* meditation.

mediterràneo, *n.m. and adj.* Mediterranean.

medusa, *n.f.* jellyfish.

megàfono, *n.m.* megaphone.

megahertz, *n.m.* megahertz.

megera, *n.f.* hag, witch, vixen.

mèglio, *adv.* better. **il m.,** (the) best.

mela, *n.f.* apple.

melagrana, *n.f.* pomegranate.

melancònico, *adj.* melancholy, dismal.

melanzana, *n.f.* eggplant.

melassa, *n.f.* molasses.

melenso, *adj.* dull; silly.

melma, *n.f.* muck, mire, ooze, slime.

melo, *n.m.* apple-tree.

melodìa, *n.f.* melody, tune.

melodioso, *adj.* melodious, tuneful.

melodramma, *n.m.* melodrama.

melone, *n.m.* melon; cantaloupe.

membrana, *n.f.* membrane.

mèmbro, *n.m.* member; limb.

memoràbile, *adj.* memorable.

mèmore, *adj.* mindful.

memòria, *n.f.* memory; memoir; record.

memoriale, *n.m.* memorial.

memorizzare, *vb.* memorize.

menare, *vb.* lead.

mènda, *n.f.* fault, defect, imperfection.

mendace, *adj.* mendacious, lying.

mendicante, *n.m. and adj.* beggar, mendicant.

mendicare, *vb.* beg.

mèndico, *n.m.* mendicant.

menefreghismo, *n.m.* couldn't-care-less attitude.

menestrèllo, *n.m.* minstrel.

meno, *adv. and prep.* minus; less. **a m. di,** without. **a m. che . . . non,** unless.

menomare, *vb.* diminish, reduce; impair.

menopàusa, *n.f.* menopause.

mensile, *adj.* monthly.

mènsola, *n.f.* shelf; bracket.

menta, *n.f.* mint.

mentale, *adj.* mental.

mentalità, *n.f.* mentality.

mente, *n.f.* mind.

mentire, *vb.* lie.

mento, *n.m.* chin.

mentòlo, *n.m.* menthol.

mentre, *conj.* while.

menù, *n.m.* menu.

menzionare, *vb.* mention.

menzione, *n.f.* mention.

menzogna, *n.f.* lie, untruth.

menzognèro, *adj.* lying, untruthful.

meramente, *adv.* merely.

meravìglia, *n.f.* marvel, wonder; amazement, astonishment.

meravigliare, *bv.* amaze, astonish; *(refl.)* be amazed, marvel, wonder.

meraviglioso, *adj.* marvelous, wonderful, amazing.

mercante, *n.m.* merchant.

mercanteggiare, *vb.* bargain, haggle.

mercantile, *adj.* mercantile.

mercanzìa, *n.f.* merchandise.

mercato, *n.m.* market.

mèrce, *n.f.* commodity; ware. *(pl.)* goods; freight.

mercé, *n.f.* favor; mercy.

mercenàrio, 1. *n.* hireling; mercenary. **2.** *adj.* mercenary.

mercerìa, *n.f.* haberdashery.

merciàio, *n.m.* haberdasher.

mercoledì, *n.m.* Wednesday.

mercùrio, *n.m.* mercury.

merènda, *n.f.* light meal, collation.

meretrice, *n.f.* harlot.
meridionale, *adj.* southern.
meringa, *n.f.* meringue.
meritare, *vb.* deserve, merit, earn.
meritévole, *adj.* deserving.
mèrito, *n.m.* merit.
meritòrio, *adj.* meritorious.
merletto, *n.m.* lace.
mèrlo, *n.m.* blackbird.
merluzzo, *n.m.* cod, codfish.
mèro, *adj.* mere.
mescere, *vb.* pour.
meschino, *adj.* mean, petty; paltry, shabby, beggarly, picayune, trivial.
mescolanza, *n.f.* mixture, admixture, blend.
mescolare, *vb.* mix, blend, mingle; alloy.
mese, *n.m.* month.
messa, *n.f.* mass.
messaggèro, *n.m.* messenger.
messàggio, *n.m.* message.
Messìa, *n.m.* Messiah.
messicano, *adj.* Mexican.
Mèssico, *n.m.* Mexico.
messinscena, *n.f.* production, staging; faking.
messo, *n.m.* messenger.
mestiere, *n.m.* job, occupation.
méstola, *n.f.* ladle.
mèstolo, *n.m.* ladle, dipper.
mestruazioni, *n.f.pl.* menstruation.
mèta, *n.f.* goal.
metà, *n.f.* half.
metabolismo, *n.m.* metabolism.
metafisica, *n.f.* metaphysics.
metàllico, *adj.* metallic.
metallo, *n.m.* metal.
metallurgìa, *n.f.* metallurgy.
metamòrfosi, *n.f.* metamorphosis.
mètano, *n.m.* methane, firedamp.
metanodotto, *n.m.* natural gas pipeline.
metèora, *n.f.* meteor.
meteorologìa, *n.f.* meteorology.
meticcio, *n.m. and adj.* half-breed.
meticoloso, *adj.* meticulous.
metòdico, *adj.* methodical.
metodista, *n.m. and n.f. and adj.* Methodist.
mètodo, *n.m.* method.

metràggio, *n.m.* length in meters; footage.
mètrico, *adj.* metric.
mètro, *n.m.* meter.
metrònomo, *n.m.* metronome.
metròpoli, *n.f.* metropolis.
metropolitana, *n.f.* subway.
metropolitano, *adj.* metropolitan.
méttere, *vb.* place, put, set, lay.
mezzadrìa, *n.f.* sharecropping.
mezzaluna, *n.f.* half-moon.
mezzanino, *n.m.* mezzanine.
mezzanòtte, *n.f.* midnight.
mezzarìa, *n.f.* center line.
mèzzo, **1.** *n.m.* middle; medium; means. **in m. a**, amid. **2.** *adj.* half; mid-.
mezzogiorno, *n.m.* noon; south.
mezzùccio, *n.m.* ruse, expedient.
mi, *pron.* me; to me.
miccia, *n.f.* fuse.
microfilm, *n.m.* microfilm.
micròfono, *n.m.* microphone.
microforma, *n.f.* microform.
microònda, *n.f.* microwave.
microscheda, *n.f.* microfiche.
microscòpico, *adj.* microscopic.
microscòpio, *n.m.* microscope.
midollo, *n.m.* marrow.
mièle, *n.m.* honey.
miètere, *vb.* reap.
miglio, *n.m.* mile.
miglioramento, *n.m.* improvement.
migliorare, *vb.* improve, better, ameliorate, amend.
migliore, *adj.* better. **il m.**, (the) best.
migrare, *vb.* migrate.
migratòrio, *adj.* migratory.
migrazione, *n.f.* migration.
milanese, *adj.* Milanese.
Milano, *n.f.* Milan.
miliare, *adj.* **pietra m.**, milestone.
milionàrio, *n.m.* millionaire.
milione, *n.m.* million.
militante, *adj.* militant.
militare, *adj.* military.
militaresco, *adj.* military.
militarismo, *n.m.* militarism.
mìlite, *n.m.* soldier.
milizia, *n.f.* militia.
miliziano, *n.m.* militiaman.
millantare, *vb.* bluster, brag.

millantatore, *n.m.* braggart.
millanterìa, *n.f.* bluster, brag.
mille, *num.* thousand.
millefòglie, *n.f.* napoleon (pastry).
millenàrio, *afj.* millenial.
millìmetro, *n.m.* millimeter.
milza, *n.f.* spleen.
mimetismo, *n.m.* mimicry; camouflage.
mimetizzare, *vb.* camouflage.
mina, *n.f.* mine.
minàccia, *n.f.* menace, threat.
minacciare, *vb.* menace, threaten.
minare, *vb.* mine.
minatore, *n.m.* miner.
minatòrio, *adj.* threatening.
minerale, *n.m. and adj.* mineral, ore.
mineràrio, *adj.* mining.
minèstra, *n.f.* soup.
mingherlino, *adj.* skinny, frail, thin.
miniatura, *n.f.* miniature.
miniaturizzare, *vb.* miniaturize.
minièra, *n.f.* mine.
minimamente, *adv.* least.
mìnimo, 1. *n.m.* minimum. **2.** *adj.* least, minimum.
ministèro, *n.m.* ministry.
ministro, *n.m.* minister.
minoranza, *n.f.* minority.
minore, *adj.* minor, lesser; younger, junior.
minorènne, *n.m. and adj.* minor.
minùgia, *n.f.pl.* catgut.
minùscolo, *adj.* tiny.
minuto, *n.m. and adj.* minute. **al m.,** at retail.
mìo, *adj.* my; mine.
mìope, *adj.* short-sighted.
miopìa, *n.f.* myopia.
miosòtide, *n.f.* forget-me-not.
mira, *n.f.* aim.
miràcolo, *n.m.* miracle.
miracoloso, *adj.* miraculous.
miràggio, *n.m.* mirage.
mirare, *vb.* aim.
mirìade, *n.f.* myriad.
mirtillo, *n.m.* blueberry.
mirto, *n.m.* myrtle.
miscèla, *n.f.* blend, mixture.
miscellàneo, *adj.* miscellaneous.
misconoscere, *vb.* disregard, ignore, deny.

miscredènte, *n. and adj.* miscreant; infidel.
miscùglio, *n.m.* mixture; medley; hodge-podge.
miseràbile, *adj.* pitiful; poor.
misèria, *n.f.* poverty, want; misery.
misericòrdia, *n.f.* mercy.
misero, *adj.* miserable, wretched.
misfatto, *n.m.* misdeed; crime.
missile, *n.m.* missile.
missionàrio, *n.m. and adj.* missionary.
missione, *n.f.* mission.
missiva, *n.f.* letter.
misterioso, *adj.* mysterious.
mistèro, *n.m.* mystery.
mìstico, *adj.* mystic.
mistificare, *vb.* mystify.
misto, *adj.* mixed; coeducational.
mistura, *n.f.* mixture.
misura, *n.f.* measure; size.
misurare, *vb.* measure, gauge.
misuratore, *adj.* measuring.
misurazione, *n.f.* measurement.
misurino, *n.m.* measuring spoon or cup.
mìte, *adj.* gentle; meek; mild.
mitemente, *adv.* mildly, gently.
mitezza, *n.f.* mildness, meekness.
mìtico, *adj.* mythical.
mitigare, *vb.* mitigate, soften, lessen, assuage.
mìtili, *n.m.pl.* mussels.
mito, *n.m.* myth.
mitologìa, *n.f.* mythology.
mitòmane, *n.m. and f.* compulsive liar.
mitràglia, *n.f.* grapeshot.
mitragliatrice, *n.f.* machine gun.
mòbile, 1. *n.m.* piece of furniture. **2.** *adj.* movable, mobile.
mobìlia, *n.f.* furnishings.
mobilitare, *vb.* mobilize.
mobilitazione, *n.f.* mobilization.
mòda, *n.f.* mode, fashion. **alla m.,** fashionable, modish.
modellare, *vb.* model, mold.
modèllo, *n.m.* model, pattern.
moderare, *vb.* moderate.
moderato, *adj.* moderate.
moderazione, *n.f.* moderation.
modèrno, *adj.* modern.
modèstia, *n.f.* modesty.

modèsto, adj. modest, demure; plain.

modificare, vb. modify.

modista, n.m. or f. milliner.

modisteria, n.f. millinery.

mòdo, n.m. manner; mode; way. **m. di vìvere,** life style.

modulare, vb. modulate.

mòdulo, n.m. blank form.

moffetta, n.f. skunk.

mògano, n.m. mahogany.

mòggio, n.m. bushel.

móglie, n.f. wife.

molare, adj. molar.

molècola, n.f. molecule.

molestare, vb. molest.

molla, n.f. spring.

molle, adj. soft.

mòlo, n.m. jetty, mole, pier.

molòsso, n.m. bulldog.

moltéplice, adj. multiple, manifold.

molteplicità, n.f. multiplicity.

moltiplicare, vb. multiply.

moltiplicazione, n.f. multiplication.

moltitùdine, n.f. multitude, host.

molto, 1. adj. much; (pl.) many, plenty of. **2.** adv. very; much.

momentàneo, adj. momentary.

momènto, n.m. moment.

mònaca, n.f. nun.

mònaco, n.m. monk.

Mònaco di Bavièra, n.m. Munich.

monarca, n.m. monarch.

monarchìa, n.f. monarchy.

monastèro, n.m. monastery.

moncone, n.m. stump.

mondano, adj. worldly.

mondare, vb. peel; cleanse.

mondiale, adj. world-wide.

mondo, n.m. world.

monèllo, n.m. gamin, urchin.

moneta, n.f. coin.

monetàrio, adj. monetary.

monile, n.m. necklace; jewel.

monìto, n.m. admonition, warning.

monitore, n.m. monitor.

monòcolo, n.m. monocle.

monogamìa, n.f. monogamy.

monòlogo, n.m. monologue.

monoplano, n.m. monoplane.

monopolizzare, vb. monopolize.

monopòlio, n.m. monopoly.

monosìllabo, n.m. monosyllable.

monòssido, n.m. monoxide.

monotonìa, n.f. monotony, dullness.

monòtono, adj. monotonous, dull, dreary, humdrum.

monsone, n.m. monsoon.

montacarichi, n.m. freight elevator.

montàggio, n.m. assembly.

montagna, n.f. mountain.

montagnoso, adj. mountainous.

montanaro, n.m. mountaineer.

montano, adj. mountain.

montare, vb. mount; set.

montatura, n.f. mounting, setting; frame; (fig.) lie.

monte, n.m. mount, mountain.

montone, n.m. ram.

montuoso, adj. mountainous.

monumentale, adj. monumental.

monumento, n.m. monument, memorial.

moquette, n.f. carpeting.

mòra, n.f. blackberry.

morale, 1. n.m. morale. **2.** n.f. and adj. moral.

moralista, n.m. moralist.

moralità, n.f. morality.

moralmente, adj. morally.

moratòria, n.f. moratorium.

mòrbido, adj. soft.

morbillo, n.m. measles.

morbo, n.m. disease; illness.

morboso, adj. morbid.

mordace, adj. scathing.

mòrdere, vb. bite.

morente, adj. dying.

morfina, n.f. morphine.

morìa, n.f. high mortality; pestilence.

mormorare, vb. murmur.

mormorìo, n.m. murmur.

morosa, n.f. sweetheart.

moroso, adj. boyfriend.

mòrso, n.m. bite; (harness) bit.

mortale, adj. mortal, deadly, deathly, fatal.

mortalità, n.f. mortality.

mòrte, n.f. death, demise.

mortificare, vb. mortify.

mòrto, *adj.* dead.
mortuàrio, *adj.* mortuary.
mosàico, *n.m.* mosaic.
mosca, *n.f.* fly. **m. cavallina,** horsefly.
moscerino, *n.m.* gnat.
mostarda, *n.f.* mustard.
mosto, *n.m.* must, new wine.
mostra, *n.f.* show, exhibit, exhibition.
mostrare, *vb.* show, exhibit.
mostro, *n.m.* monster.
mostruosità, *n.f.* monstrosity, freak.
mostruoso, *adj.* monstrous, freak.
motivare, *vb.* motivate.
motivazione, *n.f.* justification.
motivo, *n.m.* motive; motif; sake.
mòto, *n.m.* motion.
motocicletta, *n.f.* motorcycle.
motocultura, *n.f.* motorized farming.
motore, 1. *n.m.* motor. **2.** *adj.* motive.
motorizzare, *vb.* motorize.
motoscafo, *n.m.* motor-boat.
motto, *n.m.* motto, quip, slogan.
movimento, *n.m.* movement.
mozione, *n.f.* motion.
mozzare, *vb.* lop off.
mozzicone, *n.m.* stub.
mozzo, *n.m.* deck-hand.
mòzzo, *n.m.* hub.
mùcchio, *n.m.* heap, pile, stack.
muco, *n.m.* mucus.
mucoso, *adj.* mucous.
muffa, *n.f.* mold. **m. bianca,** mildew.
muffito, *adj.* moldy.
mugghiare, *vb.* bellow, low.
mùgghio, *n.m.* bellow.
muggire, *vb.* bellow.
muggito, *n.m.* bellow.
mughetto, *n.m.* lily of the valley.
mugnaio, *n.m.* miller.
mulatto, *n.m.* mulatto.
mulino, *n.m.* mill.
mulla(h), *n.m.* mullah.
mulo, *n.m.* mule.

multa, *n.f.* fine.
multare, *vb.* fine.
multicolore, *adj.* multicolored, motley.
multilaterale, *adj.* multilateral.
multinazionale, *adj.* multinational.
mùltiplo, *adj.* multiple.
mùmmia, *n.f.* mummy.
mùngere, *vb.* milk.
municipale, *adj.* municipal.
municìpio, *n.m.* city hall.
munìfico, *adj.* munificent.
munizione, *n.f.* munition, ammunition.
muòvere, *vb.* move, stir; *(refl.)* budge.
murale, *adj.* mural.
muratore, *n.m.* bricklayer, mason.
muratura, *n.f.* masonry, bricklaying.
muro, *n.m.* wall.
musa, *n.f.* muse.
muschio, *n.m.* moss.
muscolare, *adj.* muscular.
mùscolo, *n.m.* muscle.
musèo, *n.m.* museum.
museruòla, *n.f.* muzzle.
mùsica, *n.f.* music. **m. da càmera,** chamber music.
musicale, *adj.* musical.
musicista, *n.f.* musician.
muso, *n.m.* muzzle.
mussolina, *n.f.* muslin.
musulmano, *n.m. and adj.* Moslem.
muta, *n.f.* pack (of dogs).
mutabilità, *n.f.* changeability.
mutamento, *n.m.* change.
mutande, *n.f.pl.* briefs, underwear.
mutandine, *n.f.pl.* panties.
mutare, *vb.* change.
mutazione, *n.f.* mutation.
mutévole, *adj.* changeable.
mutilare, *vb.* mutilate.
mutilato, *n.m.* amputee.
muto, *adj.* mute, dumb.
mutua, *n.f.* medical insurance.
mùtuo, *adj.* mutual.

nababbo, *n.m.* nabob; rich person.

nàcchere, *n.f.pl.* castanets.

nafta, *n.f.* naphtha.

nàia, *n.f.* military service (slang.).

nàilon, *n.m.* nylon.

nanna, *n.f.* sleep (of child), beddy-bye.

nano, *n.m.* dwarf, midget.

napoletano, *adj.* Neapolitan.

Nàpoli, *n.f.* Naples.

narciso, *n.m.* narcissus, daffodil.

narcòtico, *n.m. and adj.* narcotic.

narice, *n.f.* nostril.

narrare, *vb.* narrate, relate.

narrativo, *adj.* narrative.

narrazione, *n.f.* narration, relation.

nasale, *adj.* nasal.

nàscere, *vb.* come into being; be born; arise.

nàscita, *n.f.* birth.

nascóndere, *vb.* hide; *(refl.)* lurk.

nascondiglio, *n.m.* hide-out, cache.

nascondino, *n.m.* hide-and-seek.

naso, *n.m.* nose.

nastro, *n.m.* ribbon; tape. **n. televisivo,** videotape.

natale, *adj.* natal.

Natale, *n.m.* Christmas; Noël.

natalità, *n.f.* birth rate.

natante, 1. *n.m.* craft. **2.** *adj.* floating.

nàtica, *n.f.* buttock.

natio, *adj.* native.

natività, *n.f.* nativity.

nativo, *adj.* native.

nato, *adj.* born.

natura, *n.f.* nature. **n. mòrta,** still life.

naturale, *adj.* natural.

naturalezza, *n.f.* naturalness.

naturalista, *n.m.* naturalist.

naturalizzare, *vb.* naturalize.

naturalmente, *adv.* of course; by nature, naturally.

naufragare, *vb.* wreck.

naufràgio, *n.m.* shipwreck.

nàufrago, *n.m.* castaway.

nàusea, *n.f.* nausea.

nauseante, *adj.* nauseating.

nauseare, *vb.* nauseate, disgust.

nàutico, *adj.* nautical.

navale, *adj.* naval.

navata, *n.f.* aisle; nave.

nave, *n.f.* ship, vessel.

navigàbile, *adj.* navigable.

navigare, *vb.* navigate; sail.

navigato, *adj.* experienced.

navigatore, *n.m.* navigator.

navigazione, *n.f.* navigation.

naviglio, *n.m.* fleet; canal.

nazionale, *adj.* national.

nazionalismo, *n.m.* nationalism.

nazionalità, *n.f.* nationality.

nazionalizzare, *vb.* nationalize.

nazionalizzazione, *n.f.* nationalization.

nazione, *n.f.* nation.

nazista, *n.m.f. and adj.* Nazi.

ne, *pro-phrase* (replaces phrases introduced by **di** and by **da** when meaning "from") some; any; thereof; of it (him, her); about it (him, her); from there.

nè, *conj.* neither; nor.

neanche, *adv.* not even; nor.

nébbia, *n.f.* fog, haze, mist.

nebbioso, *adj.* foggy, hazy, misty.

nebulizzare, *vb.* atomize (liquids); spray.

nebulosa, *n.f.* nebula.

nebuloso, *adj.* nebulous.

nécessaire, *n.m.* vanity case; small tool box.

necessàrio, *adj.* necessary, needful, requisite.

necessità, *n.f.* necessity.

necrològio, *n.m.* obituary.

necròsi, *n.f.* necrosis.

nefando, *adj.* nefarious.

negare, *vb.* deny.

negativo, *n.m. and adj.* negative.

negletto, *adj.* neglected; ignored.

negligènte, *adj.* remiss.

negligènza, *n.f.* oversight.

negoziante, *n.m.* dealer.

negoziare, *vb.* negotiate.

negoziazione, *n.f.* negotiation.

negòzio, *n.m.* store, shop.

negra, *n.f.* Black (woman).

negro, *n.m.* Black (man or person).

nèmesi, *n.f.* nemesis.
nemico, *n.m. and adj.* enemy, foe.
nemmeno, *adv.* not even.
nènia, *n.f.* lamentation, dirge.
nèo, *n.m.* mole; imperfection.
neòfita, *n.f.* neophyte.
nèon, *n.m.* neon.
neonato, 1. *n.m.* baby; newborn. **2.** *adj.* newborn.
nepotismo, *n.m.* nepotism.
nèrbo, *n.m.* sinew.
nero, *adj.* black.
nèrvo, *n.m.* nerve.
nervoso, *adj.* nervous, jittery.
nessuno, 1. *adj.* no; (after negative) any. **2.** *pron.* nobody, no one; none.
nettare, *vb.* clean, cleanse.
nèttare, *n.m.* nectar.
nettézza, *n.f.* cleanness. **n. urbana,** garbage collection.
netto, *adj.* clean; clear-cut; net.
netturbino, *n.m.* street cleaner.
neurologia, *n.f.* neurology.
neutralità, *n.f.* neutrality.
neutralizzare, *vb.* neutralize, counteract.
nèutro, *n.m. and adj.* neutral.
neutrone, *n.m.* neutron.
nevàio, *n.m.* snowfield; glacier.
neve, *n.f.* snow.
nevicare, *vb.* snow.
nevicata, *n.f.* snowfall, snowstorm.
nevischio, *n.m.* sleet.
nevralgia, *n.f.* neuralgia.
nevròtico, *adj.* neurotic.
nibbio, *n.m.* kite.
nicchia, *n.f.* niche.
nichel, *n.m.* nickel.
nicotina, *n.f.* nicotine.
nidiata, *n.f.* nestful.
nido, *n.m.* nest, aerie.
niènte, *pron.* nothing. **n. affatto,** *adv.* not at all.
ninfa, *n.f.* nymph.
ninna-nanna, *n.f.* lullaby.
ninnolo, *n.m.* knicknack.
nipote, *n.m. and f.* nephew; niece; grandson; granddaughter.
nitrato, *n.m.* nitrate.
nitrògeno, *n.m.* nitrogen.
nò, *interj.* no.
nòbile, *n. and adj.* noble.
nobilmente, *adv.* nobly.

nobiltà, *n.f.* nobility.
nobiluòmo, *n.m.* nobleman.
nòcca, *n.f.* knuckle; fetlock.
nocciòla, *n.f.* nut; hazelnut.
nocciolina, *n.f.* small nut. **n. americana,** peanut.
nocciòlo, *n.m.* hazel; *(fig.)* kernel.
noce, n. 1. *m.* nut-tree; walnut. **n. americano,** hickory. **2.** *f.* nut; walnut.
nocivo, *adj.* harmful, injurious.
nòdo, *n.m.* knot, gnarl, kink, node. **n. scorsòio,** slipknot; noose.
nodoso, *adj.* knotty.
noi, *pron.* we; us.
nòia, *n.f.* boredom, ennui.
noleggiare, *vb.* hire.
noléggio, *n.m.* rental.
nòlo, *n.m.* hire.
nòmade, *n.m.* nomad.
nome, *n.m.* name; given name.
nomìgnolo, *n.m.* nickname.
nòmina, *n.f.* nomimation, appointment.
nominale, *adj.* nominal.
nominare, *vb.* nominate, name, appoint.
non, *adv.* not.
non allineato, *adj.* non-aligned.
noncurante, *adj.* easy-going.
nondimeno, *adv.* nonetheless, nevertheless, all the same.
nònna, *n.f.* grandmother.
nònno, *n.m.* grandfather.
nòno, *adj.* ninth.
nonostante, *prep.* notwithstanding.
non-ti-scordar-di-mé, *n.m.* forget-me-not.
nord, *n.m.* north.
nord-èst, *n.m.* northeast.
nord-òvest, *n.m.* northwest.
nòrma, *n.f.* norm; standard.
normale, *adj.* normal; standard.
normalmente, *adv.* normally.
norvegese, *adj.* Norwegian.
Norvègia, *n.f.* Norway.
nostalgia, *n.f.* nostalgia; homesickness.
nòstro, *adj.* our; ours.
nostròmo, *n.m.* boatswain.
nòta, *n.f.* note; footnote.

notàbile, *adj.* noteworthy.
notàio, *n.m.* notary.
notare, *vb.* note.
notazione, *n.f.* notation.
nòtes, *n.m.* notepad.
notévole, *adj.* notable, noticeable, remarkable.
notificare, *vb.* notify.
notificazione, *n.f.* notification.
notìzia, *n.f.* piece of news.
notiziàrio, *n.m.* news report.
nòto, *adj.* well-known.
notorietà, *n.f.* notoriety.
notòrio, *adj.* notorious.
notte, *n.f.* night. **buona n.,** good night.
nottetempo, *adv.* at night.
notturno, 1. *n.m.* nocturne. 2. *adj.* nocturnal.
novanta, *num.* ninety.
novantésimo, *adj.* ninetieth.
nòve, *num.* nine.
novella, *n.f.* short story; good news.
novellino, 1. *n.m.* inexperienced person, beginner. 2. *adj.* inexperienced.
novellìstica, *n.f.* novel-writting, fiction.
novello, *adj.* new, tender.
novèmbre, *n.m.* November.
novèna, *n.f.* novena.
novità, *n.f.* novelty.
novìzio, *n.m.* novice.

novocaìna, *n.f.* novocaine.
nozione, *n.f.* notion.
nòzze, *n.f. pl.* wedding.
nube, *n.f.* cloud.
nucleare, *adj.* nuclear.
nùcleo, *n.m.* nucleus.
nudità, *n.f.* nudity, bareness.
nudo, *adj.* naked, nude, bare.
nulla, *pron.* nothing.
nullità, *n.f.* nonentity.
nullo, *adj.* void.
nume, *n.m.* deity.
numerare, *vb.* number.
numèrico, *adj.* numerical.
nùmero, *n.m.* number.
numeroso, *adj.* numerous.
nùnzio, *n.m.* nuncio.
nuòcere, *vb.* harm, injure.
nuòra, *n.f.* daughter-in-law.
nuotare, *vb.* swim.
nuotata, *n.f.* swim.
nuotatore, *n.m.* swimmer.
nuòvo, *adj.* new. **di n.,** anew; again.
nutrice, *n.f.* nurse.
nutrènte, *adj.* nutritious.
nutrimento, *n.m.* nourishment; feed.
nutrire, *vb.* nourish; feed.
nutrizione, *n.f.* nutrition.
nùvola, *n.f.* cloud.
nuvolosità, *n.f.* cloudiness.
nuvoloso, *adj.* cloudy.
nuziale, *adj.* nuptial, bridal.

O

o, *conj.* or. **o . . . o,** either . . . or.
oasi, *n.f.* oasis.
obbediènte, *adj.* obedient, compliant.
obbediènza, *n.f.* obedience, compliance.
obbedire, *vb.* obey, comply.
obbiettare, *vb.* object.
obbligare, *vb.* oblige.
obbligatòrio, *adj.* obligatory, binding, compulsory, mandatory.
obbligazione, *n.f.* obligation; bond, debenture.
obbròbrio, *n.m.* opprobrium, disgrace, shame.
obelisco, *n.m.* obelisk.
obèso, *adj.* obese.

òbice, *n.m.* howitzer.
obiettare, *vb.* object, demur.
obiettivo, 1. *n.m.* objective. 2. *adj.* objective; factual.
obiezione, *n.f.* objection.
obitòrio, *n.m.* morgue.
oblazione, *n.f.* fine paid voluntarily.
oblìo, *n.m.* oblivion.
obliquo, *adj.* oblique, slant.
obliterare, *vb.* obliterate.
oblò, *n.m.* porthole.
oblungo, *adj.* oblong.
òbolo, *n.m.* obol; mite.
òca, *n.f.* goose.
occasionale, *adj.* occasional.

occasione, *n.f.* occasion, opportunity, chance; bargain.
occhiali, *n.m.pl.* eyeglasses, spectacles.
occhiata, *n.f.* glance, look.
occhièllo, *n.m.* button-hole; eyelet.
òcchio, *n.m.* eye. **o. della mànica,** armhole. **o. pesto,** black eye.
occidentale, *adj.* occidental, western.
occidènte, *n.m.* Occident, west.
occulto, *adj.* occult.
occupante, *n.m.* occupant.
occupare, *vb.* occupy.
occupato, *adj.* busy.
occupazione, *n.f.* occupation, job.
ocèano, *n.m.* ocean.
oculare, *adj.* ocular. **testimone o.,** eye-witness.
oculista, *n.m.* oculist.
od, *conj.* or.
odiare, *vb.* hate.
odierno, *adj.* today's, current.
òdio, *n.m.* hate, hatred.
odioso, *adj.* hateful, invidious, odious, obnoxious.
odissea, *n.f.* odyssey.
odontoiatrìa, *f.* dentistry.
odore, *n.m.* odor, scent, smell.
offèndere, *vb.* offend.
offensiva, *n.f.* offensive.
offensivo, *adj.* offensive, objectionable.
offensore, *n.m.* offender.
offerènte, *n.m.* bidder.
offèrta, *n.f.* offer; bid.
offesa, *n.f.* offense.
officiare, *vb.* officiate.
officina, *n.f.* workshop.
offrire, *vb.* offer, tender; bid.
offuscare, *vb.* darken, obscure.
oftàlmico, *adj.* ophthalmic.
oggettività, *n.f.* objectivity.
oggètto, *n.m.* object.
òggi, *n.m.and adv.* today.
oggigiorno, *adv.* nowadays.
ogni, *adj.* each, every.
ogniqualvòlta, *adv.* whenever.
ognuno, *pron.* everybody, everyone.
Olanda, *n.f.* Holland.
olandese, 1. *n.m.* Dutchman. **2.** *adj.* Dutch.

oleificio, *n.m.* oil refinery.
oleoso, *adj.* oily.
olfattòrio, *adj.* olfactory.
oligarchìa, *n.f.* oligarchy.
olimpìadi, *n.f. pl.* Olympic Games.
òlio, *n.m.* oil.
oliva, *n.f.* olive.
olivastro, *adj.* livid; olive colored.
oliveto, *n.m.* olive yard.
olivo, *n.m.* olive-tree.
olmo, *n.m.* elm.
olocàusto, *n.m.* holocaust.
olografìa, *n.f.* holography.
ologramma, *n.m.* hologram.
oltràggio, *n.m.* outrage.
oltraggioso, *adj.* outrageous.
oltranza, *adv.* **a o.,** to the bitter end.
oltre, *adv. and prep.* beyond; besides, further.
oltremare, *adv.* overseas.
oltrepassare, *vb.* pass beyond; outrun.
omàggio, *n.m.* homage; gift, present.
ombellico, *n.m.* navel.
ombra, *n.f.* shade; shadow.
ombelico, *n.m.* navel.
ombreggiare, *vb.* shade.
ombrèllo, *n.m.* umbrella.
ombroso, *adj.* shady.
omelìa, *n.f.* homily.
omeopàtico, *adj.* homeopathic.
omertà, *n.f.* silence, code of silence.
omèttere, *vb.* omit, leave out; overlook.
omètto, *n.m.* little man; clothes hanger.
omicida, *n.m.* homicide (person).
omicìdio, *n.m.* homicide, manslaughter.
omissione, *n.f.* omission.
òmnibus, *n.m.* local (train).
omnisciente, *adj.* all-knowing.
omogèneo, *adj.* homogeneous.
omogenizzare, *vb.* homogenize.
omologare, *vb.* probate.
omologazione, *n.f.* probate.
omònimo, 1. *n.m.* homonym; namesake. **2.** *adj.* homonymous, of the same name.
omosessuale, *adj.* homosexual.
óncia, *n.f.* ounce.
onda, *n.f.* wave.

ondeggiare, *vb.* undulate.
ònere, *n.m.* burden, onus.
oneroso, *adj.* burdensome.
onestà, *n.f.* honesty, integrity.
onestamente, *adv.* honestly, decently.
onèsto, *adj.* honest, decent, above board.
onnipotènte, *adj.* almighty, omnipotent.
onorare, *vb.* honor.
onorario, 1. *n.m.* honorarium, fee. 2. *adj.* honorary.
onore, *n.m.* honor.
onorévole, *adj.* honorable, decent.
onorevolezza, *n.f.* honorableness, decency.
onta, *n.f.* shame; insult.
opacità, *n.f.* opacity.
opaco, *adj.* opaque.
opale, *n.m.* opal.
òpera, *n.f.* work; opera.
operaio, *n.m.* worker.
operare, *vb.* operate.
operativo, *adj.* operative.
operatore, *n.m.* operator.
operazione, *n.f.* operation; transaction.
operetta, *n.f.* operetta; musical comedy.
operoso, *adj.* industrious.
opinione, *n.f.* opinion.
opporre, *vb.* oppose; *(refl.)* object.
opportunamente, *adv.* advisably.
opportunismo, *n.m.* opportunism.
opportunità, *n.f.* desirability; suitability; advisability; expediency.
opportuno, *adv.* fitting; desirable; advisable; expedient.
opposizione, *n.f.* opposition.
oppressione, *n.f.* oppression.
oppòsto, *n.m. and adj.* opposite.
oppressivo, *adj.* oppressive.
opprèsso, *adj.* oppressed, downtrodden.
oppressore, *n.m.* oppressor.
opprimènte, *adj.* oppressive, burdensome.
opprimere, *vb.* oppress.
oppugnare, *vb.* attack, assail.

optare, *vb.* opt, choose.
optometria, *n.f.* optometry.
opulènto, *adj.* opulent, affluent.
opulènza, *n.f.* opulence, affluence.
opùscolo, *n.m.* pamphlet.
opzione, *n.f.* option.
ora, 1. *n.f.* hour; o'clock; time. **che o. è?** what time is it? 2. *adv.* now.
oràcolo, *n.m.* oracle.
orale, *adj.* oral.
oràrio, *n.m.* timetable, schedule.
oratore, *n.m.* orator, speaker.
oratòria, *n.f.* oratory.
orazione, *n.f.* oration.
orbare, *vb.* bereave.
òrbe, *n.f.* world.
orbene, *adv.* well.
òrbita, *n.f.* orbit; socket.
òrbo, *n.m.* (coll.) blind man.
orchèstra, *n.f.* orchestra.
orchidèa, *n.f.* orchid.
òrda, *n.f.* horde.
ordàlia, *n.f.* ordeal.
ordinamento, *n.m.* arrangement.
ordinanza, *n.f.* ordinance.
ordinare, *vb.* order, arrange, array; ordain; tidy, trim.
ordinàrio, *n.m.* ordinary.
ordinato, *adj.* orderly, tidy, trim.
ordinazione, *n.f.* ordination.
órdine, *n.m.* order; array; fiat.
ordire, *vb.* hatch (a plot); warp.
orecchino, *n.m.* ear-ring.
orécchio, *n.m.* ear.
orecchioni, *n.m.pl.* mumps.
oréfice, *n.m.* goldsmith.
òrfano, *n.m.* orphan.
orfanotròfio, *n.m.* orphanage.
organico, *adj.* organic.
organigramma, *n.m.* organization chart.
organismo, *n.m.* organism.
organista, *n.m.* organist.
organizzare, *vb.* organize.
organizzazione, *n.f.* organization.
òrgano, *n.m.* organ.
orgasmo, *n.m.* orgasm.
organza, *n.f.* organdy.
òrgia, *n.f.* orgy, debauch.
orgòglio, *n.m.* pride.
orgoglioso, *adj.* proud.
orientale, *adj.* Oriental; eastern.
orientamento, *n.m.* orientation; bearings.

orientare, *vb.* orient.
orientazione, *n.f.* orientation.
oriènte, *n.m.* Orient; east.
orifizio, *n.m.* orifice, opening.
originale, *adj.* original, novel.
originalità, *n.f.* originality.
orìgine, *n.f.* origin.
origliare, *vb.* eavesdrop.
orina, *n.f.* urine.
orinare, *vb.* urinate.
orinatòio, *n.m.* urinal.
oriundo, *adj.* native.
orizzontale, *adj.* horizontal; level.
orizzonte, *n.m.* horizon.
orlare, *vb.* hem; edge.
orlatura, *n.f.* edging.
orlo, *n.m.* brink, brim, edge, rim,
verge; hem. **o. a giorno,** hemstitch.
orma, *n.f.* footstep; footprint.
ormeggiare, *vb.* moor.
ormeggio, *n.m.* mooring.
ormone, *n.m.* hormone.
ornamentale, *adj.* ornamental.
ornamento, *n.m.* ornament.
ornare, *vb.* ornament, adorn.
ornato, *adj.* ornate.
ornitologìa, *n.f.* ornithology.
òro, *n.m.* gold.
orologiaio, *n.m.* watchmaker.
orològio, *n.m.* clock; watch. **o. a
pólvere,** hourglass.
or' ora, *adv.* just now.
oròscopo, *n.m.* horoscope.
orpello, *n.m.* Dutch gold.
orrèndo, *adj.* ghastly, gruesome.
orrìbile, *adj.* horrible, grisly.
òrrido, *adj.* horrid.
orripilante, *adj.* bloodcurdling.
orrore, *n.m.* horror.
orsachiotto, *n.m.* teddy bear.
orso, *n.m.* bear.
ortènsia, *n.f.* hydrangea.
ortica, *n.f.* nettle; hives.
orticària, *n.f.* nettle rash.
orticultura, *n.f.* horticulture.
òrto, *n.m.* orchard; garden.
ortodòsso, *adj.* orthodox.
ortografìa, *n.f.* orthography,
spelling.
ortolano, *n.m.* greengrocer.
ortopèdico, *adj.* orthopedic.
orzaiòlo, *n.m.* sty.
orzata, *n.f.* orgeat.
orzo, *n.m.* barley.

osannare, *vb.* acclaim.
osare, *vb.* dare; venture.
oscèno, *adj.* obscene.
oscillare, *vb.* oscillate, sway.
oscuramento, *n.m.* darkening;
blackout.
oscurare, *vb.* darken, obscure,
dim, shade.
oscurità, *n.f.* darkness, obscurity,
dimness, gloom.
oscuro, *adj.* dark, obscure, dim,
gloomy.
osmòsi, *n.f.* osmosis.
ospedale, *n.m.* hospital.
ospedaliere, *n.m.* hospital
worker.
ospedalizzare, *vb.* hospitalize.
ospedalizzazione, *n.f.* hospitalization.
ospitale, *adj.* hospitable.
ospitalità, *n.f.* hospitality.
òspite, *n.* 1. *m.* host; guest; visitor;
lodger. 2. *f.* hostess; guest; visitor.
ospizio, *n.m.* nursing home; hos-
pice.
ossatura, *n.f.* framework.
òsseo, *adj.* bony.
ossequiare, *vb.* pay respects to.
ossequioso, *adj.* ceremonious.
osservanza, *n.f.* observance.
osservare, *vb.* observe, notice, remark.
osservatore, *n.m.* observer.
osservatòrio, *n.m.* observatory.
osservazione, *n.f.* observation,
remark.
ossessionare, *vb.* obsess.
ossessione, *n.f.* obsession.
ossesso, *n.m.* possessed.
ossìa, *conj.* or.
ossido, *n.m.* oxide.
ossìgeno, *n.m.* oxygen.
òsso, *n.m.* bone.
ossuto, *adj.* bony.
ostacolare, *vb.* hinder, bar, block,
interfere with, obstruct.
ostàcolo, *n.m.* obstacle, bar, hindrance, block, snag.
ostàggio, *n.m.* hostage.
ostare, *vb.* hinder. **nulla osta,** no
objection.
òste, *n.m.* innkeeper.
ostensìbile, *adj.* ostensible.
ostentare, *vb.* show off, display,
flaunt.

ostentato, *adj.* ostentatious.
ostentazione, *n.f.* ostentation, display.
osteria, *n.f.* tavern.
ostètrico, 1. *n.m.* obstetrician. **2.** *adj.* obstetrical.
òstia, *n.f.* Host.
ostile, *adj.* hostile, antagonistic.
ostilità, *n.f.* hostility.
ostinato, *adj.* obstinate, dogged, headstrong; obdurate.
ostracizzare, *vb.* ostracize.
òstrica, *n.f.* oyster.
ostruire, *vb.* obstruct.
ostruzione, *n.f.* obstruction.
otorinolaringoiatra, *n.m.* ear, nose, and throat specialist.
òtre, *n.f.* wineskin.
ottàgono, *n.m.* octagon.
ottanta, *num.* eighty, fourscore.
ottantèsimo, *adj.* eightieth.
ottava, *n.f.* eight; octave.
ottavino, *n.m.* piccolo.
ottavo, *adj.* eighth.
ottemperare, *vb.* obey.
ottenebrare, *vb.* becloud.
ottenere, *vb.* obtain, get.
òttica, *n.f.* optics.
òttico, 1. *n.m.* optician. **2.** *adj.* optic.

ottimismo, *n.m.* optimism.
ottimìstico, *adj.* optimistic.
òtto, *num.* eight.
ottobre, *n.m.* October.
ottone, *n.m.* brass.
ottopode, *n.m.* octopus.
ottùndere, *vb.* dull.
otturare, *vb.* stop up; fill.
otturatore, *n.m.* shutter.
otturazione, *n.f.* filling.
ottusamente, *adv.* bluntly, obtusely.
ottusità, *n.f.* obtuseness, dullness, bluntness.
ottuso, *adj.* obtuse, dull, blunt.
ovaia, *n.f.* ovary.
ovale, *n.m.* and *adj.* oval.
ovatta, *n.f.* wadding.
ovazione, *n.f.* ovation.
òvest, *n.* west.
ovile, *n.m.* sheepcote, fold.
ovino, *n.m.* sheep.
ovunque, *adv.* wherever; everywhere.
ovvero, *conj.* or.
òvvio, *adj.* obvious.
oziare, *vb.* loaf.
òzio, *n.m.* idleness.
ozioso, *adj.* idle.
ozono, *n.m.* ozone.

P

pacare, *vb.* placate.
pacato, *adj.* serene.
pacca, *n.f.* smack.
pàcchia, *n.f.* well-being; godsend.
pacco, *n.m.* package, pack, parcel.
pace, *n.f.* peace.
pacificare, *vb.* pacify.
pacificatore, *n.m.* pacifier.
pacifico, *adj.* pacific, peaceful.
pacifismo, *n.m.* pacifism.
pacifista, *n.m.* pacifist.
padèlla, *n.f.* pan, frying pan.
padiglione, *n.m.* pavilion; stand.
Pàdova, *n.f.* Padua.
padovano, *adj.* Paduan.
padre, *n.m.* father.
padrino, *n.m.* godfather.
padrona, *n.f.* mistress; landlady.
padronanza, *n.f.* mastery.
padrone, *n.m.* boss, employer; landlord; master.

paesàggio, *n.m.* landscape, scenery.
paese, *n.m.* country.
paga, *n.f.* pay.
pagamento, *n.m.* payment.
pagano, *n.* and *adj.* pagan, heathen.
pagare, *vb.* pay, defray.
pàggio, *n.m.* page.
pàgina, *n.f.* page.
pàgine centrali, *n.f.pl.* centerfold.
pàglia, *n.f.* straw. **p. di acciàio,** *n.f.* steel wool.
pagliaccesco, *adj.* clownish.
pagliàccio, *n.m.* clown.
pagliàio, *n.m.* haystack.
pagnòtta, *n.f.* loaf.
pago, *adj.* satisfied.
pagòda, *n.f.* pagoda.
paio, *n.m.* pair, couple.

pala, *n.f.* shovel.
palafitta, *n.f.* pile.
palafrenière, *n.m.* groom.
palata, *n.f.* shovelful. **a palate,** a lot.
pàlato, *n.m.* palate.
palazzo, *n.m.* palace; large building; mansion. **p. di giustizia,** courthouse.
palco, *n.m.* antler; box (in theater).
palcoscènico, *n.m.* stage.
palesare, *vb.* disclose, reveal.
palese, *adj.* evident, obvious.
palesemente, *adv.* openly.
palèstra, *n.f.* gymnasium.
palizzata, *n.f.* fence.
palla, *n.f.* ball.
pallacanestro, *n.f.* basketball.
pallamàglio, *n.m.* croquet.
pallavolo, *n.f.* volleyball.
palliativo, *adj.* palliative.
pàllido, *adj.* pale, pallid, wan, pasty.
pallinacci, *n.m.pl.* buckshot.
pallini, *n.m.pl.* shot.
pallino, *n.m.* craze, mania; gunshot.
pallone, *n.m.* balloon.
pallore, *n.m.* paleness.
pallòttola, *n.f.* bullet; ball.
palma, *n.f.* palm.
palo, *n.m.* pole, post, stake.
pàlpebra, *n.f.* eyelid.
palpitare, *vb.* palpitate.
palude, *n.f.* swamp, bog, marsh.
panacèa, *n.f.* panacea.
pancetta, *n.f.* bacon.
pància, *n.f.* paunch, belly.
panciòtto, *n.m.* vest.
pane, *n.m.* bread, loaf. **p. abbrustolito,** toast.
pànfilo, *n.m.* yacht.
pànico, *n.m.* panic.
paniere, *n.m.* basket.
panino, *n.m.* roll.
panna, *n.f.* cream.
pannaiòlo, *n.m.* clothier; draper.
panne, *n.m.* breakdown.
pannèllo, *n.m.* panel.
pannolino, *n.m.* diaper.
panorama, *n.m.* panorama.
pantaloni, *n.m.(pl.)* trousers, pants, breeches.
pantano, *n.m.* bog.

pantèra, *n.f.* panther.
pantòfola, *n.f.* slipper.
pantomima, *n.f.* pantomime.
panzana, *n.f. (coll.)* lie, fib, humbug.
paonazzo, *adj.* purple. **divenir p.** blush.
papa, *n.m.* pope.
papà, *n.m.* papa.
papàbile, *adj.* likely to be chosen.
papale, *adj.* papal.
papavero, *n.m.* poppy.
pàpera, *n.f.* goose; slip (of the tongue).
paperetto, *n.m.* gosling.
pàpero, *n.m.* gander.
papiro, *n.m.* papyrus.
pappa, *n.f.* gruel.
pappagallo, *n.m.* parrot; parakeet.
pappare, *vb.* gulp down; gobble up while unseen.
paràbola, *n.f.* parabola.
parabrezza, *n.m.* windshield, windscreen.
paracadute, *n.m.* parachute.
paradiso, *n.m.* paradise.
paradòsso, *n.m.* paradox.
parafango, *n.m.* mudguard; fender.
paraffina, *n.f.* paraffin.
parafrasare, *vb.* paraphrase.
paràfrasi, *n.f.* paraphrase.
parafùlmine, *n.m.* lightning-rod.
parafuòco, *n.m.* firescreen.
paraggi, *n.m.pl.* environs, vicinity.
paragonàbile, *adj.* comparable.
paragonare, *vb.* compare.
paragone, *n.m.* comparison.
paràgrafo, *n.m.* paragraph.
paràlisi, *n.f.* paralysis.
paralizzare, *vb.* paralyze.
parallelo, *n.m. and adj.* parallel.
paralume, *n.m.* shade.
paramèdico, *n.m.* paramedic.
paràmetro, *n.m.* parameter.
parapiglia, *n.f.* scramble.
parare, *vb.* stop; protect; adorn, decorate.
parassita, *n.m.* parasite.
parata, *n.f.* parade.
paratìa, *n.f.* bulkhead.
paravènto, *n.m.* screen; windshield.
parchèggio, *n.m.* parking.

parco, 1. *n.m.* park. **2.** *adj.* frugal.
parécchia, *adj.* some; considerable; *(pl.)* several.
parènte, *n.m.* relative.
parentèla, *n.f.* kin, kindred; relationship.
parèntesi, *n.f.* parenthesis. **p. quadra,** bracket.
parere, 1. *n.m.* opinion. **2.** *vb.* appear, seem.
pari, 1. *n.m.* peer. **2.** *n.f.* par. **3.** *adj.* even, equal.
pària, *n.m.* pariah, outcast.
Parigi, *n.f.* Paris.
parigino, *adj.* Parisian.
parità, *n.f.* parity. **p. àurea,** gold standard.
parlamentare, 1. *adj.* parliamentary. **2.** *vb.* parley.
parlamento, *n.m.* parliament, legislature; parley.
parlare, *vb.* speak, talk.
parmigiano, *adj.* Parmesan.
parodìa, *n.f.* parody.
parodiare, *vb.* parody.
paròla, *n.f.* word.
parolàccia, *n.f.* swear word.
parolàio, *n.m.* chatter.
parossismo, *n.m.* paroxysm.
parricìdio, *n.m.* patricide.
parròcchia, *n.f.* parish.
parrocchiale, *adj.* parochial.
pàrroco, *n.m.* parish priest; parson.
parrucca, *n.f.* wig.
parrucchière, *n.m.* hairdresser; barber.
parsimònia, *n.f.* parsimony.
parisimonioso, *adj.* parsimonious.
parte, *n.f.* part; share. **a p.,** apart. **p. del discorso,** part of speech.
partecipante, *n.m.* participant.
partecipare, *vb.* participate, partake.
partecipazione, *n.f.* participation.
partecipe, *adj.* partaking; informed.
parteggiare, *vb.* to take sides.
partènza, *n.f.* departure.
particèlla, *n.f.* particle.
participio, *n.m.* participle.
particolare, 1. *adj.* particular, peculiar. **2.** *n.m.* detail.

particolareggiato, *adj.* detailed; circumstantial.
partigiano, *n.m. and adj.* partisan.
partire, *vb.* depart, leave.
partita, *n.f.* game.
partito, *n.m.* party.
partitura, *n.f.* score.
partizione, *n.f.* partition.
parto, *n.m.* childbirth.
partorire, *vb.* bear, give birth to.
parvenza, *n.f.* appearance.
parziale, *adj.* partial.
parzialità, *n.f.* partiality, bias.
pàscere, *vb.* graze.
pasciuto, *adj.* nourished, fed.
pàscolo, *n.m.* pasture; grazing.
Pasqua, *n.f.* Easter.
pasquinata, *n.f.* lampoon.
passàbile, *adj.* passable.
passàggio, *n.m.* passage; aisle; crossing. **p. a livèllo,** grade crossing.
passante, *n.m.* passer-by.
passapòrto, *n.m.* passport.
passare, *vb.* pass; spend.
passatèmpo, *n.m.* pastime.
passato, 1. *n.m.* past; purée. **2.** *adj.* past, over, bygone.
passeggiare, *vb.* walk, stroll.
passeggiata, *n.f.* walk, stroll; ride.
passeggèro, *n.m.* passenger.
passeggiatore, *n.m.* stroller.
passerèlla, *n.f.* gangway.
pàssero, *n.m.* sparrow.
passìbile, liable. **p. di,** liable to.
passione, *n.f.* passion; fondness.
passivo, *n.m. and adj.* passive.
passo, *n.m.* pass; pace; step; tread.
pasta, *n.f.* paste; dough, batter. **p. asciutta,** macaroni. **p. fròlla,** frosting.
pastello, *n.m.* pastel; crayon.
pasteurizzare, *vb.* pasteurize.
pastìccia, *n.f.* pastille, lozenge, tablet.
pasticcerìa, *n.f.* pastry; pastry-shop.
pasticcini, *n.m.pl.* pastries, cookies.
pastìccio, *n.f.* mess; pasty.
pasticcione, *n.m.* bungler, muddler.
pastìglia, *n.f.* pastille.
pasto, *n.m.* meal.

pastore, *n.m.* shepherd; pastor.
pastoso, *adj.* dense; doughy; mellow.
patata, *n.f.* potato.
patente, *n.f.* license.
paternità, *n.f.* paternity, fatherhood.
paterno, *adj.* paternal, fatherly.
patetico, *adj.* pathetic.
patibolo, *n.m.* scaffold.
patina, *n.f.* coating; film; shoe polish.
patinoso, *adj.* furry.
patologia, *n.f.* pathology.
pàtos, *n.m.* pathos.
pàtria, *n.f.* country; fatherland, homeland.
patriarca, *n.m.* patriarch.
patrigno, *n.m.* stepfather.
patrimònio, *n.m.* patrimony, inheritance; estate.
patriòta, *n.m.* patriot.
patriòttico, *adj.* patriotic.
patriottismo, *n.m.* patriotism.
patrocinare, *vb.* sponsor.
patronato, *n.m.* patronage.
patròno, *n.m.* patron.
pattinare, *vb.* skate.
pàttino, *n.m.* skate.
patto, *n.m.* pact; compact.
pattùglia, *n.f.* patrol.
pattuire, *vb.* strike a deal, agree.
paùra, *n.f.* fear. **aver p.,** be afraid.
pauroso, *adj.* fearful.
pàusa, *n.f.* pause.
paventare, *vb.* fear.
pavimentare, *vb.* pave.
pavimentazione, *n.f.* flooring.
pavimento, *n.m.* floor.
pavone, *n.m.* peacock.
pavoneggiarsi, *vb.* strut.
paziènte, *adj.* patient.
paziènza, *n.f.* patience.
pazzìa, *n.f.* insanity, madness, lunacy.
pazzo, *adj.* crazy, insane, mad.
peccaminoso, *adj.* sinful.
peccare, *vb.* sin.
peccato, *n.m.* sin; pity; shame. **che p.!** what a pity!
peccatore, *n.m.* sinner.
pece, *n.f.* pitch.
pècora, *n.f.* sheep, ewe.
pecorino, *n.m.* sheep-milk cheese.
peculato, *n.m.* embezzlement.

peculiare, *adj.* peculiar.
peculiarità, *n.f.* peculiarity.
pecuniàrio, *adj.* pecuniary.
pedàggio, *n.m.* toll.
pedagogìa, *n.f.* pedagogy.
pedagògo, *n.m.* pedagogue.
pedale, *n.m.* pedal.
pedante, *n.m.* pedant.
pedata, *n.f.* kick.
pedèstre, *adj.* pedestrian.
pediàtra, *n.m.* pediatrician.
pedina, *n.f.* pawn.
pedonale, *adj.* pedestrian.
pedone, *n.m.* pedestrian.
pedula, *n.f.* hiking boot.
pèggio, *adv.* worse. **il p.,** worst.
peggiore, *adj.* worse. **il p.,** the worst.
pegno, *n.m.* pledge; pawn.
pelapatate, *n.m.* potato peeler.
pelare, *vb.* skin, peel.
pèlle, *n.f.* skin, hide. **p. verniciata,** patent leather.
pellegrinàggio, *n.m.* pilgrimage.
pellegrino, *n.m.* pilgrim.
pellerossa, *n.m.* native American.
pellìccia, *n.f.* fur.
pellicciaio, *n.m.* furrier.
pellìcola, *n.f.* film, movie.
pelo, *n.m.* hair.
peloso, *adj.* hairy.
pelùria, *n.f.* down.
pèlvi, *n.f.* pelvis.
pena, *n.f.* pain; penalty.
penalista, *n.m.* criminalist.
penare, *vb.* suffer.
pendènte, 1. *n.m.* pendant. 2. *adj.* pending; hanging.
pendènza, *n.f.* slope.
pèndere, *vb.* hang.
pendìo, *n.m.* slope, slant, incline.
pendolare, *n.m.* commuter.
pèndolo, *n.m.* pendulum.
penetrante, *adj.* penetrating, discerning.
penetrare, *vb.* penetrate.
penetrazione, *n.f.* penetration, insight.
penicillina, *n.f.* penicillin.
penisola, *n.f.* peninsula.
penitènte, *n.m.* and *adj.* penitent.
penitènza, *n.f.* penitence.
penitenziàrio, *n.m.* prison.
penna, *n.f.* feather, plume; pen. **p. stilogràfica,** fountain pen.

pennarello, *n.m.* felt-tip pen.
pennèllo, *n.m.* brush.
pennuto, *adj.* feathered.
penombra, *n.f.* twilight, half-light.
penoso, *adj.* painful.
pensare, *vb.* think.
pensatore, *n.m.* thinker.
pensièro, *n.m.* thought.
pensilina, *n.f.* marquee.
pensionante, *n.m.* boarder.
pensionato, 1. *n.m.* retired person. **2.** *adj.* retired.
pensione, *n.f.* pension, boarding house.
pensoso, *adj.* pensive, thoughtful.
pentimento, *n.m.* repentance.
pentirsi, *vb.* repent, rue.
péntola, *n.f.* kettle, pot. **p. a pressione,** pressure cooker.
penùria, *n.f.* penury.
penzolare, *vb.* dangle.
penzoloni, *adv.* dangling, hanging.
pepe, *n.m.* pepper.
peperoncino, *n.m.* hot pepper.
peperone, *n.m.* bell pepper.
pepita, *n.f.* nugget.
per, *prep.* for; through; by; per.
pera, *n.f.* pear.
per cènto, *adv.* per cent.
percentuale, *n.m.* percentage.
percettibile, *adj.* perceptible.
percezione, *n.f.* perception.
perché, 1. *adv.* why. **2.** *conj.* because; for.
perciò, *adv.* therefore.
percome, *n.m. and conj.* wherefore.
percorrènza, *n.f.* distance travelled.
percorso, *n.m.* passage (of time); lapse; route.
percòssa, *n.f.* blow; *(pl.)* beating.
percuòtere, *vb.* hit, strike, maul; tap.
percussione, *n.f.* percussion.
pèrdere, *vb.* lose; miss; forfeit; leak.
pèrdita, *n.f.* loss; bereavement; forfeiture; leakage.
perdizione, *n.f.* perdition.
perdonare, *vb.* pardon, forgive.
perdono, *n.m.* pardon, forgiveness.

perènne, *adj.* perennial.
perentòrio, *adj.* peremptory.
perfettamente, *adv.* perfectly.
perfètto, *adj.* perfect, flawless.
perfezionare, *vb.* perfect.
perfezione, *n.f.* perfection.
perfino, *adv.* even.
perforare, *vb.* punch.
perforazione, *n.f.* perforation.
pergamena, *n.f.* parchment.
pergolato, *n.m.* arbor, bower.
pericolo, *n.m.* danger, peril, jeopardy.
pericoloso, *adj.* dangerous, perilous.
periferia, *n.f.* periphery, outskirts.
perìmetro, *n.m.* perimeter.
periòdico, 1. *n.m.* periodical, magazine. **2.** *adj.* periodical; periodic; serial.
perìodo, *n.m.* period, term.
perire, *vb.* perish.
perito, 1. *n.m.* specialist, expert. **2.** *adj.* dead.
perìzia, *n.f.* survey (by an expert).
pèrla, *n.f.* pearl.
perlaceo, *adj.* pearly.
perlomeno, *adv.* at least.
perlopiù, *adv.* in general, mostly.
permanènte, *adj.* permanent.
permanènza, *n.f.* stay.
permeare, *vb.* permeate.
permesso, *n.m.* permission, leave, license.
perméttere, *vb.* permit, let, allow.
permissìbile, *adj.* permissible.
permuta, *n.f.* exchange.
pernàcchia, *n.f.* Bronx cheer.
pernice, *n.f.* partridge.
pernicioso, *adj.* pernicious.
pèrnio, *n.m.* pivot.
pernottare, *vb.* stay overnight.
pero, *n.m.* pear-tree.
però, *adv.* however; though.
perpendicolare, *n.m. and adj.* perpendicular.
perpetrare, *vb.* perpetrate.
perpètuo, *adj.* perpetual.
perplessità, *n.f.* perplexity, bafflement, bewilderment, quandary.
perplèsso, *adj.* perplexed, baffled, bewildered.
persecuzione, *n.f.* persecution.
perseguire, *vb.* pursue.

perseguitare, vb. persecute.
perseveranza, n.f. perseverance.
perseverare, vb. persevere.
pèrsico, adj. pesce p., bass (fish); perch.
persistènte, adj. persistent.
persistere, vb. persist.
persona, n.f. person. **p. anziana**, senior citizen.
personàggio, n.m. personage.
personale, **1.** n.m. personnel, staff. **2.** adj. personal.
personalità, n.f. personality.
personalmente, adv. personally.
perspicare, adj. farsighted, shrewd, sagacious.
persuadere, vb. persuade.
persuasivo, adj. persuasive.
pèrtica, n.f. perch; pole.
pertinènte, adj. pertinent, relevant.
pertùgio, n.m. hole, perforation.
perturbare, vb. perturb.
pervàdere, vb. pervade.
perversione, n.f. perversion.
pervèrso, adj. perverse.
pervertire, vb. pervert, debauch.
pesante, adj. heavy.
pesare, vb. weigh; balance.
pesca, n.f. fishing.
pèsca, n.f. peach.
pescàggio, n.m. draft.
pescare, vb. fish; angle.
pescatore, n.m. fisherman.
pesce, n.m. fish. **p. rosso**, goldfish. **p. spada**, swordfish.
pececane, n.m. shark; profiteer.
pescheréccio, n.m. fishing boat.
peschièra, n.f. fishery.
pesciolino, n.f. minnow.
pescivèndola, n.f. fishwife.
pescivèndolo, n.m. fishmonger.
pèsco, n.m. peach-tree.
peso, n.m. weight. **p. màssimo**, heavyweight. **p. lordo**, gross weight.
pessimismo, n.m. pessimism.
pestare, vb. pound.
pèste, n.f. plague.
pestífero, adj. (col.) troublemaking; pestiferous.
pestilènza, n.f. pestilence.
pesto, adj. pounded, crushed. **òcchio p.**, black eye.
pètalo, n.m. petal.

petardo, n.m. firecracker.
petizione, n.f. petition.
pèto, n.m. fart.
petròlio, n.m. petroleum. **p. raffinato**, kerosene.
pettègola, n.f. gossip.
pettegolare, vb. gossip.
pettegolezzo, n.m. gossip.
pettégolo, **1.** n.m. gossip. **2.** adj. gossipy.
pettinare, vb. comb.
pettinatura, n.f. coiffure, hair-do.
pèttine, n.m. comb.
pettirosso, n.m. robin.
pètto, n.m. chest, bosom; (meat) brisket.
pettorale, n.m. pectoral.
petulante, adj. petulant.
petulanza, n.f. petulance, huff.
pèzza, n.f. patch.
pezzente, n.m. beggar.
pezzettino, n.m. little bit, mite.
pezzetto, n.m. scrap.
pèzzo, n.m. piece, bit, chunk. **p. di ricàmbio**, spare part. **p. gròsso**, big shot.
piacere, **1.** n.m. pleasure. **2.** vb. please.
piacévole, adj. pleasing, pleasant, agreeable, genial.
piacevolezza, n.f. pleasing quality, geniality.
piacevolmente, adv. pleasingly, agreeably, genially.
piacimento, n.m. liking, taste.
piaga, n.f. sore; wound.
piagnisteo, n.m. moaning.
piagnucolare, vb. whimper, snivel, blubber.
piagnucolone, n.m. whiner, whimperer, sniveler, complainer.
piagnucoloso, adj. maudlin.
pialla, n.f. plane.
piallàccio, n.m. veneer.
piallare, vb. plane.
pianeggiante, adj. flat, level.
pianeta, n.m. planet.
piàngere, vb. weep, cry, bewail, mourn.
pianista, n.m. pianist.
piano, **1.** n.m. plan; story, floor; plane. **2.** adj. level, flat.
pianofòrte, n.m. piano.
pianta, n.f. plant; plan, plot; map.
piantagione, n.f. plantation.

piantare, *vb.* plant.
piantonare, *vb.* guard.
piantatore, *n.m.* planter.
pianto, *n.m.* crying, weeping.
pianura, *n.f.* plain.
pianuzza, *n.f.* halibut.
piastra, *n.f.* plate.
piastrella, *n.f.* tile.
pietire, *vb.* beg.
piattaforma, *n.f.* platform, dais.
piattino, *n.m.* saucer.
piatto, 1. *n.m.* dish, plate; cymbal.
   2. *adj.* flat.
piàttola, *n.f.* roach, crab louse,
   bore.
piazza, *n.f.* square.
piazzale, *n.m.* large square.
piazzare, *vb.* place; sell.
piazzista, *n.m.* salesman.
piccante, *adj.* piquant.
picchetto, *n.m.* picket.
picchiare, *vb.* hit, smack, sock,
   clout, cuff, rap.
picchiata, *n.f.* nose dive.
picchiatore, *n.m.* divebomber.
picchio, *n.m.* blow, rap.
piccino, 1. *adj.* little. 2. *n.m.* child.
piccione, *n.m.* pigeon. **p. viaggiatore,** homing pigeon, carrier
   pigeon.
picco, *n.m.* peak, crag.
piccolo, *adj.* little, small, petty.
piccone, *n.m.* pick.
pidòcchio, *n.m.* louse.
piède, *n.m.* foot. **p. stòrto,** clubfoot.
piedestallo, *n.m.* pedestal.
pièga, *n.f.* fold, crease, pleat, tuck.
piegare, *vb.* fold, bend, crease.
piegatura, *n.f.* bending, folding.
pieghettato, *adj.* pleated.
pieghévole, *adj.* pliable, pliant;
   folding.
Piemonte, *n.m.* Piedmont.
piemontese, *adj.* Piedmontese.
pienamente, *adv.* fully.
pienezza, *n.f.* fullness.
pieno, *adj.* full.
pietà, *n.f.* mercy, pity, piety.
pietanza, *n.f.* entree (meal).
pietoso, *adj.* merciful, pitiful.
piètra, *n.f.* stone. **p. angolare,**
   cornerstone. **p. focaia,** flint.
pietrificare, *vb.* petrify.
piffero, *n.m.* fife, fifer, piper.

pigia pigia, *n.m.* crowd, crush.
pigiama, *n.m.pl.* pajamas.
pigiare, *vb.* press, crush, squeeze.
pigione, *n.f.* rent.
pigmento, *n.m.* pigment.
pignolo, *adj.* fussy, pernickety.
pignoramento, *n.m.* seizure
   (law).
pignorare, *vb.* attach, distrain,
   seize.
pigrizia, *n.f.* laziness.
pigro, *adj.* lazy.
pila, *n.f.* battery. **p. a secco,** dry
   cell.
pilastro, *n.m.* pillar.
pillola, *n.f.* pill.
pilone, *n.m.* pier; pillar.
pilòta, *n.m.* pilot.
piluccare, *vb.* nibble, pick at;
   pluck.
pinacoteca, *n.f.* picture gallery.
pineta, *n.f.* pine grove.
pingue, *adj.* corpulent; big; rich.
pinna, *n.f.* fin.
pinnàcolo, *n.m.* pinnacle.
pino, *n.m.* pine.
pinta, *n.f.* pint.
pinze, *n.f.pl.* pincers, pliers.
pinzette, *n.f.pl.* tweezers.
pio, *adj.* pious.
pioggerèlla, *n.f.* drizzle.
piòggia, *n.f.* rain.
piombo, *n.m.* lead.
pionière, *n.m.* pioneer.
piòta, *n.f.* turf, sod.
piòvere, *vb.* rain.
piovigginare, *vb.* drizzle.
piovoso, *adj.* rainy.
piovra, *n.f.* octopus.
pipa, *n.f.* pipe.
pipistrèllo, *n.m.* bat.
pira, *n.f.* pyre.
piràmide, *n.f.* pyramid.
pirata, *n.m.* pirate.
piròscafo, *n.m.* steamship.
piscina, *n.f.* swimming pool.
pisèllo, *n.m.* pea.
pisolino, *n.m.* doze, snooze, nap.
pista, *n.f.* (race) track; (race)
   course; (cinder) path. **p. d'at-
   teràggio,** landing strip, runway.
pistola, *n.f.* pistol.
pistone, *n.m.* piston.
pittore, *n.m.* painter.
pittoresco, *adj.* picturesque.

pittura, *n.f.* painting.
più, 1. *adv.* more; **per di p.,** moreover; **per lo p.,** mostly. **2.** *prep.* plus.
piuma, *n.f.* plume, feather.
piumàggio, *n.m.* plumage.
piumato, *adj.* plumed, feathered.
piumino, *n.m.* feathers.
piumoso, *adj.* feathery.
piuttosto, *adv.* rather.
pizza, *n.f.* pizza.
pizzicòtto, *n.m.* nip, pinch.
pizzo, *n.m.* lace.
placare, *vb.* appease, placate.
placatore, *n.m.* appeaser.
plàcido, *adj.* placid.
plagiare, *vb.* plagiarize.
plàgio, *n.m.* plagiarism.
planetàrio, 1. *n.m.* planetarium.
2. *adj.* planetary.
plasma, *n.m.* plasma.
plàstica, *n.f.* plastic.
plàstico, *adj.* plastic.
plàtino, *n.m.* platinum.
plausìbile, *adj.* plausible.
plebe, *n.f.* populace, humble people.
plebàglia, *n.f.* mob, rabble.
plebiscito, *n.m.* plebiscite.
plenàrio, *adj.* plenary.
plenilùnio, *n.m.* full moon.
pleurite, *n.f.* pleurisy.
plico, *n.m.* stack (of paper); file.
plotone, *n.m.* platoon.
plùmbeo, *adj.* leaden.
plurale, *n.m. and adj.* plural.
plutòcrate, *n.m.* plutocrat.
pneumàtico, 1. *n.* tire. **2.** *adj.* pneumatic.
po', *n.m.* **un p.,** a little, somewhat.
pòchi, *adj. and pron. pl.* few.
pòco, *n. and adv.* little. **fra p.,** in a short time, presently, soon.
podère, *n.m.* farm; property.
poderoso, *adj.* strong, powerful.
podismo, *n.m.* running; walking.
poèma, *n.m.* poem.
poesìa, *n.f.* poem; poetry.
poèta, *n.m.* poet.
poetéssa, *n.f.* woman poet.
poètico, *adj.* poetic.
pòi, *adv.* then.
poichè, *conj.* since.
polacca, *n.f.* polonaise.

polacco, *adj.* Polish.
polare, *adj.* polar.
polarizzere, *vb.* polarize.
polèmica, *n.f.* polemic; controversial subject.
polèmico, *adj.* polemical, controversial.
poligamìa, *n.f.* polygamy.
poliglòtto, *adj.* polyglot.
polìgono, *n.m.* polygon.
polipo, *n.m.* polyp.
polistirolo, *n.m.* polystyrene, styrofoam.
polìtica, *n.f.* politics; policy.
polìtico, 1. *n.m.* politician. **2.** *adj.* politic, political.
polizìa, *n.f.* police.
poliziòtto, *n.m.* policeman, cop.
pòlizza, *n.f.* policy.
pollàio, *n.m.* chicken coop.
pollame, *n.m.* poultry.
pòllice, *n.m.* thumb; big toe; inch.
pòlline, *n.m.* pollen.
pollo, *n.m.* chicken, fowl.
polmonare, *adj.* pulmonary.
polmone, *n.m.* lung.
polmonite, *n.f.* pneumonia.
pòlo, *n.m.* pole.
Polònia, *n.f.* Poland.
polpa, *n.f.* pulp.
polpetta, *n.f.* meat-ball; croquette.
polpettone, *n.m.* meat loaf.
polsino, *n.m.* cuff.
polso, *n.m.* wrist; pulse.
poltrona, *n.f.* armchair, easychair.
pólvere, *n.f.* dust; powder.
polverizzare, *vb.* pulverize; powder.
polveroso, *adj.* dusty.
pomeriggio, *n.m.* afternoon.
pomiciare, *vb.* spoon (slang).
pomo, *n.m.* apple.
pomodoro, *n.m.* tomato.
pompa, *n.f.* pump; pomp. **p. da incèndio,** fire engine.
pompare, *vb.* pump.
pompèlmo, *n.m.* grapefruit.
pompière, *n.m.* fireman.
pomposo, *adj.* pompous.
pònce, *n.m.* punch.
ponderare, *vb.* ponder.
ponderoso, *adj.* ponderous.
ponente, *n.m.* west.

ponte, *n.m.* bridge; deck; span. **p. levatòio,** drawbridge. **p. sospeso,** suspension bridge.

pontéfice, *n.m.* pontiff.

pontile, *n.m.* gangplank.

pontone, *n.m.* pontoon.

popelina, *n.f.* broadcloth.

popolare, *adj.* popular.

popolarità, *n.f.* popularity.

popolazione, *n.f.* population.

pòpolo, *n.m.* people, folk.

poppa, *n.f.* stern; breast.

pòrca, *n.f.* sow; ridge.

porcellana, *n.f.* porcelain, china.

porcellino, *n.m.* piglet. **p. d'India,** guinea pig.

porcile, *n.m.* sty.

pòrco, *n.m.* hog, pig, swine.

pornografìa, *n.f.* pornography.

pòro, *n.m.* pore.

poroso, *adj.* porous.

pórpora, *n.f.* purple.

porre, *vb.* put, place, set, lay.

pòrro, *n.m.* leek.

pòrta, *n.f.* door; gate; gateway; goal.

portabagagli, *n.m.* porter.

portacéneri, *n.m.* ash-tray.

portaèrei, *n.m.* aircraft carrier, flat-top.

portafògli, *n.m.* billfold, wallet; pocketbook.

portafòglio, *n.m.* wallet, portfolio.

portafortuna, *n.m.* good-luck charm; mascot.

portale, *n.m.* portal.

portamento, *n.m.* bearing, posture, conduct.

portamonete, *n.m.* wallet, purse.

portasigarette, *n.m.* cigarette-holder.

portata, *n.f.* reach; range, scope.

portàtile, *adj.* portable.

portatore, *n.m.* carrier, bearer.

portavoce, *n.m.* spokesman, mouthpiece.

portento, *n.m.* prodigy, marvel.

pòrtico, *n.m.* portico, porch.

portièra, *n.f.* door.

portière, *n.m.* goal-keeper; porter.

portinàio, *n.m.* doorman, concierge.

portinerìa, *n.f.* concierge's office.

pòrto, *n.m.* port, harbor, haven, inlet.

Portogallo, *n.m.* Portugal.

portoghese, *adj.* Portuguese.

portone, *n.m.* gate.

porzione, *n.f.* portion, helping, share.

pòsa, *n.f.* pose; exposure.

posare, *vb.* pose.

posarsi, *vb.* perch.

posata, *n.f.* silverware.

posaterìa, *n.f.* cutlery.

posato, *adj.* quiet, well behaved.

posatòio, *n.m.* perch.

poscritto, *n.m.* postscript.

positivo, *adj.* positive.

posizione, *n.f.* position.

posporre, *vb.* postpone.

possedere, *vb.* possess, own.

possènte, *adj.* powerful.

possessivo, *adj.* possessive.

possèsso, *n.m.* possession, belonging.

possessore, *n.m.* possessor, owner.

possìbile, *adj.* possible.

possibilità, *n.f.* possibility.

possibilmente, *adv.* possibly.

possidente, *n.m. and f.* proprietor; wealthy person.

pòsta, *n.f.* mail, post.

postale, *adj.* postal.

postbèllico, *adj.* postwar.

postdatare, *vb.* postdate.

posteggiare, *vb.* park.

postèggio, *n.m.* parking.

pòsteri, *n.m.pl.* posterity.

posteriore, *adj.* posterior, rear, back, hind.

posterità, *n.f.* posterity.

posticipare, *vb.* postpone, defer, reschedule.

postino, *n.m.* mailman, postman.

posto, *n.m.* place; post; room; spout.

postulante, *n.m. and f.* petitioner.

postulare, *vb.* solicit, petition, postulate.

potàssio, *n.m.* potassium.

potatura, *n.f.* pruning.

potènte, *adj.* powerful, potent, forcible, mighty.

potènza, *n.f.* power, might.
potenziale, *n.m.* and *adj.* potential.
potere, 1. *n.m.* power. **2.** *vb.* be able, can, may.
poveràccio, *n.m.* poor fellow.
pòvero, 1. *n.m.* poor man, pauper. **2.** *adj.* poor.
povertà, *n.f.* poverty.
pozione, *n.f.* potion.
pozzànghera, *n.f.* puddle.
pozzo, *n.m.* well; shaft. **p. nero,** cesspool.
prammàtica, *adj.* pragmatic.
pranzare, *vb.* dine.
pranzo, *n.m.* dinner.
prassi, *n.f.* praxis, practice.
prateria, *n.f.* prairie.
pràtica, 1. *n.f.* practice. **2.** *n.f.* file, dossier.
praticàbile, *adj.* passable; practicable.
praticamente, *adv.* practically.
praticante, 1. *adj.* practicing; **2.** *n.m.* apprentice; observant.
praticare, *vb.* practice.
pràtico, *adj.* practical, business-like. **p. di,** skilled in; acquainted with, familiar with.
praticone, *n.m.* old hand (pejorative).
prato, *n.m.* meadow, field; lawn.
preàmbolo, *n.m.* preamble.
preavvertire, *vb.* forewarn.
precàrio, *adj.* precarious.
precauzione, *n.f.* precaution.
precedènte, 1. *n.m.* precedent. **2.** *adj.* preceding, former, previous.
precedènza, *n.f.* precedence, right of way.
precèdere, *vb.* precede, go before, (in time) antedate.
precètto, *n.m.* precept.
precipitare, *vb.* precipitate; *(refl.)* rush.
precipìzio, *n.m.* precipice.
precisione, *n.f.* precision.
preciso, *adj.* precise.
preclùdere, *vb.* preclude.
precòce, *adj.* precocious.
precursore, *n.m.* precursor, fore-runner, harbinger.
prèda, *n.f.* prey.
predare, *vb.* plunder, forage.
predatòrio, *adj.* predatory.

predecessore, *n.m.* predecessor.
predestinazione, *n.f.* predestination.
predicare, *vb.* preach.
predicato, *n.m.* predicate.
predicatore, *n.m.* preacher.
predilètto, *n.* and *adj.* favorite, darling.
predilezione, *n.f.* predilection.
predire, *vb.* predict, foretell.
predisporre, *vb.* predispose, bias.
predominante, *adj.* predominant.
predomìnio, *n.m.* dominance.
predone, *n.m.* marauder, robber.
prefabbricato, *adj.* prefabricated.
prefazione, *n.f.* preface, foreword.
preferènza, *n.f.* preference.
preferìbile, *adj.* preferable.
preferire, *vb.* prefer.
prefètto, *n.m.* prefect.
prefisso, *n.m.* prefix. **p. teleselettivo,** area code.
pregare, *vb.* pray, beg.
preghièra, *n.f.* prayer, request, plea.
prègio, *n.m.* virtue, value, worth.
pregiudicare, *vb.* prejudice.
pregiudicato, *n.m.* criminal; previous offender.
pregiudìzio, *n.m.* prejudice, bias.
prègna, *adj.f.* pregnant.
prego, *interj.* Please!; You're welcome.; Come in!
pregustare, *vb.* foretaste.
pregustazione, *n.f.* foretaste.
preistòrico, *adj.* prehistoric.
prelato, *n.m.* priest.
prelazione, *n.f.* privilege; preemption.
prelevare, *v.b.* draw, withdraw; take away.
preliminare, *adj.* preliminary.
prelùdio, *n.m.* prelude.
prematuro, *adj.* premature.
premeditare, *vb.* premeditate.
prèmere, *vb.* press.
premessa, *n.f.* premise.
premiare, *vb.* award (a prize to); reward.
prèmio, *n.m.* prize, award, premium.
premonizione, *n.f.* premonition.

premunirsi, vb. (refl.) forearm, protect.

premurosamente, adv. considerately.

premuroso, adj. considerate.

prenatale, adj. prenatal.

préndere, vb. take; get; catch.

prenotare, vb. reserve.

prenotazione, n.f. reservation.

preoccupante, adj. worrisome.

preoccupare, vb. worry.

preoccupazione, n.f. worry.

preparare, vb. prepare.

preparatòrio, adj. preparatory.

preparazione, n.f. preparation.

preponderante, adj. preponderant.

preposizione, n.f. preposition.

preposto, 1. adj. responsible for.

prepotènte, 1. adj. overbearing, tyrannical. 2. n. bully.

prerogativa, n.f. prerogative.

presa, n.f. grasp, grip, hold; (electrical) outlet; socket. **p. di tèrra,** (electrical) ground.

presàgio, n.m. omen, portent.

presagire, vb. presage, predict, forebode, foreshadow, portend.

presbite, adj. farsighted.

prescritto, adj. prescribed, fixed; compulsory.

prescrivere, vb. prescribe.

prescrizione, n.f. prescription.

presentàbile, adj. presentable.

presentare, vb. present, introduce.

presentatore, n.m. announcer.

presentazione, n.f. presentation, introduction.

presènte, adj. present.

presentimento, n.m. presentiment, foreboding.

presentire, vb. forebode.

presènza, n.f. presence.

presenziare, vb. attend; be present.

preservare, vb. preserve.

preservativo, n.m. condom.

presidènte, n.m. president, chairman.

presidentessa, n.f. chairwoman.

presidènza, n.f. presidency, chairmanship.

presidio, n.m. defense garrison.

presièdere, vb. preside.

prèssa, n.f. press.

pressappòco, adv. about, approximately.

pressione, n.f. pressure.

prèsso a, prep. near; by.

prestare, vb. lend, loan.

prestigio, n.m. prestige.

prèstito, n.m. loan.

prèsto, adv. soon, quickly; early.

presùmere, vb. presume.

presuntuosità, n.f. presumptuousness, forwardness.

presuntuoso, adj. presumptuous.

presunzione, n.f. presumption.

presupporre, vb. presuppose.

prète, n.m. priest.

pretèndere, vb. pretend; claim.

pretenzioso, adj. pretentious.

pretesa, n.f. pretense.

pretèsto, n.m. pretext.

prevalènte, adj. prevalent.

prevalere, vb. prevail.

prevedere, vb. foresee, forecast.

prevedìbile, adj. foreseeable.

preventivo, 1. n.m. estimate; budget; deterrent. 2. adj. preventive.

prevenzione, n.f. prevention.

previdènza, n.f. foresight.

previsione, n.f. forecast.

prezioso, adj. precious, valuable.

prezzémolo, n.m. parsley.

prèzzo, n.m. price, charge; fare; rate.

prigione, n.f. prison, jail.

prigionìa, n.f. imprisonment, captivity.

prigionièro, n.m. and adj. prisoner, captive.

prima, 1. n. première. 2. adv. first; before; beforehand. **p. che,** conj. before. **p. di,** prep. before.

primario, 1. adj. primary. 2. n.m. head physician.

primato, n.m. record.

primavera, n.f. spring.

primaverile, adj. spring-like.

primitivo, adj. primitive; original.

primo, adj. first; foremost; prime.

primordiale, adj. primeval.

principale, adj. principal, chief, main, prime.

principalmente, adv. principally, chiefly, mainly.

principato, n.m. principality, princedom.

principe, *n.m.* prince.
principesco, *adj.* princely, luxurious.
principessa, *n.f.* princess.
principiante, *n.m.* beginner.
principiare, *vb.* begin.
principio, *n.m.* beginning; principle.
priorità, *n.f.* priority.
prisma, *n.m.* prism.
privare, *vb.* deprive, bereave.
privato, *adj.* private.
privazione, *n.f.* deprivation.
privilègio, *n.m.* privilege.
privo, *adj.* devoid, void, lacking (in); destitute.
probàbile, *adj.* probable.
probabilità, *n.f.* probability, likelihood.
probante, *adj.* probatory, constituting evidence.
probità, *n.f.* probity.
problèma, *n.m.* problem.
probo, *adj.* upright.
procace, *adj.* forward; provoking.
procèdere, *vb.* proceed.
procedimento, *n.m.* proceeding; procedure.
procedura, *n.f.* procedure.
processare, *vb.* prosecute.
processione, *n.f.* procession.
procèsso, *n.m.* process; trial.
procione, *n.m.* racoon.
proclamare, *vb.* proclaim.
proclamazione, *n.f.* proclamation.
procrastinare, *vb.* procrastinate.
procreare, *vb.* procreate, generate.
procura, *n.f.* proxy.
procurare, *vb.* procure.
procuratore, *n.m.* attorney; proxy.
prode, *adj.* brave, gallant.
prodezza, *n.f.* prowess.
prodigalità, *n.f.* prodigality, extravagance.
prodigare, *vb.* lavish.
prodigio, *n.m.* prodigy.
pròdigo, *adj.* prodigal, extravagant, lavish.
proditòrio, *adj.* treacherous.
prodotto, *n.m.* product.
produrre, *vb.* produce.
produttivo, *adj.* productive.

produzione, *n.f.* production, output, yield.
profanare, *vb.* profane, defile.
profano, *adj.* profane.
proferire, *vb.* utter.
professare, *vb.* profess.
professionale, *adj.* professional.
professione, *n.f.* profession, calling, occupation.
professionista, *n.m.* professional; practitioner.
professore, *n.m.* professor.
profèta, *n.m.* prophet.
profètico, *adj.* prophetic.
profètizzare, *vb.* prophesy.
profezìa, *n.f.* prophecy.
proficuo, *adj.* profitable.
profilassi, *n.f.* prophylaxis; prescribed cure.
profilàttico, *n.m.* condom.
profilo, *n.m.* profile.
profitto, *n.m.* profit.
proflùvio, *n.m.* overflow, flood; superabundance; *(pathology)* discharge.
profondamente, *adv.* deeply, profoundly.
profondità, *n.f.* profundity, depth.
profondo, *adj.* deep, profound; in-depth.
profumare, *vb.* perfume.
profumo, *n.m.* perfume, scent.
profuso, *adj.* profuse.
progettare, *vb.* project, plan.
progètto, *n.m.* project, plan, scheme. **p. di legge,** (legislative) bill.
prògnosi, *n.f.* prognosis.
programma, *n.m.* program.
progredire, *vb.* progress, advance.
progredito, *adj.* progressed; advanced.
progressione, *n.f.* progression.
progressivo, *adj.* progressive.
progrèsso, *n.m.* progress, headway.
proibire, *vb.* prohibit, forbid, ban.
proibitivo, *adj.* prohibitive.
proibizione, *n.f.* prohibition, band.
proiettare, *vb.* project.
proièttile, *n.m.* projectile.
proiettore, *n.m.* projector.

proiezione, *n.f.* projection.
pròle, *n.f.* offspring, issue.
proliferazione, *n.f.* proliferation.
prolìfico, *adj.* prolific.
pròlogo, *n.m.* prologue.
prolungamento, *n.m.* prolongation, extension.
prolungare, *vb.* prolong, extend.
promessa, *n.f.* promise.
prométtere, *vb.* promise.
prominènte, *adj.* prominent.
promìscuo, *adj.* promiscuous.
promontòrio, *n.m.* promontory.
promotore, *n.m.* promoter.
promozione, *n.f.* promotion.
promulgare, *vb.* promulgate.
promuòvere, *vb.* promote.
pronipote, *n.m.* great-grandchild; descendant.
prono, *adj.* prone; with the habit of.
pronome, *n.m.* pronoun.
pronosticare, *vb.* forecast.
prontamente, *adv.* readily.
pronto, **1.** *adj.* ready; prompt; quick; willing. **2.** *interj.* (telephone) hello.
prontuàrio, *n.m.* handbook, reference book, manual.
pronùncia, *n.f.* pronunciation.
pronunciare, *vb.* pronounce.
propaganda, *n.f.* propaganda.
propagare, *vb.* propagate.
propaggine, *n.f.* ramification, physical appendix.
propèndere, *vb.* incline.
propensione, *n.f.* propensity.
propènso, *adj.* inclined.
propinare, *vb.* administer, give.
propìzio, *adj.* propitious, favorable.
proponènte, *n.m.* proponent.
proporre, *vb.* propose.
proporzionato, *adj.* proportionate.
proporzione, *n.f.* proportion.
propòsito, *n.m.* purpose. **a p.**, apropos. **di p.**, on purpose.
proposizione, *n.f.* sentence.
propòsta, *n.f.* proposal; proposition.
proprietà, *n.f.* property, belongings.

proprietàrio, *n.m.* proprietor.
pròprio, **1.** *adj.* proper; own. **2.** *adv.* just; right; quite.
propugnare, *vb.* advocate.
propugnatore, *n.m.* advocate.
propugnazione, *n.f.* advocacy.
propulsione, *n.m.* propulsion.
pròra, *n.f.* prow, bow.
pròroga, *n.f.* delay; extension.
prorogare, *vb.* delay; extend.
prorómpere, *vb.* burst forth.
pròsa, *n.f.* prose.
prosàico, *adj.* prosaic.
prosciògliere, *vb.* set free; acquit, absolve.
prosciugare, *vb.* drain, dry up.
prosciutto, *n.m.* ham.
proscrìvere, *vb.* proscribe.
prosecuzione, *n.f.* prosecution; continuation.
proseguimento, *n.m.* continuation.
proseguire, *vb.* continue, follow, carry on.
prosèlito, *n.m.* proselyte.
prosperare, *vb.* prosper, thrive.
prosperità, *n.f.* prosperity, boom.
pròspero, *adj.* prosperous.
prospettiva, *n.f.* perspective.
prospettivo, *adj.* prospective.
prospètto, *n.m.* prospect.
prossimità, *n.f.* proximity, nearness, closeness.
pròssimo, **1.** *n.* neighbor. **2.** *adj.* next; nearest; forthcoming.
prostituta, *n.f.* prostitute.
prostrare, *vb.* prostrate.
prostrato, *adj.* prostrate.
protagonista, *n.m. and f.* protagonist.
protèggere, *vb.* protect, shield.
proteìna, *n.f.* protein.
protèndere, *vb.* stretch.
protèsta, *n.f.* protest.
protestante, *n.m. and adj.* Protestant.
protestántesimo, *n.m.* Protestantism.
protestare, *vb.* protest.
protettivo, *adj.* protective.
protettore, *n.m.* protector.
protezione, *n.f.* protection.
protocòllo, *n.m.* protocol.

protone, n.m. proton.
protòtipo, n.m. prototype.
protrarre, vb. protract.
protuberanza, n.f. protuberance, swelling, bulge, lump.
pròva, n.f. proof; test; ordeal; rehearsal; probation; trial. **p. conclusiva,** acid test. **p. generale,** dress rehearsal.
provare, vb. try; essay; rehearse; test.
proverbiale, adj. proverbial.
provèrbio, n.m. proverb, adage.
provìncia, n.f. province.
provinciale, adj. provincial.
provocante, adj. defiant.
provocare, vb. provoke.
provocazione, n.f. provocation.
provvedere, vb. provide, supply.
provvidènza, n.f. providence.
provvisòrio, adj. temporary, acting, interim.
provvista, n.f. provision; supply, store, stock.
prudènte, adj. prudent.
prudènza, n.f. prudence.
prùdere, vb. itch.
prudore, n.m. itch.
prugna, n.f. plum.
prurire, vb. itch.
prurito, n.m. itch.
pseudònimo, n.m. pseudonym.
psichedèlico, adj. psychedelic.
psichiatra, n.m. psychiatrist.
psichiatrìa, n.f. psychiatry.
psicoanàlisi, n.f. psychoanalysis.
psicologìa, n.f. psychology.
psicològico, adj. psychological.
psicòsi, n.f. psychosis.
ptomaìna, n.f. ptomaine.
pubblicare, vb. publish.
pubblicazione, n.f. publication.
pubblicità, n.f. publicity; advertising.
pubblicizzare, v.b. advertise.
pùbblico, n. and adj. public.
pubertà, n.f. puberty.
pudico, adj. reserved, demure; bashful.
pudore, n.m. decency; shame.
pugilato, n.m. boxing.
pugilatore, n.m. boxer.
pugilìstico, adj. pugilistic, fistic.

Pùglie, n.f.pl. Apulia.
pugliese, adj. Apulian.
pugnace, adj. pugnacious.
pugnalare, vb. stab.
pugnalata, n.f. stab.
pugnale, n.m. dagger.
pugno, n.m. fist; punch.
pula, n.f. chaff.
pulce, n.f. flea.
pulcino, n.m. chick.
puledro, n.m. colt.
pulèggia, n.f. pulley.
pulire, vb. clean; polish. **p. a secco,** dry-clean.
pulito, adj. clean; polished.
pulitore, n.m. cleaner.
pulitura, n.f. cleaning. **p. a secco,** dry-cleaning.
pulizia, n.f. cleanliness.
pullman, n.m. de luxe bus.
pùlpito, n.m. pulpit.
pulsante, n.m. push button.
pùlsar, n.m. pulsar.
pulsare, vb. pulsate.
puma, n.m. cougar.
pungènte, adj. pungent, sharp, biting.
pùngere, vb. prick, sting.
pungiglione, n.m. sting.
pùngolo, n.m. goad.
punire, vb. punish, chastise.
punitivo, adj. punitive.
punizione, n.f. punishment, chastisement.
punta, n.f. tip.
puntare, vb. point; aim; wager, stake.
puntata, n.f. installment.
punteggiare, vb. punctuate.
punteggiatura, n.f. punctuation.
puntellare, vb. prop.
puntèllo, n.m. prop.
puntìglio, n.m. stubbornness, obstinacy.
puntina, n.f. needle.
punto, n.m. point; period; dot; stitch. **p. di vista,** viewpoint; standpoint. **due punti,** colon. **p. mòrto,** stalemate, deadlock. **p. esclamativo,** exclamation point. **p. e vìrgola,** semicolon.
puntuale, adj. punctual.
puntura, n.f. puncture; sting.

pupàttola, *n.f.* doll.
pupazzo, *n.m.* puppet.
pupillo, *n.m.* ward.
pupo, *n.m.* baby.
purchè, *conj.* provided that.
pure, 1. *too, also; even.* **2.** *conj.* though.
purè, *n.m.* puree.
purezza, *n.f.* purity.
purga, *n.f.* purge.
purgante, *n.m. and adj.* purgative, laxative.
purgare, *vb.* purge.
purgativo, *adj.* cathartic.
purgatòrio, *n.m.* purgatory.

purificare, *vb.* purify.
purità, *n.f.* purity.
puritano, *adj.* puritan.
puro, *adj.* pure.
purpùreo, *adj.* purple.
putrefatto, *adj.* rotten, decayed.
putrefazione, *n.f.* rot.
pùtrido, *adj.* decayed, putrid, rotten; (egg) addled.
puttana, *n.f.* whore, tart.
puzzare, *vb.* stink, smell.
puzzo, *n.m.* stench, smell.
puzzolènte, *adj.* stinking, noisome.
puzzone, *n.m.* skunk.

Q

qua, *adv.* hither.
quadràngolo, *n.m.* quadrangle.
quadrante, *n.m.* quadrant; dial.
quadrare, *vb.* square.
quadrato, 1. *n.m.* square; ring. **2.** *adj.* square.
quadrifònico, *adj.* quadraphonic.
quadro, *n.m.* picture; table; cadre.
quadro generale, *n.m.* overview.
quadrùpede, *n.m.* quadruped.
quàglia, *n.f.* quail.
quagliare, *vb.* curdle.
quagliata, *n.f.* curd, clabber.
qualche, *adj.* some.
qualcosa, *pron.* something; anything.
qualcuno, *pron.* somebody; anybody.
quale, *adj.* which. **il q.,** which; who.
qualìfica, *n.f.* qualification.
qualificare, *vb.* qualify.
qualificazione, *n.f.* qualification.
qualità, *n.f.* quality.
qualunque, *adj.* whatever; whichever.
quando, *adv.* when. **di q. in q.,** from time to time, occasionally.
quantità, *n.f.* quantity, amount.
quanto, *adj. and adv.* how much; how many. **in q. che,** in so far as.
quantunque, *conj.* although.
quaranta, *num.* forty.
quarantésimo, *adj.* fortieth.
quarantena, *n.f.* quarantine.

quarantotto, 1. *uproar, mess.* **2.** *num.* forty-eight.
quarésima, *n.f.* Lent.
quartetto, *n.m.* quartet.
quartière, *n.m.* quarter. **q. generale,** headquarters.
quarto, 1. *n.* quarter. **2.** *adj.* fourth.
quarzo, *n.m.* quartz.
quàsar, *n.m.* quasar.
quasi, 1. *adv.* almost, nearly. **2.** *conj.* as if.
quassù, *adv.* up here.
quatto, *adj.* crouching.
quatto quatto, *adv.* stealthily, silently.
quattòrdici, *num.* fourteen.
quattrini, *n.m.pl.* money.
quattro, *num.* four.
quegli, *adj.m.pl.* those.
quei, *adj.m.pl.* those.
quel, *adj.m.sg.* that.
quella, *adj. and pron. f.sg.* that.
quelle, *adj. and pron. f.pl.* those.
quelli, *pron.m.pl.* those.
quello, 1. *adj.* that. **2.** *pron.* that one; the former.
quèrcia, *n.f.* oak.
querela, *n.f.* lawsuit, complaint.
querelare, *vb.* sue.
quesito, *n.m.* question; query; problem.
questa, *adj. and pron. f.sg.* this.
queste, *adj. and pron. f.pl.* these.
questi, *adj. and pron. m.pl.* these.

quésti, *pron. m.sg.* this man.
questionàrio, *n.m.* questionnaire.
questióne, *n.f.* question.
questo, 1. *adj.* this. **2.** *pron.* this one; the latter.
questóre, *n.m.* police commissioner.
quèstua, *n.f.* (church) collection.
questùra, *n.f.* police headquarters.
qui, *adv.* here.
quietànza, *n.f.* receipt.
quiète, *n.f.* quiet, stillness.
quièto, *adj.* quiet.
quindi, *adv.* hence, therefore.
quindicèsimo, *adj.* fifteenth.

quìndici, *num.* fifteen.
quindicinale, *adj.* fortnightly, bi-monthly.
quinte, *n.f.pl.* **dietro le q.** back-stage.
quintale, *n.m.* 100 kilograms.
quintètto, *n.m.* quintet.
quìnto, *adj.* fifth.
quisquìlia, *n.f.* trifle.
quòta, *n.f.* quota; dues; fee.
quotazióne, *n.f.* quotation (of prices).
quotidianaménte, *adv.* daily.
quotidiàno, *n.m. and adj.* daily, everyday.
quoziènte, *n.m.* quotient.

R

rabàrbaro, *n.m.* rhubarb.
rabberciàre, *vb.* botch.
ràbbia, *n.f.* anger, rage; rabies.
rabbìno, *n.m.* rabbi.
rabbióso, *adj.* rabid.
rabbrividìre, *vb.* shudder; shiver.
raccapricciante, *adj.* horrifying, bloodcurdling.
raccattàre, *vb.* pick up.
racchétta, *n.f.* racket.
raccògliere, *vb.* collect, gather; harvest, reap.
raccòlta, *n.f.* collection, gathering; harvest, crop.
raccòlto, *n.m.* crop, harvest.
raccomandàre, *vb.* recommend; commend.
raccomandazióne, *n.f.* recommendation.
raccontàre, *vb.* tell, narrate.
raccónto, *n.m.* story, tale, account, narrative.
raccorciaménto, *n.m.* abbreviation; shortening.
raccorciàre, *vb.* abbreviate; shorten.
raddrizzàre, *vb.* straighten.
ràdere, *vb.* shave.
radiatóre, *n.m.* radiator.
radicàle, *n.m. and adj.* radical.
radicchièlla, *n.f.* dandelion.
radìce, *n.f.* root.
ràdio, *n.* **1.** *m.* radium. **2.** *f.* radio, wireless.
radioattìvo, *adj.* radio-active.

radiocorrière, *n.m.* radio news.
radiofònico, *adj.* radio.
radiotelemetrìa, *n.f.* radar.
radiotelèmetro, *n.m.* radar.
rado, *adj.* sparse.
radunàre, *vb.* gather; muster.
radùno, *n.m.* rally.
radùra, *n.f.* glade, clearing.
ràfano, *n.m.* horse-radish.
raffazzonaménto, *n.m.* reworking; patchwork.
rafférmo, *adj.* stale.
ràffica, *n.f.* gust; squall; blast.
raffinàre, *vb.* refine.
raffinatézza, *n.f.* refinement.
ràffio, *n.m.* claw.
rafforzàre, *vb.* strengthen.
raffreddàre, *vb.* chill.
raffreddóre, *n.m.* cold.
raffrenàre, *vb.* restrain, curb.
ragàzza, *n.f.* girl, lass.
ragàzzo, *n.m.* boy, lad.
raggiànte, *adj.* radiant, beaming.
ràggio, *n.m.* spoke; ray, beam; shaft; radius.
raggiùngere, *vb.* arrive at, achieve, attain; reach; overtake.
raggiungìbile, *adj.* attainable.
raggiungiménto, *n.m.* achievement, attainment.
raggrumàrsi, *vb.* clot.
raggruppaménto, *n.m.* grouping.
raggruppàre, *vb.* group.
ragguàglio, *n.m.* report; information.

ragionamento, *n.m.* reasoning, argument.
ragionare, *vb.* reason; talk.
ragione, *n.f.* reason. **aver r.,** be right.
ragioneria, *n.f.* accounting.
ragionévole, *adj.* reasonable.
ragioniere, *n.m.* accountant.
ragliare, *vb.* bray.
raglio, *n.m.* bray.
ragnatela, *n.f.* cobweb.
ragno, *n.m.* spider.
ragù, *n.m.* meat sauce.
ràion, *n.m.* rayon.
rallegrare, *vb.* cheer up, rejoice.
rallentare, *vb.* slow down, slacken.
ramaiuòlo, *n.m.* ladle, scoop.
ramanzina, *n.f.* scolding.
rame, *n.m.* copper.
rammendare, *vb.* mend, darn.
rammendo, *n.m.* mend, darn.
rammentare, *vb.* remind; *(refl.)* recollect.
ramingo, *adj.* wandering, roving.
rammaricare, *vb. (refl.)* regret, be sorry.
rammollito, *adj.* soft-headed, imbecile.
ramo, *n.m.* branch, bough, limb.
ramolàccio, *n.m.* radish.
ramoscèllo, *n.m.* twig; sprig.
rana, *n.f.* frog.
ràncido, *adj.* rancid.
ràncio, *n.m.* mess.
rancore, *n.m.* rancor.
randellare, *vb.* bludgeon, cudgel, club.
randello, *n.m.* bludgeon, cudgel.
rango, *n.m.* rank.
rannicchiarsi, *vb.* huddle.
rannuvolarsi, *vb.* cloud over.
ranòcchio, *n.m.* frog.
ràntolo, *n.m.* rattle.
ranùncolo, *n.m.* buttercup.
rapa, *n.f.* turnip.
rapare, *vb.* shave.
rapidamente, *vb.* rapidly, quickly, fast.
ràpido, 1. *n.m.* limited (train). **2.** *adj.* rapid, fast, quick, speedy.
rapimento, *n.m.* abduction, kidnapping.
rapina, *n.f.* rapine, plunder. **uccèllo di r.,** *n.m.* bird of prey.

rapire, *vb.* abduct, kidnap.
rapitore, *n.m.* abductor, kidnapper.
rappacificare, *vb.* reconcile; pacify.
rappezzare, *vb.* patch.
rappòrto, *n.m.* relation; report; rapport; ratio; intercourse.
rapprendere, *vb.* congeal.
rappresàglia, *n.f.* reprisal, retaliation.
rappresentare, *vb.* represent; perform.
rappresentativo, *adj.* representative.
rappresentazione, *n.f.* representation; performance.
raramente, *vb.* rarely, seldom.
rarità, *n.f.* rarity, scarcity.
raro, *adj.* rare.
raschiare, *vb.* scrape; scratch out; erase.
raschino, *n.m.* eraser.
rasente, *adv.* close, near.
rasentare, *vb.* skirt, skim.
raso, *n.m.* satin.
rasòio, *n.m.* razor.
rassegna, *n.f.* review; exhibition.
rassegnarsi, *vb.* resign oneself.
rassegnazione, *n.f.* resignation.
rassicurare, *vb.* reassure.
rassomigliare, *vb.* resemble.
rastrellare, *vb.* rake.
rastrellièra, *n.f.* rack.
rastrèllo, *n.m.* rake.
rata, *n.f.* installment.
ratificare, *vb.* ratify.
ratto, *n.m.* rat; abduction.
rattoppare, *vb.* patch.
rattristare, *vb.* sadden.
ràuco, *adj.* hoarse, raucous.
ravanèllo, *n.m.* radish.
ravvivamento, *n.m.* revival.
ravvivare, *vb.* enliven; revive.
razionale, *adj.* rational.
razionare, *vb.* ration.
razione, *n.f.* ration.
razza, *n.f.* race, breed, kind.
razzo, *n.m.* rocket.
re, *n.m.* king.
reagire, *vb.* react.
reale, *adj.* real; royal.
realista, *n.m.* realist.
realizzare, *vb.* realize; fulfill.

realizzazione, *n.f.* realization; fulfillment.
realmente, *adv.* really.
realtà, *n.f.* reality.
reame, *n.m.* realm.
reattore, *n.m.* reactor; jet.
reazionàrio, *adj.* reactionary.
reazione, *n.f.* reaction.
recare, *vb.* reach; hand (over); *(refl.)* go, betake oneself.
recèdere, *vb.* recede.
recensione, *n.f.* review.
recensire, *vb.* review.
recènte, *adj.* recent; latter.
recentemente, *adv.* recently, lately.
recinto, *n.m.* enclosure, fence.
recipiènte, *n.m.* vessel; beaker; bin; container; holder.
recitare, *vb.* act; play; recite.
recitazione, *n.f.* recitation; acting.
reclamante, *n.m.* claimant.
reclamare, *vb.* claim.
réclame, *n.f.* advertising.
reclamizzare, *vb.* advertise.
reclamo, *n.m.* claim.
reclinare, *vb.* recline.
reclusione, *n.f.* seclusion; confinement, imprisonment.
recluso, 1. *adj.* secluded. 2. *n.m.* recluse, prisoner.
rècluta, *n.f.* recruit.
reclutare, *vb.* recruit.
recòndito, *adj.* concealed, hidden.
recriminare, *vb.* recriminate; complain.
redditìzio, *adj.* lucrative, profitable.
rèddito, *n.m.* income.
redentore, *n.m.* redeemer.
redenzione, *n.f.* redemption.
redìgere, *vb.* draw up, draft; edit.
redìmere, *vb.* redeem, reclaim.
rèdina, *n.f.* rein.
regalare, *vb.* present.
regale, *adj.* regal.
regalità, *n.f.* royalty.
regalo, *n.m.* present.
reggènte, *n.m.* regent.
règgere, *vb.* hold up; wield.
reggimento, *n.m.* regiment.
reggipètto, *n.m.* brassière.
reggiseno, *n.m.* brassière.

regime, *n.m.* regime, rule; diet.
regina, *n.f.* queen.
règio, *adj.* royal.
regione, *n.f.* region.
registrare, *vb.* register; record; (luggage) check.
registratore a filo, *n.m.* wire recorder.
registratore magnètico, *n.m.* tape recorder.
registrazione, *n.f.* registration.
registro, *n.m.* register; record.
regnare, *vb.* reign, rule.
regno, *n.m.* kingdom, realm, reign.
règola, *n.f.* rule; *(pl.)* menstruation.
regolamento, *n.m.* regulation.
regolare, 1. *adj.* regular. 2. *vb.* regulate, rule; set.
regolarità, *n.f.* regularity.
regolatore, *n.m.* regulator.
règolo, *n.m.* ruler. **r. calcolatore,** slide-rule.
regredire, *vb.* regress.
reiètto, *n.m.* outcast.
reincarnare, *vb.* reincarnate.
reintegrare, *vb.* restore, reinstate.
reiterare, *vb.* reiterate.
relatività, *n.f.* relativity.
relativo, *adj.* relative.
relazione, *n.f.* relation; liaison.
relè, *n.m.* relay.
relegare, *vb.* banish; relegate.
religione, *n.f.* religion.
religioso, *adj.* religious.
relìquia, *n.f.* relic.
remare, *vb.* row.
remata, *n.f.* row.
reminiscènza, *n.f.* reminiscence.
remissivo, *adj.* submissive.
remo, *n.m.* oar, paddle.
rèmora, *n.f.* hindrance; impediment.
remòto, *adj.* remote.
rena, *n.f.* sand.
rèndere, *vb.* render; give back. **r. conto di,** account for.
rendiconto, *n.m.* statement.
rendimento, *n.m.* output.
rène, *n.f.* kidney.
reniforme, *adj.* kidney-shaped.
renitente, *adj.* reluctant, unwilling. **r. alla leva,** draft dodger.
rènna, *n.f.* reindeer.

renoso, *adj.* sandy.
repellènte, *adj.* repulsive.
reperto, *n.m.* finding, evidence.
repentino, *adj.* sudden, unexpected.
reperìbile, *adj.* to be found; available; recoverable.
repertòrio, *n.m.* repertoire.
rèplica, *n.f.* reply, rejoinder; repeat performance.
replicare, *vb.* reply, rejoin; repeat.
repressione, *n.f.* repression.
reprìmere, *vb.* repress.
repùbblica, *n.f.* republic; commonwealth.
repubblicano, *adj.* republican.
repulsivo, *adj.* repulsive; forbidding.
reputare, *vb.* consider, deem.
requisire, *vb.* requisition, commandeer.
requisito, *n.m.* requirement, qualification.
requisizione, *n.f.* requisition.
rescìndere, *vb.* rescind.
residènte, *adj.* resident.
residènza, *n.f.* residence.
residuo, *n.m.* residue.
rèsina, *n.f.* rosin.
resistènza, *n.f.* resistance.
resìstere, *vb.* resist.
respingènte, *n.m.* bumper, buffer.
respìngere, *vb.* reject, repel, repulse.
respirare, *vb.* breathe.
respirazione, *n.f.* respiration.
respiro, *n.m.* breath, breathing.
responsàbile, *adj.* responsible, accountable, answerable, liable; amenable.
responsabilità, *n.f.* responsibility, liability.
responsivo, *adj.* responsive.
restare, *vb.* remain, stay.
restaurare, *vb.* restore.
restaurazione, *n.f.* restoration.
restituire, *vb.* restore; refund.
restituzione, *n.f.* restitution.
rèsto, *n.m.* remainder, remnant; change.
restrìngere, *vb.* restrict.
restrizione, *n.f.* restriction.
retàggio, *n.m.* inheritance.
retata, *n.f.* roundup.

rete, *n.f.* net; netting; network.
reticella, *n.f.* luggage rack.
reticènte, *adj.* reticent.
reticènza, *n.f.* reticence.
reticolato, *n.m.* grid; barbed wire.
rètina, *n.f.* retina.
retrattile, *adj.* retractable.
retribuzione, *n.f.* retribution.
retroattivo, *adj.* retroactive.
retrocèdere, *vb.* recede, retreat.
retroguàrdia, *n.f.* rear-guard.
retroscèna, *n.f.* backstage.
retrospettivo, *adj.* retrospective.
retrotèrra, *n.f.* hinterland.
retrovisore, *adj.* **specchio r.,** rear-view mirror.
rettàngolo, *n.m.* rectangle.
rettificare, *vb.* rectify.
rettificatrice, *n.f.* rectifier.
rèttile, *n.m.* reptile.
rettilìneo, *n.m.* straightaway.
rètto, *adj.* straight.
retòrica, *n.f.* rhetoric.
retòrico, *adj.* rhetorical.
reumàtico, *adj.* rheumatic.
reumatismo, *n.m.* rheumatism.
reverèndo, *adj.* reverend.
revisione, *n.f.* revision.
revisore, *n.m.* (accounts) auditor; (proof) proof-reader.
rèvoca, *n.f.* revocation.
revocare, *vb.* revoke.
riabilitare, *vb.* rehabilitate.
rialzo, *n.m.* rise; raise.
rianimare, *vb.* revive; cheer up.
riarmo, *n.m.* rearmament.
riassùmere, *vb.* make a résumé of, summarize.
riassunto, *n.m.* abstract, résumé.
ribadire, *vb.* rivet.
ribalta, *n.f.* footlights.
ribàttere, *vb.* retort.
ribellarsi, *vb.* rebel, revolt.
ribèlle, 1. *n.m.* rebel, insurgent. **2.** *adj.* rebellious, insurgent; refractory.
ribellione, *n.f.* rebellion.
ribes, *n.m.* gooseberry; currant.
ribrezzo, *n.m.* disgust.
ricadere, *vb.* relapse.
ricaduta, *n.f.* relapse.
ricamare, *vb.* embroider.
ricambiare, *vb.* reciprocate, retaliate.

ricàmbio, *n.m.* exchange. **di r.,** spare.

ricamo, *n.m.* embroidery.

ricapitolare, *vb.* recapitulate, sum up.

ricaricare, *vb.* reload.

ricattare, *vb.* blackmail.

ricattatore, *n.m.* blackmailer, extortioner.

ricatto, *n.m.* blackmail.

ricavato, *n.m.* proceeds; yield.

ricchezza, *n.f.* riches, wealth.

riccio, *n.m.* hedgehog.

ricciolo, *n.m.* curl.

ricciuto, *adj.* curly.

ricco, *adj.* rich, wealthy.

ricerca, *n.f.* search, quest; research.

ricercare, *vb.* search.

ricercato, *adj.* recherché; far-fetched.

ricètta, *n.f.* recipe.

ricettàcolo, *n.m.* receptacle.

ricettivo, *adj.* receptive.

ricevènte, *n.m.* recipient.

ricévere, *vb.* receive, get.

ricevimento, *n.m.* reception; party.

ricevitore, *n.m.* receiver.

ricevitoria, *n.f.* collection office.

ricevuta, *n.f.* receipt.

richiamare, *vb.* recall.

richiedènte, *n.m.* applicant.

richièdere, *vb.* request, ask for; demand; entail; require.

richièsta, *n.f.* request; demand.

riciclare, *vb.* recycle.

ricino, *n.m.* castor oil.

recognitore, *n.m.* scout.

ricognizione, *n.f.* reconnaissance; acknowledgment.

ricolmo, *adj.* full (of liquid).

ricompènsa, *n.f.* recompense, reward.

ricompensare, *vb.* recompense, reward.

riconciliare, *vb.* reconcile.

ricondurre, *vb.* bring back; take back; lead back.

ricongiùngersi, *vb.* rejoin.

riconoscènza, *n.f.* gratitude.

riconóscere, *vb.* recognize; acknowledge.

riconoscimento, *n.m.* recognition.

ricordare, *vb.* remember, recollect.

ricòrdo, *n.m.* remembrance, souvenir, keepsake, memento; record.

ricórrere, *vb.* recur; resort; have recourse.

ricorso, *n.m.* recourse; resort.

ricostruire, *vb.* reconstruct, rebuild.

ricoverare, *vb.* shelter; hospitalize.

ricòvero, *n.m.* shelter; hospitalization.

ricuperare, *vb.* recover, recuperate; retrieve.

ricùpero, *n.m.* recovery.

ridacchiare, *vb.* giggle, chortle.

ridere, *vb.* laugh.

ridìcolo, 1. *n.m.* ridicule. 2. *adj.* ridiculous, laughable, ludicrous.

ridire, *vb.* say again.

ridòsso, 1. *n.m.* shelter. 2. *adv.* **a r.** adjacent to a bigger object or thing.

ridotto, *n.m.* redoubt; foyer.

ridurre, *vb.* reduce, curtail; (music) arrange.

riduttore, *n.m.* adapter.

riduzione, *n.f.* reduction; (music) arrangement.

rielezione, *n.f.* reelection.

riempire, *vb.* fill.

rientranza, *n.f.* recess.

rièntro, *n.m.* reentry; recess.

riepìlogo, *n.m.* recapitulation, summary.

riesame, *n.m.* review.

riesaminare, *vb.* re-examine, review.

riesumare, *vb.* exhume; bring back.

rievocare, *vb.* recall, reminisce.

riferimento, *n.m.* reference.

riferire, *vb.* refer; (*refl.*) relate.

riffa, *n.f.* raffle.

rifiutare, *vb.* refuse, decline.

rifiuto, *n.m.* refusal.

rifiuti, *n.m.pl.* refuse, garbage. **r. nucleari,** nuclear waste.

riflessione, *n.f.* reflection.

riflèsso, *n.m.* reflection, glint; reflex.

riflèttere, *vb.* reflect.

rifluire, *vb*. ebb.

riflusso, *n.m*. ebb.

riforma, *n.f*. reform, reformation.

riformare, *vb*. reform.

rifuggire, *vb*. shrink.

rifugiarsi, *vb*. take refuge.

rifugiato, *n.m*. refugee.

rifùgio, *n.m*. refuge, shelter, asylum, haven.

riga, *n.f*. line, file, row.

rigàglie, *n.f.pl*. giblets.

rigettare, *vb*. reject.

righello, *n.m*. ruler.

rigidezza, *n.f*. rigidity, stiffness.

rìgido, *adj*. rigid, stiff.

rigo, *n.m*. line; staff.

rigoglioso, *adj*. luxuriant.

rigore, *n.m*. rigor.

rigoroso, *adj*. rigorous, stringent.

riguardare, *vb*. regard, concern.

riguardo, *n.m*. regard. **r. a**, regarding.

rilanciare, *vb*. toss back; throw again; raise (poker).

rilasciare, *vb*. release.

rilassamento, *n.m*. relaxation, laxity.

rilassato, *adj*. relaxed, lax.

rilegare, *vb*. bind.

rilegatura, *n.f*. binding.

rilevamento, *n.m*. survey.

rilevante, *adj*. relevant, germane.

rilièvo, *n.m*. relief; remark; prominence.

rilucènte, *adj*. shiny, lustrous.

riluttante, *adj*. reluctant, loath.

riluttanza, *n.f*. reluctance.

rima, *n.f*. rhyme.

rimandare, *vb*. postpone, put off.

rimando, *n.m*. reference.

rimanènte, *n.m*. remainder, rest.

rimanère, *vb*. remain, stay, abide.

rimarchévole, *adj*. noteworthy, remarkable.

rimasùglio, *n.m*. residues, leftovers.

rimare, *vb*. rhyme.

rimbalzare, *vb*. bounce, rebound.

rimbalzo, *n.m*. bounce, rebound.

rimbambimento, *n.m*. dotage.

rimbambirsi, *vb*. grow childish (in old age).

rimbeccare, *vb*. retort.

rimboccare, *vb*. tuck.

rimbombo, *n.m*. loud noise; echo.

rimborsare, *vb*. reimburse, repay.

rimborso, *n.m*. repayment, reimbursement.

rimediare, *vb*. remedy.

rimèdio, *n.m*. remedy.

rimestare, *vb*. stir.

rimmel, *n.m*. mascara.

riméttere, *vb*. put back; remit; reinstate; (*refl*.) get back.

rimodernare, *vb*. modernize, renovate.

rimorchiare, *vb*. tow.

rimorchiatore, *n.m*. tugboat.

rimòrchio, *n.m*. trailer.

rimorso, *n.m*. remorse.

rimozione, *n.f*. removal.

rimpatriare, *vb*. repatriate.

rimpiàngere, *vb*. regret.

rimpianto, *n.m*. regret.

rimpiazzare, *vb*. replace.

rimpinzare, *vb*. cram, stuff.

rimproverare, *vb*. reprove, chide, rebuke, reproach, reprimand, upbraid.

rimpròvero, *n.m*. rebuke, reproof, reproach, reprimand.

rimuòvere, *vb*. remove.

rinàscere, *vb*. be reborn.

rinascimento, *n.m*. renaissance.

rinàscita, *n.f*. rebirth.

rinato, *adj*. born-again.

rinchiùdere, *vb*. enclose.

rincréscere, *vb*. cause regret.

rincrescimento, *n.m*. regret.

rinforzare, *vb*. reinforce.

rinfòrzo, *n.m*. reinforcement.

rinfrescare, *vb*. cool; refresh; freshen.

ringhiare, *vb*. snarl.

ringhièra, *n.f*. railing, banister.

rìnghio, *n.m*. snarl.

ringiovanire, *vb*. rejuvenate.

ringraziare, *vb*. thank.

rinnovamento, *n.m*. renewal.

rinnovare, *vb*. renew.

rinoceronte, *n.m*. rhinoceros.

rinomanza, *n.f*. renown.

rinomato, *adj*. renowned.

rintocco, *n.m*. knell.

rintanare, *vb*. (*refl*.) hide.

rintontire, *vb*. stun, daze.

rintracciare, *vb*. trace.

rinùncia, *n.f*. waiver.

rinunciare, *vb*. renounce, forego; waive.

rinviare, vb. postpone; send back.
rinvìo, n.m. postponement.
rione, n.m. ward.
ripagare, vb. repay.
riparare, vb. repair, recondition.
riparazione, n.f. repair, reparation, redress.
ripercussione, n.f. repercussion.
ripètere, vb. repeat.
ripetizione, n.f. repetition.
ripetutamente, adv. repeatedly, again and again.
ripiano, n.m. ledge.
rìpido, adj. steep; abrupt.
ripièno, 1. n.m. stuffing. **2.** adj. stuffed.
riposante, adj. restful.
riposare, vb. rest, repose.
ripòso, n.m. repose, rest, leisure.
ripostìglio, n.m. closet.
riprèndere, vb. retake; resume; reprehend.
ripresa, n.f. revival; (music) repeat.
ripristinare, vb. reestablish; restore.
riprodurre, vb. reproduce.
riproduzione, n.f. reproduction.
riproduzione esatta, n.f. clone.
ripudiare, vb. repudiate.
ripùdio, n.m. repudiation.
ripugnante, adj. repugnant, abhorrent.
ripugnanza, n.f. repugnance, abhorrence, loathing.
ripulsa, n.f. rebuff, repulse.
risàia, n.f. rice field.
risanare, vb. heal.
risata, n.f. burst of laughter.
risatina, n.f. snicker.
riscaldare, vb. warm up, heat; (refl.) warm oneself; bask.
riscattare, vb. ransom.
riscatto, n.m. ransom.
rischiare, vb. risk, hazard; stake; venture.
rischio, n.m. risk, hazard, venture.
rischioso, adj. risky, hazardous.
risciacquare, vb. rinse.
riscossa, n.f. insurrection; recovery; counterattack.
riscossione, n.f. collection.
riscuòtere, vb. shake; collect; cash.

riserbo, n.m. discretion.
risèrva, n.f. reserve.
riservare, vb. reserve.
riservato, adj. reserved, aloof.
risièdere, vb. reside.
riso, n.m. laughter; rice.
risolino, n.m. giggle.
risoluto, adj. resolute, determined.
risoluzione, n.f. resolution.
risòlvere, vb. resolve, solve.
resolvìbile, adj. solvable.
risonante, adj. resonant.
risonanza, n.f. resonance.
risonare, vb. resound, ring out.
risorgènte, adj. resurgent.
risorsa, n.f. resource.
risparmiare, vb. save.
rispàrmio, n.m. saving(s).
rispettàbile, adj. respectable.
rispettare, vb. respect.
rispettivo, adj. respective.
rispètto, n.m. respect, regard.
rispettoso, adj. respectful.
risplendènte, adj. resplendent, beaming, effulgent.
risplèndere, vb. be resplendent, shine, beam, glitter.
rispóndere, vb. answer, respond, reply.
risposta, n.f. answer, response, reply.
rissa, n.f. brawl, fight, affray.
rissoso, adj. quarrelsome.
ristagnare, vb. stagnate.
ristorante, n.m. restaurant.
ristorare, vb. restore, refresh.
ristoratore, n.m. restaurant.
ristòro, n.m. refreshment.
risultare, vb. result; appear; be evident.
risultato, n.m. result, outgrowth.
risurrezione, n.f. resurrection.
risvegliare, vb. rouse.
risvòlta, n.f. lapel.
ritaglio, n.m. clipping, cutting.
ritardare, vb. delay, retard.
ritardo, n.m. delay, lag. **in r.,** delayed, late.
ritenere, vb. retain.
ritenzione, n.f. retention.
ritirare, vb. retire, withdraw; (refl.) retreat, pull back, back out; flinch.
ritirata, n.f. retreat; toilet.

rìtmico, *adj.* rhythmical.
ritmo, *n.m.* rhythm.
rito, *n.m.* rite.
ritornare, *vb.* return; revert.
ritorno, *n.m.* return.
ritrarre, *vb.* retract, pull back.
ritrasméttere, *vb.* relay.
ritrattare, *vb.* portray; retract.
ritratto, *n.m.* portrait.
ritroso, *adj.* unwilling, balky.
ritrovare, *vb.* find, discover; regain.
ritrovato, *n.m.* finding.
ritròvo, *n.m.* meeting-place, hangout. **r. notturno,** cabaret.
rituale, *n.m. and adj.* ritual.
riunione, *n.f.* reunion; meeting, assembly.
riunire, *vb.* reunite; join; assemble; *(refl.)* meet, foregather.
riuscire, *vb.* succeed; turn out.
riuscita, *n.f.* success.
riuscito, *adj.* successful.
riva, *n.f.* bank; strand.
rivale, *n. and adj.* rival.
rivaleggiare, *vb.* rival.
rivalità, *n.f.* rivalry.
rivalsa, *n.f.* revenge.
rivangare, *vb.* dig up; mull over.
rivedere, *vb.* see again; review.
rivelare, *vb.* reveal, disclose.
rivelazione, *n.f.* revelation, disclosure, exposure.
rivendicare, *vb.* claim; demand.
riverberare, *vb.* reverberate.
riverbero, *n.m.* glare.
riverènte, *adj.* reverent.
riverènza, *n.f.* reverence; bow, curtsy, obeisance.
riverire, *vb.* revere.
rivestitura, *n.f.* facing.
rivista, *n.f.* magazine; review; revue; musical comedy; muster.
rivòlgere, *vb.* turn to; address; turn around.
rivòlta, *n.f.* revolt.
rivoltare, *vb.* revolt.
rivoltèlla, *n.f.* revolver.
rivoluzionàrio, *adj.* revolutionary.
rivoluzione, *n.f.* revolution.
ròba, *n.f.* stuff. **r. da chiòdi,** junk; nonsense.
robustezza, *n.f.* hardiness.

robusto, *adj.* robust, strong, hardy, hale, stalwart, sturdy.
ròcca, *n.f.* fortress; rock.
roccafòrte, *n.f.* stronghold.
rocchetto, *n.m.* reel; spool.
ròccia, *n.f.* rock.
roccioso, *adj.* rocky.
rock, *n.m. and adj.* rock (music).
rodàggio, *n.m.* breaking in (period).
ródere, *vb.* gnaw, champ.
roditore, *n.m.* rodent.
rognone, *n.m.* kidney.
rollìo, *n.m.* roll (of ship).
Roma, *n.f.* Rome.
romano, *adj.* Roman.
romàntico, *adj.* romantic.
romanzière, *n.m.* novelist.
romanzo, *n.m.* novel; romance.
rombo, *n.m.* roar.
romitàggio, *n.m.* hermitage.
rómpere, *vb.* break.
rompibile, *adj.* breakable.
rompicapo, *n.m.* puzzle.
rompicollo, *adv.* **a r.,** breakneck.
rompistàcole, *n.m.* pest.
róndine, *n.f.* swallow.
ronzare, *vb.* buzz, drone; hum.
ronzino, *n.m.* nag.
ronzìo, *n.m.* buzz, drone, hum.
ròsa, 1. *n.f.* rose. 2. *adj.* pink.
rosàrio, *n.m.* rosary.
ròseo, *adj.* rosy.
roseto, *n.m.* rose garden.
rosicchiare, *vb.* nibble, gnaw.
rosolare, *vb.* brown, sauté.
rosolìa, *n.f.* German measles.
rospo, *n.m.* toad.
rossetto, *n.m.* lipstick; rouge.
rosso, *adj.* red.
rossore, *n.m.* blush.
rosticcerìa, *n.f.* grillroom.
rotàia, *n.f.* rail.
rotatòrio, *adj.* rotatory.
rotazione, *n.f.* rotation.
rotèlla, *n.f.* roller. **r. del ginócchio,** knee-cap.
rotolare, *vb.* roll.
ròtolo, *n.m.* roll; scroll.
rotondo, *adj.* round.
rotta, *n.f.* rout.
rottame, *n.m.* scrap, wreck.
rotto, *adj.* broken.
rottura, *n.f.* break, breakage; rupture.

ròtula, *n.f.* kneecap.

rovesciare, *vb.* reverse; spill.

rovèscio, *n.m.* reverse; downpour. **a r.,** backhand.

rovina, *n.f.* ruin, downfall, wreck.

rovinare, *vb.* ruin, wreck.

rovinoso, *adj.* ruinous.

rovente, *adj.* red-hot.

ròvo, *n.m.* briar.

rozzo, *adj.* rough.

rubacchiare, *vb.* pilfer.

rubare, *vb.* rob, steal, burglarize, filch.

rubicondo, *adj.* rubicund, ruddy, florid.

rubinetto, *n.m.* faucet; tap; cock.

rubino, *n.m.* ruby.

rude, *adj.* rude, rough, curt, abrupt, blunt.

rùdere, *n.m.* ruin.

rudezza, *n.f.* roughness, curtness, abruptness.

rudimento, *n.m.* rudiment.

ruga, *n.f.* wrinkle.

rùggine, *n.f.* rust.

rugginoso, *adj.* rusty.

ruggire, *vb.* roar.

ruggito, *n.m.* roar.

rugiada, *n.f.* dew.

rugiadoso, *adj.* dewy.

rullare, *vb.* roll.

rullìo, *n.m.* roll.

rullo, *n.m.* roller.

ruminare, *vb.* chew the cud.

rumore, *n.m.* noise, clatter, din.

rumoroso, *adj.* noisy, blatant.

ruòlo, *n.m.* list, roll; rôle.

ruòta, *n.f.* wheel.

ruotare, *vb.* rotate.

rupe, *n.f.* cliff, rock.

rurale, *adj.* rural.

ruscèllo, *n.m.* brook.

ruspa, *n.f.* excavator.

ruspante, *adj.* scratching about. **pollo r.,** barnyard chicken.

russare, *vb.* snore.

Rùssia, *n.f.* Russia.

russo, *adj.* Russian.

rùstico, *n.m. and adj.* rustic.

ruttare, *vb.* belch.

rutto, *n.m.* belch.

rùvido, *adj.* rough.

S

sàbato, *n.m.* Saturday.

sàbbia, *n.f.* sand; grit.

sabbiature, *n.f.pl.* sand baths.

sabbioso, *adj.* sandy.

sabotàggio, *n.m.* sabotage.

sabotare, *vb.* sabotage.

sabotatore, *n.m.* saboteur.

saccarina, *n.f.* saccharine.

saccarino, *adj.* saccharine.

saccheggiare, *vb.* sack, pillage, plunder.

acchèggio, *n.m.* sack, pillage.

sacco, *n.m.* sack, bag. **s. ad aria,** (automobile) airbag. **s. da montagna,** backpack.

sacerdote, *n.m.* clergyman.

sacramento, *n.m.* sacrament.

sacrificare, *vb.* sacrifice.

sacrificio, *n.m.* sacrifice.

sacrilègio, *n.m.* sacrilege.

sacrìlego, *adj.* sacrilegious.

sacro, *adj.* sacred.

sadismo, *n.m.* sadism.

saétta, *n.f.* stroke of lightning.

sagace, *adj.* sagacious.

saggezza, *n.f.* wisdom.

saggiare, *vb.* sample, try, assay, test.

sàggio, 1. *n.m.* essay; sample; specimen; assay, test. **2.** *adj.* wise, sage.

saggista, *n.m.* essayist.

sàgoma, *n.f.* loading gauge.

sagrestano, *n.m.* sacristan, sexton.

sagrestìa, *n.f.* sacristy, vestry.

saia, *n.f.* denim.

sàio, *n.m.* habit (of monk), frock.

sala, *n.f.* hall; room.

salame, *n.m.* salami; bologna.

salamòia, *n.f.* pickle.

salare, *vb.* salt.

salàrio, *n.m.* wages.

salato, *adj.* salty; briny.

saldare, *vb.* solder; *(comm.)* settle; balance.

saldatura, *n.f.* solder.

saldo, 1. *n.m. (comm.)* balance. **2.** *adj.* steady, steadfast.

sale, *n.m.* salt.

sàlice, *n.m.* willow.
saliente, *adj.* salient.
salire, *vb.* go up, ascend, mount.
saliscendi, *n.m.* latch.
salita, *n.f.* ascent.
saliva, *n.f.* saliva.
salma, *n.f.* corpse, body.
salmastro, *adj.* briny, salty.
salmì, *n.m.* **in s.,** in a stew.
salmo, *n.m.* psalm.
salmone, *n.m.* salmon.
salone, *n.m.* salon; lounge.
salottino, *n.m.* boudoir.
salòtto, *n.m.* parlor.
salpare, *vb.* set sail.
salsa, *n.f.* sauce.
salsedine, *n.f.* airborne saltiness.
salsiccia, *n.f.* sausage.
salsiera, *n.f.* gravy boat.
salso, *adj.* salt, salty.
saltare, *vb.* jump, leap, bound, hop, gambol, skip, spring, vault.
saltimbanco, *n.m.* acrobat, tumbler; street performer.
salto, *n.m.* jump, leap, bound, hop, gambol, spring, vault. **s. mortale,** somersault.
saltuàrio, *adj.* desultory.
salubre, *adj.* salubrious, healthful.
salumeria, *n.f.* pork butcher shop; delicatessen.
salutare, 1. *adj.* salutary, beneficial. **2.** *vb.* greet, salute, hail.
salutazione, *n.f.* salutation.
salute, *n.f.* health.
saluto, *n.m.* greeting, salute, salutation.
salvagente, *n.m.* life-buoy; life-preserver. **isolòtto s.,** safety island.
salvare, *vb.* save, salvage.
salvaguardare, *vb.* safeguard.
salvaguàrdia, *n.f.* safeguard.
salvatàggio, *n.m.* salvage.
salvatore, *n.m.* savior.
salvezza, *n.f.* salvation.
sàlvia, *n.f.* sage.
salvo, 1. *adj.* safe. **2.** *prep.* except, but, save.
sambuco, *n.m.* elder tree.
sanatòrio, *n.m.* sanatorium.
sàndalo, *n.m.* sandal.
sangue, *n.m.* blood; gore.
sanguinare, *vb.* bleed.

sanguinàrio, *adj.* bloodthirsty, sanguinary.
sanguinoso, *adj.* bloody.
sanguisuga, *n.f.* leech.
sanità, *n.f.* sanity.
sanitàrio, *adj.* sanitary.
sano, *adj.* healthy, sound, sane, wholesome.
santificare, *vb.* sanctify, hallow.
santità, *n.f.* holiness, sanctity.
santo, 1. *n.* saint. **2.** *adj.* holy, sainted.
santuàrio, *n.m.* sanctuary, shrine.
sanzionare, *vb.* sanction.
sanzione, *n.f.* sanction.
sapere, *vb.* know; know how to; savor, taste.
sapiente, 1. *adj.* sage; wise. **2.** *n.m.* wise man.
sapone, *n.m.* soap.
sapore, *n.m.* taste, flavor, savor.
saporito, *adj.* savory, tasty.
saporoso, *adj.* tasty, luscious.
sarcasmo, *n.m.* sarcasm.
sarcàstico, *adj.* sarcastic.
sarcòfago, *n.m.* sarcophagus.
Sardegna, *n.f.* Sardinia.
sardèlla, sardina, *n.f.* sardine.
sardo, *adj.* Sardinian.
sarta, *n.f.* dressmaker.
sarto, *n.m.* tailor.
sassata, *n.f.* throwing of a stone; pelt of a stone.
sasso, *n.m.* rock, boulder, stone.
sassoso, *adj.* stony.
Satana, *n.m.* Satan.
satanasso, *n.m.* devil.
satèllite, *n.m.* satellite.
sàtira, *n.f.* satire.
satireggiare, *vb.* satirize.
satollo, *adj.* sated, full.
saturare, *vb.* saturate.
saturazione, *n.f.* saturation, glut.
saziare, *vb.* satiate, sate, cloy.
sbadato, *adj.* careless, heedless.
sbadigliare, *vb.* yawn.
sbadiglio, *n.m.* yawn.
sbagliare, *vb.* err, blunder, make a mistake, slip.
sbàglio, *n.m.* mistake.
sbalordire, *vb.* astound, dumbfound.
sballottare, *vb.* toss.
sbalzo, *n.m.* leap; climb; relief; sudden change.

sbandare, vb. disband.
sbandato, adj. stray; alienated; skidding.
sbarazzare, vb. rid.
sbarcare, vb. disembark, land.
sbarco, n.m. disembarkation, landing.
sbarra, n.f. bar, rail.
sbarramento, n.m. **fuòco di s.,** barrage.
sbarrare, vb. bar.
sbàttere, vb. slam, bang.
sbavare, vb. drivel.
sbirciare, vb. peek, look sideways.
sbirro, n.m. cop.
sbloccare, vb. unblock.
sbocco, n.m. outlet.
sborsare, vb. disburse, pay out.
sbraitare, vb. squall.
sbranare, vb. eat by tearing to pieces.
sbriciolare, vb. crumble.
sbrigare, vb. expedite.
sbrinamento, n.m. defrosting (refrigerator).
sbrinare, vb. defrost (refrigerator).
sbronzare, vb. refl. get drunk.
sbucciare, vb. peel, pare.
sbuffare, vb. puff, chug.
sbuffo, n.m. puff, chug.
scabroso, adj. rugged.
scacchi, n.m.pl. chess.
scacchièra, n.f. chessboard, checkerboard.
scacco, n.m. chessman. **s. matto,** checkmate.
scadènza, n.f. maturity.
scadere, vb. fall due.
scaffale, n.m. shelf; bookcase.
scafo, n.m. hull.
scagliare, vb. hurl, sling.
scaglione, n.m. echelon.
scala, n.f. staircase; scale. **s. a piòli,** ladder.
scalare, vb. scale, climb.
scalèo, n.m. stepladder.
scalo, n.m. station. **s. mèrci,** freight station. **s. di smistamento,** marshalling yards, freight yard.
scalzo, adj. barefoot.
scambiàbile, adj. exchangeable.
scambiare, vb. exchange.
scàmbio, n.m. exchange; (railroad) switch; points.

scampanare, vb. chime, peal.
scampanellata, n.f. ring.
scampanìo, n.m. chime, peal.
scampo, n.m. escape.
scandagliare, vb. take soundings, sound out, fathom.
scàndalo, n.m. scandal.
scandaloso, adj. scandalous.
scandire, vb. scan (poetry).
scanso, n.m. avoidance. **a s. di,** so as to avoid.
scapaccione, n.m. cuff.
scappare, vb. escape.
scappata, n.f. escapade.
scappatòia, n.f. means of escape, loophole.
scarafàggio, n.m. beetle.
scaramùccia, n.f. skirmish.
scaramucciare, vb. skirmish.
scàrica, n.f. discharge.
scaricare, vb. unload, discharge, dump.
scàrico, n.m. discharge; spillway.
scarlattina, n.f. scarlet fever.
scarlatto, n.m. and adj. scarlet.
scarpa, n.f. shoe.
scarponi, n.m.pl. heavy boots.
scarseggiare, vb. be scarce.
scarsezza, n.f. scarcity, dearth.
scarsità, n.f. scarcity, dearth.
scarso, adj. scarce, meager, scant.
scartamento, n.m. gauge.
scartare, vb. discard, scrap.
scarti, n.m.pl. rubbish.
scartòffie, n.f.pl. papers.
scassare, vb. break.
scassinare, vb. burglarize; break open; pick the lock.
scatenare, vb. unleash; excite; trigger, provoke.
scàtola, n.f. box; can.
scattare, vb. spring up; burst forth; spurt; dash.
scatto, n.m. spring; spurt; dash.
scavare, vb. excavate, dig out; burrow, delve.
scavezzacollo, n.m. daredevil.
scavo, n.m. excavation.
scégliere, vb. choose, pick, select.
scelta, n.f. choice, selection; triage.
scelto, adj. select, choice.
scémpio, n.m. ruin; slaughter.
scèna, n.f. scene.
scenàrio, n.m. scenario.

scéndere, vb. descend, go down, get down, alight.

scervellato, adj. harebrained, madcap.

scèttico, 1. n. skeptic. **2.** adj. skeptical.

scèttro, n.m. scepter.

scevro, adj. free, exempt.

scheda, n.f. card; form; ballot.

schedàrio, n.m. card-file.

schedina, n.f. (filing) card.

scheggia, n.f. chip, splinter.

scheggiare, vb. chip, splinter.

schèletro, n.m. skeleton.

schema, n.m. diagram; draft; plan.

scherma, n.f. fencing.

schermidore, n.m. fencer.

schermire, vb. fence.

schermo, n.m. screen.

schernire, vb. mock, scoff at, taunt.

scherno, n.m. mockery.

scherzare, vb. joke, jest, banter.

scherzo, n.m. joke, jest, banter; play; (music) scherzo.

scherzoso, adj. joking, playful.

schiaccianoci, n.m. nutcracker.

schiacciare, vb. crush, mash.

schiaffeggiare, vb. slap, buffet, smack.

schiaffo, n.m. slap, buffet.

schiappa, n.m. bungler.

schiarire, vb. clear up.

schiavitù, n.f. slavery.

schiavo, n.m. slave.

schièna, n.f. back.

schifoso, adj. loathsome.

schioccare, vb. snap.

schiuma, n.f. foam, froth, lather, suds. **s. per capelli,** hairspray.

schivare, vb. avoid, dodge, shun.

schizzare, vb. sketch; squirt.

schizzinoso, adj. squeamish.

schizzo, n.m. splash, splotch, dab; sketch, outline.

sci, n.m. ski.

scìa, n.f. wake.

sciàbola, n.f. saber.

sciacallo, n.m. jackal.

sciagura, n.f. calamity.

scialacquare, vb. squander.

scialle, n.m. shawl.

sciamare, vb. swarm.

sciame, n.m. swarm.

sciampo, n.m. shampoo.

sciancato, 1. n. cripple. **2.** adj. crippled.

sciare, vb. ski.

sciarpa, n.f. scarf, muffler.

sciàtica, n.f. sciatica.

sciatto, adj. sloppy; dowdy.

scìbile, n.m. knowledge.

scientìfico, adj. scientific.

scïènza, n.f. science.

scienziato, n.f. scientist.

scìmmia, n.f. ape; monkey.

scimpanzè, n.m. chimpanzee.

scìndere, vb. split.

scintilla, n.f. spark.

scintillare, vb. sparkle, glitter, glisten.

scintillìo, n.m. sparkle, glitter.

sciòcco, adj. stupid, foolish, dumb, silly.

sciògliere, vb. untie; loosen; resolve; dissolve; melt.

scioglimento, n.m. dénouement.

sciolina, n.f. ski wax.

sciòlto, adj. loose.

scioperante, n.m. and f. striker.

scioperare, vb. strike.

scioperato, adj. lazy, idle.

sciòpero, n.m. strike.

sciròppo, n.m. syrup.

scissione, n.f. division; cleavage; split.

sciupare, vb. spoil; waste; fritter away.

sciupone, n.m. spendthrift.

scivolare, vb. slip; slide; glide.

scivolone, n.m. slip.

scodèlla, n.f. bowl.

scòglio, n.m. reef.

scoiàttolo, n.m. squirrel.

scolare, vb. drain.

scolaro, n.m. pupil.

scollato, adj. décolleté.

scolorimento, n.m. discoloration.

scolorire, vb. discolor.

scolpire, vb. carve.

scommessa, n.f. bet, wager.

scomméttere, vb. bet, wager.

scomodare, vb. inconvenience, disturb.

scomodità, n.f. inconvenience.

scompagnato, adj. odd.

scomparire, vb. disappear.

scomparsa, n.f. disappearance.

scompartimento, *n.m.* compartment.

scompigliare, *vb.* disarrange.

scompiglio, *n.m.* disarray.

scomposto, *adj.* unseemly. **stare s.,** slouch.

scomùnica, *n.f.* excommunication.

scomunicare, *vb.* excommunicate.

sconcertante, *adj.* disconcerting, upsetting, bewildering.

sconcertare, *vb.* disconcert, upset, faze, abash.

sconfìggere, *vb.* defeat.

sconfinato, *adj.* unbounded.

sconfitta, *n.f.* defeat, discomfiture.

scongiurare, *vb.* conjure.

sconnèsso, *adj.* disconnected, disjointed.

sconnèttere, *vb.* disconnect.

sconosciuto, *adj.* unknown.

sconsolato, *adj.* disconsolate, comfortless.

scontare, *vb.* discount.

scontentare, *vb.* discontent.

scontènto, 1. *n.m.* discontent. **2.** *adj.* discontented, disgruntled.

sconto, *n.m.* discount, rebate.

scontrarsi, *vb.* collide.

scontrino, *n.m.* check.

scontro, *n.m.* collision.

sconveniènte, *adj.* unbecoming, improper, unseemly.

sconvòlgere, *vb.* upset, overturn; overthrow; derange; unsettle.

sconvolgimento, *n.m.* upset, overturn; overthrow; derangement.

scopa, *n.f.* broom.

scopare, *vb.* sweep; (coll.) to have sexual intercourse.

scopèrta, *n.f.* discovery.

scopèrto, *adj.* uncovered, bare.

scopetta, *n.f.* whisk-broom.

scòpo, *n.m.* purpose, aim.

scoppiare, *vb.* burst, explode.

scoppiettare, *vb.* pop.

scòppio, *n.m.* outbreak; explosion.

scoprimento, *n.m.* uncovering.

scoprire, *vb.* discover, uncover, bare, detect.

scopritore, *n.m.* discoverer.

scoraggiamento, *n.m.* discouragement, dejection.

scoraggiare, *vb.* discourage, dishearten.

scoraggiato, *adj.* discouraged, dejected, downhearted.

scorato, *adj.* broken-hearted.

scorciatòia, *n.f.* shortcut.

scordare, *vb.* forget.

scòrgere, *vb.* perceive, discern.

scorpacciata, *n.f.* gorge; gluttonous eating. **fare una s.,** pig out (coll.).

scórrere, *vb.* flow; peruse.

scorrerìa, *n.f.* foray.

scorrettezza, *n.f.* impropriety.

scorrévole, *adj.* fluent.

scorrevolezza, *n.f.* fluency.

scorso, *adj.* past, last.

scorsòio, *adj.* running.

scòrta, *n.f.* escort.

scortare, *vb.* escort.

scortese, *adj.* discourteous, impolite.

scortesìa, *n.f.* discourtesy.

scorticare, *vb.* flay.

scorza, *n.f.* bark.

scosceso, *adj.* steep.

scòssa, *n.f.* jolt; shake; shock.

scossone, *n.m.* jerk, jolt.

scostare, *vb.* shift, move away.

scostumato, *adj.* bad-mannered; dissolute.

scotennare, *vb.* scalp; skin.

scottare, *vb.* scald.

scottatura, *n.f.* scald.

scovare, *vb.* find, discover.

Scòzia, *n.f.* Scotland.

scozzese, *adj.* Scotch.

screditare, *vb.* discredit, debunk.

scremare, *vb.* skim.

screpolare, *vb.* chap.

screpolatura, *n.f.* chapping; crevice.

scrèzio, *n.m.* tiff, disagreement.

scriba, *n.m.* scribe.

scribacchiare, *vb.* scribble.

scricchiolare, *vb.* creak.

scrigno, *n.m.* strong-box, safe, coffer.

scritto, *n.m.* writing.

scrittòio, *n.m.* writing desk.

scrittore, *n.m.* writer.

scrittura, *n.f.* writing; scripture.

scritturare, *vb.* engage.

scrivanìa, *n.f.* desk.
scrìvere, *vb.* write.
scrofa, *n.f.* sow.
scròscio, *n.m.* gust.
scrostare, *vb.* scale.
scrùpolo, *n.m.* scruple.
scrupoloso, *adj.* scrupulous.
scrutare, *vb.* scrutinize, scan.
scudo, *n.m.* shield, escutcheon.
sculacciare, *vb.* spank.
sculacciata, *n.f.* spanking.
scultore, *n.m.* sculptor, carver.
scultura, *n.f.* sculpture, carving.
scuòla, *n.f.* school.
scuòtere, *vb.* shake, jog, jar; wag; *(refl.)* bestir oneself.
scuretto, *n.m.* shutter.
scusa, *n.f.* excuse, apology.
scusàbile, *adj.* excusable.
scusare, *vb.* excuse; *(refl.)* apologize.
sdegno, *n.m.* indignation.
sdentato, *adj.* toothless.
sdraiarsi, *vb.* stretch out, sprawl.
sdrucciolare, *vb.* slide, slip.
sdrucciolévole, *adj.* slippery.
sdrucire, *vb.* tear, rip, rend.
se, *conj.* if; whether.
sè, *pron.* himself; herself; itself; themselves.
sebbène, *conj.* although.
sebo, *n.m.* sebum, tallow.
secca, *n.f.* sandbank.
seccare, *vb.* dry; bore; hassle.
seccatura, *n.f.* bore, nuisance; hassle.
secchezza, *n.f.* dryness.
sécchia, *n.f.* bucket, pail, hod.
secco, *adj.* dry.
secolare, *adj.* secular; century-long.
sècolo, *n.m.* century.
secondàrio, *adj.* secondary.
secondo, 1. *n.* second; halfback; mate. **2.** *adj.* second. **3.** *prep.* according to.
secrezione, *n.f.* secretion.
sèdano, *n.m.* celery.
sedativo, *n.m. and adj.* sedative.
sede, *n.f.* seat. **Santa S.,** Holy See.
sedere, *vb.* sit.
sèdia, *n.f.* chair, seat. **s. a dòndolo,** rocker.
sedicèsimo, *adj.* sixteenth.

sédici, *num.* sixteen.
seducènte, *adj.* seductive, alluring.
sedurre, *vb.* seduce.
seduta, *n.f.* sitting.
seduzione, *n.f.* seduction.
sega, *n.f.* saw.
ségale, *n.f.* rye.
segare, *vb.* saw.
sèggio, *n.m.* seat. **s. elettorale,** voting polls.
seggiovìa, *n.f.* ski-lift.
seghettato, *adj.* jagged.
segmento, *n.m.* segment.
segnalare, *vb.* signal.
segnale, *n.m.* signal.
segnalibro, *n.m.* bookmark.
segnare, *vb.* mark; score.
segno, *n.m.* sign, cue, mark, token.
sego, *n.m.* tallow.
segregare, *vb.* segregate.
segretària, *n.f.* secretary.
segretàrio, *n.m.* secretary.
segreto, *n.m. and adj.* secret.
seguace, *n.m.* follower, hanger-on.
seguènte, *adj.* next.
segùgio, *n.m.* bloodhound.
seguire, *vb.* follow.
sèguito, *n.m.* retinue, suite.
sèi, *num.* six.
selce, *n.f.* flint.
selciato, *n.m.* pavement.
selettivo, *adj.* selective.
selezione, *n.f.* selection.
sèlla, *n.f.* saddle.
sellare, *vb.* saddle.
selva, *n.f.* forest.
selvaggina, *n.f.* game.
selvàggio, *n.m. and adj.* savage, wild.
selvàtico, *adj.* wild.
selvaticume, *n.m.* wildlife.
semàforo, *n.m.* traffic light.
semàntica, *n.f.* semantics.
semàntico, *adj.* semantic.
sembrare, *vb.* seem.
seme, *n.m.* seed.
semèstre, *n.m.* semester.
semicérchio, *n.m.* semicircle.
semidìo, *n.m.* demigod.
seminare, *vb.* sow.
seminàrio, *n.m.* seminary.
seminterrato, *n.m.* basement.

semmài, *conj.* if ever.
semolino, *n.m.* semolina.
sempitèrno, *adj.* everlasting.
sémplice, *adj.* simple, plain; no-frills.
semplicemente, *adv.* simply.
semplicità, *n.f.* simplicity.
semplificare, *vb.* simplify.
sèmpre, *adv.* always, ever; still, yet.
sempreverde, *adj.* evergreen.
sènape, *n.f.* mustard.
senato, *n.m.* senate.
senatore, *n.m.* senator.
senile, *adj.* senile.
senno, *n.m.* sense.
seno, *n.m.* breast, bosom. **s. frontale,** sinus.
senonché, *conj.* except that, but.
sensale, *n.m.* broker.
sensato, *adj.* reasonable, sensible.
sensazionale, *adj.* sensational, lurid.
sensazione, *n.f.* sensation.
senserìa, *n.f.* brokerage.
sensìbile, *adj.* sensitive, sympathetic.
sensitivo, *adj.* sensitive.
sènso, *n.m.* sense; direction. **s. unico,** one-way (street).
sensuale, *adj.* sensual.
sentièro, *n.m.* path, trail.
sentimentale, *adj.* sentimental.
sentimento, *n.m.* feeling, sentiment.
sentire, *vb.* feel; hear.
sènza, *prep.* without. **s. piombo,** unleaded (gasoline).
separare, *vb.* separate, part.
separato, *adj.* separate.
separazione, *n.f.* separation, parting.
sepolcro, *n.m.* grave.
sepoltura, *n.f.* burial, interment.
seppellire, *vb.* bury, entomb, inter.
séppia, *n.f.* cuttlefish.
sequela, *n.f.* series, succession.
sequenza, *n.f.* sequence, succession.
sequèstro, *n.m.* lien.
sera, *n.f.* evening.
serbare, *vb.* keep, preserve.
serbatòio, *n.m.* reservoir; cistern; tank.

serenata, *n.f.* serenade.
serenità, *n.f.* serenity.
sereno, 1. *n.f.* clear sky. **2.** *adj.* serene; clear; cloudless.
sergènte, *n.m.* sergeant.
seriamente, *adv.* seriously.
sèrie, *n.f.* series; row; array; set; suite; succession.
serietà, *n.f.* seriousness, earnestness.
sèrio, *adj.* serious, earnest. **sul s.,** earnestly.
sermone, *n.m.* sermon.
sèrpe, *n.m.* snake.
serpènte, *n.m.* serpent.
sèrra, *n.f.* greenhouse, hothouse.
serràglio, *n.m.* menagerie.
serranda, *n.f.* shutter, gate.
serrata, *n.f.* lockout.
serrato, *adj.* locked; compact; quick.
serratura, *n.f.* lock.
servile, *adj.* servile, menial, subservient.
servitù, *n.f.* servitude, bondage; servants.
serviziévole, *adj.* helpful, obliging.
servìzio, *n.m.* service; employ.
sèrvo, *n.m.* servant.
servosterzo, *n.m.* power steering.
sessanta, *num.* sixty.
sessantésimo, *adj.* sixtieth.
sessione, *n.f.* session.
sessismo, *n.m.* sexism.
sessista, *adj.* sexist.
sèsso, *n.m.* sex.
sessuale, *adj.* sexual.
sèsto, *adj.* sixth.
seta, *n.f.* silk.
setàceo, *adj.* silken.
sete, *n.f.* thirsty.
sétola, *n.f.* bristle.
setoloso, *adj.* bristly.
sètta, *n.f.* sect, denomination.
settanta, *num.* seventy.
settantésimo, *adj.* seventieth.
sètte, *num.* seven.
settèmbre, *n.m.* September.
settentrionale, *adj.* northern.
settimana, *n.f.* week.
settimanale, *n.m. and adj.* weekly.
sèttimo, *adj.* seventh.
severità, *n.f.* severity.

severo, *adj.* severe, dour, stern, strict.

seviziare, *vb.* torture, torment.

sezionale, *adj.* sectional.

sezione, *n.f.* section.

sfaccendato, *n.m.* loafer.

sfacelo, *n.m.* breakdown, ruin, debacle.

sfamare, *vb.* feed, nourish; *(refl.)* feed.

sfarzo, *n.m.* pomp, ostentation; magnificence, luxury.

sfarzoso, *adj.* magnificent, gorgeous.

sfavore, *n.m.* disfavor, disgrace.

sfavorevole, *adj.* unfavorable.

sfèra, *n.f.* sphere.

sferza, *n.f.* whip, scourge, lash.

sferzare, *vb.* lash, whip, scourge.

sfida, *n.f.* challenge, dare, defiance.

sfidante, *n.m.* defier, challenger.

sfidare, *vb.* defy, challenge, dare.

sfiducia, *n.f.* distrust.

sfilare, *vb.* defile; file off.

sfinito, *adj.* tired out; jaded.

sfiorare, *vb.* touch lightly, brush against, dab at, skim.

sfitto, *adj.* untenanted.

sfociare, *vb.* flow; lead to.

sfogare, *vb.* vent.

sfogo, *n.m.* expression; outlet; scope; vent.

sfondo, *n.m.* background.

sfortuna, *n.f.* misfortune, bad luck.

sfortunato, *adj.* unfortunate.

sforzare, *vb.* strain.

sforzarsi, *vb.* make an effort, endeavor, strive.

sforzo, *n.m.* effort, endeavor, exertion; stress.

sfottere, *vb.* tease, harass.

sfracellare, *vb.* smash, crash.

sfregiare, *vb.* deface.

sfrontatezza, *n.f.* effrontery.

sfruttamento, *n.m.* exploitation.

sfruttare, *vb.* exploit.

sfuggire, *vb.* escape.

sfumatura, *n.f.* nuance.

sgabello, *n.m.* stool; footstool.

sgarbería, *n.f.* indignity.

sgargiante, *adj.* flamboyant, garish.

sghignazzare, *vb.* guffaw.

sghignazzata, *n.f.* guffaw.

sgomberare, *vb.* clear.

sgombro, *n.m.* mackerel.

sgonfiare, *vb.* deflate.

sgòrbio, *n.m.* blotch; daub; scrawl.

sgorgare, *vb.* empty, disgorge; gush, well forth.

sgradévole, *adj.* disagreeable.

sgranocchiare, *vb.* munch.

sgravare, *vb.* relieve, ease; lessen.

sgraziato, *adj.* graceless.

sgretolare, *vb.* crumble.

sgridare, *vb.* scold, bawl out, berate, chide.

sguardo, *n.m.* look, glance.

sguattero, *n.m.* servant, busboy.

si, *pron.* himself; herself; itself; themselves; yourself; yourselves.

sì, *interj.* yes.

sia, *conj.* either; or.

sibilare, *vb.* hiss.

sibilo, *n.m.* hiss.

sicario, *n.m.* hired killer.

siccità, *n.f.* dryness, drought.

Sicilia, *n.f.* Sicily.

siciliano, *adj.* Sicilian.

sicura, *n.f.* safety lock.

sicuramente, *adv.* surely; securely; assuredly.

sicurezza, *n.f.* safety, security, surety.

sicuro, *adj.* sure; secure; assured; safe.

sidro, *n.m.* cider.

sièpe, *n.f.* hedge.

sièro, *n.m.* buttermilk; whey; serum.

sifilide, *n.f.* syphilis.

sifilitico, *adj.* syphilitic.

sifone, *n.m.* syphon.

Sig., *n.m.* (abbr. for Signore) Mr.

sigaretta, *n.f.* cigarette.

sigaro, *n.m.* cigar.

sigillare, *vb.* seal.

sigillo, *n.m.* seal; cachet.

significare, *vb.* signify, mean, betoken, purport.

significativo, *adj.* significant.

significato, *n.m.* significance, meaning, import, purport.

signora, *n.f.* lady; Mrs.; madam.

signore, *n.f.pl.* (on toilets) ladies.

signore, *n.m.* gentleman; lord; Mr.; sir.

signorìa, *n.f.* lordship.

silenziatore, *n.m.* silencer, muffler.

silènzio, *n.m.* silence.

silenzioso, *adj.* silent, quiet, noiseless.

sìllaba, *n.f.* syllable.

silo, *n.m.* silo.

silòfono, *n.m.* xylophone.

silurare, *vb.* undermine.

siluro, *n.m.* torpedo.

silvicultore, *n.m.* forester.

silvicultura, *n.f.* forestry.

simbòlico, *adj.* symbolic.

sìmbolo, *n.m.* symbol.

similcuòio, *n.m.* artificial leather.

sìmile, *adj.* similar, alike, like.

similmente, *adv.* similarly, alike, likewise.

simmetrìa, *n.f.* symmetry.

simpatìa, *n.f.* sympathy.

simpàtico, *adj.* likeable, aggreable, pleasant, congenial.

simpatizzare, *vb.* sympathize.

simpòsio, *n.m.* symposium.

simulare, *vb.* simulate.

simultàneo, *adj.* simultaneous.

sinagoga, *n.f.* synagogue.

sinceramente, *adv.* sincerely.

sincerità, *n.f.* sincerity.

sincèro, *adj.* sincere, heartfelt.

sincronizzare, *vb.* synchronize.

sìncrono, *adj.* synchronous.

sindacato, *n.m.* union.

sìndaco, *n.m.* mayor.

sìndrome, *n.f.* syndrome.

sinfonìa, *n.f.* symphony; overture.

sinfònico, *adj.* symphonic.

singhiozzare, *vb.* sob.

singhiozzo, *n.m.* sob.

singolare, *adj.* singular.

sìngolo, *adj.* single; unique.

singulto, *n.m.* hiccup.

sinistra, *n.f.* left.

sinistro, 1. *n.m.* accident. **2.** *n.m.* left; sinister.

sinistròrso, *adj. and adv.* counterclockwise.

sino, *prep.* as far as, up to, till. **s. da,** since.

sinònimo, 1. *n.m.* synonym. **2.** *adj.* synonymous.

sintassi, *n.f.* syntax.

sìntesi, *n.f.* synthesis.

sintètico, *adj.* synthetic.

sìntomo, *n.m.* symptom.

sintonìa, *n.f.* harmony, accord; tuning (radio).

sintonizzare, *vb.* tune in.

sinuoso, *adj.* sinuous.

sipàrio, *n.m.* curtain.

sirèna, *n.f.* siren; mermaid.

siringa, *n.f.* syringe.

sisma, *n.m.* earthquake.

sistèma, *n.m.* system.

sistemare, *vb.* put in order, arrange, settle, fix up.

sistemàtico, *adj.* systematic.

sistemazione, *n.f.* arrangement; settlement; solution.

sito, *n.m.* site.

situare, *vb.* situate.

situazione, *n.f.* situation, location.

slacciare, *vb.* unlace, untie, unfasten, unbutton, undo.

slanciarsi, *vb.* rush, dash.

slancio, *n.m.* rush, dash; impetus; élan.

slavo, *adj.* Slavic.

sleale, *adj.* disloyal.

slealtà, *n.f.* disloyalty.

slitta, *n.f.* sleigh, sled.

slittamento, *n.m.* skid.

slittare, *vb.* slide, skid.

slogare, *vb.* dislocate.

sloggiare, *vb.* dislodge.

smacchiatore, *n.m.* stain remover.

smagliante, *adj.* bright, dazzling, resplendent.

smagliatura, *n.f.* run (in stockings); imperfection; stretch mark.

smagrire, *vb.* become thin or lean, lose weight.

smaltare, *vb.* enamel, glaze.

smalto, *n.m.* enamel, glaze.

smantellare, *vb.* dismantle.

smarrire, *vb.* mislay, misplace, lose.

smarrito, *adj.* stray.

smascherare, *vb.* unmask.

smembrare, *vb.* dismember.

smemorato, *adj.* forgetful, absent-minded.

smentire, *vb.* give the lie to, belie.

smeraldo, *n.m.* emerald.

smeriglio, *n.m.* emery.

sméttere, *vb.* stop, quit.

smilitarizzare, *vb.* demilitarize.

smilzo, *adj.* gangling.
smobilitare, *vb.* demobilize.
smobilitazione, *n.f.* demobilization.
smontare, *vb.* dismount, alight, disassemble.
smòrfia, *n.f.* grimace.
smorzare, *vb.* attenuate, extinguish; diminish, lessen; tone down, taper.
snaturare, *vb.* denaturalize.
snervamento, *n.m.* enervation.
snervare, *vb.* enervate.
sobbalzare, *vb.* jounce, jolt; throb.
sobbalzo, *n.m.* jounce, jolt.
sobborgo, *n.m.* suburb, *(pl.)* outskirts.
sòbrio, *adj.* sober, somber.
socchiuso, *adj.* half-closed, ajar.
soccómbere, *vb.* succumb.
soccórrere, *vb.* succor, relieve.
soccorso, *n.m.* succor, relief.
sociale, *adj.* social.
socialismo, *n.m.* socialism.
socialista, *n. and adj.* socialist.
società, *n.f.* society; company. **S. delle Nazioni,** League of Nations.
sociévole, *adj.* sociable, companionable.
sòcio, *n.m.* member; fellow; partner.
sociologìa, *n.f.* sociology.
sòda, *n.f.* soda.
soddisfacènte, *adj.* satisfactory.
soddisfare, *vb.* satisfy.
soddisfazione, *n.f.* satisfaction.
sòdio, *n.m.* sodium.
sòdo, *adj.* hard-boiled.
sofà, *n.m.* sofa.
sofaletto, *n.m.* davenport.
soffiare, *vb.* blow.
soffietto, *n.m.* bellows.
soffitta, *n.f.* attic, garret.
soffitto, *n.m.* ceiling.
soffocare, *vb.* suffocate, choke, smother, stifle.
soffrigere, *vb.* sauté, fry lightly.
soffrire, *vb.* suffer, tolerate, put up with.
sofisma, *n.m.* chicanery.
sofisticato, *adj.* sophisticated.
soggètto, 1. *n.m.* subject. **2.** *adj.* subject, liable.

soggezione, *n.f.* awe; uneasiness.
sogghignare, *vb.* sneer.
sogghigno, *n.m.* sneer.
soggiogare, *vb.* subjugate, subdue.
soggiornare, *vb.* sojourn, stay.
soggiorno, *n.m.* sojourn, stay.
sòglia, *n.f.* doorsill; threshhold, entrance.
sògliola, *n.f.* sole.
sognare, *vb.* dream.
sognatore, *n.m.* dreamer.
sogno, *n.m.* dream.
sòia, *n.f.* soy.
solaio, *n.m.* loft.
solamente, *vb.* only, alone.
solare, *adj.* solar.
solatìo, *adj.* sunny.
solcare, *vb.* furrow, groove; plow.
solco, *n.m.* furrow; groove; rut.
soldato, *n.m.* soldier. **s. sémplice,** private.
sòldo, *n.m.* penny.
sole, *n.m.* sun; sunshine.
solènne, *adj.* solemn.
solennità, *n.f.* solemnity.
solere, *vb.* be in the habit of, be accustomed to.
solerte, *adj.* diligent, zealous, industrious.
solidarietà, *n.f.* solidarity.
solidificare, *vb.* solidify.
solidità, *n.f.* solidity.
sòlido, *n.m. and adj.* solid.
solista, *n.m. or f.* soloist.
solitàrio, *adj.* solitary, lone, lonely, lonesome.
sòlito, *adj.* usual, habitual, accustomed.
solitùdine, *n.f.* solitude, privacy.
sollazzo, *n.m.* amusement, pastime.
sollecitare, *vb.* solicit; urge.
sollecitazione, *n.f.* urging, solicitation.
sollécito, *adj.* solicitous.
solleticare, *vb.* ticklish.
sollevamento, *n.m.* lifting, raising.
sollevare, *vb.* raise, lift, heave; relieve, ease.
sollevazione, *n.f.* uprising.
sollièvo, *n.m.* relief.
solo, *adj.* alone, sole, only, single.
soltanto, *adv.* only.
solùbile, *adj.* soluble.

soluzione, n.f. solution.
solvènte, n.m. and adj. solvent.
sòmaro, n.m. donkey.
somiglianza, n.f. likeness, similarity.
somma, n.f. sum, amount, quantity.
sommare, vb. sum up, add.
sommàrio, n.m. and adj. summary.
sommèrgere, vb. submerge.
sommergìbile, n.m. submarine.
sommesso, adj. subdued, submissive.
sommità, n.f. summit, top.
sondare, vb. probe; sound.
sonnecchiare, vb. doze, nap, drowse.
sonnellino, n.m. nap, doze.
sonno, n.m. sleep, slumber.
sonnolènto, adj. somnolent, drowsy, sleepy.
sonnolènza, n.f. somnolence, drowsiness.
sontuoso, adj. sumptuous.
sopire, vb. appease, pacify; make drowsy.
sopore, n.m. drowsiness, stupor.
soporìfero, adj. soporific, sedative.
soppiantare, vb. supplant, supersede.
soppiatto, adj. di s., stealthily.
sopportàbile, adj. bearable.
sopportare, vb. support, bear; abide, endure.
sopportazione, n.f. endurance.
soppressione, n.f. suppression.
sopprìmere, vb. suppress, put down, quell.
sopra, adv. and prep. over, above; upon.
sopràbito, n.m. overcoat, topcoat.
sopraccìglio, n.m. eyebrow.
sopraffare, vb. overcome, overwhelm.
sopraindicato, adj. aforementioned.
soprammòbile, n.m. knicknack.
soprannaturale, adj. supernatural.
soprannome, n.m. nickname.
soprappensiero, adv. absent minded, distracted.

sopratutto, adv. above all.
sopravvivènza, n.f. survival.
sopravvivère, vb. survive, outlive.
sorbetto, n.m. sherry.
sórcio, n.m. mouse.
sòrdido, adj. sordid.
sordità, n.f. deafness.
sordo, adj. deaf.
sordomuto, n.m. deaf-mute.
sorèlla, n.f. sister.
sorellastra, n.f. stepsister.
sorgènte, n.f. source; spring; headwater(s).
sórgere, vb. rise, spring.
sormontare, vb. surmount.
sornione, adj. sneaky, cunning, sly.
sorpassare, vb. pass; surpass; cross over.
sorpasso, n.m. passing.
sorprèndere, vb. surprise.
sorpresa, n.f. surprise, astonishment.
sorrèggere, vb. sustain, support.
sorrìdere, vb. smile.
sorriso, n.m. smile.
sorsata, n.f. sip; gulp down.
sorseggiare, vb. sip.
sorso, n.m. swallow; sip.
sòrta, n.f. sort.
sòrte, n.f. luck; lot.
sortèggio, n.m. drawing.
sortilègio, n.m. sorcery magic; spell.
sorveglianza, n.f. surveillance, supervision.
sorvegliare, vb. oversee, supervise.
sorvolare, vb. flyover.
sòsia, adj. look alike.
sospèndere, vb. suspend, discontinue.
sospensione, n.f. suspension; abeyance; stay.
sospettare, vb. suspect.
sospètto, 1. n.m. suspicion, hunch. **2.** adj. suspicious, suspect.
sospettosamente, adv. suspiciously, askance.
sospettoso, adj. suspicious, distrustful.
sospìngere, vb. push, drive.
sospirare, vb. sigh.
sospiro, n.m. sigh.

sòsta, *n.f.* stopping.
sostantìvo, *n.m.* noun.
sostanza, *n.f.* substance.
sostanziale, *adj.* substantial.
sostare, *vb.* stop.
sostegno, *n.m.* backing, support; foothold.
sostenere, *vb.* uphold, sustain; maintain; support, back (up).
sostenitore, *n.m.* upholder, backer, sponsor.
sostituire, *vb.* substitute, replace.
sostituto, *n.m.* substitute, alternate.
sostrato, *n.m.* substratum.
sostituzione, *n.f.* substitution.
sottana, *n.f.* petticoat; skirt.
sotterfùgio, *n.m.* subterfuge.
sotterràneo, *adj.* underground.
sottile, *adj.* subtle; thin, slim.
sotto, *adv. and prep.* under, underneath, below, beneath.
sottolineare, *vb.* underline.
sottomarino, *adj.* submarine.
sottométtere, *vb.* submit.
sottomissione, *n.f.* submission.
sottopassàggio, *n.m.* underpass.
sottoporre, *vb.* subject.
sottoposto, 1. *adj.* subject to. 2. *n.m.* subordinate.
sottoprodotto, *n.m.* by-product.
sottoscritto, *adj.* undersigned.
sottoscrìvere, *vb.* subscribe; sign.
sottosopra, *adv.* upside down, topsy-turvy.
sottotenènte, *n.m.* second lieutenant.
sottovalutare, *vb.* underestimate.
sottovènto, 1. *n.m.* lee. 2. *adv.* leeward.
sottovèste, *n.f.* slip; *(pl.)* underwear.
sottrarre, *vb.* subtract, deduct; *(refl.)* get out of, shirk.
sottufficiale, *n.m.* non-commissioned officer.
sovente, *adv.* often.
soviètico, *adj.* soviet.
sovraccàrico, *adj.* overloaded.
sovranità, *n.f.* sovereignty.
sovrano, *n.m. and adj.* sovereign, ruler.
sovrintendènte, *n.m.* superintendent.
sovrumano, *adj.* superhuman.

sovenzionare, *vb.* subsidize.
sovvenzione, *n.f.* subvention.
sovversivo, *adj.* subversive.
sovvertire, *vb.* subvert; overthrow.
sozzo, *adj.* dirty, filthy.
spaccare, *vb.* split.
spacciare, *vb.* sell (dope), deal; pretend to be *(refl.)*.
spàccio, *n.m.* sale; shop.
spacconata, *n.f.* brag.
spada, *n.f.* sword.
spadroneggiare, *vb.* act as if one owned the place; be bossy, domineer.
spaghetti, *n.m.pl.* spaghetti.
Spagna, *n.f.* Spain.
spagnuòlo, 1. *n.m.* Spaniard. 2. *adj.* Spanish.
spago, *n.m.* twine.
spalancare, *vb.* open wide.
spalla, *n.f.* shoulder.
spalleggiare, *vb.* back (up).
spalmare, *vb.* smear.
spanna, *n.f.* span.
sparare, *vb.* fire, shoot.
spàrgere, *vb.* scatter.
sparire, *vb.* disappear.
sparlare, *vb.* speak ill.
sparo, *n.m.* shot.
sparpagliare, *vb.* scatter, disseminate.
sparuto, *adj.* haggard.
spasimare, *vb.* long for; suffer; writhe.
spàsimo, *n.m.* spasm, pang.
spasmòdico, *adj.* spasmodic.
spassionato, *adj.* dispassionate.
spassoso, *adj.* amusing, funny.
spauràcchio, *n.m.* scarecrow.
spavaldo, *adj.* bold, audacious.
spaventare, *vb.* frighten, alarm, appal, scare.
spavènto, *n.m.* fright, scare.
spaventoso, *adj.* fearful, frightful.
spàzio, *n.m.* space.
spazioso, *adj.* spacious, capacious; roomy, commodious.
spazzacamino, *n.m.* chimneysweep.
spazzamine, *n.m.* nave s., minesweeper.
spazzaneve, *n.m.* snowplow.
spazzare, *vb.* sweep.

spazzatura, *n.f.* sweepings, dust.
spazzino, *n.m.* street-cleaner; scavenger.
spàzzola, *n.f.* brush.
spazzolare, *vb.* brush.
spècchio, *n.m.* mirror, looking-glass.
speciale, *adj.* special, especial.
specialista, *n.m.* specialist.
specialità, *n.f.* specialty.
specialmente, *adv.* specially, especially.
spècie, *n.f.* species.
specificare, *vb.* specify.
specifico, *adj.* specific.
speculare, *vb.* speculate.
speculazione, *n.f.* speculation.
spedire, *vb.* send, despatch, ship; remit.
speditore, *n.m.* sender, shipper, dispatcher.
spedizione, *n.f.* expedition; despatch; shipment; remittance.
spedizionière, *n.m.* shipping agent.
spègnere, *vb.* put out; douse; switch off.
spellare, *vb.* skin, flay.
spèndere, *vb.* spend; expend.
spennare, *vb.* pluck.
spennellare, *vb.* dab, smear.
spensieratamente, *adv.* thoughtlessly, heedlessly, carelessly.
spensieratezza, *n.f.* thoughtlessness, heedlessness, carelessness.
spensierato, *adj.* thoughtless, heedless, careless, happy-go-lucky.
speranza, *n.f.* hope.
sperare, *vb.* hope.
spergiurare, *vb.* perjure oneself.
spergiuro, *n.m.* perjury.
sperimentale, *adj.* experimental; tentative.
sperimentare, *vb.* experiment.
speróne, *n.m.* spur.
spesa, *n.f.* expense, expenditure.
spesso, **1.** *adj.* thick. **2.** *adv.* often.
spessore, *n.m.* thickness.
spettacolare, *adj.* spectacular.
spettàcolo, *n.m.* spectacle, show.
spettatore, *n.m.* spectator, onlooker, bystander.
spettegolare, *vb.* gossip.
spettinare, *vb.* muss (hair).

spettinato, *adj.* uncombed, ungroomed.
spèttro, *n.m.* specter, ghost; spectrum.
spèzie, *n.f.pl.* spice.
spezzare, *vb.* break, fracture.
spezzatino, *n.m.* stew.
spiacciare, *vb.* squash.
spiacévole, *adj.* unpleasant.
spiàggia, *n.f.* beach, shore.
spia, *n.f.* spy.
spiano, *n.m.* levelling, smoothing. **a tutto s.,** at full blast; profusely.
spiare, *vb.* spy.
spiccàgnolo, *adj.* freestone.
spidocchiare, *vb.* delouse.
spiedino, *n.m.* skewer, kebab.
spiedo, *n.m.* spit, skewer. **allo s.,** barbecued.
spiegare, *vb.* explain; spread; unfold; unfurl.
spiegazione, *n.f.* explanation.
spiegazzare, *vb.* crinkle, crease, crumple.
spietato, *adj.* pitiless, merciless, ruthless.
spiga, *n.f.* ear (of grain).
spilla, *n.f.* brooch.
spillo, *n.m.* pin. **s. di sicurezza,** safety-pin.
spina, *n.f.* thorn; spine; (electric) plug. **s. dorsale,** backbone.
spinaci, *n.m.pl.* spinach.
spinetta, *n.f.* spinet.
spìngere, *vb.* push, jostle, shove; thrust; urge.
spinta, *n.f.* push, shove; thrust.
spionàggio, *n.m.* espionage.
spione, *n.m.* spy.
spira, *n.f.* spire, coil.
spiràglio, *n.m.* opening, aperture.
spirale, *n.m. and adj.* spiral.
spiritismo, *n.m.* spiritualism.
spirito, *n.m.* spirit; wit.
spiritoso, *adj.* witty.
spirituale, *adj.* spiritual.
splèndere, *vb.* shine.
splèndido, *adj.* splendid, gorgeous.
splendore, *n.m.* splendor, brilliance.
spodestare, *vb.* dispossess.
spogliare, *vb.* unclothe; divest, despoil, strip; harry.
spoletta, *n.f.* fuse.

sponda, *n.f.* shore.
spontaneità, *n.f.* spontaneity.
spontàneo, *adj.* spontaneous.
spopolare, *vb.* depopulate.
spòra, *n.f.* spore.
sporàdico, *adj.* sporadic.
sporcare, *vb.* foul, soil.
spòrco, *adj.* dirty, foul, soiled.
spòrgere, *vb.* put out; project.
sporta, *n.f.* shopping bag.
sportello, *n.m.* door; window
(bank, station, post office).
sportivo, 1. *n.* sportsman. **2.** *adj.*
sport.
sposa, *n.f.* bride, spouse.
sposalìzio, *n.m.* wedding, espousal.
sposare, *vb.* marry, espouse.
sposi, *n.m.pl.* bride and groom;
newlyweds.
sposo, *n.m.* bridegroom, spouse.
spostamento, *n.m.* displacement.
spostare, *vb.* displace.
sprecare, *vb.* waste.
sprèco, *n.m.* waste.
spregévole, *adj.* contemptible,
despicable, mean.
spregiare, *vb.* despise.
sprègio, *n.m.* scorn, contempt,
disdain.
spregiudicato, *adj.* broadminded.
sprèmere, *vb.* squeeze.
spremuta, *n.f.* squash.
sprezzante, *adj.* contemptuous,
despising, scornful.
sprezzantemente, *adv.* contemptuously.
sprezzo, *n.m.* disdain.
sprigionare, *vb.* release.
sprizzare, *vb.* spray.
sprofondarsi, *vb.* subside; sink.
sprolòquio, long, rambling
speech.
spronare, *vb.* spur.
sprone, *n.m.* spur.
sproporzionato, *adj.* disproportionate.
sproporzione, *n.f.* disproportion.
spropòsito, *n.m.* mistaken, slip. **a
s.** *adv.* out of place.
spruzzare, *vb.* spout; spurt;
splash; spatter.
spruzzo, *n.m.* splash, spatter.

spudorato, *adj.* shameless, brazen.
spugna, *n.f.* sponge.
spugnoso, *adj.* spongy.
spuma, *n.f.* foam, froth.
spuntare, *vb.* appear; dawn.
spuntino, *n.m.* snack.
spùrio, *adj.* spurious.
sputacchièra, *n.f.* spittoon, cuspidor.
sputare, *vb.* spit.
squadra, *n.f.* squad, gang; team.
squadrone, *n.m.* squadron.
squalìfica, *n.f.* disqualification.
squalificare, *vb.* disqualify.
squàllido, *adj.* squalid, bleak.
squallore, *n.m.* squalor, bleakness.
squama, *n.f.* scale.
squarciare, *vb.* gash, slash.
squàrcio, *n.m.* gash, slash.
squillare, *vb.* blare.
squillo, *n.m.* blare.
squisitezza, *n.f.* exquisiteness,
daintiness, delicacy.
squisito, *adj.* exquisite, dainty,
delicate.
Sra., *n.f.* (abbr. for Signora) Mrs.
sradicare, *vb.* eradicate; uproot.
sradicatore, *n.m.* eradicator.
sregolatezza, *n.f.* dissipation, de-
bauchery.
stàbile, *adj.* stable.
stabilimento, *n.m.* establishment.
stabilire, *vb.* establish; set; appoint; settle.
stabilità, *n.f.* stability.
stabilizzare, *vb.* stabilize.
staccare, *vb.* detach, sever.
stacciare, *vb.* sift.
stàccio, *n.m.* sieve.
stàdio, *n.m.* stadium; stage.
staffétta, *n.f.* courier; relay race.
staffière, *n.m.* footman; groom.
staffilata, *n.f.* lash, whip.
stagione, *n.f.* season.
stagliare, *vb.* mangle; (*refl.*)
stand out.
stagnante, *adj.* stagnant.
stagnare, *vb.* stagnate.
stagnino, *n.m.* tinsmith; plumber.
stagno, *n.m.* pond; pool; tin.
stalla, *n.f.* stable.
stallo, *n.m.* stall.
stallone, *n.m.* stallion.

stame, *n.m.* stamen.

stamigna, *n.f.* bunting.

stampa, *n.f.* press; printing.

stampare, *vb.* print.

stampatello, *n.m.* block letters.

stampèlla, *n.f.* crutch.

stampino, *n.m.* stencil.

stampo, *n.m.* stamp; mold; die.

stancare, *vb.* tire.

stanco, *adj.* tired, fagged, weary.

standardizzare, *vb.* standardize.

stanga, *n.f.* shaft.

stangata, *n.f.* blow, strike.

stanghetta, *n.f.* hang-over.

stantuffo, *n.m.* piston.

stanza, *n.f.* room. **s. da bagno,** bathroom. **s. da lètto,** bedroom.

stanziamento, *n.m.* appropriation.

stanziare, *vb.* appropriate.

stappare, *vb.* uncork.

stare, *vb.* stand; be.

starnutire, *vb.* sneeze.

starnuto, *n.m.* sneeze.

stasera, *adv.* tonight.

stasi, *n.f.* standstill, stasis.

stàtico, *adj.* static.

statìstica, *n.f.* statistics.

stato, *n.m.* state; estate.

stàtua, *n.f.* statue.

statura, *n.f.* stature.

statuto, *n.m.* statute.

stazionàrio, *adj.* stationary.

stazione, *n.f.* station; resort. **s. balneare,** bathing resort.

stecca, *n.f.* stick; cue; slat; splint.

stella, *n.f.* star.

stellare, *adj.* stellar.

stelo, *n.m.* stem.

stèmma, *n.m.* coat of arms.

stèndere, *vb.* extend; spread; draw up; *(refl.)* span.

stenògrafa, *n.f.* stenographer.

stenografìa, *n.f.* stenography, shorthand.

stentatamente, *adv.* with difficulty.

stento, *n.m.* hardship, difficulty; privation. **a s.,** hardly.

stèrco, *n.m.* dung.

stereofònico, *adj.* stereophonic.

stereotipìa, *n.f.* stereotype.

stèrile, *adj.* sterile, barren.

sterilità, *n.f.* sterility, barrenness.

sterilizzare, *vb.* sterilize.

sterlina, *n.f.* pound sterling.

sterminare, *vb.* exterminate.

stermìnio, *n.m.* extermination.

sterno, *n.m.* breastbone, sternum.

sterzata, *n.f.* swerve, veer.

sterzo, *n.m.* steering wheel.

stesso, *adj.* same; self.

stetoscòpio, *n.m.* stethoscope.

stìa, *n.f.* hen-coop.

stigma, *n.m.* stigma.

stile, *n.m.* style.

stiletto, *n.m.* dagger.

stillare, *vb.* ooze, exude, drip.

stima, *n.f.* esteem, estimate, appraisal.

stimàbile, *adj.* estimable.

stimare, *vb.* esteem, estimate, appraise, deem, value.

stìmmate, *n.f.pl.* stigmata.

stimolante, *n.m.* and *adj.* stimulant.

stimolare, *vb.* stimulate, goad.

stìmolo, *n.m.* stimulus, goad.

stinco, *n.m.* shin.

stìngere, *vb.* discolor, fade.

stipèndio, *n.m.* salary.

stipettaio, *n.m.* cabinetmaker.

stìpite, *n.m.* jamb.

stipo, *n.m.* cabinet.

stipulare, *vb.* stipulate.

stirare, *vb.* iron.

stirpe, *f.* lineage; stock.

stitichezza, *n.f.* constipation.

stìtico, *adj.* constipated.

stiva, *n.f.* hold (of boat).

stivale, *n.m.* boot.

stivare, *vb.* stow.

stivatore, *n.m.* stevedore.

stizza, *n.f.* upset, annoyance, anger.

stizzoso, *adj.* peevish.

Stoccarda, *n.f.* Stuttgart.

Stoccolma, *n.f.* Stockholm.

stòffa, *n.f.* cloth, stuff, material, fabric.

stòico, 1. *n.* stoic, **2.** *adj.* stoical.

stòla, *n.f.* stole.

stòlido, *adj.* stolid.

stolto, 1. *n.m.* fool, dunce. **2.** *adj.* foolish.

stomachévole, *adj.* sickening.

stòmaco, *n.m.* stomach.

stòrcere, *vb.* sprain.

stordimento, *n.m.* dizziness.

stordire, *vb.* stun.

stordito, *adj.* stunned, dizzy.
stòria, *n.f.* history; story, yarn.
stòrico, 1. *n.* historian. **2.** *adj.* historic, historical.
storione, *n.m.* sturgeon.
stormo, *n.m.* swarm, flock.
stornare, *vb.* turn away; divert.
storpiare, *vb.* maim.
stòrta, *n.f.* sprain.
stòrto, *adj.* crooked.
stovìglie, *n.f.pl.* earthenware, pottery.
stra-, *prefix,* extra-.
stràbico, *adj.* cross-eyed.
stràccio, *n.m.* rag; clout.
straccione, *n.m.* ragamuffin.
stracotto, *adj.* overcooked; stew.
strada, *n.f.* road, street. **s. maestra,** highway.
stradale, *adj.* pertaining to roads.
strafalcione, *n.m* blunder, blooper.
strafare, *vb.* overdo.
strafottènte, *adj.* inconsiderate.
strale, *n.m.* arrow; shaft.
stralunato, *adj.* upset; wild-eyed; troubled.
stranezza, *n.f.* strangeness, oddity.
strangolare, *vb.* strangle, choke.
straniero, 1. *n.* stranger; foreigner. **2.** *adj.* strange; foreign.
strano, *adj.* strange, odd, peculiar, queer, quaint, weird.
straordinàrio, *adj.* extraordinary; extra.
strappare, *vb.* tear, rip, rend; snatch, wrench.
strapazzate, *adj.* **uòva s.,** scrambled eggs.
straripare, *vb.* overflow.
stratagèmma, *n.m.* stratagem.
strategìa, *n.f.* strategy.
stratègico, *adj.* strategic.
strato, *n.m.* stratum, layer; coating.
stratosfèra, *n.f.* stratosphere.
strattone, *n.m.* jerk.
stravagante, *adj.* extravagant.
stravaganza, *n.f.* extravagance.
straziante, *adj.* heart-rending.
straziato, *adj.* heartbroken.
strega, *n.f.* witch, hag.
stregare, *vb.* bewitch.
stregone, *n.m.* wizard.

stregonerìa, *n.f.* sorcery.
strènuo, *adj.* strenuous.
streptocòcco, *n.m.* streptococcus.
stretta, *n.f.* clasp; squeeze. **s. di mano,** hand-shake.
stretto, 1. *n.m.* strait. **2.** *adj.* narrow, tight.
strìa, *n.f.* streak.
stridore, *n.m.* shriek; squeak.
strìdulo, *adj.* shrill, strident.
strigliare, *vb.* curry.
strillare, *vb.* scream, shriek.
strillo, *n.m.* scream, shriek.
striminzito, *adj.* small; shrunken; skinny.
strinare, *vb.* singe.
strìngere, *vb.* hold tight; clasp; clench; squeeze; press; tighten. **s. la mano a,** shake hands with.
strìscia, *n.f.* strip; stripe; band; slip.
strisciare, *vb.* creep.
striscione, *n.m.* banner, festoon.
stritolare, *vb.* crush, mash.
strofinàccio, *n.m.* wiper; dustcloth; dishcloth.
strofinare, *vb.* rub; wipe.
stroncare, *vb.* break down; repress; slash.
strozzare, *vb.* strangle.
strozzino, *n.m.* loan shark.
strumentale, *adj.* instrumental.
strumento, *n.m.* instrument; implement.
strutto, *n.m.* lard.
struttura, *n.f.* structure.
struzzo, *n.m.* ostrich.
stucco, *n.m.* stucco.
studènte, *n.m.* student.
studentessa, *n.f.* student.
studiare, *vb.* study.
stùdio, *n.m.* study; studio.
studioso, *adj.* studious.
stufa, *n.f.* stove.
stufare, *vb.* stew.
stufato, *n.m.* stew.
stufo, *adj.* fed up, sick and tired.
stuòia, *n.f.* mat.
stuoìno, *n.m.* door-mat.
stuòlo, *n.m.* group, throng, crowd; company.
stupèndo, *adj.* stupendous.
stupidità, *n.f.* stupidity, dumbness, backwardness.

stùpido, *adj.* stupid, dumb, backward.

stupire, *vb.* amaze, astonish, astound, surprise, daze.

stupirsi, *vb.* be amazed, be astonished, be surprised.

stupore, *n.m.* daze, stupor; astonishment, amazement, wonder.

sturare, *vb.* uncork.

su, *prep. and adv.* on; upon; up.

subcosciènte, *adj.* subconscious.

subire, *vb.* undergo.

sùbito, *adv.* immediately.

sublimare, *vb.* sublimate.

sublimato, *n.m. and adj.* sublimate.

sublime, *adj.* sublime.

subnormale, *adj.* subnormal.

subodorare, *vb.* sense, suspect.

subordinato, *n.m. and adj.* subordinate.

succèdere, *vb.* succeed; happen; occur.

successione, *n.f.* succession.

successivo, *adj.* successive; subsequent.

succèsso, *n.m.* success.

successore, *n.m.* successor.

succhiare, *vb.* suck.

succhièllo, *n.m.* auger, gimlet.

succinto, *adj.* concise; scarce.

succo, *n.m.* juice.

succoso, *adj.* juicy.

succursale, *n.f.* branch.

sud, *n.m.* south. **polo s.,** South Pole.

sudare, *vb.* sweat, perspire, swelter.

sudàrio, *n.m.* shroud.

suddetto, *adj.* aforesaid.

suddividere, *vb.* subdivide.

sùddito, *n.m.* subject.

sud-èst, *n.m.* southeast.

sùdicio, *adj.* dirty, dingy, filthy, grimy.

sudiciume, *n.m.* dirt, filth, grime.

sudore, *n.m.* sweat, perspiration.

sud-òvest, *n.m.* southwest.

sufficiènte, *adj.* sufficient, adequate, enough.

sufficientemente, *adv.* sufficiently, adequately.

sufficiènza, *n.f.* sufficiency, adequacy.

suffisso, *n.m.* suffix.

suffragare, *vb.* substantiate, corroborate.

suffràgio, *suffrage.*

suggellare, *vb.* seal.

suggèllo, *n.m.* seal.

suggerimento, *n.m.* suggestion.

suggerire, *vb.* suggest.

suggeritore, *n.m.* prompter.

sùghero, *n.m.* cork.

sugo, *n.m.* sauce. **s. di carne,** gravy.

sugoso, *adj.* juicy.

suicidarsi, *vb.* commit suicide.

suicìdio, *n.m.* suicide.

suindicato, *adj.* aforementioned.

suino, **1.** *n.m.* swine. **2.** *adj.* of pork, swinish.

sultanina, *adj.* uva s., sultana raisin.

sunto, *n.m.* abstract, résumé.

suo, *adj.* his; her; hers; its; your; yours.

suòcera, *n.f.* mother-in-law.

suòcero, *n.m.* father-in-law.

suòla, *n.f.* sole.

suòlo, *n.m.* soil.

suonare, *vb.* sound; ring; play.

suonatore, *n.m.* player.

suòno, *n.m.* sound; ring.

suòra, *n.f.* nun, sister.

superare, *vb.* overcome; surpass, exceed; excel; top; pass (exam.).

supèrbia, *n.f.* haughtiness, pride.

supèrbo, *adj.* haughty, proud; superb.

superficiale, *adj.* superficial.

superficie, *n.f.* surface.

supèrfluo, *adj.* superfluous.

superiore, *adj.* superior; upper.

superiorità, *n.f.* superiority.

superlativo, *n.m. and adj.* superlative.

supermercato, *n.m.* supermarket.

supèrstite, **1.** *adj.* surviving. **2.** *n.m. and f.* survivor.

superstizione, *n.f.* superstition.

superstizioso, *adj.* superstitious.

superuòmo, *n.m.* superman.

supino, *adj.* supine, lying down.

supplemento, *n.m.* supplement.

sùpplica, *n.f.* supplication, entreaty.

supplicare, *vb.* supplicate, beseech, entreat.

supplichévole, *adj.* beseeching.

supplichevolmente, *adv.* beseechingly.

supplire, *vb.* replace; make up for; eke out.

supplízio, *n.m.* torture, torment, agony.

supporre, *vb.* suppose.

supposizione, *n.f.* supposition, assumption.

suppurare, *vb.* suppurate, fester.

supremazia, *n.f.* supremacy, ascendancy.

suprèmo, *adj.* supreme, paramount.

surclassare, *vb.* outclass.

surgelamento, *n.m.* deep freeze.

surrenale, *adj.* adrenal.

surriscaldare, *vb.* overheat.

surrogato, *n.m.* surrogate, substitute; makeshift.

susina, *n.f.* plum.

susino, *n.m.* plum-tree.

sussidiare, *vb.* subsidize.

sussidio, *n.m.* subsidy.

sussultare, *vb.* start.

sussulto, *n.m.* start.

svaligiare, *vb.* rob completely.

svalutare, *vb.* devalue.

svanire, *vb.* vanish.

svantàggio, *n.m.* disadvantage, drawback, handicap.

svariato, *adj.* varied.

svedese, 1. *n.* Swede. **2.** *adj.* Swedish.

svegliare, *vb.* awaken, wake up, arouse; *(refl.)* awake.

svéglio, *adj.* awake.

svelto, *adj.* quick; slender.

svenimento, *n.m.* faint, swoon.

svenire, *vb.* faint, swoon.

sventolare, *vb.* wave; fan.

sventura, *n.f.* misfortune, bad luck.

sventurato, *adj.* unfortunate, unlucky, miserable.

svergognato, *adj.* shameless, impudent.

svernare, *vb.* winter; hibernate.

svestire, *vb.* undress; *(refl.)* disrobe.

Svèzia, *n.f.* Sweden.

svignàrsela, *vb. (fam.)* abscond.

sviluppare, *vb.* develop.

sviluppatore, *n.m.* developer.

sviluppo, *n.m.* development, growth.

sviscerare, *vb.* eviscerate; dissect.

svista, *n.f.* blunder.

Svizzera, *n.f.* Switzerland.

svizzero, *n. and adj.* Swiss.

svogliato, *adj.* listless.

svolazzare, *vb.* flutter.

svòlgere, *vb.* unfold; develop; occur, happen.

svòlta, *n.f.* turn.

T

tabacco, *n.m.* tobacco.

tabellone, *n.m.* (bulletin) board.

tabernàcolo, *n.m.* tabernacle.

tacca, *n.f.* nick, notch.

taccagno, *adj.* niggardly.

tacchino, *n.m.* turkey, gobbler.

tacco, *n.m.* heel.

taccuino, *n.m.* note-book.

tacere, *vb.* be quiet, keep quiet.

tachimetro, *n.m.* speedometer.

taciturno, *adj.* taciturn, silent.

tafano, *n.m.* gadfly.

tafferùglio, *n.m.* scuffle, scrap.

tàglia, *n.f.* size, measure; ransom, reward.

tagliando, *n.m.* coupon.

tagliare, *vb.* cut; carve; chop; clip; hack; hew.

tagliatèlle, *n.f.pl.* noodles.

tagliatore, *n.m.* cutter.

tàglio, *n.m.* cut.

tale, *adj.* such.

talènto, *n.m.* talent.

talloncino, *n.m.* stub, coupon.

tallone, *n.m.* heel.

talpa, *n.f.* mole.

tamburo, *n.m.* drum; drummer. **t. maggiore,** drum major.

tamponare, *vb.* tampon; hit from rear.

tana, *n.f.* burrow, den, lair.

tànghero, *n.m.* boor, cold.

tangibile, *adj.* tangible.

tantino, *n.m.* a bit, a little.

tanto, 1. *adj.* much. **2.** *adv.* very; very much, a lot.

tappare, *vb.* plug, stop up.
tappeto, *n.m.* carpet, rug.
tappezzare, *vb.* upholster.
tappezzeria, *n.f.* tapestry, hanging; wallcovering.
tappezziere, *n.m.* upholsterer.
tappo, *m.* cork, stopper, plug.
tarchiato, *adj.* squat, stocky.
tardi, *adv.* late.
tardivo, *adj.* tardy, late.
tardo, *adj.* late.
targa, *n.f.* plate.
tariffa, *n.f.* tariff; fare.
tarma, *n.f.* moth.
tarpare, *vb.* clip, cut.
tartagliare, *vb.* stutter.
tartaruga, *n.f.* turtle.
tasca, *n.f.* pocket.
tascàbile, *adj.* pocket size.
tassa, *n.f.* tax; fee. **t. di scambio,** sales tax.
tassèllo, *n.m.* dowel.
tassì, *n.m.* taxicab.
tasso, *n.m.* badger.
tastièra, *n.f.* keyboard.
tasto, *n.m.* key.
tastoni, *adv.* **andare a t.,** grope.
tatto, *n.m.* tact; feel.
tàvola, *n.f.* table; board; plank.
tavoletta, *n.f.* tablet.
tavolòzza, *n.f.* palette.
tazza, *n.f.* cup.
te, *pron.* 2. *sg.* thee; you.
tè, *n.m.* tea.
teatro, *n.m.* theater.
tèca, *n.f.* case.
tècnica, *n.f.* technique.
tècnico, *adj.* technical.
tedesco, *n.* and *adj.* German.
tediare, *vb.* bore.
tèdio, *n.m.* tedium.
tedioso, *adj.* tedious.
tegame, *n.m.* pan, casserole dish.
tégola, *n.f.* tile.
teièra, *n.f.* tea-pot.
tela, *n.f.* cloth; web. **t. cerata,** oil-cloth. **t. da fusto,** buckram.
telaio, *n.m.* loom; frame; chassis.
telefonare, *vb.* telephone.
telefonata, *n.f.* telephone call.
telèfono, *n.m.* telephone.
telegrafare, *vb.* telegraph.
telègrafo, *n.m.* telegraph.
telegramma, *n.m.* telegram.

teleschermo, *n.m.* television screen.
telescòpio, *n.m.* telescope.
telescrivènte, *n.f.* teletype.
televisione, *n.f.* television.
televisore, *n.m.* television set.
tèma, *n.m.* theme.
temerarietà, *n.f.* rashness, foolhardiness.
temeràrio, 1. *n.m.* daredevil. **2.** *adj.* rash, foolhardy.
temere, *vb.* fear, dread.
temperamento, *n.m.* temperament.
temperanza, *n.f.* temperance.
temperare, *vb.* temper.
temperato, *adj.* temperate.
temperatura, *n.f.* temperature.
temperino, *n.m.* pen-knife.
tempèsta, *n.f.* tempest, storm, gale.
tempestare, *vb.* pound, storm; harass, assail.
tempestivo, *adj.* timely, opportune.
tempestoso, *adj.* tempestuous, stormy, gusty.
tèmpia, *n.f.* temple.
tèmpio, *n.m.* temple.
tèmpo, *n.m.* time; weather.
temporàneo, *adj.* temporary.
temprare, *vb.* harden.
tenace, *adj.* tenacious, dogged.
tènda, *n.f.* tent; awning; booth.
tendènte, *adj.* tending, conducive.
tendènza, *n.f.* tendency, trend.
tèndere, *vb.* tend, conduce; stretch.
tèndine, *n.m.* tendon.
tendòpoli, *n.f.* tent city, encampment.
tènebre, *n.f.pl.* darkness.
tenebroso, *adj.* dark.
tenènte, *n.m.* lieutenant.
teneramente, *adv.* tenderly, fondly.
tenere, *vb.* hold; keep.
tenerezza, *n.f.* tenderness, fondness.
tènero, *adj.* tender, fond.
tènia, *n.f.* tapeworm.
tenore, *n.m.* tenor.
tensione, *n.f.* tension, strain, stress.

tentàcolo, n.m. tentacle.

tentare, vb. attempt, try; tempt.

tentativo, 1. n.m. attempt. **2.** adj. tentative.

tentazione, n.f. temptation.

tènue, adj. tenuous, flimsy.

teologia, n.f. theology.

teòlogo, n.m. theologian.

teorèma, n.m. theorem.

teorìa, n.f. theory.

teòrico, adj. theoretical.

tepore, n.m. warmth.

teppista, n.m. hoodlum.

terapìa, n.f. therapy.

tergicristallo, n.m. windshield-wiper.

terminale, adj. terminal.

terminare, vb. terminate, end, finish.

tèrmine, n.m. end; terminus; term; deadline; abutment.

termòmetro, n.m. thermometer.

termosifone, n.m. heating system.

tèrra, n.f. earth, ground, land.

terrazza, n.f. terrace.

terremòto, n.m. earthquake.

terreno, 1. n.m. soil, terrain; lot. **2.** adj. earthy, earthly.

terribile, adj. terrible, awful, frightful, dire, dreadful.

terribilmente, adv. terribly, awfully, dreadfully.

terriccio, n.m. loam.

terrificare, vb. horrify.

territòrio, n.m. territory.

terrore, n.m. terror, fear, awe.

terrorismo, n.m. terrorism.

terso, adj. terse, clear.

tèrzo, adj. third.

Terzo Mondo, n.m. Third World.

tesa, n.f. (hat) brim.

teso, adj. tight, taut, tense, uptight.

tesorière, n.m. treasurer.

tesòro, n.m. treasure; treasury.

tèssera, n.f. card; ticket.

tèssere, vb. weave.

tèssile, adj. textile.

tessitore, n.m. weaver.

tessitura, n.f. texture; weaving.

tessuto, n.m. tissue; textile.

tèsta, n.f. head. **t. di sbarco,** bridgehead. **tener t. a,** cope with.

testamento, n.m. testament, will.

testardo, adj. stubborn, headstrong, self-willed.

testata càrica, n.f. warhead.

testàtico, n.m. poll-tax.

testé, adv. just now, just; soon.

testimòne, n.m. witness. **t. oculare,** eyewitness.

testimonianza, n.f. testimony.

testimoniare, vb. testify.

tèsto, n.m. text.

testone, n.m. headstrong person; dolt.

testuale, adj. verbatim, precise.

tètano, n.m. tetanus, lockjaw.

tetraone, n.m. grouse.

tètto, n.m. roof.

tettòia, n.f. shed.

thè, n.m. tea.

ti, pron. 2. sg. thee; you.

tiépido, adj. tepid, lukewarm.

tifo, n.m. typhus.

tifoidèo, adj. typhoid.

tifoso, n.m. fan, enthusiast.

tìglio, n.m. lime-tree; linden.

tiglioso, adj. tough, leathery.

tigre, n.f. tiger.

timbrare, vb. stamp.

timbro, n.m. stamp.

timidamente, adv. timidly, shyly, bashfully.

timidezza, n.f. timidity, shyness, bashfulness.

tìmido, adj. timid, shy, bashful, coy; chicken-hearted; diffident.

timone, n.m. helm; rudder; (wagon) pole.

timonière, n.m. steersman, helmsman; coxswain.

timore, n.m. fear, apprehension, dread.

timoroso, adj. timorous, fearful, apprehensive.

tìmpano, n.m. ear-drum; kettledrum.

tìngere, vb. dye.

tino, n.m. vat.

tinca, n.f. tench.

tinello, n.m. pantry.

tinta, n.f. tint, shade.

tintinnare, vb. tinkle, jingle.

tintore, n.m. dyer; dry-cleaner.

tintura, n.f. dye.

tìpico, adj. typical.

tipo, n.m. type.

tirabaci, n.m. spitcurl.

tirannìa, *n.f.* tyranny.

tiranno, *n.m.* tyrant.

tirante, *n.m.* rod; tightening; brace.

tirare, *vb.* draw, pull, tag.

tirata, *n.f.* pull.

tiratura, *n.f.* printing.

tìrchio, *adj.* stingy.

tiro, *n.m.* trick.

tirocìnio, *n.m.* internship.

tìsi, *n.f.* consumption, tuberculosis.

tìsico, *adj.* consumptive.

titolare, 1. *n.* incumbent. **2.** *adj.* titular.

tìtolo, *n.m.* title, headline, heading, caption.

tìzio, *n.m.* chap, fellow, guy.

toccante, *adj.* touching, moving, poignant.

toccare, *vb.* touch.

toccasana, *n.m.* cure, panacea.

tocco, *n.m.* touch.

toga, *n.f.* gown.

tògliere, *vb.* take away, remove.

tollerante, *adj.* tolerant.

tolleranza, *n.f.* tolerance.

tollerare, *vb.* tolerate, stand.

tomba, *n.f.* tomb, grave.

tombale, *adj.* pertaining to a tomb or grave.

tombino, *n.m.* sewer cap, manhole.

tondo, *adj.* round.

tonfo, *n.m.* splash; thud.

tònica, *n.f.* (music) tonic.

tònico, *n.m. and adj.* tonic.

tonnellata, *n.f.* ton.

tonno, *n.m.* tuna.

tòno, *n.m.* tone, pitch.

tonsilla, *n.f.* tonsil.

tonto, *adj.* dumb, dull.

topo, *n.m.* mouse.

torace, *n.m.* thorax.

tòrcere, *vb.* twist, wring.

torinese, *adj.* Turinese.

Torino, *n.f.* Turin.

tormenta, *n.f.* snowstorm, blizzard.

tormentare, *vb.* torment; fret; nag; tease.

tormento, *n.m.* torment.

tormentoso, *adj.* excruciating.

tornaconto, *n.m.* profit, advantage.

tornare, *vb.* return.

tornasole, *n.m.* litmus.

tórnio, *n.m.* lathe.

tòro, *n.m.* bull.

torre, *n.f.* tower.

torrefazione, *n.f.* roasting (of coffee).

torrènte, *n.m.* torrent; mountain stream.

torretta, *n.f.* turret.

tórsolo, *n.m.* core.

torta, *n.f.* cake, tart, pie.

tòrto, *n.m.* wrong. **aver t.,** be wrong.

tortuóso, *adj.* tortuous, winding, twisted; ambiguous.

tortura, *n.f.* torture.

torturare, *vb.* torture.

tosare, *vb.* clip, shear.

tosatore, *n.m.* clipper.

tosatura, *n.f.* clipping.

Toscana, *n.f.* Tuscany.

toscano, *adj.* Tuscan.

tosse, *n.f.* cough.

tòssico, 1. *n.m. (coll.)* drug addict. **2.** *adj.* toxic.

tossicòmane, *n.m.* drug addict.

tossire, *vb.* cough.

tot, *n.m.* so much; a specific amount.

totale, *n.m. and adj.* total.

totalità, *n.f.* totality, entirety.

totalitàrio, *adj.* totalitarian.

tovàglia, *n.f.* tablecloth.

tovagliolino, *n.m.* little napkin; doily.

tovagliòlo, *n.m.* napkin.

tòzzo, *adj.* stocky, chunky.

tra, *prep.* between, among, amid.

traballare, *vb.* reel, stagger, lurch.

traboccare, *vb.* overflow.

tràccia, *n.f.* trace.

tradimento, *n.m.* betrayal, treason.

tradire, *vb.* betray.

traditore, *n.m.* traitor.

tradizionale, *adj.* traditional.

tradizione, *n.f.* tradition.

tradurre, *vb.* translate.

traduzione, *n.f.* translation.

tràffico, *n.m.* traffic.

trafiggere, *vb.* transfix, spear.

traforare, *vb.* pierce; tunnel.

traforo, *n.m.* tunnel.

tragèdia, *n.f.* tragedy.

traghetto, n.m. ferry.
tràgico, adj. tragic.
traguardo di puntamento, n.m. bombsight.
tram, n.m. street-car, trolley-car.
trambusto, n.m. flurry.
tramestìo, n.m. bustle.
tramezzino, n.m. sandwich.
trampolino, n.m. springboard.
tramutare, vb. transform, change.
trangugiare, vb. gulp.
tranne, prep. except.
tranquillità, n.f. tranquillity.
tranquillo, adj. tranquil, quiet, peaceful.
transatlàntico, 1. n.m. liner **2.** adj. transatlantic.
transizione, n.f. transition.
transvestito, n.m. transvestite.
trantran, n.m. routine.
tranvia, n.f. tramway, streetcar line.
tranviàrio, adj. tramway.
trapanare, vb. drill.
tràpano, n.m. drill.
trapassare, vb. pierce through; pass through; pass away.
trapasso, n.m. death, passage; (property) conveyance.
trapelare, vb. ooze, leak through.
tràppola, n.f. pitfall, snare, trap.
trapunta, n.f. quilt.
trarre, vb. get; take; pull, drag; draw; lead; heave.
trasalire, vb. give a start.
trasandato, adj. sloppy.
trascinare, vb. drag, haul, lug.
trascinarsi, vb. crawl.
trascórrere, vb. elapse, pass.
trascuràbile, adj. negligible.
trascurare, vb. neglect, disregard, ignore, overlook.
trascuratamente, adv. negligently, carelessly.
trascuratezza, n.f. negligence, carelessness.
trascurato, adj. negligent, careless, frowzy, sloppy, slovenly.
trasferimento, n.m. transfer.
trasferire, vb. transfer.
trasferta, n.f. transfer; business trip.
trasformare, vb. transform.
trasfusione, n.f. transfusion.

traslòco, n.m. move; (household goods) moving.
trasméttere, vb. transmit, broadcast, convey.
trasmettitore, n.m. transmitter, broadcaster.
trasmissione, n.f. transmission. **t. radiofònica,** broadcast.
trasparènte, adj. transparent.
trasportare, vb. transport, carry, haul, convey.
trasportatore, n.m. conveyor.
traspòrto, n.m. transport; carriage; cartage; haulage.
trastullare, vb. amuse; (refl.) toy.
trastullo, n.m. toy.
trasudare, vb. ooze, seep.
tratta, n.f. draft.
trattàbile, adj. negotiable; tractable, manageable, friendly.
trattamento, n.m. treatment.
trattare, vb. treat; deal.
trattativa, n.f. negotiation.
trattato, n.m. treaty; treatise.
trattenere, vb. entertain; refrain; restrain; withhold; (refl.) forbear.
trattenuta, n.f. withholding.
trattino, n.m. hyphen; dash.
tratto, n.m. trait; feature; dash; stretch; tract. **t. d'unione,** hyphen.
trattore, n.m. restaurant-keeper.
trattoria, n.f. restaurant.
trattrice, n.f. tractor.
traumatizzare, vb. traumatize.
travaglio, n.m. labor.
travasare, vb. scoop; pour off.
trave, n.f. beam, girder.
travèrso, adv. **di travèrso,** awry.
travestimento, n.m. disguise; travesty.
travestire, vb. disguise; travesty.
travicèllo, n.m. joist, rafter.
travisare, vb. distort, misunderstand.
travòlgere, vb. overwhelm; sweep away; knock over; overturn.
tre, num. three.
tréccia, n.f. braid.
tredicésimo, adj. thirteenth.
trédici, num. thirteen.
trégua, n.f. truce; respite.
tremare, vb. tremble, quake, shake.

tremèndo, *adj.* tremendous; awesome.

trèmito, *n.m.* trembling, quake.

tremolare, *vb.* tremble, flicker, quaver.

tremolìo, *n.m.* trembling, flicker.

treno, *n.m.* train.

trenta, *num.* thirty.

trentésimo, *adj.* thirtieth.

trepidare, *vb.* fear; fret, worry.

tresca, *n.f.* intrigue; (illicit) love affair.

trescone, *n.m.* reel (dance).

triàngolo, *n.m.* triangle.

tribade, *n.f.* Lesbian.

tribolare, *vb.* trouble, suffer; worry.

tribolazione, *n.f.* tribulation.

tribordo, *n.m.* starboard.

tribù, *n.f.* tribe, clan.

tribuna, *n.f.* stand, grandstand.

tributàrio, *n.m. and adj.* tributary.

tributo, *n.m.* tribute.

trichèco, *n.m.* walrus.

trifòglio, *n.m.* clover.

trimestrale, *adj.* every three months, quarterly.

trimèstre, *n.m.* three-month period, quarter; (school) term.

trincèa, *n.f.* trench; cutting.

trincerare, *vb.* entrench.

trinciante, *n.m.* carving-knife.

trinciare, *vb.* carve, cut up.

trionfale, *adj.* triumphal.

trionfante, *adj.* triumphal.

trionfare, *vb.* triumph.

trionfo, *n.m.* triumph

triplicare, *vb.* triple.

trìplice, *adj.* triple.

trippa, *n.f.* tripe; (coll.) fat.

tripudiare, *vb.* exult.

tripùdio, *n.m.* exultation, happiness.

triste, *adj.* sad, gloomy, depressed, doleful, glum.

tristezza, *n.f.* sadness, gloom, glumness.

tritacarne, *n.m.* meat grinder.

tritare, *vb.* pound, mangle.

trito, *adj.* trite.

tritòlo, *n.m.* T.N.T.

triturare, *vb.* mince.

trivèllo, *n.m.* auger, borer.

trofèo, *n.m.* trophy.

trògolo, *n.m.* trough.

tròia, *n.f.* sow.

tromba, *n.f.* trumpet.

trombettière, *n.m.* trumpeter.

tronco, *n.m.* trunk; log.

trónfio, *adj.* haughty, conceited.

tròno, *n.m.* throne.

tròpico, **1.** *n.m.* tropic. **2.** *adj.* tropical.

troppo, **1.** *adj.* too many; too much. **2.** *adv.* too.

tròta, *n.f.* trout.

trottare, *vb.* trot.

tròtto, *n.m.* trot.

trovare, *vb.* find, locate; *(refl.)* be; be located; happen to be.

trovata, *n.f.* find; invention; idea; trick.

trovatèllo, *n.m.* foundling.

trucco, *n.m.* trick.

trucidare, *vb.* slay.

truffare, *vb.* cheat, swindle.

truffatore, *n.m.* cheater, swindler.

truppa, *n.f.* troop.

tu, *pron.* 2. *sg.* thou; you.

tubercolosi, *n.f.* tuberculosis.

tubo, *n.m.* tube, pipe.

tuffare, *vb.* plunge; dip; dunk; *(refl.)* dive.

tuffatore, *n.m.* diver; dive-bomber.

tuffo, *n.m.* dive, plunge.

tugùrio, *n.m.* hovel.

tulipano, *n.m.* tulip.

tumefazione, *n.m.* tumefaction, swelling.

tumore, *n.m.* tumor.

tùmulo, *n.m.* mound.

tumulto, *n.m.* tumult, uproar, hubbub, riot.

tùnica, *n.f.* tunic, gown.

tuo, *adj.* thy; your.

tuonare, *vb.* thunder.

tuòno, *n.m.* thunder.

tuórlo, *n.m.* yolk.

turbante, *n.m.* turban.

turbare, *vb.* upset; disturb; trouble, perturb.

turbina, *n.f.* turbine.

turbinare, *vb.* whirl, gyrate, swirl.

tùrbine, *n.m.* whirlwind.

turbo-èlica, *n.f.* turbo-prop.
turbolènto, *adj.* turbulent; boisterous.
turboreattore, *n.m.* turbojet.
Turchìa, *n.f.* Turkey.
turco, 1. *n.m.* Turk. **2.** *adj.* Turkish.
tùrgido, *adj.* turgid.
turismo, *n.m.* sightseeing, tourism.
turista, *n.m.* tourist.

turìstico, *adj.* tourist.
turno, *n.m.* turn, shift.
turpe, *adj.* abject; ugly; vile.
tuta, *n.f.* overalls; dungarees.
tutèla, *n.f.* guardianship.
tutore, *n.m.* guardian.
tuttavìa, *adv.* however; yet.
tutto, 1. *adj.* all; whole. **t. a un tratto,** all of a sudden. **2.** *pron.* everything.
tuttóra, *adv.* yet, still, even now.

U

ubbidire, *vb.* obey.
ubriachezza, *n.f.* drunkenness, intoxication.
ubriaco, *adj.* drunk, drunken.
ubriacone, *n.m.* drunkard, inebriate.
uccellièra, *n.f.* bird-house, aviary.
uccellino, *n.m.* fledgling.
uccèllo, *n.m.* bird. **u. di rapina,** bird of prey.
uccìdere, *vb.* kill.
uccisore, *n.m.* killer.
udìbile, *adj.* audible.
udiènza, *n.f.* audience, interview, hearing.
udire, *vb.* hearing.
uditivo, *adj.* auditory.
udito, *n.m.* hearing.
uditore, *n.m.* hearer, auditor.
uditòrio, *n.m.* audience.
uditrice, *n.f.* hearer, auditor.
ufficiale, 1. *n.m.* officer, official. **2.** *adj.* official.
uffìcio, *n.m.* office, bureau.
ufficioso, *adj.* unofficial.
ufo, a u., *adv.* free; parasitically.
ùgola, *n.f.* uvula.
uguaglianza, *n.f.* equality.
uguagliare, *vb.* equal, equalize, equate, match.
uguale, *adj.* equal.
ùlcera, *n.f.* ulcer.
ulivo, *n.m.* olive tree.
ulteriore, *adj.* ulterior, further.
ùltimo, *adj.* last, end, hindmost, ultimate.
ultraterreno, *adj.* unearthly.
ultravioletto, *n.m.* ultraviolet.
ululare, *vb.* howl.
umanamente, *adv.* humanly.

umanésimo, *n.m.* humanism.
umanista, *n.m.* humanist.
umanità, *n.f.* humanity, mankind.
umanitàrio, *adj.* humanitarian, humane.
umano, *adj.* human.
umbro, *adj.* Umbrian.
umidità, *n.f.* dampness, humidity, moisture.
ùmido, *adj.* damp, humid, moist, wet.
ùmile, *adj.* humble, lowly.
umiliare, *vb.* humiliate, humble; *(refl.)* grovel.
umiliazione, *n.f.* humiliation.
umiltà, *n.f.* humility.
umore, *n.m.* humor.
umorismo, *n.m.* humor.
umorista, *n.m.* humorist.
umorìstico, *adj.* humorous, jocular.
un, *art.* a, an.
unànime, *adj.* unanimous.
uncinare, *vb.* hook.
uncino, *n.m.* hook, grapple.
undicésimo, *adj.* eleventh.
ùndici, *num.* eleven.
ùngere, *vb.* grease; smear; anoint; oil.
ungherese, *adj.* Hungarian.
Ungherìa, *n.f.* Hungary.
ùnghia, *n.f.* fingernail.
unguènto, *n.m.* unguent, salve, ointment.
ùnico, *adj.* only; unique; single; sole.
unificare, *vb.* unify.
uniforme, 1. *n.m.* uniform. **2.** *adj.* uniform, even.

uniformità, *n.f.* uniformity, evenness.
unilaterale, *adj.* unilateral, one-sided.
unione, *n.f.* union.
unire, *vb.* unite.
unisessuale, *adj.* unisex.
unità, *n.f.* unity; unit.
universale, *adj.* universal.
università, *n.f.* university, college.
universitàrio, *adj.* pertaining to a university, collegiate.
univèrso, *n.m.* universe.
uno, *m.,* **una** *f.* **1.** *art.* a, an. **2.** *num.* one.
unto, *adj.* oily, greasy.
untuoso, *adj.* greasy.
uòmo, *n.m.* man.
uòpo, *n.m.* purpose.
uòvo, *n.m.* egg. **u. affogato,** poached egg.
uragano, *n.m.* hurricane.
uraninite, *n.f.* pitchblende.
urbano, *adj.* urban.
urgènte, *adj.* urgent, pressing.
urgènza, *n.f.* urgency.
urina, *n.f.* urine.
urlare, *vb.* yell, holler, bawl, shout, cry, howl.
urlo, *n.m.* yell, shout, howl.
urna, *n.f.* urn.

urtare, *vb.* bump; shock; clash.
urto, *n.m.* bump; shock; impact; clash.
usanza, *n.f.* usage.
usare, *vb.* use.
usato, 1. *adj.* used. **2.** *n.m.* second-hand, vintage.
uscente, *adj.* ending, closing, terminating.
uscière, *n.m.* usher; bailiff.
ùscio, *n.m.* door.
uscita, *n.f.* exit; airport gate.
usignuòlo, *n.m.* nightingale.
uso, *n.m.* use; custom.
ustione, *n.f.* burn.
usuale, *adj.* usual.
usufruire, *vb.* have the use of, use; benefit.
usura, *n.f.* usury.
usurpare, *vb.* usurp, encroach upon.
utènsile, *n.m.* utensil, tool.
utènte, *n.m.* user.
ùtero, *n.m.* uterus, womb.
ùtile, *adj.* useful, helpful.
utilità, *n.f.* utility, usefulness, helpfulness.
utilitària, *n.f.* economy car.
utilizzare, *vb.* utilize.
utopia, *n.f.* utopia.
uva, *n.f.* grape.
ùzzolo, *n.m.* whim; impulse.

V

va bene, *interj.* O.K.
vacante, *adj.* vacant.
vacanza, *n.f.* holiday, *(pl.)* vacation.
vacca, *n.f.* cow.
vaccaro, *n.m.* cowboy, cowhand.
vacchetta, *n.f.* cowhide.
vaccinare, *vb.* vaccinate.
vaccinazione, *n.f.* vaccination.
vaccìnio, *n.m.* huckleberry.
vaccino, *n.m.* vaccine.
vacillante, *adj.* vacillating, flickening, unstable.
vacillare, *vb.* vacillate, waver.
vacuità, *n.f.* vacuity, emptiness.
vàcuo, *adj.* vacuous.
vademecum, *n.m.* handbook.
vagabondo, *n.m.* vagabond, hobo, bum, tramp.

vagare, *vb.* wander around, gallivant, ramble, roam.
vàglia, *n.m.* money-order.
vàglio, *n.m.* sieve.
vago, *adj.* vague, dreamy, hazy; (poetical) charming.
vagone, *n.m.* car; coach. **v. ristorante,** dining car. **v. lètti,** sleeper.
vaiòlo, *n.m.* smallpox.
valanga, *n.f.* avalanche.
valere, *vb.* be worth.
valico, *n.m.* mountain pass.
vàlido, *adj.* valid.
valigetta, *n.f.* little suitcase; handbag.
valìgia, *n.f.* suitcase, valise.
valle, *n.f.* valley.
valletta, *n.f.* vale, dale, glen.

valore, *n.m.* valor; value, worth.
valorizzare, *vb.* value; exploit.
valoroso, *adj.* valiant.
valuta, *n.f.* currency.
valutare, *vb.* evaluate, estimate, value.
valutazione, *n.f.* evaluation, estimate.
vàlvola, *n.f.* valve; (radio) tube.
vàlzer, *n.m.* waltz.
vampiro, *n.m.* vampire.
vanaglorioso, *adj.* vainglorious, boastful.
vàndalo, *n.m.* vandal.
vanga, *n.f.* spade.
vangèlo, *n.m.* gospel.
vaniglia, *n.f.* vanilla.
vanità, *n.f.* vanity, conceit.
vanitoso, *adj.* vain, conceited.
vano, 1. *n.m.* room. **2.** *adj.* vain.
vantàggio, *n.m.* advantage, benefit, profit. **trarre v. da,** benefit by.
vantaggiosamente, *adv.* advantageously.
vantaggioso, *adj.* advantageous, beneficial, profitable.
vantare, *vb.* boast.
vanterìa, *n.f.* boast, boasting, boastfulness.
vanto, *n.m.* boast.
vànvera, *adv. at random.* **parlare a v.,** ramble.
vapore, *n.m.* vapor, steam.
varare, *vb.* launch.
variàbile, *n.f. and adj.* variable.
variare, *vb.* vary.
variazione, *n.f.* variation.
varicèlla, *n.f.* chicken-pox.
variegato, *adj.* variegated.
varietà, *n.f.* variety.
vàrio, *adj.* various.
variopinto, *adj.* multicolored.
varo, *n.m.* launching.
vasca, *n.f.* tub.
vascello, *n.m.* vessel, ship.
vasellame, *n.m.* crockery, earthenware.
vasectomìa, *n.f.* vasectomy.
vaso, *n.m.* vase. **v. da nòtte,** chamber-pot.
vassallo, *n.m.* vassal.
vassòio, *n.m.* tray.
vasto, *adj.* vast.
vècchia, *n.f.* old woman, crone.
vècchio, *adj.* old, aged, elderly.

vece, *n.m.* behalf. **in v. di,** on behalf of.
vedere, *vb.* see, behold.
védova, *n.f.* widow.
védovo, *n.m.* widower.
veduta, *n.f.* view.
veemènte, *adj.* vehement.
veemènza, *n.f.* vehemence.
vegetale, *adj.* vegetable.
vegetariano, *adj.* vegetarian.
vegetazione, *n.f.* vegetation.
vègeto, *adj.* vigorous, strong.
vèggente, *n.m. and f.* seer; prophet.
véglia, *n.f.* vigil; wake.
vegliare, *vb.* be awake.
vegliardo, *n.m.* old man.
veicolo, *n.m.* vehicle.
vela, *n.f.* sail.
velato, *adj.* veiled, filmy.
veleno, *n.m.* poison, venom.
velenoso, *adj.* poisonous, venomous.
vèllo, *n.m.* fleece.
velluto, *n.m.* velvet.
velo, *n.m.* veil.
veloce, *adj.* swift, fleet, speedy.
velocista, *n.m.* sprinter.
velocità, *n.f.* velocity, speed.
velòdromo, *n.m.* bicycle ring.
vena, *n.f.* vein.
venale, *adj.* venal.
venato, *adj.* veined; streaked, variegated.
vendémmia, *n.f.* vintage.
véndere, *vb.* sell.
vendetta, *n.f.* revenge, vengeance.
vendicare, *vb.* avenge, revenge.
vendicativo, *adj.* vindictive, vengeful.
vendicatore, *n.m.* avenger.
véndita, *n.f.* sale. **v. all'asta,** auction.
venerdì, *n.m.* Friday. **v. santo,** Good Friday.
venèreo, *adj.* venereal.
Venèzia, *n.f.* Venice.
veneziano, *adj.* Venetian.
venire, *vb.* come.
ventàglio, *n.m.* fan.
ventèsimo, *adj.* twentieth.
venti, *num.* twenty.
ventilare, *vb.* ventilate.
ventilazione, *n.f.* ventilation.
ventina, *n.f.* score.

vènto, *n.m.* wind.
ventoso, *adj.* windy, breezy.
vèntre, *n.m.* belly.
ventriglio, *n.m.* gizzard.
ventura, *n.f.* venture.
venuta, *n.f.* coming.
veramente, *adv.* truly, really, actually.
veranda, *n.f.* porch.
verbale, 1. *n.m.* minutes. **2.** *adj.* verbal.
vèrbo, *n.m.* verb.
verboso, *adj.* verbose, wordy.
verde, *adj.* green. **al v.,** broke, penniless.
verdetto, *n.m.* verdict.
verdura, *n.f.* vegetables.
verga, *n.f.* rod, switch.
vérgine, *n.f.* virgin.
vergogna, *n.f.* shame.
vergognarsi di, *vb.* be ashamed of.
vergognoso, *adj.* ashamed; shameful.
verídico, *adj.* truthful.
verífica, *n.f.* verification, check, audit.
verificare, *vb.* verify, check, audit.
verità, *n.f.* truth, reality, actuality.
veritiero, *adj.* truthful, earnest.
vèrme, *n.m.* worm.
vermíglio, *adj.* vermilion.
vernàcolo, *n.m. and adj.* vernacular.
vernice, *n.f.* varnish, glaze.
verniciare, *vb.* varnish, glaze.
vero, *adj.* true, real, actual; very.
verosímile, *adj.* likely, probable.
vèrro, *n.m.* boar.
verruca, *n.f.* wart.
versamento, *n.m.* payment.
versare, *vb.* pour; pay in; shed.
versàtile, *adj.* versatile.
versato, *adj.* versed, conversant.
versificare, *vb.* versify.
versione, *n.f.* version.
vèrso, 1. *n.m.* verse; song; (hen, goose) cackle. **2.** *prep.* toward.
versucci, *n.m.pl.* doggerel.
vèrtebra, *n.f.* vertebra.
vertebrato, *n.m. and adj.* vertebrate.
vèrtenza, *n.f.* quarrel, dispute, controversy.

verticale, *adj.* vergical.
vèrtice, *n.m.* vertex, top; summit.
vertigine, *n.f.* vertigo, dizziness.
vertiginoso, *adj.* vertiginous, dizzy.
verza, *n.f.* cabbage.
verzura, *n.f.* greenery.
vescica, *n.f.* bladder; blister.
vescovato, *n.m.* bishopric.
véscovo, *n.m.* bishop.
vèspa, *n.f.* wasp.
vespasiano, *n.m.* public urinal.
vèspri, *n.m.pl.* vespers.
vessillo, *n.m.* flag, emblem.
vestàglia, *n.f.* dressing-gown, bathrobe, negligée.
vèste, *n.f.* dress, garb, apparel, robe.
vestíbolo, *n.m.* vestibule, hallway.
vestígia, *n.f.pl.* vestiges.
vestire, *vb.* dress, clothe, garb, apparel.
vestito, 1. *n.m.* dress, suit, garment; *(pl.)* clothes, clothing. **2.** *adj.* clad, clothed.
Vesùvio, *n.m.* Vesuvius.
veterano, *n.m.* veteran.
veterinàrio, *n.m. and adj.* veterinary.
vèto, *n.m.* veto.
vetràio, *n.m.* glazier.
vetrina, *n.f.* shop window; showcase.
vetro, *n.m.* glass, pane.
vetroresina, *n.m.* fiberglass.
vetroso, *adj.* glassy.
vetta, *n.f.* summit.
vettovàglie, *n.f.pl.* victuals.
vettura, *n.f.* carriage; car.
vezzeggiare, *vb.* fondle, coddle, pet.
vézzo, *n.m.* habit, quirk.
vi, *pron.* **2.** *pl.* you.
vi, *pro-phrase* (replaces phrases introduced by prepositions of place) there; to it; at it.
vìa, 1. *n.f.* way, road, street. **2.** *adv.* away; off. **3.** *prep.* via.
viadotto, *n.m.* viaduct.
viaggiare, *vb.* journey, travel, tour, voyage.
viaggiatore, *n.m.* traveller.
viàggio, *n.m.* journey, trip, travel, tour, voyage.

viale, *n.m.* avenue, boulevard; drive(way); (in garden) alley.

viandante, *n.m.* wayfarer, wonderer.

viavài, *n.m.* bustle, coming and going.

vibrare, *vb.* vibrate.

vibrazione, *n.f.* vibration.

vicàrio, *n.m.* vicar.

vicenda, 1. *n.f.* story, vicissitude. **2.** *adv.* **av.,** alternatively, reciprocally.

vicinanza, *n.f.* neighborhood, vicinity.

vicinato, *n.m.* neighborhood.

vicino, 1. *n.m.* neighbor. **2.** *adj.* nearby, neighboring, close. **vicino a,** *prep.* near, about. **3.** *adv.* near, close.

vico, *n.m.* hamlet.

vìcolo, *n.m.* alley. **v. cièco,** blind alley, dead end.

videocassetta, *n.f.* videotape.

videodisco, *n.m.* videodisc.

vidimare, *vb.* validate, authenticate.

vietare, *vb.* forbid, veto.

vietato, *adj.* forbidden.

vigilante, *adj.* vigilant, alert, watchful.

vigilare, *vb.* watch, look out.

vìgile, *n.m.* policeman.

vigilia, *n.f.* vigil; eve.

vigliaccherìa, *n.f.* cowardice.

vigliacco, *n.m.* cad.

vigna, *n.f.* vineyard.

vigneto, *n.m.* vineyard.

vignetta, *n.f.* cartoon.

vigore, *n.m.* vigor, force.

vigoroso, *adj.* vigorous, forceful, lusty.

vile, *adj.* vile.

vilipèndere, *vb.* scorn, despise, insult.

villàggio, *n.m.* village.

villano, *adj.* inconsiderate.

villetta, *n.f.* cottage.

villoso, *adj.* fleecy, hairy.

vincere, *vb.* conquer, overcome, overpower, beat, vanquish, win.

vincìbile, *adj.* conquerable.

vincitore, *n.m.* victor, conqueror, winner.

vincolare, *vb.* bind.

vincolo, *n.m.* bind, link.

vinile, *n.m.* vinyl.

vino, *n.m.* wine. **v. di Xeres,** sherry.

viòla, *n.f.* viola; viol; violet.

violare, *vb.* violate; rape.

violatore, *n.m.* violator.

violazione, *n.f.* violation, breach.

violento, *adj.* violent.

violènza, *n.f.* violence.

violino, *n.m.* violin, fiddle.

violoncellista, *n.m.* cellist.

violoncèllo, *n.m.* cello.

viòttolo, *n.m.* byway, lane.

vìpera, *n.f.* adder, viper.

virare, *vb.* tack, veer.

vìrgola, *n.f.* comma.

virile, *adj.* virile, manly.

virilità, *n.f.* virility, manhood.

virtù, *n.f.* virtue.

virtuale, *adj.* virtual.

virtuosismo, *n.m.* virtuosity.

virtuoso, *adj.* virtuous.

virulento, *adj.* virulent, deadly.

vìscere, *n.f.pl.* viscera, guts, bowels.

vìschio, *n.m.* bird-lime; mistletoe.

viscoso, *adj.* viscous, sticky.

visìbile, *adj.* visible.

visiera, *n.f.* visor.

visione, *n.f.* vision.

visita, *n.f.* visit.

visitare, *vb.* visit.

visivo, *adj.* of vision.

viso, *n.m.* face, countenance.

visone, *n.m.* mink.

vispo, *adj.* brisk, lively; attentive.

vista, *n.f.* sight; eyesight; view.

vistare, *vb.* visa.

visto, *n.m.* visa.

vistosamente, *adv.* gaudily.

vistosità, *n.f.* flashiness, gaudiness.

vistoso, *adj.* flashy, gaudy.

visuale, *adj.* visual.

vita, *n.f.* life; livelihood; living; waist.

vitale, *adj.* vital.

vitalità, *n.f.* vitality.

vitalìzio, *adj.* for life.

vitamina, *n.f.* vitamin.

vite, *n.f.* vine; grapevine; screw.

vitèllo, *n.m.* calf; veal.

vitìccio, *n.m.* tendril.

vìtreo, *adj.* glassy, of glass.

vìttima, n.f. victim.
vitto, n.m. food, victuals, board.
vittòria, n.f. victory.
vittorioso, adj. victorious.
viuzza, n.f. narrow street.
viva, interj. hurrah (for).
vivace, adj. vivacious, lively, brisk.
vivacemente, adv. vivaciously, briskly.
vivacità, n.f. vivacity, liveliness, briskness.
vivàio, n.m. hatchery, nursery.
vivanda, n.f. food, dish.
vivènte, adj. living, alive.
vivere, vb. live, be alive.
vìvido, adj. vivid.
vivo, adj. live.
viziare, vb. vitiate.
vìzio, n.m. vice.
vizioso, adj. vicious.
vizzo, adj. withered; flabby.
vocabolàrio, n.m. vocabulary.
vocale, 1. n.f. vowel. 2. adj. vocal.
vocazione, n.f. vocation, calling.
voce, n.f. voice; word, rumor, report.
vociare, vb. vociferate.
voga, n.f. vogue.
vòglia, n.f. wish, desire; birth-mark.
voi, pron. 2. pl. you.
volante, n.m. steering-wheel; flounce.
volantino, n.m. flier.
volare, vb. fly.
volerci, vb. be necessary.
volgare, adj. vulgar; common; vernacular.

volgarità, n.f. vulgarity, commonness.
volgo, n.m. rabble.
volo, n.m. flight. v. noleggiato, charter flight.
volontà, n.f. will.
volontàrio, 1. n.m. volunteer. 2. adj. voluntary.
volpe, n.f. fox.
volpino, adj. foxy.
vòlta, n.f. time; vault.
voltafàccia, n.m. about-face.
voltagabbana, n.m. turncoat, traitor.
voltàggio, n.m. voltage.
voltastòmaco, n.m. revulsion, nausea.
volteggiare, vb. hover; turn; vault.
volume, n.m. volume, bulk.
voluminoso, adj. voluminous, bulky.
voluttà, n.f. pleasure, delight.
vòmere, n.m. coulter; plowshare.
vomitare, vb. vomit, disgorge.
vòmito, n.m. vomit.
vorace, adj. voracious.
vòrtice, n.m. vortex, whirlpool, eddy.
vòstro, adj. your; yours.
votante, n.m. voter.
votare, vb. vote.
votazione, n.f. voting, ballot.
voto, n.m. vow; wish; mark; grade.
vulcano, n.m. volcano.
vulneràbile, adj. vulnerable.
vuotare, vb. empty.
vuòto, 1. n.m. emptiness; vacuum. 2. adj empty, blank, vacant.

W, X, Z

W., abbr. for **evviva** hurrah for.
W.C., abbr. for water-closet (toilet).
xenòfobo, adj. xenophobe.
zabaiòne, n.m. eggnog.
zaffiro, n.m. sapphire.
zàino, n.m. knapsack.
zampa, n.f. paw.
zampillare, vb. gush; squirt.
zampogna, n.f. bagpipe.
zàngola, n.f. churn.

zanna, n.f. fang.
zanzara, n.f. mosquito.
zanzarièra, n.f. mosquito-net.
zappa, n.f. hoe.
zappare, vb. hoe.
zar, n.m. czar.
zàttera, n.f. raft.
zavorra, n.f. ballast.
zèbra, n.f. zebra.
zecca, n.f. mint.

zecchino, *n.m.* first-quality gold, pure gold; sequin.
zèffiro, *n.m.* zephyr.
zelante, *n.m.* zealous.
zèlo, *n.m.* zeal.
zènzero, *n.m.* ginger.
zeppo, *adj.* chock full.
zèro, *n.m.* zero; cipher.
zìa, *n.f.* aunt.
zibellino, *n.m.* sable.
zigrinare, *vb.* grain, groove; mill, knurl.
zimbello, *n.m.* laughing stock.
zinco, *n.m.* zinc.
zingara, *n.f.* gypsy woman.
zingaro, *n.m.* gypsy.
zio, *n.m.* uncle.
zitèlla, *n.f.* old maid, spinster.
zittire, *fb.* shut up, silence; hiss.

zitto, *adj.* silent.
zòccolo, *n.m.* hoof; wooden shoe; baseboard.
zòlla, *n.f.* clod, sod.
zòna, *n.f.* zone.
zoològico, *adj.* zoological.
zoologìa, *n.f.* zoology.
zoppicamento, *n.m.* limp.
zoppicare, *vb.* limp, hobble.
zòppo, *adj.* lame.
zòtico, 1. *n.* boor. **2.** *adj.* boorish.
zoticone, *n.m.* lout.
zucca, *n.f.* gourd, pumpkin, squash.
zùcchero, *n.m.* sugar.
zuppa, *n.f.* soup.
Zurigo, *n.m.* Zurich.
zuzzerellone, *n.m.* hobblede-hoy.

A

a, *art.* un *m.,* una *f.*
aback, *adv.* all'indietro.
abacus, *n.* àbaco *m.*
abandon, 1. *n.* abbandono *m.* **2.** *vb.* abbandonare.
abandoned, *adj.* abbandonato.
abandonment, *n.* abbandono *m.*
abase, *vb.* abbassare, avvilire.
abasement, *n.* abbassamento *m.,* avvilimento *m.*
abash, *vb.* sconcertare.
abate, *vb.* diminuire.
abatement, *n.* diminuzione *f.*
abbacy, *n.* abbazia *f.*
abbess, *n.* badessa *f.*
abbey, *n.* badia *f.,* abbazia *f.*
abbot, *n.* abate *m.*
abbreviate, *vb.* abbreviare, raccorciare.
abbreviation, *n.* abbreviatura *f.,* raccorciamento *m.*
abdicate, *vb.* abdicare.
abdication, *n.* abdicazione *f.*
abdomen, *n.* addòme *m.*
abdominal, *adj.* addominale.
abduct, *vb.* rapire.
abduction, *n.* rapimento *m.,* ratto *m.*
abductor, *n.* rapitore *m.*
abed, *adv.* a letto.
aberrant, *adj.* aberrante.
aberration, *n.* aberrazione *f.*
abet, *vb.* incoraggiare.
abetment, *n.* incoraggiamento *m.*
abettor, *n.* incoraggiatore *m.*
abeyance, *n.* sospensione *f.*
abhor, *vb.* aborrire, detestare.
abhorrence, *n.* aborrimento *m.,* ripugnanza *f.*
abhorrent, *adj.* ripugnante.
abide, *vb.* (dwell) abitare; (remain) rimanere; (tolerate) sopportare.
abiding, *adj.* permanènte, costante.
ability, *n.* abilità *f.,* capacità *f.*
abject, *adj.* abiètto.
abjuration, *n.* abiura *f.*
abjure, *vb.* abiurare.
abjurer, *n.* chi abiura.
ablative, *adj. and n.* ablativo *(m.).*

ablaze, *adj.* in fiamme.
able, *adj.* àbile, capace (di); **(be a.)** potere.
able-bodied, *adj.* forte, robusto.
abloom, *adj.* in fiore.
ablution, *n.* abluzione *f.*
ably, *adv.* abilmente.
abnegate, *vb.* abnegare.
abnegation, *n.* abnegazione *f.*
abnormal, *adj.* anormale.
abnormality, *n.* anormalità *f.*
abnormally, *adv.* anormalmente.
aboard, 1. *adv. (naut.)* a bordo; **(all a.)** in carrozza. **2.** *prep.* a bordo di.
abode, *n.* dimora *f.*
abolish, *vb.* abolire.
abolishment, *n.* abolimento *m.*
abolition, *n.* abolizione *f.*
A-bomb, *n.* bomba atòmica *f.*
abominable, *adj.* abominévole.
abominate, *vb.* abominare.
abomination, *n.* abominazione *f.*
aboriginal, *adj.* indigeno, aborìgeno.
aborigine, *n.* indigeno *m,* aborìgeno *m.*
aborning, *adj.* nascente.
abort, *vb.* abortire.
abortion, *n.* aborto *m.*
abortive, *adj.* abortivo.
abound, *vb.* abbondare.
about, 1. *adv.* (approximately) pressappòco, all'incirca: (around) intorno; **(be a. to)** stare per. **2.** *prep.* (concerning; around) intorno a; (near) vicino a.
about-face, *n.* voltafàccia *m.*
above, *adv. and prep.* sopra.
aboveboard, 1. *adj.* sincèro, onèsto. **2.** *adv.* apertamente, onestamente.
above-mentioned, *adj.* summenzionato.
abrasion, *n.* abrasione *f.*
abrasive, *n. and adj.* abrasivo *(m.).*
abreast, *adv. and prep.* di fianco (a).
abridge, *vb.* abbreviare.
abridgment, *n.* abbreviamento *m.*
abroad, *adv.* all'èstero.

abrogate, *vb.* abrogare.
abrogation, *n.* abrogazione *f.*
abrupt, *adj.* (sudden) improvviso; (steep) rípido; (curt) rude.
abruptly, *adv.* (suddenly) all'improvviso, improvvisamente; (curtly) rudemente.
abruptness, *n.* rudezza *f.*
abscess, *n.* ascèsso *m.*
abscissa, *n.* ascissa *f.*
abscond, *vb.* sparire; (*fam.*) svignàrsela.
absence, *n.* assènza *f.*
absent, *adj.* assènte.
absentee, *n.* assènte *m.*
absenteeism, *n.* assenteismo *m.*
absent-minded, *adj.* distratto.
absinthe, *n.* assènzio *m.*
absolute, *adj.* assoluto.
absolutely, *adv.* assolutamente.
absoluteness, *n.* assolutezza *f.*
absolution, *n.* assoluzione *f.*
absolutism, *n.* assolutismo *m.*
absolve, *vb.* assòlvere.
absorb, *vb.* assorbire.
absorbed, *adj.* (*lit.*) assorbìto; (*fig.*) assorto.
absorbent, *n. and adj.* assorbènte *m.*
absorbing, *adj.* assorbènte.
absorption, *n.* assorbimento *m.*
abstain, *vb.* astenersi.
abstemious, *adj.* astèmio.
abstinence, *n.* astinènza *f.*
abstract, 1. *n.* (book, article) riassunto *m.*, sunto *m.* **2.** *adj.* astratto. **3.** *vb.* astrarre, riassùmere.
abstracted, *adj.* astratto.
abstraction, *n.* astrazione *f.*
abstruse, *adj.* astruso.
absurd, *adj.* assurdo.
absurdity, *n.* assurdità *f.*, assurdo *m.*
absurdly, *adv.* assurdamente.
abundance, *n.* abbondanza *f.*
abundant, *adj.* abbondante.
abundantly, *adv.* abbondantemente.
abuse, 1. *n.* (misuse) abuso *m.*; (insult) insulto *m.*, ingiùria *f.* **2.** *vb.* abusare (di), insultare, ingiuriare.
abusive, *adj.* (misusing) abusivo; (insulting) insolente, ingiurioso.
abusively, *adv.* abusivamente, insolentemente, ingiuriosamente.

abut, *vb.* confinare con.
abutment, *n.* tèrmine *m.*
abysmal, *adj.* abissale.
abyss, *n.* abisso *m.*
Abyssinia, *n.* Abissínia *f.*
Abyssinian, *n. and adj.* abissíno.
acacia, *n.* acàcia *f.*
academic, *adj.* accadèmico.
academic freedom, *n.* libertà d'insegnamento *f.*
academic year, *n.* anno accadèmico *m.*
academy, *n.* accadèmia *f.*
acanthus, *n.* acanto *m.*
accede, *vb.* consentire.
accelerate, *vb.* accelerare.
acceleration, *n.* accelerazione *f.*
accelerator, *n.* acceleratore *m.*
accent, *n.* accènto *m.*
accentuate, *vb.* (*lit.*) accentare; (*fig.*) accentuare.
accept, *vb.* accettare.
acceptability, *n.* accettabilità.
acceptable, *adj.* accètto, accettàbile, gradévole.
acceptably, *adv.* accettabilmente.
acceptance, *n.* accettazione *f.*
access, *n.* accèsso *m.*
accessible, *adj.* accessíbile.
accessory, *n. and adj.* accessòrio (*m.*).
accident, *n.* incidènte *m.*, sinistro *m.*; (by a.) per caso.
accidental, *adj.* accidentale.
accidentally, *adv.* accidentalmente.
acclaim, *vb.* acclamare.
acclamation, *n.* acclamazione *f.*
acclimate, *vb.* acclimare, acclimatare.
acclivity, *n.* acclività *f.*
accolade, *n.* accollata *f.*
accommodate, *vb.* accomodare; (lodge) alloggiare.
accommodating, *adj.* accomodante, cortese.
accommodation, *n.* accomodazione *f.*; (lodging) allòggio *m.*
accompaniment, *n.* accompagnamento *m.*
accompanist, *n.* accompagnatore *m.*
accompany, *vb.* accompagnare.
accomplice, *n.* còmplice *m. and f.*
accomplish, *vb.* compire.

accomplished, *adj.* compito.
accomplishment, *n.* compimento *m.*
accord, *n.* accòrdo *m.*
accordance, *n.* conformità *f.*; **(in a. with)** conforme a.
accordingly, *adv.* (correspondingly) conformemente; (therefore) dunque.
according to, *prep.* secondo.
accordion, *n.* fisarmònica *f.*
accost, *vb.* abbordare.
account, *n.* (comm.) conto *m.*; (narrative) racconto *m.*
accountable for, *adj.* responsàbile di.
accountant, *n.* ragioniere.
account for, *vb.* rèndere conto di.
accounting, *n.* (occupation) ragioneria *f.*; (procedure) contabilità *f.*
accouter, *vb.* abbigliare.
accoutrements, *n.* abbigliatura *f.sg.*
accredit, *vb.* accreditare.
accretion, *n.* accrescimento *m.*
accrual, *n.* accrescimento *m.*
accrue, *vb.* accréscere.
accumulate, *vb.* accumulare.
accumulation, *n.* accumulazione *f.*
accumulative, *adj.* accumulativo.
accumulator, *n.* accumulatore *m.*
accuracy, *n.* accuratezza *f.*
accurate, *adj.* accurato.
accursed, *adj.* maledetto.
accusation, *n.* accusa *f.*
accusative, *n. and adj.* accusativo *(m.).*
accuse, *vb.* accusare, incolpare, imputare.
accused, *n.* accusato *m.*, incolpato *m.*
accuser, *n.* accusatore *m.*, incolpatore *m.*
accustom, *vb.* abituare.
accustomed, *adj.* sòlito, abituale; (be accustomed to) solere; (become accustomed to) abituarsi a.
ace, *n.* asso *m.* **(a. in the hole)** asso nella manica
acerbity, *n.* acerbità *f.*
acetate, *n.* acetato *m.*
acetic, *adj.* acètico.

acetify, *vb.* acidificare.
acetone, *n.* acetone *m.*
acetylene, *n.* acetilène *m.*
ache, *n.* dolore *m.*, male *m.*
achieve, *vb.* compire, raggiùngere.
achievement, *n.* compimento *m.*, raggiungimento *m.*
Achilles' heel, *n.* tallone d'Achille *m.*
acid, *n. and adj.* àcido *(m.).*
acidify, *vb.* acidificare.
acidity, *n.* acidità *f.*
acidosis, *n.* acidòsi *f.*
acid test, *n.* prova del fuoco *f.*
acidulous, *adj.* acídulo.
acknowledge, *vb.* (recognize) riconóscere; **(a. receipt of)** accusare, dichiarare ricevuta di.
acme, *n.* acme *f.*, punto culminante *m.*
acne, *n.* acne *f.*
acolyte, *n.* accòlito *m.*
acorn, *n.* ghianda *f.*
acoustics, *n.* acùstica *f.sg.*
acquaint, *vb.* informare, far sapere; (be acquainted with) conóscere.
acquaintance, *n.* conoscènza *f.*
acquainted, *adj.* conosciuto, familiare.
acquiesce, *vb.* acquietarsi, consentire tacitamente.
acquiescence, *n.* acquiescenza *f.*
acquire, *vb.* acquistare.
acquisition, *n.* acquisto *m.*
acquisitive, *adj.* acquisitivo.
acquit, *v.* assòlvere.
acquittal, *n.* assoluzione *f.*
acre, *n.* acro *m.*
acreage, *n.* estensione di terra *f.*
acrid, *adj.* acre.
acrimonious, *adj.* acre.
acrimony, *n.* acrèdine *f.*, acrimònia *f.*
acrobat, *n.* acròbata *m. and f.*
acrobatics, *n.* acròbàtica *f.*
acronym, *n.* acrònimo *m.*
acropolis, *n.* acròpoli, *f.*
across, *adv. and prep.* attraverso. **(a. the board)** generalizzato.
acrostic, *n.* acròstico *n.*
act, **1.** *n.* atto *m.* **2.** *vb.* agire; (stage) recitare; (behave) comportarsi.

acting, 1. n. recitazione f. **2.** adj. provvisòrio.
actinium, n. attínio m.
action, n. azione f.
activate, vb. attivare.
activation, n. attivazione f.
activator, n. attivatore m.
active, adj. attivo.
activism, n. attivismo m.
activity, n. attività f.
actor, n. attore m.
actress, n. attrice f.
actual, adj. vero.
actuality, n. verità f.
actually, adv. veramente.
actuary, n. attuàrio m.
actuate, vb. attuare.
acumen, n. acume m.
acupuncture, n. agopuntura f.
acute, adj. acuto.
acutely, adv. acutamente.
acuteness, n. acutezza f.
adage, n. adàgio m., màssima f., provèrbio m.
Adam, Adamo.
adamant, adj. adamantino.
Adam's apple, n. pomo d'Adamo m.
adapt, vb. addattare.
adaptability, n. adattabilità f.
adaptable, adj. adattàbile.
adaptation, n. adattamento m.
adapter, n. riduttore m.
adaptive, adj. adattévole.
add, vb. (join) aggiùngere; (arith.) sommare, addizionare.
addendum, n. addendo m.
adder, n. vípera f.
addict, n. dipendente m.; (drug a.) tossicòmane m.
addict oneself to, vb. dedicarsi a.
adding machine, n. calcolatrice f.
addition, n. addizione f.
additional, adj. addizionale.
additive, n. additivo m.
addle, vb. confondere; (egg) imputridirsi.
addled, adj. confuso; (egg) màrcio, pùtrido.
address, 1. n. (on letters, etc.) indirizzo m.; (speech) discorso m. **2.** vb. (a letter) indirizzare; (a person) indirizzarsi a.
addressee, n. destinatàrio m.
adduce, vb. addurre.

adenoid, 1. n. vegetazione adenòide f. **2.** adj. adenòide.
adept, adj. dèstro, àbile.
adeptly, adv. destramente, abilmente.
adeptness, n. destrezza f., abilità f.
adequacy, n. sufficiènza f.
adequate, adj. adeguato, sufficiènte.
adequately, adv. adeguatamente, sufficientemente.
adhere, vb. aderire.
adherence, n. aderènza f.
adherent, n. aderènte m.
adhesion, n. adesione f.
adhesive, n. and adj. adesivo (m.).
adhesiveness, n. adesività f.
adieu, interj. addío.
adjacent, adj. adiacènte.
adjustable, adj. regolàbile.
adjective, n. aggettivo m.
adjoin, vb. essere adiacènte a.
adjoining, adj. adiacènte.
adjourn, vb. aggiornare.
adjournment, n. aggiornamento m.
adjunct, n. and adj. aggiunto, accessòrio.
adjust, vb. aggiustare.
adjuster, n. aggiustatore, m.
adjustment, n. (action) aggiustamento m.; (money) aggiusstatura f.
adjutant, n. aiutante m., assistènte m.
ad-lib, vb. improvvisare.
administer, vb. amministrare.
administration, n. amministrazione f.
administrative, adj. amministrativo.
administrator, n. amministratore m.
admirable, adj. ammirévole, ammiràbile.
admirably, adv. ammirabilmente.
admiral, n. ammiràglio m.
admiralty, n. ammiragliato m., ministero della marina m.
admiration, n. ammirazione f.
admire, vb. ammirare.
admirer, n. ammiratore m.

admiringly, *adv.* con ammirazione.

admissible, *adj.* ammissíbile.

admission, *n.* (entrance) ammissione *f.*; (entry) entrata *f.*; (confession) confessione *f.*

admit, *vb.* amméttere.

admittance, *n.* ammissione *f.*; (entry) entrata *f.*

admittedly, *adv.* ammettendo.

admixture, *n.* mescolanza *f.*

admonish, *vb.* ammonire.

admonition, *n.* ammonizione *f.*

ado, *n.* fracasso *m.*

adobe, *n.* mattone crudo *m.*

adolescence, *n.* adolescènza *f.*

adolescent, *n. and adj.* adolescènte (*m.*).

adopt, *vb.* adottare.

adoption, *n.* adozione *f.*

adorable, *adj.* adoràbile.

adoration, *n.* adorazione *f.*

adore, *vb.* adorare.

adorn, *vb.* adornare, ornare.

adorned, *adj.* adorno.

adornment, *n.* adornamento *m.*

adrenal glands, *n.* ghiàndole surrenali *f.pl.*

adrenalin, *n.* adrenalina *f.*

Adriatic, *adj.* Adriatico.

adrift, *adv.* alla deriva.

adroit, *adj.* destro, àbile.

adulate, *vb.* adulare.

adulation, *n.* adulazione *f.*

adult, *n. and adj.* adulto.

adulterant, *n. and adj.* adulterante.

adulterate, *vb.* adulterare.

adulterer, *n.* adùltero *m.*

adulteress, *n.* adùltera *f.*

adultery, *n.* adultèrio *m.*

advance, 1. *n.* progresso *m.*; (pay) anticípo *m.*; (in a.) in anticípo. 2. *vb.* avanzare, progredire; (pay) anticipare.

advanced, *adj.* avanzato, progredito.

advancement, *n.* avanzamento *m.*

advantage, *n.* vantàggio *m.*

advantageous, *adj.* vantaggioso.

advantageously, *adv.* vantaggiosamente.

advent, *n.* avvènto *m.*

adventitious, *adj.* avventízio.

adventure, 1. *n.* avventura *f.* 2. *vb.* avventurare, rischiare.

adventurer, *n.* avventurière *m.*

adventurous, *adj.* avventuroso.

adventurously, *adv.* avventurosamente.

adverb, *n.* avvèrbio *m.*

adverbial, *adj.* avverbiale.

adversary, *n.* avversàrio *m.*

adverse, *adj.* avvèrso.

adversely, *adv.* avversamente.

adversity, *n.* avversità *f.*

advert, *vb.* avvertire.

advertise, *vb.* far réclame per, reclamizzare.

advertisement, *n.* réclame *f.*, pubblicità *f.*; (newspaper) annunzio *m.*, inserzione *f.*

advertiser, *n.* inserzionista *m.*

advertising, *n.* réclame *f.*, pubblicità *f.* (a. agent) *n.* pubblicista *m. and f.*; (a. campaign) *n.* campagna pubblicitaria *f.*

advice, *n.* consiglio *m.*; (news) avviso *m.*

advisability, *n.* convenienza *f.*, opportunità *f.*

advisable, *adj.* conveniente, opportuno.

advisably, *adv.* opportunamente.

advise, *adv.* consigliare; (inform) avvisare.

advisedly, *adv.* consigliatamente, apposta.

advisement, *n.* deliberazione *f.*

adviser, *n.* consigliere *m.*

advisory, *adj.* consultivo.

advocacy, *n.* difesa *f.*, propugnazione *f.*

advocate, 1. *n.* (law) avvocato *m.*; (defender) difensore *m.*, propugnatore *m.* 2. *vb.* propugnare, difèndere.

aegis, *n.* ègida *f.*

aerate, *vb.* aerare.

aeration, *n.* aerazione *f.*

aerial, *adj.* aèreo.

aerially, *adv.* per ària.

aerie, *n.* nido *m.*

aerodynamic, *adj.* aerodinàmico.

aeronautics, *n.* aeronàutica *f.*

aerosol bomb, *n.* bomboletta nebulizzante *f.*

aesthete, *n.* esteta *m. and f.*

aesthetic, *adj.* estètico.

aesthetics, n. estètica f.
afar, adv. lontano.
affability, n. affabilità f.
affable, adj. affàbile.
affably, adv. affabilmente.
affair, n. affare m.
affect, vb. (move) commuovere; (concern) interessare; (pretend) affettare.
affectation, n. affettazione f.
affected, adj. affettato.
affecting, adj. commovènte.
affection, n. affezione f.
affectionate, adj. affetuoso.
affectionately, adv. affettosamente.
afferent, adj. afferènte.
affiance, vb. fidanzare.
affidavit, n. dichiarazione giurata f.
affiliate, vb. affiliare, associare.
affiliation, n. affiliazione f., associazione f.
affinity, n. affinità f.
affirm, vb. affermare.
affirmation, n. affermazione f.
affirmative, adj. affermativo.
affirmatively, adv. affermativamente.
affix, 1. n. affisso m. 2. vb. affissare.
afflict, vb. affliggere.
affliction, n. afflizione f.
affluence, n. opulènza f.
affluent, adj. opulento.
afford, vb. (have the means to) avere i mezzi di.
affray, n. lite f., rissa f.
affront, 1. n. affronto m. 2. vb. affrontare.
afield, adv. (far a.) lontano.
afire, adj. in fiamme.
aflame, adj. in fiamme.
afloat, adv. a galla.
afoot, adj. a piedi.
aforementioned, adj. sopraindicato, suindicato.
aforesaid, adj. sopraddetto, suddetto.
afraid, pred.adj. (be a.) aver paùra.
afresh, adv. di nuovo, da capo, daccapo.
Africa, n. Àfrica f.
African, n. and adj. africano (m.)

aft, adv. indiètro.
after, 1. prep. dopo. 2. conj. dopo che.
aftereffect, n. effètto m.
afterlife, n. al-di-là m.
aftermath, n. conseguènze f. (pl.)
afternoon, n. pomeriggio m.
aftershave, n. dopobarba m.
afterthought, n. (as an a.) ripensàndoci.
afterward, adv. dopo.
afterwards, adv. dopo.
again, adv. di nuòvo; (again and again) ripetutamente.
against, prep. contro.
agape, adv. a bocca aperta.
agate, n. àgata f.
age, 1. n. età f. 2. vb. invecchiare.
aged, adj. vècchio.
ageism, n. discriminazione basata sull'età f.
ageless, adj. che non invècchia.
agency, n. agenzia f.
agenda, n. òrdine del giorno m.
agent, n. agènte m.
agglutinate, vb. agglutinare.
agglutination, n. agglutinazione f.
aggrandize, vb. ingrandire.
aggrandizement, n. ingrandimento m.
aggravate, vb. aggravare.
aggravation, n. aggravamento m.
aggregate, 1. n. aggregato m. 2. vb. aggregare.
aggregation, n. aggregazione f.
aggression, n. aggressione f.
aggressive, adj. aggressivo.
aggressively, adv. aggressivamente.
aggressiveness, n. aggressività f.
aggressor, n. aggressore m.
aghast, adj. sbalordito.
agile, adj. àgile.
agility, n. agilità f.
agitate, vb. agitare.
agitation, n. agitazione f.
agitator, n. agitatore m.
agnostic, n. and adj. agnòstico (m.)
ago, adv. fa (always follows).
agonize, vb. agonizzare; (refl.) angosciarsi.
agonized, adj. agonizzante.

agony, n. agonía f.; **(be in a.)** agonizzare.

agrarian, adj. agràrio.

agree, vb. concordare, èssere d'accordo.

agreeable, adj. piacévole, gradévole; (of persons) simpàtico.

agreeably, adv. piacevolmente, gradevolmente.

agreeing, adj. concòrde.

agreement, n. accòrdo m.

agribusiness, n. agricultura, orticultura f.

agriculture, n. agricultura f.

agronomy, n. agronomia f.

ahead, adv. avanti; **(straight a.)** sèmpre diritto.

aid, 1. n. aiuto m. 2. vb. aiutare.

aide, n. aiutante m.

AIDS, n. aids. f. (sindrome di immunodeficenza aggravata).

ail, vb. èssere malato.

ailing, adj. malato.

ailment, n. malattía f.

aim, 1. n. mira; (purpose) scòpo. 2. vb. (point) puntare; (direct) dirigere; (look toward) mirare.

aimless, adj. senza scòpo.

aimlessly, adv. senza scòpo.

air, 1. n. ària f. 2. vb. aerare.

airbag, n. (in automobiles) sacco ad aria m.

air base, n. base aèrea f.

airborne, adj. aviotrasportato.

air-conditioned, vb. installare un impianto di condizionamento di ària in.

air-conditioned, adj. ad ària condizionata.

air-conditioning, n. aria condizionata f.

aircraft, n. aèreo m.

aircraft-carrier, n. portaèrei m.

air fleet, n. flotta aèrea f.

air gun, n. fucile ad ària compressa m.

airing, n. (walk) passeggiata f.

airline, n. aviolínea f.

air liner, n. aeroplano m.

air mail, n. posta aèrea f.

airplane, n. aeroplano m.

air pollution, n. inquinamento dell'aria m.

airport, n. aeropòrto m., aeroscalo m.; (for seaplanes) idroscalo m.

air pressure, n. pressione dell'ària f.

air raid, n. attacco aèreo m.

air-sick, adj. **(be a.)** sentir nàusea (in un aeroplano).

airtight, adj. impermeàbile all'aria.

airy, adj. arioso.

aisle, n. passaggio m.; (church) navata f.

ajar, adj. socchiuso.

akin, adj. affine.

alacrity, n. alacrità f.

alarm, 1. n. allarme m. 2. vb. allarmare, spaventare.

alarmist, n. allarmista m.

albino, n. and adj. albino (m.).

album, n. album m.

albumen, n. albume m.

alchemy, n. alchimia f.

alcohol, n. àlcool m.

alcoholic, adj. alc(o)òlico.

alcove, n. alcòva f.

ale, n. birra f.

alert, 1. n. allarme m. 2. adj. vigilante; (keen) acuto. 3. vb. avvertire.

alfalfa, n. alfalfa f.

algae, n. alghe f.pl.

algebra, n. àlgebra f.

alias, adv. àlias.

alibi, n. àlibi m.

alien, n. and adj. alièno (m.); (foreign) straniero (m.), forestiero (m.).

alienate, vb. alienare.

alight, 1. vb. (dismount) smontare; (get down) scéndere 2. adj. acceso.

align, vb. allineare.

alike, 1. adj. símile. 2. adv. similmente.

alimentary, adj. alimentare.

alimentary canal, n. canale alimentàrio m.

alimony, n. alimenti m.pl.

alive, adj. vivente; **(be a.)** vívere.

alkali, n. àlcali m.

alkaline, adj. alcalino.

all, adj. tutto; **(above a.)** sopratutto; **(a. at once)** tutt'un tratto; **(a. the same)** nondimeno;

(a. of you) voi tutti; **(not at a.)** niente affatto.

allay, *vb.* alleviare; (lessen) diminuire.

allegation, *n.* accusa *f.*

allege, *vb.* accusare.

allegiance, *n.* fedeltà *f.*

allegory, *n.* allegoría *f.*

allergy, *n.* allergía *f.*

alleviate, *vb.* alleviare.

alley, *n.* vícolo *m.;* (in garden) viale *m.*

alliance, *n.* alleanza *f.*

allied, *adj.* alleato; (related) affine.

alligator, *n.* alligatore *m.*

allocate, *vb.* assegnare.

allot, *vb.* assegnare, dividere.

allotment, *n.* assegnazione *f.*

allow, *vb.* (permit) perméttere; (admit) ammméttere; (grant) concédere; **(a. for)** far débito conto di.

allowance, *n.* (money) assegno *m.;* (permission) permesso *m.;* (reduction) riduzione *f.*

alloy, 1. *n.* lega *f.* **2.** *vb.* mescolare.

all right, *interj.* va bène.

all-time, *adj.* senza precedenti.

allude, *vb.* allúdere.

allure, *vb.* affascinare, adescare.

alluring, *adj.* adescatore, seducènte.

allusion, *n.* allusione *f.*

ally, 1. *n.* alleato *m.* **2.** *vb.* alleare.

almanac, *n.* almanacco *m.*

almighty, *adj.* onnipotente.

almond, *n.* màndorla *f.*

almond-tree, *n.* màndorlo *m.*

almost, *adv.* quasi.

alms, *n.* elemòsina *f. (sg.)*

aloft, *adv.* in alto.

alone, 1. *adj.* solo; **(let a.)** lasciare in pace. **2.** *adv.* solamente.

along, *prep.* lungo; **(come a.!)** venite dunque!

alongside, 1. *adv.* accanto. **2.** *prep.* accanto a.

aloof, 1. *adj.* riservato. **2.** *adv.* in disparte.

aloud, *adv.* ad alta voce.

alpaca, *n.* alpaca *m.*

alphabet, *n.* alfabèto *m.*

alphabetical, *adj.* alfabètico.

alphabetize, *vb.* méttere in òrdine alfabètico.

alpine, *adj.* alpino.

Alps, *n.* Alpi *f. pl.*

already, *adv.* già, di già.

also, *adv.* anche.

also-ran, *adj.* non-piazzato, perdente.

altar, *n.* altare *m.*

alter, *vb.* alterare.

alteration, *n.* alterazione *f.*

alternate, 1. *n.* sostituto *m.* **2.** *adj.* alternativo. **3.** *vb.* alternare.

alternating current, *n.* corrente alternata *f.*

alternative, 1. *n.* alternativa *f.* **2.** *adj.* alternativo.

although, *conj.* benchè, quantunque, sebbene.

altitude, *n.* altitùdine *f.*

alto, *n.* contralto *m.*

altogether, *adv.* completamente.

altruism, *n.* altruismo *m.*

aluminum, *n.* alluminio *m.*

altruism, *n.* altruismo *m.*

always, *adv.* sèmpre.

amalgam, *n.* amàlgama *m.*

amalgamate, *vb.* amalgamare.

amass, *vb.* ammassare.

amateur, *n.* dilettante *m. and f.*

amaze, *vb.* meravigliare, stupire; **(be a.d.)** meravigliarsi, stupirsi.

amazement, *n.* meraviglia *f.,* stupore *m.*

amazing, *adj.* meraviglioso.

ambassador, *n.* ambasciatore *m.*

amber, *n.* ambra *f.*

ambidextrous, *adj.* ambidèstro.

ambiguity, *n.* ambiguità *f.*

ambiguous, *adj.* ambìguo.

ambition, *n.* ambizione *f.*

ambitious, *adj.* ambizioso.

amble, *vb.* camminare senza fretta.

ambulance, *n.* ambulanza *f.*

ambulatory, *n. and adj.* ambulatòrio *(m.)*.

ambush, 1. *n.* imboscata *f.* **2.** *vb.* tendere un'imboscata.

ameliorate, *vb.* migliorare.

amen, *interj.* amen, così sia.

amenable, *adj.* responsàbile, governàbile, dòcile.

amend, *vb.* emendare, corrèggere, migliorare.

amendment, *n.* emendamento *m.*

amenity, *n.* amenità *f.*

America, *n.* Amèrica *f.*

American, *n. and adj.* americano (*m*).

amethyst, *n.* ametista *f.*

amiable, *adj.* amàbile.

amicable, *adj.* amichévole.

amid, *prep.* fra, tra, in mèzzo a.

amidships, *adv.* nel mezzo della nave.

amiss, *adv.* che non va bene; (be a.) non andar bene.

amity, *n.* amicizia *f.*

ammonia, *n.* ammoníaca *f.*

ammunition, *n.* munizione *f.*

amnesia, *n.* amnesía *f.*

amnesty, *n.* amnistía *f.*

amniocentesis, *n.* amniocèntesi *f.*

amoeba, *n.* amèba *f.*

among, *prep.* fra, tra.

amoral, *adj.* amorale.

amorous, *adj.* amoroso.

amorphous, *adj.* amorfo.

amortize, *vb.* ammortizzare.

amount, **1.** *n.* somma *f.*, quantità *f.* **2.** *vb.* ammontare.

ampere, *n.* ampère *m.*

amphibian, *n.* anfibio *m.*

amphibious, *adj.* anfibio.

amphitheater, *n.* anfiteatro *m.*

ample, *adj.* àmpio.

amplify, *vb.* ampliare, amplificare.

amputate, *vb.* amputare.

amputee, *n.* amputato *m.*, mutilato *m.*

amuse, *vb.* divertire.

amusement, *n.* divertimento *m.*

an, *art.* un *m.*, una *f.*

anachronism, *n.* anacronismo *m.*

anagram, *n.* anagramma *m.*

analogous, *adj.* anàlogo.

analogy, *n.* analogía *f.*

analysis, *n.* anàlisi *f.*

analyst, *n.* analista *m.*

analytic, *adj.* analítico.

analyze, *vb.* analizzare.

anarchy, *n.* anarchía *f.*

anathema, *n.* anatema *m.*

anatomy, *n.* anatomía *f.*

ancestor, *n.* antenato *m.*

ancestral, *adj.* degli antenati.

ancestry, *n.* lignàggio *m.*

anchor, **1.** *n.* àncora *f.* **2.** *vb.* ancorare.

anchorage, *n.* ancoràggio *m.*

anchovy, *n.* acciuga *f.*

ancient, *adj.* antico.

and, *conj.* e; (before vowels) ed.

anecdote, *n.* anèddoto *m.*

anemia, *n.* anemía *f.*

anesthesia, *n.* anestesía *f.*

anesthetic, *n. and adj.* anestètico (*m.*).

anesthetist, *n.* anestesista *f.*

anew, *adv.* di nuòvo.

angel, *n.* àngelo *m.*

anger, *n.* ira *f.*, ràbbia *f.*

angle, **1.** *n.* àngolo *m.* **2.** *vb.* (fish) pescare.

angry, *adj.* adirato, arrabiato; (get a.) adirarsi, arrabbiarsi.

anguish, *n.* angòscia *f.*

angular, *adj.* angolare.

aniline, *n.* anilina *f.*

animal, *n. and adj.* animale (*m.*).

animate, *vb.* animare.

animated, *adj.* animato.

animated cartoon, *n.* disegno animato *m.*

animation, *n.* animazione *f.*

animosity, *n.* animosità *f.*

animus, *n.* ànimo *m.*

anise, *n.* ànice *m.*

ankle, *n.* caviglia *f.*

annals, *n.* annali *m.* (*pl.*)

annex, **1.** *n.* annèsso *m.* **2.** *vb.* annèttere.

annexation, *n.* annessione *f.*

annihilate, *vb.* annichilire.

anniversary, *n.* anniversàrio *m.*

annotate, *vb.* annotare.

annotation, *n.* annotazione *f.*

announce, *vb.* annunziare, annunciare.

announcement, *n.* annùncio *m.*

announcer, *n.* annunciatore *m.*, annunciatrice *f.*

annoy, *vb.* infastidire.

annoyance, *n.* fastídio *m.*

annual, *n. and adj.* ànnuo (*m.*), annuale (*m.*).

annuity, *n.* annualità *f.*

annul, *vb.* annullare.

annunciate, *vb.* annunciare.

anode, *n.* ànodo *m.*

anoint, *vb.* ùngere.

anomalous, *adj.* anòmalo.

anomaly, n. anomalía f.
anonymity, n. anonimità f.
anonymous, adj. anònimo.
anorexia, n. anoressia f.
anorexic, adj. anorèssico.
another, adj. un altro m., un'altra f.; (one a.) l'un l'altro.
answer, 1. n. risposta f. **2.** vb. rispóndere.
answerable adj. responsàbile.
ant, n. formica f.
antacid, 1. n. antàcido m. **2.** adj. antiàcido.
antagonism, n. antagonismo m.
antagonist, n. antagonista m.
antagonistic, adj. ostile.
antagonize, vb. réndere ostile.
antarctic, n. and adj. antàrtico (m.).
antecede, vb. precèdere.
antecedent, adj. antecedènte.
antedate, vb. precédere.
antelope, n. antìlope f.
antenna, n. antenna f.
anterior, adj. anteriore.
anteroom, n. anticàmera f.
anthem, n. (church music) antifona f.; **(national a.)** inno nazionale m.
anthill, n. formicaio m.
anthology, n. antologìa f.
anthracite, n. antracite f.
anthropological, adj. antropològico.
anthropology, n. antropologìa f.
antiaircraft, adj. antiaèreo.
antibody, n. anticòrpo m.
antic, n. buffonata f.
anticipate, vb. anticipare.
anticipation, n. anticipazione f.
anticlerical, adj. anticlericale.
anticlimax, n. delusione f.
Antichrist, n. Anticristo m.
antidote, n. antídoto m.
antimony, n. antimònio m.
antinuclear, adj. antinucleare.
antipathy, n. antipatìa f.
antiquated, adj. antiquato.
antique, 1. n. oggetto antico m. **2.** adj. antico.
antiquity, n. antichità f.
antiseptic, n. and adj. antisèttico (m.).
antisocial, adj. antisociale.
antitoxin, n. antitossina f.

antler, n. palco m.
anvil, n. incùdine f.
anxiety, n. ànsia f., ansietà f.
anxious, adj. ansioso.
any, 1. adj. (in questions, for "some") del, dello, dell' m.sg., della, dell' f.sg., dei, degli m.pl., delle f.pl; **(not . . . any)** non . . . nessun; (no matter which) non impòrta quale; (every) ogni. **2.** pron. (any of it, any of them, with verb) ne.
anybody, pron. qualcuno; (after negative) nessuno; (no matter who) non importa chi.
anyhow, adv. in qualche manièra, a ogni modo.
anyone, pron. see anybody.
anything, pron. qualcosa, qualche còsa; (after negation) niènte; (no matter) non impòrta che còsa.
anyway, adv. see anyhow.
anywhere, adv. non impòrta dove.
apart, adv. a parte.
apartheid, n. segregazione razziale f.
apartment, n. appartamento m.
apathetic, adj. apàtico.
apathy, n. apatìa f.
ape, n. scimmia f.
aperture, n. apertura f.
apex, n. àpice m.
aphorism, n. aforismo m.
apiary, n. apiàrio m.
apiece, adj. l'uno, cadaùno.
apogee, n. apogèo m.
apologetic, adj. **(be a.)** scusarsi.
apologize for, vb. scusarsi di.
apology, n. (defense) apologìa f.; (excuse) scusa f.
apoplectic, adj. apoplèttico.
apoplexy, n. apoplessia f.
apostasy, n. apòstasi f.
apostate, n. apòstata m.
apostle, n. apòstolo m.
apostolic, adj. apostólico.
apostrohe, n. apòstrofo m.
apotheosis, n. apoteòsi f.
Appalachians, n. Appalacchi m.pl.
appall, vb. spaventare.
apparatus, n. apparato m., apparècchio m.

apparel, 1. n. vèste f., vestimento m. **2.** vb. vestire.

apparent, adj. apparènte.

apparition, n. apparizione f.

appeal, 1. n. appèllo m. **2.** vb. appellare.

appear, vb. parere; (become visible) apparire; (seem) sembrare; (be evident) risultare.

appearance, n. apparènza f.; (looks) aspètto m.

appease, vb. placare, acquetare.

appeasement, n. rappacificazione f.

appeaser, n. pacificatore m.

appellant, n. appellante m.

appellate, adj. d'appèllo.

appendage, n. appendice f.

appendectomy, n. appendectomia f.

appendicitis, n. appendicite f.

appendix, n. appendice f.

appetite, n. appetito m.

appetizer, n. antipasto m.

appetizing, adj. gustoso.

applaud, vb. applaudire.

applause, n. applàuso m.

apple, n. pomo m., mela f.

apple pie, n. torta di mele f.

applesauce, n. (lit.) consèrva di mele f.; (nonsense) fròttola f.

apple-tree, n. melo m.

appliance, n. apparècchio m.

appliances, n. (electric) elettrodomèstici m.pl.

applicable, adj. applicàbile.

applicant, n. richiedènte m.

application, n. (putting on) applicazione f.; (request) domanda f.

appliqué, adj. applicato; **(a. work)** ricamo applicato m.

apply, vb. (put on) applicare; (request) richièdere, fare una domanda.

appoint, vb. (a person) nominare; (time, place) fissare, stabilire.

appointment, n. (nomination) nòmina f.; (date) appuntamento m.

apportion, vb. distribuire.

appose, vb. giustapporre.

apposite, adj. appòsito.

apposition, n. apposizione f.

appraisal, n. stima f.

appraise, vb. stimare.

appreciable, adj. apprezzàbile.

appreciate, vb. apprezzare, tenere in giusto conto.

appreciation, n. apprezzamento m.

apprehend, vb. (fear) temere; (catch) arrestare.

apprehension, n. timore m.

apprehensive, adj. timoroso.

apprentice, n. apprendista m.

apprise, vb. informare.

approach, 1. n. accèsso m. **2.** vb. avvicinarsi a.

approachable, adj. avvicinàbile.

approbation, n. approvazione f.

appropriate, 1. adj. appropriato. **2.** vb. (take for oneself) appropriarsi; (set aside funds) stanziare.

appropriation, n. stanziamento m.

approval, n. approvazione f.

approve, vb. approvare.

approximate, 1. vb. approssimare. **2.** adj. approssimativo.

approximately, adv. approssimativamente.

approximation, n. approssimazione f.

appurtenance, n. appartenènza f.

apricot, n. albicòcca f.

April, n. aprile m.

apron, n. grembiule m.

apropos, adv. a propòsito.

apse, n. àbside f.

apt, adj. atto; (quick at) pronto a.

aptitude, n. attitùdine f.

Apulia, n. le Pùglie f.pl.

Apulian, adj. pugliese.

aquarium, n. acquàrio m.

aquatic, adj. acquàtico.

aqueduct, n. acquedotto m.

aqueous, adj. àcqueo.

aquiline, adj. aquilino.

Arab, n. àrabo m.

Arabic, adj. àrabo.

arable, adj. aràbile.

arbiter, n. àrbitro m.

arbitrary, adj. arbitràrio.

arbitrate, vb. arbitrare.

arbitration, n. arbitrato m.

arbitrator, n. àrbitro m.

arbor, n. pergolato m.

arboreal, adj. arbòreo.

arc, n. arco m.

arcade, *n.* galleria *f.*

arch, *n.* arco *m.*

archaeology, *n.* archeología *f.*

archaic, *adj.* arcàico.

archbishop, *n.* arcivéscovo *m.*

archdiocese, *n.* arcidiòcesi *f.*

archduke, *n.* arciduca *m.*

archer, *n.* arcière *m.*

archery, *n.* tiro dell'arco *m.*

archetype, *n.* archètipo *m.*

archipelago, *n.* arcipèlago *m.*

architect, *n.* architetto *m.*

architectural, *adj.* architettònico.

architecture, *n.* architettura *f.*

archives, *n.* archívio *m. (sg.)*

archway, *n.* pòrtico *m.*

arctic, *adj.* àrtico.

Arctic Circle, *n.* círcolo polare.

ardent, *adj.* ardènte.

ardor, *n.* ardore *m.*

arduous, *adj.* àrduo.

area, *n.* àrea *f.*

area code, *n.* prefisso teleselettivo *m.*

arena, *n.* arena *f.*

Argentine, 1. *n.* Argentina *f.* **2.** *adj.* argentino.

argue, *vb.* (draw a conclusion) arguire; (quarrel) bisticciarsi.

argument, *n.* (in debate) argomento *m.;* (quarrel) bistíccio *m.*

argumentative, *adj.* litigioso.

aria, *n.* ària *f.*

arid, *adj.* àrido.

aridity, *n.* aridità *f.*

arise, *vb.* (get up) levarsi; (come into being) nàscere.

aristocracy, *n.* aristocrazía *f.*

aristocrat, *n.* aristocràtico *m.*

aristocratic, *adj.* aristocràtico.

Aristotelian, *adj.* aristotèlico.

arithmetic, *n.* aritmètica *f.*

arithmetician, *n.* aritmetico *m.*

ark, *n.* arca *f.*

arm, 1. *n.* (body part) bràccio *m.;* (weapon) arma *f.* **2.** *vb.* armare.

armament, *n.* armamento *m.*

armature, *n.* armatura *f.*

armchair, *n.* poltrona *f.*

armful, *n.* bracciata *f.*

armhole, *n.* òcchio della mànica *m.*

armistice, *n.* armistízio *m.*

armlet, *n.* bracciale *m.*

armor, *n.* armatura *f.*

armored, *adj.* blindato.

armory, *n.* armería *f.;* magazzino *m.*

armpit, *n.* ascèlla *f.*

arms, *n.* (weapons) armi *f.pl.*

army, *n.* esèrcito *m.*

arnica, *n.* àrnica *f.*

aroma, *n.* aròma *m.*

aromatic, *adj.* aromàtico.

around, 1. *adv.* intorno. **2.** *prep.* intorno a.

arouse, *vb.* svegliare.

arraign, *vb.* accusare.

arrange, *vb.* ordinare, disporre, sistemare; (music) ridurre.

arrangement, *n.* ordinamento *m.;* (music) riduzione *f.*

array, 1. *n.* órdine *m.,* sèrie *f.* **2.** *vb.* ordinare.

arrears, *n.* arretrati *m.pl.*

arrest, 1. *n.* arrèsto *m.* **2.** *vb.* arrestare.

arrival, *n.* arrivo *m.*

arrive, *vb.* arrivare, giùngere.

arrogance, *n.* arroganza *f.*

arrogant, *adj.* arrogante.

arrogate, *vb.* arrogarsi.

arrow, *n.* fréccia *f.,* strale *m.*

arrowhead, *n.* punta di fréccia *f.*

arsenal, *n.* arsenale *m.*

arsenic, *n.* arsènico *m.*

arson, *n.* incèndio doloso *m.*

art, *n.* arte *f.;* (fine arts) bèlle arti *f.pl.*

arterial, *adj.* arteriale.

arteriosclerosis, *n.* arterioscleròsi *f.*

artery, *n.* artèria *f.*

artesian well, *n.* pozzo artesiano *m.*

artful, *adj.* astuto.

arthritic, *adj. and n.* artritico *m.*

arthritis, *n.* artrite *f.*

artichoke, *n.* carciòfo *m.*

article, *n.* artícolo *m.*

articulate, 1. *adj.* articolato. **2.** *vb.* articolare.

articulation, *n.* articolazione *f.*

artifice, *n.* artifício *m.*

artificial, *adj.* artificiale.

artificiality, *n.* artificialità *f.*

artillery, *n.* artiglierìa *f.*

artisan, *n.* artigiano *m.*

artist, *n.* artista *m., f.*

artistic, *adj.* artístico.

artistry, *n.* arte *f.*
artless, *adj.* ingènuo, senz'arte.
as, *prep. and conj.* come; **(as if)** quasi.
asbestos, *n.* asbèsto *m.*
ascend, *vb.* salire.
ascendancy, *n.* supremazìa *f.*
ascendant, *adj.* suprèmo.
ascent, *n.* salita *f.*
ascertain, *vb.* accertarsi.
ascetic, *n. and adj.* ascètico *(m.).*
ascribe, *vb.* ascrìvere.
ash, *n.* (tree) fràssino *m.*
ashamed, *adj.* vergognoso; **(be a. of)** vergognarsi di.
ashen, *adj.* di cénere.
ashes, *n.* cénere *f. (sg.).*
ashore, *adv.* a terra.
ash-tray, *n.* portacénere *m.*
Ash Wednesday, *n.* Mercoledì delle Ceneri *m.*
Asia, *n.* Àsia *f.*
Asian, *adj.* asiàtico.
aside, *adv.* a parte.
asinine, *adj.* asinino.
ask, *vb.* (question) domandare; (request) chièdere; (invite) invitare.
askance, *adv.* sospettosamente.
asleep, *adj.* addormentato; **(fall a.)** addormentarsi.
asparagus, *n.* aspàrago *m.,* spàragi *m.pl.*
aspect, *n.* aspètto *m.*
asperity, *n.* asperità *f.*
aspersion, *n.* denigrazione *f.*
asphalt, *n.* asfalto *m.*
asphyxia, *n.* asfissìa *f.*
asphyxiate, *vb.* asfissiare.
aspirant, *n.* aspirante *m.*
aspirate, 1. *n.* aspirata *f.* **2.** *adj.* aspirato. **3.** *vb.* aspirare.
aspiration, *n.* aspirazione *f.*
aspirator, *n.* aspiratore *m.*
aspire, *vb.* aspirare.
aspirin, *n.* aspirina *f.*
ass, *n.* àsino *m.;* sedere *m.*
assail, *vb.* assalire, attaccare.
assailable, *adj.* attaccàbile.
assailant, *n.* assalitore *m.*
assassin, *n.* assassino *m.*
assassinate, *vb.* assassinare.
assassination, *n.* assassìnio *m.*
assault, 1. *n.* assalto *m.* **2.** *vb.* assaltare.

assay, 1. *n.* sàggio *m.* **2.** *vb.* saggiare, assaggiare.
assemblage, *n.* riunione *f.*
assemble, *vb.* (bring together) riunire; (come together) riunirsi.
assembler, *n.* montatore *m.*
assembly, *n.* riunione *f.,* assemblèa *f.;* (autos, etc.) montàggio *m.*
assembly line, *n.* catena di montaggio *f.*
assent, 1. *n.* assènso *m.* **2.** *vb.* assentire.
assert, *vb.* asserire.
assertion, *n.* asserzione *f.*
assertive, *adj.* dogmàtico.
assertiveness, *n.* dogmaticità *f.*
assess, *vb.* (a fine) fissare (una multa); (property) stimare.
assessment, *n.* valutazione *f.,* giudìzio *m.*
assessor, *n.* assessore *m.*
asset, *n.* (possession) bène *m.;* (in accounting) attivo *m.*
asseverate, *vb.* asseverare.
asseveration, *n.* asseverazione *f.*
assiduity, *n.* assiduità *f.,* frequenza *f.*
assiduous, *adj.* assìduo.
assiduously, *adv.* assiduamente.
assign, *vb.* assegnare.
assignable, *adj.* assegnàbile.
assignation, *n.* assegnazione *f.;* (date) appuntamento *m.*
assigned, *adj.* addetto.
assignee, *n.* ricevitore *m.,* incaricato *m.*
assignment, *n.* assegnamento *m.,* assegnazione *f.,* incàrico *m.;* (school) cómpito *m.*
assimilable, *adj.* assimilabile.
assimilate, *vb.* assimilare.
assimilation, *n.* assimilazione *f.*
assimilative, *adj.* assimilativo.
assist, *vb.* aiutare.
assistance, *n.* aiuto *m.*
assistant, *n. and adj.* assistènte *(m.).*
assistantship, *n.* (academic) incarico di assistente *m.*
associate, *vb.* associare, *tr.;* associarsi, *intr.*
association, *n.* associazione *f.*
assonance, *n.* assonanza *f.*
assort, *vb.* assortire.
assorted, *adj.* assortito.

assortment, n. assortimento m.

assuage, vb. (pain) mitigare; (desire) soddisfare.

assume, vb. assùmere; (appropriate) arrogarsi; (feign) fìngere; (suppose) supporre.

assuming, adj. arrogante, presuntuoso.

assumption, n. supposizione f.; (eccles.) Ascensione f.

assurance, n. assicurazione f.

assure, vb. assicurare.

assured, adj. assicurato, sicuro.

assuredly, adv. sicuramente.

aster, n. astro m.

asterisk, n. asterisco m.

astern, adv. a poppa.

asteroid, n. asterôide m.

asthma, n. asma m.

astigmatism, n. astigmatismo m.

astir, adv. in mòto.

astonish, vb. sorprèndere, meravigliare.

astonishment, n. sorpresa f., meraviglia f.

astound, vb. stupire; **(be a.ed)** stupirsi.

astral, adj. astrale.

astray, 1. adj. sviato. **2.** vb. **(go a.)** sviarsi.

astride, adv. a cavalcioni; prep. a cavalcioni di.

astringent, adj. astringènte.

astrology, n. astrologia f.

astronaut, n. astronàuta m. and f.

astronautical, adj. astronautico.

astronomical, adj. astronòmico.

astronomy, n. astronomia f.

astrophysics, n. astrofìsica f.

astute, adj. astuto.

asunder, adv. (in twain) in due; (in pieces) a pèzzi.

aswarm, adj. pieno di.

asylum, n. (refuge) rifùgio m.; (madhouse) manicòmio m.

asymmetry, n. asimmetria f.

at, prep. (time, place, price) ad (before vowels), a (before vowels or consonants); (at someone's house, shop, etc.) da.

ataxia, n. atassia f.

atheist, n. àteo m.

athlete, n. atlèta m.

athletic, adj. atlètico.

athletics, n. atletismo m.

athwart, adv. attravèrso.

Atlantic, adj. atlàntico.

Atlantic Ocean, n. Ocèano atlàntico m.

atlas, n. atlante m.

atmosphere, n. atmosfèra f.

atmospheric, adj. atmosfèrico.

atoll, n. atòllo m.

atom, n. àtomo m.

atomic, adj. atòmico.

atomic age, n. era atòmica f.

atomic bomb, n. bomba atòmica f.

atomic energy, n. energia atòmica f.

atomize, vb. (liquids) nebulizzare.

atonal, adj. atonale.

atone for, vb. espiare.

atonement, n. espiazione f.

atonic, adj. atònico.

atrium, n. atrio m.

atrocious, adj. atroce.

atrocity, n. atrocità f.

atrophy, n. atrofìa f.

atropine, n. atropìna f.

attach, vb. attaccare.

attaché, n. addetto m.

attachment, n. (lit.) attaccamento m.; (liking) affezione f.; (equipment) accessòrio m.

attack, 1. n. attacco m. **2.** vb. attaccare.

attacker, n. assalitore m.

attain, vb. raggiùngere.

attainable, adj. raggiungìbile.

attainment, n. raggiungimento m.

attempt, 1. n. tentativo m. **2.** vb. tentare.

attend, vb. (give heed to) prestare attenzione a; (medical) curarsi di; (serve) servire; (meeting) assìstere a; (lectures) frequentare; (see to) occuparsi di.

attendance, n. assistènza f.

attendant, n. and adj. assistènte (m.).

attendee, n. assistito m.

attention, n. attenzione f.; **(pay a.)** fare attenzione.

attentive, adj. attènto.

attentively, adv. attentamente.

attenuate, vb. attenuare.

attenuation, *n.* attenuazione *m.*

attest, *vb.* attestare.

attic, *n.* soffitta *f.*

attire, 1. *n.* abbigliamento *m.* **2.** *vb.* abbigliare.

attitude, *n.* atteggiamento *m.;* **(take an a.)** atteggiarsi.

attorney, *n.* procuratore *m.*

attract, *vb.* attrarre.

attraction, *n.* attrazione *f.*

attractive, *adj.* attraènte.

attributable, *adj.* attribuíbile.

attribute, *vb.* attribuire.

attribution, *n.* attribuzione *f.*

attrition, *n.* attrito *m.*

attune, *vb.* armonizzare; **(an instrument)** accordare.

auction, *n.* véndita all'asta *f.*

auctioneer, *n.* banditore *f.*

audacious, *adj.* audace.

audacity, *n.* audàcia *f.*

audible, *adj.* udíbile.

audience, *n.* (listeners) uditòrio *m.;* (interview) udiènza *f.*

audiovisual, *adj.* audiovisivo.

audit, 1. *n.* verifica *f.,* contròllo *m.* **2.** *vb.* verificare, controllare.

audition, *n.* audizione *f.*

auditor, *n.* uditore *m.,* uditrice *f.;* (accounts) revisore *m.,* controllore *m.*

auditorium, *n.* auditòrio *m.*

auditory, *adj.* uditivo.

auger, *n.* succhièllo *m.,* trivèllo *m.*

augment, *vb.* aumentare.

augur, *vb.* augurare.

august, *adj.* augusto.

August, *n.* agosto *m.*

aunt, *n.* zía *f.*

auricular, *adj.* auricolare.

auspice, *n.* auspício *m.*

auspicious, *adj.* favorévole.

austere, *adj.* austèro.

austerity, *n.* austerità *f.*

Austria, *n.* Àustria *f.*

Austrian, *adj.* austríaco.

authentic, *adj.* autèntico.

authenticate, *vb.* autenticare.

authenticity, *n.* autenticità *f.*

author, *n.* autore *m.*

authoritarian, *adj.* autoritàrio.

authoritative, *adj.* autorévole.

authoritatively, *adv.* autorevolmente.

authority, *n.* autorità *f.*

authorization, *n.* autorizzazione *f.*

authorize, *vb.* autorizzare.

autism, *n.* autismo *m.*

auto, *n.* àuto *m.*

autobiographical, *adj.* autobio-gràfico.

autobiography, *n.* autobiografía *f.*

autocracy, *n.* autocrazía *f.*

autocrat, *n.* autòcrate *m.*

autograph, *n.* autògrafo *m.*

automatic, *adj.* automàtico.

automatically, *adv.* automatica-mente.

automaton, *n.* autòma *m.*

automobile, *n.* automòbile *f.*

automotive, *adj.* automobilís-tico.

autonomous, *adj.* autònomo.

autonomy, *n.* autonomía *f.*

autopsy, *n.* autopsía *f.*

autumn, *n.* autunno *m.*

auxiliary, *n. and adj.* ausiliare (*m.*)

avail, *vb.* servire; **(be of no a.)** non servire a nulla.

available, *adj.* disponíbile.

avalanche, *n.* valanga *f.*

avarice, *n.* avarízia *f.*

avaricious, *adj.* avaro.

avenge, *vb.* vendicare.

avenger, *n.* vendicatore *m.*

avenue, *n.* viale *m.*

average, 1. *n.* mèdia *f.* **2.** *adj.* mèdio. **3.** *vb.* fare la mèdia di.

averse, *adj.* avvèrso.

aversion, *n.* avversione *f.*

avert, *vb.* impedire.

aviary, *n.* aviàrio *m.,* uccellièra *f.*

aviation, *n.* aviazione *f.*

aviator, *n.* aviatore *m.*

aviatrix, *n.* aviatrice *f.*

avid, *adj.* àvido.

avocation, *n.* divertimento *m.*

avoid, *vb.* evitare, scansare; **(so as to a.)** a scanso di.

avoidable, *adj.* evitàbile.

avoidance, *n.* scanso *m.*

avow, *vb.* confessare.

avowal, *n.* confessione *f.*

avowedly, *adv.* lo confèsso.
await, *vb.* aspettare.
awake, 1. *adj.* svéglio. **2.** *vb.* svegliare, *tr.;* svegliarsi, *intr.*
awaken, *vb.* see **awake.**
award, 1. *n.* prèmio *m.* **2.** *vb.* conferire; **(a. a prize to)** premiare.
aware, *adj.* consapévole, cònscio.
awash, *adj.* al livéllo dell'acqua.
away, *adv.* via, lontano; **(go a.)** andàrsene.
awe, 1. *n.* terrore *m.,* soggezione *f.* **2.** *vb.* ispirare terrore a.
awesome, *adj.* tremèndo.
awful, *adj.* terribile.
awhile, *adv.* per un momento.
awkward, *adj.* gòffo; (difficult) difficile.
awning, *n.* tènda *f.*
awry, *adv.* di travèrso.
axe, *n.* àscia *f.*
axiom, *n.* assiòma *m.*
axis, *n.* asse *m.*
axle, *n.* asse *m.*
ayatollah, *n.* ayatollah *m.*
azure, *adj.* azzurro.

babble, 1. *n.* balbettío *m.* **2.** *vb.* balbettare.
babbler, *n.* balbuziènte *m.*
babe, *n.* bimbo *m.;* (girl) ragazza *f.*
baboon, *n.* babbuino *m.*
baby, *n.* bambino *m.,* bimbo *m.;* **(b.-carriage)** carrozzèlla *f.*
babyish, *adj.* bambinesco, infantile.
bachelor, *n.* scàpolo *m.;* (degree) baccellière *m.*
bacillus, *n.* bacillo *m*
back, 1. *n.* dòsso *m.,* dòrso *m.,* schièna *f.* **2.** *adj.* posteriore. **3.** *vb.* (go backwards) indietreggiare; (support) appoggiare, sostenere, spalleggiare; **(b. down)** cédere. **4.** *adv.* indiètro.
backbone, *n.* spina dorsale *f.*
backer, *n.* sostenitore *m.*
backfire, *vb.* scoppiare.
background, *n.* sfondo *m.*
backhand, *n.* rovèscio *m.*
backing, *n.* appòggio *m.,* sostegno *m.*
backlash, *n.* reazione conservatrice *f.*
backlog, *n.* risèrve *f.pl.*
back out, *vb.* ritirarsi.
backpack, *n.* sacco da montagna *m.*
backstage, *n.* retroscèna *f.*
backward, 1. *adj.* stùpido. **2.** *adv.* indiètro.
backwardness, *n.* stupidità *f.*
backwards, *adv.* indiètro.
backwater, *n.* acqua stagnante *f.*
backwoods, *n.* retrotèrra *f.*

backyard, *n.* giardino privato *m.*
bacon, *n.* pancetta *f.*
bacteria, *n.* battèri *m.pl.*
bactericide, *adj. and n.* battericida *(m.)*
bacteriologist, *n.* batteriòlogo *m.*
bacteriology, *n.* batteriología *f.*
bacterium, *n.* battèrio *m.*
bad, *adj.* cattivo.
badge, *n.* emblèma *f.,* distintivo *m.*
badger, *n.* tasso *m.*
badly, *adv.* male, malamente.
badmouth, *vb.* criticare, diffamare.
badness, *n.* cattivèria *f.*
bad-tempered, *adj.* di cattivo umore.
baffle, *vb.* (hinder) impedire; (perplex) rèndere perplèsso.
bafflement, *n.* perplessità *f.*
bag, 1. *n.* sacco *m.,* borsa *f.;* (woman's purse) borsetta *f.* **2.** *vb.* (get) ottenere; **(put in a b.)** insaccare.
baggage, *n.* bagàglio *m.;* **(b. check)** scontrino per bagagli *m.*
baggage cart, *n.* (airport) carretta per bagagli *f.*
baggy, *adj.* gónfio.
bagpipe, *n.* cornamusa *f.,* zampogna *f.*
baguette, *n.* baguette *f.,* ciabatta *f.*
bail, *n.* cauzione *f.,* garanzía *f.*
bailiff, *n.* usciere *m.*
bail out, *vb.* (set free) fornire garanzía per; (water) vuotare.

bait, n. esca f.

bake, vb. cuòcere al forno.

baker, n. fornaio m.

bakery, n. forno m.

baking, n. cottura al forno m.

baking powder, n. polvere di amido e diossido di carbonio f.

baking soda, n. bicarbonato di sodio m.

balance, 1. n. (equilibrium) equilìbrio m.; (comm.) saldo m.; (scales) bilància f. **2.** vb. bilanciare; (weigh) pesare; (make of equal weight) equilibrare; (comm.) saldare.

balance sheet, n. bilancio m.

balcony, n. balcone m.

bald, adj. calvo.

baldness, n. calvìzie f.sg.

bale, n. balla f.

baleful, adj. minacciante.

balk, vb. (hinder) impedire; (refuse to move) essere ritroso.

Balkans, n. i Balcani m.pl.

balky, adj. ritroso.

ball, n. palla f.; (bullet) pallòttola f.; (dance) ballo m.

ballad, n. ballata f.

ballade, n. ballata f.

ballast, n. zavorra f.

ball bearing, n. cuscinetto a sfere m.

ballerina, n. ballerina f.

ballet, n. ballo m.

ballistics, n. balìstica f.

balloon, n. pallone m.

ballot, n. (voting) votazione f; (paper) scheda f.

ballot box, n. urna f.

ballpoint, n. penna a sfera f.

ballroom, n. sala da ballo f.

balm, n. bàlsamo m.

balmy, adj. balsàmico.

balsam, n. bàlsamo m.

baluster, n. balaustra f.

balustrade, n. balaùstra f., balaustrata f.

bamboo, n. bambù m.

bamboozle, vb. truffare.

ban, 1. n. proibizione f. **2.** vb. proibire.

banal, adj. banale.

banana, n. banana f.

band, n. (group, including musical band) banda f.; (headband) benda f.; (ribbon) striscia f.

bandage, n. benda f.

bandanna, n. fazzoletto multicolore m.

bandbox, n. cappellièra f.

bandit, n. bandito m.

bandmaster, n. capobanda m., maestro di banda m.

bandsaw, n. sega a nastro f.

bandsman, n. bandista m.

bandstand, n. palco della banda musicale f.

baneful, adj. dannoso.

bang, 1. n. (hair-do) frangia f.; (blow) colpo m. **2.** vb. sbàttere. **3.** interj. pum!

banish, vb. bandire, esiliare.

banishment, n. bando, esilio m.

banister, n. ringhièra , f.

bank, 1. n. (institution) banca f., banco m.; (edge of water) riva f. **2.** vb. (rely on) contare su; (airplane) inclinare.

bankbook, n. libretto di depòsito m.

banker, n. banchière m.

banking, 1. n. operazioni bancàrie f.pl. **2.** adj. bancàrio.

bank note, n. banconota f.

bankrupt, 1. adj. fallito. **2.** vb. far fallire; (go b.) fallire.

bankruptcy, n. fallimento m., bancarotta f.

banner, n. bandièra f.

banns, n. bandi matrimoniali m.pl.

banquet, n. banchetto m.

banter, 1. n. scherzo m., cèlia f. **2.** vb. scherzare, celiare.

baptism, n. battésimo m.

baptismal, adj. battesimale.

Baptist, n. battista m.

baptistery, n. battistèro m.

baptize, vb. battezzare.

bar, 1. n. sbarra f.; (obstacle) ostàcolo m.; (for drinks) bar m. **2.** vb. sbarrare; ostacolare.

bar association, n. ordine degli avvocati m.

barb, n. punta ricurva f.

barbarian, n. bàrbaro m.

barbaric, adj. barbarico.

barbarism, n. barbàrie f.; (gram.) barbarismo m.
barbarous, adj. bàrbaro m.
barbecue, vb. cucinare alla brace.
barbed, adj. pungente, spinoso.
barbed wire, n. filo spinato m.
barber, n. barbière m., parrucchière m.
barbiturate, n. barbitùrico m.
bare, 1. adj. nudo, scopèrto. **2.** vb. scoprire.
bareback, adv. sènza sèlla.
barefoot, adj. scalzo.
barely, adv. appena.
bareness, n. nudità f.
bargain, 1. n. affare m.; (cheap purchase) occasione f. **2.** vb. mercanteggiare.
barge, n. chiatta f.
baritone, n. and adj. barítono (m.).
barium, n. bàrio m.
bark, 1. n. (of tree) scorza f., cortéccia f.; (of dog) abbaiamento m. **2.** vb. abbaiare.
barley, n. orzo m.
barn, n. granaio m.
barnacle, n. cirrìpede m.
barnyard, n. cortile m.
barometer, n. baròmetro m.
barometric, adj. barométrico.
baron, n. barone m.
baroness, n. baronessa f.
baronial, adj. baronale.
baroque, adj. baròcco.
barracks, n. casèrma f.sg.
barrage, n. fuoco di sbarramento m.
barred, adj. sbarrato; (excluded) escluso; (forbidden) vietato.
barrel, n. barile m.
barren, adj. stèrile.
barrenness, n. sterilità f.
barricade, n. barricata f.
barrier, n. barrièra f.
barroom, n. béttola f., bar m.
bartender, n. barista m.
barter, 1. n. baratto m. **2.** vb. barattare.
base, 1. n. base f. **2.** adj. basso. **3.** vb. basare.
baseball, n. baseball m.
baseboard, n. zòccolo m.
Basel, n. Basilèa f.
basement, n. cantina f.

baseness, n. bassezza f.
bashful, adj. tímido.
bashfully, adv. timidamente.
bashfulness, n. timidezza f.
basic, adj. fondamentale.
basin, n. catino m.
basis, n. base f.
bask, vb. riscaldarsi, godersi.
basket, n. cesta f.
basketball, n. pallacanestro m.
bass, n. (voice) basso m.; (fish) pesce pèrsico m.
bassinet, n. culla f.
bassoon, n. fagòtto m.
bastard, n. and adj. bastardo (m.).
baste, vb. (sewing) imbastire; (cooking) ammorbidire.
bat, n. (animal) pipistrèllo m.; (baseball) bastone m.
batch, n. infornata f.
bate, vb. diminuire.
bath, n. bagno m.
bathe, vb. (tr.) bagnare; (intr.) fare il bagno.
bather, n. bagnante m. or f.
bathing resort, n. stazione balneare f.
bathing suit, n. costume da bagno m.
bathrobe, n. vestàglia f.
bathroom, n. stanza da bagno f.
bathtub, n. vasca da bagno f.
baton, n. (military) bastone m.; (conductor's) bacchetta f.
battalion, n. battaglione m.
batter, 1. n. (cooking) pasta f. **2.** vb. bàttere.
battery, n. batteria f., pila f.
batting, n. imbottitura f.
battle, 1. n. battàglia f. **2.** vb. combàttere.
battlefield, n. campo di battàglia m.
battleship, n. nave da guèrra f.
bauxite, n. bauxite m.
bawl, vb. urlare; (b. out) sgridare.
bay, 1. n. (geography) bàia f.; (plant) làuro m.; (howl) latrato m.; (at b.) a bada. **2.** adj. (color) baio. **3.** vb. latrare; abbaiare.
bayonet, n. baionetta f.
bazaar, n. bazàr m.
be, vb. èssere; (health) stare.
beach, n. spiàggia f., lido m.

beachhead, n. tèsta di ponte f.

beach robe, n. accappatòio m.

beach umbrella, n. ombrellone m.

beacon, n. faro m.

bead, 1. n. grano m. **2.** vb. ornare di grani.

beading, n. ornamento di grani m.

beady, adj. a forma di grano.

beagle, n. segugio m.

beak, n. becco m.

beaker, n. recipiènte m.

beam, 1. n. (construction) trave f.; (light) ràggio m. **2.** vb. irradiare, risplèndere.

beaming, adj. raggiante, risplendènte.

bean, n. fagiòlo m., fava f.

bear, 1. n. (animal) orso m. **2.** vb. (carry) portare; (endure) sopportare; (give birth to) partorire.

bearable, adj. sopportàbile.

beard, n. barba f.

bearded, adj. barbuto.

beardless, adj. imbèrbe.

bearer, n. portatore m.

bearing, n. (behavior) condotta f.; (position) orientamento m.; (machinery) cuscinetto m.

bearish, adj. orsesco; al ribasso (financial).

bearskin, n. pèlle d'orso f.

beast, n. bèstia f.

beastly, adj. bestiale.

beat, 1. n. bàttito m. **2.** vb. bàttere; (conquer) vìncere.

beaten, adj. battuto.

beaten path, n. la via nota f.; sentiero marcato m.

beater, n. frullatore m.

beatify, vb. beatificare.

beating, n. percosse f.pl; (defeat) disfatta f.

beatitude, n. beatitùdine f.

beau, n. (fop) damerino m.; (wooer) corteggiatore m.

beautician, n. estetista m. and f.

beautiful, adj. bèllo; (excellent) eccellènte.

beautifully, adv. in bel modo, bène, eccellentemente.

beautify, vb. abbellire.

beauty, n. bellezza f.; (b. parlor) salone di bellezza m.

beaver, n. castòro m.

becalm, vb. abbonacciare.

because, conj. perché; **(b. of)** a causa di.

beckon, vb. far cenno, accennare.

becloud, vb. annebbiare; confondere.

become, vb. divenire, diventare; (be suitable for) convenire a; (be attractive on) stare bène a.

becoming, adj. grazioso.

bed, n. lètto m.; (for animals) lettièra f.

bed and board, n. vitto e allòggio m.

bedbug, n. cìmice f.

bedclothes, n. lenzuòla f.pl.

bedding, n. letterecci m.pl.

bedevil, vb. tormentare; confondere.

bedfellow, n. compagno di lètto m.

bedizen, vb. ornare.

bedridden, adj. degènte.

bedroom, n. stanza da lètto f.

bedside, n. **(at the b. of)** al capezzale di.

bedsore, n. piaga f.

bedspread, n. copèrta da lètto f.

bedstead, n. lettièra f.

bedtime, n. ora d'andare a lètto m.

bee, n. ape f.

beech, n. faggio m.

beef, n. bue m.

beefsteak, n. bistecca f.

beef stew, n. stufato di manzo m.

beehive, n. alveare m.

beer, n. birra f.

beeswax, n. cera f.

beet, n. barbabiètola f.

beetle, n. scarafàggio m.

befall, vb. accadere, capitare.

befit, vb. convenire a.

befitting, adj. conveniènte.

before, 1. adv. (in front) avanti, davanti; (earlier) prima. **2.** prep. avanti, davanti a, prima di. **3.** conj. prima che.

beforehand, adv. prima, in anticipo.

befriend, vb. aiutare.

befuddle, vb. confóndere.

beg, vb. (ask alms) mendicare; (request) chièdere; (implore) pregare; implorare.

beget, vb. generare.

beggar, n. mendicante m.

beggarly, adj. meschino.

begin, vb. cominciare, incominciare, iniziare.

beginner, n. principiante m.

beginning, n. princípio m., cominciamento m., inízio m.

begrudge, vb. invidiare.

beguile, vb. ingannare.

behalf, n. favore m.; **(on b. of)** da parte di; **(in b. of)** a favore di.

behave, vb. comportarsi, condursi.

behavior, n. comportamento m., condotta f.

behead, vb. decapitare.

behest, n. ordine m., comando m.

behind, 1. adv. indiètro. 2. prep. diètro a.

behold, vb. vedere.

beige, adj. beige, avana.

being, n. èssere m.; (existence) esistènza f.

bejewel, vb. ornare di gioièlli.

belated, adj. tardivo.

belch, 1. n. rutto m. 2. vb. ruttare.

belfry, n. campanile m.

Belgian, n. and adj. bèlga.

Belgium, n. il Bèlgio m.

belie, vb. smentire.

belief, n. credènza f., opinione f., fede f.

believable, adj. credíbile.

believe, vb. crédere; (make believe) fíngere.

believer, n. credènte m.

belittle, vb. denigrare.

bell, n. (house) campanèllo m.; (church) campana f.

bellboy, n. camerière m.

bell buoy, n. bòa a campana f.

bellglass, n. campana di vetro f.

bellicose, adj. bellicoso, battagliéro.

belligerence, n. belligeranza f.

belligerent, adj. belligerante, bellicoso.

belligerently, adv. bellicosamente.

bellringer, n. campanaro m.

bellow, 1. n. mùgghio m., muggito m. 2. vb. muggire, mugghiare.

bellows, n. (large) màntice m.; (small) soffietto m.

bell-tower, n. campanile m.

belly, n. vèntre m., pància f.

belong, vb. appartenere.

belongings, n. possessi m.pl. proprietà f.sg.

beloved, adj. amato, dilètto.

below, adv. and prep. sotto.

belt, n. cintura f.

bench, n. banco m.

bend, vb. piegare; (curve) curvare.

beneath, adv. and prep. sotto.

benediction, n. benedizione f.

benefactor, n. benefattore m.

benefactress, n. benefattrice f.

beneficent, adj. benèfico.

beneficial, adj. vantaggioso, salutare.

beneficiary, n. beneficiàrio m.

benefit, 1. n. benefício m., vantaggio m. 2. vb. beneficare, trarre vantaggio da (intr.).

benevolence, n. benevolènza f.

benevolent, adj. benèvolo, caritatévole.

benevolently, adv. benevolmente, caritatevolmente.

benign, adj. benigno.

benignity, n. benignità f.

bent, adj. piegato, curvo.

benzine, n. benzina f.

bequeath, vb. legare.

bequest, n. legato m.

berate, vb. sgridare.

bereave, vb. orbare, privare.

bereavement, n. pèrdita f.

beriberi, n. beri-bèri m.

Bern, n. Berna f.

berry, n. bacca f.

berth, n. cuccetta f.

beseech, vb. supplicare.

beseeching, adj. supplichévole.

beseechingly, adv. supplichevolmente.

beset, vb. assalire, assediare.

beside, prep. accanto a.

besides, 1. adv. inoltre. 2. prep. oltre.

besiege, vb. assediare.

besieger, n. assediante m.

besmirch, vb. insudiciare; (dishonor) disonorare.

best, 1. adj. il migliore. 2. adv. il mèglio. 3. vb. víncere.

bestial, adj. bestiale.

bestir oneself, vb. scuòtersi.

best man, n. testimone dello sposo m.
bestow, vb. conferire.
bestowal, n. concessione f.
bet, 1. n. scommessa f. 2. vb. scomméttere.
betake (oneself), vb. recarsi, andare.
betoken, vb. significare.
betray, vb. tradire.
betrayal, n. tradimento m.
betroth, vb. fidanzare.
betrothal, n. fidanzamento m.
better, 1. adj. migliore. 2. adv. mèglio. 3. vb. migliorare.
between, prep. fra, tra.
bevel, n. inclinazione f.
beverage, n. bevanda f.
bewail, vb. lamentare, piàngere.
beware, vb. guardarsi.
bewilder, vb. confóndere, rèndere perplèsso.
bewildered, adj. confuso, perplèsso.
bewildering, adj. sconcertante.
bewilderment, n. confusione f., perplessità f.
bewitch, vb. ammaliare, stregare.
beyond, 1. adv. al di là, oltre. 2. prep. al di là di, oltre.
biannual, adj. biennale.
bias, 1. n. parzialità f., pregiudizio m.; **(on the b.)** disbieco. 2. vb. predisporre.
bib, n. bavaglino m.
Bible, n. Bìbbia f.
Biblical, adj. bíblico.
bibliography, n. bibliografía f.
bibliophile, n. bibliofilo m.
bicarbonate, n. bicarbonato m.
bicentennial, adj. bicentennale.
biceps, n. bíceps m.
bicker, vb. litigare, bisticciarsi.
bicycle, n. bicicletta f.
bicyclist, n. ciclista m. or f.
bid, 1. n. (offer) offèrta f.; (invitation) invito m. 2. vb. (offer) offrire; (command) comandare.
bidder, n. offerènte m.
bidding, n. ordine m.; offerte f.pl.
bide, vb. aspettare.
biennial, adj. biennale.
bier, n. bara f.
bifocal, adj. bifocale.
big, adj. grande, gròsso; (preg-

nant) gràvida f.; **(b. shot)** pèzzo gròsso m.
bigamist, n. bígamo m.
bigamous, adj. bígamo.
bigamy, n. bigamía f.
big game, n. caccia grossa f.
big-hearted, adj. buono; magnanimo.
bigmouthed, adj. sbraitante.
bigot, n. bigòtto m.
bigoted, adj. bigòtto.
bigotry, n. bigottería f., bigottismo m.
big shot, n. pezzo grosso m., alto papavero m.
big toe, n. alluce m.
bike, n. bicicletta f.
bilateral, adj. bilaterale.
bile, n. bile f.
bilingual, adj. bilingue.
bilious, adj. (pertaining to bile) biliare; (temperament) bilioso.
bilk, vb. defraudare.
bill, n. (bird) becco m.; (money) biglietto m.; (sum owed) conto m.; (legislative) progètto di legge m.; **(b. of fare)** lista f.
billboard, n. cartèllo pubblicitàrio m.
billet, 1. n. allòggio m. 2. vb. alloggiare.
billfold, n. portafògli m.
billiard ball, n. palla da biliardo f.
billiards, n. biliardo m.sg.
billion, n. bilione m.
bill of health, n. certificato mèdico m.
bill of lading, n. polizza di càrico f.
bill of rights, n. dichiarazione dei diritti.
bill of sale, n. manifèsto di véndita m.
billow, n. maroso m.
bimetallic, adj. bimetàllico.
bimonthly, adj. (twice a month) bimensile, quindicinale; (every two months) bimestrale.
bin, n. recipiènte m.
bind, vb. legare; (oblige) obbligare; (a book) rilegare.
binder, n. rilegatore m.
bindery, n. legatoría f.
binding, 1. n. (book) rilegatura f. 2. adj. obbligatòrio.

bingo, n. tombola f.

binocular, 1. n. binòcolo m. **2.** adj. binoculare.

biochemical, adj. biochímico.

biochemistry, n. biochímica f.

biodegradable, adj. biodegradàbile.

biofeedback, n. feedback biològico m. biofeedback m.

biographer, n. biògrafo m.

biographical, adj. biogràfico.

biography, n. biografía f.

biological, adj. biológico.

biologically, adv. biologicamente.

biology, n. biología f.

bipartisan, adj. di tutti e due i partiti.

biped, n. and adj. bípede (m.).

bird, n. uccèllo m.

birdlike, adj. come un uccèllo, uccellescamente.

bird of prey, n. uccèllo di rapina m., repace m.

birth, n. nàscita f.

birth control, n. controllo delle nàscite m.

birthday, n. compleanno m.

birthmark, n. vòglia f.

birthplace, n. luògo di nàscita m.

birth rate, n. natalità f.

birthright, n. diritto di primogenitura m.

biscuit, n. (roll) panino m.; (cracker) biscòtto m.

bisect, vb. bisecare.

bishop, n. véscovo m.

bishopric, n. vescovato m., dócesi f.

bismuth, n. bismuto m.

bison, n. bisonte m.

bisulfate, n. bisolfato m.

bit, n. (piece) pèzzo m.; (a b. of) un po' di; (harness) mòrso m.; (computer) síngola unità d'informazione f.

bitch, n. cagna f.; donnaccia f.

bite, 1. n. mòrso m. **2.** vb. mòrdere.

biting, adj. pungènte.

bitter, adj. amaro.

bitterly, adv. amaramente.

bitterness, n. amarezza f.

bittersweet, adj. agrodolce, dolceamaro.

bivouac, n. bivacco m.

biweekly, adj. (twice a week) bisettimanale; (every two weeks) quindicinale.

biyearly, adj. biennale; semestrale.

bizarre, adj. bizzarro.

black, adj. nero.

Black, (n. and adj.) (person) negro m.; negra f.

blackberry, n. mòra f.

blackbird, n. mèrlo m.

blackboard, n. lavagna f.

Black Death, n. peste bubbònica f.

blacken, vb. annerire.

black eye, n. òcchio pesto m.

blackguard, n. mascalzone m.; furfante m.

blackish, adj. nerastro.

black magic, n. magia nera f.

blackmail, 1. n. ricatto m. **2.** vb. ricattare.

blackmailer, n. ricattatore m.

black market, n. mercato nero m.

blackout, n. oscuramento m.

blacksmith, n. fabbro ferraio m.

bladder, n. vescica f.

blade, n. (of cutting tool) lama f.; (grass) fòglia f.

blame, 1. n. biàsimo m. **2.** vb. biasimare.

blameless, adj. innocènte.

blanch, vb. impallidire.

bland, adj. blando.

blandish, vb. blandire.

blank, 1. n. (empty space) spàzio bianco m.; (form) mòdulo m. **2.** adj. (page) bianco; (empty) vuòto.

blank check, n. assegno in bianco m.

blanket, n. copèrta f.

blank verse, n. verso sciolto m.

blare, 1. n. squillo m. **2.** vb. squillare.

blaspheme, vb. bestemmiare.

blasphemer, n. bestemmiatore m.

blasphemous, adj. émpio.

blasphemy, n. bestémmia f.

blast, 1. n. (of wind) ràffica f.; (explosion) esplosione f. **2.** vb. far saltare.

blast furnace, n. altoforno m.

blastoff, n. lancio (of rocket) m.

blatant, adj. clamoroso, rumoroso.

blaze, 1. n. fiamma f.; (fire) fuòco m. 2. vb. fiammeggiare.

bleach, vb. imbiancare.

bleachers, n. tribune f.pl.

bleak, adj. squàllido.

bleakness, n. squallore m.

bleary, adj. cisposo; poco chiaro.

bleed, vb. sanguinare.

blemish, n. màcchia f.

blend, 1. n. mescolanza f. 2. vb. mescolare.

bless, vb. benedire.

blessed, adj. benedetto, beato.

blessing, n. benedizione f.

blight, 1. n. malattìa f. 2. vb. (be b.ed) ammalare.

blind, 1. adj. cièco. 2. vb. accecare.

blindfold, 1. n. benda f. 2. adj. bendato. 3. vb. bendare.

blindly, adv. ciecamente.

blindness, n. cecità f.

blink, vb. sbàttere le pàlpebre.

blinker, n. (signal) lampeggiatore m.

bliss, n. beatitùdine f.

blissful, adj. beato.

blissfully, adv. beatamente.

blister, n. vescica f.

blithe, adj. gaio, gioioso.

blizzard, n. tempèsta di neve f.

bloat, vb. gonfiare.

bloc, n. blòcco m.

block, 1. n. blòcco m., ostàcolo m. 2. vb. bloccare, ostacolare.

blockade, n. blòcco m.

blond, adj. biondo.

blood, n. sangue m.

bloodhound, n. cane poliziòtto m.

bloodless, adj. esangue, senza sangue.

blood plasma, n. plasma m.

blood poisoning, n. avvelenamento del sangue m.

blood pressure, n. pressione del sangue f.

bloodshed, n. spargimento di sangue m.

bloodshot, adj. infiammato.

bloodthirsty, adj. sanguinàrio.

bloody, adj. sanguinoso.

bloom, 1. n. fiore m. 2. vb. fiorire.

blossom, 1. n. fiore m. 2. vb. fiorire.

blot, 1. n. màcchia f. 2. vb. macchiare; (dry ink) asciugare.

blotch, n. (spot) màcchia f.; sgòrbio m.

blotchy, adj. macchiato.

blotter, n. carta assorbente f.

blouse, n. blusa f.

blow, 1. n. colpo m. 2. vb. soffiare.

blowout, n. scòppio d'un pneumàtico m.

blubber, 1. n. (whale) grasso di balena f. 2. vb. piagnucolare.

bludgeon, n. mazza f.

blue, adj. azzurro, blu; (gloomy) triste.

blueberry, n. mirtillo m.

bluebird, n. uccèllo azzurro m.

blue cheese, n. gorgonzola m.

blue chip, n. azioni leader (financial).

blue jeans, n. blue jeans m.pl.

blueprint, n. eliotipìa f.; (plan) piano m.

bluff, 1. n. (cliff) rupe scoscesa f.; (cards) bluff m.; (trickery) inganno m. 2. adj. franco. 3. vb. bluffare, ingannare.

bluffer, n. bluffatore m.

bluing, n. anile m.

bluish, adj. bluastro.

blunder, 1. n. errore m.; svista f. 2. vb. sbagliare.

blunderer, n. stordito m.

blunt, adj. (dull) ottuso; (curt) rude.

bluntly, adv. ottusamente.

bluntness, n. ottusità f.

blur, 1. n. confusione f. 2. vb. rèndere indistinto.

blush, 1. n. rossore m. 2. vb. arrossire.

bluster, 1. n. millantería f. 2. vb. millantare.

boar, n. vèrro m.

board, 1. n. (plank) asse f., tàvola f.; (food) vitto m.; (committee) comitato m.; (council) consiglio m.; (of ship) bordo m. 2. vb. (go on b.) andare a bordo.

boarder, n. pensionante m.

boarding house, n. pensione f.

boarding pass, n. carta d'imbarco f.

boarding school, n. collegio m.

board of directors, n. consíglio d'amministrazione m.

board of health, n. ufficio d'igiene m.

board of trade, n. càmera di commèrcio f.

boast, 1. n. vanto m., vantería f. **2.** vb. vantare, tr.

boaster, n. vantatore m.

boastful, adj. vanaglorioso.

boastfulness, n. vantería f.

boat, n. barca f., battèllo m.

boathouse, n. tettòia per barche.

boatswain, n. nostròmo m.

bob, vb. tagliare corto.

bobbin, n. bobina f.

bobby pin, n. forcina f.

bode, vb. presagire.

bodice, n. busto m.

bodily, adj. corpòreo.

body, n. còrpo m.

bodyguard, n. guàrdia del còrpo f.

bog, 1. n. pantano m., palude f. **2.** vb. **(b. down)** impantanarsi.

Bohemian, n. and adj. boemo (m.).

boil, 1. n. (med.) forùncolo m. **2.** vb. bollire.

boiler, n. caldaia f.

boisterous, adj. impetuoso, turbolènto.

boisterously, adv. impetuosamente.

bold, adj. ardito; **(be b.)** ardire.

boldface, n. (type) caràtteri grassi m.pl.

boldly, adv. arditamente.

boldness, n. ardimento m.

Bolivian, adj. boliviano.

bologna, n. salsíccia f., salame m.

bolster, vb. appoggiare.

bolster up, vb. tenere su.

bolt, 1. n. catenàccio m. **2.** vb. (shut) chiùdere a catenàccio; (run away) fuggire.

bomb, n. bomba f.

bombard, vb. bombardare.

bombardier, n. bombardière m.

bombardment, n. bombardamento m.

bomber, n. bombardière m.

bombproof, adj. a pròva di bomba.

bombshell, n. bomba f.

bombsight, n. traguardo di puntamento m.

bonbon, n. dolce m.

bond, n. legame m., obbligazione f., vìncolo m., buòno m.

bondage, n. servitù f.

bonded, adj. vincolato.

bone, n. òsso m.

boneless, adj. sènza òssa.

bonfire, n. falò m.

bonnet, n. (headdress) cappèllo m.; (motor-car) còfano m.

bonus, n. gratificazione f.

bony, adj. ossuto.

book, n. libro m.

bookbinder, n. legatore m.

bookbindery, n. legatoría f.

bookcase, n. scaffale m.

bookkeeper, n. contàbile m.

bookkeeping, n. contabilità f.

booklet, n. libretto m.

bookmaker, n. (bets) allibratore m.

bookmark, n. segnalibro m.

bookseller, n. libraio m.

bookshelf, n. scaffale m.

bookstore, n. librería f.

boom, n. prosperità f.

boon, n. dono m.

boor, n. zòtico m.

boorish, adj. zòtico.

boost, 1. n. (increase) accrescimento m.; (push) spinta f. **2.** vb. (increase) accréscere; (push) spíngere; (praise) lodare.

booster, n. (telephone) amplificatore m.; (person) entusiasta m.

boot, n. stivale m.

bootblack, n. lustrascarpe m.

booth, n. tènda f.

booty, n. bottino m.

booze, vb. ubriacarsi.

border, 1. n. confine m., frontièra f. **2.** vb. confinare.

borderline, 1. n. línea di confine f. **2.** adj. marginale.

bore, 1. n. (hole) foro m.; (annoyance) seccatura f. **2.** vb. (make a hole) forare; (annoy) seccare.

boredom, n. nòia f.

boric, adj. bòrico.

boring, 1. n. (hole) foro m. **2.** adj. seccante.

born, adj. nato; **(be b.)** nàscere.

born-again, *adj.* rinato.
borough, *n.* borgo *m.*
borrow, *vb.* prendere in prèstito.
borrower, *n.* chi prende a prèstito.
bosom, *n.* pètto *m.,* seno *m.*
boss, *n.* padrone *m.*
bossy, *adj.* spadroneggiante.
botanical, *adj.* botànico.
botany, *n.* botànica *f.*
botch, *vb.* rabberciare.
both, *adj. and pron.* ambedue.
bother, 1. *n.* fastídio *m.* **2.** *vb.* infastidire.
bothersome, *adj.* fastidioso.
bottle, *n.* bottíglia *f.*
bottom, *n.* fondo *m.*
bottomless, *adj.* sènza fondo.
boudoir, *n.* salottino *m.*
bough, *n.* ramo *m.*
bouillon, *n.* bròdo *m.*
boulder, *n.* sasso *m.*
boulevard, *n.* viale *m.*
bounce, 1. *n.* rimbalzo *m.* **2.** *vb.* rimbalzare.
bound, 1. *n.* límite *m.; (jump)* balzo *m.,* salto *m.* **2.** *vb.* balzare, saltare.
boundary, *n.* confine *m.*
bound for, *adj.* diretto a.
boundless, *adj.* illimitato.
boundlessly, *adv.* illimitatamente.
bounteous, *adj.* liberale.
bounty, *n.* liberalità *f.*
bouquet, *n.* mazzo di fiori *m.*
bourgeois, *adj.* borghese.
bout, *n. (boxing)* assalto *m.*
bovine, *adj.* bovino.
bow, 1. *n. (for arrows, violin)* arco *m.; (greeting)* inchino *m.; (of boat)* pròra *f.* **2.** *vb.* inchinarsi.
bowels, *n.* budella *f.pl.,* intestini *m.pl.*
bower, *n.* pergolato *m.*
bowl, 1. *n. (vessel)* scodèlla *f.* **2.** *vb.* giocare alle bocce.
bowlegged, *adj.* colle gambe ad archetto.
bowler, *n.* giocatore di bocce.
bowling, *n.* giòco delle bocce *f.*
box, 1. *n.* scàtola *f.,* cassetta *f.; (theater)* palco *m.; (P.O.)* casèlla postale *f.* **2.** *vb.* fare del pugilato.
boxcar, *n.* vagone mèrci *m.*
boxer, *n.* pugilatore *m.*

boxing, *n.* pugilato *m.*
box office, *n.* botteghino *m.*
boy, *n.* ragazzo *m.,* fanciullo *m.*
boycott, 1. *n.* boicottàggio *m.* **2.** *vb.* boicottare.
boyhood, *n.* fanciullezza *f.*
boyish, *adj.* fanciullesco.
boyishly, *adv.* fanciullescamente.
brace, 1. *n.* sostegno *m.* **2.** *vb.* sostenere.
bracelet, *n.* braccialetto *m.*
bracket, *n.* mènsola *f.; (group)* gruppo *m.; (typography)* parèntesi quadra *f.*
brag, *vb.* millantare.
braggart, *n.* millantatore *m.*
braid, 1. *n.* tréccia *f.* **2.** *vb.* intrecciare.
brain, *n.* cervèllo *m.*
brainy, *adj.* intelligènte.
brake, 1. *n.* freno *m.* **2.** *vb.* frenare.
bran, *n.* crusca *f.*
branch, *n.* ramo *m.; (comm.)* succursale *f.*
brand, *n.* marca *f.*
brandish, *vb.* brandire.
brand-new, *adj.* nuovíssimo.
brandy, *n.* acquavite *f.*
brash, *adj.* impertinènte.
brass, *n.* ottone *m.*
brassiere, *n.* reggipètto *m.,* reggiseno *m.*
brassy, *adj.* d'ottone; sfacciato.
brat, *n.* marmòcchio *m.*
bravado, *n.* bravata *f.*
brave, *adj.* coraggioso.
bravery, *n.* coràggio *m.*
brawl, *n.* lite *f.,* rissa *f.*
brawn, *n.* fòrza muscolare *f.*
bray, 1. *n.* ràglio *m.* **2.** *vb.* ragliare.
braze, *vb.* brasare.
brazen, *adj.* di ottone; (insolent) insolènte.
Brazil, *n.* il Brasile *m.*
Brazilian, *adj.* brasiliano.
breach, *n.* bréccia *f.; (of law)* violazione *f.*
bread, *n.* pane *m.; (b. crumbs)* pangrattato *m.; (b. stick)* grissino *m.*
breaded, *adj.* impanato.
breadth, *n.* larghezza *f.,* ampiezza *f.*
bread winner, *n.* sostegno della famiglia *m.*

break, 1. *n.* rottura *f.;* interruzione *f.* **2.** *vb.* rómpere.
breakable, *adj.* rompíbile.
breakage, *n.* rottura *f.*
breaker, *n.* frangente *m.*
breakfast, *n.* prima colazione *f.*
breakneck, *adv.* a rompicollo.
breakwater, *n.* frangi-onde *m.*
breast, *n.* seno *m.,* mammèlla *f.,* poppa *f.;* (chest) pètto *m.*
breath, *n.* fiato *m.,* respiro *m.*
breathe, *vb.* respirare.
breathing, *n.* respiro *m.*
breathless, *adj.* sènza fiato; ansante.
breathlessly, *adv.* ansando.
breeches, *n.* brache *f.pl.,* pantaloni *m.pl.*
breed, 1. *n.* razza *f.* **2.** *vb.* (beget) generare; (train) educare; (raise) allevare.
breeder, *n.* generatore *m.,* allevatore *m.*
breeding, *n.* educazione *f.*
breeze, *n.* brezza *f.*
breezy, *adj.* (windy) ventoso; (cool) fresco.
brevity, *n.* brevità *f.*
brew, *vb.* fabbricare la birra.
brewer, *n.* birràio *m.,* fabbricante di birra *m.*
brewery, *n.* fàbbrica di birra *f.*
briar, *n.* rovo *m.*
bribe, *vb.* corrómpere.
briber, *n.* corruttore *m.*
bribery, *n.* corruzione *f.*
brick, *n.* mattone *m.*
bricklayer, *n.* muratore *m.*
bricklaying, *n.* muratura *f.*
bricklike, *adj.* come un mattone.
bridal, *adj.* nuziale.
bride, *n.* sposa *f.*
bridegroom, *n.* sposo *m.*
bridesmaid, *n.* damigèlla d'onore *f.*
bridge, *n.* ponte *m.*
bridged, *adj.* connèsso.
bridgehead, *n.* tèsta di ponte *f.*
bridle, *n.* bríglia *f.*
brief, *adj.* brève.
brief case, *n.* borsa *f.*
briefly, *adv.* brevemente.
briefness, *n.* brevità *f.*
brier, *n.* rovo *m.*
brig, *n.* brigantino *m.*

brigade, *n.* brigata *f.*
bright, *adj.* chiaro; luminoso.
brighten, *vb.* illuminare.
brightness, *n.* chiarore *m.*
brilliance, *n.* splendore *m.*
brilliant, *adj.* brillante.
brim, *n.* (cup) orlo *m.;* (hat) tesa *f.*
brimstone, *n.* zolfo *m.*
brine, *n.* acqua salata *f.*
bring, *vb.* portare; apportare; **(b. about)** causare.
brink, *n.* orlo *m.;* bordo *m.*
briny, *adj.* salato.
brisk, *adj.* vivace.
brisket, *n.* (meat) pètto *m.*
briskly, *adv.* vivacemente.
briskness, *n.* vivacità *f.*
bristle, 1. *n.* sétola *f.* **2.** *vb.* arruffare.
bristly, *adj.* setoloso.
Britain, *n.* **(Great B.)** la Gran Bretagna *f.*
British, *adj.* britànnico.
Briton, *n.* Brètone *m.*
brittle, *adj.* frágile.
broad, *adj.* largo, àmpio.
broadcast, 1. *n.* trasmissione radiofònica *f.* **2.** *vb.* trasméttere.
broadcaster, *n.* trasmettitore *m.*
broadcloth, *n.* popelina *f.*
broaden, *vb.* allargare.
broadly, *adv.* largamente.
broadminded, *adv.* spregiudicato.
broadside, *n.* bordata *f.*
brocade, *n.* broccato *m.*
brocaded, *adj.* di broccato.
broil, *adv.* mettere alla graticola.
broiler, *n.* graticola *f.*
broke, *adj.* al verde.
broken, *adj.* rotto.
broken-down, *adj.* avvilito; rovinato.
broken-hearted, *adj.* scorato.
broker, *n.* sensale *m.*
brokerage, *n.* sensería *f.*
bronchial, *adj.* bronchiale.
bronchitis, *n.* bronchite *f.*
bronco, *n.* puledro brado *m.*
bronze, *n.* bronzo *m.*
brooch, *n.* spilla *f.*
brood, 1. *n.* covata *f.,* famìglia *f.* **2.** *vb.* covare.
brook, *n.* ruscèllo *m.*
broom, *n.* scopa *f.*

broomstick, n. mànico della scopa f.

broth, n. bròdo m.

brothel, n. bordèllo m.

brother, n. fratèllo m.

brotherhood, n. fratellanza f.

brother-in-law, n. cognato m.

brotherly, adj. fratèrno.

brow, n. fronte f.

browbeat, vb. intimorire.

brown, adj. bruno.

browse, vb. brucare.

bruise, 1. n. ammaccatura f. **2.** vb. ammaccare.

brunette, n. bruna f.

brunt, n. urto m.

brush, 1. n. spàzzola f.; (artist's) pennèllo m. **2.** vb. spazzolare; **(b. against)** sfiorare.

brush-off, n. scortesia f.

brushwood, n. màcchia f.

brusque, adj. brusco.

brusquely, adv. bruscamente.

brutal, adj. brutale.

brutality, n. brutalità f.

brutalize, vb. maltrattare.

brute, n. and adj. bruto (m.).

bubble, n. bolla f.

buck, n. dàino m.; (male) màschio m.

bucket, n. sécchia f.

buckle, 1. n. fìbbia f. **2.** vb. affibbiare.

buckram, n. tela da fusto f.

bucksaw, n. sega intelaiata f.

buckshot, n. pallinacci m.pl.

buckwheat, n. grano saraceno m.

bud, 1. n. gèmma f. **2.** vb. gemmare.

Buddhism, n. buddismo m.

buddy, n. amico m., compagno m.

budge, vb. muòversi.

budget, n. preventivo m.

buff, adj. bruno-giallastro.

buffalo, n. bùfalo m.

buffer, n. respingènte m.; **(b. state)** stato cuscinetto m.

buffet, 1. n. (slap) schiaffo m.; (eating place) caffè m. **2.** vb. schiaffeggiare.

buffoon, n. buffone m.

bug, n. insètto m.

bugle, n. bùccina f.

build, vb. costruire, fabbricare.

builder, n. costruttore m.

building, n. edificio m.

buildup, n. concentrazione f.; sviluppo m.; preparazione f.

built-in, adj. incorporato.

bulb, n. (of plant) bulbo m.; (electric light) lampadina f.

bulge, 1. n. protuberanza f. **2.** vb. gonfiarsi.

bulk, n. volume m., massa f.

bulkhead, n. paratìa f.

bulky, adj. voluminoso.

bull, n. tòro m.

bulldog, n. molòsso m.

bulldozer, n. livellatrice f.

bullet, n. pallòttola f.

bulletin, n. bollettino m.

bulletproof, adj. a pròva di fucile.

bullfight, n. corrida f.

bullfinch, n. ciuffolòtto m.

bullion, n. (gold) oro in lingotti m.

bullock, n. manzo m.

bullring, n. arena f.

bully, n. prepotènte m.

bulwark, n. baluardo m.

bum, n. vagabondo m.

bumblebee, n. calabrone m.

bump, 1. n. urto m. **2.** vb. urtare.

bumper, n. respingènte m.

bun, n. panino m.

bunch, n. mazzo m., gràppolo m.

bundle, n. fàscio m.

bungle, vb. abborracciare.

bunion, n. infiammazione del pòllice del piède f.

bunk, n. (bed) cuccetta f.; (nonsense) fròttole f.pl.

bunny, n. coniglietto m.

bunting, n. stamigna f.

buoy, n. bòa f.

buoyant, adj. che può galleggiare; (cheerful) allegro.

burden, n. fardèllo m.; **(b. of proof)** ònere della pròva m.

burdensome, adj. opprimènte, oneroso.

bureau, n. ufficio m.

burglar, n. ladro m.

burglarize, vb. rubare.

burglary, n. furto m.

burial, n. sepoltura f.

burlap, n. canovàccio rozzo m.

burly, adj. corpulènto.

burn, 1. n. bruciatura f. **2.** vb. bruciare, àrdere.

burner, n. bècco m.

burning, adj. bruciante, ardènte.

burnish, vb. brunire.

burrow, 1. n. tana f. **2.** vb. scavare.

burst, 1. n. scatto m. **2.** vb. scoppiare; (dash) scattare; **(b. forth)** prorómpere.

bury, vb. seppellire.

bus, n. àutobus m.; **(trolley b.)** filobus m.; **(de luxe b.)** pullman m.; **(b. line)** autolínea f.

bus driver, n. conducente d'autobus m.

bush, n. cespùglio m.

bushel, n. mòggio m.

bushy, adj. cespuglioso; (thick) folto.

busily, adv. attivamente.

business, n. affare m.; affari m.pl.

businesslike, adj. prático.

businessman, n. uòmo d'affari m.

businesswoman, n. dònna d'affari f.

buss, n. bacio con schiocco m.

bus stop, n. fermata d'autobus f.

bust, n. busto m.

bustle, n. tramestío m.

busy, adj. occupato, affaccendato, attivo.

busybody, n. faccendière m.

but, 1. prep. eccètto, salvo. **2.** conj. ma.

butcher, 1. n. macellaio m. **2.** vb. macellare.

butchery, n. macèllo m.

butler, n. maggiordòmo m.

butt, n. estremità f.; (of gun) càlcio m.

butter, n. burro m.

buttercup, n. ranùncolo m.

butterfat, n. grasso del latte m.

butterfly, n. farfalla f.

buttermilk, n. sièro m.

buttock, n. nàtica f.

button, n. bottone m.

buttonhole, n. occhièllo m.

buttress, n. contrafforte m.

buxom, adj. grassòccio.

buy, vb. comprare.

buyer, n. compratore m.

buzz, 1. n. ronzío m. **2.** vb. ronzare.

buzzard, n. poiana f.

buzzer, n. campanèllo m.

buzz saw, n. sega circolare f.

by, prep. (through) per; (near) prèsso a; (at) a; (indicating agent) da.

by-and-by, adv. fra pòco.

bygone, adj. passato.

by-law, n. legge particolare f.

by-pass, vb. evitare.

by-path, n. sentiero secondario m.; strada privata f.

by-product, n. prodotto secondàrio m.

bystander, n. spettatore m.

byte, n. byte f.

byway, n. viòttolo m.

C

cab, n. tassi m.

cabaret, n. ritròvo notturno m.

cabbage, n. càvolo m.

cabin, n. capanna f.; (on boat) cabina f.

cabin boy, n. mozzo m.

cabinet, n. (furniture) stipo m.; (politics) gabinetto m.

cabinetmaker, n. stipettaio m.

cable, n. cavo m.

cable car, n. teleferica f.

cablegram, n. cablogramma f.

cableway, n. funivia f.

cache, n. nascondíglio m.

cachet, n. sigillo m.

cackle, 1. n. vèrso m. **2.** vb. cantare.

cacophony, n. cacofonía f.

cactus, n. cactus m.

cad, n. vigliacco m.

cadaver, n. cadàvero m.

cadaverous, adj. cadavèrico.

cadet, n. cadetto m.

cadence, n. cadènza f.

caddie, n. portamazze m.

cadmium, n. càdmio m.

cadre, n. quadro m.

café, n. caffè m.

café society, n. bel mondo m.

caffeine, n. caffeína f.

cage, 1. n. gàbbia f. **2.** vb. ingabbiare.

caisson, n. cassone m.

cajole, vb. lusingare.

cake, *n.* tòrta *f.*, focàccia *f.*
calamitous, *adj.* calamitoso.
calamity, *n.* calamità *f.*
calcify, *vb.* calcificare.
calcium, *n.* càlcio *m.*
calculable, *adj.* calcolàbile.
calculate, *vb.* calcolare.
calculating, *adj.* calcolatore; **(c. machine)** màcchina calcolatrice *f.*
calculation, *n.* càlcolo *m.*
calculus, *n.* càlcolo *m.*
caldron, *n.* caldaia *f.*
calendar, *n.* calendàrio *m.*
calf, *n.* vitèllo *m.*
calfskin, *n.* pèlle di vitèllo *f.*
caliber, *n.* càlibro *m.*
calibrate, *vb.* calibrare.
calico, *n.* calicò *m.*
caliper, *n.* càlibro *m.*
caliph, *n.* califfo *m.*
calisthenic, *adj.* ginnàstico.
calisthenics, *n.* ginnàstica *f.*
calk, *vb.* calafatare.
calker, *n.* calafato *m.*
call, 1. *n.* chiamata *f.*, appèllo *m.* **2.** *vb.* chiamare.
caller, *n.* chiamante *m.*; visitatore *m.*
calligraphy, *n.* calligrafìa *f.*
calling, *n.* vocazione *f.*, professione *f.*
calling card, *n.* biglietto da vìsita *m.*; carta telefònica *f.*
callous, *adj.* calloso; (unfeeling) insensìbile.
callousness, *n.* callosità *f.*, insensibilità *f.*
callow, *adj.* inespèrto.
call to arms, *n.* chiamata alle armi *f.*
callus, *n.* callo *m.*
calm, 1. *n.* calma *f.* **2.** *adj.* calmo. **3.** *vb.* calmare.
calmly, *adv.* con calmo.
calmness, *n.* calma *f.*
caloric, *adj.* calòrico.
calorie, *n.* caloria *f.*
calorimeter, *n.* calorímetro *m.*
calumniate, *vb.* calunniare.
calumny, *n.* calùnnia *f.*
Calvary, *n.* Calvàrio *m.*
calve, *vb.* partorire.
calyx, *n.* càlice *m.*
camaraderie, *n.* cameratismo *m.*
camber, *n.* curvatura *f.*

cambric, *n.* cambrì *m.*
camel, *n.* cammèllo *m.*
camelia, *n.* camèlia *f.*
camel's hair, *n.* peli di cammèllo *m.pl.*
cameo, *n.* cammèo *m.*
camera, *n.* màcchina fotogràfica *f.*
camomile, *n.* camomilla *f.*
camouflage, 1. *n.* camuffamento *m.*, mimetismo *m.* **2.** *vb.* camuffare, mimetizzare.
camp, 1. *n.* accampamento *m.* **2.** *vb.* accamparsi; (sport) campeggiare.
campaign, *n.* campagna *f.*
camper, *n.* campeggiatore *m.*
camphor, *n.* cánfora *f.*
camping, *n.* campèggio *m.*
campus, *n.* città universitària *f.*
camshaft, *n.* albero a camme *m.*; distribuzione *f.*
can, 1. *n.* (tin) scàtola *f.*; (large) bidone *m.* **2.** *vb.* (be able) potere.
Canada, *n.* il Canadà *m.*
Canadian, *adj.* canadese.
canal, *n.* canale *m.*
canalize, *vb.* canalizzare.
canapé, *n.* crostino *m.*
canard, *n.* fròttola *f.*
canary, *n.* canarino *m.*
Canary Islands, *n.* Canàrie *f.pl.*
cancel, *vb.* annullare, cancellare, disdire.
cancellation, *n.* annullamento *m.*
cancer, *n.* cancro *m.*
candelabrum, *n.* candelabro *m.*
candid, *adj.* càndido, franco.
candidacy, *n.* candidatura *f.*
candidate, *n.* candidato *m.*
candidly, *adv.* candidamente, francamente.
candidness, *n.* franchezza *f.*, candore *m.*
candied, *adj.* candito.
candle, *n.* candela *f.*
candlestick, *n.* candelière *f.*
candor, *n.* candore *m.*
candy, *n.* dolciumi *m.pl.*; caramella *f.*
cane, *n.* bastone *m.*; (plants) canna *f.*
cane seat, *n.* sedia impagliata *f.*
cane sugar, *n.* zucchero di canna *m.*
canine, *adj.* canino.

canister, *n.* scàtola *f.*

canker, *n.* cancro *m.*

cankerworm, *n.* bruco *m.*

canned, *adj.* in scàtola.

canner, *n.* fabbricante di consèrve alimentari *m.*

cannery, *n.* stabilimento dí consèrve alimentari *m.*

cannibal, *n.* cannibale *m.*

canning, *n.* preparazione di consèrve alimentari *f.*

cannon, *n.* cannone *m.*

cannonade, *n.* cannoneggiamento *m.*

cannoneer, *n.* cannonière *m.*

cannot, *vb.* non potere.

canny, *adj.* astuto.

canoe, *n.* canòa *f.*

canon, *n.* (rule, law) cànone *m.;* (person) canònico *m.*

canonical, *adj.* canònico.

canonize, *vb.* canonizzare.

canon law, *n.* diritto canonico *m.*

can-opener, *n.* apriscàtole *m.*

canopy, *n.* baldacchino *m.*

cant, *n.* ipocrisìa *f.*

can't, *vb.* non potere.

cantaloupe, *n.* melone *m.*

canteen, *n.* cantina *f.*

canter, *vb.* andare al píccolo galòppo.

cantonment, *n.* accantonamento *m.*

canvas, *n.* canovàccio *m.*

canvass, 1. *n.* esame *m.* **2.** *vb.* esaminare.

canyon, *n.* burrone *m.*

cap, *n.* berretto *m.*

capability, *n.* capacità *f.*

capable, *adj.* capace, àbile.

capably, *adv.* abilmente.

capacious, *adj.* spazioso.

capacity, *n.* capacità *f.*

caparison, 1. *n.* bardatura *f.* **2.** *vb.* bardare.

cape, *n.* cappa *f.*

caper, 1. *n.* capriòla *f.* **2.** *vb.* far capriòle.

capillary, *adj.* capillare.

capital, 1. *n.* (money) capitale *m.;* (city) capitale *f.* **2.** *adj.* capitale.

capital punishment, *n.* pena capitale *f.;* pena di morte *f.*

capitalism, *n.* capitalismo *m.*

capitalist, *n.* capitalista *m.*

capitalistic, *adj.* capitalístico.

capitalization, *n.* capitalizzazione *f.*

capitalize, *vb.* capitalizzare.

capitulate, *vb.* capitolare.

capon, *n.* cappone *m.*

caprice, *n.* capríccio *m.*

capricious, *adj.* capriccioso.

capriciously, *adv.* capricciosamente.

capriciousness, *n.* capricciosità *f.*

capsize, *vb.* capovòlgere.

capsule, *n.* càpsula *f.*

captain, *n.* capitano *m.*

caption, *n.* títolo *m.*

captious, *adj.* capzioso.

captivate, *vb.* affascinare.

captive, *n. and adj.* prigionièro (*m.*).

captivity, *n.* prigionìa *f.*

captor, *n.* catturatore *m.*

capture, 1. *n.* cattura *f.* **2.** *vb.* catturare.

car, *n.* carro *m.,* vettura *f.;* (auto) automòbile *f.;* (railroad) vagone *m.*

caracul, *n.* lince persiana *f.*

carafe, *n.* caraffa *f.*

caramel, *n.* caramèlla *f.*

carat, *n.* carato *m.*

caravan, *n.* carovana *f.*

caraway, *n.* cumino *m.*

carbide, *n.* carburo *m.*

carbine, *n.* carabina *f.*

carbohydrate, *n.* idrato di carbònio *m.*

carbon, *n.* carbònio *m.*

carbon dioxide, *n.* biòssido di carbònio *m.*

carbon monoxide, *n.* monòssido di carbònio *m.*

carbon paper, *n.* carta carbone *f.*

carbuncle, *n.* carbónchio *m.*

carburetor, *n.* carburatore *m.*

carcass, *n.* carcassa *f.*

carcinogenic, *adj.* carcinògeno.

card, *n.* carta *f.,* biglietto *m.;* (filing) schedina *f.*

cardboard, *n.* cartone *m.;* (thin) cartoncino *m.*

card-carrying, *adj.* tesserato, socio.

card holder, *n.* tesserato *m.,* socio *m.*

cardiac, *adj.* cardíaco.

cardigan, n. golf m.

cardinal, adj. and n. cardinale (m).

cardsharp, n. baro m.

care, 1. n. cura f. **2.** vb. curarsi; **(take c. of)** curare.

careen, vb. carenare.

career, n. carrièra f.

carefree, adj. sènza preoccupazioni.

careful, adj. accurato, attento.

carefully, adv. accuratamente, attentamente.

carefulness, n. accuratezza f., attenzione f.

careless, adj. spensierato, trascurato.

carelessly, adv. spensieratamente, trascuratamente.

carelessness, n. spensieratezza f., trascuratezza f.

caress, 1. n. carezza f. **2.** vb. accarezzare.

caretaker, n. guardiano m.

carfare, n. spìccioli per il tram m.pl.

cargo, n. càrico m.

caricature, n. caricatura f.

caries, n. càrie f.

carillon, n. carillón m.

carload, n. carrettata f.

carnage, n. carneficina f.

carnal, adj. carnale.

carnation, n. garòfano m.

carnival, n. carnevale m.

carnivorous, adj. carnivoro.

carol, 1. n. canto di Natale m. **2.** vb. cantare.

carouse, vb. far baldòria.

carousel, n. carosèllo m.

carpenter, n. falegname m.

carpet, n. tappeto m.

carpeting, n. stoffa per tappeti f.

car pool, n. consòrzio automobilìstico m.

carriage, n. (vehicle) vettura f.; (transportation) traspòrto m.

carrier, n. portatore m.

carrier pigeon, n. piccione viaggiatore m.

carrot, n. caròta f.

carry, vb. portare; **(c. on)** continuare; **(c. out)** eseguire; **(c. through)** condurre a buon fine.

cart, n. carro m.

cartage, n. traspòrto m.

carte blanche, n. carta bianca f.

cartel, n. cartèllo m.

carter, n. carrettiere m.

cart horse, n. cavallo da tiro m.

cartilage, n. cartilàgine f.

carton, n. scàtola di cartone f.

cartoon, n. (sketch) cartone m.; (picture) disegno m.

cartoonist, n. disegnatore m., vignettista m.

cartridge, n. cartùccia f.

carve, vb. (art) scolpire; (meat) tagliare, trinciare.

carver, n. scultore m.

carving, n. scultura f.

carving-knife, n. trinciante m.

cascade, n. cascata f.

case, n. (instance; state of things) caso m.; (law) càusa f.; (packing) cassa f.; (holder) astùccio m.; **(in any c.)** in ogni caso.

case study, n. casìstica f.

cash, 1. n. contanti m.pl. **2.** vb. (cheque) riscuòtere.

cashew, n. anacardio m.; mandorla indiana f.

cashier, n. cassière m.; (cashier's desk) cassa f.

cashmere, n. casimiro f.

casing, n. copertura f.

casino, n. casino m.

cask, n. barile m.

casket, n. cassettina f.

casserole, n. casseruòla f.

cassette, n. cassette f.

cast, 1. n. (throw) gètto m. **2.** vb. gettare; (metal) fóndere.

castanets, n. nàcchere f.pl.

castaway, n. nàufrago m.

caste, n. casta f.

caster, n. fonditore m.

castigate, vb. castigare.

cast iron, n. ghisa f.

castle, n. castèllo m.

castoff, adj. abbandonato.

castrate, vb. castrare.

casual, adj. (accidental) casuale; (nonchalant) indifferente.

casually, adv. casualmente, indifferentemente.

casualness, n. indifferenza f.

casualty, n. (accident) disgràzia f.; (injured person) ferito m.

cat, n. gatto m., gatta f.

cataclysm, n. cataclisma m.
catacomb, n. catacomba f.
catalogue, n. catàlogo m.
catapult, n. catapulta f.
cataract, n. cateratta f.
catarrh, n. catarro m.
catastrophe, n. catàstrofe f.
catch, vb. afferrare; (sickness) prèndere.
catcher, n. chi affèrra, chi prende.
catchword, n. parola di richiamo f.
catchy, adj. melodioso.
catechism, n. catechismo m.
catechize, vb. catechizzare.
categorical, adj. categòrico.
category, n. categoría f.
cater, vb. provvedere a.
caterpillar, n. bruco m.
catgut, n. minùgia f.pl.
catharsis, n. catarsi f.
cathartic, adj. purgativo.
cathedral, n. cattedrale f.
catheter, n. catètere m.
cathode, n. càtodo m.
Catholic, adj. cattòlico.
Catholicism, n. cattolicismo m.
cat nap, n. pisolino m.
catsup, n. salsa di pomodoro f.
cattle, n. bestiame m.
cattleman, n. bovaro m.
catwalk, n. ballatòio m.
cauliflower, n. cavolfiore m.
causation, n. causalità f.
cause, 1. n. càusa f. 2. vb. causare, cagionare.
causeway, n. strada selciata f.
caustic, adj. càustico, sarcàstico.
cauterize, vb. cauterizzare.
cautery, n. cautèrio m.
caution, 1. n. cautèla f. 2. vb. ammonire.
cautious, adj. càuto.
cavalcade, n. cavalcata f.
cavalier, n. cavalière m.
cavalry, n. cavallería f.
cave, n. cavèrna f.
cave-in, n. crollo m.
cavern, n. cavèrna f.
caviar, n. caviale m.
cavity, n. cavità f.
caw, vb. gracchiare.
cayman, n. caimano m.
cease, vb. cessare.
ceasefire, n. cessate il fuoco m.

ceaseless, adj. incessante.
cedar, n. cedro m.
cede, vb. cédere.
ceiling, n. soffitto m.
celebrant, n. celebrante m.
celebrate, vb. celebrare.
celebrated, adj. (famous) cèlebre.
celebration, n. celebrazione f.
celebrity, n. celebrità f.
celerity, n. celerità f.
celery, n. sèdano m.
celestial, adj. celèste.
celibacy, n. celibato m.
celibate, adj. cèlibe.
cell, n. (room) cèlla f.; (biology) cèllula f.
cellar, n. cantina f.
cellist, n. violoncellista m.
cello, n. violoncèllo m.
cellophane, n. cèllofane m.
cellular, adj. cellulare.
celluloid, n. cellulòide f.
cellulose, n. cellulosa f.
Celtic, adj. cèltico.
cement, 1. n. cemento m. 2. vb. cementare.
cemetery, n. cimitèro m., camposanto m.
censor, 1. n. censore m. 2. vb. censurare.
censorious, adj. censòrio.
censorship, n. censura f.
censure, n. censura f.
census, n. censimento m.
cent, n. centèsimo m.
centaur, n. centàuro m.
centenary, adj. and n. centenàrio (m.)
centennial, adj. and n. centennale (m.)
center, n. cèntro m.
centerfold, n. pàgine centrali f.pl.
centerpiece, n. centro da tàvola m; centrino m.
centigrade, adj. centígrado.
central, adj. centrale.
centralize, vb. centralizzare.
century, n. sècolo m.
century plant, n. àgave f.
ceramic, adj. ceràmico.
ceramics, n. ceràmica f.
cereal, n. and adj. cereale (m.)
cerebral, adj. cerebrale.
ceremonial, adj. cerimoniale.
ceremonious, adj. cerimonioso.

ceremony, *n.* cerimònia *f.*

certain, *adj.* cèrto.

certainly, *adv.* certamente.

certainty, *n.* certezza *f.*

certificate, *n.* certificato *m.*

certification, *n.* certificazione *f.*

certified, *adj.* garantito; **(c. check)** assegno a copertura garantita *m.*; **(c. copy)** còpia conforme *f.*

certify, *vb.* certificare.

certitude, *n.* certezza *f.*

cervical, *adj.* cervicale.

cervix, *n.* cervice *f.*

cesarean section, *n.* taglio cesàreo *m.*

cessation, *n.* cessazione *f.*

cession, *n.* cessione *f.*

cesspool, *n.* pozzo nero *m.*

chafe, *vb.* (warm) riscaldare; (irritate) irritare.

chaff, **1.** *n.* pula *f.*, lòppa *f.*; (banter) cèlia *f.* **2.** *vb.* celiare.

chagrin, *n.* crùccio *m.*

chain, **1.** *n.* catena *f.* **2.** *vb.* incatenare.

chain reaction, *n.* reazione a catena *f.*

chain saw, *n.* motosega *f.*

chain smoke, *vb.* fumarne una via l'altra.

chair, *n.* sèdia *f.*

chairman, *n.* presidènte *m.*

chairmanship, *n.* presidènza *f.*

chairperson, *n.* presidènte *m.*; presidèntessa *f.*

chairwoman, *n.* presidentessa *f.*

chalice, *n.* càlice *f.*

chalk, *n.* gesso *m.*

chalky, *adj.* gessoso.

challenge, **1.** *n.* sfida *f.* **2.** *vb.* sfidare.

challenger, *n.* sfidante *m.*

chamber, *n.* càmera *f.*; **(c.-pot)** vaso da nòtte *m.*

chamber of commerce, *n.* camera di commercio *f.*

chamberlain, *n.* ciambellano *m.*

chambermaid, *n.* camerièra *f.*

chamber music, *n.* mùsica da càmera *f.*

chameleon, *n.* camaleonte *m.*

chamois, *n.* camòscio *m.*

champ, *vb.* ròdere.

champagne, *n.* champagne *f.*

champion, *n.* campione *m.*

championship, *n.* campionato *m.*

chance, **1.** *n.* caso *m.*; (opportunity) occasione *f.*; **(by c.)** per caso. **2.** *adj.* fortùito.

chancel, *n.* còro *m.*

chancellery, *n.* cancellería *f.*

chancellor, *n.* cancellière *m.*

chandelier, *n.* lampadàrio *m.*

change, **1.** *n.* cambio *m.*, cambiamento *m.*, mutamento *m.*; (small coins) moneta spícciola *f.*; (money due) rèsto *m.* **2.** *vb.* cambiare, mutare.

changeability, *n.* mutabilità *f.*

changeable, *adj.* mutévole.

change of heart, *n.* pentimento *m.*; conversione *f.*

change of life, *n.* menopausa *f.*

changer, *n.* (money-changer) cambiavalute *m.*

channel, *n.* canale *m.*

chant, **1.** *n.* canto *m.* **2.** *vb.* cantare.

chaos, *n.* càos *m.*

chaotic, *adj.* caòtico.

chap, **1.** *n.* (on skin) screpolatura *f.*; (fellow) tízio *m.* **2.** *vb.* screpolare.

chapel, *n.* cappèlla *f.*

chaplain, *n.* cappellano *m.*

chapter, *n.* capítolo *m.*

char, *vb.* carbonizzare.

character, *n.* caràttere *m.*

characteristic, **1.** *n.* caratterística *f.* **2.** *adj.* caratterístico.

chracteristically, *adv.* caratteristicamente.

characterization, *n.* caratterizzazione *f.*

characterize, *vb.* caratterizzare.

charcoal, *n.* carbone di legna *m.*

charge, **1.** *n.* (load) càrico *m.*; (attack; gun) càrica *f.* (price) prèzzo *m.*; (custody) custòdia *f.* **2.** *vb.* (load) caricare; (set a price) far pagare.

charger, *n.* cavallo da guerra *m.*

chariot, *n.* carro *m.*

charioteer, *n.* auriga *m.*

charisma, *n.* carisma *m.*

charitable, *adj.* caritatévole.

charitableness, *n.* carità *f.*

charitably, *adv.* caritatevolmente.

charity, *n.* carità *f.*

charlatan, *n.* ciarlatano *m.*

charlatanism, *n.* ciarlatanismo *m.*

charm, 1. *n.* incanto *m.;* (good-luck c.) portafortuna *m.* **2.** *vb.* incantare, affascinare.

charmer, *n.* incantatore *m.*, incantatrice *f.*

charming, *adj.* affascinante

chart, *n.* (map) carta *f.;* (graph) gráfico *m.*

charter, *n.* carta *f.*

charter flight, *n.* volo noleggiato *m.*

charter member, *n.* sòcio fondatore *m.*

charwoman, *n.* domèstica *f.*

chase, 1. *n.* càccia *f.* **2.** *vb.* cacciare.

chaser, *n.* cacciatore *m.*

chasm, *n.* abisso *m.*

chassis, *n.* telaio *m.*

chaste, *adj.* casto.

chasten, *vb.* castigare.

chasteness, *n.* castità *f.*

chastise, *vb.* castigare, punire.

chastisement, *n.* castigo *m.*, punizione *f.*

chastity, *n.* castità *f.*

chat, 1. *n.* chiàcchiera *f.* **2.** *vb.* chiacchierare.

château, *n.* castèllo *m.*

chattel, *n.* bène mòbile *m.*

chatter, 1. *n.* chiàcchiera *f.* **2.** *vb.* chiacchierare.

chatterbox, *n.* chiacchierone *m.*

chauffeur, *n.* autista *m.*

cheap, *adj.* a buòn mercato, econòmico.

cheapen, *vb.* (prices) calare; (depreciate) deprezzare.

cheaply, *adv.* a buòn mercato, economicamente.

cheapness, *n.* buòn mercato *m.*

cheat, *vb.* ingannare, truffare.

cheater, *n.* ingannatore *m.*, truffatore *m.*

check, 1. *n.* (restraint) freno *m.;* (verification) contròllo *m.;* (theater) contromarca *f.;* (clothes, luggage) scontrino *m.;* (bill) conto *m.;* (bank) assegno *m.* **2.** *vb.* (restrain) frenare; (verify) controllare; (luggage) registrare.

checkbook, *n.* libretto per gli assegni *m.*

checker, *n.* scacco *m.*

checkerboard, *n.* scacchièra *f.*

checkered, *adj.* (career) vissuta; (color) variegato.

checkers, *n.* dama *f.*

checking account, *n.* conto corrente *m.*, c.c. *m.*

checkmate, *n.* scacco matto *m.*

checkout, *n.* (hotel) partenza *f.*

checkpoint, *n.* posto d'ispezione *m.*

checkroom, *n.* guardaroba *m.*

checkup, *n.* ispezione *m.;* visita mèdica *f.*

cheek, *n.* guància *f.*

cheekbone, *n.* zigomo *m.*

cheer, 1. *n.* applàuso *m.* **2.** *vb.* applaudire; (c. up) rallegrare, *tr.*

cheerful, *adj.* allegro.

cheerfulness, *n.* allegría *f.*

cheerless, *adj.* triste.

cheery, *adj.* allegro.

cheese, *n.* càcio *m.*, formàggio *m.*

cheesecloth, *n.* garza *f.*

cheesy, *adj.* di qualità inferiore.

chef, *n.* cuòco *m.*

chemical, *adj.* chímico.

chemically, *adv.* chimicamente.

chemist, *n.* chímico *m.*

chemistry, *n.* chímica *f.*

chemotherapy, *n.* chemioterapía *f.*

chenille, *n.* ciniglia *f.*

cheque, *n.* assegno *m.*

cherish, *vb.* tener caro.

cherry, *n.* ciliègia *f.*

cherry-tree, *n.* ciliègio *m.*

cherub, *n.* cherubino *m.*

chess, *n.* scacchi *m.pl.*

chessboard, *n.* scacchièra *f.*

chessman, *n.* scacco *m.*

chest, *n.* (box) cassa *f.;* (body) pètto *m.*

chestnut, *n.* (nut) castagna *f.;* (tree) castagno *m.*

chevron, *n.* gallone *m.*

chew, *vb.* masticare.

chewer, *n.* masticatore *m.*

chewing gum, *n.* gomma da masticare *f.*

chic, *adj.* alla mòda.

chicanery, *n.* sofisma *m.*

chick, *n.* pulcino *m.*

chicken, n. pollo m.
chicken-hearted, adj. tímido.
chicken-pox, n. varicèlla f.
chickpea, n. cece m.
chicory, n. cicòria f.
chide, vb. rimproverare, sgridare.
chief, 1. n. capo m. **2.** adj. principale.
chief executive, n. capo del governo m.
chief justice, n. presidente della corte suprema m.
chiefly, adv. principalmente.
chief of staff, n. capo di stato maggiore m.
chieftain, n. capo m.
chiffon, n. mussolina leggeríssima f.
chilblain, n. gelone m.
child, n. bambino m., bambina f.
childbirth, n. parto m.
childhood, n. infànzia f.
childish, adj. infantile.
childishness, n. infantilità f.
childless, adj. sènza figli.
childlessness, n. mancanza di prole f.
childlike, adj. infantile.
chill, 1. n. freddo m.; (shiver) brívido m. **2.** vb. raffreddare.
chilliness, n. freddo m.
chilly, adj. freddo, gélido.
chime, 1. n. scampanío m. **2.** vb. scampanare.
chimney, n. camino m.
chimney-sweep, n. spazzacamino m.
chimpanzee, n. scimpanzè m.
chin, n. mento m.
China, n. (la) Cina f.
china, n. porcellana f.
chinaware, n. porcellane f.pl.
chinchilla, n. cincillà m.
Chinese, adj. cinese.
chink, n. crèpa f.
chintz, n. indiana f.
chip, 1. n. schéggia f. **2.** vb. scheggiare.
chiropodist, n. callista m.
chiropractor, n. callista m.
chirp, 1. n. cinguettío m. **2.** vb. cinguettare.
chisel, 1. n. cesèllo m. **2.** vb. cesellare.
chivalrous, adj. cavalleresco.

chivalry, n. cavallería f.
chive, n. cipolla f.
chloride, n. cloruro m.
chlorine, n. clòro m.
chloroform, n. cloroförmio m.
chlorophyll, n. clorofilla f.
chock full, adj. pieno zeppo.
chocolate, n. cioccolato m.
choice, 1. n. scelta f. **2.** adj. scelto.
choir, n. còro m.
choke, vb. soffocare, strangolare.
choker, n. cravatta f.
choler, n. còllera f.
cholera, n. colèra f.
choleric, adj. collèrico.
choose, vb. scégliere.
chop, 1. n. (meat) costoletta f. **2.** vb. tagliare.
chopper, n. (knife) mannaia f.
choppy, adj. (of sea) corto.
chopstick, n. bacchetta f.
choral, adj. corale.
chord, n. (string) còrda f.; (harmony) accòrdo m.
chore, n. lavoro di casa m.; corvè f.
choreographer, n. coreògrafo m.
choreography, n. coreografia f.
chorister, n. corista m.
chortle, vb. ridacchiare.
chorus, n. còro m.
chowder, n. minestra di pesce f.
Christ, n. Cristo m.
christen, vb. battezzare.
Christendom, n. cristianità f.
christening, n. battésimo m.
Christian, n. and adj. cristiano.
Christianity, n. cristianésimo m.
Christmas, n. Natale m.
chromatic, adj. cromàtico.
chrome, chromium, n. cròmo m.
chromosome, n. cromosòma m.
chronic, adj. crònico.
chronically, adv. cronicamente.
chronicle, n. crònaca f.
chronological, adj. cronològico.
chronology, n. cronología f.
chrysalis, n. crisàlide f.
chrysanthemum, n. crisantèmo m.
chubby, adj. grassetto.
chuck, vb. (cluck) chiocciare; (throw) lanciare.
chuckle, vb. ridere sotto voce.

chug, 1. n. sbuffo m. **2.** vb. sbuffare.

chum, n. compagno m.

chummy, adj. intimo.

chump, n. ciocco m., ceppo, m.

chunk, n. pèzzo m.

chunky, adj. tozzo.

church, n. chièsa f.

churchman, n. prète m.

churchyard, n. cimitèro m., camposanto m.

churlish, adj. villano.

churn, n. zàngola f.

chute, n. canale di scolo m.

cicada, n. cicala f.

cider, n. sidro m.

cigar, n. sígaro m.

cigarette, n. sigaretta f.; **(c. butt)** cicca f.

cigar store, n. tabaccheria f.

cilia, n. cíglio m.

ciliary, adj. ciliare.

cinch, n. còsa cèrta f.

cinchona, n. cincona f.

cinder, n. brùscolo m.

cinema, n. cínema m., cinematògrafo m.

cinematic, adj. cinematogràfico.

cinnamon, n. (tree) cinnamòmo m.; (spice) cannèlla f.

cipher, n. (zero) zèro m.; (figure, secret writing) cifra f.

circle, n. (figure) cérchio m.; (group) circolo m.

circuit, n. circùito m.; **(short c.)** corto circùito m.

circuitous, adj. indiretto.

circuitously, adv. indirettamente.

circuitry, n. schema di montaggio m.; circuitazione f.

circular, n. and adj. circolare (m.).

circularize, vb. mandare dei circolari a.

circulate, vb. circolare.

circulation, n. circolazione f.

circulatory, adj. circolatòrio.

circumcise, vb. circoncídere.

circumcision, n. circoncisione f.

circumference, n. circonferènza f.

circumflex, adj. circonflesso.

circumlocution, n. circonlocuzione f.

circumscribe, vb. circonscrívere.

circumspect, adj. circospètto.

circumstance, n. circostanza f.

circumstantial, adj. circostanziale; (detailed) particolareggiato.

circumstantially, adv. circostanziatamente.

circumvent, vb. circonvenire, impedire.

circumvention, n. circonvenzione f.

circus, n. circo m.

cirrhosis, n. cirròsi f.

cistern, n. cistèrna f., serbatòio m.

citadel, n. cittadèlla f.

citation, n. citazione f.

cite, vb. citare.

citizen, n. cittadino m., cittadina f.

citizenry, n. cittadinanza f.

citizenship, n. cittadinanza f.

citric, adj. cítrico.

citron, n. cedro m.

city, n. città f.; **(small c.)** cittadina f.

city council, n. consiglio municipale m.

city editor, n. capo cronista m.

city hall, n. municipio m.

city planning, n. urbanistica f.

city room, n. redazione f.

civic, adj. cívico.

civil, adj. civile.

civilian, n. and adj. civile.

civility, n. civiltà f.

civilization, n. civiltà f.

civilize, vb. civilizzare.

civilized, adj. civile.

clabber, n. quagliata f.

clad, adj. vestito.

claim, 1. n. reclamo m. **2.** vb. reclamare.

claimant, n. reclamante m.

clairvoyance, n. chiaroveggènza f.

clairvoyant, n. and adj. chiaroveggènte m. and f.

clamber, vb. arrampicarsi.

clammy, adj. freddo e ùmido.

clamor, n. clamore m.

clamorous, adj. clamoroso.

clamp, n. grappa f.

clan, n. clan m., tribù f.; (clique) cricca f.

clandestine, adj. clandestino.

clandestinely, *adv.* clandestinamente.
clang, *n.* fragore *m.*
clangor, *n.* clangore *m.*
clap, *vb.* (applaud) applaudire; (hands) bàttere le mani.
clapboard, *n.* tégola di legno *f.*
clapper, *n.* battàglio *m.*
claret, *n.* claretto *m.*
clarification, *n.* chiarificazione *f.*
clarify, *vb.* chiarificare.
clarinet, *n.* clarinetto *m.*
clarinetist, *n.* clarinettista *m.*
clarion, *n.* chiarina *f.*
clarity, *n.* chiarità *f.*
clash, 1. *n.* urto *m.* **2.** *vb.* urtarsi.
clasp, 1. *n.* gàncio *m.;* (hand) stretta di mano *f.;* (embrace) abbràccio *m.* **2.** *vb.* agganciare, stringere, abbracciare.
class, 1. *n.* classe *f.;* (social) cèto *m.* **2.** *vb.* classificare.
classic, classical, *adj.* clàssico.
classicism, *n.* classicismo *m.*
classifiable, *adj.* classificàbile; (secret) segreto.
classification, *n.* classificazione *f.*
classified, *adj.* segreto.
classify, *vb.* classificare.
classmate, *n.* compagno di classe *m.*
classroom, *n.* àula *f.*
classy, *adj.* di classe.
clatter, *n.* rumore *m.*
clause, *n.* clàusola *f.*
claustrophobia, *n.* claustrofobìa *f.*
clavicle, *n.* clavìcola *f.*
claw, *n.* artìglio *m.,* ràffio *m.*
claw-hammer, *n.* martèllo a ràffio *m.*
clay, *n.* argilla *f.,* creta *f.*
clayey, *adj.* argilloso.
clean, 1. *adj.* pulito, netto. **2.** *vb.* pulire.
clean-cut, *adj.* netto.
cleaner, *n.* pulitore *m.*
cleanliness, cleanness, *n.* pulizìa *f.*
cleanse, *vb.* pulire.
clean-shaven, *adj.* appenarasato.
cleanup, *n.* pulizìa *f.*
clear, 1. *adj.* chiaro. **2.** *vb.* (clear up) chiarire; (profit) guadagnare; (pass beyond) sorpassare;

(weather, *refl.*) schiarirsi; (leave free) sgomberare.
clearance, *n.* permesso di partire *m.*
clear-cut, *adj.* netto.
clearing, *n.* radura *f.*
clearing house, *n.* stanza di compensazione *f.*
clearly, *adv.* chiaramente.
clearness, *n.* chiarezza *f.*
cleat, *n.* bietta *f.*
cleavage, *n.* fessura *f.,* scissione *f.*
cleave, *vb.* fèndere.
cleaver, *n.* mannaia *f.*
clef, *n.* chiave *f.*
cleft, *n.* fenditura *f.*
clemency, *n.* clemènza *f.*
clement, *adj.* clemente.
clench, *vb.* stringere.
clergy, *n.* clèro *m.*
clergyman, *n.* ecclesiàstico *m.*
clerical, *adj.* clericale.
clericalism, *n.* clericalismo *m.*
clerk, *n.* (clergyman) ecclesiàstico *m.;* (employee) impiegato *m.*
clerkship, *n.* posto d'impiegato *m.*
clever, *adj.* àbile, ingegnoso.
cleverly, *adv.* abilmente, ingegnosamente.
cleverness, *n.* abilità *f.,* ingegnosità *f.*
clew, *n.* filo *m.*
cliché, *n.* luògo comune *m.*
click, *n.* rumore secco *m.*
client, *n.* cliènte *m.*
clientele, *n.* clientèla *f.*
cliff, *n.* rupe *f.*
climactic, *adj.* culminante.
climate, *n.* clima *f.*
climatic, *adj.* climàtico.
climax, *n.* cùlmine *m.*
climb, *vb.* scalare, arrampicarsi su.
climber, *n.* arrampicatore *m.;* (social) arrivista *m. or f.*
clinch, *vb.* (grasp) afferrare; (confirm) confermare; (conclude) conclùdere.
cling, *vb.* aderire.
clinic, *n.* clìnica *f.*
clinical, *adj.* clìnico.
clinically, *adv.* clinicamente.
clinician, *n.* clìnico *m.*
clip, 1. *n.* gàncio *m.* **2.** *vb.* (hair) ta-

gliare; (wool) tosare; (plants) cimare.

clipper, n. tosatore m.

clipping, n. tosatura f.

clique, n. cricca f.

cloak, n. mantéllo m.; (cloakroom) guardaróba f.

clock, n. orológio m.; (two o'c.) le due.

clockwise, adj. and adv. destròrso.

clockwork, n. meccanismo d'orologería m.

clod, n. zòlla f.; (person) tànghero m.

clog, 1. n. (wooden shoe) zòccolo m. 2. vb. ingombrare.

cloister, n. chiòstro m.

clone, n. riproduzione esatta f.

close, 1. adj. (closed) chiuso; (narrow) stretto; (near) vicino; (secret) riservato; 2. vb. chiùdere. 3. adv. vicino. 4. prep. (c. to) vicino a.

close call, n. rischio scampato appena m.

closed chapter, n. affare chiuso m.

close-lipped, adj. riservato.

closely, adv. da vicino.

closeness, n. prossimità f; (weather) pesantezza f.; (secrecy) riservatezza f.

closet, n. (toilet) gabinetto m.; (clothes) armàdio m.

close-up, n. primo piano m.

closing, n. fine f.

closure, n. chiusura f.

clot, 1. n. grumo m. 2. vb. raggrumarsi.

cloth, n. stòffa f., tela f.

clothe, vb. vestire.

clothes, n. vestiti m.pl.

clothespin, n. ferma biancheria f.

clothes tree, n. attaccapanni m.

clothier, n. pannaiòlo m.

clothing, n. vestiti m.pl.

cloud, 1. n. nùvola f., nube f. 2. vb. (c. over) rannuvolarsi.

cloudburst, n. acquazzone m.

cloud-capped, adj. coperto.

cloudiness, n. nuvolosità f.

cloudless, adj. senza nùvole, sereno.

cloudy, adj. nuvoloso.

clout, 1. n. (blow) colpo m.; (rag) stràccio m. 2. vb. picchiare.

clove, n. chiodo di garófano m.

cloven-hoofed, adj. satanico.

clover, n. trifóglio m.

clown, n. pagliàccio m.

clownish, adj. pagliaccesco.

cloy, vb. saziare.

club, 1. n. (group) círcolo m.; (stick) bastone m. 2. vb. bastonare.

clubfoot, n. piede stòrto m.

clubs, n. (cards) fiori m.pl.

clue, n. filo m.

clump, n. gruppo m.

clumsiness, n. goffàggine f.

clumsy, adj. goffo.

cluster, 1. n. gràppolo m.; (people) gruppo m. 2. vb. raggruppare.

clutch, 1. n. (claw) artíglio m.; (automobile) frizione f. 2. vb. afferrare.

clutter, vb. ingombrare.

coach, 1. n. (carriage) carrozza f.; (horse-drawn) còcchio m.; (train) vagone m.; (sports) allenatore m. 2. vb. (sports) allenare; (school) dare lezioni private a.

coach house, n. rimessa f.

coachman, n. cocchière f.

coagulate, vb. coagulare.

coagulation, n. coagulazione f.

coal, n. carbone fòssile m.

coalesce, vb. coalizzarsi.

coalition, n. coalizione f.

coal oil, n. petròlio m.

coal tar, n. catrame m.

coarse, adj. grossolano.

coarsen, vb. rèndere grossolano.

coarseness, n. grossolanità f.

coast, n. còsta f.

coastal, adj. costièro.

coaster, n. (ship) nave costièra f.

coast guard, n. milízia guardacòste f.

coat, n. (of suit) giacca f.; (overcoat) sopràbito m.

coating, n. strato m.

coat of arms, n. insegna f., stèmma m.

coax, vb. blandire.

cobalt, n. cobalto m.

cobbler, n. ciabattino m., calzolàio m.

cobblestone, n. ciòttolo m.

cobra, n. còbra m.

cobweb, n. ragnatela f.

cocaine, n. cocaína f.

cock, 1. n. (rooster) gallo m.; (male) maschio m.; (of gun) cane m.; (tap) rubinetto m.

cocker spaniel, n. cocker m.

cockeyed, adj. (lit.) stràbico; (crazy) matto, pazzo.

cockhorse, n. cavallo a dóndolo m.

cockpit, n. carlinga f.

cockroach, n. blatta f.

cocksure, adj. presuntuoso.

cocktail, n. còctail m.

cocky, adj. impudènte.

cocoa, n. cacao m.

coconut, n. noce di còcco f.

cocoon, n. bòzzolo m.

cod, n. merluzzo m.

C.O.D., adv. contro assegno.

coddle, vb. vezzeggiare.

code, n. (law) còdice m.; (secret) cifràrio m.

codeine, n. codeína f.

codfish, n. merluzzo m.

codger, n. (old c.) vecchietto m.

codify, vb. codificare.

cod-liver oil, n. òlio di fégato di merluzzo m.

coed, adj. misto.

coeducation, n. insegnamento misto m.

coeducational, adj. misto.

coequal, adj. coeguale.

coerce, vb. costringere.

coercion, n. coercizione f.

coercive, adj. coercitivo.

coexist, vb. coesistere.

coffee, n. caffè m.; (c. shop) caffè m.

coffee maker, n. macchina per il caffè f.

coffee pot, n. caffettiera f.

coffer, n. còfano m.; scrigno m.

coffin, n. cassa da mòrto f.

cog, n. dente m.; (c. railway) ferrovia a cremagliera f.

cogent, adj. convincente.

cogitate, vb. cogitare.

cognac, n. cognac m.

cognizance, n. conoscènza f.; (legal) competènza f.

cognizant, adj. competènte.

cogwheel, n. ruòta dentata f.

cohabit, vb. coabitare.

cohere, vb. èssere coerènte.

coherent, adj. coerènte.

cohesion, n. coesione f.

cohesive, adj. coesivo.

cohort, n. coòrte f.

coiffeur, n. parrucchiere per signora m.

coiffure, n. pettinatura f.

coil, 1. n. spira f.; (electr.) bobina f.; (induction c.) bobina d'induzione f. 2. vb. arrotolare.

coil spring, n. molla a spirale f.

coin, 1. n. moneta f. 2. vb. coniare.

coinage, n. cònio m.

coincide, vb. coincidere.

coincidence, n. coincidènza f.

coincident, adj. coincidènte.

coincidental, adj. coincidènte.

coincidentally, adv. per coincidènza.

coke, n. coca f.

colander, n. colatòio m.

cold, 1. n. (temperature) freddo m.; (med.) raffreddore m. 2. adj. freddo; (it is c.) fa freddo; (feel c.) aver freddo.

cold-blooded, adj. a sangue freddo.

cold comfort, n. magra consolazione f.

cold cuts, n. affettati m.pl.

coldly, adv. freddamente.

coldness, n. freddezza f.

collaborate, vb. collaborare.

collaboration, n. collaborazione f.

collaborator, n. collaboratore m.

collapse, 1. n. cròllo m.; (med.) collasso m. 2. vb. crollare.

collar, n. colletto m.; (dog's, priest's) collare m.

collarbone, n. clavicola f.

collate, vb. collezionare.

collateral, n. and adj. collaterale m.

collation, n. (comparison) confronto m.; (meal) merènda f.

colleague, n. collèga m.

collect, vb. raccògliere; (money) riscuòtere.

collection, n. raccòlta f., collezione f.; (church) quèstua f.

collective, adj. collettivo.

collectively, adv. collettivamente.

collector, n. (art) collezionista m.; (tickets) controllore m.

college, n. università f.

collegiate, adj. universitario.

collide, n. collusione f.

colliery, n. miniera di carbone f.

collision, n. scontro m.

colloquial, adj. colloquiale.

colloquialism, n. colloquialismo m.

colloquially, adv. colloquialmente.

colloquy, n. collòquio m.

collusion, n. collusione f.

Cologne, n. Colònia f.

colon, n. (writing) due punti m.pl.

colonel, n. colonnèllo m.

colonial, adj. coloniale.

colonist, n. colòno m.

colonization, n. colonizzazione f.

colonize, vb. colonizzare.

colony, n. colònia f.

color, 1. n. colore m. 2. vb. colorire.

coloration, n. colorazione f.

colored, adj. di colore.

colorful, adj. pittoresco.

coloring, n. coloritura f.

colorless, adj. sènza colore.

colossal, adj. colossale.

colt, n. puledro m.

column, n. colonna f.

columnist, n. cronista m.

coma, n. còma m.

comb, 1. n. pèttine m.; (rooster) cresta f. 2. vb. pettinare.

combat, 1. n. combattimento m. 2. vb. combàttere.

combatant, n. combattènte m.

combative, adj. battaglièro.

combination, n. combinazione f.

combination lock, n. serratura a combinazioni f.

combine, vb. combinare.

combustible, adj. combustìbile.

combustion, n. combustione f.

come, vb. venire; (c. about) accadere; (c. across) incontrare, trovare; (c. away) andàrsene; (c. back) tornare; (c. down) scéndere; (c. in) entrare; (c. out) uscire; (c. up) salire.

comedian, n. còmico m.

comedienne, n. attrice còmica f.

comedy, n. commèdia f.

come in!, interj. avanti!

comely, adj. grazioso.

comet, n. cometa f.

comfort, 1. n. confòrto m. 2. vb. confortare, consolare.

comfortable, adj. còmodo.

comfortably, adv. comodamente.

comforter, n. confortatore m., consolatore m.; coperta f.

comfortingly, adv. in modo consolatore.

comfortless, adj. sconsolato.

comic, comical, adj. còmico.

comic book, n. giornalino a fumetti m.

comic strip, n. fumetto m.

coming, n. venuta f.

comma, n. vìrgola f.

command, 1. n. comando m. 2. vb. comandare.

commandeer, vb. requisire.

commander, n. comandante m.

commander in chief, n. comandante in capo m.

commandment, n. comandamento m.

commemorate, vb. commemorare.

commemoration, n. commemorazione f.

commemorative, adj. commemorativo.

commence, vb. cominciare.

commencement, n. esòrdio m.

commend, vb. raccomandare, lodare.

commendable, adj. lodévole.

commendably, adv. lodevolmente.

commendation, n. lòde f.

commensurate, adj. commisurato.

comment, 1. n. commento m. 2. vb. commentare.

commentary, n. commento m.

commentator, n. (radio) cronista m.

commerce, n. commèrcio m.

commercial, adj. commerciale.

commercialism, n. commercialismo m.

commercialize, vb. commercializzare.

commercially, adv. commercialmente.

commiserate, *vb.* commiserare.

commissary, *n.* commissariato *m.*

commission, **1.** *n.* (committee, percentage) commissione *f.*; (assignment) incàrico *m.*; mandato *m.* **2.** *vb.* incaricare.

commissioner, *n.* commissàrio *m.*

commit, *vb.* comméttere.

commitment, *n.* impegno *m.*

committee, *n.* comitato *m.*, commissione *f.*

commodious, *adj.* spazioso.

commodity, *n.* mèrce *f.*

common, *n.* comune; (vulgar) volgare.

common law, *n.* diritto consuetudinario *m.*

commonly, *adv.* comunemente.

commonness, *n.* volgarità *f.*

commonplace, **1.** *n.* luògo comune *m.* **2.** *adj.* banale.

common sense, *n.* senso comune *m.*

common-sense, *adj.* giudizioso.

commonwealth, *n.* repùbblica *f.*

commotion, *n.* commozione *f.*

communal, *adj.* comunale.

commune, *vb.* comunicare.

communicable, *adj.* comunicàbile.

communicant, *n.* comunicante *m.*

communicate, *vb.* comunicare.

communication, *n.* comunicazione *f.*

communicative, *adj.* comunicativo.

communion, *n.* comunione *f.*; (take c.) comunicarsi.

communiqué, *n.* comunicato *m.*

communism, *n.* comunismo *m.*

communist, *n.* comunista *m.* or *f.*

communistic, *adj.* comunìstico.

community, *n.* comunità *f.*

community center, *n.* centro sociale *m.*

community chest, *n.* fondo di beneficenza *m.*

commutation, *n.* commutazione *f.*; (c. ticket) biglietto d'abbonamento *m.*

commute, *vb.* pendolare; (travel) viaggiare regolarmente, fare il pendolare.

commuter, *n.* pendolare *m.* or *f.*

compact, **1.** *n.* accòrdo *m.*, patto *m.* **2.** *adj.* compatto.

compactness, *n.* compattezza *f.*

companion, *n.* compagno *m.*, compagna *f.*

companionable, *adj.* sociévole.

companionship, *n.* compagnìa *f.*

company, *n.* compagnìa *f.*, società *f.*

comparable, *adj.* paragonàbile, comparàbile.

comparative, *adj.* comparativo.

comparatively, *adv.* comparativamente.

compare, *vb.* paragonare, confrontare, comparare.

comparison, *n.* paragone *m.*, confronto *m.*

compartment, *n.* scompartimento *m.*

compass, *n.* (naut.) bùssola *f.*; (geom.) compasso *m.*

compass card, *n.* rosa dei venti *f.*

compassion, *n.* compassione *f.*

compassionate, *adj.* compassionévole.

compassionately, *adv.* compassionevolmente.

compatible, *adj.* compatìbile.

compatriot, *n.* compatriòta *m.*, compaesano *m.*

compel, *vb.* costrìngere.

compelling, *adj.* imperioso; inevitàbile; necessario.

compensate, *vb.* compensare.

compensation, *n.* compènso *m.*

compensatory, *adj.* compensativo.

compete, *vb.* compètere, concórrere, gareggiare.

competence, *n.* competènza *f.*

competent, *adj.* competènte.

competently, *adv.* competentemente.

competition, *n.* concorso *m.*, gara *f.*; (comm.) concorrènza *f.*

competitive, *adj.* di concorso, di concorrènza.

competitor, *n.* concorrènte *m.*

compilation, *n.* compilazione *f.*; collezione *f.*

compile, *vb.* compilare.

complacency, *n.* contentezza di sè stesso *f.*

complacent, *adj.* contento di sè stesso.

complain, *vb.* lagnarsi, dolersi.

complainant, *n.* querelante *m.*

complainer, *n.* piagnucolone *m.*

complainingly, *adv.* lagnàndosi.

complaint, *n.* lagnanza *f.;* (sickness) malattìa *f.*

complaisance, *n.* compiacenza *f.*

complement, *n.* complemento *m.*

complete, 1. *adj.* complèto. **2.** *vb.* completare.

completely, *adv.* completamente.

completeness, *n.* completezza *f.*

completion, *n.* completamento *m.*

complex, *n. and adj.* complèsso *(m.).*

complexion, *n.* colorito *m.*

complexity, *n.* complessità *f.*

compliance, *n.* obbediènza *f.*

compliant, *adj.* obbediènte.

complicate, *vb.* complicare.

complicated, *adj.* complicato.

complication, *n.* complicazione *f.*

complicity, *n.* complicità *f.*

compliment, 1. *n.* complimento *m.* **2.** *vb.* complimentare, felicitare.

complimentary, *adj.* gratùito.

comply, *vb.* obbedire.

component, *n. and adj.* componènte *(m.).*

comport oneself, *vb.* comportarsi.

compose, *vb.* comporre.

composed, *adj.* (made of) composto di; (calm) calmo.

composer, *n.* compositore *m.*

composite, *adj.* composto.

composition, *n.* composizione *f.*

compositor, *n.* compositore *m.*

compost, *n.* concime *m.*

composure, *n.* compostezza *f.;* calma *f.*

compote, *n.* consèrva *f.*

compound, *n. and adj.* composto *(m.)*

comprehend, *vb.* comprèndere.

comprehensible, *adj.* comprensibile.

comprehension, *n.* comprensione *f.*

comprehensive, *adj.* comprensivo.

compress, *vb.* comprìmere.

compressed, *adj.* comprèsso.

compression, *n.* compressione *f.*

compressor, *n.* compressore *m.*

comprise, *vb.* comprèndere.

compromise, 1. *n.* compromesso *m.* **2.** *vb.* accomodarsi; (endanger) comprométtere.

comptroller, *n.* economo *m.;* amministratore *m.;* controllore *m.*

compulsion, *n.* costrizione *f.*

compulsive, *adj.* coercitivo; (involuntary) involontàrio.

compulsory, *adj.* obbligatòrio.

compunction, *n.* compunzione *f.*

computation, *n.* computazione *f.*

compute, *vb.* computare.

computer, *n.* calcolatrice elettrònica *f.;* calcolatore *m.*

computer science, *n.* informàtica *f.*

computerize, *v.* informatizzare.

comrade, *n.* camerata *m.*

comradeship, *n.* cameratismo *m.*

concave, *adj.* còncavo.

conceal, *vb.* celare.

concealment, *n.* occultamento *m.*

concede, *vb.* concèdere.

conceit, *n.* vanità *f.*

conceited, *adj.* vanitoso.

conceivable, *adj.* concepìbile.

conceivably, *adv.* concepibilmente.

conceive, *vb.* concepire.

concentrate, *vb.* concentrare.

concentration, *n.* concentrazione *f.,* concentramento *m.*

concentration camp, *n.* campo di concentramento *m.*

concept, *n.* concètto *m.*

conception, *n.* concezione *f.*

concern, 1. *n.* (affair) affare *m.;* (interest) interèsse *m.;* (firm) aziènda *f.;* (worry) ansietà *f.* **2.** *vb.* concèrnere, interessare, riguardare; **(c. oneself with)** interessarsi di; **(be c.ed over)** inquietarsi di.

concerning, *prep.* riguardo a, concernènte.

concert, 1. *n.* concèrto *m.* **2.** *vb.* concertare.

concertmaster, *n.* primo violino *m.*

concession, n. concessione f.
conch-shell, n. conchíglia f.
concierge, n. portinaio m.; **(c.'s office)** portineria f.
conciliate, vb. conciliare.
conciliation, n. conciliazione f.
conciliator, n. conciliatore m.
conciliatory, adj. conciliativo.
concise, adj. conciso.
concisely, adv. concisamente.
conciseness, n. concisione f., concisione f.
conclave, n. conclave m.
conclude, vb. conclùdere.
conclusion, n. conclusione f.
conclusive, adj. conclusivo.
conclusively, adv. conclusivamente.
concoct, vb. concuòcere.
concoction, n. concozione f.
concomitant, adj. concomitante.
concord, n. accòrdo m.
concordance, n. concòrde.
concordat, n. concordato m.
concourse, n. concorso m.
concrete, 1. n. cemento m. **2.** adj. concrèto.
concretely, adv. concretamente.
concrete mixer, n. betoniera m.
concreteness, n. concretezza f.
concubine, n. concubina f.
concur, vb. (events) concórrere; (persons) essere d'accòrdo.
concurrence, n. concorrènza f.; (agreement) consènso m.
concurrent, adj. concorrènte.
concussion, n. concussione f.
condemn, vb. condannare.
condemnable, adj. condannàbile.
condemnation, n. condanna f.
condensation, n. condensazione f.
condense, vb. condensare.
condenser, n. condensatore m.
condescend, vb. accondiscéndere.
condescending, adj. condiscendente.
condescendingly, adv. con accondiscendènza.
condescension, n. accondiscendènza f.
condiment, 1. n. condimento m. **2.** vb. condire.

condition, 1. n. condizione f. **2.** vb. condizionare.
conditional, adj. condizionale.
conditionally, adv. condizionalmente.
condole, vb. condolersi.
condolence, n. condoglianza f.
condom, n. preservativo m.
condominium, n. condomínio m.
condone, vb. condonare.
conduce, vb. condurre, tèndere.
conducive, adj. tendènte.
conduct, 1. n. condotta f. **2.** vb. condurre.
conductive, adj. conduttivo.
conductivity, n. conduttività f.
conductor, n. conduttore m.; (orchestra) direttore m.; (train) capotreno m.; (tram, bus) bigliettaio m.
conduit, n. condotto m.
cone, n. còno m.
confection, n. (dress) confezione f.; (candy) confetto m.; confettura f.
confectioner, n. confettière m.; **(c. shop)** confettería f.
confectionery, n. (store) confettería f.
confederacy, n. confederazione f.
confederate, 1. n. confederato m. **2.** vb. confederarsi.
confederation, n. confederazione f.
confer, vb. conferire.
conference, n. conferènza f.
confess, vb. confessare.
confession, n. confessione f.
confessional, n. and adj. confessionale (m.).
confession of faith, n. professione di fede f.
confessor, n. confessore m.
confetti, n. coriàndoli m.pl.
confidant, n. confidènte m.
confidante, n. confidènte f.
confide, vb. confidare.
confidence, n. confidènza f.
confident, adj. confidènte.
confidential, adj. confidenziale.
confidentially, adv. in confidènza.
confidently, adv. confidentemente.
confine, vb. confinare.
confirm, vb. confermare.

confirmation, n. conferma f.
confirmed, adj. confermato.
confiscate, vb. confiscare.
confiscation, n. confisca f.
conflagration, n. conflagrazione f.
conflict, 1. n. conflitto m. 2. vb. venire a conflitto.
conflicting, adj. contrastante, contradittório.
confluence, n. confluenza f.
conform, vb. conformarsi.
conformation, n. conformazione f.
conformer, **conformist**, n. conformista m.
conformity, n. conformità f.
confound, vb. confóndere.
confounded, adj. maledetto, odioso.
confront, vb. confrontare.
confrontation, n. contestazione f.
confuse, vb. confóndere.
confusion, n. confusione f.
congeal, vb. congelare.
congealment, n. congelamento m.
congenial, adj. simpàtico.
congenital, adj. congènito.
congenitally, adv. congenitamente.
congest, vb. congestionare.
congestion, n. congestione f.
conglomerate, 1. n. and adj. conglomerato (m.). 2. vb. conglomerare.
conglomeration, n. conglomerazione f.
congratulate, vb. felicitare, congratularsi con.
congratulation, n. felicitazione f., congratulazione f.
congratulatory, adj. congratulatòrio.
congregate, vb. congregarsi.
congregation, n. congregazione f.
congress, n. congrèsso m., parlamento m.
congressional, adj. parlamentare.
congressman, n. parlamentare al congresso degli S.U. m.

congresswoman, n. parlamentare al congresso degli S.U. f.
conic, adj. cònico.
conjecture, 1. n. congettura f. 2. vb. congetturare.
conjugal, adj. coniugale.
conjugate, vb. coniugare.
conjugation, n. coniugazione f.
conjunction, n. congiunzione f.
conjunctive, adj. congiuntivo.
conjunctivitis, n. congiuntivite f.
conjure, vb. scongiurare.
connect, vb. collegare, connèttere; (transport) coincídere.
connecting rod, n. biella f.
connection, n. collegamento m., connessione f.; (transport) coincidènza f.
connivance, n. connivènza f.
connive, vb. essere connivènte.
connoisseur, n. conoscitore m.
connotation, n. connotazione f.
connote, vb. connotare.
connubial, adj. connubiale.
conquer, vb. víncere, conquistare.
conquerable, adj. vincíbile, conquistàbile.
conqueror, n. vincitore m., conquistatore m.
conquest, n. conquista f.
conscience, n. coscènza f.
conscientious, adj. coscienzioso.
conscientiously, adv. coscienziosamente.
conscientious objector, n. obiettore di coscienza m.
conscious, adj. cònscio, consapévole.
consciously, adv. consciamente.
consciousness, n. coscènza f.
conscript, n. coscritto m.
conscription, n. coscrizione f.
consecrate, vb. consacrare.
consecration, n. consacrazione f.
consecutive, adj. consecutivo.
consecutively, adv. consecutivamente.
consensus, n. consènso m.
consent, 1. n. consènso m. 2. vb. consentire, acconsentire.
consequence, n. conseguenza f.
consequent, adj. conseguènte.
consequential, adj. conseguenziale.

consequently, adv. conseguentemente, per conseguènza.

conservation, n. conservazione f.

conservative, n. and adj. conservatore (m.).

conservatism, n. conservatorismo m.

conservatory, n. conservatòrio m.

conserve, vb. conservare.

consider, vb. considerare.

considerable, adj. considerévole, consideràbile; (a fair amount) parécchio.

considerably, adv. considerabilmente.

considerate, vb. premuroso.

considerately, adv. premurosamente.

consideration, n. considerazione f.

considering, adv. considerando.

consign, vb. consegnare.

consignment, n. consegna f.

consist, vb. consistere.

consistency, n. consistènza f.

consistent, adj. coerènte.

consolation, n. consolazione f.

console, vb. consolare.

consolidate, vb. consolidare.

consommé, n. bròdo ristretto m.

consonant, n. and adj. consonante (f.).

consort, n. consòrte m. and f.

conspicuous, adj. cospícuo.

conspicuously, adv. cospicuamente.

conspicuousness, n. cospicuità f.

conspiracy, n. congiura f.

conspirator, n. congiurato m.

conspire, vb. congiurare.

constancy, n. costanza f.

constant, adj. costante.

constantly, adv. costantemente.

constellation, n. costellazione f.

consternation, n. costernazione f.

constipate, vb. costipare.

constipated, adj. stítico.

constipation, n. stitichezza f.

constituency, n. votanti m.pl.

constituent, adj. costituènte.

constitute, vb. costituire.

constitution, n. costituzione f.

constitutional, adj. costituzionale.

constrain, vb. costríngere.

constraint, n. costrizione f.

constrict, vb. costríngere.

construct, vb. costruire.

construction, n. costruzione f.; (interpretation) interpretazione f.

constructive, adj. costruttivo.

constructively, adv. costruttivamente.

constructor, n. costruttore m.

construe, vb. interpretare.

consul, n. cònsole m.

consular, adj. consolare.

consulate, n. consolato m.

consulship, n. consolato m.

consult, vb. consultare.

consultant, n. consultatore m.

consultation, n. consultazione f., consulto m.

consume, vb. consumare.

consumer, n. consumatore m.

consumer goods, n. merci di consumo f.pl.

consumerism, n. consumismo m.

consummate, adj. consumato.

consummation, n. consumazione f.

consumption, n. consumo m.; (tuberculosis) tisi f.; tuberculosi f.

consumptive, adj. tísico.

contact, 1. n. contatto m. 2. vb. venire a contatto con.

contact lenses, n. lenti a contatto f.pl.

contagion, n. contàgio m.

contagious, adj. contagioso.

contain, vb. contenere.

container, n. recipiènte m.

contaminate, vb. contaminare.

contamination, n. contaminazione f.

contemplate, vb. contemplare.

contemplation, n. contemplaziane f.

contemplative, n. contemplativo.

contemporaneous, adj. contemporaneo.

contemporary, adj. contemporàneo.

contempt, n. disprèzzo m.

contemptible, adj. spregévole.

contempt of court, n. oltraggio alla giuria m.

contemptuous, adj. sprezzante.

contemptuously, adv. sprezzantemente.

contend, vb. contèndere; (affirm) sostenere.

contender, n. contendènte m.

content, 1. adj. contento. 2. vb. accontentare.

contented, adj. contento.

contention, n. contenzione f.

contentment, n. accontentamento m.

contest, 1. n. contesa f., gara f. 2. vb. contestare.

contestable, adj. contestàbile.

contestant, n. gareggiante m.

context, n. contèsto m.

contiguous, adj. contíguo.

continence, n. continènza f.

continent, n. and adj. continènte (m.).

continental, adj. continentale.

contingency, n. contingènza f.

contingent, adj. contingènte.

continual, adj. contínuo.

continuance, n. (law) rinvío m.

continuation, n. continuazione f.

continue, vb. continuare.

continuity, n. continuità f.

continuous, adj. contínuo.

continuous showing, n. spettacolo permanente m.

continuously, adv. continuamente.

contort, vb. contòrcere.

contortion, n. contorsione f.

contortionist, n. contorsionista m.

contour, n. contorno m.

contraband, n. contrabbando m.

contrabass, n. contrabasso m.

contraception, n. controllo delle nàscite m.

contraceptive, n. and adj. contraccettivo (m.)

contract, 1. n. contratto m. 2. vb. contrarre; (agree) contrattare.

contraction, n. contrazione f.

contractor, n. contrattatore m., imprenditore m.

contradict, vb. contraddire.

contradictable, adj. contraddicíbile.

contradiction, n. contraddizione f.

contradictory, adj. contraddittòrio.

contralto, n. contralto m.

contraption, n. congegno m.

contrary, adj. contrário.

contrast, 1. n. contrasto m. 2. vb. contrastare, intr.

contravene, vb. contravvenire.

contribute, vb. contribuire; (newspaper) collaborare.

contribution, n. contributo m., contribuzione f.

contributive, adj. contributivo.

contributor, n. contributore m.; (newspaper) collaboratore m.

contributory, adj. contributòrio.

contrite, adj. contrito.

contrition, n. contrizione f.

contrivance, n. congegno m.

contrive, vb. (invent) inventare; (bring about) effettuare.

control, 1. n. controllo m. 2. vb. controllare.

controllable, adj. controllàbile.

controller, n. controllore m.

controlling interest, n. maggioranza delle azioni f.

control stick, n. leva di comando f.

controversial, adj. controvèrso.

controversy, n. controvèrsia f.

contumacious, adj. ribelle, contumace.

contumacy, n. contumàcia f.

contusion, n. contusione f.

conundrum, n. indovinèllo m.

convalesce, vb. rimèttersi in salute.

convalescence, n. convalescènza f.

convalescent, adj. convalescènte.

convene, vb. convenire.

convenience, n. conveniènza f.

convenient, adj. conveniènte.

conveniently, adv. convenientemente.

convent, n. convènto m.

convention, n. convenzione f.; (meeting) congrèsso m.

conventional, adj. convenzionale.

conventionally, adv. convenzionalmente.

converge, vb. convèrgere.
convergence, n. convergènza f.
convergent, adj. convergènte.
conversant with, adj. versato in, pràtico di.
conversation, n. conversazione f.
conversational, adj. di conversazione.
conversationalist, n. conversatore m.
converse, 1. adj. convèrso. **2.** vb. conversare.
conversely, adv. per convèrso.
conversion, n. conversione f.
convert, vb. convertire.
converter, n. convertitrice f.
convertible, adj. convertíbile.
convex, adj. convèsso.
convey, vb. trasméttere, trasportare.
conveyance, n. traspòrto m.; (property) trapasso di proprietà m.
conveyor, n. trasportatore m.
conveyor belt, n. nastro trasportatore m.
convict, 1. n. condannato m. **2.** vb. dichiarare colpévole.
conviction, n. (belief) convinzione f.; (law) condanna f.
convince, vb. convíncere.
convincing, adj. convincènte.
convincingly, adv. in modo convincènte.
convivial, adj. conviviale.
convocation, n. convocazione f.
convoke, vb. convocare.
convoy, 1. n. convòglio m. **2.** vb. convogliare.
convulse, vb. méttere in convulsioni.
convulsion, n. convulsione f.
convulsive, adj. convulsivo.
coo, vb. tùbare, gèmere.
cook, 1. n. cuòco m. **2.** vb. cucinare.
cookbook, n. libro di cucina m.
cookie, n. biscòtto m.
cookout, n. picnic m.
cool, 1. adj. fresco. **2.** vb. rinfrescare.
coolant, n. antigelo m.
cooler, n. frigorífero m.
cool-headed, adj. calmo, imperturbabile.

coolish, adj. freschetto.
coolness, n. fresco m.; (fig.) indifferènza f.
coop, n. stía f.
cooper, n. bottaio m.
cooperate, vb. cooperare.
cooperation, n. cooperazione f.
cooperative, 1. n. cooperativa f. **2.** adj. cooperativo.
cooperatively, adv. cooperativamente.
coordinate, vb. coordinare.
coordination, n. coordinazione f.
coordinator, n. coordinatore m.
coot, n. fòlaga f.; vècchio pazzo m.
cop, n. poliziòtto m.
copartner, n. sòcio m.
cope, vb. lottare; **(c. with)** tener tèsta a.
copier, n. macchina copiatrice f.; fotocopiatrice f.
copilot, n. copilota m.
copious, adj. copioso.
copiously, adv. copiosamente.
copiousness, n. copiosità f., còpia f.
copper, n. rame m.
copperplate, n. calligrafía f.
copulate, vb. copulare.
copy, 1. n. còpia f.; (of book) esemplare m. **2.** vb. copiare.
copyist, n. copista m.
copyright, n. diritti d'autore m.pl.
copywriter, n. redattore m.
coquetry, n. civetteria f.
coquette, 1. n. civetta f. **2.** vb. civettare.
coquettish, adj. civettuolo.
coral, n. corallo m.
coral reef, n. barriera corallina f.
cord, n. còrda f.
cordial, n. and adj. cordiale (m.).
cordiality, n. cordialità f.
cordially, adv. cordialmente.
cordon, n. cordone m.
cordovan, n. cordovano m.
core, n. (fruit) tórsolo m.; (heart) cuòre m.
cork, n. súghero m.; (of bottle) tappo m.
corkscrew, n. cavatappi m. (sg.).
corn, n. (grain) granturco m.; (on foot) callo m.

corn bread, *n.* pane di farina gialla *m.*

cornea, *n.* còrnea *f.*

corner, **1.** *n.* àngolo *m.*, canto *m.* **2.** *vb.* (*comm.*) accaparrare.

cornerstone, *n.* piètra angolare *f.*

cornet, *n.* cornetta *f.*

cornetist, *n.* cornettista *m.*

corn exchange, *n.* borsa dei cereali *f.*

cornflakes, *n.* fiocchi di granturco *m.pl.*

corn flour, *n.* farina di granturco *f.*

cornice, *n.* cornicione *m.*

corn-plaster, *n.* callifugo *m.*

cornstarch, *n.* farina di granturco *f.*

cornucopia, *n.* cornucòpia *m.* or *f.*

corollary, *n.* corollàrio *m.*

coronary, *adj.* coronàrio.

coronation, *n.* incoronazione *f.*

coronet, *n.* (noble's) corna nobiliare *f.*; (headdress) diadèma *f.*

corporal, **1.** *n.* caporale *m.* **2.** *adj.* corporale.

corporate, *adj.* corporato.

corporation, *n.* corporazione *f.*

corps, *n.* còrpo *m.*

corpse, *n.* cadàvere *m.*

corpulent, *adj.* corpulènto.

corpuscle, *n.* corpùscolo *m.*

correct, **1.** *adj.* corrètto. **2.** *vb.* corrèggere.

correction, *n.* correzione *f.*

corrective, *adj.* correttivo.

correctly, *adv.* correttamente.

correctness, *n.* correttezza *f.*

correlate, *vb.* méttere in correlazione.

correlation, *n.* correlazione *f.*

correspond, *vb.* corrispóndere.

correspondence, *n.* corrispondènza *f.*

correspondent, *n. and adj.* corrispondènte (*m.*).

corridor, *n.* corridòio *m.*

corroborate, *vb.* corroborare.

corroboration, *n.* corroborazione *f.*

corroborative, *adj.* corroborativo.

corrode, *vb.* corródere.

corrosion, *n.* corrosione *f.*

corrugate, *vb.* corrugare.

corrupt, *vb.* corrómpere.

corrupter, *n.* corruttore *m.*

corruptible, *adj.* corruttibile.

corruption, *n.* corruzione *f.*

corruptive, *adj.* corruttivo.

corsage, *n.* fiori *m.pl.*

corset, *n.* busto *m.*

Corsican, *adj.* còrso.

cortège, *n.* cortèo *m.*

corvette, *n.* corvetta *f.*

cosmetic, *n. and adj.* cosmètico (*m.*).

cosmic, *adj.* còsmico.

cosmopolitan, *adj.* cosmopolita.

cosmos, *n.* còsmo *m.*

cost, **1.** *n.* costo *m.* **2.** *vb.* costare.

costliness, *n.* costosità *f.*

costly, *adj.* costoso.

costume, *n.* costume *m.*

costumer, *n.* vestiarista *m.*

cot, *n.* lettino *m.*

coterie, *n.* combriccola *f.*, cenàcolo *m.*

cotillion, *n.* cotiglione *m.*

cottage, *n.* villetta *f.*, casetta *f.*

cotton, *n.* cotone *m.*

cottonseed, *n.* seme di cotone *m.*

couch, *n.* lètto *m.*

cough, **1.** *n.* tosse *f.* **2.** *vb.* tossire.

could, *vb.* use past or conditional of potere.

coulter, *n.* vòmere *m.*

council, *n.* consiglio *m.*

councilman, *n.* consiglière *m.*

counsel, **1.** *n.* consiglio *m.* **2.** *vb.* consigliare.

counselor, *n.* consiglière *m.*

count, **1.** *n.* conto *m.*; (noble) conte *m.* **2.** *vb.* contare.

countenance, **1.** *n.* viso *m.* **2.** *vb.* approvare.

counter, *n.* banco *m.*

counteract, *vb.* neutralizzare.

counteraction, *n.* controazione *f.*

counterattack, *n.* contrattacco *m.*

counterbalance, *n.* contrappeso *m.*

counter-clockwise, *adj. and adv.* sinistròrso.

counterfeit, **1.** *n. and adj.* falso (*m.*). **2.** *vb.* contraffare, falsificare.

countermand, vb. contromandare.

counteroffensive, n. controffensiva f.

counterpart, n. contropartita f.

Counter-Reformation, n. Controriforma f.

countess, n. contessa f.

countless, adj. innumerévole.

country, n. (nation) paese m.; (opposed to city) campagna f.; (native land) pàtria f.

countryman, n. (of same country) compatriòta m.; (rustic) contadino m.

countryside, n. campagna f.

county, n. contèa f.

coupé, n. cupè m.

couple, 1. n. cóppia f., paio m. **2.** vb. accoppiare.

coupon, n. tagliando m., cèdola f.

courage, n. coràggio m.

courageous, adj. coraggioso.

courier, n. corrière m.

course, n. corso m.; (for races) pista f.

court, 1. n. corte f. **2.** vb. corteggiare, far la corte a.

courteous, adj. cortese.

courtesan, n. cortigiana f.

courtesy, n. cortesía f.

courthouse, n. palazzo di giustízia m.

courtier, n. cortigiano m.

courtly, adj. cerimonioso.

courtmartial, n. corte marziale f.

courtroom, n. aula di udiènza f.

courtship, n. corteggiamento m.

courtyard, n. cortile m.

cousin, n. cugino m., cugina f.

covenant, n. convenzione f.

cover, 1. n. copertura f., (book) copertina f. **2.** vb. coprire.

covering, n. copertura f.

covet, vb. bramare.

covetous, adj. bramoso.

cow, 1. n. vacca f., mucca f. **2.** vb. intimidire.

coward, n. codardo m.

cowardice, n. codardía f.

cowardly, adj. codardo.

cowboy, n. vaccaro m.; cowboy m.

cower, vb. rannicchiarsi.

cow hand, n. vaccaro m.

cowhide, n. vacchetta f.

coxswain, n. timonière m.

coy, adj. tímido.

crab, n. grànchio m.

crack, 1. n. fenditura f. **2.** vb. fèndere.

cracked, adj. fesso.

cracker, n. biscòtto m.

crackup, n. incidènte m.

cradle, 1. n. culla f. **2.** vb. cullare.

craft, n. arte f.

craftsman, n. artigiano m.

craftsmanship, n. arte f.

crafty, adj. furbo.

crag, n. picco m.

cram, vb. rimpinzare, infarcire.

cramp, n. crampo m.

crane, n. gru f.

cranium, n. crànio m.

crank, 1. n. (handle) manovella f.; (crackpot) pazzo m. **2.** vb. girare.

cranky, adj. capriccioso.

cranny, n. fessura f.

crapshooter, n. giocatore di dadi m.

craps, n. giòco dei dadi m.

crash, 1. n. cròllo m. **2.** vb. crollare.

crate, n. gabbietta da imballàggio f.

crater, n. cratère m.

crave, vb. bramare.

craven, adj. codardo.

craving, n. brama f.

craw, n. gozzo m.

crawl, vb. trascinarsi.

crayfish, n. aragosta f.; gambero m.

crayon, n. pastello m.

crazed, adj. pazzo.

craze, n. mania f.; moda f.

crazy, adj. pazzo, fòlle.

creak, vb. cigolare, scricchiolare.

creaky, adj. cigolante, scricchiolante.

cream, n. crèma f., panna f.

creamery, n. cremería f.

cream puff, n. bignè m.

creamy, adj. ricco di panna.

crease, 1. n. pièga f. **2.** vb. (fold) piegare; (crinkle) spiegazzare.

create, vb. creare.

creation, n. creazione f.

creative, adj. creativo.

creator, n. creatore m.

creature, n. creatura f.

credence, n. credènza f.

credentials, n. credenziali f.pl.

credibility, n. credibilità f.

credible, adj. credíbile.

credit, n. crèdito m.

creditable, adj. soddisfacènte.

creditably, adv. in modo soddisfacènte.

credit card, n. carta di crèdito f.

creditor, n. creditore m.

credo, n. crèdo m.

credulity, n. credulità f.

credulous, adj. crèdulo.

creed, n. crèdo m.; fede f.

creek, n. ruscello m.; **(mountain c.)** torrènte m.

creep, vb. strisciare, arrampicarsi.

cremate, vb. cremare.

cremation, n. cremazione f.

crematory, 1. adj. crematòrio. **2.** n. forno crematòrio m.

creosote, n. creosòto m.

crepe, n. crespo m.

crescent, n. mezzaluna f.

cress, n. crescione m.

crest, n. cresta f.

crestfallen, adj. a cresta bassa, scoraggiato.

cretonne, n. cotonina f.

crevasse, n. crepàccio m.

crevice, n. screpolatura f.

crew, n. equipàggio m.

crew cut, n. capelli a spazzola m.pl.

crib, n. lettino da bimbo m.

cricket, n. grillo m.

crier, n. banditore m.

crime, n. delitto m.

criminal, n. and adj. criminale (m.).

criminologist, n. criminòlogo m.

criminology, n. criminologia f.

crimp, n. pièga f.

crimson, adj. crèmisi.

cringe, vb. piegarsi.

crinkle, vb. spiegazzare.

cripple, 1. n. sciancato. **2.** vb. rendere sciancato.

crippled, adj. sciancato.

crisis, n. crisi f.

crisp, adj. crespo; **(bread, etc.)** croccante.

crisscross, adj. incrociato.

criterion, n. critèrio m.

critic, n. crítico m.

critical, adj. crítico.

criticism, n. crítica f.

criticize, vb. criticare.

critique, n. crítica f.

croak, vb. gracidare.

crochet, vb. lavorare all'uncinetto.

crock, n. vaso di terracotta m.

crockery, n. vasellame m.

crocodile, n. coccodrillo m.

crocodile tears, n. làcrime di coccodrillo f.pl.

crocus, n. croco m.

crone, n. vècchia f.

crony, n. compare m.

crook, n. **(bend)** curvatura f.; **(scoundrel)** mascalzone m.

crooked, adj. stòrto.

croon, vb. canticchiare.

crop, n. raccòlta f., raccólto m.

croquet, n. pallamàglio m.

croquette, n. crocchetta f., polpetta f.

cross, 1. n. croce f.; **(mixture)** incròcio m. **2.** adj. irritato, adirato. **3.** vb. attraversare; **(mix)** incrociare.

crossbones, n. tèschio con tíbie incrociate m.; il símbolo dei pirati m.

crossbow, n. balestra f.

crossbreed, 1. n. incròcio di razze m. **2.** adj. di razza incrociata.

cross-country, adj. campestre.

cross-examine, vb. esaminare in contraddittòrio.

cross-eyed, adj. stràbico.

cross-fertilization, n. ibridazione f.

crossing, n. incròcio m.; **(grade c.)** passàggio a livèllo m.

cross-purposes, be at, vb. fraintèndersi.

cross-reference, n. richiamo m.; rimando m.

crossroads, n. crocícchio m., crocevía f.

cross section, n. sezione f.

crossword puzzle, n. crucivèrba m.

crotch, n. **(tree)** biforcazione f.; **(human body)** inforcatura f.

crouch, vb. accucciarsi.

croup, n. crup m.

crouton, n. crostino m.
crow, 1. n. còrvo m. **2.** vb. cantare.
crowd, 1. n. fòlla f. **2.** vb. affollare; (push) spingere.
crowded, adj. affollato.
crown, 1. n. corona f. **2.** vb. incoronare.
crown prince, n. príncipe ereditàrio m.
crow's-foot, n. zampa di gallina f.
crow's-nest, n. còffa f.
crucial, adj. cruciale.
crucible, n. crogiòlo m.
crucifix, n. crocefisso m.
crucifixion, n. crocefissione f.
crucify, vb. crocefiggere.
crude, adj. crudo.
crudeness, n. crudezza f.
crudity, n. crudezza f.
cruel, adj. crudèle.
cruelty, n. crudeltà f.
cruet, n. olièra f.
cruise, 1. n. crocièra f. **2.** vb. incrociare.
cruiser, n. incrociatore m.
crumb, n. briciola f.
crumble, vb. sbriciolare.
crummy, adj. sporco; pòvero.
crumple, vb. spiegazzare.
crunch, vb. schiacciare rumorosamente.
crusade, n. crociata f.
crusader, n. crociato m.
crush, 1. n. fòlla f. **2.** vb. schiacciare.
crust, n. crosta f.
crustacean, n. and adj. crostàceo (m.).
crusty, adj. crostoso; (manners) irritàbile.
crutch, n. grùccia f., stampèlla f.
cry, 1. n. grido m. **2.** vb. (shout) gridare, urlare; (weep) piàngere.
crybaby, n. piagnone m.; lamentoso m.
crying, n. pianto m.
cryosurgery, n. criochirurgia f.
crypt, n. cripta f.
cryptic, adj. breve ed oscuro.
cryptography, n. crittografia f.
crystal, n. cristallo m.
crystalline, adj. cristallino.
crystallize, vb. cristallizzare.
cub, n. piccolo m.

cubbyhole, n. nascondíglio m.
cube, n. cubo m.
cubic, adj. cùbico.
cubicle, n. cubícolo m.
cubism, n. cubismo m.
cuckold, 1. adj. cornuto becco. **2.** n. cornuto m.
cuckoo, 1. n. cúculo m. **2.** adj., pazzo.
cucumber, n. cetriòlo m.
cud, n. bòlo m.; (chew the c.) ruminare.
cuddle, vb. accarezzare.
cudgel, n. clava f., mazza f.
cue, n. segno m.; (billiards) stecca f.
cuff, 1. n. (shirt) polsino m.; (blow) scapaccione m. **2.** vb. picchiare.
cuisine, n. cucina f.
culinary, adj. culinàrio.
cull, vb. cògliere.
culminate, vb. culminare.
culmination, n. culminazione f.
culpable, adj. colpévole.
culprit, n. colpévole m.
cult, n. culto m.
cultivate, vb. coltivare.
cultivated, adj. colto.
cultivation, n. coltivazione f.
cultivator, n. coltivatore m.
cultural, adj. culturale.
culture, n. cultura f.
cultured, adj. colto.
cumbersome, adj. ingombrante.
cumulative, adj. cumulativo.
cunning, 1. n. abilità f. **2.** adj. astuto, àbile; (attractive) attraènte, bellino.
cup, n. tazza f.
cupboard, n. credènza f.
cupidity, n. cupidígia f.
cupola, n. cùpola f.
curable, adj. guaríbile.
curator, n. curatore m.
curb, 1. n. (sidewalk) cordone m.; **2.** vb. raffrenare.
curbstone, n. bordo di piètre m.
curd, n. quagliata f.
curdle, vb. quagliare.
cure, 1. n. cura f., guarigione f. **2.** vb. guarire.
curfew, n. coprifuòco m.
curio, n. curiosità f.
curiosity, n. curiosità f.

curious, *adj.* curioso; (queer) strano.

curl, 1. *n.* rícciolo *m.* **2.** *vb.* arricciare.

curly, *adj.* ricciuto.

currant, *n.* ribes *m.*

currency, *n.* circolazione *f.;* (money) valuta *f.*

current, *n. and adj.* corrènte (*f.*).

currently, *adv.* correntemente.

curriculum, *n.* currícolo *m.*

curry, *vb.* (horse) strigliare.

curse, 1. *n.* maledizione *f.* **2.** *vb.* maledire.

cursed, *adj.* maledetto.

curse-word, *n.* bestémmia *f.*

cursive, *n. and adj.* corsivo *m.*

cursory, *adj.* frettoloso.

curt, *adj.* asciutto, breve.

curtail, *vb.* accorciare, ridurre.

curtain, *n.* cortina *f.;* (theater) sipàrio *m.*

curtain raiser, *n.* avanspettacolo *m.*

curtsy, *n.* riverènza *f.*

curvature, *n.* curvatura *f.*

curve, 1. *n.* curva *f.* **2.** *vb.* curvare.

curved, *adj.* curvo, ricurvo; curvato.

cushion, *n.* cuscino *m.*

cuspidor, *n.* sputacchièra *f.*

cuss, *vb.* maledire; bestemmiare.

custard, *n.* crema caramella *f.*

custodian, *n.* custòde *m.*

custody, *n.* custòdia *f.*

custom, *n.* costume *m.,* consuetùdine *f.,* uso *m.*

customary, *adj.* consuèto.

custom-built, *adj.* fatto su misura.

customer, *n.* cliènte *m.;* (regular c.) avventore *m.*

customs-house, customs, *n.* dogana *f.*

customs-officer, *n.* doganière *m.*

cut, 1. *n.* tàglio *m.* **2.** *vb.* tagliare.

cut-and-dried, *adj.* monòtono; preparato in anticipo.

cutaneous, *adj.* cutàneo.

cutback, *n.* tàglio *m.;* riduzione *f.*

cute, *adj.* attraènte, bellino.

cut glass, *n.* cristallo *m.*

cuticle, *n.* cutícola *f.*

cutlass, *n.* sciàbola *f.*

cutlet, *n.* costoletta *f.*

cutlery, *n.* posatería *f.*

cutoff, *n.* tàglio *m.;* scorciatòia *f.*

cutout, *n.* interruttore *m.*

cut-rate, *adj.* scontato.

cutter, *n.* tagliatore *m.;* (boat) cottro *m.*

cutthroat, *n.* assassino *m.*

cutting, *n.* (railway) trincèa *f.;* (newspaper) ritàglio *m.*

cuttlefish, *n.* sèppia *f.*

cyclamate, *n.* ciclamato *m.*

cycle, 1. *n.* ciclo *m.;* (bicycle) bicicletta *f.* **2.** *vb.* andare in bicicletta.

cyclist, *n.* ciclista *m.*

cyclone, *n.* ciclone *m.*

cyclotron, *n.* ciclotrone *m.*

cylinder, *n.* cilindro *m.*

cylindrical, *adj.* cilíndrico.

cymbal, *n.* piatto *m.,* cimbali *m.pl.*

cynic, *n.* cínico *m.*

cynical, *adj.* cínico.

cynicism, *n.* cinismo *m.*

cypress, *n.* ciprèsso *m.*

cyst, *n.* ciste *f.*

czar, *n.* zar *m.*

D

dab, 1. *n.* schizzo *m.* **2.** *vb.* sfiorare.

dabble, *vb.* essere un dilettante.

dad, *n.* babbo *m.*

daddy, *n.* papà *m.;* babbo *m.*

daffodil, *n.* narciso *m.*

daffy, *adj.* pazzo.

dagger, *n.* daga *f.,* pugnale *m.*

dahlia, *n.* dàlia *f.*

daily, 1. *n.* (newspaper) giornale *m.* **2.** *adj.* giornalièro, quotidiano. **3.** *adv.* quotidianamente.

daintiness, *n.* squisitezza *f.*

dainty, *adj.* squisito, delicato.

dairy, *n.* lattería *f.*

dairymaid, *n.* lattàia *f.*

dairyman, *n.* lattàio *m.*

dais, *n.* piattaforma *f.*

daisy, *n.* margherita *f.*

dale, *n.* valletta *f.*

dally, *vb.* indugiare.

dam, *n.* diga *f.*

damage, 1. *n.* danno *m.,* avaria *f.* **2.** *vb.* danneggiare, avariare.

damask, *n.* damasco *m.*

damn, *vb.* dannare; (curse) maledire.

damnation, *n.* dannazione *f.*

damned, *adj.* dannato; maledetto.

damp, 1. *n.* umidità *f.* **2.** *adj.* ùmido.

dampen, *vb.* inumidire.

dampness, *n.* umidità *f.*

damsel, *n.* damigèlla *f.*

dance, 1. *n.* ballo *m.,* danza *f.;* **(d. tune)** ballàbile *m.* **2.** *vb.* ballare, danzare.

dance floor, *n.* pista da ballo *f.*

dancer, *n.* ballerino *m.,* ballerina *f.*

dancing, *n.* ballo *m.*

dandelion, *n.* radicchièlla *f.*

dandruff, *n.* fórfora *f.*

dandy, 1. *n.* damerino *m.,* bellimbusto *m.* **2.** *adj.* òttimo.

danger, *n.* perícolo *m.*

dangerous, *adj.* pericoloso.

dangle, *vb.* penzolare.

Danish, *adj.* danese.

dapper, *adj.* píccolo e vivace.

dappled, *adj.* macchiettato.

dare, 1. *n.* sfida *f.* **2.** *vb.* osare; (challenge) sfidare.

daredevil, *n.* temeràrio *m.*

daring, 1. *n.* audàcia *f.* **2.** *adj.* audace.

dark, 1. *n.* oscurità *f.* **2.** *adj.* oscuro, bùio, tenebroso.

darken, *vb.* oscurare.

dark horse, *n.* candidato sconosciuto *m.*

darkly, *adv.* oscuramente; segretamente.

darkness, *n.* oscurità *f.,* bùio *m.,* tènebre *f.pl.*

darkroom, *n.* càmera oscura *f.*

darling, *n. and adj.* prediletto.

darn, 1. *n.* rammendatura *f.* **2.** *vb.* rammendare. **3.** *interj.* accidenti!

darning needle, *n.* ago da rammendo *m.*

dart, 1. *n.* dardo *m.;* (movement) balzo *m.* **2.** balzare.

dash, 1. *n.* (energy) slàncio *m.,*

scatto *m.;* (pen) tratto *m.* **2.** *vb.* (throw) gettare; (destroy) distrùggere; (rush) slanciarsi; (spurt) scattare.

dashboard, *n.* cruscòtto *m.*

dashing, *adj.* impetuoso.

dastardly, *adj.* vile; codardo.

data, *n.* dati *m.pl.*

data processing, *n.* elaborazione dati *f.*

date, 1. *n.* data *f.;* (appointment) appuntamento *m.;* (fruit) dàttero *m.* **2.** *vb.* datare.

date line, *n.* línea del cambiamento di data *f.*

daub, 1. *n.* imbrattatura *f.* **2.** *vb.* imbrattare.

daughter, *n.* fíglia *f.*

daughter-in-law, *n.* nuòra *f.*

daunt, *vb.* intimidire.

dauntless, *adj.* intrèpido.

dauntlessly, *adv.* intrepidamente.

davenport, *n.* divano *m.,* sofaletto *m.*

daw, *n.* cornàcchia *f.*

dawdle, *vb.* indugiare.

dawn, 1. *n.* alba *f.* **2.** *vb.* spuntare.

day, *n.* giorno *m.;* (span of day) giornata *f.*

daybreak, *n.* alba *f.*

daydream, *n.* fantasticheria *f.*

daylight, *n.* luce del giorno *f.*

daylight-saving time, *n.* ora d'estate *f.*

daze, 1. *n.* stupore *m.* **2.** *vb.* stupire.

dazzle, *vb.* abbagliare.

deacon, *n.* diàcono *m.*

dead, *n. and adj.* mòrto (*m.*).

deaden, *vb.* ammortire.

dead end, *n.* vícolo cièco *m.*

dead letter, *n.* léttera mòrta *f.*

deadline, *n.* límite *m.*

deadlock, *n.* punto mòrto *m.*

deadly, *adj.* mortale.

deadwood, *n.* legno mòrto *m.*

deaf, *adj.* sordo.

deafen, *vb.* assordare.

deaf-mute, *n. and adj.* sordomuto (*m.*).

deafness, *n.* sordità *f.*

deal, 1. *n.* (amount) quantità *f.;* (business) affare *m.;* (cards) dis-

tribuzione *f.* 2. *vb.* **(d. with)** trattare con; **(d. out)** distribuire.
dealer, *n.* negoziante *m.*
dean, *n.* decano *m.*
dear, *adj.* caro.
dearly, *adv.* caramente.
dearth, *n.* scarsezza *f.*, scarsità *f.*
death, *n.* mòrte *f.*
deathless, *adj.* immortale, imperituro.
deathly, *adj.* mortale.
débâcle, *n.* sfacèlo *m.*, disastro *m.*
debase, *vb.* abbassare, avvilire.
debatable, *adj.* discutibile.
debate, 1. *n.* dibattimento *m.* 2. *vb.* dibàttere.
debater, *n.* dibattènte *m.*
debauch, 1. *n.* òrgia *f.*, sregolatezza *f.* 2. *vb.* pervertire.
debenture, *n.* obbligazione *f.*
debilitate, *vb.* debilitare.
debit, *n.* dèbito *m.*
debonair, *adj.* gaio.
debris, *n.* detriti *m.pl.*
debt, *n.* dèbito *m.*
debtor, *n.* debitore *m.*
debunk, *vb.* screditare.
debut, *n.* debutto *m.*
debutante, *n.* debuttante *f.*
decade, *n.* decènnio *m.*
decadence, *n.* decadènza *f.*
decadent, *adj.* decadènte.
decaffeinated, *adj.* decaffeinizzato.
decalcomania, *n.* decalcomanía *f.*
decanter, *n.* caraffa *f.*
decapitate, *vb.* decapitare.
decay, 1. *n.* decadènza *f.*, decomposizione *f.*; (teeth) càrie *f.* 2. *vb.* decadere, decomporre, marcire; (teeth) cariarsi.
deceased, *n. and adj.* deceduto *(m.)*, defunto *(m.)*
deceit, *n.* inganno *m.*
deceitful, *adj.* ingannatore.
deceive, *vb.* ingannare.
deceiver, *n.* ingannatore *m.*
decelerate, *vb.* decelerare.
December, *n.* dicèmbre *m.*
decency, *n.* (modesty) decènza *f.*; (honorable behavior) onorevolezza *f.*
decent, *adj.* (modest) decènte; (honorable) onorévole.

decentralization, *n.* decentramento *m.*
decentralize, *vb.* decentrare.
deception, *n.* inganno *m.*
deceptive, *adj.* ingannévole.
decibel, *n.* dècibel *m.*
decide, *vb.* decídere.
deciduous, *adj.* decíduo.
decimal, *adj.* decimale.
decimal point, *n.* vírgola dei decimali *f.*
decimate, *vb.* decimare.
decipher, *vb.* decifrare.
decision, *n.* decisione *f.*
decisive, *adj.* decisivo.
deck, *n.* ponte *m.*
deck chair, *n.* sèdia a sdràio *f.*
deck-hand, *n.* mozzo *m.*
declaim, *vb.* declamare.
declamation, *n.* declamazione *f.*
declaration, *n.* dichiarazione *f.*
declarative, *adj.* dichiarativo.
declare, *vb.* dichiarare.
declension, *n.* declinazione *f.*
declination, *n.* declinazione *f.*
decline, 1. *n.* decadènza *f.* 2. *vb.* declinare; (refuse) rifiutare; (decay) decadere.
declivity, *n.* declivio *m.*; pendice *f.*
decode, *vb.* decifrare.
décolleté, *adj.* scollato.
decompose, *vb.* decomporre.
decomposition, *n.* decomposizione *f.*
decongestant, *adj.* decongestionante.
décor, *n.* messa in scena *f.*
decorate, *vb.* decorare.
decoration, *n.* decorazione *f.*
decorative, *adj.* decorativo.
decorator, *n.* decoratore *m.*
decorous, *adj.* decoroso.
decorum, *n.* decòro *m.*
decoy, *vb.* attirare.
decrease, 1. *n.* diminuzione *f.* 2. *vb.* diminuire.
decree, 1. *n.* decreto *m.* 2. *vb.* decretare.
decrepit, *adj.* decrèpito.
decry, *vb.* deprecare.
dedicate, *vb.* dedicare.
dedication, *n.* dèdica *f.*
deduce, *vb.* dedurre.
deduct, *vb.* dedurre, sottrarre.
deductible, *adj.* (tax) deducibile.

deduction, *n.* deduzione *f.*
deductive, *adj.* deduttivo.
deed, *n.* atto *m.*, fatto *m.*
deem, *vb.* giudicare, stimare.
deep, *adj.* profondo.
deepen, *vb.* approfondire.
deep freeze, *n.* surgelamento *m.*
deeply, *adv.* profondamente.
deep-rooted, *adj.* profondamente radicato.
deep-seated, *adj.* profondo, connaturato.
deer, *n.* cèrvo *m.*
deerskin, *n.* pèlle di dàino *f.*
deface, *vb.* sfregiare.
defamation, *n.* diffamazione *f.*
defame, *vb.* diffamare.
default, 1. *n.* contumàcia *f.* 2. *n.* rèndersi contumace; *(comm.)* mancar di pagare.
defaulting, *adj.* contumace.
defeat, 1. *n.* sconfitta *f.*, disfatta *f.* 2. *vb.* sconfiggere.
defeatism, *n.* disfattismo *m.*
defect, *n.* difètto *m.*, mènda *f.*
defection, *n.* defezione *f.*
defective, *adj.* difettoso.
defend, *vb.* difèndere.
defendant, *n.* imputato *m.*
defender, *n.* difensore *m.*
defense, *n.* difesa *f.*
defenseless, *adj.* sènza difesa.
defensible, *adj.* difensìbile.
defensive, *adj.* difensivo.
defer, *vb.* (put off) differire; (conform) conformarsi.
deference, *n.* deferènza *f.*
deferential, *adj.* deferènte.
defiance, *n.* sfida *f.*
defiant, *adj.* provocante.
deficiency, *n.* deficiènza *f.*
deficient, *adj.* deficiènte.
deficit, *n.* dèficit *m.*
defile, *vb.* (march) sfilare; (foul) profanare.
define, *vb.* definire.
definite, *adj.* definito.
definitely, *adj.* definitivamente.
definition, *n.* definizione *f.*
definitive, *adj.* definitivo.
deflate, *vb.* sgonfiare; *(econ.)* deflazionare.
deflation, *n.* deflazione *f.*
deflect, *vb.* deflèttere.
deflower, *vb.* deflorare.

deforest, *vb.* disboscare.
deform, *vb.* deformare.
deformed, *adj.* deforme.
deformity, *n.* deformità *f.*
defraud, *vb.* defraudare.
defray, *vb.* pagare.
defrost, *vb.* scongelare.
defroster, *n.* (auto) cruscotto tèrmico *m.*
defrosting, *n.* (refrigerator) sbrinamento *m.*
deft, *adj.* dèstro, àbile.
defunct, *adj.* defunto.
defy, *vb.* sfidare.
degenerate, 1. *n. and adj.* degenerato *(m.).* 2. *vb.* degenerare.
degeneration, *n.* degenerazione *f.*
degradation, *n.* degradazione *f.*
degrade, *vb.* degradare.
degrading, *adj.* degradante.
degree, *n.* grado *m.*; (university) làurea *f.*
dehydrate, *vb.* disidratare.
deice, *vb.* sgelare; sghiacciare.
deify, *vb.* deificare.
deign, *vb.* degnarsi.
deity, *n.* deità *f.*
dejected, *adj.* scoraggiato.
dejection, *n.* scoraggiamento *m.*, abbattimento *m.*
delay, 1. *n.* indùgio *m.*, ritardo *m.* 2. *vb.* indugiare, ritardare.
delectable, *adj.* dilettévole.
delegate, 1. *n.* delegato *m.* 2. *vb.* delegare.
delegation, *n.* delegazione *f.*
delete, *vb.* cancellare.
deliberate, 1. *adj.* deliberato. 2. *vb.* deliberare.
deliberately, *adv.* deliberatamente, appòsta.
deliberation, *n.* deliberazione *f.*
deliberative, *adj.* deliberativo.
delicacy, *n.* delicatezza *f.*
delicate, *adj.* delicato.
delicious, *adj.* delizioso.
delight, *n.* dilètto *m.*
delightful, *adj.* dilettévole.
delineate, *vb.* delineare.
delinquency, *n.* delinquènza *f.*
delinquent, *n. and adj.* delinquènte *(m.).*
delirious, 1. *adj.* delirante. 2. *vb.* (be d.) delirare.

delirium, n. delírio m.

deliver, vb. (set free) liberare; (hand over) consegnare.

deliverance, n. liberazione f.

delivery, n. consegna f.

deliveryman, n. fattorino m.

delivery room, n. sala parto f.

delivery truck, n. furgoncino m.

delouse, vb. spidocchiare.

delude, vb. delùdere.

deluge, n. dilùvio m.

delusion, n. delusione f.

de luxe, adj. di lusso.

delve, vb. scavare.

demagnetize, vb. smagnetizzare.

demagogue, n. demagògo m.

demand, 1. n. domanda f., richièsta f. **2.** vb. domandare, richièdere, esigere.

demanding, adj. esigente; impregnativo.

demarcate, vb. demarcare, marcare.

demarcation, n. demarcazione f.

demean (oneself), vb. abbassarsi.

demeanor, n. condotta f.

demented, adj. demènte.

demerit, n. demèrito m.

demigod, n. semidío m.

demilitarize, vb. smilitarizzare.

demise, n. mòrte f.

demobilization, n. smobilitazione f.

demobilize, vb. smobilitare.

democracy, n. democrazía f.

democrat, n. democràtico m.

democratic, adj. democràtico.

demolish, vb. demolire.

demolition, n. demolizione f.

demon, n. demònio m.

demonstrable, adj. dimostràbile.

demonstrate, vb. dimostrare.

demonstration, n. dimostrazione f.

demonstrative, adj. dimostrativo.

demonstrator, n. dimostratore m.

demoralize, vb. demoralizzare.

demote, vb. degradare.

demotion, n. retrocessione f.

demur, vb. obiettare.

demure, adj. modesto.

den, n. tana f., covo m.

denaturalize, vb. snaturare.

denature, vb. denaturare.

denial, n. diniègo m.

denim, n. saia f.

denizen, n. abitante m. and f.

Denmark, n. Danimarca f.

denomination, n. denominazione f.; (church) sètta f.

denominator, n. denominatore m.

denote, vb. denotare.

dénouement, n. scioglimento m.

denounce, vb. denunciare.

dense, adj. dènso.

density, n. densità f.

dent, n. incavo m.

dental, adj. dentale.

dentifrice, n. dentifrício m.

dentist, n. dentista m.

dentistry, n. odontoiatría f.

denture, n. dentièra f.

denude, vb. denudare.

denunciation, n. denùncia f.

deny, vb. negare.

deodorant, n. and adj. deodorante (m.).

deodorize, vb. deodorare.

depart, vb. partire.

department, n. dipartimento m.

departmental, adj. dipartimentale.

department store, n. grande magazzino m.

departure, n. partènza f.

depend, vb. dipèndere.

dependability, n. dipendibilità f., fidùcia f.

dependable, adj. fidato.

dependence, n. dipendènza f.

dependency, n. dipendenza f.; possessione f.

dependent, n. and adj. dipendènte (m.).

depict, vb. dipìngere.

depiction, n. rappresentazione f.

deplete, vb. esaurire.

deplorable, adj. deplorévole.

deplore, vb. deplorare.

deploy, vb. (military) spiegare, disporre.

deployment, n. spiegamento m.

depolarize, vb. depolarizzare.

depopulate, vb. spopolare.

deport, vb. deportare.

deportation, n. deportazione f.

deportee, *n.* deportato *m.*

deportment, *n.* condotta *f.*

depose, *vb.* deporre.

deposit, 1. *n.* depòsito. **2.** *vb.* depositare.

deposition, *n.* deposizione *f.*

depositor, *n.* depositante *m.*, correntista *m.*

depository, *n.* depòsito *m.*

depot, *n.* (military) depòsito *m.*; (railroad) stazione *f.*

deprave, *vb.* depravare.

depravity, *n.* depravazione *f.*

deprecate, *vb.* deprecare.

depreciate, *vb.* deprezzare.

depreciation, *n.* deprezzamento *m.*

depredation, *n.* depredamento *m.*

depress, *vb.* deprímere.

depression, *n.* depressione *f.*

deprivation, *n.* privazione *f.*

deprive, *vb.* privare.

depth, *n.* profondità *f.*

depth charge, *n.* bomba di profondità *f.*

deputy, *n.* deputato *m.*

derail, *vb.* deragliare.

derailment, *n.* deragliamento *m.*

derange, *vb.* far impazzire.

deranged, *adj.* impazzito.

derangement, *n.* disordine *m.*; pazzia *f.*

derelict, *adj.* derelitto.

dereliction, *n.* negligènza del dovere *f.*

deride, *vb.* derídere.

derision, *n.* derisione *f.*

derisive, *adj.* ridicolizzante.

derivation, *n.* derivazione *f.*

derivative, *adj.* derivato.

derive, *vb.* derivare.

dermatology, *n.* dermatología *f.*

derogatory, *adj.* dispregiativo.

derrick, *n.* gru *f.*

desalinization, *n.* desalinizzazione *f.*

descend, *vb.* scéndere.

descendant, *n.* discendènte *m.*

descendent, *adj.* discendente.

descent, *n.* discesa *f.*

describe, *vb.* descrivere.

description, *n.* descrizione *f.*

descriptive, *adj.* descrittivo.

desecrate, *vb.* profanare, dissacrare.

desegregate, *vb.* desegregare.

desensitize, *vb.* desensibilizzare.

desert, 1. *n.* desèrto *m.*; (merit) mèrito *m.* **2.** *vb.* disertare.

deserter, *n.* disertore *m.*

desertion, *n.* diserzione *f.*

deserve, *vb.* meritare.

deserving, *adj.* meritévole.

design, 1. *n.* disegno *m.* **2.** *vb.* disegnare.

designate, *vb.* designare.

designation, *n.* designazione *f.*

designedly, *adv.* intenzionalmente.

designer, *n.* disegnatore *m.*

designing, *adj.* astuto.

desirability, *n.* desiderabilità *f.*

desirable, *adj.* desideràbile.

desire, 1. *n.* desidèrio *m.* **2.** *vb.* desiderare.

desirous, *adj.* desideroso.

desist, *vb.* desistere.

desk, *n.* scrivania *f.*

desolate, 1. *adj.* desolato. **2.** *vb.* desolare.

desolation, *n.* desolazione *f.*

despair, 1. *n.* disperazione *f.* **2.** *vb.* disperare.

despatch, dispatch, 1. *n.* spedizione *f.*; (speed) prontezza *f.* **2.** *vb.* spedire.

desperado, *n.* disperato *m.*

desperate, *adj.* disperato.

desperation, *n.* disperazione *f.*

despicable, *adj.* spregévole.

despise, *vb.* disprezzare, spregiare.

despite, *prep.* malgrado.

despondent, *adj.* abbattuto.

despot, *n.* dèspota *m.*

despotic, *adj.* dispòtico.

despotism, *n.* dispotismo *m.*

dessert, *n.* dessért *m.* (French pronunciation).

destination, *n.* destinazione *f.*

destine, *vb.* destinare.

destiny, *n.* destino *m.*

destitute, *adj.* destituito.

destitution, *n.* destituzione *f.*

destroy, *vb.* distrùggere.

destroyer, *n.* cacciatorpedinière *m.*

destructible, *adj.* distruttíbile.

destruction, *n.* distruzione *f.*

destructive, *adj.* distruttivo.

desultory, *adj.* saltuàrio.
detach, *vb.* staccare, distaccare.
detachable, *adj.* staccàbile, separàbile.
detachment, *n.* distacco *m.; (mil.)* distaccamento *m.*
detail, 1. *n.* dettaglio *m.* **2.** *vb.* dettagliare.
detain, *vb.* detenere.
detect, *vb.* scoprire.
detection, *n.* scoprimento *m.*
detective, *n.* detective *m.* (English pron.).
detective story, *n.* giallo *m.*
detente, *n.* distensione *f.*
detention, *n.* detenzione *f.*
deter, *vb.* distògliere.
detergent, *n.* and *adj.* detergènte *(m.)*
deteriorate, *vb.* deteriorare.
deterioration, *n.* deteriorazione *f.*
determination, *n.* determinazione *f.*
determine, *vb.* determinare.
determined, *adj.* risoluto.
determinism, *n.* determinismo *m.*
deterrence, *n.* preventivo *m.*
detest, *vb.* detestare.
detestation, *n.* fastidio *m.*, odio *m.*
dethrone, *vb.* detronizzare.
detonate, *vb.* detonare.
detonation, *n.* detonazione *f.*
detonator, *n.* detonatore *m.*
detour, *n.* deviazione *f.*
detract, *vb.* detrarre.
detractor, *n.* detrattore *m.*
detriment, *n.* detrimento *m.*, danno *m.*
detrimental, *adj.* dannoso.
devaluate, *vb.* svalutare.
devaluation, *n.* svalutazione *f.*
devastate, *vb.* devastare.
devastating, *adj.* devastante.
devastation, *n.* devastazione *f.*
develop, *vb.* sviluppare.
developer, *n.* sviluppatore *m.*
developing nation, *n.* nazione in via di sviluppo *f.*
development, *n.* sviluppo *m.*
deviate, *vb.* deviare.
deviation, *n.* deviazione *f.*
device, *n.* congegno *m.*
devil, *n.* diàvolo *m.*

devilish, *adj.* diabòlico.
devious, *adj.* deviato, tortuoso, traverso.
devise, *vb.* escogitare.
devitalize, *vb.* devitalizzare.
devoid, *adj.* privo.
devote, *vb.* dedicare.
devoted, *adj.* devòto.
devotee, *n.* entusiasta *m.* or *f.*
devotion, *n.* devozione *f.*
devour, *vb.* divorare.
devout, *adj.* devòto.
dew, *n.* rugiada *f.*
dewy, *adj.* rugiadoso.
dexterity, *n.* destrezza *f.*
dexterous, *adj.* dèstro.
diabetes, *n.* diabète *m.*
diabolic, *adj.* diabòlico.
diadem, *n.* diadèma *m.*
diagnose, *vb.* diagnosticare.
diagnosis, *n.* diàgnosi *f.*
diagnostic, *adj.* diagnòstico.
diagonal, *adj.* diagonale.
diagonally, *adv.* diagonalmente.
diagram, *n.* diagramma *m.*
dial, 1. *n.* quadrante *m.;* (telephone) disco combinatore *m.* **2.** *vb.* (telephone) formare (un nùmero).
dialect, *n.* dialètto *m.*
dialogue, *n.* diàlogo *m.*
dial tone, *n.* segnale di via libera *m.*
diameter, *n.* diàmetro *m.*
diametrical, *adj.* diametrale.
diamond, *n.* diamante *m.*
diaper, *n.* pannilino *m.*, pannolino *m.*
diaphragm, *n.* diaframma *m.*
diarrhea, *n.* diarrèa *f.*
diary, *n.* diàrio *m.*
diathermy, *n.* diatermìa *f.*
diatribe, *n.* diatriba *f.*
dice, *n.* dadi *m.pl.*
dickens (the), *interj.* diàmine!
dicker, *vb.* mercanteggiare.
dictaphone, *n.* dittàfono *m.*
dictate, *vb.* dettare.
dictation, *n.* dettatura *f.*
dictator, *n.* dittatore *m.*
dictatorial, *adj.* dittatoriale.
dictatorship, *n.* dittatura *f.*
diction, *n.* dizione *f.*
dictionary, *n.* dizionàrio *m.*
didactic, *adj.* didàttico.

die, 1. *n.* (gaming cube) dado *m.;* (stamper) stampo *m.* **2.** *vb.* morire.

die-hard, *adj.* intransigente.

diet, *n.* dièta *f.,* regime *m.*

dietary, *adj.* dietético.

dietetic, *adj.* dietético.

dietetics, *n.* dietética *f.*

dietitian, *n.* dietista *m.*

differ, *vb.* differire.

difference, *n.* differènza *f.*

different, *adj.* differènte, divèrso.

differential, *adj.* differenziale.

differentiate, *vb.* differenziare.

difficult, *adj.* difficile.

difficulty, *n.* difficoltà *f.*

diffident, *adj.* tímido.

diffuse, 1. *adj.* diffuso. **2.** *vb.* diffóndere.

diffusion, *n.* diffusione *f.*

dig, *vb.* scavare.

digest, *vb.* digerire.

digestible, *adj.* digeríbile.

digestion, *n.* digestione *f.*

digestive, *adj.* digestivo.

digital, *adj.* digitale.

digitalis, *n.* digitale *f.*

dignified, *adj.* dignitoso.

dignify, *vb.* nobilitare.

dignitary, *n.* dignitàrio *m.*

dignity, *n.* dignità *f.*

digress, *vb.* digredire.

digression, *n.* digressione *f.*

dike, *n.* diga *f.*

dilapidated, *adj.* dilapidato.

dilapidation, *n.* dilapidazione *f.*

dilate, *vb.* dilatare.

dilatory, *adj.* dilatòrio.

dilemma, *n.* dilèmma *m.*

dilettante, *n.* dilettante *m.*

diligence, *n.* diligènza *f.*

diligent, *adj.* diligènte.

dill, *n.* anèto *m.*

dilute, *vb.* diluire.

dilution, *n.* diluizione *f.*

dim, 1. *adj.* oscuro. **2.** *vb.* oscurare.

dime, *n.* moneta da dieci centesimi *f.*

dimension, *n.* dimensione *f.*

diminish, *vb.* diminuire, menomare.

diminution, *n.* diminuzione *f.*

diminutive, *n. and adj.* diminutivo (*m.*)

dimly, *adv.* indistintamente.

dimmer, *n.* smorzatore *m.*

dimness, *n.* oscurità *f.*

dimple, *n.* fossetta *f.*

din, *n.* rumore *m.*

dine, *vb.* pranzare.

diner, *n.* vettura ristorante *f.*

dining-car, *n.* vagone ristorante *m.*

dining room, *n.* sala da pranzo *f.*

dingy, *adj.* sùdicio.

dinner, *n.* pranzo *m.*

dinner set, *n.* servizio da tàvola *m.*

dinosaur, *n.* dinosàuro *m.*

dint, *n.* tacca *f.;* ammaccatura *f.*

diocese, *n.* diòcesi *f.*

diode, *n.* diodo *m.*

dioxide, *n.* biòssido *m.*

dip, *vb.* immèrgere, tuffare.

diphtheria, *n.* difterite, *f.*

diphthong, *n.* dittongo *m.*

diploma, *n.* diplòma *m.*

diplomacy, *n.* diplomazía *f.*

diplomat, *n.* diplomàtico *m.*

diplomatic, *adj.* diplomàtico.

dipper, *n.* mèstolo *m.*

dire, *adj.* terríbile.

direct, 1. *adj.* dirètto. **2.** *vb.* dirigere.

direct current, *n.* corrènte contínua *f.*

direction, *n.* direzione *f.,* sènso *m.*

directional, *adj.* direttivo.

directive, *adj.* direttivo.

directly, *adv.* direttamente, immediatamente.

directness, *n.* franchezza *f.*

direct object, *n.* complemento oggetto *m.*

director, *n.* direttore *m.*

directorate, *n.* direttorato *m.*

directory, *n.* guida *f.;* (telephone d.) elènco telefònico *m.*

dirge, *n.* canto funebre *m.*

dirigible, *n. and adj.* dirigíbile (*m.*).

dirt, *n.* sudiciume *m.*

dirt road, *n.* strada in terra battuta *f.*

dirty, *adj.* sùdicio, sporco.

dirty trick, *n.* tiro mancino *m.*

disability, *n.* incapacità *f.*

disable, *vb.* rèndere incapace.

disabled, *adj.* invàlido.

disabuse, *vb.* disingannare.

disadvantage, *n.* svantàggio *m.*

disagree, *vb.* discordare, dissentire.

disagreeable, *adj.* sgradévole, antipàtico.

disagreement, *n.* dissènso *m.*

disallow, *vb.* rifiutare; non consentire.

disappear, *vb.* sparire, scomparire.

disappearance, *n.* scomparsa *f.*

disappoint, *vb.* delùdere.

disappointment, *n.* delusione *f.*

disapproval, *n.* disapprovazione *f.*

disapprove, *vb.* disapprovare.

disarm, *vb.* disarmare.

disarmament, *n.* disarmo *m.*

disarming, *adj.* simpatico; accattivante.

disarrange, *vb.* scompigliare.

disarray, *n.* scompíglio *m.*

disassemble, *vb.* smontare.

disaster, *n.* disastro *m.*

disastrous, *adj.* disastroso.

disavow, *vb.* disconóscere.

disavowal, *n.* disconoscimento *m.*

disband, *vb.* sbandare.

disbar, *vb.* cancellare dall'albo dell'avvocatura.

disbelieve, *vb.* non credere.

disburse, *vb.* sborsare.

discard, *vb.* scartare.

discern, *vb.* discèrnere, scòrgere.

discernible, *adj.* discernibile.

discerning, *adj.* penetrante.

discernment, *n.* giudízio *m.*

discharge, 1. *n.* scàrico *m.*; (gun) scàrica *f.*; (mil., job) licenziamento *m.* 2. *vb.* scaricare; (mil., job) licenziare.

disciple, *n.* discépolo *m.*

disciplinary, *adj.* disciplinare.

discipline, 1. *n.* disciplina *f.* 2. *vb.* disciplinare.

disclaim, *vb.* disconóscere.

disclaimer, *n.* disconoscimento *m.*

disclose, *vb.* rivelare.

disclosure, *n.* rivelazione *f.*

disco, *n.* (musicaccia) disco *f.*

discolor, *vb.* scolorire.

discoloration, *n.* scolorimento *m.*

discomfit, *vb.* sconcertare; frustrare.

discomfiture, *n.* sconfitta *f.*

discomfort, *n.* disàgio *m.*

disconcert, *vb.* sconcertare.

disconnect, *vb.* sconnèttere.

disconsolate, *adj.* sconsolato.

discontent, 1. *n.* scontènto *m.* 2. *vb.* scontentare.

discontented, *adj.* scontènto.

discontinue, *vb.* interrómpere, sospèndere.

discord, *n.* discòrdia *f.*; (music) disaccòrdo *m.*

discordant, *adj.* discordante.

discothèque, *n.* discotèca *f.*

discount, 1. *n.* sconto *m.* 2. *vb.* scontare.

discourage, *vb.* scoraggiare.

discouragement, *n.* scoraggiamento *m.*

discourse, 1. *n.* discorso *m.* 2. *vb.* discórrere.

discourteous, *adj.* scortese.

discourtesy, *n.* scortesía *f.*

discover, *vb.* scoprire.

discoverer, *n.* scopritore *m.*

discovery, *n.* scopèrta *f.*

discredit, 1. *n.* discrèdito *m.* 2. *vb.* screditare.

discreditable, *adj.* disonorévole.

discreet, *adj.* discreto.

discrepancy, *n.* discrepanza *f.*

discrepant, *adj.* discrepante.

discretion, *n.* discrezione *f.*

discriminate, *vb.* discriminare.

discrimination, *n.* discriminazione *f.*

discriminatory, *adj.* discriminante.

discursive, *adj.* digressivo.

discuss, *vb.* discùtere.

discussion, *n.* discussione *f.*

disdain, 1. *n.* disdegno *m.* 2. *vb.* disdegnare; sdegnare.

disdainful, *adj.* sdegnoso.

disease, *n.* malattía *f.*

disembark, *vb.* sbarcare.

disembarkation, *n.* sbarco *m.*

disembodied, *adj.* incorpòreo.

disembowel, *vb.* sventrare; sbudellare.

disenchantment, *n.* disincanto *m.*

disengage, *vb.* disimpegnare.

disentangle, *vb.* districare.

disfavor, *n.* sfavore *m.*

disfigure, *vb.* sfigurare, deturpare.

disfranchise, *vb.* privare della franchígia.

disgorge, *vb.* vomitare; *(intr.)* sgorgare.

disgrace, 1. *n.* disgràzia *f.*, sfavore *m.*, disonore *m.* **2.** *vb.* disonorare.

disgraceful, *adj.* disonorante.

disgruntle, *vb.* seccare, irritare.

disgruntled, *adj.* scontento.

disguise, 1. *n.* travestimento *m.* **2.** *vb.* travestire.

disgust, 1. *n.* disgusto *m.* **2.** *vb.* disgustare.

disgusting, *adj.* disgustante, disgustoso.

dish, *n.* piatto *m.*

dishcloth, *n.* strofinàccio (per piatti) *m.*

dishearten, *vb.* scoraggiare.

dishonest, *adj.* disonèsto.

dishonesty, *n.* disonestà *f.*

dishonor, 1. *n.* disonore *m.* **2.** *vb.* disonorare.

dishonorable, *adj.* disonorèvole.

dish-towel, *n.* asciugapiatti *m.*

disillusion, 1. *n.* disillusione *f.* **2.** *vb.* disillùdere.

disinfect, *vb.* disinfettare.

disinfectant, *n.* disinfettante *m.*

disinherit, *vb.* diseredare.

disintegrate, *vb.* disintegrare.

disinterested, *adj.* disinteressato.

disjointed, *adj.* sconnèsso.

disk, *n.* disco *m.*

dislike, 1. *n.* antipatía *f.* **2.** *vb.* non piacere (with English subject as indirect object).

dislocate, *vb.* slogare.

dislodge, *vb.* sloggiare.

disloyal, *adj.* sleale.

disloyalty, *n.* slealtà *f.*

dismal, *adj.* melancònico.

dismantle, *vb.* smantellare.

dismay, 1. *n.* costernazione *f.* **2.** *vb.* costernare.

dismember, *vb.* smembrare.

dismiss, *vb.* congedare, diméttere.

dismissal, *n.* congedo *m.*

dismount, *vb.* smontare.

disobedience, *n.* disubbidiènza *f.*

disobedient, *adj.* disobbediènte.

disobey, *vb.* disubbidire.

disorder, 1. *n.* disòrdine *m.* **2.** *vb.* disordinare.

disorderly, *adj.* disordinato.

disorganize, *vb.* disorganizzare.

disoriented, *adj.* disorientato.

disown, *vb.* disconóscere.

disparage, *vb.* disprezzare.

disparagement, *n.* discrédito *m.*

disparate, *adj.* disparato.

disparity, *n.* disparità *f.*

dispassionate, *adj.* spassionato.

dispatch, see **despatch.**

dispatcher, *n.* spedizioniere *m.*

dispel, *vb.* dissipare.

dispensable, *adj.* dispensàbile.

dispensary, *n.* dispensàrio *m.*

dispensation, *n.* dispensa *f.*

dispense, *vb.* dispensare; **(d. from)** esentare da.

dispenser, *n.* distributore *m.*

dispersal, *n.* dispersione *f.*

disperse, *vb.* dispèrdere.

dispersion, *n.* dispersione *f.*

dispersive, *adj.* dispersivo.

dispirit, *vb.* scoraggiare.

displace, *vb.* spostare.

displaced person, *n.* rifugiato *m.*

displacement, *n.* spostamento *m.*; (ship) dislocamento *m.*

display, 1. *n.* esibizione *f.*; (showing off) ostentazione *f.* **2.** *vb.* esibire, ostentare.

displease, *vb.* dispiacere (a).

displeasing, *adj.* spiacevole.

displeasure, *n.* dispiacere *m.*

disposable, *adj.* disponíbile.

disposal, *n.* disposizione *f.*

dispose, *vb.* disporre.

disposition, *n.* disposizione *f.*

dispossess, *vb.* spodestare.

disproof, *n.* confutazione *f.*

disproportion, *n.* sproporzione *f.*

disproportionate, *adj.* sproporzionato.

disprove, *vb.* confutare.

disputable, *adj.* disputàbile.

dispute, 1. *n.* disputa *f.* **2.** *vb.* disputare.

disqualification, *n.* squalífica *f.*

disqualify, *vb.* squalificare.

disquiet, 1. *n.* inquietúdine *f.* **2.** *vb.* turbare, inquietare.

disquisition, *n.* disquisizione *f.*

disregard, 1. *n.* indifferènza *f.* **2.** *vb.* trascurare.

disrepair, n. dilapidazione f.
disreputable, adj. disonorévole.
disrespect, n. mancanza di rispètto f.
disrespectful, adj. irrispetoso.
disrobe, vb. svestirsi.
disrupt, vb. interròmpere, mandare a monte.
disruption, n. interruzione f.; disarticolazione f.
dissatisfaction, n. insoddisfazione f.
dissatisfy, vb. non soddisfare.
dissect, vb. sezionare.
dissection, n. dissezione f.
dissemble, vb. dissimulare.
disseminate, vb. disseminare.
dissension, n. dissènso m.
dissent, 1. n. dissènso m. 2. vb. dissentire.
dissertation, n. dissertazione f.; tesi f.
disservice, n. disservízio m.
dissidence, n. dissidenza f.
dissimilar, adj. dissímile.
dissimulate, vb. dissimulare.
dissipate, vb. dissipare.
dissipated, adj. dissoluto.
dissipation, n. dissipazione f., dissolutezza f.
dissociate, vb. dissociare.
dissolute, adj. dissoluto.
dissoluteness, n. dissolutezza f.
dissolution, n. dissoluzione f.
dissolve, vb. dissòlvere, sciògliere.
dissonance, n. dissonanza f.
dissonant, adj. dissonante.
dissuade, vb. dissuadere.
distance, n. distanza f.
distant, adj. distante, lontano; (be d.) distare.
distaste, n. disgusto m.
distasteful, adj. disgustoso.
distemper, n. indisposizione f.
distend, vb. distèndere.
distill, vb. distillare.
distillation, n. distillazione f.
distiller, n. distillatore m.
distillery, n. distilleria f.
distinct, adj. distinto.
distinction, n. distinzione f.
distinctive, adj. distintivo.
distinctly, adv. distintamente.
distinguish, vb. distínguere.
distinguished, adj. distinto.

distort, vb. distòrcere.
distract, vb. distrarre.
distraction, n. distrazione f.
distraught, adj. pazzo.
distress, 1. n. afflizione f. 2. vb. affliggere.
distribute, vb. distribuire.
distribution, n. distribuzione f.
distributor, n. distributore m.
district, n. distretto m.
distrust, 1. n. sfidùcia f. 2. vb. non fidarsi di.
distrustful, adj. sospettoso.
disturb, vb. disturbare.
disturbance, n. disturbo m.
disunite, vb. disunire.
disuse, n. disuso m.
ditch, n. fosso m., fossato m.
dither, n. agitazione f.
ditto, n. lo stesso m.
diva, n. diva f.
divan, n. divano m.
dive, 1. n. tuffo m. 2. vb. tuffarsi.
dive-bomber, n. picchiatore m., tuffatore m.
diver, n. tuffatore m.
diverge, vb. divèrgere.
divergence, n. divergènza f.
divergent, adj. divergènte.
diverse, adj. divèrso.
diversify, vb. diversificare.
diversion, n. diversione f.
diversity, n. diversità f.
divert, vb. (turn away) stornare; (amuse) divertire.
divest, vb. spogliare.
divide, vb. dividere.
dividend, n. dividèndo m.
divine, 1. adj. divino. 2. vb. divinare.
diving board, n. trampolino m.
divinity, n. divinità f.
divisible, adj. divisíbile.
division, n. divisione f., scissione f.
divorce, 1. n. divòrzio m. 2. vb. divorziare.
divorcée, n. divorziata f.
divulge, vb. divulgare.
dizziness, n. vertigine f., stordimento m.
dizzy, adj. vertiginoso, stordito.
do, vb. fare; (how do you do?) come sta?
docile, adj. dòcile.

dock, *n.* bacino *m.*

dockage, *n.* attracco *m.*

docket, *n.* etichetta *f.;* (legal) elenco *m.*

dockyard, *n.* arsenale *m.*

doctor, *n.* dottore *m.,* mèdico *m.*

doctorate, *n.* dottorato *m.*

doctrinaire, *adj.* dottrinàrio.

doctrine, *n.* dottrina *f.*

document, 1. *n.* documento *m.* 2. *vb.* documentare.

documentary, *adj.* documentàrio.

documentation, *n.* documentazione *f.*

doddering, *adj.* tremante; rimbambito.

dodge, *vb.* elùdere, schivare.

doe, *n.* cèrva *f.*

doeskin, *n.* pelle di cèrva *f.*

dog, *n.* cane *m.*

dogged, *adj.* ostinato, tenace.

doggerel, *n.* versucci *m.pl.*

doghouse, *n.* canile *m.*

dogma, *n.* dògma *f.*

dogmatic, *adj.* dogmàtico.

dogmatism, *n.* dogmatismo *m.*

doily, *n.* tovagliolino *m.*

doldrum, *n.* **(in the d.s)** *adj.* calmo.

dole, 1. *n.* elemòsina *f.* 2. *vb.* **(d. out)** distribuire.

doleful, *adj.* triste.

doll, *n.* bàmbola *f.,* pupàttola *f.*

dollar, *n.* dòllaro *m.*

dolorous, *adj.* doloroso.

dolphin, *n.* delfino *m.*

domain, *n.* domínio *m.*

dome, *n.* cùpola *f.*

domestic, *adj.* domèstico.

domesticate, *vb.* domesticare.

domicile, *n.* domicílio *m.*

dominance, *n.* predomínio *m.*

dominant, *adj.* dominante.

dominate, *vb.* dominare.

domination, *n.* dominazione *f.*

domineer, *vb.* spadroneggiare.

dominion, *n.* domínio *m.*

don, *vb.* indossare.

donate, *vb.* donare.

donation, *n.* donazione *f.*

done, *adj.* fatto; (food) còtto.

donkey, *n.* àsino *m.,* somaro *m.*

don't, *vb.* non fare.

doom, 1. *n.* (condemnation) con-

danna *f.;* (fate) destino *m.* 2. *vb.* condannare.

doomsday, *n.* giorno del giudízio universale *m.*

door, *n.* pòrta *f.;* (auto) portièra *f.*

doorman, *n.* portinaio *m.*

door-mat, *n.* stuoíno *m.*

doorstep, *n.* gradino della pòrta *m.*

doorway, *n.* vano della pòrta *m.*

dope, *n.* (drug) narcòtico *m.;* (fool) imbecille *m.*

dormant, *adj.* inattivo.

dormer, *n.* abbaíno *m.*

dormitory, *n.* dormitòrio *m.*

dosage, *n.* dosatura *f.*

dose, 1. *n.* dòse *f.* 2. *vb.* dosare.

dossier, *n.* incartamento *m.*

dot, *n.* punto *m.*

dotage, *n.* rimbambimento *m.*

dotard, *n.* vecchio rimbambito *m.*

dote, *vb.* esser rimbambito; **(d. upon)** adorare.

double, 1. *n. and adj.* dóppio *(m.).* 2. *vb.* doppiare.

double bass, *n.* contrabbasso *m.*

double-breasted, *adj.* a dóppio pètto.

double-cross, *vb.* ingannare.

double-dealing, *n.* duplicità *f.*

double-decker, *n.* àutobus a due piani *m.*

double-jointed, *adj.* snodato.

double-park, *vb.* parcheggiare in doppia fila.

double standard, *n.* due pesi e due misure *m.pl.*

double time, *n.* passo di càrica *m.*

doubly, *adv.* doppiamente.

doubt, 1. *n.* dùbbio *m.* 2. *vb.* dubitare.

doubter, *n.* scèttico *m.*

doubtful, *adj.* dùbbio, dubbioso.

doubtless, *adv.* senza dùbbio.

dough, *n.* pasta *f.*

doughnut, *n.* ciambella *f.*

doughy, *adj.* pastoso, molle.

dour, *adj.* severo.

douse, *vb.* spègnere.

dove, *n.* colombo *m.*

dowager, *n.* vècchia ricca e tirànnica *f.*

dowdy, *adj.* sciatto.

dowel, *n.* tassèllo *m.*

down, 1. *n.* (on face; bird) pelùria

f.; (feathers) piumino *m.* **2.** *adv.* giù. **3.** *prep.* giù per.

downcast, *adj.* abbassato.

downfall, *n.* rovina *f.*

downhearted, *adj.* scoraggiato.

downhill, *adv.* in discesa.

down payment, *n.* antícipo *m.*

downpour, *n.* rovèscio di piòggia *m.*

downright, *adj.* chiaro, completo.

downstairs, *adv.* giù per le scale.

downstream, *adv.* a valle.

downtown, *n.* centro della città *m.*

downtrend, *n.* tendenza al ribasso *f.*

downtrodden, *adj.* opprèsso.

downward, *adv.* in giù.

downy, *adj.* coperto di pelúria.

dowry, *n.* dòte *f.*

doze, **1.** *n.* sonnellino *m.*, pisolino *m.* **2.** *vb.* sonnecchiare.

dozen, *n.* dozzina *f.*

drab, *adj.* grígio.

draft, **1.** *n.* (plan) abbozzo *m.;* (money) tratta *f.;* (ship) pescàggio *m.;* (air) corrènte d'aria *f.;* (military service) servízio militare *m.* **2.** *vb.* (draw up) redígere.

draft beer, *n.* birra alla spina *f.*

draft dodger, *n.* renitente alla leva *m.;* imboscato *m.*

draftee, *n.* rècluta *f.*

draftsman, *n.* disegnatore *m.*

drafty, *adj.* pièno di corrènti d'ària.

drag, *vb.* trascinare.

dragnet, *n.* giàcchio *m.*

dragon, *n.* dragone *m.*

drain, **1.** *n.* fogna *f.* **2.** *vb.* scolare.

drainage, *n.* drenàggio *m.*

dram, *n.* dramma *m.*

drama, *n.* dramma *m.*

dramatic, *adj.* drammàtico.

dramatics, *n.* drammàtica *f.*

dramatist, *n.* drammaturgo *m.*

dramatize, *vb.* drammatizzare.

dramaturgy, *n.* drammaturgía *f.*

drape, **1.** *n.* drappéggio *m.* **2.** *vb.* drappeggiare.

drapery, *n.* drappéggio *m.*

drastic, *adj.* dràstico.

draught, see **draft.**

draw, *vb.* (pull) tirare; (picture) disegnare; (**d. back**) ritirarsi; (**d. up**) stèndere.

drawback, *n.* svantàggio *m.*

drawbridge, *n.* ponte levatòio *m.*

drawer, *n.* cassetto *m.*

drawing, *n.* (picture) disegno *m.;* (lottery) sortéggio *m.*

drawl, *vb.* parlare lentamente.

dray, *n.* carro *m.*

drayhorse, *n.* cavallo da tiro *m.*

drayman, *n.* carrettiere *m.*

dread, **1.** *n.* timore *m.* **2.** *vb.* temere.

dreadful, *adj.* terríbile.

dreadfully, *adv.* terribilmente.

dream, **1.** *n.* sogno *m.* **2.** *vb.* sognare.

dreamer, *n.* sognatore *m.*

dreamy, *adj.* vago.

dreary, *adj.* fosco.

dredge, **1.** *n.* draga *f.* **2.** *vb.* dragare.

dregs, *n.* fèccia *f.sg.*

drench, *vb.* inzuppare.

dress, **1.** *n.* vestito *m.*, àbito *m.* **2.** *vb.* vestire.

dresser, *n.* credènza *f.*

dressing, *n.* (food) condimento *m.;* (medical) bende *f.pl.*

dressing gown, *n.* vestàglia *f.*

dressmaker, *n.* sarta da dònna *f.*

dress rehearsal, *n.* pròva generale *f.*

drier, *n.* essiccatòio *m.*

drift, **1.** *n.* deriva *f.* **2.** *vb.* andare alla deriva.

driftwood, *n.* legno flottante *m.*

drill, **1.** *n.* (tool) tràpano *m.;* (practice) esercitazione *f.* **2.** *vb.* trapanare; esercitare.

drink, **1.** *n.* bevanda *f.*, bíbita *f.* **2.** *vb.* bere.

drinkable, *adj.* bevíbile.

drinker, *n.* bevitore *m.*

drinking water, *n.* àcqua potàbile *f.*

drip, **1.** *n.* gocciolío *m.* **2.** *vb.* gocciolare.

drive, **1.** *n.* (ride) passeggiata in carrozza *f.;* (avenue) viale *m.* **2.** *vb.* costríngere; (auto) guidare.

drivel, **1.** *n.* bava *f.* **2.** *vb.* sbavare.

driver, *n.* conducènte *m.*, autista *m.*

driver's license, n. patente di guida f.

driveway, n. passo carràbile m.

drizzle, 1. n. pioggerèlla f. **2.** vb. piovigginare.

droll, adj. buffo, spassoso.

dromedary, n. dromedàrio m.

drone, 1. n. (bee) fuco m.; (hum) ronzio m. **2.** vb. ronzare.

drool, vb. sbavare.

droop, vb. abbàttersi.

drop, 1. n. góccia f. **2.** vb. (fall) cadere; (let fall) lasciar cadere.

dropout, n. studente che lascia definitivamente la scuola f.

dropper, n. contagocce m.

dropsy, n. idropisìa f.

dross, n. scòria f.

drought, n. siccità f.

drove, n. màndria f.

drown, vb. annegare.

drowse, vb. sonnecchiare, assopirsi.

drowsiness, n. sonnolènza f.

drowsy, adj. sonnolènto.

drub, vb. battere.

drudge, vb. lavorare duramente.

drudgery, n. lavoro monòtono m.

drug, n. dròga f.

drug addict, n. tòssico dipendente m.

druggist, n. farmacista m.

drug store, n. farmacìa f.

drug traffic, n. narcotràffico m.

drum, n. tamburo m.

drum major, n. tamburo maggiore m.

drummer, n. tamburo m.

drumstick, n. (lit.) bacchetta del tamburo m.; (chicken) gamba di pollo f.

drunk, adj. ubriaco.

drunkard, n. ubriacone. m.

drunken, adj. ubriaco.

drunkenness, n. ubriachezza f.

dry, 1. adj. secco, asciutto. **2.** vb. seccare, asciugare.

dry cell, n. pila a secco f.

dry-clean, vb. lavare a secco.

dry-cleaner, n. tintore m.

dry-cleaning, n. lavàggio a secco m.

dry dock, n. bacino di carenàggio m.

dry goods, n. stoffe f.pl.; tessuti m.pl.

dry law, n. legge proibizionista f.

dryness, n. secchezza f.

dry run, n. esercitazione f.

dual, n. and adj. duale (m.).

dualism, n. dualismo m.

dubbing, n. doppiàggio m.

dubious, adj. dùbbio.

duchess, n. duchessa f.

duchy, n. ducato m.

duck, 1. n. ànitra f. **2.** vb. tuffare.

duct, n. canale m.

ductile, adj. dùttile.

dud, n. bomba inesplòsa f.; (failure) fiasco m.

due, adj. dèbito, dovuto; (fall d.) scadere.

duel, 1. n. duèllo m. **2.** vb. duellare.

duelist, n. duellante m.

dues, n. quòta f.; (tax) diritti m.

duet, n. duetto m.

duffle bag, n. zàino m.

dugout, n. trincèa f.

duke, n. duca m.

dukedom, n. ducato m.

dulcet, adj. armonioso.

dull, 1. adj. monòtono, ottuso, insulso. **2.** vb. ottùndere.

dullard, n. stùpido m.

dullness, n. monotonìa f., ottusità f.

duly, adv. debitamente.

dumb, adj. muto; (stupid) sciocco.

dumbfound, vb. sbalordire.

dumbwaiter, n. calapranzi m., calapiatti m.

dummy, n. fantòccio m.

dump, vb. scaricare.

dumpling, n. gnòcco m.

dun, adj. grigio fosco.

dunce, n. stolto m.

dune, n. duna f.

dung, n. stèrco m.; letame m.

dungarees, n. tuta f.sg.

dungeon, n. prigione sotterrànea f.

dunk, vb. tuffare, inzuppare.

dupe, n. credulone m.

duplex, n. dóppio.

duplicate, vb. duplicare.

duplication, n. duplicazione f.

duplicity, n. duplicità f.

durable, adj. duràbile.

durability, n. durabilità f.

duration, *n.* durata *f.*
duress, *n.* coercizione *f.*
during, *prep.* durante.
dusk, *n.* crepùscolo *m.*
dusky, *adj.* fosco.
dust, *n.* pólvere *m.;* (sweepings) spazzatura *f.*
dustpan, *n.* paletta per spazzature *f.*
dusty, *adj.* polveroso.
Dutch, *adj.* olandese.
Dutchman, *n.* olandese *m.*
dutiful, *adj.* obbediènte.
dutifully, *adv.* con ubbidiènza.
duty, *n.* dovere *m.;* (tax) imposta *f.*
duty-free, *adj.* esente da dogana.
dwarf, *n.* nano *m.*

dwell, *vb.* abitare; (d. upon) diffóndersi su.
dweller, *n.* abitante *m.*
dwelling, *n.* abitazione *f.,* dimora *f.*
dwindle, *vb.* diminuire.
dye, 1. *n.* tintura *f.* **2.** *vb.* tíngere.
dyer, *n.* tintore *m.*
dyestuff, *n.* matèria colorante *f.*
dynamic, *adj.* dinàmico.
dynamics, *n.* dinàmica *f.*
dynamite, *n.* dinamite *f.*
dynamo, *n.* dínamo *f.*
dynasty, *n.* dinastìa *f.*
dysentery, *n.* dissenterìa *f.*
dyslexia, *n.* dislessìa *f.*
dyspepsia, *n.* dispepsia *f.*
dyspeptic, *adj.* dispèptico.

E

each, *adj.* ogni.
each one, *pron.* ciascuno, cadaùno.
each other, *pron.* l'un l'altro; or use reflexive.
eager, *adj.* bramoso, impaziènte.
eagerly, *adv.* bramosamente, impazientemente.
eagerness, *n.* brama *f.,* impaziènza *f.*
eagle, *n.* àquila *f.*
eaglet, *n.* aquilòtto *m.*
ear, *n.* orécchio *m.;* (grain) spiga *f.*
earache, *n.* mal d'orecchi *(m.)*
eardrum, *n.* tìmpano *m.*
earflap, *n.* paraorecchi *m.*
earl, *n.* conte *m.*
early, *adv.* di buon'ora, prèsto.
early bird, *n.* persona mattiniera *f.*
earmark, *vb.* riservare.
earn, *vb.* guadagnare; (deserve) meritare.
earnest, *adj.* sèrio; (in e.) sul sèrio.
earnestly, *adv.* seriamente.
earnestness, *n.* serietà *f.*
earnings, *n.* guadagni *m.pl.*
earphone, *n.* cùffia *f.*
earring, *n.* orecchino *m.*
earshot, *n.* portata di voce *f.*
earsplitting, *adj.* assordante.
earth, *n.* tèrra *f.*

earthenware, *n.* stovìglie *f.pl.*
earthling, *n.* terrestre *m.*
earthly, *adj.* terreno.
earthmover, *n.* ruspa *f.*
earthquake, *n.* terremòto *m.*
earthworm, *n.* lombrico *m.*
earthy, *adj.* terreno.
earwax, *n.* cerume *m.*
ease, 1. *n.* àgio *m.,* còmodo *m.* **2.** *vb.* sollevare.
easel, *n.* cavalletto *m.*
easily, *adv.* facilmente.
easiness, *n.* facilità *f.*
east, *n.* èst *m.,* oriènte *m.*
Easter, *n.* Pasqua *f.*
easterly, *adj.* ad est, da est.
eastern, *adj.* orientale.
eastward, *adv.* vèrso èst.
easy, *adj.* fàcile.
easygoing, *adj.* noncurante.
eat, *vb.* mangiare.
eatable, *adj.* mangiàbile.
eaves, *n.* gronda *f.sg.*
eavesdrop, *vb.* origliare.
ebb, 1. *n.* riflusso *m.;* (ebb-tide) bassa marèa *f.* **2.** *vb.* rifluire.
ebony, *n.* èbano *m.*
ebullient, *adj.* esuberante.
eccentric, *adj.* eccèntrico.
eccentricity, *n.* eccentricità *f.*
ecclesiastic, *n. and adj.* ecclesiàstico *(m.)*
ecclesiastical, *adj.* ecclesiastico.

echelon, n. scaglione m.
echo, 1. n. èco m. **2.** vb. echeggiare.
eclipse, 1. n. eclissi f. **2.** vb. eclissare.
ecology, n. ecología f.
ecological, adj. ecológico.
economic, adj. econòmico.
economical, adj. econòmico.
economics, n. economía política f.
economist, n. economista m.
economize, vb. economizzare.
economy, n. economía f.
ecru, n. (colore di) seta cruda.
ecumenical, adj. ecumènico.
ecstasy, n. èstasi f.
eczema, n. eczèma m.
eddy, n. vòrtice m.
edge, n. bordo m., màrgine m.; orlo m.
edging, n. orlatura f.
edgy, adj. irritàbile.
edible, adj. mangiàbile.
edict, n. editto m.
edifice, n. edifício m.
edify, vb. edificare.
edifying, adj. edificante.
edit, vb. dirígere; (book) curare l'edizione di.
edition, n. edizione f.
editor, n. (journal) direttore m.
editorial, 1. n. artícolo di fondo m. **2.** adj. editoriale.
educate, vb. educare.
education, n. educazione f.
educational, adj. educativo.
educator, n. educatore m.
eel, n. anguilla f.
eerie, adj. spettrale.
efface, vb. cancellare.
effect, 1. n. effètto m.; **(in e.)** effettivamente. **2.** vb. effettuare.
effective, adj. effettivo.
effectively, adv. effettivamente.
effectiveness, n. effettività f.
effectual, adj. efficace.
effeminate, adj. effeminato.
effervescence, n. effervescènza f.
effete, adj. effeminato.
efficacious, adj. efficace.
efficacy, n. efficàcia f.
efficiency, n. efficiènza f.
efficient, adj. efficiènte.
efficiently, adv. efficientemente.

effigy, n. effígie f.
effort, n. sforzo m.; **(make an e.)** sforzarsi.
effortless, adj. sènza sforzo.
effrontery, n. sfrontatezza f.
effulgent, adj. risplendènte.
effusive, adj. espansivo.
egg, n. uòvo m.
eggplant, n. melanzana f.
ego, n. ío m.
egoism, n. egoísmo m.
egotism, n. egoísmo m.
egotist, n. egoísta m.
Egypt, n. l'Egitto m.
Egyptian, adj. egiziano.
eight, num. òtto.
eighteen, num. diciòtto.
eighteenth, adj. diciottèsimo, decimottavo.
eighth, adj. ottavo.
eightieth, adj. ottantèsimo.
eighty, num. ottanta.
either, 1. pron. l'uno o l'altro. **2.** conj. o; od; sia; **(either . . . or)** o . . . o; sia . . . che.
ejaculate, vb. (med.) eiaculare; (fig.) esclamare.
eject, vb. espèllere.
ejection, n. espulsione f.
eke out, vb. supplire a.
elaborate, 1. adj. elaborato. **2.** vb. elaborare.
elapse, vb. trascórrere.
elastic, n. and adj. elàstico (m.)
elasticity, n. elasticità f.
elate, vb. esaltare.
elated, adj. esaltato.
elation, n. esaltazione f.
elbow, n. gómito m.
elbowroom, n. spàzio líbero m.
elder, 1. n. (older person) maggiore m.; (tree) sambuco m. **2.** adj. maggiore.
elderberry, n. frutto del sambuco m.
elderly, adj. vècchio.
eldest, adj. (il) maggiore.
elect, vb. elèggere.
election, n. elezione f.
electioneer, vb. cercare voti.
elective, adj. elettivo.
electorate, n. votanti m.pl.
electric, electrical, adj. elèttrico.
electric eel, n. anguilla elèttrica f.; gimnòto m.

electrician, n. elettricista m.
electricity, n. elettricità f.
electrocardiogram, n. elettrocardiogramma m.
electrocution, n. elettrocuzione f.
electrode, n. elèttrodo m.
electrolysis, n. elettròlisi f.
electron, n. elettrone m.
electronic, adj. elettrònico.
electronics, n. elettrònica f.
electroplating, n. galvanoplàstica f.
elegance, n. eleganza f.
elegant, adj. elegante.
elegiac, adj. elegíaco.
elegy, n. elegia f.
element, n. elemento m.
elemental, elementary, adj. elementare.
elephant, n. elefante m.
elephantine, adj. elefantesco.
elevate, vb. elevare.
elevation, n. elevazione f.
elevator, n. ascensore m.
eleven, num. ùndici.
eleventh, adj. undicésimo.
eleventh hour, n. ultimo momento m.; zona cesarini f.
elf, n. folletto m.
elfin, adj. di folletto.
elicit, vb. cavar fuòri.
elide, vb. elìdere.
eligibility, n. eleggibilità f.
eligible, adj. eleggìbile.
eliminate, vb. eliminare.
elimination, n. eliminazione f.
elision, n. elisione f.
elite, adj. eletto; d'elite.
elixir, n. elisìr m.
elk, n. alce m.
ellipse, n. elissi f.
elliptic, adj. elittico.
elm, n. olmo m.
elocution, n. elocuzione f.
elongate, vb. allungare.
elope, vb. fuggire.
eloquence, n. eloquènza f.
eloquent, adj. eloquènte.
eloquently, adv. eloquentemente.
else, 1. adj. altro. **2.** adv. altrimenti.
elsewhere, adv. altrove.
elucidate, vb. elucidare.
elude, vb. elùdere.

elusive, adv. elusivo.
emaciated, adj. emaciato.
emanate, vb. emanare.
emancipate, vb. emancipare.
emancipation, n. emancipazione f.
emancipator, n. emancipatore m.
emasculate, vb. castrare.
embalm, vb. imbalsamare.
embankment, n. àrgine m.
embargo, n. embargo m.
embark, vb. imbarcare.
embarrass, vb. imbarazzare.
embarrassing, adj. imbarazzante.
embarrassment, n. imbarazzo m.
embassy, n. ambasciata f.
embed, vb. incassare.
embellish, vb. abbellire.
embellishment, n. abbellimento m.
embers, n. brace f.sg.
embezzle, vb. appropriarsi fraudolentemente.
embezzlement, n. malversazione f., peculato m.
embitter, vb. amareggiare.
emblazon, vb. adornare, illustrare.
emblem, n. emblèma m.
emblematic, adj. emblemàtico.
embody, vb. incorporare.
embolden, vb. imbaldanzire.
emboss, vb. stampare in rilièvo.
embrace, 1. n. abbràccio m.; (sexual) amplèsso m. **2.** vb. abbracciare.
embroider, vb. ricamare.
embroidery, n. ricamo m.
embroil, vb. imbrogliare.
embryo, n. embrione m.
embryology, n. embriologia f.
embryonic, adj. embrionale.
emend, vb. emendare.
emerald, n. smeraldo m.
emerge, vb. emèrgere.
emergency, n. emergènza f.
emergent, adj. emergènte.
emery, n. smeriglio m.
emetic, n. and adj. emètico (m.)
emigrant, n. and adj. emigrante (m.)
emigrate, vb. emigrare.
emigration, n. emigrazione f.
eminence, n. eminènza f.

eminent, adj. eminènte.

emissary, n. emissàrio m.

emission controls, n.pl. apparècchio per limitare l'emissione di fumi nocivi m.

emit, vb. eméttere.

emollient, n. and adj. emolliènte (m.)

emolument, n. emolumento m.

emotion, n. emozione f.

emotional, adj. emotivo; (easily moved) emozionàbile.

emperor, n. imperatore m.

emphasis, n. ènfasi f.

emphasize, vb. méttere in rilièvo.

emphatic, adj. enfàtico.

empire, n. impèro m.

empirical, adj. empírico.

employ, 1. n. impiègo m., servízio m. **2.** vb. impiegare.

employed, adj. addetto.

employee, n. impiegato m., impiegata f.

employer, n. datore di lavoro m.; (boss) padrone m.

employment, n. impiègo m.

empower, vb. autorizzare.

empress, n. imperatrice f.

emptiness, n. vuòto m.

empty, 1. adj. vuòto. **2.** vb. vuotare.

emulate, vb. emulare.

emulsion, n. emulsione f.

enable, vb. méttere in grado di.

enact, vb. decretare.

enactment, n. decreto m.

enamel, 1. n. smalto m. **2.** vb. smaltare.

enamor, vb. innamorare.

encamp, vb. accamparsi.

encampment, n. accampamento m.

encephalitis, n. encefalite f.

encephalon, n. encèfalo m.

enchant, vb. incantare.

enchanting, adj. incantévole.

enchantment, n. incanto m.

encircle, vb. accerchiare.

enclose, vb. rinchiùdere; (with letter) acclùdere.

enclosure, n. recinto m.

encompass, vb. (surround) circondare; (cause) causare.

encore, n. bis m.

encounter, 1. n. incontro m. **2.** vb. incontrare.

encourage, vb. incoraggiare, confortare.

encouragement, n. incoraggiamento m.

encroach upon, vb. usurpare.

encumber, vb. ingombrare.

encyclical, n. encíclica f.

encyclopaedia, n. enciclopedia f.

end, 1. n. fine f., tèrmine m.; (aim) scòpo m. **2.** adj. último. **3.** vb. finire, terminare.

endanger, vb. méttere in perícolo.

endear, vb. rèndere caro.

endearment, n. carezza f.

endeavor, 1. n. sforzo m. **2.** vb. sforzarsi.

endemic, adj. endèmico.

ending, n. fine f.; (gram.) desinènza f.

endive, n. indivia f.

endless, adj. sènza fine.

endocrine, adj. endòcrino.

endorse, vb. firmare; (cheques, etc.) girare.

endorsee, n. giratàrio m.

endorsement, n. girata f.

endorser, n. girante m.; responsàbile m.

endow, vb. dotare.

endowment, n. dotazione f.

endurance, n. sopportazione f.

endure, vb. sopportare; (last) durare.

enduring, adj. durévole.

enema, n. clistère m.; (colonic irrigation) enteroclisma m.

enemy, n. and adj. nemico (m.)

energetic, adj. enèrgico.

energy, n. energía f.

enervate, vb. snervare.

enervation, n. snervamento m.

enfeeble, vb. indebolire.

enfold, vb. avvòlgere.

enforce, vb. eseguire.

enforcement, n. esecuzione f.

enfranchise, vb. affrancare.

engage, vb. (hire) prèndere a nolo; (attention) attrarre; (to get married) fidanzare.

engaged, adj. (to get married) fidanzato.

engagement, *n.* (to get married) fidanzamento *m.;* (date) appuntamento *m.*

engaging, *adj.* attraènte.

engender, *vb.* generare.

engine, *n.* màcchina *f.;* (locomotive) locomotiva *f.*

engineer, *n.* ingegnère *m.;* (train driver) macchinista *m.*

engineering, *n.* ingegnería *f.,* gènio *m.*

England, *n.* Inghilterra *f.*

English, *adj.* inglese.

Englishman, *n.* inglese *m.*

Englishwoman, *n.* inglese *f.*

engrave, *vb.* incidere.

engraver, *n.* incisore *m.*

engraving, *n.* incisione *f.*

engross, *vb.* (absorb) assorbire; (copy) copiare.

engrossing, *adj.* assorbente.

engulf, *vb.* sommergere.

enhance, *vb.* aumentare, accréscere.

enigma, *n.* enigma *m.*

enigmatic, *adj.* enigmàtico.

enjoin, *vb.* (command) ingiùngere; (forbid) vietare.

enjoy, *vb.* godere.

enjoyable, *adj.* godìbile, piacévole.

enjoyment, *n.* godimento *m.*

enlace, *vb.* allacciare.

enlarge, *vb.* aumentare; ingrandire.

enlargement, *n.* ingrandimento *m.*

enlarger, *n.* ingranditore *m.*

enlighten, *vb.* illuminare.

enlightenment, *n.* chiarimento *m.*

enlist, *vb.* arruolare.

enlisted man, *n.* uòmo di truppa *m.*

enlistment, *n.* arruolamento *m.*

enliven, *vb.* ravvivare.

enmesh, *vb.* invilupparre.

enmity, *n.* inimicízia *f.*

ennoble, *vb.* innobilire; nobilitare.

ennui, *n.* nòia *f.*

enormity, *n.* enormità *f.*

enormous, *adj.* enòrme.

enormously, *adv.* enormemente.

enough, 1. *adj.* sufficiènte. 2. *adv.* abbastanza. 3. *vb.* (be e.) bastare.

enrage, *vb.* far arrabbiare.

enrapture, *vb.* estasiare.

enrich, *vb.* arricchire.

enroll, *vb.* iscrìvere, registrare; (mil.) arruolare.

enrollment, *n.* iscrizione *f.,* registrazione *f.*

en route, *adv.* in cammino.

ensemble, *n.* insième *m.*

enshrine, *vb.* méttere in un reliquàrio.

ensign, *n.* (flag) bandièra *f.,* insegna *f.;* (rank) alfière *m.*

enslave, *vb.* asservire.

enslavement, *n.* asservimento *m.*

ensnare, *vb.* prèndere in tràppola.

ensue, *vb.* (follow) seguire; (happen) accadere.

ensuing, *adj.* risultante, conseguente.

ensure, *vb.* garantire.

entail, *vb.* comportare, richièdere.

entailment, *n.* conseguènza *f.,* deduzione *f.*

entangle, *vb.* aggrovigliare.

entanglement, *n.* groviglio *m.*

enter, *vb.* entrare.

enterprise, *n.* impresa *f.*

enterprising, *adj.* avventuroso.

entertain, *vb.* trattenere; (guests) accògliere; (amuse) divertire.

entertainment, *n.* trattenimento *m.;* (amusement) divertimento *m.*

enthrall, *vb.* incantare.

enthusiasm, *n.* entusiasmo *m.*

enthusiast, *n.* entusiasta *m.*

enthusiastic, *adj.* entusiàstico.

entice, *vb.* adescare.

entire, *adj.* intero.

entirely, *adj.* interamente.

entirety, *n.* totalità *f.*

entitle, *vb.* intitolare; (authorize) autorizzare.

entity, *n.* entità *f.*

entomb, *vb.* seppellire.

entombment, *n.* sepoltura *f.*

entrails, *n.* interiora *f.pl.*

entrain, *vb.* prèndere il treno.

entrance, *n.* entrata *f.,* ingrèsso *m.*

entrant, *n.* concorrènte *m.*

entrap, *vb.* intrappolare.

entreat, *vb.* supplicare.

entreaty, *n.* sùpplica *f.*

entree, *n.* entrata *f.;* portata *f.*

entrench, vb. trincerare.
entrepreneur, n. imprenditore m.
entrust, vb. affidare.
entry, n. entrata f., ingresso m.
enumerate, vb. enumerare.
enumeration, n. enumerazione f.
enunciate, vb. enunciare.
enunciation, n. enunciazione f.
envelop, vb. avviluppare.
envelope, n. busta f.
enviable, adj. invidiàbile.
envious, adj. invidioso.
environment, n. ambiente m.
environmentalist, n. fautore della preservazione dell'ambiente m.
environmental protection, n. protezione dell'ambiente f.
environs, n. dintorni m.pl.
envisage, vb. figurarsi.
envoy, n. inviato m.
envy, 1. n. invidia f. 2. vb. invidiare.
eon, n. eternità f.
ephemeral, adj. effìmero.
epic, 1. n. epopèa f. 2. adj. èpico.
epicure, n. epicurèo m.
epidemic, 1. n. epidemia f. 2. adj. epidèmico.
epidermis, n. epidèrmide f.
epigram, n. epigramma m.
epilepsy, n. epilessia f.
epilogue, n. epìlogo m.
episode, n. episòdio m.
epistle, n. epìstola f.
epitaph, n. epitàffio m.
epithet, n. epìteto m.
epitome, n. epìtome f.
epitomize, vb. epitomare.
epoch, n. època f.
equable, adj. èquo.
equal, 1. adj. uguale, pari. 2. vb. uguagliare.
equality, n. uguaglianza f.
equalize, vb. uguagliare.
equanimity, n. equanimità f.
equate, vb. uguagliare.
equation, n. equazione f.
equator, n. equatore m.
equatorial, adj. equatoriale.
equestrian, adj. equèstre.
equidistant, adj. equidistante.
equilateral, adj. equilaterale.
equilibrate, vb. equilibrare.
equilibrium, n. equilìbrio m.

equinox, n. equinòzio m.
equip, vb. corredare, fornire.
equipment, n. equipàggio m., corrèdo m.
equitable, adj. èquo.
equity, n. equità f.
equivalent, adj. equivalente; (be e.) equivalere.
equivocal, adj. equìvoco.
equivocate, vb. giocare sull'equìvoco.
era, n. èra f.
eradicate, vb. sradicare.
eradicator, n. sradicatore m.
erase, vb. cancellare, raschiare.
eraser, n. raschino m., cancellino m.
erasure, n. cancellatura f.
erect, 1. adj. erètto. 2. vb. erìgere, costruire.
erection, n. erezione f., costruzione f.
erectness, n. posizione erètta f.
ermine, n. ermellino m.
erode, vb. eròdere.
erosion, n. erosione f.
erosive, adj. erosivo.
erotic, adj. eròtico.
err, vb. errare.
errand, n. commissione f.
errand boy, n. fattorino m.; messo m.
errant, adj. errante.
erratic, adj. erràtico.
erroneous, adj. erròneo.
error, n. errore m.
erudite, adj. erudito.
erudition, n. erudizione f.
erupt, vb. eruttare.
eruption, n. eruzione f.
escalate, vb. aumentare.
escalator, n. scala mòbile f.
escapade, n. scappatella f.
escape, 1. n. fuga f., scampo m. 2. vb. sfuggire, scappare.
escapism, n. desidèrio di sfuggire alla realtà m.
escarpment, n. scarpata f.
eschew, vb. evitare.
escort, 1. n. scòrta f. 2. vb. scortare.
esculent, adj. esculènto.
escutcheon, n. scudo m.
esophagus, n. esòfago m.
esoteric, adj. esotèrico.

espalier, n. spalliera f.
especial, adj. speciale.
especially, adv. specialmente.
espionage, n. spionàggio m.
esplanade, n. spianata f.; piazzale m.
espousal, n. sposalízio m.
espouse, vb. sposare.
essay, 1. n. sàggio m. 2. vb. provare.
essayist, n. saggista m.
essence, n. essènza f.
essential, adj. essenziale.
essentially, adv. essenzialmente.
establish, vb. stabilire.
establishment, n. stabilimento m.
estate, n. (inheritance) patrimònio m.; (possessions) bèni m.pl.; (condition) condizione f., stato m.
esteem, 1. n. stima f. 2. vb. stimare.
esthete, n. esteta m.
esthetic, adj. estético.
estimable, adj. stimàbile.
estimate, 1. n. valutazione f., stima f. 2. vb. valutare, stimare.
estimation, n. stima f., valutazione f.
estrange, vb. alienare.
estrangement, n. disaffezione m.
estuary, n. estuàrio m.
etching, n. acquafòrte f.
eternal, adj. etèrno.
eternity, n. eternità f.
ether, n. ètere m.
ethereal, adj. etèreo.
ethical, adj. ètico.
ethics, n. ètica f.
ethnic, adj. ètnico.
etiquette, n. galatèo m.
etymology, n. etimología f.
eucalyptus, n. eucalipto m.
eugenic, adj. eugènico.
eugenics, n. eugenètica f.
eulogize, vb. elogiare.
eulogy, n. elògio m.
eunuch, n. eunuco m.
euphonious, adj. eufònico.
Europe, n. Europa f.
European, n. and adj. europèo (m.)
euthanasia, n. eutanasía f.
evacuate, vb. evacuare.
evade, vb. evitare, elùdere.

evaluate, vb. valutare.
evaluation, n. valutazione f.
evanescent, adj. evanescènte.
evangelist, n. evangelista m.
evaporate, vb. evaporare.
evaporation, n. evaporazione f.
evasion, n. evasione f.
evasive, adj. evasivo.
eve, n. vigilia f.
even, 1. adj. pari, giusto, uniforme. 2. adv. anche, perfino.
evening, n. sera f.
evenness, n. uniformità f.
event, n. avvenimento m.
eventful, adj. pièno di avvenimenti.
eventual, adj. finale.
ever, adv. sèmpre, mai.
everglade, n. palude f.
evergreen, adj. sempreverde.
everlasting, adj. sempitèrno.
every, adj. ogni.
everybody, pron. ognuno.
everyday, adj. quotidiano.
everyone, pron. ognuno.
everything, pron. tutto.
everywhere, adv. dappertutto.
evict, vb. espèllere.
eviction, n. espulsione f.
evidence, n. evidènza f.
evident, adj. evidènte; (be e.) risultare.
evidently, adv. evidentemente.
evil, 1. n. male m. 2. adj. cattivo.
evildoer, n. malvagio m.
evil eye, n. malòcchio m.
evil-minded, adj. malintenzionato.
evince, vb. manifestare.
eviscerate, vb. sviscerare.
evoke, vb. evocare.
evolution, n. evoluzione f.
evolutionist, n. evoluzionista m.
evolve, vb. evòlvere.
ewe, n. pècora f.
exacerbate, vb. esacerbare.
exact, 1. adj. esatto. 2. vb. esìgere.
exacting, adj. esigente.
exaction, n. esazione f.
exactly, adv. esattamente.
exaggerate, vb. esagerare.
exaggeration, n. esagerazione f.
exalt, vb. esaltare.
exaltation, n. esaltazione f.
examination, n. esame m.

examine, vb. esaminare.

example, n. esèmpio m.

exasperate, vb. esasperare.

exasperation, n. esasperazione f.

excavate, vb. scavare.

excavation, n. scavo m.

exceed, vb. eccèdere, superare.

exceedingly, adv. estremamente.

excel, vb. eccèllere, superare.

excellence, n. eccellènza f.

Excellency, n. Eccellènza f.

excellent, adj. eccellènte.

except, 1. vb. eccettuare. **2.** prep. eccètto, salvo, tranne; **(e. for)** all'infuòri di.

exception, n. eccezione f.

exceptional, adj. eccezionale.

excerpt, n. brano m.

excess, n. eccèsso m.

excess fare, n. supplemento m.

excessive, adj. eccessivo.

exchange, 1. n. scàmbio m. **2.** vb. scambiare.

exchangeable, adj. scambiàbile.

excise, n. dàzio m.

excitable, adj. eccitàbile.

excite, vb. eccitare.

excitement, n. eccitamento m., eccitazione f.

exclaim, vb. esclamare.

exclamation, n. esclamazione f.

exclamation point or mark, n. punto esclamativo m.

exclude, vb. esclùdere.

exclusion, n. esclusione f.

exclusive, adj. esclusivo.

excogitate, vb. escogitare.

excommunicate, vb. scomunicare.

excommunication, n. scomùnica f.

excoriate, vb. escoriare.

excrement, n. escremento m.

excruciating, adj. tormentoso.

exculpate, vb. discolpare.

excursion, n. escursione f.

excusable, adj. scusàbile.

excuse, 1. n. scusa f. **2.** vb. scusare.

execrable, adj. esecràbile.

execute, vb. eseguire; (kill legally) giustiziare.

execution, n. esecuzione f.; (legal killing) esecuzione capitale f.

executioner, n. bòia m., carnéfice m.

executive, 1. n. amministratore m. **2.** adj. esecutivo.

executor, n. esecutore m.

exemplary, adj. esemplare.

exemplify, vb. esemplificare.

exempt, 1. adj. esènte. **2.** vb. esentare.

exercise, 1. n. esercízio m. **2.** vb. esercitare.

exert, vb. esercitare.

exertion, n. sforzo m.

exhale, vb. esalare.

exhaust, vb. esaurire.

exhaustion, n. esaurimento m.

exhaustive, adj. esauriente.

exhibit, 1. n. mostra f. **2.** vb. esibire, mostrare.

exhibition, n. esibizione f., mostra f.

exhibitionism, n. esibizionismo m.

exhibitor, n. espositore m.

exhilarating, adj. esilarante.

exhilarate, vb. esilarare.

exhort, vb. esortare.

exhortation, n. esortazione f.

exhume, vb. esumare.

exigency, n. esigènza f.

exile, 1. n. esilio m.; (person) fuoruscito m. **2.** vb. esiliare.

exist, vb. esistere.

existence, n. esistènza f.

existent, adj. esistènte.

existing, adj. esistente.

exit, n. uscita f.

exodus, n. èsodo m.

exonerate, vb. esonerare.

exorbitant, adj. esorbitante.

exorcise, vb. esorcizzare; (chase away) scacciare.

exotic, adj. esòtico.

expand, vb. espàndere.

expanse, n. distesa f.

expansion, n. espansione f.

expansive, adj. espansivo.

expatiate, vb. diffóndersi.

expatriate, n. espatriato m.

expect, vb. aspettarsi.

expectancy, n. aspettativa f.

expectation, n. aspettativa f.

expectorate, vb. espettorare.

expediency, n. opportunità f.

expedient, 1. n. espediènte m. **2.** adj. espediènte, opportuno.

expedite, vb. sbrigare.

expedition, n. spedizione f.

expeditious, adj. sbrigativo, spiccio.

expel, vb. espèllere.

expend, vb. spèndere, consumare.

expendable, adj. spendìbile; sacrificàbile.

expenditure, n. spesa f.

expense, n. spesa f.

expensive, adj. costoso.

expensively, adv. costosamente.

experience, 1. n. esperiènza f. **2.** vb. sperimentare.

experienced, adj. espèrto.

experiment, 1. n. esperimento m. **2.** vb. sperimentare.

experimental, adj. sperimentale.

expert, n. and adj. espèrto (m.).

expertise, n. maestrìa .

expiate, vb. espiare.

expiation, n. espiazione. f.

expiration, n. espirazione f.

expire, vb. espirare, morire.

explain, vb. spiegare.

explainable, adj. spiegàbile.

explanation, n. spiegazione f.

explanatory, adj. esplicativo.

expletive, 1. n. bestémmia f. **2.** adj. espletivo.

explicit, adj. esplicito.

explode, vb. esplòdere, scoppiare.

exploit, vb. sfruttare.

exploitation, n. sfruttamento m.

exploration, n. esplorazione f.

exploratory, adj. esplorativo.

explore, vb. esplorare.

explorer, n. esploratore.

explosion, n. esplosione f., scòppio m.

explosive, n. and adj. esplosivo (m.)

exponent, n. esponènte m.

export, 1. n. esportazione f. **2.** vb. esportare.

exportation, n. esportazione f.

exporter, n. esportatore m.

expose, vb. esporre.

exposé, n. esposto m., esposizione f.

exposition, n. esposizione f.

expository, adj. espositivo.

expostulate, vb. far rimostranze.

exposure, n. esposizione f., rivelazione f.; (photography) pòsa f.

expound, vb. esporre.

express, 1. n. esprèsso m.; (train) direttìssimo m. **2.** adj. esprèsso. **3.** vb. esprímere.

expressage, n. spese di traspòrto f.pl.

expression, n. espressione f.; (outlet) sfògo m.

expressive, adj. espressivo.

expressly, adv. espressamente.

expressman, n. impiegato della compagnìa di traspòrti m.

expressway, n. autostrada f.

expropriate, vb. espropriare.

expulsion, n. espulsione f.

expunge, vb. espùngere.

expurgate, vb. espurgare.

exquisite, adj. squisito.

extant, adj. esistènte.

extemporaneous, adj. estemporàneo.

extemporize, vb. improvvisare.

extend, vb. estèndere; (in time) prolungare; prorogare.

extended, adj. esteso; allungato.

extension, n. estensione f.; (in time) prolungamento m.; pròroga f.

extensive, adj. esteso.

extensively, adv. estesamente.

extent, n. estensione f., distesa f.

extenuate, vb. estenuare.

exterior, adj. esteriore.

exterminate, vb. sterminare.

extermination, n. stermínio m.

external, adj. estèrno; (foreign) èstero.

extinct, adj. estinto.

extinction, n. estinzione f.

extinguish, vb. estínguere.

extinguisher, n. estintore m.

extirpate, vb. estirpare.

extol, vb. elogiare.

extort, vb. estòrcere.

extortion, n. estorsione f.

extortioner, n. ricattatore m.

extra, adj. extra, aggiunto, straordinàrio.

extra-, prefix. estra-, stra-.

extract, 1. n. estratto. **2.** vb. estrarre.

extraction, n. estrazione f.; (race) stirpe f.
extracurricular, adj. fuoriprogramma.
extradite, vb. estradare.
extradition, n. estradizione f.
extramarital, adj. extraconiugale.
extraneous, adj. estràneo.
extraordinary, adj. straordinàrio.
extrapolate, vb. estrapolare.
extravagance, n. stravaganza f., prodigalità f.
extravagant, adj. stravagante, pròdigo.
extravaganza, n. rivista frívola f.
extreme, adj. estrèmo.
extremely, adv. estremamente.
extremist, n. and adj. estremista m. and f.
extremity, n. estremità f.
extricate, vb. districare.
extrinsic, adj. estrinseco.
extrovert, adj. estroverso.
exuberant, adj. esuberante.

exudation, n. trasudazione f.
exude, vb. trasudare.
exult, vb. esultare.
exultant, adj. esultante.
eye, n. òcchio m.
eyeball, n. glòbo dell'òcchio m.
eyebrow, n. sopracciglio m.
eyedropper, n. contagócce m.
eyeful, n. vista f.; colpo d'òcchio m.
eyeglass, n. lènte f.
eyeglasses, n. occhiali m.pl.
eyelash, n. ciglio m.
eyelet, n. occhièllo m.
eyelid, n. pàlpebra f.
eyeshade, n. visiera f.
eyeshadow, n. rimmel m.
eyesight, n. vista f.
eyesore, n. cosa brutta o spiacevole f.; (coll.) pugno nell'occhio m.
eyetooth, n. dente canino m.
eyewitness, n. testimòne oculare m.

F

fable, n. fàvola f.
fabric, n. (cloth) stòffa f.; (architecture) fàbbrica f.
fabricate, vb. fabbricare.
fabrication, n. fabbricazione f.; (lie) bugía f.
fabulous, adj. favoloso.
façade, n. facciata f.
face, 1. n. faccia f., viso m. 2. vb. fronteggiare, affrontare.
face-lift, n. plàstica facciale m.
face powder, n. cipria f.
facet, n. faccetta f.
facetious, adj. facèto.
face value, n. valore nominale m.
facial, adj. del viso, facciale.
facile, adj. fàcile.
facilitate, vb. facilitare.
facility, n. facilità f.
facing, 1. n. rivestimento f. 2. adv. dirimpètto. 3. prep. dirimpètto a.
facsimile, n. facsimile m.
fact, n. fatto m.
faction, n. fazione f.
factor, n. fattore m.
factory, n. fàbbrica f.
factual, adj. obiettivo.

faculty, n. facoltà f.
fad, n. manía f.
fade, vb. appassire; (lose color) impallidire.
faeces, n. fècce f.pl.
fagged, adj. stanco.
fail, vb. fallire, mancare; (in examination) èsser bocciato.
failing, 1. n. debolezza f. 2. prep. in mancanza di.
faille, n. fàglia f.
failure, n. fiasco m., mancanza f.; (bankruptcy) fallimento m.
faint, 1. n. svenimento m. 2. adj. dèbole. 3. vb. svenire.
faintly, adv. debolmente.
fair, 1. n. fièra f. 2. adj. bèllo; (blond) biondo; (just) giusto, èquo.
fairly, adj. giustamente; (moderately) abbastanza.
fairness, n. giustezza f.
fairy, n. fata f.
fairyland, n. paese delle fate m.
faith, n. fede f.
faithful, adj. fedele.
faithfulness, n. fedeltà f.

faithless, *adj.* sènza fede.
fake, 1. *n.* falso *m.* **2.** *vb.* falsificare.
faker, *n.* falsificatore *m.*
falcon, *n.* falcone *m.*
falconry, *n.* falconería *f.*
fall, 1. *n.* caduta *f.;* (autumn) autunno *m.* **2.** *vb.* cadere; **(f. asleep)** addormentarsi; **(f. due)** scadere; **(f. in love)** innamorarsi; **(f. upon)** attaccare.
fallacious, *adj.* fallace.
fallacy, *n.* fallàcia *f.*
fallible, *adj.* fallibile.
fallout, *n.* pioggia radioattiva *f.*
fallow, *adj.* a maggese; **(f. field)** maggese *n.m.*
false, *adj.* falso.
false-hearted, *adj.* pèrfido.
falsehood, *n.* bugia *f.*
falseness, *n.* falsità *f.*
falsetto, *n.* falsetto *m.*
falsification, *n.* falsificazione *f.*
falsify, *vb.* falsificare.
falter, *vb.* esitare, incespicare.
fame, *n.* fama *f.*
famed, *adj.* famoso.
familiar, *adj.* familiare; **(f. with)** pràtico di.
familiarity, *n.* familiarità *f.*
familiarize, *vb.* familiarizzare.
family, *n.* famiglia *f.;* **(f. tree)** àlbero genealògico *m.*
famine, *n.* carestía *f.*
famished, *adj.* affamato.
famous, *adj.* famoso.
fan, 1. *n.* ventàglio *m.;* (enthusiast) tifoso *m.* **2.** *vb.* sventolare.
fanatic, *n. and adj.* fanàtico (*m.*).
fanatical, *adj.* fanàtico.
fanaticism, *n.* fanatismo *m.*
fancied, *adj.* immaginàrio.
fanciful, *adj.* immaginoso, capriccioso.
fancy, 1. *n.* immaginazione *f.* **2.** *adj.* di fantasía. **3.** *vb.* immaginare.
fanfare, *n.* fanfara *f.*
fang, *n.* zanna *f.*
fantastic, *adj.* fantàstico.
fantasy, *n.* fantasía *f.*
far, *adj. and adv.* lontano; **(as far as)** fino a; **(by far)** di gran lunga; **(how far?)** fino dove?; **(in so far as)** in quanto che; **(so far)** finora.
faraway, *adj. and adv.* lontano.

farce, *n.* farsa *f.*
farcical, *adj.* farsesco.
fare, 1. *n.* (price) tariffa *f.;* (passenger) passeggièro *m.;* (food) cibo *m.* **2.** *vb.* andare.
farewell, *n. and interj.* addio (*m.*)
far-fetched, *adj.* ricercato.
far-flung, *adj.* esteso.
farina, *n.* farina *f.*
farm, *n.* fattoría *f.*
farmer, *n.* agricoltore *m.*, colòno *m.*
farmhouse, *n.* casa colònica *f.*
farming, *n.* agricultura *f.*
farmyard, *adj.* cortile.
far-reaching, *adj.* esteso.
far-sighted, be, *vb.* aver vista lunga.
farther, *adv.* più lontano.
farthest, *adv.* il più lontano.
fascinate, *vb.* affascinare.
fascination, *n.* fàscino *m.*
fascism, *n.* fascismo *m.*
fascist, *n. and adj.* fascista (*m.* and *f.*)
fashion, *n.* mòda *f.;* (manner) manièra *f.*
fashionable, *adj.* alla mòda.
fast, 1. *n.* digiuno *m.* **2.** *adj.* (speedy) ràpido; (firm) fermo; (of clock) avanti. **3.** *vb.* digiunare. **4.** *adv.* (quickly) rapidamente; (firmly) fermamente.
fasten, *vb.* attaccare, fissare.
fastener, fastening, *n.* chiusura *f.*, fermatura *f.*
fastidious, *adj.* fastidioso.
fat, *n. and adj.* grasso (*m.*)
fatal, *adj.* fatale; (deadly) mortale.
fatality, *n.* fatalità *f.*
fatally, *adv.* fatalmente.
fate, *n.* fato *m.*
fateful, *adj.* fatale.
father, *n.* padre *m.*
fatherhood, *n.* paternità *f.*
father-in-law, *n.* suòcero *m.*
fatherland, *n.* pàtria *f.*
fatherless, *adj.* òrfano di padre.
fatherly, *adj.* patèrno.
fathom, 1. *n.* bràccio *m.* **2.** *vb.* scandagliare.
fatigue, 1. *n.* fatica *f.* **2.** *vb.* affaticare.
fatten, *vb.* ingrassare.
fatty, *adj.* grasso.

fatuous, adj. fàtuo.

faucet, n. rubinetto m.

fault, n. colpa f.; (defect) difetto m., mènda f.

faultfinding, n. crítica f.

faultless, adj. irreprensíbile.

faultlessly, adv. irreprensibilmente.

faulty, adj. difettoso.

favor, 1. n. favore m. 2. vb. favorire.

favorable, adj. favorévole, propízio.

favorite, n. and adj. favorito (m.).

favoritism, n. favoritismo m.

fawn, 1. n. cerbiàtto m. 2. vb. (f. upon) adulare.

faze, vb. sconcertare.

fear, 1. n. paùra f., timore m. 2. vb. temere, aver paùra di.

fearful, adj. (person) pauroso, timoroso; (thing) spaventoso.

fearless, adj. intrèpido.

fearlessness, n. intrepidezza f.

feasible, adj. fattíbile.

feast, n. fèsta f.; (banquet) banchetto m.

feat, n. fatto m.; impresa f.

feather, n. penna f., piuma f.

feather, n. penna f., piuma f.

feathered, adj. pennuto, piumato.

feathery, adj. piumoso.

feature, n. tratto m.

February, n. febbraio m.

fecund, adj. fecondo.

federal, adj. federale.

federation, n. federazione f.

fedora, n. cappèllo flòscio m.

fee, n. (for professional services) onoràrio m.; (membership) quòta f.; (school) tassa f.

feeble, adj. débole.

feeble-minded, adj. débole di cervèllo.

feebleness, n. debolezza f.

feed, 1. n. nutrimento m. 2. vb. nutrire, alimentare.

feedback, n. feedback m.

feed pump, n. pompa d'alimentazione f.

feel, 1. n. tatto m. 2. vb. sentire.

feeler, n. sondàggio m.

feeling, n. sentimento m.

feign, vb. fíngere.

feint, 1. n. finta f. 2. vb. fare una finta.

felicitate, vb. felicitare.

felicitous, adj. felice.

felicity, n. felicità f.

feline, adj. felino.

fell, 1. adj. malvàgio. 2. vb. abbàttere.

fellow, n. individuo m.; (associate) sòcio m.

fellowship, n. borsa f.

felon, n. fellone m.

felony, n. fellonía f.

felt, n. feltro m.

felt-tip pen, n. pennarello m.

female, 1. n. fèmmina f. 2. adj. femminile.

feminine, adj. femminile.

femininity, n. femminilità f.

fence, 1. n. recinto m. 2. vb. chiùdere con un recinto; (sword, foil) schermire.

fencer, n. schermidore m.

fencing, n. scherma f.

fend, vb. (f. off) parare; (f. for oneself) badare a se stesso.

fender, n. (auto) parafango m.

fennel, n. finòcchio m.

ferment, 1. n. fermento m. 2. vb. fermentare.

fermentation, n. fermentazione f.

fern, n. felce f.

ferocious, adj. feroce.

ferociously, adv. ferocemente.

ferocity, n. feròcia f.

ferry, n. traghetto m.

fertile, adj. fèrtile.

fertility, n. fertilità f.

fertilization, n. fertilizzazione f.

fertilize, vb. fertilizzare.

fertilizer, n. fertilizzante m.

fervency, n. fervore m.

fervent, adj. fervènte.

fervently, adv. ferventemente.

fervid, adj. fèrvido.

fervor, n. fervore m.

fester, vb. suppurare.

festival, n. fèsta f.

festive, adj. festivo.

festivity, n. festività f.

festoon, n. festone m.

fetal, adj. fetale.

fetch, vb. (go and get) andare a cercare; (bring) apportare.

fetching, adj. attraènte.

fête, n. fèsta f.

fetid, adj. fètido.

fetish, n. feticcio m.

fetlock, n. nòcca f.

fetters, n. ceppi m.pl.

fetus, n. fèto m.

feud, n. inimicízia f.; (historical) fèudo m.

feudal, adj. feudale.

feudalism, n. feudalismo m.

fever, n. fèbbre f.

feverish, adj. febbrile.

feverishly, adv. febbrilmente.

few, adj. and pron. pòchi pl.

fiancé, n. fidanzato m.

fiancée, n. fidanzata f.

fiasco, n. fiasco m.

fiat, n. órdine m.

fib, n. fandònia f.

fiber, n. fibra f.

fiberglass, n. vetrorèsina f.

fibrous, adj. fibroso.

fickle, adj. incostante.

fickleness, n. incostanza f.

fiction, n. finzione f.; (novel-writing) novellística f.

fictional, adj. finto.

fictitious, adj. fittízio.

fictitiously, adv. fittiziamente.

fiddle, 1. n. violino m. **2.** vb. suonare il violino.

fiddler, n. violinista m.

fiddlesticks, interj. fandònie!

fidelity, n. fedeltà f.

fidget, vb. agitarsi.

fief, n. fèudo m.

field, n. campo m.

fiend, n. demònio m.

fiendish, adj. demoníaco.

fierce, adj. feroce.

fiery, adj. focoso.

fife, n. piffero m.

fifteen, num. quíndici.

fifteenth, adj. quindicésimo.

fifth, adj. quinto.

fifty, num. cinquanta.

fig, n. fico m.

fight, 1. n. combattimento m.; (struggle) lotta f.; (quarrel) lite f. **2.** vb. combàttere.

fighter, n. combattènte m.; (plane) càccia m.

figment, n. finzione f.

figurative, adj. figurato.

figuratively, adv. figuratamente.

figure, 1. n. figura f.; (of body) línea f.; (math.) cifra f. **2.** vb. figurare, calcolare.

figurehead, n. prestanome m., fantòccio m.

figure of speech, n. figura retòrica f.

figurine, n. figurina f.

figure skating, n. pattinàggio artístico m.

filament, n. filamento m.

filch, vb. rubare.

file, 1. n. (tool) lima f.; (row) fila f.; riga f.; (papers, etc.) filza f.; archívio m.; (cards) schedàrio m. **2.** vb. (tool) limare; (papers) archiviare; (f. off) sfilare.

filet, n. filetto m.

filial, adj. filiale.

filiation, n. filiazione f.; (business) filiale f.

filibuster, n. (politics) ostruzionismo m.; filibustiere m.

filigree, n. filigrana f.

filing cabinet, n. schedàrio m.

filings, n. limatura f.sg.

fill, vb. riempire; (tooth) otturare.

fillet, n. (band) banda f.; (meat) filetto m.; (fish) fetta f.

filling, n. (of tooth) otturazione f.

filling station, n. stazione di servízio f.

fillip, n. stimolo m.; colpetto m.

film, n. pellícola f.

filmy, adj. velato.

filter, 1. n. filtro m. **2.** vb. filtrare.

filtering, n. filtràggio m.

filth, n. sudiciume m.

filthy, adj. sùdicio.

fin, n. pinna f.

final, adj. finale.

finale, n. finale m.

finalist, n. finalista m.

finality, n. finalità f.

finally, adv. finalmente.

finance, n. finanza f.

financial, adj. finanziàrio.

financier, n. finanzière m.

financing, n. finanziamento m.

find, vb. trovare.

finding, n. ritrovato m.

fine, 1. n. multa f. ammènda f.; (voluntary) oblazione f. **2.** adj. (beautiful) bèllo; (pure) fino; (excellent) bravo. **3.** vb. multare.

fine arts, n. bèlle arti f.pl.

fine-print, n. (business) dettagli contrattuàli m.pl.

finery, n. vestiti eleganti m.pl.

finesse, n. finezza f.

finger, n. dito m.

fingernail, n. ùnghia f.

fingerprint, n. impronta digitale f.

finicky, adj. affettato.

finish, 1. n. fine f. 2. vb. finire, terminare.

finite, adj. definito.

fir, n. abete m.

fire, 1. n. fuòco m.; (burning of house, etc.) incèndio m. 2. vb. (weapon) sparare; (deprive of job) licenziare.

fire alarm, n. allarme d'incendio m.

firearm, n. arma da fuòco f.

firecracker, n. petardo m.

firedamp, n. grisou m., mètano m.

fire engine, n. pompa da incèndio f.

fire escape, n. uscita di sicurezza f.

fire extinguisher, n. estintore m.

firefly, n. lùcciola f.

fireman, n. pompière m.; (locomotive) fuochista m.

fireplace, n. focolare m.

fireproof, adj. ignifugo.

firescreen, n. parafuòco m.

fireside, n. cantùccio del focolare m.

firewood, n. legna f.

fireworks, n. fuòchi d'artificio m.pl.

firm, 1. n. ditta f. 2. adj. fermo.

firmness, n. fermezza f.

first, adj. primo.

first aid, n. pronto soccorso m.

first-class, adj. di prima classe.

first-hand, adj. di prima mano.

first-rate, adj. di prima qualità.

fiscal, adj. fiscale.

fish, 1. n. pesce m. 2. vb. pescare.

fisherman, n. pescatore m.

fishery, n. peschièra f.

fishhook, n. amo m.

fishing, n. pesca f.

fishmonger, n. pescivéndolo m.

fishwife, n. pescivéndola f.

fishy, adj. di pesce; (strange) strano.

fission, n. fissione f.

fissure, n. fessura f.

fist, n. pugno m.

fistic, adj. pugilistico.

fit, 1. n. accèsso m. 2. adj. adatto, idòneo. 3. vb. (befit) convenire a; (clothes) andar bène; (adapt) adattare.

fitful, adj. irregolare; spasmodico.

fitness, n. idoneità f.; (health) salute f.

fitting, 1. n. adattamento m. 2. adj. conveniènte.

five, num. cinque.

fix, 1. n. impíccio m. 2. vb. acconciare; (repair) riparare; (set) fissare; (f. up) sistemare.

fixation, n. fissazione f.

fixed, adj. fisso.

fixing, adj. fissante.

fixture, n. infisso m.

fizz, n. effervescenza f.

flabbergast, vb. sbalordire.

flabby, adj. flòscio.

flaccid, adj. flàccido.

flag, n. bandièra f.; (stone) lastra di ròccia f.

flagellant, n. flagellante m.

flagellate, vb. flagellare.

flagging, adj. indebolito.

flagman, n. manovratore m.

flagon, n. coppa f.

flagpole, n. asta di bandièra f.

flagrant, adj. flagrante.

flagrantly, adv. flagrantemente.

flagship, n. nave ammiràglia f.

flagstone, n. lastra di ròccia f.

flail, n. coreggiato m.

flair, n. fiuto m.; (ability) abilità f.

flake, n. fiòcco m.

flaky, adj. a falde.

flamboyant, adj. sgargiante.

flame, 1. n. fiamma f.; (burst into f.s) divampare. 2. vb. fiammeggiare.

flame thrower, n. lanciafiamme m.

flaming, adj. fiammante.

flamingo, n. fiammingo m., fenicòttero m.

flammable, adj. infiammabile.

flank, 1. n. fianco m. 2. vb. fiancheggiare.

flannel, n. flanèlla f.
flap, n. (wing) colpo m.; (envelope) lembo di chiusura m.
flare, vb. fiammeggiare.
flare-up, n. scòppio d'ira m.
flash, 1. n. baleno m. 2. vb. balenare.
flashback, n. flashback m.
flashcube, n. cubo per flash m.
flashiness, n. vistosità f.
flashlight, n. lampadina tascàbile f.
flashy, adj. vistoso.
flask, n. fiasco m.
flat, 1. n. appartamento m.; (music) bemòlle m. 2. adj. piatto, piano; (f. tire) gomma a terra f.
flatboat, n. chiatta f.
flatcar, n. carro piatto m.
flatness, n. monotonía f.
flatten, vb. appiattire.
flatter, vb. adulare, lusingare.
flatterer, n. adulatore m., lusingatore m.
flattering, adj. lusinghièro.
flattery, n. adulazione f., lusinghe f.pl.
flat-top, n. portaèrei m.
flatware, n. argentería f.
flaunt, vb. ostentare.
flavor, 1. n. (taste) sapore m.; (odor) aròma m. 2. vb. insaporire.
flavoring, n. aròma artificiale m.
flavorless, adj. sènza sapore.
flaw, n. difetto m.
flawless, adj. perfètto.
flawlessly, adv. perfettamente.
flax, n. lino m.
flay, vb. scorticare.
flea, n. pulce f.
fleck, n. macchietta f.
fledgling, n. uccellino m.
flee, vb. fuggire.
fleece, n. vèllo m.
fleecy, adj. velloso.
fleet, 1. n. fiòtta f. 2. adj. veloce.
fleeting, adj. fugace.
Fleming, n. fiammingo m.
Flemish, adj. fiammingo.
flesh, n. carne f.
fleshy, adj. carnoso.
flex, vb. flèttere.
flexibility, n. flessibilità f.
flexible, adj. flessíbile.

flicker, 1. n. tremolío m. 2. vb. tremolare.
flier, n. aviatore m.
flight, n. volo m.
flight attendant, n. camerière m.; camerièra f. assistente di volo m. and f.
flighty, adj. capriccioso.
flimsy, adj. tènue.
flinch, vb. ritirarsi.
fling, vb. lanciare.
flint, n. (lighter) piètra focaia f.; (stone) selce f.
flip, vb. gettare.
flippant, adj. leggero.
flippantly, adv. leggermente.
flirt, 1. n. civetta f. 2. vb. civettare, flirtare.
flirtation, n. flirt m.
float, vb. galleggiare.
flock, 1. n. gregge m. 2. vb. affollarsi.
flog, vb. fustigare.
flood, 1. n. inondazione f. 2. vb. inondare.
floodgate, n. cateratta f.
floodlight, n. riflettore elèttrico m.
floor, n. pavimento m.; (story) piano m.; **(take the f.)** prèndere la paròla.
flooring, n. pavimentazione f.
floorwalker, n. ispettore di magazzino m.
flop, 1. n. (failure) fiasco m.; (thud) tonfo m. 2. vb. muòversi goffamente; (fail) far fiasco.
floral, adj. floreale.
Florence, n. Firènze f.
Florentine, adj. fiorentino.
florescence, n. infiorescenza f.
florid, adj. rubicondo.
florist, n. fioraio m.
floss, n. lanugine f.
flounce, 1. n. volante m. 2. vb. dimenarsi.
flounder, vb. dibàttersi.
flour, n. farina f.
flourish, vb. fiorire; (wave around) agitare.
floury, adj. farinoso.
flow, vb. scórrere.
flower, 1. n. fiore m. 2. vb. fiorire.
flowerpot, n. vaso per fiori m.
flowery, adj. fiorito.

flu, *n.* influenza *f.*

fluctuate, *vb.* fluttuare.

fluctuation, *n.* fluttuazione *f.*

flue, *n.* conduttura *f.*

fluency, *n.* scorrevolezza *f.*

fluent, *adj.* scorrévole.

fluently, *adv.* scorrevolmente.

fluffy, *adj.* lanuginoso.

fluid, *n. and adj.* flùido *(m.)*

fluidity, *n.* fluidità *f.*

flunk, *vb.* bocciare.

flunkey, *n.* lacchè *m.*

fluorescent, *adj.* fluorescènte.

fluoroscope, *n.* fluoroscòpio *m.*

flurry, *n.* trambusto *m.*

flush, 1. *adj.* a livèllo di. **2.** *vb.* (f. the toilet) tirare lo sciacquone.

flute, *n.* flàuto *m.*

flutist, *n.* flautista *m. and f.*

flutter, *vb.* svolazzare.

flux, *n.* flusso *m.*

fly, 1. *n.* mosca *f.* **2.** *vb.* volare.

flycatcher, *n.* pigliamosche *m.*

flywheel, *n.* volano *m.*

foam, 1. *n.* schiuma *f.*, spuma *f.* **2.** *vb.* spumare.

foamy, *adj.* schiumoso.

focal, *adj.* focale.

focus, *n.* fuòco *m.*

fodder, *n.* foràggio *m.*

foe, *n.* nemico *m.*

fog, *n.* foschìa *f.*

foggy, *adj.* nebbioso.

foil, 1. *n.* (fencing) fiorètto *m.*; (metal) fòglia *f.* **2.** *vb.* frustrare.

foist, *vb.* far accettare.

fold, 1. *n.* pièga *f.* **2.** *vb.* piegare.

folder, *n.* cartèlla *f.*

foliage, *n.* fogliame *m.*

folio, *n.* fòglio *m.*

folk, *n.* pòpolo *m.*

folklore, *n.* folclore *m.*

folks, *n.* la gènte *f.*

follicle, *n.* follìcolo *m.*

follow, *vb.* seguire; (pursue) inseguire.

follower, *n.* seguace *m.*

folly, *n.* follìa *f.*

foment, *vb.* fomentare.

fond, *adj.* amante, tènero.

fondant, *n.* fondènte *m.*

fondle, *vb.* accarezzare.

fondly, *adv.* teneramente.

fondness, *n.* tenerezza *f.*, passione *f.*

food, *n.* cibo *m.*, alimento *m.*, vitto *m.*

foodstuffs, *n.* gèneri alimentari *m.pl.*

fool, 1. *n.* citrullo *m.*, sciòcco *m.*, stolto *m.* **2.** *vb.* ingannare.

foolhardiness, *n.* temerarietà *f.*

foolhardy, *adj.* temeràrio.

foolish, *adj.* sciòcco, stolto.

foolproof, *adj.* assolutamente sicuro.

foolscap, *n.* carta formato protocòllo *f.*

foot, *n.* piède *m.*

footage, *n.* metràggio *m.*

football, *n.* (soccer) càlcio *m.*

foothill, *n.* collina bassa *f.*

foothold, *n.* appòggio *m.*, sostegno *m.*

footing, *n.* appòggio *m.*, base *f.*

footlights, *n.* ribalta *f.sg.*

footman, *n.* staffière *m.*

footnote, *n.* nòta *f.*

footprint, *n.* orma *f.*

footsore, be, *vb.* aver male ai piedi.

footstep, *n.* orma *f.*

footstool, *n.* sgabèllo *m.*

fop, *n.* damerino *m.*

for, 1. *prep.* per. **2.** *conj.* perchè, chè.

forage, 1. *n.* foràggio *m.* **2.** *vb.* predare.

foray, *n.* scorrerìa *f.*

forbear, *vb.* trattenersi.

forbearance, *n.* paziènza *f.*

forbid, *vb.* proibire, vietare.

forbidding, *adj.* repulsivo.

force, 1. *n.* fòrza *f.*, vigore *m.* **2.** *vb.* forzare.

forceful, *adj.* vigoroso.

forcefulness, *n.* vigore *m.*

forceps, *n.* fòrcipe *m.* (*sg.*)

forcible, *adj.* forzato; (powerful) potènte.

ford, *n.* guado *m.*

fore, *adj.* anteriore.

fore and aft, *adv.* a pròra e a poppa.

forearm, *n.* avambràccio *m.*

forebears, *n.* antenati *m.pl.*

forebode, *vb.* presentire.

foreboding, *n.* presentimento *m.*

forecast, 1. *n.* previsione *f.* **2.** *vb.* prevedere, pronosticare.

forecaster, n. pronosticatore m.
forecastle, n. castèllo di prua m.
foreclose, vb. preclùdere.
foreclosure, n. graduazione f.
foredoom, vb. condannare all'insuccesso.
forefather, n. antenato m.
forefinger, n. indice m.
forefront, n. primo piano m.
forego, vb. rinunziare a.
foregoing, adj. anteriore.
foregone, adj. anticipato.
foreground, n. primo piano m.
forehanded, adj. previdente.
forehead, n. fronte f.
foreign, adj. stranièro, èstero.
foreign aid, n. aiuto ai paesi èsteri m.
foreigner, n. stranièro m.
foreleg, n. gamba anteriore f.
foreman, n. capo operaio m.
foremost, 1. adj. primo. 2. adv. in avanti.
forenoon, n. mattina f.
forensic, adj. forènse.
forerunner, n. precursore m.
foresee, vb. prevedere.
foreseeable, adj. prevedíbile.
foreshadow, vb. presagire.
foreshorten, vb. scorciare.
foresight, n. previdènza f.
foresighted, adj. previdente.
foreskin, n. prepùzio m.
forest, n. forèsta f.
forestall, vb. impedire.
forester, n. silvicultore m.; (guard) guàrdia forestale f.
forestry, n. silvicultura f.
foretaste, 1. n. pregustazione f. 2. vb. pregustare.
foretell, vb. predire.
forethought, n. premeditazione f.
forever, adv. per sèmpre.
forevermore, adv. eternamente.
forewarn, vb. preavvertire.
foreword, n. prefazione f.
forfeit, vb. demeritare, pèrdere.
forfeiture, n. pèrdita f.
forgather, vb. riunirsi.
forge, 1. n. fucina f. 2. vb. (make) foggiare; (falsify) contraffare.
forger, n. contraffattore m.
forgery, n. contraffazione f.
forget, vb. dimenticare.
forgetful, adj. diméntico.

forget-me-not, n. miosòtide f., non ti scordar di me m.
forgive, vb. perdonare.
forgiveness, n. perdono m.
forgo, vb. rinunziare a.
fork, n. forchetta f.; (in road) bívio m.
forlorn, adj. disperato.
form, 1. n. forma f.; (blank) mòdulo m. 2. vb. formare.
formal, adj. formale.
formaldehyde, n. formaldèide f.
formality, n. formalità f.
formally, adv. formalmente.
format, n. formato m.
formation, n. formazione f.
formative, adj. formativo.
former, 1. adj. precedènte. 2. pron. quello.
formerly, adv. anticamente, già.
formidable, adj. formidàbile.
formless, adj. informe.
formula, n. fòrmula f.
formulate, vb. formulare.
formulation, n. formulazione f.
forsake, vb. abbandonare.
forsythia, n. forsízia f.
fort, n. fortezza f.
forte, n. fòrte m.
forth, adv. (out) fuòri; (onward) via; (and so f.) e così via.
forthcoming, adj. pròssimo.
forthright, adj. onèsto.
forthwith, adv. immediatamente.
fortieth, adj. quarantésimo.
fortification, n. fortificazione f.
fortify, vb. fortificare.
fortissimo, adv. fortíssimo.
fortitude, n. fortezza f.
fortnight, n. quíndici giorni m.pl.
fortress, n. fortezza f., ròcca f.
fortuitous, adj. fortùito.
fortunate, adj. fortunato.
fortune, n. fortuna f.
fortune-teller, n. chiaroveggènte m.
forty, num. quaranta.
forum, n. fòro m.
forward, adv. avanti.
forwardness, n. presuntuosità f.
fossil, n. and adj. fòssile (m.)
fossilize, vb. fossilizzare, tr.
foster, vb. (raise) allevare; (nourish) nutrire.

foul, 1. adj. spòrco; (unfair) disonèsto. **2.** vb. sporcare.
foulmouthed, adj. oscèno.
foul play, n. reàto m.
found, vb. fondare.
foundation, n. (building) fondamento m.; (fund) fondazione f.
founder, n. fondatore m.
foundling, n. trovatèllo m.; **(f. hospital)** brefotròfio m.
foundry, n. fonderìa f.
fount, n. fonte f.
fountain, n. fontana f.
fountainhead, n. sorgente f.
fountain pen, n. penna stilogràfica f.
four, num. quattro.
four-cylinder, adj. a quattro cilìndri.
four-flush, vb. millantare crèdito.
four-flusher, n. millantatore m.
four-footed, adj. quadrùpede.
four-in-hand, n. cravatta f.
fourscore, num. ottanta.
foursome, n. gruppo di quattro persone m.
fourteen, num. quattòrdici.
fourth, adj. quarto.
fowl, n. pollo m.
fox, n. volpe f.
foxglove, n. digitale f.
foxhole, n. trincèa f.
foxy, adj. volpino.
foyer, n. ingresso m.; (theater) ridotto m.
fracas, n. fracasso m.
fraction, n. frazione f.
fracture, 1. n. frattura f. **2.** vb. fratturare.
fragile, adj. fràgile.
fragment, n. frammento m.
fragmentary, adj. frammentàrio.
fragrance, n. fragranza f.
fragrant, adj. fragrante.
frail, adj. fràgile; (morally) dèbole.
frailty, n. debolezza f.
frame, 1. n. cornice m. **2.** vb. incorniciare.
framework, n. ossatura f.
France, n. Frància f.
franchise, n. diritto di voto m.
frank, adj. franco.
frankfurter, n. salsìccia f.
frankincense, n. incènso m.
frankly, adv. francamente.

frankness, n. franchezza f.
frantic, adj. frenètico.
fraternal, adj. fratèrno.
fraternally, adv. fraternamente.
fraternity, n. fraternità f.
fraternize, vb. fraternizzare.
fratricide, n. (act) fratricídio m.; (person) fratricida m.
fraud, n. fròde f.
fraudulent, adj. fraudolento.
fraudulently, adv. fraudolentemente.
fraught, adj. càrico m.
fray, n. combattimento m.
freak, 1. n. mostruosità f. **2.** adj. mostruoso.
freckle, n. lentìggine f.
freckled, adj. lentigginoso.
free, 1. adj. lìbero; (without cost) gratùito. **2.** vb. liberare.
freedom, n. libertà f.
free lance, n. giornalista o politicante indipendènte m.
freestone, adj. spiccàgnolo.
freeze, vb. gelare.
freezer, n. frigorífero m.; congelatore m.
freezing, n. congelamento m.; **(f. point)** punto di congelamento m.
freight, n. càrico m.; **(f. train)** treno mèrci m.; **(f. station)** scalo mèrci m.
freightage, n. spese di trasporto f.pl.
freighter, n. nave mercantile m.
French, adj. francese.
Frenchman, n. francese m. or f.
frenzied, adj. frenètico.
frenzy, n. frenesìa f.
frequency, n. frequènza f.
frequency modulation, n. modulazione di frequènza f.
frequent, 1. adj. frequènte. **2.** vb. frequentare.
frequently, adv. frequentemente.
fresco, n. affresco m.
fresh, adj. fresco; (impudent) impudènte.
freshen, vb. rinfrescare.
freshman, n. matrìcola f.
freshness, n. freschezza f.
fresh-water, adj. d'acqua dolce.
fret, vb. tormentare, tr., irritare, tr.
fretful, adj. irritàbile.

fretfully, *adv.* irritabilmente.
fretfulness, *n.* irritabilità *f.*
friar, *n.* frate *m.*
fricassee, *n.* fricassèa *f.*
friction, *n.* frizione *f.*
Friday, *n.* venerdì *m.*
friend, *n.* amico *m.,* amica *f.*
friendless, *adj.* sènza amici.
friendliness, *n.* amichevolezza *f.*
friendly, *adj.* amichévole, amico.
friendship, *n.* amicízia *f.*
frieze, *n.* frégio *m.*
frigate, *n.* fregata *f.*
fright, *n.* spavènto *m.*
frighten, *vb.* spaventare.
frightful, *adj.* spaventoso.
frigid, *adj.* frígido.
frigidity, *n.* frigidità *f.*
Frigid Zone, *n.* zona glaciale *f.*
frill, *n.* gala *f.,* affettazione *f.*
frilly, *adj.* increspato.
fringe, *n.* frángia *f.*
fringe benefits, *n.* incentivi *m.pl.*
frippery, *n.* fronzoli *m.pl.*
frisky, *adj.* allegro.
fritter, 1. *n.* frittèlla *f.* **2.** *vb.* **(f. away)** sciupare.
frivolity, *n.* frivolezza *f.*
frivolous, *adj.* frívolo.
frivolousness, *n.* frivolezza *f.*
frizzle, *n.* ricciolo *m.*
frizzly, *adj.* crespo, riccio.
frock, *n.* àbito da donna *m.*
frog, *n.* ranòcchio *m.,* rana *f.*
frogman, *n.* sommozzatore *m.*
frolic, *vb.* far capriòle.
frolicsome, *adj.* scherzoso.
from, *prep.* da.
front, *n.* fronte *m.;* parte anteriore *f.;* davanti *m.;* **(in f.)** davanti *m.;* **(in f. of)** davanti a.
frontage, *n.* facciata *f.*
frontal, *adj.* frontale.
frontier, *n.* frontièra *f.*
frost, *n.* brina *f.*
frostbite, *n.* congelamento *m.*
frosting, *n.* glassa *f.*
frosty, *adj.* gèlido.
froth, *n.* schiuma *f.,* spuma *f.*
froward, *adj.* indòcile.
frown, *vb.* aggrottare le ciglia.
frowzy, *adj.* trascurato.
frozen foods, *n.* cibi surgelati *m.pl.*
fructify, *vb.* fruttificare.

frugal, *adj.* frugale.
frugality, *n.* frugalità *f.*
fruit, *n.* frutto *m.*
fruitful, *adj.* fruttuoso.
fruition, *n.* fruizione *f.*
fruitless, *adj.* infruttuoso.
fruit salad, *n.* macedònia *f.*
fruit stand, *n.* fruttivèndolo *m.*
frustrate, *vb.* frustrare.
frustration, *n.* frustrazione *f.*
fry, *vb.* friggere.
fryer, *n.* (chicken) pollo gióvane *m.*
frying-pan, *n.* padèlla *f.*
fuchsia, *n.* fùcsia *f.*
fudge, 1. *n.* fondènte *m.* **2.** *interj.* sciocchezze!
fuel, *n.* combustíbile *m.;* **(motor f.)** carburante *m.*
fuel cell, *n.* unità elettrògena *f.*
fugitive, *n. and adj.* fuggitivo *(m.)*
fugue, *n.* fuga *f.*
fulcrum, *n.* fulcro *m.*
fulfill, *vb.* realizzare.
fulfillment, *n.* realizzazione *f.*
full, *adj.* pieno.
fullback, *n.* estrèmo *m.*
full dress, *n.* àbito da cerimònia *m.*
fullness, *n.* pienezza *f.*
fully, *adv.* pienamente.
fulminate, *vb.* fulminare.
fulmination, *n.* folgorazione *f.*
fumble, *vb.* lasciar cadere.
fume, *n.* esalazione *f.*
fumigate, *vb.* fumigare.
fumigator, *n.* fumigatore *m.*
fun, *n.* divertimento *m.*
function, 1. *n.* funzione *f.* **2.** *vb.* funzionare.
functional, *adj.* funzionale.
functionary, *n.* funzionàrio *m.*
fund, *n.* fondo *m.*
fundamental, *adj.* fondamentale.
funeral, 1. *n.* funerale *m.* **2.** *adj.* fùnebre.
funereal, *adj.* funereo.
fungicide, *n.* fungicida *m.*
fungus, *n.* fungo *m.*
funnel, *n.* imbuto *m.;* (smoke-stack) ciminièra *f.*
funny, *adj.* còmico.
fur, *n.* pellíccia *f.*
furious, *adj.* furioso.

furlough, n. licènza f.
furnace, n. fornace m., caldaia f.
furnish, vb. fornire; (house) ammobiliare.
furnishings, n. mobilia f.
furniture, n. mòbili m.pl.
furor, n. furore m.
furred, adj. copèrto di pellìccia.
furrier, n. pellicciaio m.
furrow, n. solco m.
furry, adj. copèrto di pellìccia; (tongue) patinoso.
further, 1. adj. ulteriore. 2. adv. oltre, più avanti.
furtherance, n. appòggio m.
furthermore, adv. inoltre.
fury, n. fùria f., furore m.

fuse, 1. n. (electricity) fusíbile m.; (explosives) spoletta f. 2. vb. fóndere.
fuselage, n. fusolièra f.
fusillade, n. fucileria f.
fusion, n. fusione f.
fuss, n. chiasso m.
fussy, adj. difficoltoso.
futile, adj. fùtile.
futility, n. futilità f.
future, 1. n. futuro m., avvenire m. 2. adj. futuro.
futurity, n. avvenire m.
futurology, n. futurologìa f.
fuzz, n. lanùgine f.
fuzzy, adj. lanuginoso; (confused) confuso.

G

gab, vb. chiacchierare.
gabardine, n. gabardina f.
gable, n. (architecture) timpano m.
gadabout, n. bighellone m.
gadfly, n. tafano m.
gadget, n. congegno m.
gaff, n. arpione m.
gag, 1. n. bavàglio m.; (joke) trovata còmica f. 2. vb. imbavagliare.
gage, n. pegno m.; sfida f.
gaiety, n. gaiezza f.
gaily, vb. gaiamente.
gain, 1. n. guadagno m. 2. vb. guadagnare.
gainful, adj. lucroso.
gainfully, adv. lucrosamente.
gainsay, vb. contraddire.
gait, n. andatura f.
gaiter, n. ghetta f.
gala, 1. n. gala f. 2. adj. di gala.
galaxy, n. galàssia f.
gale, n. tempèsta f.
gall, 1. n. (bile) fièle m.; (insolence) sfacciatàggine f. 2. vb. irritare.
gallant, adj. galante, coraggioso.
gallantly, adv. coraggiosamente.
gallantry, n. coràggio m.
gall bladder, n. vescica del fièle m.
gall bladder attack, n. travaso di bile m.
galleon, n. galeone m.

gallery, n. galleria f.; (top g., theater) loggione m.
galley, n. (ship) galèa f.; (kitchen) cucina f.; (typogr.) colonna f.
galley proof, n. bòzze in colonna f.pl.
Gallic, adj. gàllico.
gallivant, vb. vagare.
gallon, n. gallone m.
gallop, 1. n. galòppo m. 2. vb. galoppare.
gallows, n. forca f.
gallstone, n. càlcolo biliare m.
galore, adv. a bizzèffe.
galosh, n. galòscia f.
galvanize, vb. galvanizzare.
gamble, vb. giocare d'azzardo.
gambler, n. giocatore d'azzardo m.
gambling, n. gиòco d'azzardo m.
gambol, 1. n. salto m. 2. vb. saltare.
game, 1. n. gioco m.; (sports encounter) partita f.; (hunting) selvaggina f. 2. adj. coraggioso.
gamely, adv. coraggiosamente.
gameness, n. coràggio m.
gamin, n. monèllo m.
gamut, n. gamma f.
gamy, adj. alquanto putrefatto.
gander, n. pàpero m.
gang, n. gruppo m., squadra f.
gangling, adj. smilzo.
gangplank, n. pontile m.

gangrene, n. cancrena f.
gangrenous, adj. cancrenoso.
gangster, n. gangster m.
gangway, n. passerèlla f.
gap, n. apertura f.
gape, vb. spalancare la bocca.
garage, n. autorimessa f.
garb, n. costume m.
garbage, n. rifiuti f.pl.
garble, vb. ingarbugliare.
garden, n. giardino m.
gardener, n. giardinière m.
gardenia, n. gardènia f.
gargle, 1. n. gargarismo m. **2.** vb. gargarizzare.
gargoyle, n. grondàia a forma di testa grottesca f.
garish, adj. sgargiante.
garland, n. ghirlanda f.
garlic, n. àglio m.
garment, n. vestito m.
garner, vb. cògliere.
garnet, n. granato m.
garnish, vb. guarnire.
garnishee, vb. méttere il fermo su.
garnishment, n. guarnizione f.
garret, n. soffitta f.
garrison, n. guarnigione f.
garrote, n. garrota f.
garrulous, adj. gàrrulo.
garter, n. giarrettièra f.
gas, n. gas m.; (gasoline) benzina f.
gaseous, adj. gassoso.
gash, 1. n. squàrcio m. **2.** vb. squarciare.
gasket, n. guarnizione f.
gasless, adj. sènza gas, sènza benzina.
gas mask, n. màschera antigas f.
gas meter, n. contatore del gas m.
gasohol, n. benzina ricavata da prodotti alcòlici f.
gasoline, n. benzina f.
gasoline dealer, n. benzinàio m.
gasp, 1. n. boccheggiamento m. **2.** vb. boccheggiare.
gas stove, n. cucina a gas f.
gassy, adj. gassoso.
gastric, adj. gàstrico.
gastric juice, n. succo gàstrico m.
gastritis, n. gastrite f.
gastronomical, adj. gastronòmico.
gastronomy, n. gastronomía f.

gate, n. (city) pòrta f.; (apartment house) portone m.; (fence) cancèllo m.; (airport) uscita f.
gatekeeper, n. portiere m.; guardiano m.
gateway, n. pòrta m., entrata f.
gather, vb. raccògliere, radunare; (infer) desùmere.
gathering, n. adunata f., assemblèa f.
gaudily, adv. vistosamente.
gaudiness, n. vistosità f.
gaudy, adj. vistoso.
gauge, n. apparécchio misuratore m.; (track) scartamento m.; (loading g.) sàgoma f. **2.** vb. misurare, stimare.
gaunt, adj. magro.
gauntlet, n. guanto m.
gauze, n. garza f.
gavel, n. martellino m.
gavotte, n. gavòtta f.
gawk, vb. guardare fissamente.
gawky, adj. goffo.
gay, 1. adj. gaio; (homosexual) omosessuale. **2.** n. finòcchio m.
gaze, vb. guardare.
gazelle, n. gazzèlla f.
gazette, n. gazzetta f.
gazetteer, n. dizionàrio geogràfico m.
gear, n. ingranàggio m.; (harness) finimenti m.pl.; (g. lever) lèva del cambio f.
gear box, n. scàtola del cambio màrcia m.
gearing, n. ingranàggio m.
gearshift, n. càmbio di velocità m.
gelatine, n. gelatina f.
gelatinous, adj. gelatinoso.
geld, vb. castrare.
gelding, n. castrato m.
gem, n. gèmma f.
gender, n. gènere m.
gene, n. gène m.
genealogical, adj. genealògico.
genealogy, n. genealogía f.
general, n. and adj. generale (m.)
generality, n. generalità f.
generalization, n. generalizzazione f.
generalize, vb. generalizzare.
generally, adv. generalmente.

generalship, n. qualità da generale f.pl.

general staff, n. stato maggiore m.

generate, vb. generare.

generation, n. generazione f.

generator, n. generatore m.

generic, adj. genèrico.

generosity, n. generosità f.

generous, adj. generoso.

generously, adv. generosamente.

genesis, n. gènesi f.

genetic, adj. genètico.

genetics, n. genètica f.

Geneva, n. Ginèvra f.

Genevan, adj. ginevrino.

genial, adj. piacévole, cordiale.

geniality, n. piacevolezza f., cordialità f.

genially, adv. piacevolmente, cordialmente.

genital, adj. genitale.

genitals, n. genitali m.pl.

genitive, n. and adj. genitivo (m.)

genius, n. gènio m.

Genoa, n. Gènova f.

Genoese, adj. genovese.

genocide, n. genocidio m.

genre, n. gènere m.

genteel, adj. eccessivamente raffinato.

gentian, n. genziana f.

gentile, n. and adj. gentile (m.); non israelítico.

gentility, n. raffinatezza eccessiva f.

gentle, adj. mite.

gentleman, n. signore m., gentiluòmo m.

gentlemanly, adj. da gentiluòmo.

gentlemen's agreement, n. impegno d'onore m.

gentleness, n. mitezza f.

gently, adv. mitemente, adagio.

gentry, n. piccola nobiltà f.; (ironical) gènte f.

genuflect, vb. genuflèttersi.

genuine, adj. genuíno.

genuinely, adv. genuinamente.

genuineness, n. genuinità f.

genus, n. gènere m.

geographer, n. geògrafo m.

geographical, adj. geogràfico.

geography, n. geografia f.

geometric, adj. geomètrico.

geometry, n. geometría f.

geopolitics, n. geopolítica f.

geranium, n. gerànio m.

geriatrics, n. geriatría f.

germ, n. gèrme m.

German, n. and adj. tedesco (m.)

germane, adj. rilevante.

Germanic, adj. germànico.

German measles, n. rosolía f.

Germany, n. Germània f.

germicidal, adj. germicida.

germicide, n. germicida m.

germinal, adj. germinale.

germinate, vb. germinare.

germ warfare, n. guerra batteriològica f.

gerontology, n. gerontologia f.

gerund, n. gerùndio m.

gestate, vb. portare nell'ùtero m.

gestation, n. gestazione f.

gesticulate, vb. gesticolare.

gesticulation, n. gesticolazione f.

gesture, n. gèsto m.

get, vb. (obtain) ottenere; (receive) ricévere; (take) prénder e; (become) divenire, diventare; (arrive) arrivare; (g. in) entrare; (g. off) scéndere; (g. on, agree) intèndersi; (g. on, go up) montare; (g. out) uscire; (g. up) alzarsi.

getaway, n. fuga f.

get-together, n. riunione f.

geyser, n. geyser m.

ghastly, adj. orrèndo.

ghetto, n. ghetto m.

ghost, n. spèttro m., larva f.

ghost writer, n. collaboratore anònimo m.

giant, n. and adj. gigante (m.)

gibberish, n. borbottamento m.

gibbon, n. gibbone m.

gibe at, vb. beffarsi di.

giblets, n. rigàglie f.pl.

giddiness, n. vertigine f.

giddy, adj. stordito.

gift, n. dono m.

gifted, adj. dotato.

gigantic, adj. gigantesco.

giggle, vb. ridere scioccamente.

gigolo, n. cicisbèo m.

gild, vb. dorare, indorare.

gill, n. brànchia f.

gilt, 1. n. doratura f. 2. adj. dorato.

gilt-edged, adj. sicuro.

gimcrack, n. cianfrusàglia f.

gimlet, *n.* succhièllo *m.*

gin, *n.* gin *m.*

ginger, *n.* zènzero *m.*

gingerly, *adj.* càuto.

gingham, *n.* ghingano *m.*

giraffe, *n.* giraffa *f.*

gird, *vb.* cíngere, *tr.*

girder, *n.* trave *f.*

girdle, *n.* cintura *f.*

girl, *n.* ragazza *f.*, fanciulla *f.*

girlish, *adj.* da ragazza.

girth, *n.* circonferènza *f.*

gist, *n.* contenuto essenziale *m.*

give, *vb.* dare; **(g. back)** rèndere; **(g. in)** cédere; **(g. out)** distribuire; **(g. up)** rinunziare a.

give-and-take, *n.* scàmbio *m.*

given name, *n.* nome di battésimo *m.*

giver, *n.* datore *m.*, donatore *m.*

gizzard, *n.* ventríglio *m.*

glacé, *adj.* lùcido.

glacial, *adj.* glaciale.

glacier, *n.* ghiacciaio *m.*

glad, *adj.* contènto, lièto.

gladden, *vb.* allietare.

glade, *n.* radura *f.*

gladiolus, *n.* gladiòlo *m.*

gladly, *adv.* lietamente, con piacere.

gladness, *n.* contentezza *f.*

glamor, *n.* fàscino *m.*

glamorous, *adj.* affascinante.

glance, *n.* sguardo *m.*, occhiata *f.*

gland, *n.* ghiàndola *f.*

glandular, *adj.* ghiandolare.

glare, *n.* bagliore *m.*

glaring, *adj.* abbagliante.

glass, *n.* vetro *m.*; **(drinking-g.)** bicchière *m.*

glass-blowing, *n.* soffiatura del vetro *f.*

glasses, *n.* occhiali *m.*

glassful, *n.* bicchière *m.*

glassware, *n.* cristallerie *f.pl.*

glassy, *adj.* vetroso, vítreo.

glaucoma, *n.* glaucòma *f.*

glaze, 1. *n.* (enamel) smalto *m.;* (varnish) vernice *f.* **2.** *vb.* smaltare, verniciare.

glazier, *n.* vetràio *m.*

gleam, *n.* barlume *m.*

glee, *n.* giòia *f.*

glee club, *n.* còro maschile *m.*

gleeful, *adj.* gioioso.

glen, *n.* valletta *f.*

glib, *adj.* fluènte.

glide, *vb.* scivolare.

glider, *n.* aliante *m.*

glimmer, 1. *n.* barlume *m.* **2.** *vb.* mandare una luce incèrta.

glimmering, 1. *n.* barlume *m.* **2.** *adj.* incèrto.

glimpse, *vb.* intravedere.

glint, *n.* riflèsso *m.*

glisten, *vb.* scintillare.

glitter, 1. *n.* scintillío *m.* **2.** *vb.* scintillare, rispléndere.

gloaming, *n.* crepuscolo *m.*

gloat, *vb.* gioire.

global, *adj.* globale.

globe, *n.* glòbo *m.*

globe-trotter, *n.* giramondo *m.*

globular, *adj.* globulare.

globule, *n.* glòbulo *m.*

glockenspiel, *n.* campanette *f.pl.*

gloom, *n.* (darkness) oscurità *f.;* (sadness) tristezza *f.*

gloomy, *adj.* oscuro, triste.

glorification, *n.* glorificazione *f.*

glorify, *vb.* glorificare.

glorious, *adj.* glorioso.

glory, 1. *n.* glòria *f.* **2.** *vb.* gloriarsi.

gloss, 1. *n.* lucidità *f.;* (explanation) chiòsa *f.* **2.** *vb.* lucidare; chiosare.

glossary, *n.* glossàrio *f.*

glossy, *adj.* lùcido.

glottis, *n.* glòttide *f.*

glove, *n.* guanto *m.*

glow, 1. *n.* incandescènza *f.* **2.** *vb.* èssere incandescènte.

glowing, *adj.* incandescènte.

glowworm, *n.* lùcciola *f.*

glucose, *n.* glucòsio *m.*

glue, 1. *n.* còlla *f.* **2.** *vb.* incollare.

gluey, *adj.* appiccicaticcio, attaccaticcio.

glum, *adj.* (frowning) acciigliato; (sad) triste.

glumness, *n.* tristezza *f.*

glut, *n.* saturazione *f.*

glutinous, *adj.* glutinoso.

glutton, *n.* ghiottone *m.*

gluttonous, *adj.* ghiotto.

glycerine, *n.* glicerina *f.*

gnarl, *n.* nodo *m.*

gnash, *vb.* digrignare.

gnat, *n.* moscerino *m.*

gnaw, *vb.* ródere.

gnome, n. gnomo m.

go, vb. andare; (become) diventare; **(g. away)** andàrsene; **(g. back)** tornare; **(g. by)** passare; **(g. down)** scèndere; **(g. in)** entrare; **(g. on)** continuare; **(g. out)** uscire; **(g. up)** salire; **(g. without)** fare a meno di.

goad, 1. n. pùngolo m., stímolo m. 2. vb. stimolare.

goal, n. mèta f.; (soccer) pòrta f.

goalie, n. portiere m.

goal-keeper, n. portière m.

goat, n. capra f.

goatee, n. barbetta f.

goatherd, n. capraio m.

goatskin, n. pèlle di capra f.

gob, n. massa informe f.

gobble, vb. ingollare.

gobbler, n. tacchino m.

go-between, n. intermediàrio m.

goblet, n. coppa f.

goblin, n. folletto m.

go-cart, n. carrettino m.

god, n. dio m., iddío m.

godchild, n. figliòccio m.

goddess, n. dèa f.

godfather, n. padrino m., compare m.

God-fearing, adj. timorato di Dio.

Godforsaken, adj. miseràbile.

godless, adj. àteo; (impious) émpio.

godlike, adj. divino.

godly, adj. devòto, pío.

godmother, n. madrina f., comare f.

godsend, n. dòno del cièlo m.

Godspeed, n. buona sorte f.

go-getter, n. arrivista m.

goiter, n. gozzo m.

gold, n. òro m.

golden, adj. d'òro, àureo.

gold-filled, adj. (tooth) otturato d'òro.

goldfinch, n. cardellino m.

goldfish, n. pesce rosso m.

goldilocks, n. bionda f.

goldleaf, n. fòglia d'òro f.

goldsmith, n. oréfice m.

gold-plate, vb. dorare.

gold standard, n. parità àurea f.

golf, n. golf m.

gondola, n. góndola f.

gondolier, n. gondolière m.

gone, adj. (vanished) sparito; (departed) partito.

gong, n. gong m.

gonorrhea, n. gonorrèa f.

good, 1. n. bène m.; (g.s) mèrci f.pl. 2. adj. buòno.

good-by, n. and interj. addío (m.)

Good Friday, n. venerdí santo m.

good-hearted, adj. di buòn cuòre.

good-humored, adj. di buòn umore.

good-looking, adj. bellino.

good-natured, adj. di buòn temperamento.

goodness, n. bontà f.

good will, n. buona volontà f.

goose, n. òca f., pàpera f.

gooseberry, n. ribes m.

gooseneck, n. collo di cigna m.

goose step, n. passo d'òca m.

gore, n. sangue m.

gorge, n. gola f.

gorgeous, adj. splèndido.

gorilla, n. gorilla m.

gory, adj. insanguinato.

gosling, n. paperetto m.

gospel, n. vangèlo m.

gossamer, n. garza sottile f.

gossip, 1. n. (talk) diceria f., pettegolezzo m.; (person) pettégolo m., pettégola f. 2. vb. pettegolare.

gossipy, adj. pettégolo.

Gothic, adj. gòtico.

gouge, n. sgòrbia f.

gourd, n. zucca f.

gourmand, n. ghiottone m.

gourmet, n. buongustaio m.

govern, vb. governare.

governess, n. governante f.

government, vb. govèrno m.

governmental, adj. governativo.

governor, n. governatore m.

governorship, n. governatorato m.

gown, n. gonnèlla f.

grab, vb. arraffare, carpire.

grace, n. gràzia f.

graceful, adj. grazioso.

gracefully, adv. graziosamente.

graceless, *adj.* sgraziato.
grace note, *n.* *(music)* appoggiatura *f.*
gracious, *adj.* grazioso.
grackel, *n.* gràcchio *m.*
grade, 1. *n.* grado *m.;* (quality) qualità *f.;* (mark) voto *m.* **2.** *vb.* classificare.
grade crossing, *n.* passàggio a livèllo *m.*
gradual *adj.* graduale.
gradually, *adv.* gradualmente.
graduate, *vb.* graduare; (university) laurearsi.
graduate school, *n.* scuòla di studi superiori *f.*
graft, 1. *n.* innèsto *m.;* (fraud) corruzione *f.* **2.** *vb.* innestare.
graham flour, *n.* farina integrale *f.*
grail, *n.* gradale *m.*
grain, *n.* grano *m.;* (single) chicco *m.*
grain alcohol, *n.* àlcol etilico *m.*
graining, *n.* ventura *f.*
gram, *n.* grammo *m.*
grammar, *n.* grammàtica *f.*
grammarian, *n.* grammàtico *m.*
grammar school, *n.* scuòla elementare *f.*
grammatical, *adj.* grammaticale.
gramophone, *n.* grammòfono *m.*
granary, *n.* granàio *m.*
grand, *adj.* grande, grandioso.
grandchild, *n.* nipote *m. or f.*
granddaughter, *n.* nipote *f.*
grandeur, *n.* grandezza *f.*
grandfather, *n.* nònno *m.*
grandiloquent, *adj.* magniloquente.
grandiose, *adj.* grandioso.
grandly, *adj.* grandiosamente.
grandmother, *n.* nònna *f.*
grandparents, *n.* nònni *m.pl.*
grandson, *n.* nipote *m.*
grandstand, *n.* tribuna *f.*
grange, *n.* fattoria *f.*
granger, *n.* fattore *m.*
granite, *n.* granito *m.*
granny, *n.* vècchia *f.*
grant, 1. *n.* concessione *f.;* (gift) dono *m.* **2.** *vb.* concèdere.
grantee, *n.* beneficiàrio *m.*

granular, *adj.* granulare.
granulate, *vb.* granulare.
granulation, *n.* granulazione *f.*
granule, *n.* granèllo *m.*
grape, *n.* uva *f.;* **(g. juice)** spremuta d'uva *f.*
grapefruit, *n.* pompèlmo *m.*
grapeshot, *n.* mitràglia *f.*
grapevine, *n.* vite *f.*
graph, *n.* gràfico *m.*
graphic, *adj.* gràfico, vívido.
graphite, *n.* grafite *f.*
graphology, *n.* grafología *f.*
grapple, 1. *n.* uncino *m.*, lotta *f.* **2.** *vb.* venire alle prese.
grasp, 1. *n.* presa *f.* **2.** *vb.* afferrare.
grasping, *adj.* avaro.
grass, *n.* èrba *f.;* (marijuana) marijuana *f.*
grasshopper, *n.* cavalletta *f.*
grassy, *adj.* erboso.
grate, 1. *n.* graticola *f.* **2.** *vb.* (cheese, etc.) grattugiare; (irritate) irritare.
grateful, *adj.* grato.
grater, *n.* grattùgia *f.*
gratify, *vb.* gratificare.
grating, *n.* inferriata *f.*
gratis, 1. *adj.* gratùito. **2.** *adv.* gratuitamente.
gratitude, *n.* gratitùdine *f.*
gratuitous, *adj.* gratùito.
gratuity, *n.* mància *f.*
grave, 1. *n.* tomba *f.* **2.** *adj.* grave.
gravel, *n.* ghiaia *f.*
gravely, *adj.* gravemente.
gravestone, *n.* piètra tombale *f.*
graveyard, *n.* camposanto *m.*
gravitate, *vb.* gravitare.
gravitation, *n.* gravitazione *f.*
gravity, *n.* gravità *f.*
gravure, *n.* incisione *f.*
gravy, *n.* sugo di carne *m.*
gravy boat, *n.* salsiera *f.*
gray, *adj.* grígio.
gray-haired, *adj.* canuto.
grayhound, *n.* levriere *m.*
grayish, *adj.* grigiastro.
gray matter, *n.* cervèllo *m.*
graze, *vb.* pàscere.
grazing, *n.* pàscolo *m.*
grease, 1. *n.* grasso *m.* **2.** *vb.* ùngere, lubrificare.

greasy, *adj.* grasso; untuoso.
great, *adj.* grande.
greatness, *n.* grandezza *f.*
Greece, *n.* Grècia *f.*
greed, *n.* cupidígia *f.*
greediness, *n.* ghiottoneria *f.*
greedy, *adj.* ghiottone.
Greek, *adj.* grèco.
green, *adj.* verde.
greenery, *n.* verzura *f.*
greenhouse, *n.* sèrra *f.*
green thumb, *n.* pòllice verde *m.*
greet, *vb.* salutare.
greeting, *n.* saluto *m.*
greeting card, *n.* biglietto d'auguri *m.*
gregarious, *adj.* gregàrio.
grenade, *n.* granata *f.*
grenadine, *n.* granatina *f.*
greyhound, *n.* levrière *m.*
grid, *n.* graticola *f.;* (electric power) rete *f.*
griddle, *n.* graticola *f.*
gridiron, *n.* graticola *f.*
grief, *n.* dolore *m.*
grievance, *n.* lagnanza *f.*
grieve, *vb.* addolorare, *tr.*
grievous, *adj.* doloroso, grave.
griffin, *n.* grifo *m.,* grifone *f.*
grill, *n.* graticola *f.*
grillroom, *n.* rosticceria *f.*
grim, *adj.* fosco.
grimace, *n.* smòrfia *f.*
grime, *n.* sudiciume *m.*
grimy, *adj.* sùdicio.
grin, *n.* sorrìdere da un orécchio all'altro.
grind, *vb.* macinare.
grinder, *n.* macinino *m.*
grindstone, *n.* màcina *f.*
grip, 1. *n.* presa *f.;* (suitcase) valígia *f.* **2.** *vb.* afferrare.
gripe, 1. *n.* lagnanza *f.* **2.** *vb.* lagnarsi.
grippe, *n.* influènza *f.*
gripping, *adj.* molto intrigante, affascinante.
grisly, *adj.* orrìbile.
grist, *n.* grano da macinare *m.*
gristle, *n.* cartilàgine *f.*
grit, *n.* sàbbia *f.*
grizzled, *adj.* grígio.
groan, 1. *n.* gèmito *m.* **2.** *vb.* gèmere.

grocer, *n.* negoziante di gèneri alimentari *m.*
grocery, *n.* negòzio di gèneri alimentari *m.*
grog, *n.* gròg *m.*
groggy, *adj.* intontito.
groin, *n.* inguine *m.*
groom, *n.* palafrenière *m.;* (footman) staffière *m.;* (bridegroom) sposo *m.*
groove, *n.* solco *m.*
grope, *vb.* andare a tastoni.
gropingly, *adv.* a tastoni.
grosgrain, *n.* grana grossa *f.*
gross, *adj.* grossolano; (blunder) madornale; (weight) lordo.
grossly, *adv.* grossolanamente; (wholly) totalmente.
grossness, *n.* grossolanità *f.*
grotesque, *adj.* grottesco.
grotto, *n.* grotta *f.*
grouch, 1. *n.* (person) brontolone *m.* **2.** *vb.* brontolare.
ground, 1. *n.* tèrra *f.;* (reason) motivo *m.;* (basis) base *f.;* (electrical) presa a tèrra *f.* **2.** *vb.* basare.
ground hog, *n.* marmotta *f.*
groundless, *adj.* sènza base.
ground swell, *n.* mareggiata *f.*
groundwork, *n.* fondamento *m.*
group, 1. *n.* gruppo *m.* **2.** *vb.* raggruppare, *tr.*
groupie, *n.* membro di un gruppo di ragazze *m.*
grouse, *n.* gallo cedrone *m.*
grove, *n.* boschetto *m.*
grovel, *vb.* umiliarsi.
grow, *vb.* créscere; (raise) coltivare.
growl, 1. *n.* brontolio *m.* **2.** *vb.* brontolare.
grown, *adj.* maturo.
grown-up, *n.* and *adj.* adulto *(m.)*
growth, *n.* créscita *f.,* sviluppo *m.*
grub, 1. *n.* larva *f.;* (food) cibo *m.* **2.** *vb.* scavare.
grubby, *adj.* sporco.
grudge, *n.* àstio *m.*
grudgingly, *adv.* controvoglia.
gruel, *n.* pappa *f.*
gruesome, *adj.* orrèndo.
gruff, *adj.* bùrbero.
grumble, *vb.* brontolare.
grumpy, *adj.* scontènto.

grunt, 1. *n.* grugnito *m.* **2.** *vb.* grugnire.

guarantee, 1. *n.* garanzía *f.* **2.** *vb.* garantire.

guarantor, *n.* mallevadore *m.*

guaranty, *n.* garanzía *f.*

guard, 1. *n.* guàrdia *f.* **2.** *vb.* custodire, guardarsi.

guarded, *adj.* guardingo.

guardhouse, *n.* guardina *f.*

guardian, *n.* guardiano *m.;* (legal) tutore *m.*

guardian angel, *n.* àngelo custode *m.*

guardianship, *n.* tutèla *f.*

guardrail, *n.* parapetto *m.*

guardsman, *n.* guàrdia *f.*

gubernatorial, *adj.* gubernatoriale.

guerilla, *n.* (war) guerríglia *f.;* (fighter) guerriglière *m.*

guess, *vb.* indovinare.

guesswork, *n.* congettura *f.*

guest, *n.* òspite *m.;* (hotel, etc.) cliènte *m.*

guffaw, 1. *n.* sghignazzata *f.* **2.** *vb.* sghignazzare.

guidance, *n.* guida *f.*

guide, 1. *n.* guida *f.* **2.** *vb.* guidare.

guidebook, *n.* guida *f.*

guide dog, *n.* caneguida per ciechi *m.*

guideline, *n.* direttiva *f.;* línea di condotta *f.;* línea.

guidepost, *n.* palo indicatore *m.*

guild, *n.* arte *f.,* corporazione *f.*

guile, *n.* astùzia *f.*

guileful, *adj.* astuto.

guileless, *adj.* sincero.

guillotine, *n.* ghigliottina *f.*

guilt, *n.* colpa *f.*

guiltily, *adv.* colpevolmente.

guiltless, *adj.* sènza colpa.

guilty, *adj.* colpévole.

guinea fowl, *n.* faraona *f.*

guinea pig, *n.* porcellino d'India *m.*

guise, *n.* apparènza *f.;* (shape) fòggia *f.*

guitar, *n.* chitarra *f.*

guitarist, *n.* chitarrista *m.*

gulch, *n.* burrone *m.*

gulf, *n.* golfo *m.*

gull, *n.* gabbiano *m.*

gullet, *n.* gola *f.*

gullible, *adj.* crèdulo.

gully, *n.* burrone *m.*

gulp, *vb.* inghiottire; **(g. down)** ingollare.

gum, *n.* gomma *f.;* **(chewing-g.)** gomma da masticare *f.*

gummy, *adj.* gommoso.

gun, *n.* pistola *f.;* fucile *m.;* (cannon) cannone *m.*

gunboat, *n.* cannonièra *f.*

guncotton, *n.* fulmicotone *m.*

gunman, *n.* bandito armato *m.*

gunner, *n.* artiglière *m.*

gunpowder, *n.* pólvere da sparo *m.*

gunshot, *n.* portata di un fucile *f.*

gunwale, *n.* parapètto *m.*

gurgle, 1. *n.* gorgoglio *m.* **2.** *vb.* gorgogliare.

guru, *n.* guru *m.*

gush, *vb.* sgorgare, zampillare.

gusher, *n.* sorgènte di petròlio *f.*

gushing, *adj.* zampillante, sgorgante.

gusset, *n.* gherone *m.*

gust, *n.* ràffica *f.;* (rain) scròscio *m.*

gustatory, *adj.* gustativo.

gusto, *n.* gusto *m.*

gusty, *adj.* tempestoso.

guts, *n.* intestino *m.,* minùgia *f.;* (courage) fégato *m.*

gutter, *n.* (street) cunetta *f.;* (house) grondaia *f.*

guttural, *adj.* gutturale.

guy, *n.* tízio *m.*

guzzle, *vb.* ingozzare.

gym, *n.* palèstra *f.*

gymnasium, *n.* palèstra *f.;* (school) ginnàsio *m.*

gymnast, *n.* ginnasta *m.*

gymnastic, *adj.* di ginnàstica.

gymnastics, *n.* ginnàstica *f.*

gynaecology, *n.* ginecología *f.*

gypsum, *n.* gesso *m.*

gypsy, *n.* zíngaro *m.,* zíngara *f.*

gyrate, *vb.* turbinare.

gyroscope, *n.* giroscòpio *m.*

haberdasher, *n*. merciàio *m*.
haberdashery, *n*. merceria *f*.
habiliments, *n*. vestimenta *f.pl*.
habit, *n*. abitùdine *f*.; (dress) àbito *m*.
habitable, *adj*. abitàbile.
habitat, *n*. ambiènte *f*.
habitation, *n*. abitazione *f*.
habitual, *adj*. abituale.
habituate, *vb*. abituare.
habitué, *n*. frequentatore *m*.
hack, 1. *n*. cavallo da dipòrto *m*. 2. *vb*. tagliare.
hackneyed, *adj*. banale.
hacksaw, *n*. sega per metalli *f*.
haft, *n*. mànico *m*.
hag, *n*. strega *f*.
haggard, *adj*. sparuto.
haggle, *vb*. mercanteggiare.
hag-ridden, *adj*. tormentato da streghe.
Hague, The, *n*. l'Aia *f*.
hail, 1. *n*. gràndine *f*. 2. *vb*. grandinare; (call to) salutare.
Hail Mary, *n*. avemaria *f*.
hailstone, *n*. chicco di gràndine *m*.
hailstorm, *n*. grandinata *f*.
hair, *n*. capelli *m.pl*., crine, *f*.; (single, on head) capello *m*.; (body, animals) pelo *m*.
hairbrush, *n*. spàzzola per capelli *f*.
haircut, *n*. tàglio di capelli *m*.
hairdo, *n*. pettinatura *f*., acconciatura *f*.
hairdresser, *n*. parrucchière *m*.
hair dryer, *n*. asciuga-capelli *m*., phon *m*.
hair dye, *n*. tintura per capelli *f*.
hairless, *adj*. pelato; calvo; rasato.
hairline, *n*. linea sottilissima *f*.
hairpin, *n*. forcina *f*.
hair-raising, *adj*. orrèndo.
hair remover, *n*. depilatore *m*.
hair restorer, *n*. rigeneratore del pelo *m*.
hair's-breadth, *n*. grossezza di un capello *f*.
hairsplitting, *adj*. pignolo.
hairspray, *n*. schiuma per capelli *f*.

hairy, *n*. peloso.
halcyon, *adj*. felice.
hale, *adj*. robusto.
half, 1. *n*. metà *f*. 2. *adj*. mèzzo. 3. *adv*. a metà.
half-and-half, *adv*. metà e metà.
halfback, *n*. secondo *m*.
half-baked, *adj*. immaturo, imperfètto.
half-breed, *n*. meticcio *m*.
half-brother, *n*. fratellastro *m*.
half-dollar, *n*. mèzzo dòllaro *m*.
half-hearted, *adj*. sènza entusiasmo.
half-mast, *adv*. a mezz'asta.
half-staff, **(at h.)**, *adv*. a mezz'asta.
halfway, *adv*. a mèzza via.
half-wit, *n*. imbecille *m*.
halibut, *n*. pianuzza *f*.
hall, *n*. sala *f*., àula *f*.; (hallway) vestibolo *m*., corridoio *m*.
hallmark, *n*. màrchio *m*.
hallow, *vb*. santificare.
Halloween, *n*. la véglia di Ognissanti *f*.
hallucination, *n*. allucinazione *f*.
hallway, *n*. vestibolo *m*., corridoio *m*.
halo, *n*. auréola *f*.
halt, 1. *n*. fermata *f*. 2. *vb*. fermare, *tr*. 3. *interj*. alt!
halter, *n*. cavezza *f*., capestro *m*.
halve, *vb*. dimezzare.
halyard, *n*. drizza *f*.
ham, *n*. prosciutto *m*.
Hamburg, *n*. Amburgo *m*.
hamlet, *n*. frazione *f*.; paesino *m*.
hammer, 1. *n*. martèllo *m*. 2. *vb*. martellare.
hammock, *n*. amaca *f*.
hamper, 1. *n*. cesta *f*. 2. *vb*. impedire.
hamster, *n*. criceto *m*.
hamstring, *vb*. ostacolare.
hand, *n*. mano *f*.
handbag, *n*. (lady's) borsetta *f*.; (suitcase) valigetta *f*.
hand baggage, *n*. bagaglio a mano *m*.
handbook, *n*. manuale *m*.
handcuffs, *n*. manette *f.pl*.

handful, n. manciata f.
handicap, n. svantàggio m.
handicraft, n. lavoro manuale f.
handiwork, n. òpera f.
handkerchief, n. fazzoletto m.
handle, 1. n. mànico m., maníglia f., manovèlla f. **2.** vb. maneggiare.
handle bar, n. manùbrio m.
hand-made, adj. fatto a mano.
handmaid, n. ancella f.
handorgan, n. organetto a mano-vèlla m.
handout, n. (alms) elemosina f.; sintesi di articolo f.
hand-pick, vb. scégliere con cura.
hand-rail, n. passomano m.
handsome, adj. bèllo.
hand-to-hand, adj. còrpo a còrpo.
handwriting, n. calligrafia f.
handy, adj. (person) dèstro; (thing) còmodo; (at hand) a por-tata di mano.
handy-man, n. factotum m.
hang, vb. pèndere; (execute) im-piccare.
hangar, n. angar m.
hangdog, adj. con una fàccia patibolare.
hanger, n. gàncio m.; (coat-h.) at-taccapanni m.
hanger-on, n. seguace m.
hang glider, n. deltaplano m.
hanging, n. (execution) impiccag-ione f.; (tapestry) tappezzería f.
hangman, n. impiccatore m.
hangnail, n. pipita f.
hangout, n. ritròvo m.
hang-over, n. stanghetta f.
hangup, n. difficoltà psicològica f.
hank, n. matassa f.
hanker, vb. bramare.
haphazard, adv. a casàccio.
hapless, adj. sfortunato.
happen, vb. (take place) accadere, succédere; (chance to be) trovarsi.
happening, n. avvenimento m.
happily, adv. felicemente.
happiness, n. felicità f.
happy, adj. felice.
happy-go-lucky, adj. spen-sierato.
harakiri, n. karakiri m.
harangue, 1. n. arringa f. **2.** vb. ar-ringare.

harass, vb. annoiare.
harbinger, n. precursore m.
harbor, n. (refuge) rifùgio m.; (port) pòrto m.
hard, 1. adj. duro; (difficult) diffic-ile. **2.** adv. fortemente, duramente.
hard-and-fast, adj. inflessíbile.
hard-bitten, adj. tenace.
hard-boiled, adj. sòdo.
hard cash, n. denaro contante m.
hard coal, n. antracite f.
harden, vb. indurire.
hard-fought, adj. accanito.
hard-headed, adj. pràtico.
hard-hearted, adj. di cuòre duro.
hardiness, n. robustezza f.
hard labor, n. lavori forzati m.pl.
hardly, adv. (with difficulty) sten-tatamente; (scarely) appena; **(h. ever)** quasi mai.
hardness, n. durezza f.
hard-of-hearing, adj. duro d'o-recchi.
hardship, n. avversità f.
hardware, n. ferramenta f.pl.
hard-won, adj. conquistato con fatica.
hardwood, n. legno duro m.
hardy, adj. robusto.
hare, n. lèpre f.
hare-brained, adj. scervellato.
hare-lip, n. labbro leporino m.
harem, n. àrem m.
hark, vb. ascoltare.
Harlequin, n. Arlecchino m.
harlot, n. meretrice f.
harm, 1. n. danno m. **2.** vb. dan-neggiare, nuòcere.
harmful, adj. dannoso, nocivo.
harmless, adj. innòcuo, in-nocènte.
harmonic, adj. armònico.
harmonica, n. armònica f.
harmonious, adj. armonioso.
harmonize, vb. armonizzare.
harmony, n. armonía f.
harness, 1. n. bardatura f. **2.** vb. bardare.
harp, n. arpa f.
harpoon, 1. n. fiòcina f. **2.** vb. fi-ocinare.
harpsichord, n. clavicémbalo m.
harridan, n. vecchiàccia f.
harrow, 1. n. èrpice m. **2.** vb. er-picare.

harry, vb. spogliare.

harsh, adj. aspro.

harshness, n. asprezza f.

harvest, 1. n. raccòlta f. **2.** vb. raccògliere.

hash, n. guazzabùglio m.

hashish, n. hascisc m.

hasn't, vb. non à.

hassle, vb. seccare n., seccatura f.

hassock, n. cuscino m.

haste, 1. n. fretta m. **2.** vb. affrettarsi.

hasten, vb. affrettare tr.

hastily, adv. affrettatamente, frettolosamente.

hasty, adj. affrettato, frettoloso.

hat, n. cappèllo m.

hatch, 1. n. (boat) boccapòrto m. **2.** vb. (hen) covare; (egg) schiudersi; aprirsi.

hatchery, n. vivaio m.

hatchet, n. accetta f.

hate, 1. n. òdio m. **2.** vb. odiare.

hateful, adj. odioso.

hatred, n. òdio m.

haughtiness, n. supèrbia f.

haughty, adj. supèrbo.

haul, vb. trascinare, trasportare.

haunch, n. anca f.

haunt, vb. frequentare.

have, vb. avere; **(h. to,** necessity) dovere.

haven, n. pòrto m.; (refuge) rifùgio m.

haven't, vb. non ho, etc.

havoc, n. devastazione f.

hawk, n. falco m.

hawker, n. venditore ambulante m.

hawser, n. alzaia f., gòmena f.

hawthorn, n. biancospino m.

hay, n. fièno m.

hay fever, n. asma del fièno m.

hayfield, n. campo da fièno m.

hayloft, n. fienile m.

haystack, n. covone m.

hazard, 1. n. rischio m. **2.** vb. rischiare.

hazardous, adj. rischioso.

haze, n. nébbia f.

hazel, n. (plant) nocciòlo m.; (nut) nocciòla f.

hazy, adj. nebbioso, vago.

he, pron. egli, lùi.

head, n. tèsta f., capo m.

headache, n. mal di tèsta m.

headband, n. bènda f., diadèma m.

headfirst, adv. colla tèsta in avanti; di testa.

headgear, n. acconciatura del capo f.

head-hunting, n. càccia alle tèste f.

heading, n. titolo m.

headland, n. promontòrio m.

headless, adj. acefalo; senza testa.

headlight, n. fanale anteriore m.

headline, n. titolo m.

headlong, adv. a capofitto.

head-man, n. capo m.

headmaster, n. direttore m.

head-on, adj. frontale.

headquarters, n. quartière generale m.

headset, n. cùffia f.

headstone, n. piètra tombale f.

headstrong, adj. ostinato, testardo.

headwaters, n. sorgènti f.pl.

headway, n. progrèsso m.; (trains, etc.) intervallo m.

head-work, n. lavoro intellettuale m.

heady, adj. impetuoso, inebriante.

heal, vb. guarire, risanare.

healer, n. guaritore m.

health, n. salute f.; (skoal) brindisi m.

healthful, adj. salubre.

health insurance, n. assicurazione malattia f.

healthy, adj. sano.

heap, 1. n. mùcchio m. **2.** vb. ammucchiare.

hear, vb. sentire, udire.

hearer, n. ascoltatore m.

hearing, n. (sense) udito m.; (audience) udiènza f.

hearken to, vb. ascoltare.

hearsay, n. (by h.) per sentito dire.

hearse, n. carro fùnebre m.

heart, n. cuòre m.

heartache, n. angòscia f.

heart attack, n. attacco cardiaco, m., infarto m.

heart-break, n. crepacuòre m.

heartbreaker, n. rubacuori m.

heartbroken, *adj.* straziato.
heartburn, *n.* bruciore di stòmaco *m.*
hearten, *vb.* rincuorare.
heartfelt, *adj.* sincèro.
hearth, *n.* focolare *m.*
heartily, *adv.* di cuore.
heartless, *adj.* sènza cuòre.
heart-rending, *adj.* straziante.
heart-sick, *adj.* scoraggiato.
heart-stricken, *adj.* colpito al cuòre.
heart-to-heart, *adj.* íntimo.
hearty, *adj.* cordiale.
heat, 1. *n.* calore *m.,* caldo *m.* **2.** *vb.* riscaldare.
heated, *adj.* (dwelling-place) riscaldato; (discussion) infiammato.
heater, *n.* calorífero *m.*
heath, *n.* brughièra *f.*
heathen, *n. and adj.* pagano *(m.)*
heather, *n.* èrica *f.*
heating, *n.* riscaldamento *m.*
heat-stroke, *n.* colpo di calore *m.*
heat wave, *n.* ondata di caldo *f.*
heave, *vb.* sollevare; (utter) eméttere.
heaven, *n.* cièlo *m.*
heavenly, *adj.* celèste.
heavy, *adj.* pesante.
heavyweight, *n. and adj.* peso màssimo *(m.)*
Hebrew, *n. and adj.* ebrèo *(m.);* ebràico *(m.)*
heckle, *vb.* fare domande imbarazzanti.
hectare, *n.* èttaro *m.*
hectic, *adj.* febbrile.
hectogram, *n.* ètto *m.,* ettogramma *m.*
hedge, *n.* sièpe *f.*
hedgehog, *n.* ríccio *m.*
hedge-hop, *vb.* volare rasentando la tèrra.
hedgerow, *n.* sièpe di cespùgli o di àlberi.
hedonism, *n.* edonismo *m.*
heed, *vb.* badare a, prestare attenzione a.
heedless, *adj.* spensierato.
heel, *n.* calcagno *m.,* tallone *m.;* (shoes) tacco *m.*
hefty, *adj.* pesante, vigoroso.
hegemony, *n.* egemonía *f.*
heifer, *n.* giovènca *f.*

height, *n.* altezza *f.;* (high place) altura *f.*
heighten, *vb.* (raise) innalzare; (increase) accréscere.
heinous, *adj.* atroce.
heir, *n.* erède *m.*
heir apparent, *n.* erède legíttimo *m.*
heirloom, *n.* oggètto antico di famíglia *m.*
heir presumptive, *n.* presunto erède *m.*
helicopter, *n.* elicòttero *m.*
heliocentric, *adj.* eliocèntrico.
heliograph, *n.* eliògrafo *m.*
heliotrope, *n.* eliotròpio *m.*
helium, *n.* èlio *m.*
hell, *n.* infèrno *m.*
Hellenic, *adj.* ellènico.
Hellenism, *n.* ellenismo *m.*
hellish, *adj.* infernale.
hello, *interj.* buòn giorno, buòna sera; (telephone) pronto.
helm, *n.* timone *m.*
helmet, *n.* èlmo *m.*
helmsman, *n.* timonière *m.*
help, 1. *n.* aiuto *m.* **2.** *vb.* aiutare; (at table) servire.
helper, *n.* aiutante *m.*
helpful, *adj.* (person) serviziévole; (thing) útile.
helpfulness, *n.* utilità *f.*
helping, *n.* porzione *f.*
helpless, *adj.* impotènte.
helter-skelter, *adv.* a casàccio.
hem, 1. *n.* orlo *m.* **2.** *vb.* orlare.
hematite, *n.* ematite *f.*
hemisphere, *n.* emisfèro *m.*
hemline, *n.* orlo della gonna *m.*
hemlock, *n.* cicuta *f.*
hemoglobin, *n.* emoglobina *f.*
hemophilia, *n.* emofilía *f.*
hemorrhage, *n.* emorragía *f.*
hemorrhoid, *n.* emorròide *f.*
hemp, *n.* cànapa *f.*
hemstitch, *n.* orlo a giorno *m.*
hen, *n.* gallina *f.*
hence, *adv.* (time, place) di qui; (therefore) quindi.
henceforth, *adv.* d'ora in pòi.
henchman, *n.* bravo *m.*
henhouse, *n.* pollàio *m.*
henna, *n.* enné *m.*
henpecked, *adj.* dominato dalla móglie.

hepatic, *adj.* epàtico.
hepatica, *n.* epàtica *f.*
her, 1. *adj.* suo, di lèi. **2.** *pron.* (direct) la; (indirect) le; (alone, stressed, or with prep.) lèi.
herald, *n.* araldo *m.*
heraldic, *adj.* aràldico.
heraldry, *n.* aràldica *f.*
herb, *n.* èrba *f.*
herbaceous, *adj.* erbàceo.
herbarium, *n.* erbàrio *m.*
herculean, *adj.* ercùleo.
herd, *n.* gregge *m.*; màndria *f.*
here, *adv.* qui; **(h. is)** ècco.
hereabout, *adv.* qui vicino.
hereafter, *adv.* d'ora in pòi.
hereby, *adv.* con questo.
hereditary, *adj.* ereditàrio.
heredity, *n.* eredità *f.*
herein, *adv.* qui dentro.
hereof, *adv.* di questo.
hereon, *adv.* in questo; su questo.
heresy, *n.* eresìa *f.*
heretic, *n.* erètico *m.*
heretical, *adj.* erètico.
hereto, *adv.* a questo.
heretofore, *adv.* finora.
herewith, *adv.* con questo.
heritage, *n.* eredità *f.*
hermetic, *adj.* ermètico.
hermit, *n.* eremita *m.*
hermitage, *n.* eremitàggio *m.*, romitàggio *m.*
hernia, *n.* èrnia *f.*
hero, *n.* eròe *m.*
heroic, *adj.* eròico.
heroically, *adv.* eroicamente.
heroin, *n.* eroìna *f.*
heroine, *n.* eroìna *f.*
heroism, *n.* eroìsmo *m.*
heron, *n.* airone *m.*
herpes, *n.* èrpete *m.*; herpes *f.*
herring, *n.* aringa *f.*
herringbone, *n.* lisca d'aringa *f.*
hers, *pron.* suo, di lèi.
herself, *pron.* sè stessa.
hertz, *n.* hertz *m.*
hesitancy, *n.* esitazione *f.*
hesitant, *adj.* esitante.
hesitate, *vb.* esitare.
hesitation, *n.* esitazione *f.*
heterodox, *adj.* eterodòsso.
heterodoxy, *n.* eterodossìa *f.*
heterogeneous, *adj.* eterogèneo.
heterosexual, *adj.* eterosessuale.

hew, *vb.* tagliare.
hex, *n.* strega *f.*
hexagon, *n.* esàgono *m.*
heyday, *n.* apogèo *m.*
hi!, interj. ciao.
hiatus, *n.* iato *m.*
hibernate, *vb.* svernare.
hibernation, *n.* ibernazione *f.*
hibiscus, *n.* ibìsco *m.*
hiccup, *n.* singulto *m.*
hick, *n.* rùstico.
hickory, *n.* noce americano *m.*
hidden, *adj.* nascosto.
hide, 1. *n.* pèlle *f.* **2.** *vb.* nascóndere *tr.*
hide-and-seek, *n.* nascondino *m.*
hideous, *adj.* spaventoso.
hide-out, *n.* nascondìglio *m.*
hiding place, *n.* nascondìglio *m.*
hierarchical, *adj.* geràrchico.
hierarchy, *n.* gerarchìa *f.*
hieroglyphic, *adj.* geroglìfico.
high, *adj.* alto, elevato; (in price) caro.
highbrow, *n. and adj.* intellettuale *(m. or f.)*
high fidelity, *n.* alta fedeltà *f.*
high-handed, *adj.* arbitràrio.
high-hat, *vb.* trattare dall'alto in basso.
highland, *n.* regione montuosa *f.*
highlight, *vb.* mèttere in rilièvo.
highly, *adv.* altamente, estremamente.
high-minded, *adj.* magnànimo.
Highness, *n.* Altezza *f.*
high noon, *n.* mezzogiorno in punto *m.*
high-pitched, *adj.* acuto; intenso.
high-rise, *n.* costruzione a molti piani *f.*
high school, *n.* lìceo *m.*, ginnàsio *m.*
high seas, *n.* alto mare *m. (sg.).*
high-spirited, *adj.* vivace.
high-strung, *adj.* eccitàbile.
high tide, *n.* alta marèa *f.*
high time, *n.* tempo *m.*; **(it is h.),** é ora.
highway, *n.* strada maestra *f.*; **(h. robber)** grassatore *m.*
hijacker, *n.* dirottatore *m.*
hike, 1. *n.* gita a pièdi *f.* **2.** *vb.* fare una gita a pièdi.
hilarious, *adj.* ìlare.

hilarity, *n.* ilarità *f.*
hill, *n.* collina *f.*
hillside, *n.* pendìo *m.*
hilltop, *n.* cima *f.*
hilly, *adj.* collinoso.
hilt, *n.* èlsa *f.*
him, *pron.* (direct) lo; (indirect) gli; (alone, stressed, or with prep.) lùi.
himself, *pron.* sè stesso; *(refl.)* si.
hind, 1. *n.* cèrva *f.*, dàina *f.* 2. *adj.* posteriore.
hinder, *vb.* impedire, ostacolare.
hindmost, *adj.* ultimo.
hindrance, *n.* impedimento *m.*, ostàcolo *m.*, intràlcio *m.*
hindsight, *n.* senno di poi *m.*
hinge, *n.* càrdine *m.*, gànghero *m.*
hint, 1. *n.* cenno *m.* 2. *vb.* accennare.
hinterland, *n.* retrotèrra *f.*
hip, *n.* anca *f.*, fianco *m.*
hippie, *n.* hippie *m.*, capellone *m.*
hippodrome, *n.* ippòdromo *m.*
hippopotamus, *n.* ippopòtamo *m.*
hire, 1. *n.* nòlo *m.* 2. *vb.* noleggiare.
hireling, *n.* mercenàrio *m.*
his, *adj. and pron.* suo, di lùi.
Hispanic, *adj.* ispànico.
hiss, 1. *n.* sìbilo *m.* 2. *vb.* sibilare.
historian, *n.* stòrico *m.*
historic, historical, *adj.* stòrico.
history, *n.* stòria *f.*
histrionic, *adj.* istriònico.
histrionics, *n.* istriònica *f.*
hit, 1. *n.* colpo *m.*; (success) succèsso *m.* 2. *vb.* colpire; percuòtere; picchiare.
hitch, 1. *n.* (obstacle) ostàcolo *m.* 2. *vb.* attaccare.
hitchhike, *vb.* fare l'autostòp.
hitchhiker, *n.* autostoppista *m. and f.*
hither, *adv.* qua.
hitherto, *adv.* finora.
hive, *n.* alveare *m.*
hives, *n.* eruzione cutànea *f.*
hoard, 1. *n.* ammasso *m.* 2. *vb.* ammassare.
hoarse, *adj.* fiòco, ràuco.
hoary, *adj.* canuto, incanutito.
hoax, 1. *n.* inganno *m.* 2. *vb.* ingannare.
hobble, *vb.* zoppicare.

hobby, *n.* passione *f.*
hobby-horse, *n.* cavallo a dòndolo *m.*
hobgoblin, *n.* folletto *m.*
hobnail, *n.* chiòdo gròsso *m.*
hobnob with, *vb.* frequentare.
hobo, *n.* vagabondo *m.*
hock, *vb.* impegnare.
hockey, *n.* hockey *m.*
hocus-pocus, *n.* inganno *m.*
hod, *n.* sècchia *f.*
hodge-podge, *n.* miscùglio *m.*
hoe, 1. *n.* zappa *f.* 2. *vb.* zappare.
hog, *n.* pòrco *m.*, maiale *m.*
hog-tie, *vb.* legare bene.
hogshead, *n.* botte *f.*
hoist, *vb.* innalzare.
hold, 1. *n.* presa *f.*; (boat) stiva *f.* 2. *vb.* tenere; (contain) contenere; **(h. up,** support) règgere.
holder, *n.* recipiènte *m.*; **(cigarette-h.)** portasigarette *f.*
holdup, *n.* grassazione *f.*
hole, *n.* buco *m.*
holiday, *n.* giorno festivo *m.*; vacanza *f.*, fèsta *f.*
holiness, *n.* santità *f.*
Holland, *n.* Olanda *f.*
hollow, *n. and adj.* cavo *(m.)*.
holly, *n.* agrifòglio *m.*
hollyhock, *n.* malvaròsa *f.*
holocaust, *n.* olocàusto *m.*
hologram, *n.* ologramma *m.*
holography, *n.* olografìa *f.*
holster, *n.* fondina *f.*
holy, *adj.* santo.
holy day, *n.* fèsta ecclesiàstica *f.*
Holy See, *n.* Santa Sede *f.*
Holy Spirit, *n.* Spírito Santo *m.*
Holy Week, *n.* settimana santa *f.*
homage, *n.* omàggio *m.*
home, 1. *n.* casa *f.* 2. *adj.* casalingo. 3. *adv.* a casa.
homeland, *n.* pàtria *f.*
homeless, *adj.* sènza tètto.
homelike, *adj.* casalingo.
homely, *adj.* brutto.
home-made, *adj.* fatto in casa.
home rule, *n.* autonomìa *f.*
homesick, be, *vb.* soffrire di nostalgìa.
homesickness, *n.* nostalgìa *f.*
home-spun, *adj.* filato in casa.
homestead, *n.* fattorìa *f.*

homestretch, n. diritture d'arrivo f.
hometown, n. città natale f.
homeward, adv. vèrso casa.
homework, n. còmpiti m.pl.
homey, adj. intimo, còmodo.
homicide, n. (act) omicídio m.; (person) omicida m.
homily, n. omelía f.
homing pigeon, n. piccione viaggiatore m.
hominy, n. semolino di granturco f.
homogeneity, n. omogeneità f.
homogeneous, adj. omogèneo.
homogenize, vb. omogenizzare.
homonym, n. omònimo m.
homonymous, adj. omònimo.
homosexual, adj. omosessuale.
hone, n. còte f.
honest, adj. onèsto.
honestly, adv. onestamente.
honesty, n. onestà f.
honey, n. mièle m.
honey-bee, n. ape da mièle f.
honeycomb, n. favo m.
honeyed, adj. mielato.
honeymoon, n. luna di mièle m.
honeysuckle, n. caprifòglio m.
honk, vb. (auto horn) suonare.
honor, 1. n. onore m. 2. vb. onorare.
honorable, adj. onorévole.
honorary, adj. onoràrio.
hood, n. cappùccio m.; (auto) còfano m.
hoodlum, n. teppista m.
hoodwink, vb. ingannare.
hoof, n. zòccolo m.
hook, 1. n. uncino m.; (fishh.) amo m. 2. vb. uncinare; (catch) prèndere all'amo.
hookworm, n. anchilòstoma m.
hoop, n. cérchio m.
hop, 1. n. (plant) lùppolo m.; (jump) salto m. 2. vb. saltare.
hope, 1. n. speranza f. 2. vb. sperare.
hopeful, adj. pieno di speranza.
hopeless, adj. disperato.
hopelessness, n. disperazione f.
horde, n. òrda f.
horehound, n. marrùbio m.
horizon, n. orizzonte m.
horizontal, adj. orizzontale.

hormone, n. ormone m.
horn, n. còrno m.; (auto) clàcson m.
hornet, n. calabrone m.
horny, adj. calloso.
horoscope, n. oròscopo m.
horrendous, adj. orrèndo.
horrible, adj. orríbile.
horrid, adj. òrrido.
horrify, vb. far inorridire; (be horrified) inorridire.
horror, n. orrore m.
horse, n. cavallo m.; (cavalry) cavallería f.
horseback, on, adv. a cavallo.
horsefly, n. mosca cavallina f.
horsehair, n. crine di cavallo f.
horseman, n. cavalière m.
horsemanship, n. equitazione f.
horseplay, n. giòco rozzo m.
horse-power, n. cavallovapore m.
horse-radish, n. ràfano m.
horseshoe, n. fèrro di cavallo m.
horsewhip, n. frustino m.
hortatory, adj. esortativo.
horticulture, n. orticultura f.
hose, n. (tube) tubo flessíbile m.; (stockings) calze f.pl.
hosiery, n. calzetteria f.
hospitable, adj. ospitale.
hospital, n. ospedale m.
hospitality, n. ospitalità f.
hospitalization, n. ospedalizzazione f.
hospitalize, vb. ospedalizzare.
host, n. (giver of hospitality) òspite m.; (innkeeper) òste m.; (crowd) moltitùdine f.; (Eucharist) òstia f.
hostage, n. ostàggio m.
hostel, n. albèrgo m.
hostelry, n. albèrgo m.
hostess, n. òspite f.; hostess f.
hostile, adj. ostile.
hostility, n. ostilità f.
hot, adj. caldo; (on water faucets) C.
hotbed, n. terreno concimato m.; (fig.) focolare m.
hot dog, n. salsiccia f.
hotel, n. albèrgo m.
hot-headed, adj. eccitàbile.
hothouse, n. sèrra f.
hound, n. cane m.
hour, n. ora f.

hourglass, n. clessidra f.
hourly, adv. ogni ora.
house, n. casa f.; (legislative) càmera f.
housefly, n. mosca f.
household, n. famíglia f.
housekeeper, n. massaia f.
housekeeping, n. economía domèstica f.
housemaid, n. domèstica f.
house painter, n. imbianchino m.
housewarming, n. festa di inaugurazione f.
housewife, n. massaia f.
housework, n. lavoro domèstico m.
housing, n. allòggio m.; **(h. office),** n. ufficio allocazione alloggi m.
hovel, n. tugùrio m.
hover, vb. volteggiare.
hovercraft, n. aliscafo m.
how, adv. come; **(h. far)** fin dove; **(h. long)** fino a quando; **(h. many, h. much)** quanti, quanto.
however, adv. comunque, però, tuttavía.
howitzer, n. òbice m.
howl, 1. n. urlo m. 2. vb. urlare.
howsoever, adv. comunque.
hub, n. mòzzo m.; (fig.) cèntro m.
hubbub, n. tumulto m.
huckleberry, n. mirtillo m.
huckster, n. trafficante m.
huddle, 1. n. consultazione f. 2. vb. rannicchiarsi; **(go into a h.)** tenere una consultazione.
hue, n. sfumatura f.
huff, n. petulanza f.
hug, 1. n. abbràccio m. 2. vb. abbracciare.
huge, adj. immane.
hulk, n. carcassa f.
hulking, adj. grosso e goffo.
hull, n. (boat) scafo m.; (fruit) bùccia f.
hullabaloo, n. chiasso m.
hum, 1. n. ronzío n 2. vb. (insect) ronzare; (sing) canticchiare.
human, adj. umano.
human being, n. essere umano m.
humane, adj. umanitàrio.
humanism, n. umanésimo m.
humanist, n. umanista m.
humanitarian, adj. umanitàrio.

humanity, n. umanità f.
humankind, n. gènere umano m.
humanly, adv. umanamente.
humble, 1. adj. ùmile. 2. vb. umiliare.
humbug, n. impostura f.
humdrum, adj. monòtono.
humid, adj. ùmido.
humidifier, n. umidificatore m.
humidify, vb. umidire.
humidity, n. umidità f.
humidor, n. scàtola per inumidire i sígari f.
humiliate, vb. umiliare.
humiliating, adj. umiliante.
humiliation, n. umiliazione f.
humility, n. umiltà f.
humor, n. umore m.; (wit) umorismo m.
humorist, n. umorista m.
humorous, adj. umorístico.
hump, n. gobba f.
humpback, n. gobbo m., gobba f.
humus, n. humus m.
hunch, 1. n. gobba f.; (suspicion) sospètto n. 2. vb. curvare, tr.
hunchback, n. gobbo m., gobba f.
hundred, num. cènto; (group of a hundred) centinaio n.m.
hundredth, adj. centésimo.
Hungarian, adj. ungherese.
Hungary, n. Ungheria f.
hunger, n. fame f.
hunger strike, n. sciòpero della fame m.
hungry, be, vb. aver fame.
hunk, n. pèzzo m.
hunt, 1. n. càccia f. 2. vb. cacciare; **(h. for)** cercare.
hunter, n. cacciatore m.
hunting, n. càccia f.
huntress, n. cacciatrice f.
hurdle, 1. n. (hedge) sièpe f.; (obstacle) ostàcolo m. 2. vb. saltare.
hurl, vb. lanciare, scagliare.
hurrah for, interj. viva, evviva (often written W).
hurricane, n. uragano m.
hurry, 1. n. fretta f. 2. vb. affrettare tr.
hurt, 1. n. danno m.; (wound) ferita f. 2. vb. far male a.
hurtful, adj. dannoso.
hurtle, vb. precipitarsi.
husband, n. marito m.

husbandry, n. amministrazione f.
hush, 1. vb. far tacere. **2.** interj. zitto!
husk, n. bùccia f.
husky, adj. (strong) fòrte; (hoarse) ràuco.
hustle, 1. n. fretta f. **2.** vb. (shove) spìngere; (hurry) affrettare, tr.
hut, n. casùpola f.
hutch, n. coniglièra f.
hyacinth, n. giacinto m.
hybrid, adj. ìbrido.
hydrangea, n. ortènsia f.
hydrant, n. idrante m.
hydraulic, adj. idràulico.
hydrochloric, adj. idroclòrico.
hydroelectric, adj. idroelèttrico.
hydrogen, n. idrògeno m.
hydrophobia, n. idrofobìa f.
hydroplane, n. idrovolante m.
hydrotherapy, n. idroterapèutica f.
hyena, n. ièna f.
hygiene, n. igiène f.
hygienic, adj. igiènico.
hymn, n. inno m.
hymnal, n. innàrio m.

hyperacidity, n. iperacidità f.
hyperbole, n. ipèrbole f.
hypercritical, adj. ipercrìtico.
hypersensitive, adj. ipersensitivo.
hypertension, n. ipertensione f.
hyphen, n. tratto d'unione m.
hyphenate, vb. scrìvere con tratto d'unione.
hypnosis, n. ipnòsi f.
hypnotic, adj. ipnòtico.
hypnotism, n. ipnotismo m.
hypnotize, vb. ipnotizzare.
hypochondria, n. ipocondrìa f.
hypochondriac, n. and adj. ipocondrìaco (m.)
hypocrisy, n. ipocrisìa f.
hypocrite, n. ipòcrita m.
hypocritical, adj. ipòcrito.
hypodermic, adj. ipodèrmico.
hypotenuse, n. ipotenusa f.
hypothesis, n. ipòtesi f.
hypothetical, adj. ipotètico.
hysterectomy, n. isterectomìa f.
hysteria, hysterics, n. isterismo m.
hysterical, adj. istèrico.

I

I, pron. io.
iambic, adj. giàmbico.
ice, n. ghiàccio m.
ice age, n. glaciazione f., era glaciale f.
ice-berg, n. borgognone m.
icebound, adj. intrappolato nel ghiaccio.
ice-box, n. ghiacciaia f.
icebreaker, n. rompighiaccio m.
ice-cream, n. gelato m.
ice-skate, n. pàttino m.
ichthyology, n. ittiologìa f.
icicle, n. ghiacciolo m.
icing, n. glassa f.
icon, n. icòne f.
icy, adj. gelato, ghiacciato.
idea, n. idèa f.
ideal, adj. ideale.
idealism, n. idealismo m.
idealist, n. idealista m.
idealistic, adj. idealìstico.
idealize, vb. idealizzare.
ideally, adv. idealmente.

identical, adj. idèntico.
identifiable, adj. identificàbile.
identification, n. identificazione f.
identify, vb. identificare.
identity, n. identità f.
ideology, n. ideologìa f.
idiocy, n. idiozìa f.
idiom, n. idiòma m.
idiomatic, adj. idiomàtico.
idiosyncrasy, n. idiosincrasìa f.
idiosyncratic, adj. idiosincràtico.
idiot, n. idiòta m.
idiotic, adj. idiòta.
idle, adj. ozioso.
idleness, n. òzio m.
idler, n. lazzarone m.
idol, n. ìdolo m.
idolator, n. idolatra m. or f.
idolatry, n. idolatrìa f.
idolize, vb. idolatrare.
idyl, n. idìllio m.
idyllic, adj. idilliaco.
if, conj. se; **(as if)** quasi, come se.

ignite, vb. accèndere.
ignition, n. accensione f.
ignition key, n. chiavetta d'accensione f.
ignoble, adj. ignòbile.
ignominious, adj. ignominioso.
ignoramus, n. ignorantone m.
ignorance, n. ignoranza f.
ignorant, adj. ignorante, ignaro.
ignore, vb. trascurare.
ill, adj. malato.
illegal, adj. illegale.
illegible, adj. illeggìbile.
illegibly, adv. illeggibilmente.
illegitimacy, n. illegittimità f.
illegitimate, adj. illegìttimo.
illicit, adj. illécito.
illiteracy, n. analfabetismo m.
illiterate, n. and adj. analfabèta (m. or f.)
illness, n. malattia f., malore m.
illogical, adj. illògico.
ill-omened, adj. infausto.
illuminate, vb. illuminare.
illumination, n. illuminazione f.
illusion, n. illusione f.
illusive, illusory, adj. illusòrio.
illustrate, vb. illustrare.
illustration, n. illustrazione f.
illustrative, adj. illustrativo.
illustrious, adj. illustre.
ill will, n. cattiva volontà f.
image, n. immàgine f.
imagery, n. figure retòriche f.pl.
imaginable, adj. immaginàbile.
imaginary, adj. immaginàrio.
imagination, n. fantasia f., immaginazione f.
imaginative, adj. immaginativo.
imagine, vb. immaginare, tr., figurarsi.
imam, n. imam m.
imbecile, n. and adj. imbecille (m. or f.)
imitate, vb. imitare.
imitation, n. imitazione f.
imitative, adj. imitativo.
imitator, n. imitatore m.
immaculate, adj. immacolato.
immanent, adj. immanènte.
immaterial, adj. immateriale.
immature, adj. immaturo.
immeasurable, adj. non misuràbile, inconmensuràbile.
immediacy, n. immediatezza f.

immediate, adj. immediato.
immediately, adv. immediatamente, sùbito.
immemorial, adj. immemoràbile.
immense, adj. immènso.
immerse, vb. immèrgere.
immersion, n. immersione f.
immigrant, n. and adj. immigrante.
immigrate, vb. immigrare.
imminent, adj. imminènte.
immobile, adj. immòbile.
immobilize, vb. immobilizzare.
immoderate, adj. immoderato.
immodest, adj. immodèsto, impùdico.
immodesty, n. immodèstia f., impudicìzia f.
immoral, adj. immorale.
immorality, n. immoralità f.
immorally, adv. immoralmente.
immortal, adj. immortale.
immortality, n. immortalità f.
immortalize, vb. immortalare.
immovable, adj. immòbile.
immune, adj. immune, esento.
immunity, n. immunità f.
immunize, vb. immunizzare.
immutable, adj. immutàbile.
imp, n. diavoletto m.
impact, n. urto m.
impair, vb. menomare.
impale, vb. impalare.
impart, vb. impartire.
impartial, adj. imparziale.
impasse, n. impasse f.; vìcolo cieco m.
impassible, adj. impassìbile.
impassioned, adj. caloroso, appassionato.
impassive, adj. impassibile.
impatience, n. impaziènza f.
impatient, adj. impaziènte.
impatiently, adv. impazientemente.
impeach, vb. imputare.
impede, vb. impedire.
impediment, n. impedimento m.
impel, vb. impèllere.
impenetrable, adj. impenetràbile.
impenitent, adj. impenitènte.
imperative, n. and adj. imperativo (m.)
imperceptible, adj. impercettìbile.

imperfect, *adj.* imperfètto.

imperfection, *n.* imperfezione *f.*

imperial, *adj.* imperiale.

imperialism, *n.* imperialismo *m.*

imperil, *vb.* méttere in perícolo.

imperious, *adj.* imperioso.

impersonal, *adj.* impersonale.

impersonate, *vb.* impersonare, contraffare.

impersonation, *n.* contraffazione *f.*

impersonator, *n.* impersonatore *m.*

impertinence, *n.* impertinènza *f.*

impertinent, *adj.* impertinènte.

impervious, *adj.* impèrvio.

impetuous, *adj.* impetuoso.

impetus, *n.* ímpeto *m.*

implacable, *adj.* implacàbile.

implant, *vb.* innestare.

implement, *n.* strumento *m.*

implicate, *vb.* implicare.

implication, *n.* implicazione *f.*

implicit, *adj.* implícito.

implied, *adj.* implícito.

implore, *vb.* implorare.

imply, *vb.* implicare; (suggest) suggerire; (insinuate) insinuare.

impolite, *adj.* scortese.

imponderable, *adj.* imponderàbile.

import, **1.** *n.* importazione *f.*; (meaning) significato *m.* **2.** *vb.* importare.

importance, *n.* importanza *f.*

important, *adj.* importante; (be i.) importare.

importation, *n.* importazione *f.*

importer, *n.* importatore *m.*

importune, **1.** *adj.* importuno. **2.** *vb.* importunare.

impose, *vb.* imporre.

imposition, *n.* imposizione *f.*

impossibility, *n.* impossibilità *f.*

impossible, *adj.* impossíbile.

impotence, *n.* impotènza *f.*

impotent, *adj.* impotènte.

impoverish, *vb.* impoverire.

impregnable, *adj.* inespugnàbile.

impregnate, *vb.* impregnare, ingravidare.

impresario, *n.* impresàrio *m.*

impress, *vb.* (imprint) imprímere; (affect) impressionare.

impression, *n.* impressione *f.*

impressive, *adj.* impressionante.

imprison, *vb.* imprigionare.

imprisonment, *n.* prigionía *f.*

improbable, *adj.* improbàbile.

impromptu, **1.** *n.* improvviso *m.* **2.** *adj.* improvvisato; estempo-ràneo.

improper, *adj.* impròprio, sconveniènte.

improve, *vb.* migliorare.

improvement, *n.* miglioramento *m.*

improvident, *adj.* imprevidente.

improvise, *vb.* improvvisare.

imprudence, *n.* imprudenza *f.*

imprudent, *adj.* imprudente.

impudence, *n.* sfrontatezza *f.*; sfacciatàggine *f.*

impudent, *adj.* impudènte.

impugn, *vb.* impugnare.

impulse, *n.* impulso *m.*

impulsive, *adj.* impulsivo.

impunity, *n.* impunità *f.*

impure, *adj.* impuro.

impurity, *n.* impurità *f.*

impute, *vb.* imputare.

in, *prep.* in; (within, of time) entro.

inadvertent, *adj.* disattento, distratto.

inalienable, *adj.* inalienàbile.

inane, *adj.* inane, fùtile.

inaugural, *adj.* inaugurale; (speech) discorso inaugurale *n.m.*

inaugurate, *vb.* inaugurare.

inauguration, *n.* inaugurazione *f.*

inborn, *adj.* innato, congènito.

inbreeding, *n.* incrocio fra animali e piante affini *m.*

incandescence, *n.* incandescènza *f.*

incandescent, *adj.* incandescènte.

incantation, *n.* incantamento *m.*

incapacitate, *vb.* rèndere incapace.

incapacity, *n.* incapacità *f.*

incarcerate, *vb.* incarcerare.

incarnate, *adj.* incarnato.

incarnation, *n.* incarnazione *f.*

incendiary, *n. and adj.* incendiàrio (*m.*).

incense, *n.* incènso *m.*

incentive, *n.* incentivo *m.*

inception, *n.* inízio *m.*

incessant, *adj.* incessante.

incest, n. incèsto m.

inch, n. pòllice m.

incidence, n. incidènza f.

incident, n. incidènte m.

incidental, adj. incidentale.

incidentally, adv. incidentalmente.

incipient, adj. incipiènte.

incise, vb. incìdere.

incision, n. incisione f.

incisive, adj. incisivo.

incisor, n. dènte incisivo m.

inclination, n. inclinazione f.

incline, 1. n. pendìo m. **2.** vb. inclinare; (fig.) propèndere.

inclined, adj. (disposed) propènso.

inclose, vb. rinchiùdere; (in letter) acclùdere.

include, vb. inclùdere.

including, prep. compreso (adj., agrees with following noun).

inclusive, adj. inclusivo.

incognito, n. incògnito.

income, n. rèddito m.

incomparable, adj. incomparàbile.

inconsiderate, adj. strafottènte; villano.

inconstant, adj. inconstante.

inconvenience, 1. n. scomodità f. **2.** vb. incomodare.

inconvenient, adj. incòmodo.

incorporate, vb. incorporare tr.

incorrigible, adj. incorreggìbile.

increase, 1. n. aumento m. **2.** vb. accréscere, aumentare.

incredible, adj. incredìbile.

incredulity, n. incredulità f.

incredulous, adj. incrèdulo.

increment, n. incremento m.

incriminate, vb. incriminare.

incrimination, n. incriminazione f.

incrust, vb. incrostare.

incubator, n. incubatrice f.

inculcate, vb. inculcare.

incumbency, n. durata in càrica f.

incumbent, 1. n. titolare m. **2.** adj. incombènte.

incur, vb. incórrere tr.

incurable, adj. incuràbile.

indebted, adj. indebitato.

indeed, adv. davvero.

indefatigable, adj. infaticàbile.

indefinite, adj. indefinito.

indefinitely, adv. indefinitamente.

indelible, adj. indelèbile.

indemnify, vb. indennizzare.

indemnity, n. indennità f.

indent, vb. dentellare; (paragraph) allineare all'interno; (coastline) frastagliare.

indentation, n. dentallatura f.

independence, n. indipendènza f.

independent, adj. indipendènte.

in-depth, adj. profondo; esauriente.

index, n. índice m.

India, n. Indìa f.

Indian, 1. n. indiano; (American Indian) pellirossa m. **2.** adj. indiano; dei pellirossa.

Indian wrestling, n. braccio di ferro m.

indicate, vb. indicare.

indication, n. indicazione f.

indicative, n. and adj. indicativo (m.)

indicator, n. indicatore m.

indict, vb. accusare.

indictment, n. accusa f.

indifference, n. indifferènza f.

indifferent, adj. indifferènte.

indigenous, adj. indígeno.

indigent, adj. indigènte.

indigestion, n. indigestione f.

indignant, adj. indignato.

indignation, n. indignazione f.

indignity, n. indegnità f., sgarberìa f.

indigo, n. indaco m.

indirect, adj. indiretto.

indiscreet, adj. indiscreto.

indiscretion, n. indiscrezione f.

indispensable, adj. indispensàbile.

indispose, vb. indisporre.

indisposed, adj. indisposto.

indisposition, n. indisposizione f.

indissoluble, adj. indissolùbile.

individual, 1. n. individuo m. **2.** adj. individuale.

individuality, n. individualità f.

individually, adj. individualmente.

indivisible, adj. indivisìbile.

Indochina, n. indocina f.

indoctrinate, vb. indottrinare.
indolent, adj. indolènte.
Indonesia, n. Indonèsia f.
indoor, adj. al coperto.
indoors, adv. al coperto; a casa.
indorse, vb. firmare; (check, etc.) girare.
induce, vb. indurre.
inducement, n. incentivo m.
induct, vb. (into army) arruolare.
induction, n. induzione f.
inductive, adj. induttivo.
indulge, vb. indùlgere.
indulgence, n. indulgènza f.
indulgent, adj. indulgènte.
industrial, adj. industriale.
industrialist, n. industriale m.
industrious, adj. industrioso, operoso.
industry, n. indùstria f.
inebriate, 1. n. ubriacone m. **2.** adj. inebriare.
ineligible, adj. ineleggìbile, inàbile.
inept, adj. inètto.
inert, adj. inèrte.
inertia, n. inèrzia f.
inescapable, adj. ineluttàbile.
inevitable, adj. inevitàbile.
inexact, adj. inesatto.
inexorable, adj. inesoràbile.
inexpensive, adj. a buòn mercato.
inexplicable, adj. inesplicàbile.
infallible, adj. infallìbile.
infamous, adj. infame.
infamy, n. infàmia f.
infancy, n. infànzia f.
infant, n. infante m.
infantile, adj. infantile.
infantry, n. fanterìa f.
infantryman, n. fante m.
infatuated, adj. innamorato, infatuato.
infatuate, vb. infatuare.
infect, vb. infettare.
infected, adj. infètto.
infection, n. infezione f.
infectious, adj. infettivo.
infer, vb. inferire, desùmere.
inference, n. inferènza f.
inferior, adj. inferiore.
inferiority, n. inferiorità f.; **(i. complex)** complesso d'inferiorità.
infernal, adj. infernale.

inferno, n. infèrno m.
infest, vb. infestare.
infidel, n. and adj. infedele; miscredènte.
infidelity, n. infedeltà f.
infiltrate, vb. infiltrare, tr.
infinite, 1. n. and adj. infinito (m.).
infinitesimal, adj. infinitesimale.
infinitive, n. infinito m.
infinity, n. infinità f.
infirm, adj. infermo; (weak) dèbole; (unsure) irresoluto.
infirmary, n. infermerìa f.
infirmity, n. infermità f.
inflame, vb. infiammare.
inflammable, adj. infiammàbile.
inflammation, n. infiammazione f.
inflammatory, adj. infiammatòrio.
inflate, vb. gonfiare.
inflation, n. gonfiamento m.; (financial) inflazione f.
inflection, n. inflessione f.; (gram.) flessione f.
inflict, vb. infliggere.
infliction, n. inflizione f.
influence, n. influènza f., influsso m.
influential, adj. influènte.
influenza, n. influènza f.
inform, vb. informare.
informal, adj. senza cerimònie, informale.
information, n. informazioni f.pl.
informed sources, n. fonti accreditate f.pl.
informer, n. informatore m.
infraction, n. infrazione f.
infrared, 1. n. infrarosso m. **2.** adj. all'infrarosso.
infrequent, adj. infrequente.
infringe, vb. infràngere.
infuriate, vb. far infuriare; **(become i.d)** infuriare.
ingenious, adj. ingegnoso.
ingenuity, n. ingegnosità f.
ingredient, n. ingrediènte m.
inhabit, vb. abitare.
inhabitant, n. abitante m.
inhale, vb. inalare.
inherent, adj. inerènte.
inherit, vb. ereditare.
inheritance, n. eredità f., retàggio m.

inhibit, vb. inibire.
inhibition, n. inibizione f.
inhuman, adj. inumano.
inimical, adj. nemico.
inimitable, adj. inimitàbile.
iniquity, n. iniquità f.
initial, n. and adj. iniziale (f.)
initiate, vb. iniziare.
initiation, n. iniziazione f.
initiative, n. iniziativa f.
inject, vb. iniettare.
injection, n. iniezione f.
injunction, n. ingiunzione f.
injure, vb. (harm) danneggiare, nuòcere; (wound) ferire.
injurious, adj. dannoso, nocivo.
injury, n. danno m., ferita f.
injustice, n. ingiustizia f.
ink, n. inchiòstro m.
inland, 1. adj. intèrno; 2. adv. vèrso l'intèrno.
inlet, n. pòrto m., canale m.
inmate, n. paziènte n.
inn, n. locanda f.
inner, adj. interiore, intèrno.
innermost, adj. più íntimo.
innocence, n. innocènza f.
innocent, adj. innocènte.
innocuous, adj. innòcuo.
innovation, n. innovazione f.
innuendo, n. insinuazione f.
innumerable, adj. innumerévole.
inoculate, vb. inoculare.
inoculation, n. inoculazione f.
input, n. entrata f.; informazioni fornite f.pl.
inquest, n. inchièsta f.
inquire, vb. informarsi.
inquiry, n. ricerca d'informazioni f., investigazione f., inchièsta f.
inquisition, n. inquisizione f.
inquisitive, adj. eccessivamente curioso.
inroad, n. incursione f.
insane, adj. insano, pazzo.
insanity, n. insània f., pazzía f.
insatiable, adj. insaziàbile.
inscribe, vb. iscrìvere.
inscription, n. iscrizione f.
insect, n. insètto m.
insecticide, n. pólvere insetticida m
insecure, adj. insicuro.
insensible, adj. insensíbile.
insensitive, adj. insensíbile.

insensitivity, n. insensibilità f.
inseparable, adj. inseparàbile.
insert, 1. n. insèrto m. 2. vb. inserire.
insertion, n. inserzione f.
inshore, adj. and adv. presso la spiàggia.
inside, 1. n. intèrno m. 2. adj. intèrno, interiore. 3. adv., prep. dentro.
insidious, adj. insidioso.
insight, n. penetrazione f.
insignia, n. insegne f.pl.
insignificance, n. insignificanza f.
insignificant, adj. insignificante.
insinuate, vb. insinuare.
insinuation, n. insinuazione f.
insipid, adj. insípido; (dull) insulso.
insist, vb. insistere.
insistence, n. insistènza f.
insistent, adj. insistènte.
insolence, n. insolènza f.
insolent, adj. insolènte.
insolently, adv. insolentemente.
insomnia, n. insònnia f.
inspect, vb. ispezionare.
inspection, n. ispezione f.
inspector, n. ispettore m.
inspiration, n. ispirazione f.
inspire, vb. ispirare.
install, vb. installare; (a person) insediare.
installation, n. installazione f.; (of a person) insediamento m.; (industrial) impianto m.
installment, n. (payment) rata f.; (story, etc.) puntata f.
instance, n. istanza f.; (example) esèmpio m.; (request) richièsta f.; (for i.) per esèmpio.
instant, 1. n. istante m., àttimo m. 2. adj. immediato; (date) corrènte.
instantaneous, adj. istantàneo.
instantly, adv. immediatamente.
instead, adv. invece di; (i. of) invece di.
instigate, vb. istigare.
instill, vb. istillare.
instinct, n. istinto m.
instinctive, adj. istintivo.
institute, n. istituto m.
institution, n. istituzione f.
instruct, vb. istruire.

instruction, n. istruzione f.
instructive, adj. istruttivo.
instructor, n. istruttore m.
instructress, n. istruttrice f.
instrument, n. strumento m.
instrumental, adj. strumentale.
insufferable, adj. intolleràbile.
insufficient, adj. insufficiènte.
insular, adj. insulare.
insulate, vb. isolare.
insulation, n. isolamento m.
insulator, n. isolatore m.
insulin, n. insulina f.
insult, 1. n. insulto m., ingiùria f.
2. vb. insultare, ingiurare.
insulting, adj. insultante, ingiurioso.
insuperable, adj. insuperàbile.
insurance, n. assicurazione f.
insure, vb. assicurare, tr.
insurer, n. assicuratore m.
insurgent, n. and adj. ribèlle (m.)
insurmountable, adj. insormontàbile.
insurrection, n. insurrezione f.
intact, adj. intatto.
intake, n. ammissione f.; immissione f.
intangible, adj. intangíbile.
integer, n. nùmero intero m.
integral, adj. integrale.
integrate, vb. integrare.
integrity, n. integrità f.
intellect, n. intellètto m.
intellectual, adj. intellettuale.
intelligence, n. intelligènza f.
intelligent, adj. intelligènte.
intelligentsia, n. intellighènzia f.
intelligible, adj. intelligíbile.
intend, vb. intèndere.
intended, adj. inteso, promesso.
intense, adj. intènso.
intensify, vb. intensificare.
intensity, n. intensità f.
intensive, adj. intensivo.
intent, 1. n. intènto m., intendimento m. **2.** adj. intènto; **(i. on)**
intènto a.
intention, n. intenzione f.,
propósito m.
intentional, adj. intenzionale.
intentionally, adv. intenzionalmente, apposta.
inter, vb. seppellire.
interact, vb. interagire.

interaction, n. interazione f.
interbreed, vb. incrociare.
intercede, vb. intercèdere.
intercept, vb. intercettare.
interchange, 1. n. interscambio
m.; svíncolo m. **2.** vb. interscambiare.
intercourse, n. rappòrto m.
interdict, 1. n. interdetto m. **2.** vb.
interdire.
interest, 1. n. interèsse m. **2.** vb.
interessare; **(be i.ed in)** interessarsi di.
interesting, adj. interessante.
interface, n. interfàccia f.
interfere, vb. **(i. in)** immischiarsi
in, intervenire in; **(i. with)** ostacolare, interferire.
interference, n. ingerènza f.;
(physics) interferènza f.
interim, 1. n. frattèmpo m. **2.** adj.
provvisòrio.
interior, n. and adj. interiore (m.)
interject, vb. inframettere.
interjection, n. interiezione f.
interlude, n. interlùdio m.
intermarry, vb. fare matrimoni
misti.
intermediary, n. and adj. intermediàrio (m.)
intermediate, adj. intermèdio.
interment, n. sepoltura f.
intermission, n. intermissione f.,
intervallo m.
intermittent, adj. intermittènte.
intern, vb. internare.
internal, adj. intèrno.
Internal Revenue Service, n.
Fisco m. (coll.)
international, adj. internazionale.
internationalism, n. internazionalismo m.
interne, n. mèdico intèrno m.
interpose, vb. interporre.
interpret, vb. interpretare.
interpretation, n. interpretazione
f.
interpreter, n. intèrprete m.
interrogate, vb. interrogare.
interrogation, n. interrogazione
f.
interrogative, adj. interrogativo.
interrupt, vb. interrómpere.
interruption, n. interruzione f.

intersect, *vb.* intersecare, *tr.*; (cross) incrociarsi.

intersection, *n.* intersezione, *f.*; (crossing) incrócio *m.*

intersperse, *vb.* cospàrgere.

interval, *n.* intervallo *m.*

intervene, *vb.* intervenire.

intervention, *n.* intervènto *m.*

interview, 1. *n.* intervista *f.* **2.** *vb.* intervistare.

intestine, *n. and adj.* intestino (*m.*)

intimacy, *n.* intimità *f.*

intimate, *adj.* íntimo.

intimidate, *vb.* intimidire.

intimidation, *n.* intimidazione *f.*

into, *prep.* in.

intolerant, *adj.* intollerante.

intonation, *n.* intonazione *f.*

intone, *vb.* intonare.

intoxicant, 1. *n.* sostanza tossica *f.*; bevanda alcolica *f.* **2.** *adj.* intossicante.

intoxicate, *vb.* (poison) intossicare; (get drunk) inebriare.

intoxication, *n.* intossicazione *f.*, ubriachezza *f.*

intransigent, *n.m. and f. and adj.* intransigente.

intransitive, *adj.* intransitivo.

intravenous, *adj.* endovenoso.

intrepid, *adj.* intrèpido.

intrepidity, *n.* intrepidità *f.*

intricacy, *n.* complicazione *f.*

intricate, *adj.* intricato, complicato.

intrigue, 1. *n.* intrigo *m.*; (love affair) tresca *f.* **2.** *vb.* intrigare.

intrinsic, *adj.* intrínseco.

introduce, *vb.* introdurre; (persons) presentare.

introduction, *n.* introduzione *f.*, presentazione *f.*

introductory, *adj.* introduttivo.

introspection, *n.* introspezione *f.*

introvert, *n.m.* introverso.

introverted, *adj.* introverso, introvertito.

intrude, *vb.* intrufolarsi, *tr.*

intruder, *n.* intruso *m.*

intuition, *n.* intuizione *f.*

intuitive, *adj.* intuitivo.

inundate, *vb.* inondare.

invade, *vb.* invàdere.

invader, *n.* invasore *m.*

invalid, *n. and adj.* invàlido (*m.*)

invariable, *adj.* invariàbile.

invasion, *n.* invasione *f.*

invective, *n.* invettiva *f.*

inveigle, *vb.* sedurre, adescare.

invent, *vb.* inventare.

invention, *n.* invenzione *f.*

inventive, *adj.* inventivo.

inventor, *n.* inventore *m.*

inventory, *n.* inventàrio *m.*

inverse, *adj.* invèrso.

invertebrate, *n. and adj.* invertebrato (*m.*)

invest, *vb.* investire.

investigate, *vb.* investigare.

investigation, *n.* investigazione *f.*

investment, *n.* investimento *m.*

inveterate, *adj.* inveterato.

invidious, *adj.* odioso.

invigorate, *vb.* invigorire.

invincible, *adj.* invincíbile.

invisible, *adj.* invisíbile.

invitation, *n.* invito *m.*

invite, *vb.* invitare.

invocation, *n.* invocazione *f.*

invoice, 1. *n.* fattura *f.* **2.** *vb.* fatturare.

invoke, *vb.* invocare.

involuntary, *adj.* involontàrio.

involve, *vb.* coinvòlgere, implicare.

involved, *adj.* complicato.

invulnerable, *adj.* invulneràbile.

inward, 1. *adj.* íntimo. **2.** *adv.* vèrso l'interno.

inwardly, *adv.* intimamente.

iodine, *n.* iòdio *m.*

Iran, *n.* Iran *m.*

Iraq, *n.* Iràk *m.*

irate, *adj.* irato.

ire, *n.* ira *f.*

Ireland, *n.* Irlanda *f.*

iridium, *n.* irídio *m.*

iris, *n.* íride (*f.*); (flower) íris *f.*

Irish, *adj.* irlandese.

irk, *vb.* infastidire.

iron, 1. *n.* fèrro *m.*; **(flat-i.)** fèrro da stiro. **2.** *adj.* di fèrro, fèrreo. **3.** *vb.* stirare.

ironical, *adj.* irònico.

ironworks, *n.* ferrièra *f.sg.*

irony, *n.* ironía *f.*

irrational, *adj.* irrazionale.

irrefutable, *adj.* irrefutàbile.

irregular, *adj.* irregolare.
irregularity, *n.* irregolarità *f.*
irrelevant, *adj.* non pertinènte, irrilevante.
irreprehensible, *adj.* irreprensibile.
irreprehensibly, *adv.* irreprensibilmente.
irresistible, *adj.* irresistibile.
irresponsible, *adj.* irresponsàbile.
irreverent, *adj.* irriverènte.
irrevocable, *adj.* irrevocàbile.
irrigate, *vb.* irrigare.
irrigation, *n.* irrigazione *f.*
irritability, *n.* irritabilità *f.*
irritable, *adj.* irritàbile.
irritant, *adj.* irritante.
irritate, *vb.* irritare.
irritation, *n.* irritazione *f.*
island, *n.* ìsola *f.*
isolate, *vb.* isolare.
isolation, *n.* isolamento *m.*
isolationist, *n.* isolazionista *m.*
isosceles, *adj.* isòscele.
Israel, *n.* Israèle *m.*
Israeli, *n.* israeliano.

Israelite, 1. *n.* israelita *f.* 2. *adj.* israelítico.
issuance, *n.* emissione *f.*
issue, 1. *n.* (offspring) pròle *f.*; (bonds, etc.) emissione *f.*; (river) foce *f.*; (magazine) nùmero *m.* 2. *vb.* (come out) uscire; (publish) pubblicare.
isthmus, *n.* istmo *m.*
it, *pron.* ciò; (subject) esso; (direct object) lo, la.
Italian, *adj.* italiano.
Italic, *adj.* itàlico.
italics, *n.* corsivo *m.sg.*
Italy, *n.* Itàlia *f.*
itch, 1. *n.* prudore *m.*, prurito *m.* 2. *vb.* prùdere.
itchy, *adj.* che prude.
item, *n.* artícolo *m.*
itemize, *vb.* elencare.
itinerant, *adj.* girovago.
itinerary, *n.* itineràrio *m.*
its, *adj.* suo.
itself, *pron.* esso stesso.
ivory, *n.* avòrio *m.*
ivy, *n.* édera *f.*

J

jab, *vb.* pugnalare.
jabber, *vb.* borbottare.
jack, *n.* binda *f.*, cricco *m.*, martinèllo *m.*
jack-of-all-trades, *n.* factotum *m.*
jackal, *n.* sciacallo *m.*
jackass, *n.* àsino *m.*
jacket, *n.* giacca *f.*, giacchetta *f.*
jackhammer, *n.* martello pneumàtico *m.*
jack-knife, *n.* coltèllo a serramànico *m.*
jade, *n.* giada *f.*
jaded, *adj.* sfinito.
jagged, *adj.* seghettato.
jaguar, *n.* giaguaro *m.*
jail, *n.* càrcere *m.*, prigione *f.*
jailer, *n.* carcerière *m.*
jam, *n.* marmellata *f.*; (trouble) impiccio *m.*
jamb, *n.* stìpite *m.*
jangle, *n.* rumore aspro *m.*
janitor, *n.* bidèllo *m.*
January, *n.* gennaio *m.*

Japan, *n.* il Giappone *m.*
Japanese, *adj.* giapponese.
jar, 1. *n.* giara *f.*; (glass) bottíglia *f.* 2. *vb.* scuòtere; (displease) offèndere.
jargon, *n.* gèrgo *m.*
jasmine, *n.* gelsomino *m.*
jaundice, *n.* itterízia *f.*
jaunt, *n.* escursione *f.*
jaunty, *adj.* disinvolto.
javelin, *n.* giavellòtto *m.*
jaw, *n.* mascèlla *f.*
jawbreaker, *n.* scioglilingua *f.*
jay, *n.* ghiandaia *f.*
jaywalk, *vb.* attraversare la strada all'infuòri dei passaggi pedonali.
jazz, *n.* jazz *m.* (pronounced giazz)
jealous, *adj.* geloso.
jealousy, *n.* gelosía *f.*
jeans, *n.* jeans *m.pl.*
jeep, *n.* gip *f.*, jeep *f.*
jeer (at), *vb.* beffarsi (di).
Jehovah's Witnesses, *n.* Testimoni di Gèova *m.pl.*

jelly, n. gelatina f.

jelly-fish, n. medusa f.

jeopardize, vb. méttere in pericolo.

jeopardy, n. pericolo m.

jerk, 1. n. strattone m., sbalzellone m. **2.** vb. tirare con strattoni.

jerked beef, n. carne essiccata f.

jerkin, n. giubbotto m.

jerky, adj. a strattoni.

jersey, n. màglia f.

Jerusalem, n. Gerusalèmme f.

jest, 1. n. scherzo m. **2.** vb. scherzare.

jester, n. buffone m.

Jesuit, n. gesuita m.

Jesus Christ, n. Gesù Cristo m.

jet, 1. n. (black substance) giavazzo m.; (emission) gètto m.; (plane) reattore m., aviogètto m. **2.** adj. a reazione. **3.** vb. sgorgare.

jet lag, n. sfasamento prodotto dal passaggio attraverso parecchi fusi orari m.; jet lag m.

jetsam, n. relitto m.

jettison, vb. gettare in mare.

jetty, n. mòlo m.

Jew, n. ebrèo m., giudèo m.

jewel, n. gioièllo m.

jewel case, n. scrigno m.; portagiòie m.

jeweler, n. gioiellière m.

jewelry, n. gioiellería f.

Jewish, adj. ebrèo, ebràico.

jib, 1. n. fiòcco m. **2.** vb. (horse) recalcitrare; (refuse) rifiutarsi.

jibe, 1. n. bèffa f. **2.** vb. (j. at) beffarsi di.

jiffy, n. istante m.

jig, n. giga f.

jigsaw, n. rompicapo m.

jilt, vb. abbandonare.

jingle, vb. tintinnare.

jinx, n. malaugùrio m.

jittery, adj. nervoso.

job, n. impiègo m., occupazione f.

jobber, n. commerciante all'ingròsso m.

jobless, adj. disoccupato.

jockey, n. fantino m.

jocular, adj. umorístico.

jocund, adj. giocondo.

jog, vb. scuòtere.

joggle, n. caletta f.

Johnny-come-lately, n. ritardatario m.

join, 1. n. congiunzione f. **2.** vb. congiùngere; (associate with) associarsi con; (j. up) arruolarsi.

joiner, n. (carpenter) falegname m.

joint, 1. n. giuntura f., articolazione f. **2.** adj. congiunto, collettivo.

jointly, adv. collettivamente, congiuntamente.

joist, n. travicèllo m.

joke, 1. n. schérzo m.; (trick) burla f. **2.** vb. scherzare.

joker, n. burlone m.

jolly, adj. allegro.

jolt, 1. n. scòssa f., sobbalzo m. **2.** vb. sobbalzare.

jonquil, n. giunchìglia f.

josh, vb. canzonare.

jostle, vb. spíngere.

jounce, 1. n. sobbalzo m. **2.** vb. sobbalzare.

journal, n. giornale m.

journalism, n. giornalismo m.

journalist, n. giornalista m.

journey, 1. n. viàggio m. **2.** vb. viaggiare.

journeyman, n. operaio espèrto m.

jovial, adj. gioviale.

jowl, n. guància f.

joy, n. giòia f.

joyful, adj. gioioso.

joyous, adj. gioioso.

jubilant, adj. giubilante.

jubilee, n. giubilèo m.

Judaism, n. giudaismo m.

judge, 1. n. giùdice m. **2.** vb. giudicare.

judgment, n. giudízio m.

judicial, adj. giudiziàrio; (impartial) imparziale.

judiciary, 1. n. magistratura f. **2.** adj. giudiziàrio.

judicious, adj. giudizioso.

jug, n. bròcca f.

juggle, vb. far giòchi di prestígio.

juggler, n. prestigiatore m.

jugular, adj. giugulare.

juice, n. succo m.

juicy, adj. succoso.

July, n. lùglio m.

jumble, n. confusione f.

jumbo, adj. enorme.

jump, 1. n. salto m. **2.** vb. saltare.

jump seat, n. spuntino m., strapuntino m.

junction, n. bívio m., diramazione f., biforcazione f.

juncture, n. giuntura f.

June, n. giugno m.

jungle, n. giungla f.

junior, adj. minore; (in names) iuniore.

junior college, n. primo biènnio universitario m.

junior high school, n. scuola media f.

juniper, n. ginepro m.

junk, n. roba vecchia f.; cianfrusaglie f.pl.

junket, n. (food) giuncata f.; (trip) escursione f.

jurisdiction, n. giurisdizione f.

jurisprudence, n. giurisprudenza f.

jurist, n. giurista m.

juror, n. giurato m.

jury, n. giuria f.

just, 1. adj. giusto **2.** adv. pròprio; (j. now) or'ora.

justice, n. giustízia f.

justifiable, adj. giustificàbile.

justification, n. giustificazione f.

justify, vb. giustificare.

jut, vb. proiettarsi, spòrgere.

jute, n. iuta f.

juvenile, adj. giovanile.

juxtapose, vb. giustapporre.

K

kale, n. càvolo m.

kaleidoscope, n. caleidoscòpio m.

kangaroo, n. canguro m.

karakul, n. lince persiana f.

karat, n. carato m.

karate, n. karate m.

keel, n. chíglia f.

keen, adj. acuto.

keep, vb. conservare, serbare, mantenere, tenere; (stay) tenersi.

keeper, n. custòde m.

keepsake, n. ricòrdo m.

keg, n. bariletto m.

kennel, n. canile m.

kerchief, n. fazzoletto m.

kernel, n. gheríglio m.; (fig.) nòcciolo m.

kerosene, n. petròlio raffinato m., cherosene m.

ketchup, n. salsa di pomodoro f.

kettle, n. péntola f.

kettledrum, n. tímpano m.

key, n. chiave f.; (piano) tasto m.; (musical structure) tonalità f.

keyboard, n. tastièra f.

keyhole, n. buco della serratura f.

keynote, n. (music) tono m.; (speech) principio chiave m.

keypunch, vb. perforare.

keyring, n. portachiavi m.

keystone, n. chiave di volta f.

keyword, n. parola chiave f.

khaki, n. cachi m.

kick, 1. n. calcio m. **2.** vb. tirar calci (a).

kid, 1. n. (goat) capretto m.; (child) ragazzo m., ragazza f. **2.** vb. prèndere in giro.

kidnap, vb. rapire.

kidnapper, n. rapitore m.

kidnapping, n. rapimento m.

kidney, n. rène f.; (as food) rognone m.

kidney bean, n. fagiolo reniforme m.

kill, vb. uccídere.

killer, n. uccisore m.

kiln, n. fornace f.

kilocycle, n. chilociclo m.

kilogram, n. chilogramma m.; chilo m.; (abbr.) kg.

kilohertz, n. kilohertz m.

kilometer, n. chilòmetro m.; (abbr.) km.

kilowatt, n. chilowatt m.; (abbr.) kw.

kilt, n. gonnellino m.; kilt m.

kimono, n. chimono m.

kin, n. parentela f.

kind, 1. n. gènere m., razza f. **2.** adj. gentile.

kindergarten, n. giardino d'infànzia m.
kindle, vb. accèndere.
kindling, n. legna minuta f.
kindly, adj. benèvolo.
kindness, n. gentilezza f.
kindred, 1. n. parentela f. **2.** adj. imparentato; (alike) affine.
kinetic, adj. cinètico.
king, n. re m.
kingdom, n. regno m.
kingly, adj. reale, maestoso.
king-size, adj. extra grande.
kink, n. nodo m.
kiosk, n. chiòsco m.
kiss, 1. n. bàcio m. **2.** vb. baciare.
kitchen, n. cucina f.
kitchenware, n. utènsili da cucina m.pl.
kite, n. aquilone m.; (bird) níbbio m.
kitten, n. gattino m.
kleptomania, n. cleptomanía f.
kleptomaniac, n. cleptòmane m.
knack, n. facoltà m.
knapsack, n. zàino m.
knead, vb. impastare.

knee, n. ginócchio m.
knee-cap, n. rotèlla del ginócchio f.
kneel, vb. inginocchiarsi.
knell, n. rintocco m.
knickers, n. pantaloni m.pl.
knife, n. coltèllo m.
knight, n. cavalière m.; (chess) cavallo m.
knit, vb. lavorare a maglia; (k. one's brows) aggrottare le cíglia.
knock, vb. **1.** n. bussata f. **2.** vb. bussare; (strike) colpire; (k. down) abbàttere.
knot, n. nodo m.
knotty, adj. nodoso.
know, vb. (from outside in) conoscere; (from inside out) sapere; (k. how to) sapere.
knowledge, n. conoscènza f.; (without the k. of) all'insaputa di.
knuckle, n. nòcca f.
kodak, n. kodak f.
Korea, n. Corèa f.
kosher, adj. secondo la norma della religione ebraica; (coll.) autentico.

L

label, n. etichetta f.
labor, 1. n. lavoro m.; (workers) manodòpera f. **2.** vb. lavorare.
laboratory, n. laboratòrio m.
laborer, n. lavoratore m.
laborious, adj. laborioso.
labor union, n. sindacato operaio m.
laburnum, n. avornièllo m.
labyrinth, n. labirinto m.
lace, n. merletto m., pizzo m.
lacerate, vb. lacerare.
laceration, n. lacerazione f.
lack, 1. n. mancanza f. **2.** vb. mancare.
lackadaisical, adj. lànguido.
lackey, n. lacchè m.
laconic, adj. lacònico.
lacquer, 1. n. lacca f. **2.** vb. laccare.
lactic, adj. làttico.
lactose, n. lattòsio m.
lacy, adj. leggèro come merletti.

lad, n. ragazzo m.
ladder, n. scala a pioli f.; (stocking) cordiglièra f.
ladies, n. signore f.pl.
ladle, n. mèstolo m., ramaiuòlo m.
lady, n. signora f.
ladybug, n. coccinèlla f.
lag, 1. n. ritardo m. **2.** vb. indugiare.
lag behind, vb. restare indiètro.
lager beer, n. birra stagionata f.
laggard, n. pigro m.
lagoon, n. laguna f.
laid-back, adj. calmo.
lair, n. covo m., tana f.
laity, n. laicato m.
lake, 1. n. lago m. **2.** adj. lacuale.
lamb, n. agnèllo m.; (meat) abbàcchio m.
lambast, vb. sferzare, stroncare.
lame, adj. zòppo.
lament, 1. n. lamento m. **2.** vb. lamentare.

lamentable, *adj.* lamentévole.
lamentation, *n.* lamentazione *f.*
laminate, *vb.* laminare.
lamp, *n.* làmpada *f.*
lampoon, *n.* pasquinata *f.*
lance, 1. *n.* lància *f.* **2.** *vb.* tagliare colla lancetta *f.*
land, 1. *n.* tèrra *f.;* (country) paese *m.* **2.** *vb.* (from boat) sbarcare; (plane) atterrare.
landfall, *n.* avvistamento di terre *m.;* (landslide) frana *f.,* slavina *f.*
landholder, *n.* proprietàrio di terre *m.;* latifondista *m.*
landing, *n.* sbarco *m.;* (plane) atterràggio *m.*
landlady, *n.* padrona *f.*
landlord, *n.* padrone *m.*
landmark, *n.* monumento *m.*
landscape, *n.* paesaggio *m.*
landslide, *n.* frana *f.*
landward, *adv.* vèrso tèrra.
lane, *n.* viòttolo *m.*
language, *n.* lingua *f.;* (manner of talking) linguaggio *m.*
languid, *adj.* lànguido.
languish, *vb.* languire.
languor, *n.* languore *m.*
lanky, *adj.* alto e smilzo.
lanolin, *n.* lanolina *f.*
lantern, *n.* lantèrna *f.*
lap, 1. *n.* grembo *m.* **2.** *vb.* lambire.
lapel, *n.* risvòlta *f.*
lapin, *n.* coníglio *m.*
lapse, 1. *n.* (mistake) errore *m.;* (time) percorso *m.* **2.** *vb.* decadere.
larceny, *n.* furto *m.*
lard, *n.* strutto *m.*
large, *adj.* grande.
largely, *adv.* in gran parte.
largo, *n., adj., adv.* largo *(m.)*
lariat, *n.* làccio *m.*
lark, *n.* allòdola *f.;* (fun) divertimento *m.*
larkspur, *n.* consòlida reale *f.*
larva, *n.* larva *f.*
laryngitis, *n.* laringite *f.*
larynx, *n.* laringe *f.*
lascivious, *adj.* lascivo.
laser, *n.* làser *m.*
lash, 1. *n.* frusta *f.,* sfèrza *f.* **2.** *vb.* frustare, sferzare.
lass, *n.* ragazza *f.*
lassitude, *n.* indolenza *f.*
lasso, *n.* làccio *m.*

last, 1. *n.* forma *f.* **2.** *adj.* ùltimo. **3.** *vb.* durare.
lasting, *adj.* durévole.
latch, *n.* saliscendi *m.*
late, 1. *adj.* tardo, tardívo. **2.** *adv.* tardi; (delayed) in ritardo.
lately, *adv.* recentemente.
latent, *adj.* latènte.
lateral, *adj.* laterale.
lath, *n.* listèllo *m.*
lathe, *n.* tórnio *m.*
lather, *n.* schiuma *f.*
Latin, *n. and adj.* latino *(m.)*
latitude, *n.* latitùdine *f.*
Latium, *n.* Làzio *m.;* (of L.) laziale.
latrine, *n.* latrina *f.*
latter, 1. *adj.* recènte. **2.** *pron.* (opposed to *former*) questo.
lattice, *n.* grata *f.*
laud, *vb.* lodare.
laudable, *adj.* lodévole.
laudanum, *n.* làudano *m.*
laudatory, *adj.* elogiativo.
laugh, 1. *n.* riso *m.* **2.** *vb.* ridere; (l. at) derídere.
laughable, *adj.* ridícolo.
laughter, *n.* riso *m.;* (burst of l.) risata *f.*
launch, 1. *n.* lància *f.* **2.** *vb.* (throw) lanciare; (boat) varare.
launching, *n.* varo *m.*
launder, *vb.* lavare.
laundress, *n.* lavandaia *f.*
laundry, *n.* (clothes) bucato *m.;* (establishment) lavandería *f.*
laundryman, *n.* lavandaio *m.*
laureate, *adj.* laureato.
laurel, *n.* allòro *m.,* làuro *m.*
lava, *n.* lava *f.*
lavallière, *n.* pendènte *m.*
lavatory, *n.* latrina *f.*
lavender, *n.* lavanda *f.*
lavish, 1. *adj.* pròdigo. **2.** *vb.* prodigare.
law, *n.* legge *f.,* diritto *m.*
lawful, *adj.* legale, legittimo.
lawless, *adj.* fuori legge.
lawmaker, *n.* legislatore *m.*
lawn, *n.* prato *m.*
lawn mower, falciatrice *f.*
lawsuit, *n.* càusa *f.*
lawyer, *n.* avvocato *m.*
lax, *adj.* rilassato.

laxative, n. and adj. lassativo (m.), purgante (m.).
laxity, n. rilassamento m.
lay, 1. adj. làico. **2.** vb. méttere, porre, deporre.
lay brother, n. converso m.
layer, n. strato m.
layman, n. làico m.
layout, n. piano m.; menabò m.
lazy, adj. pigro.
laziness, n. pigrizia f.
lead, 1. n. direzione f.; (metal) piombo m. **2.** vb. menare; condurre.
leaden, adj. di piombo, plùmbeo.
leader, n. capo m.; (Fascist) duce m.
leadership, n. guida f.
lead pencil, n. matita f.
leaf, n. fòglia f.
leafless, adj. privo di foglie.
leaflet, n. fogliolina f.
leafy, adj. fogliuto.
league, n. lega f.
League of Nations, n. Società delle Nazioni f.
leak, 1. n. falla f. **2.** vb. (lose water) pèrdere; (let water in) far acqua.
leakage, n. infiltrazione f.; (loss) pèrdita f.
leaky, adj. che pèrde, che ha falle.
lean, 1. adj. magro. **2.** vb. appoggiare, tr.
leaning, adj. inclinato, pendente.
leap, 1. n. salto m. **2.** vb. saltare.
leap year, n. anno bisestile m.
learn, vb. imparare.
learned, adj. dòtto.
learner, n. apprendista m. and f.
learning, n. dottrina f.
lease, 1. n. affitto m.; (contract) contratto d'affitto m. **2.** vb. affittare.
leash, n. guinzàglio m.
least, 1. adj. mínimo. **2.** adv. minimamente.
leather, n. cuòio m.; (artificial l.) similcuòio m.
leathery, adj. tiglioso.
leave, 1. n. (departure) commiato m.; congedo m.; (permission) permesso m.; (furlough) licénza f. **2.** vb. lisciare; (depart) partire; (go away) andàrsene; (l. out) omèttere.
leaven, n. lièvito m.

lecherous, adj. lascivo.
lecture, n. conferènza f.
lecturer, n. conferenzière m.
ledge, n. ripiano m.
ledger, n. libro mastro m.
lee, n. sottovènto m.
leech, n. sanguisuga f.
leek, n. pòrro m.
leer, vb. guardare lascivamente.
leeward, adv. sottovènto.
left, 1. n. sinistra f. **2.** adj. sinistro; (departed) partito. **3.** adv. a sinistra.
left-handed, adj. mancino.
leftist, adj. di sinistra.
left-over, n. avanzo m.
leg, n. gamba f.
legacy, n. làscito m.
legal, adj. legale.
legalize, vb. legalizzare.
legation, n. legazione f.
legend, n. leggènda f.
legendary, adj. leggendàrio.
Leghorn, n. Livorno f.
legible, adj. leggìbile.
legion, n. legione f.
legislate, vb. fare leggi.
legislation, n. legislazione f.
legislator, n. legislatore m.
legislature, n. parlamento m.
legitimate, adj. legìttimo.
legume, n. legume m.
leisure, n. àgio m., riposo m., còmodo m.
leisurely, adj. còmodo.
lemon, n. limone m.
lemonade, n. limonata f.
lend, vb. prestare.
length, n. lunghezza f.
lengthen, vb. allungare, tr.
lengthwise, adv. per il lungo.
lengthy, adj. molto lungo.
lenient, adj. clemènte.
lens, n. lènte f.
Lent, n. quarésima f.
Lenten, adj. di quarésima.
lentil, n. lenticchia f.
lento, adv. lènto.
leopard, n. leopardo m.
leper, n. lebbroso m.
leperous, adj. lebbroso.
leprosy, n. lebbra f.
lesbian, adj. lèsbico n., lèsbica f.; tribade f.
lesion, n. lesione f.

less, 1. *adj.* minore. 2. *adv. and prep.* meno.

lessen, *vb.* diminuire.

lesser, *adj.* minore.

lesson, *n.* lezione *f.*

lest, *conj.* affinché . . . non.

let, *vb.* (allow) lasciare, perméttere; (lease) affittare; **(l. alone)** lasciar stare; **(l. up)** diminuire.

letdown, *n.* allentamento *m.*

lethal, *adj.* letale.

lethargic, *adj.* letàrgico.

lethargy, *n.* letargia *f.*

letter, *n.* léttera *f.*

letter carrier, *n.* postino *m.*

letterhead, *n.* carta intestata *f.*

lettuce, *n.* lattuga *f.*

letup, *n.* pàusa *f.*, sosta *f.*

leukemia, *n.* leucèmia *f.*

levee, *n.* diga *f.*

level, 1. *n.* livéllo *m.* 2. *adj.* orizzontale, equilibrato. 3. *vb.* livellare.

lever, *n.* lèva *f.*

leverage, *n.* fozza di una leva *f.;* potere *m.*

levitation, *n.* levitazione *f.*

levity, *n.* leggerezza *f.*

levy, 1. *n.* lèva *f.;* (tax) imposta *f.* 2. *vb.* arruolare; (tax) imporre.

lewd, *adj.* impùdico.

lexical, *adj.* lessicale.

lexicon, *n.* lèssico *m.*

liability, *n.* responsabilità *f.*

liable, *adj.* responsàbile, soggètto.

liaison, *n.* (mil.) collegamento *m.;* (love affair) relazione *f.*

liar, *n.* bugiardo *m.*

libation, *n.* libagione *f.*

libel, 1. *n.* libèllo *m.* 2. *vb.* diffamare.

libelous, *adj.* diffamatòrio.

liberal, *n. and adj.* liberale (m.)

liberalism, *n.* liberalismo *m.*

liberality, *n.* liberalità *f.*

liberate, *vb.* liberare.

liberation, *n.* liberazione *f.*

liberator, *n.* liberatore *m.*

libertine, *n. and adj.* libertino *m.*

liberty, *n.* libertà *f.*

libidinous, *adj.* libidinoso.

libido, *n.* libido *f.*

librarian, *n.* bibliotecàrio *m.*

library, *n.* bibliotèca *f.*

libretto, *n.* libretto *m.*

license, *n.* licènza *f.*, permesso *m.;* (driver's) patènte *f.*

licentious, *adj.* licenzioso.

lick, *vb.* leccare.

licorice, *n.* liquirízia *f.*

lid, *n.* copèrchio *m.;* (eye) pàlpebra *f.*

lie, 1. *n.* bugìa *f.;* menzogna *f.* 2. *vb.* (tell untruths) mentire; (recline) giacere.

lien, *n.* sequèstro *m.*

lieutenant, *n.* tenènte *f.;* **(second l.)** sottotenènte *m.*

life, 1. *n.* vita *f.* 2. *adj.* **(for l.)** vitalízio.

life-boat, *n.* barca di salvatàggio *f.*

life-buoy, *n.* salvagente *m.*

life-guard, *n.* bagnino *m.*

life insurance, *n.* assicurazione sulla vita *f.*

lifeless, *adj.* sènza vita.

life-preserver, *n.* (belt) cintura di salvatàggio *f.;* salvagènte *m.*

life style, *n.* modo di vívere.

life-time, *n.* durata della vita *f.*

lift, 1. *n.* ascensore *m.* 2. *vb.* sollevare.

ligament, *n.* legamento *m.*

ligature, *n.* legatura *f.*

light, 1. *n.* luce *f.* 2. *adj.* luminoso; (not heavy) leggièro. 3. *vb.* accèndere; **(l. up)** illuminare, *tr.*

lighten, *vb.* (make less heavy) alleggerire; (flash) lampeggiare.

lighter, *n.* (cigar, cigarette) accendisìgaro *m.;* accendino *m.*

light-house, *n.* faro *m.*

lightly, *adv.* leggieramente.

lightness, *n.* leggerezza *f.*

lightning, *n.* lampo *m.*, fùlmine *m.;* **(l.-rod)** parafùlmine *m.*

lightship, *n.* nave faro *f.*

lignite, *n.* lignite *f.*

Ligurian, *adj.* lígure.

like, 1. *adj.* símile. 2. *vb.* (use piacere with English subject as indirect object). 3. *prep.* come.

likeable, *adj.* amàbile, simpàtico.

likelihood, *n.* probabilità *f.*

likely, *adj.* probàbile.

liken, *vb.* assomigliare.

likeness, *n.* somiglianza *f.*

likewise, *adv.* similmente.

lilac, *n.* lillà *m.*

lilt, n. canto m.

lily, n. giglio m.

lily of the valley, n. mughetto m.

limb, n. (of body) arto m.; mèmbro m.; (of tree) ramo m.

limber, vb. rèndere flessibile.

limbo, n. (of) limbo m.

lime, n. calce f.; **(bird-l.)** vischio f.; (fruit) limone f.; (tree) tíglio m.

limelight, n. bagliore m.

limestone, n. pietra calcare f.

lime-water, n. acqua di calce f.

limit, 1. n. límite m. 2. vb. limitare.

limitation, n. limitazione f.

limited, n. (train) ràpido m.

limited company, n. società a responsabilità limitata f.

limited monarchy, n. monarchìa costituzionale f.

limitless, adj. illimitato.

limousine, n. limousine f.

limp, 1. n. zoppicamento m. 2. adj. fiacco, flessibile. 3. vb. zoppicare.

limpid, adj. límpido.

linden, n. tíglio m.

line, 1. n. línea f.; (row) fila f.; (writing) riga f.; rigo m. 2. vb. **(l. up)** allineare, tr.

lineage, n. lignàggio m., stirpe f.

lineal, adj. diretto.

linear, adj. lineare.

linen, 1. n. (cloth) tela di lino f.; **(household l.)** biancherìa f. 2. adj. di lino.

liner, n. (boat) transatlàntico m.

linger, vb. indugiare.

lingerie, n. biancheria intima f.

linguist, n. linguìsta m. and f.

linguistic, adj. linguístico.

linguistics, n. linguística f.

liniment, n. lenitivo m.

lining, n. fòdera f.

link, 1. n. (bond) legame m., vínculo m., (in chain) anèllo m. 2. vb. collegare, tr.

linoleum, n. linòleum m.

linseed, n. seme di lino m.

lint, n. filàccia inglese f.

lion, n. leone m.

lip, n. labbro m.

lipread, vb. lèggere le labbra.

lipservice, n. omaggio ipòcrita m.

lip-stick, n. rossetto m.

liquefy, vb. liquefare, tr.

liqueur, n. liquore m.

liquid, n. and adj. liquido (m.)

liquidate, vb. liquidare.

liquidation, n. liquidazione f.

liquor, n. liquore m.

lira, n. lira f.

lisle, n. filo di cotone mercerizzato m.

lisp, 1. n. pronùncia blesa f. 2. vb. essere bleso.

lisping, adj. bleso.

lissome, adj. flessibile, agile.

list, 1. n. lista f., elenco m., ruòlo m.; (slant) inclinazione f. 2. vb. elencare; (slant) inclinarsi.

listen (to), vb. ascoltare.

listless, adj. svogliato.

litany, n. litanìa f.

liter, n. litro m.

literacy, n. alfabetismo m.; alfabetizzazione f.; istruzione f.

literal, adj. letterale.

literary, adj. letteràrio.

literate, adj. letterato.

literature, n. letteratura f.

lithe, adj. flessuoso.

lithograph, 1. n. litografìa f. 2. vb. litografare.

lithography, n. litografìa f.

litigant, n. litigante m.

litigation, n. càusa f.

litmus, n. tornasole m.

litter, 1. n. (mess) disórdine m.; (stretcher) barella f.; (animal's bed) lettièra f.; (kittens, puppies) figliata f. 2. vb. méttere in confusione; (have kittens) figliare.

little, 1. n. poco 2. adj. piccolo 3. adv. poco.

little finger, n. mignolo m.

little people, n. fate f.pl.; folletti m.pl.

liturgical, adj. litùrgico.

liturgy, n. liturgìa f.

livable, adj. abitàbile; sociévole.

live, 1. adj. vivo 2. vb. vivere.

livelihood, n. vita f.

lively, adj. vivace, brioso.

liven, vb. ravvivare, tr.

liver, n. fégato m.

livery, n. livrèa f.

livestock, n. bestiame m.

livid, adj. lívido.

living, 1. n. vita f. 2. adj. vivènte.

lizard, n. lucèrtola f.

lo, interj. ècco.

load, 1. *n.* càrico *m.* 2. *vb.* caricare.
loaf, 1. *n.* pagnòtta *f.*, pane *m.* 2. *vb.* oziare.
loafer, *n.* bighellone *m.*; (slipper) pantòfola *f.*
loam, *n.* terríccio *m.*
loan, 1. *n.* prèstito *m.* 2. *vb.* prestare.
loath, *adj.* riluttante.
loathe, *vb.* abominare.
loathing, *n.* ripugnanza *f.*
loathsome, *adj.* schifoso.
lobby, *n.* corridòio *m.*
lobe, *n.* lòbo *m.*
lobster, *n.* aragosta *f.*
local, 1. *n.* (train) òmnibus *m.*; accelerato *m.* 2. *adj.* locale.
locale, *n.* località *f.*
locality, *n.* località *f.*
localize, *vb.* localizzare.
locate, *vb.* collocare; (find) trovare; **(be l.d)** trovarsi.
location, *n.* situazione *f.*, posto *m.*
lock, 1. *n.* serratura *f.*; (canal) chiusa *f.* 2. *vb.* chiùdere a chiave.
locker, *n.* armadietto *m.*; (baggage) depòsito bagagli automàtico *m.*
locket, *n.* medaglione *m.*
lockjaw, *n.* tètano *m.*
lockout, *n.* serrata *f.*
locksmith, *n.* fabbro di serrature *m.*
locomotion, *n.* locomozione *f.*
locomotive, *n.* locomotiva *f.*, locomotore *m.*
locust, *n.* locusta *f.*
locution, *n.* locuzione *f.*
lode, *n.* filone *m.*
lodestar, *n.* stella polare *f.*
lodge, 1. *n.* casetta *f.* 2. *vb.* alloggiare.
lodger, *n.* òspite *m.*
lodging, *n.* allòggio *m.*
loft, *n.* solàio *m.*; (warehouse) magazzino *m.*
lofty, *adj.* alto.
log, *n.* ciòcco *m.*, ceppo *m.*; (tree-trunk) tronco d'àlbero *m.*
logarithm, *n.* logaritmo *m.*
loge, *n.* loggione *m.*
logic, *n.* lògica *f.*
logical, *adj.* lògico.
logistic, *adj.* logistico.
logistics, *n.* logistica.

loin, *n.* lombo *m.*; (food) lombata *f.*
loincloth, *n.* perizoma *m.*
loiter, *vb.* andare a zonzo.
lollipop, *n.* lecca-lecca *m.*
Lombard, *adj.* lombardo.
Lombardy, *n.* Lombardia *f.*
London, *n.* Londra *f.*; **(of L.)** londinese.
lone, lonely, lonesome, *adj.* solitàrio.
loneliness, *n.* solitùdine *f.*
long, 1. *adj.* lungo. 2. *vb.* **(l. for)** bramare. 3. *adv.* lungamente.
long-distance, *adj.* (telephone) interurbano, in teleselezione.
longevity, *n.* longevità *f.*
longing, *n.* brama *f.*
longitude, *n.* longitùdine *f.*
longitudinal, *adj.* longitudinale.
long-lived, *adj.* longèvo.
look, 1. *n.* sguardo *m.*; (appearance) aspètto *m.* 2. *vb.* guardare; **(l. out,** take care) badare, vigilare.
looking glass, *n.* spècchio *m.*
loom, *n.* telàio *m.*
loop, *n.* càppio *m.*, làccio *m.*
loophole, *n.* feritòia *f.*; (way out) scappatòia *f.*
loose, 1. *adj.* sciòlto. 2. *vb.* sciògliere.
loosen, *vb.* allentare, *tr.*, sciògliere, *tr.*
loot, *n.* bottino *m.*
lop off, *vb.* mozzare.
lopsided, *adj.* mal equilibrato.
loquacious, *adj.* loquace.
lord, *n.* signore *m.*
lordship, *n.* signoría *f.*
lorry, *n.* autocarro *m.*
lose, *vb.* pèrdere; (mislay) smarrire.
loss, *n.* pèrdita *f.*
lot, *n.* (fate) sòrte *f.*; (drawing) sortéggio *m.*; (group) lotto *m.*; (land) terreno *m.*; **(a l. of, l.s of)** molto *adj.*
lotion, *n.* lozione *f.*
lottery, *n.* lotteria *f.*
lotus, *n.* lòto *m.*
loud, 1. *adj.* alto, fòrte. 2. *adv.* fòrte.
loud-speaker, *n.* altoparlante *m.*
lounge, 1. *n.* divano *m.*, salone *m.* 2. *vb.* andare a zonzo.

louse, *n.* pidòcchio *m.*

lout, *n.* zoticone *m.*

louver, *n.* ventilatore *m.*

lovable, *adj.* amàbile.

love, 1. *n.* amore *m.* **2.** *vb.* amare.

lovely, *adj.* bèllo, leggiadro.

lover, *n.* amante *m. or f.*

low, 1. *adj.* basso. **2.** *vb.* mugghiare.

lowbrow, *adj.* poco intelligènte.

lower, 1. *adj.* inferiore. **2.** *vb.* abbassare, *tr.*

lowly, *adj.* ùmile.

loyal, *adj.* leale.

loyalist, *n.* lealista *m.*

loyalty, *n.* lealtà *f.*

lozenge, *n.* losanga *f.*; (pastille) pasticca *f.*

lubricant, *n. and adj.* lubrificante (*m.*)

lubricate, *vb.* lubrificare.

lucid, *adj.* chiaro.

luck, *n.* fortuna *f.*, sòrte *f.*; **(bad l.)** sfortuna *f.*

lucky, *adj.* fortunato.

lucrative, *adj.* lucroso.

ludicrous, *adj.* ridícolo.

lug, *vb.* trascinare.

luggage, *n.* bagagli *m.pl.*, bagaglio *m.*

lukewarm, *adj.* tièpido.

lull, *vb.* cullare.

lullaby, *n.* ninna-nanna *f.*

lumbago, *n.* lombàggine *f.*

lumber, *n.* legname *m.*

luminous, *adj.* luminoso.

lump, 1. *n.* massa *f.*, protuberanza *f.* **2.** *vb.* ammassare.

lumpish, *adj.* grumoso; goffo.

lump sum, *n.* somma complessiva *f.*, ammontare complessivo *m.*

lumpy, *adj.* pieno di protuberanze.

lunacy, *n.* pazzìa *f.*

lunar, *adj.* lunare.

lunatic, *n. and adj.* lunàtico (*m.*)

lunch, *n.* colazione *f.*

luncheon, *n.* colazione *f.*

luncheon meat, *n.* insaccati *m.pl.*

lung, *n.* polmone *m.*

lunge, *vb.* lanciarsi.

lurch, *vb.* traballare.

lure, *vb.* adescare.

lurid, *adj.* sensazionale.

lurk, *vb.* nascóndersi.

luscious, *adj.* saporito.

lush, *adj.* lussureggiante.

lust, *n.* concupiscènza *f.*

luster, *n.* lustro *m.*

lustful, *adj.* concupiscènte.

lustrous, *adj.* lustro.

lusty, *adj.* vigoroso.

lute, *n.* liuto *m.*

Lutheran, *adj.* luterano.

luxuriant, *adj.* lussureggiante, rigoglioso.

luxurious, *adj.* lussuoso.

luxury, *n.* lusso *m.*

lying, *adj.* menzognèro, bugiardo, mendace.

lymph, *n.* linfa *f.*

lymphatic, *adj.* linfàtico.

lynch, *vb.* linciare.

lynching, *n.* linciàggio *m.*

lynx, *n.* lince *f.*

lyre, *n.* lira *f.*

lyric, *adj.* lírico.

lyricism, *n.* liricismo *m.*

M

macabre, *adj.* màcabro.

macaroni, *n.* pasta asciutta *f.*, maccheroni *m.pl.*

mace, *n.* mazza *f.*

machine, *n.* màcchina *f.*

machine gun, *n.* mitragliatrice, *f.*

machinery, *n.* meccanismo *m.*

machinist, *n.* macchinista *m.*

machismo, *n.* gallismo *m.*

macho, *adj.* fallòcrate.

mackerel, *n.* sgombro *m.*

mackinaw, *n.* impermeàbile *m.*

mackintosh, *n.* impermeàbile *m.*

mad, *adj.* pazzo; (angry) furioso.

madam, *n.* signora *f.*

madcap, *n. and adj.* scervellato (*m.*)

madden, *vb.* far impazzire.

made-to-order, *adj.* fatto su misura.

made-up, *adj.* inventato.

madness, *n.* pazzìa *f.*

madrigal, *n.* madrigale *m.*

maelstrom, *n.* vòrtice *m.*

mafia, n. mafia f.

magazine, n. periòdico m., rivista f.

magic, 1. n. magìa f. **2.** adj. màgico.

magician, n. mago m.

magistrate, n. magistrato m.

magistrature n. magistratura f.

magnanimous, adj. magnànimo.

magnate, n. magnate m.

magnesium, n. magnèsio m.

magnet, n. magnète m.

magnetic, adj. magnètico.

magnificence, n. magnificènza f.

magnificent, adj. magnìfico.

magnify, vb. ingrandire.

magnitude, n. grandezza f.

mahogany, n. mògano m.

maid, n. domèstica f.; (old m.) zitèlla f.

maiden, n. fanciulla f.

mail, 1. n. pòsta f. **2.** vb. impostare.

mail-box, n. buca per lettere f.

mailman, n. postino m.

maim, vb. storpiare.

main, adj. principale.

mainframe, n. parte centrale di una calcolatrice f.

mainland, n. tèrra ferma f.

mainspring, n. molla principale f.

maintain, vb. mantenere; (in argument) sostenere.

maintenance, n. mantenimento m.

maize, n. granturco m.

majestic, adj. maestoso.

majesty, n. maestà f.

major, n. and adj. maggiore (m.).

majority, n. maggioranza f.

make, vb. fare.

make-believe, 1. n. finta f. **2.** adj. finto. **3.** vb. fìngere.

maker, n. fattore m.

makeshift, n. espediènte m.

make-up, n. belletto m.

malady, n. malattìa f.

malaria, n. malària f.

male, n. and adj. màschio (m.).

malevolent, adj. malèvolo.

malice, n. malevolènza f.

malicious, adj. maligno.

malign, 1. adj. maligno. **2.** vb. diffamare.

malignant, adj. maligno.

malleable, adj. malleàbile.

malnutrition, n. malnutrizione f.

malt, n. malto m.

maltreat, vb. maltrattare.

mammal, n. mammífero m.

mammoth, n. mammut m.

man, n. uòmo m.

manage, vb. amministrare, dirígere.

manageable, adj. maneggèvole; risolvibile.

management, n. amministrazione f., direzione f.

manager, n. amministratore m., direttore m.

mandate, n. mandato m.

mandatory, adj. obbligatòrio.

mandolin, n. mandolino m.

mandrake, n. mandràgola f.

mane, n. crinièra f.

maneuver, 1. n. manòvra f. **2.** vb. manovrare.

manganese, n. manganese m.

manger, n. mangiatoia f.

mangle, vb. tritare.

manhandle, vb. malmenare.

manhood, n. virilità f.

mania, n. manìa f.

maniac, n. and adj. manìaco (m.).

manicure, n. manicure f.

manifest, 1. adj. manifèsto. **2.** vb. manifestare.

manifesto, n. manifèsto m.

manifold, adj. moltéplice.

manikin, n. manichino m.

manipulate, vb. manipolare.

mankind, n. umanità f.

manly, adj. virile.

manner, n. manièra f., mòdo m.

mannerism, n. manierismo m.

manor, n. maniero m.; fèudo m.; proprietà f.

mansion, n. palazzo m.

manslaughter, n. omicìdio m.

mantelpiece, n. cornice f.

mantle, n. mantèllo m.

Mantua, n. Màntova f.

Mantuan, n. and adj. mantovano (m.)

manual, n. and adj. manuale (m.)

manufacture, n. fabbricazione f.

manufacturer, n. fabbricante m.

manufacturing, adj. industriale.

manure, n. concime m.

manuscript, *n. and adj.* manoscritto *(m.)*

many, *adj.* molti *m.pl.;* molte *f.pl.*

map, *n.* carta *f.*

maple, *n.* àcero *m.*

mar, *vb.* danneggiare, guastare.

marble, *n.* marmo *m.*

march, 1. *n.* màrcia *f.* 2. *vb.* marciare.

March, *n.* marzo *m.*

mare, *n.* cavalla *f.*

margarine, *n.* margarina *f.*

margin, *n.* màrgine *m.*

marginal, *adj.* marginale.

marijuana, *n.* marijuana *f.*

marinate, *vb.* marinare.

marine, *adj.* marino, maríttimo.

mariner, *n.* marinaio *m.*

marionette, *n.* marionetta *f.*

marital, *adj.* maritale.

maritime, *adj.* maríttimo.

mark, 1. *n.* segno *m.* 2. *vb.* marcare, segnare.

market, *n.* mercato *m.*

market place, *n.* piazza del mercato *m.*

marmalade, *n.* marmellata *f.*

maroon, *n.* (color) marrone *m.*

marquee, *n.* pensilina *f.*

marquis, *n.* marchese *m.*

marriage, *n.* matrimònio *m.*

marrow, *n.* midollo *m.*

marry, *vb.* sposare, *tr.;* (woman) maritare, *tr.*

Marseilles, *n.* Marsiglia *f.*

marsh, *n.* palude *f.*

marshal, *n.* maresciallo *m.*

marital, *adj.* marziale.

martinet, *n.* tiranno *m.*

martyr, *n.* màrtire *m.*

martyrdom, *n.* martírio *m.*

marvel, 1. *n.* meraviglia *f.* 2. *vb.* meravigliarsi.

marvelous, *adj.* meraviglioso.

mascot, *n.* portafortuna *m.*

masculine, *adj.* maschile.

mash, *vb.* schiacciare.

mask, 1. *n.* màschera *f.* 2. *vb.* mascherare.

mason, *n.* muratore *m.*

masquerade, 1. *n.* mascherata *f.* 2. *vb.* mascherarsi.

mass, *n.* massa *f.;* (church) messa *f.*

massacre, 1. *n.* massacro *m.* 2. *vb.* massacrare.

massage, 1. *n.* massaggio *m.* 2. *vb.* massaggiare.

masseur, *n.* massaggiatore *m.*

massive, *adj.* massíccio.

mass meeting, *n.* assemblèa *f.*

mast, *n.* àlbero *m.*

master, *n.* (boss) padrone *m.;* (great artist) maestro *m.;* (workman) mastro *m.*

master-key, *n.* comunèlla *f.,* passe-par-tout *m.*

masterpiece, *n.* capolavoro *m.*

mastery, *n.* padronanza *f.*

masticate, *vb.* masticare.

mat, *n.* stuòia *f.*

match, 1. *n.* (light) fiammífero *m.;* (contest) incontro *m.;* (equal) uguale *m.;* (marriage) matrimònio *m.* 2. *vb.* uguagliare.

matchless, *adj.* senza pari.

mate, 1. *n.* (spouse) consòrte *m.* or *f.;* (pal) compagno *m.;* (second in command) secondo *m.;* (assistant) assistènte *m.* 2. *vb.* accoppiare, *tr.*

material, *n. and adj.* materiale *(m.).*

materialism, *n.* materialismo *m.*

materialize, *vb.* materializzare.

maternal, *adj.* matèrno.

maternity, *n.* maternità *f.*

maternity ward, *n.* reparto maternità *m.*

mathematical, *adj.* matemàtico.

mathematician, *n.* matemàtico *m.*

mathematics, *n.* matemàtica *f.*

matinée, *n.* mattinata *f.*

matriarchy, *n.* matriarcato *m.*

matricide, *n.* matricidio *m.*

matriculation, *n.* immatricolazione *f.*

matrimony, *n.* matrimònio *m.*

matron, *n.* matrona *f.*

matter, 1. *n.* matèria *f.;* (pus) pus *m.* 2. *vb.* importare.

matter of fact, n. (as a m.) *adv.* in realtà.

mattress, *n.* materasso *m.*

mature, 1. *adj.* maturo. 2. *vb.* maturare; (fall due) scadere.

maturity, *n.* maturità *f.;* (financial) scadènza *f.*

maudlin, *adj.* piagnucoloso.

maul, vb. percuòtere.
mausoleum, n. mausolèo m.
maxim, n. màssima f.
maximum, n. and adj. màssimo (m.).
may, vb. potere.
May, n. màggio m.
maybe, adv. forse.
mayhem, n. danni m.pl.
mayonnaise, n. maionese f.
mayor, n. síndaco m.
maze, n. labirinto m.
me, pron. me, mi.
meadow, n. prato m.
meadowland, n. prateria f.
meager, adj. magro, scarso.
meal, n. pasto m.; (flour) farina f.
mean, 1. n. mèdia f. **2.** adj. (in the middle) mèdio; (base) meschino, spregévole. **3.** vb. significare, voler dire.
meander, n. meandro m.
meaning, n. significato m.
meaningful, adj. significativo.
meaningless, adj. insensato.
means, n. mèzzo m.sg.
meantime, meanwhile, n. frattèmpo m.
measles, n. morbillo m.
measurable, adj. misuràbile.
measure, 1. n. misura f. **2.** vb. misurare.
measurement, n. misuramento m.
measuring, adj. misuratore.
meat, n. carne f.
meat grinder, n. tritacarne m.
meaty, adj. polposo; in carne.
mechanic, n. meccànico m.
mechanical, adj. meccànico.
mechanism, n. meccanismo m.
mechanize, vb. meccanizzare.
medal, n. medàglia f.
meddle, vb. immischiarsi.
mediaeval, adj. medioevale.
median, adj. mediano.
mediate, vb. fare da intermediàrio.
mediator, n. intermediàrio m.
medical, adj. mèdico.
medicate, vb. medicare.
medicine, n. medicina f.
mediocre, adj. mediòcre.
mediocrity, n. mediocrità f.
meditate, vb. meditare.

meditation, n. meditazione f.
Mediterranean, n. and adj. mediterràneo (m.).
medium, 1. n. mèzzo m. **2.** adj. mèdio.; (meat) còtto moderatamente.
medley, n. miscùglio m.
meek, adj. mite.
meekness, n. mitezza f.
meet, vb. incontrare tr.
meeting, n. riunione f., assemblèa f.; (m.-place) ritròvo m.
megahertz, n. megahertz m.
megaphone, n. megàfono m.
melancholy, 1. n. malinconía f. **2.** adj. malincònico, melancònico.
mellow, adj. maturato.
melodious, adj. melodioso.
melodrama, n. melodramma m.
melody, n. melodía f.
melon, n. melone m.
melt, vb. fóndere tr., sciògliere tr.
meltdown, n. fusione f.
member, n. sòcio m., membro m.
membership, n. affiliati m.pl.
membrane, n. membrana f.
memento, n. ricòrdo m.
memoir, n. memòria f.
memorable, adj. memoràbile.
memorandum, n. memorandum m.
memorial, 1. n. monumento m., memoriale m. **2.** adj. commemorativo.
memorize, vb. imparare a memòria.
memory, n. memòria f.
menace, 1. n. minàccia f. **2.** vb. minacciare.
menagerie, n. serràglio m.
mend, vb. accomodare.
mendacious, adj. mendace.
mendicant, 1. n. mèndico m. **2.** adj. mendicante.
menial, adj. servile.
menopause, n. menopàusa f.
menses, n. mestruazioni f.pl.
menstruation, n. mestruazione f.; régole f.pl.
menswear, n. abbigliamento maschile m.
mental, adj. mentale.
mentality, n. mentalità f.
menthol, n. mentòlo m.

mention, 1. *n.* menzione *f.* **2.** *vb.* menzionare.
menu, *n.* lista *f.*
meow, 1. *n.* miagolio *m.* **2.** *vb.* miagolare.
mercantile, *adj.* mercantile.
mercenary, *adj.* mercenàrio.
merchandise, *n.* mercanzia *f.*
merchant, *n.* mercante *m.*
merchant marine, *n.* marina mercantile *f.*
merciful, *adj.* pietoso.
merciless, *adj.* spietato.
mercury, *n.* mercùrio *m.*
mercy, *n.* pietà *f.*, misericòrdia *f.*
mere, *adj.* mèro, sémplice.
merely, *adj.* meramente, semplicemente.
merge, *vb.* assorbire.
merger, *n.* fusione *f.*
meringue, *n.* meringa *f.*
merit, 1. *n.* mèrito *m.* **2.** *vb.* meritare.
meritorious, *adj.* meritòrio.
mermaid, *n.* sirena *f.*
merriment, *n.* allegrezza *f.*
merry, *adj.* allegro.
merry-go-round, *n.* carosèllo *m.*
mesh, 1. *n.* (fabric) màglia *f.* **2.** *vb.* (gears) ingranare.
mesmerize, *vb.* ipnotizzare.
mess, *n.* pasticcio *m.*, confusione *f.*; (soldiers' meals) ràncio *m.*
message, *n.* messàggio *m.*, ambasciata *f.*
messenger, *n.* messaggèro *m.*
messy, *adj.* confuso, disordinato.
metabolism, *n.* metabolismo *m.*
metal, *n.* metallo *m.*
metallic, *adj.* metàllico.
metamorphosis, *n.* metamòrfosi *f.*
metaphor, *n.* metàfora *f.*
metaphysics, *n.* metafisica *f.*
meteor, *n.* metèora *f.*
meteorology, *n.* meteorologìa *f.*
meter, *n.* (recording device) contatore *m.*; (unit of measure) mètro *m.*
method, *n.* mètodo *m.*
meticulous, *adj.* meticoloso.
metric, *adj.* mètrico.
metropolis, *n.* metròpoli *f.*
metropolitan,   *adj.*   metropolitano.

mettle, *n.* coràggio *f.*
mettlesome, *adj.* brìoso.
Mexican, *adj.* messicano.
Mexico, *n.* il Mèssico *m.*
mezzanine, *n.* mezzanino *m.*
microbe, *n.* micròbio *m.*
microfiche, *n.* microscheda *f.*
microfilm, *n.* mìcrofilm *m.*
microform, *n.* microforma *f.*
microphone, *n.* micròfono *m.*
microscope, *n.* microscòpio *m.*
microscopic, *adj.* microscòpico.
mid-, *adj.* mèdio.
middle, 1. *n.* mèzzo *m.* **2.** *adj.* mèdio, intermèdio, mèzzo.
middle-aged, *adj.* di mèzza età.
Middle Ages, *n.* medioèvo *m.*
middle class, *n.* borghesìa *f.*, ceto mèdio *m.*, classe mèdia *f.*
Middle East, *n.* Medio Oriente *m.*
midget, *n.* nano *m.*
midnight, *n.* mezzanòtte *f.*
midriff, *n.* diaframma *f.*
midwife, *n.* levatrice *f.*
mien, *n.* aspètto *m.*, cera *f.*
might, 1. *n.* potènza *f.* **2.** *vb.* use conditional of potere.
mighty, *adj.* potènte.
migraine, *n.* emicrània *f.*
migrate, *vb.* migrare.
migration, *n.* migrazione *f.*
migratory, *adj.* migratòrio.
Milan, *n.* Milano *f.*
Milanese, *adj.* milanese.
mild, *adj.* mite.
mildew, *n.* muffa bianca *f.*
mildness, *n.* mitezza *f.*
mile, *n.* mìglio *m.*
mileage, *n.* chilometràggio *m.*
milestone, *n.* piètra miliare *f.*
militant, *adj.* militante.
militarism, *n.* militarismo *m.*
military, *adj.* militare.
militia, *n.* milìzia *f.*
milk, 1. *n.* latte *m.* **2.** *vb.* mùngere.
milk-bar, *n.* latterìa *f.*
milkman, *n.* lattaio *m.*
milky, *adj.* làtteo.
Milky Way, *n.* Via Latea *f.*
mill, 1. *n.* mulino *m.*; (factory) fàbbrica *f.* **2.** *vb.* macinare.
millenium, *n.* millènio *m.*
miller, *n.* mugnaio *m.*
milligram, *n.* milligrammo *m.*
millimeter, *n.* millìmetro *m.*

milliner, n. modista m. or f.
millinery, n. modisteria f.
milling, 1. n. macinatura f.; **(m. machine)** n. fresatrice f.
million, n. milione m.
millionaire, n. milionàrio m.
mimic, 1. n. imitatore m. 2. adj. imitato. 3. vb. imitare.
mimicry, n. mimetismo m.
minaret, n. minareto m.
mince, vb. triturare.
mind, 1. n. mente f., ànimo m. 2. vb. badare a; (obey) ubbidire a; **(never m.)** non impòrta.
mindful, adj. mèmore.
mine, 1. n. minièra f.; (explosive) mina f. 2. adj. mío. 3. vb. minare.
mine field, n. campo minato m.
miner, n. minatore m.
mineral, n. and adj. minerale (m.).
mine-sweeper, n. nave spazzamine f.
mingle, vb. mescolare, tr.
miniature, n. miniatura f.
miniaturize, vb. miniaturizzare.
minimal, adj. mínimo.
minimize, vb. ridurre al mínimo.
minimum, n. and adj. mínimo (m.).
minimum wage, n. salàrio mínimo m.
mining, 1. n. coltivazione delle minière f. 2. adj. minerário.
miniskirt, n. minigonna f.
minister, 1. n. ministro m. 2. vb. ministrare.
ministry, n. ministèrio m.
mink, n. visone m.
minnow, n. pesciolino m.
minor, 1. n. (person under 21) minorènne. 2. adj. minore, minorènne.
minority, n. minoranza f.; (age) minor età f.
minstrel, n. menestrèllo m.
mint, 1. n. (plant) menta f.; (coin factory) zecca f. 2. vb. coniare.
minus, prep. meno.
minute, 1. n. minuto m.; (of meeting) verbale m. 2. adj. minuto.
miracle, n. miràcolo m.
miraculous, adj. miracoloso.
mirage, n. miràggio m.
mire, n. fango m.

mirror, n. spècchio m.
mirth, n. allegrìa f.
misadventure, n. disgràzia f.
misappropriate, vb. appropriare indebitamente.
misbehave, vb. comportarsi male.
miscalculation, n. càlcolo sbagliato m.
miscarriage, n. (justice) errore giudiziario m.; (medicine) aborto spontàneo m.
miscellaneous, adj. miscellàneo.
mischief, n. cattivèria f., malízia f.
mischievous, adj. cattivo, malizioso.
misconception, n. fraintendimento m.
misconstrue, vb. fraintèndere.
miscreant, n. and adj. miscredènte.
misdemeanor, n. contravvenzione f.
miser, n. avaro m.
miserable, adj. mísero.
miserly, adj. avaro.
misery, n. misèria f.
misfit, n. persona inadatta f.
misfortune, n. sfortuna f.
misgiving, n. apprensione f., dùbbio m.
mishap, n. disgràzia f.
mislay, vb. smarrire.
mislead, vb. ingannare.
misplace, vb. smarrire.
misplaced, adj. fuòri di propòsito.
mispronounce, vb. pronunziar male.
miss, 1. n. (unsuccessful shot) colpo mancato m. 2. vb. mancare, pèrdere; (feel the lack of) sentire la mancanza di.
Miss, n. signorina f.
missile, n. missile m.
mission, n. missione f.
missionary, n. and adj. missionàrio (m.).
misspell, vb. scrívere scorrettamente.
mist, n. nébbia f.
mistake, 1. n. sbàglio m. 2. vb. sbagliare.
mistaken, adj. errato, erròneo, sbagliato.

mister, n. signore m.

mistletoe, n. vischio m.

mistreat, vb. maltrattare, bistrattare.

mistress, n. padrona f.; (lover) amante f.

mistrust, 1. n. sfidùcia f. 2. vb. diffidare di.

misty, adj. nebbioso.

misunderstand, vb. fraintèndere.

misuse, vb. abusare di.

mite, n. (coin) òbolo m.; (small piece) pezzettino m.; (tot) piccino m.

mitigate, vb. mitigare.

mitten, n. guanto m.

mix, vb. mescolare, tr.

mixed, adj. misto, assortito.

mixed feelings, n. ambivalenza f.

mixture, n. mescolanza f., mistura f.

mix-up, n. confusione f.

moan, 1. n. gèmito m. 2. vb. gèmere.

moat, n. fòssa f.

mob, n. fòlla f., plebàglia f.

mobile, adj. mòbile.

mobility, n. mobilità f.

mobilization, n. mobilitazione f.

mobilize, vb. mobilitare.

mobster, n. criminale m.; gangster m.

moccasin, n. mocassino m.

mock, 1. adj. finto. 2. vb. deridere, beffarsi di, schernire.

mockery, n. derisione f., scherno m.

mod, adj. moderno.

mode, n. (way) mòdo m.; (fashion) mòda f.

model, 1. n. modèllo m. 2. vb. modellare.

moderate, 1. adj. moderato. 2. vb. moderare.

moderation, n. moderazione f.

modern, adj. modèrno.

modernize, vb. rimodernare, tr.

modest, adj. modèsto.

modesty, n. modèstia f.

modify, vb. modificare.

modish, adj. alla mòda.

modulate, vb. modulare.

moist, adj. ùmido.

moisten, vb. inumidire.

moisture, n. umidità f.

molar, adj. molare.

molasses, n. melassa f.

mold, 1. n. forma f., stampo m.; (must) muffa f. 2. vb. formare, modellare.

moldy, adj. ammuffito.

mole, n. (animal) talpa f.; (pier) mòlo m.

molecule, n. molècola f.

molest, vb. molestare.

mollify, vb. ammollire.

molten, adj. fuso.

moment, n. momènto m.

momentary, adj. momentàneo.

momentous, adj. importante.

monarch, n. monarca m.

monarchy, n. monarchìa f.

monastery, n. monastèro m.

Monday, n. lunedì m.

monetary, adj. monetàrio.

money, n. denaro m.

money-order, n. vàglia m.

mongrel, n. and adj. bastardo (m.).

monitor, n. monitore m.

monk, n. mònaco m.

monkey, n. scìmmia f.

monocle, n. monòcolo m.

monologue, n. monòlogo m.

monoplane, n. monoplano m.

monopolize, vb. monopolizzare.

monopoly, n. monopòlio m.

monosyllable, n. monosìllabo m.

monotone, n. tono uniforme m.

monotonous, adj. monòtono.

monotony, adj. monotonìa f.

monoxide, n. monòssido m.

monsoon, n. monsone m.

monster, 1. n. mostro m. 2. adj. (huge) immènso.

monstrosity, n. mostruosità f.

monstrous, adj. mostruoso.

month, n. mese m.

monthly, adj. mensile.

monument, n. monumento m.

monumental, adj. monumentale.

mood, n. stato d'ànimo m.

moody, adj. triste.

moon, n. luna f.

moonlight, n. chiaro di luna m.

moor, 1. n. brughièra f. 2. vb. ormeggiare.

mooring, n. ormèggio m.

moot, adj. discusso.

mop, n. scopa di stracci f.

moped, n. ciclomotore m.
moral, n. and adj. morale (f.).
morale, n. morale m.
moralist, n. moralista m.
morality, n. moralità f.
morally, adv. moralmente.
morbid, adj. morboso.
more, adv. più; **(m. and m.)** sempre più.
moreover, adv. per di più.
mores, n. costumi m.pl.
morgue, n. càmera mortuària f.
morning, n. mattina f., mattino m.
moron, n. imbecille m.
morose, adj. poco sociévole.
morphine, n. morfina f.
Morse code, n. còdice Morse m.
morsel, n. (food) boccone m.; (piece) frammento m.
mortal, n. and adj. mortale (m.).
mortality, n. mortalità f.
mortar, n. calcina f.
mortgage, 1. n. ipotèca f. **2.** vb. ipotecare.
mortician, n. imprenditore di pompe funebri m.
mortify, vb. mortificare.
mortuary, adj. mortuàrio.
mosaic, n. mosàico m.
Moscow, Mosca.
Moslem, n. and adj. mussulmano (m.)
mosque, n. moschèa f.
mosquito, n. zanzara f.; **(m. net)** zanzarièra f.
moss, n. mùschio m.
most, 1. adj. la maggior parte di. **2.** adj. maggiormente.
mostly, adv. per lo più.
motel, n. motèl m.
moth, n. tarma f.
moth-eaten, adj. tarmato.
mother, n. madre f., mamma f.
mother country, n. màdre patria f.
motherhood, n. maternità f.
mother-in-law, n. suòcera f.
motif, n. motivo m.
motion, n. mòto m.; (parliamentary) mozione f.
motionless, adj. immòbile.
motion-picture, n. pellícola f.
motivate, vb. motivare.
motive, 1. n. motivo m. **2.** adj.

motore; **(m. power)** fòrza motrice.
motley, n. eterogèneo, multicolore.
motor, n. motore m.
motorboat, n. motoscafo m.
motorcycle, n. motocicletta f.
motorist, n. automobilista m.
motorize, vb. motorizzare.
motorized farming, n. motocultura f.
motto, n. motto m.
mound, n. tùmulo m.
mount, vb. montare, salire.
mountain, n. montagna f., monte m.
mountaineer, n. montanaro m.
mountainous, adj. montagnoso, montuoso.
mountebank, n. ciarlatano m.
mourn, vb. piàngere.
mournful, adj. doloroso.
mourning, n. lutto m.
mouse, n. sórcio m., tòpo m.
mouth, n. bocca f.
mouthpiece, n. (instrument) imboccatura f.; (spokesman) portavoce m.
movable, adj. mòbile.
move, 1. n. (household goods) traslòco m. **2.** vb. muòvere, tr.
movement, n. movimento m.
movie, n. cínema m., film m.
moving, 1. n. (household goods) traslòco m. **2.** adj. commovènte.
moving staircase, n. scala mòbile f.
mow, vb. falciare.
Mr., n. Sig. m. (abbr. for Signore).
Mrs., n. Sra. f. (abbr. for Signora).
much, adj. and adv. molto.
mucilage, n. gomma líquida f.
muck, n. letame m., melma f.
muckrake, vb. sollevare scàndali.
mucous, adj. mucoso.
mucus, n. muco m.
mud, n. fango m., lòto m.
muddy, adj. fangoso.
mudslide, n. smottamento m.
muff, 1. n. manicotto m. **2.** vb. sbagliare.
muffle, vb. (wrap up) imbacuccare, tr.; (silence) attutire.
muffler, n. (scarf) sciarpa f.; (auto) silenziatore dello scàrico m.

mug, *n.* coppa *f.*
mulatto, *n.* mulatto *m.*
mulberry, *n.* gelso *m.*
mule, *n.* mulo *m.*
mullah, *n.* mulla(h) *m.*
multicolored, *adj.* multicolore.
multinational, *adj.* multinazionale.
multiple, *adj.* mùltiplo.
multiplication, *n.* moltiplicazione *f.*
multiplicity, *n.* molteplicità *f.*
multiply, *vb.* moltiplicare, *tr.*
multitude, *n.* moltitùdine *f.*
mummy, *n.* mùmmia *f.*
mumps, *n.* orecchioni *m.pl.*
munch, *vb.* sgranocchiare.
Munich, *n.* Mònaco di Bavièra *m.*
municipal, *adj.* municipale.
munificent, *adj.* munificènte.
munition, *n.* munizione *f.*
mural, *adj.* murale.
murder, *n.* assassínio *m.*
murderer, *n.* assassino *m.*
murmur, 1. *n.* mormorío *m.* **2.** *vb.* mormorare.
muscle, *n.* mùscolo *m.*
muscular, *adj.* muscolare.
muse, 1. *n.* musa *f.* **2.** *vb.* meditare.
museum, *n.* musèo *m.*
mushroom, *n.* fungo *m.*
music, *n.* mùsica *f.*
musical, *adj.* musicale.
musical comedy, *n.* operetta *f.*, rivista *f.*
music hall, *n.* sala di concerti *f.*
musician, *n.* musicista *f.*
musk, *n.* mùschio *m.*

muslin, *n.* mussolina *f.*
must, *n.* use present of dovere.
mustache, *n.* baffi *m.pl.*
mustard, *n.* sènape *f.*, mostarda *f.*
muster, 1. *n.* rivista *f.* **2.** *vb.* radunare.
musty, *adj.* ammuffito.
mutation, *n.* mutazione *f.*
mute, *adj.* muto.
mutilate, *vb.* mutilare.
mutiny, 1. *n.* ammutinamento *m.* **2.** *vb.* ammutinarsi.
mutter, *vb.* borbottare.
mutton, *n.* carne di montone *f.*
mutual, *adj.* mùtuo.
mutual fund, *n.* fondo comune d'investimento *m.*
muzzle, *n.* (gun) bocca *f.*; (animal's mouth) muso *m.*; (mouth covering) museruòla *f.*
my, *adj.* mío.
myopia, *n.* miopía *f.*
myriad, 1. *n.* miríade *f.* **2.** *adj.* innumerévole.
myrrh, *n.* mirra *f.*
myrtle, *n.* mirto *m.*
myself, *pron.* me stesso; **(I m.)** ío stesso.
mysterious, *adj.* misterioso.
mystery, *n.* mistèro *m.*
mystic, *adj.* místico.
mysticism, *n.* misticismo *m.*
mystification, *n.* mistificazione *f.*
mystify, *vb.* mistificare.
myth, *n.* mito *m.*
mythical, *adj.* mítico.
mythology, *n.* mitología *f.*

N

nag, 1. *n.* ronzino *m.* **2.** *vb.* tormentare.
nail, 1. *n.* chiòdo *m.*; (of finger, toe) unghia *f.* **2.** *vb.* inchiodare.
naïve, *adj.* ingènuo.
naked, *adj.* nudo.
name, 1. *n.* nome *m.*; **(family n.)** cognome *m.* **2.** *vb.* chiamare; (nominate) nominare.
namely, *adv.* cioè.
namesake, *n.* omònimo *m.*
nap, 1. *n.* pisolino *m.*, sonnellino *m.* **2.** *vb.* sonnecchiare.

naphtha, *n.* nafta *f.*
napkin, *n.* tovagliòlo *m.*
Naples, *n.* Nàpoli *f.*
narcissus, *n.* narciso *m.*
narcotic, *n. and adj.* narcòtico (*m.*).
narrate, *vb.* narrare.
narrative, 1. *n.* racconto *m.* **2.** *adj.* narrativo.
narration, *n.* narrazione *f.*
narrow, *adj.* stretto.
nasal, *adj.* nasale.
nasty, *adj.* disgustoso, antipàtico.

natal, *adj.* natale.
nation, *n.* nazione *f.*
national, *adj.* nazionale.
nationalism, *n.* nazionalismo *m.*
nationality, *n.* nazionalità *f.*
nationalization, *n.* nazionalizzazione *f.*
nationalize, *vb.* nazionalizzare.
native, 1. *n.* indígeno *m.* 2. *adj.* nativo, indígeno.
nativity, *n.* nativítà *f.*
natural, *adj.* naturale.
naturalist, *n.* naturalista *m.*
naturalize, *vb.* naturalizzare.
naturalness, *n.* naturalezza *f.*
nature, *n.* natura *f.*
naughty, *adj.* birichino.
nausea, *n.* nàusea *f.*
nauseating, *adj.* nauseante.
nautical, *adj.* nàutico.
naval, *adj.* navale.
nave, *n.* navata *f.*
navel, *n.* ombellico *m.*
navigable, *adj.* navigàbile.
navigate, *vb.* navigare.
navigation, *n.* navigazione *f.*
navigator, *n.* navigatore *m.*
navy, *n.* marina *f.*
navy yard, *n.* arsenale *m.*
Neapolitan, *adj.* napoletano.
near, 1. *adj.*, *adv.* vicino. 2. *prep.* vicino a.
nearby, *adv.* vicino.
nearly, *adv.* quasi.
near-sighted, *adj.* miope.
neat, *adj.* lindo, pulito.
neatness, *n.* pulizia *f.*
nebula, *n.* nebulosa *f.*
nebulous, *adj.* nebuloso.
necessary, *adj.* necessàrio; **(be n.)** bisognare, volerci.
necessity, *n.* necessità *f.*
neck, *n.* collo *m.*
necklace, *n.* collana *f.*
necktie, *n.* cravatta *f.*
nectar, *n.* nèttare *m.*
need, 1. *n.* bisogno *m.* 2. *vb.* aver bisogno di.
needful, *adj.* necessário.
needle, *n.* ago *m.*; (phonograph) puntina *f.*
needless, *adj.* inùtile.
needy, *adj.* bisognoso.
nefarious, *adj.* malvàgio, sùbdolo.

negate, *vb.* negare.
negation, *n.* negazione *f.*
negative, 1. *n.* negativa *f.* 2. *adj.* negativo.
neglect, *vb.* trascurare.
neglectful, *adj.* negligente, trascurato.
negligée, *n.* vestàglia *f.*
negligent, *adj.* trascurato.
negligible, *adj.* trascuràbile.
negotiable, *adj.* negoziàbile.
negotiate, *vb.* negoziare.
negotiation, *n.* negoziazione *f.*
Negro, *n.* negro *m.*
neighbor, *n.* vicino *m.*, pròssimo *m.*
neighborhood, *n.* vicinanza *f.*
neither, *conj.* nè.
neologism, *n.* neologismo *m.*
neon, *n.* nèon *m.*
neophyte, *n.* neòfita *m.*
nephew, *n.* nipote *m.*
nepotism, *n.* nepotismo *m.*
nerve, *n.* nèrvo *m.*; (effrontery) sfrontatezza *f.*
nervous, *adj.* nervoso.
nest, *n.* nido *m.*
nest egg, *n.* grùzzolo *m.*
nestle, *vb.* annidarsi.
net, *n.* rete *f.*
netting, *n.* rete *f.*
nettle, 1. *n.* ortica *f.* 2. *vb.* irritare.
network, *n.* rete *f.*
neuralgia, *n.* nevralgía *f.*
neurology, *n.* neurología *f.*
neurotic, *adj.* nevròtico.
neutral, *n.* and *adj.* nèutro (*m.*).
neutrality, *n.* neutralità *f.*
neutralize, *vb.* neutralizzare.
neutron, *n.* neutrone *m.*
neutron bomb, *n.* bomba al neutrone *f.*
never, *adv.* mai.
nevertheless, *adv.* nondimeno.
new, *adj.* nuòvo.
newborn, *n.* neonato *m.*
news, *n.* notízie *f.pl.*
news-boy, *n.* giornalaio *m.*
newscast, *n.* radiocorrière *m.*
newspaper, *n.* giornale *m.*
newsreel, *n.* attualità *f.pl.*
next, *adj.* pròssimo, seguènte.
nibble, *vb.* rosicchiare.
nice, *adj.* gentile, buòno.
nick, *n.* tacca *f.*

nickel, n. níchel m.
nickname, n. nomígnolo m.
nicotine, n. nicotina f.
niece, n. nipote f.
niggardly, adj. taccagno.
night, n. nòtte f.
night club, n. ritròvo notturno m., nightclub m.
nightgown, n. camícia da nòtte f.
nightingale, n. usignuòlo m.
nightly, adv. ogni nòtte.
nightmare, n. íncubo m.
night-stick, n. clava f.
nimble, adj. àgile.
nine, num. nòve.
nineteen, num. diciannòve.
nineteenth, adj. dècimo nòno, diciannovèsimo.
ninetieth, adj. novantèsimo.
ninety, num. novanta.
ninth, adj. nòno.
nip, n. pizzicòtto m.
nipple, n. capézzolo m.
nitrate, n. nitrato m.
nitrogen, n. nitrògeno m.
no, 1. adj. nessuno. 2. interj. nò.
nobility, n. nobiltà f.
noble, n. and adj. nòbile (m.).
nobleman, n. nobiluòmo m.
nobly, adv. nobilmente.
nobody, pron. nessuno.
nocturnal, adj. notturno.
nocturne, n. notturno m.
nod, 1. n. cenno d'assenso col capo m. 2. fare un cenno col capo.
node, n. nòdo m.
no-frills, adj. sémplice.
noise, n. rumore m.
noiseless, adj. silenzioso.
noisome, adj. puzzolènte.
noisy, adj. rumoroso.
nomad, n. nòmade m.
nominal, adj. nominale.
nominate, vb. nominare, designare.
nomination, n. nòmina f.
nominee, n. designato m., candidato m.
nonaligned, adj. non allineato.
nonchalant, adj. incurante.
noncombatant, n. and adj. non combattènte (m.).
non-commissioned officer, n. sottufficiale m.

noncommittal, adj. che non si compromette, disimpegnato.
nondescript, adj. sènza caratteristiche speciali.
none, adj. and pron. nessuno.
nonentity, n. nullità f.
nonpartisan, adj. nèutro.
nonresident, adj. non residènte.
nonsense, n. assurdità f., fandònie f.pl.
nonstop, adj. sènza fermate.
noodles, n. tagliatèlle f.pl.
nook, n. cantùccio m.
noon, n. mezzogiorno m.
no one, pron. nessuno.
noose, n. nodo scorsoio m.
nor, conj. nè.
norm, n. nòrma f.
normal, adj. normale.
normally, adv. normalmente.
north, 1. n. nord m. 2. adj. settentrionale.
northeast, n. nord-èst m.
northern, adj. settentrionale.
North Pole, n. polo nord m.
northwest, n. nord-òvest m.
Norway, n. Norvègia f.
Norwegian, adj. norvegese.
nose, n. naso m.
nosebleed, n. emorragia nasale f.
nose dive, n. picchiata f.
nostalgia, n. nostalgìa f.
nostril, n. narice f.
nostrum, n. rimèdio empírico m.
nosy, adj. ficcanaso.
not, adv. non.
notable, adj. notévole.
notary, n. notaio m.
notation, n. notazione f.
notch, 1. n. tacca f. 2. vb. intaccare.
note, 1. n. nòta f.; (short letter) biglietto m. 2. vb. notare.
notebook, n. agènda f., taccuino m.
noted, adj. nòto.
notepaper, n. carta da lèttera f.
noteworthy, adj. rimarchévole.
nothing, pron. niente, nulla.
notice, 1. n. avviso m., attenzione f. 2. vb. osservare.
noticeable, adj. notévole.
notification, n. notificazione f., avviso m.
notify, vb. notificare.

notion, n. nozione f.
notoriety, n. notorietà f.
notorious, adj. famigerato, notòrio.
notwithstanding, prep. nonostante.
nougat, n. torrone f.
noun, n. sostantivo m.
nourish, vb. nutrire.
nourishment, n. nutrimento m.
novel, 1. n. romanzo m. **2.** adj. originale.
novelist, n. romanziere m.
novelty, n. novità f.
November, n. novèmbre m.
novena, n. novèna f.
novice, n. novìzio m.
Novocaine, n. novocaína f.
now, adv. ora, adèsso.
nowadays, adv. di questi tempi.
noway(s), adv. in nessun modo.
nowhere, adv. in nessun luògo.
noxious, adj. nocivo.
nozzle, n. imboccatura f.
nuance, n. sfumatura f.
nuclear, adj. nucleare.
nuclear warhead, n. testata càrica nucleare f.
nuclear waste, n. rifiuti nucleari m.pl.
nucleus, n. nùcleo m.

nude, adj. nudo.
nudge, n. colpetto di gòmito m.
nugget, n. pepita f.
nudist, n. and adj. nudista m. and f.
nuisance, n. fastidio m., seccatura f.
nuke, 1. n. arma atòmica f. **2.** vb. bombardare con l'atòmica.
nullify, vb. annullare.
numb, adj. intorpidito.
number, 1. n. nùmero m. **2.** vb. numerare.
numerical, adj. numèrico.
numerous, adj. numeroso.
nun, n. mònaca f., suòra f.
nuncio, n. nùnzio m.
nuptial, adj. nuziale.
nurse, 1. n. (hospital) infermièra f.; (wet-nurse) nutrice f., bàlia f.; (baby-tender) bambinaia f. **2.** vb. curare.
nursery, n. stanza dei bambini f.; (plants) vivaio m.
nurture, vb. allevare, curare.
nut, n. nocciòla f.
nut-cracker, n. schiaccianoci m.
nutrition, n. nutrizione f.
nutritious, adj. nutriènte.
nutshell, n. gùscio di noce m.
nylon, n. nàilon m.
nymph, n. ninfa f.

O

oak, n. quèrcia f.
oar, n. remo m.
oasis, n. òasi f.
oath, n. (solemn) giuramento m.; (swear-word) bestémmia f.
oatmeal, n. fiocchi d'avena m.pl.
oats, n. avena f.sg.
obdurate, adj. ostinato.
obedience, n. obbediènza f.
obedient, adj. obbediènte.
obeisance, n. riverènza f.
obelisk, n. obelisco m.
obese, adj. obèso.
obey, vb. ubbidire, obbedire.
obfuscate, vb. offuscare.
obituary, n. necrològio m.
object, 1. n. oggetto m. **2.** vb. opporsi, obiettare.
objection, n. obiezione f.
objectionable, adj. offensivo.

objective, n. and adj. obiettivo (m.)
obligate, vb. obbligare.
obligation, n. òbbligo m., obbligazione f.
obligatory, adj. obbligatòrio.
oblige, vb. obbligare.
obliging, adj. serviziévole.
oblique, adj. obliquo.
obliterate, vb. cancellare.
oblivion, n. oblío m.
oblivious, adj. dimèntico, ignaro.
oblong, adj. oblungo.
obnoxious, adj. odioso.
oboe, n. òboe m.
obscene, adj. oscèno.
obscenity, n. oscenità f.
obscure, adj. oscuro.
obscurity, n. oscurità f.
obsequious, adj. ossequioso.

observance, n. osservanza f.
observation, n. osservazione f.
observatory, n. osservatòrio m.
observe, vb. osservare.
observer, n. osservatore m.
obsess, vb. ossessionare.
obsession, n. ossessione f.
obsolete, adj. caduto in disuso.
obstacle, n. ostàcolo m.
obstetrical, adj. ostètrico.
obstetrician, n. ostètrico m.
obstinate, adj. ostinato.
obstreperous, adj. clamoroso, chiassoso.
obstruct, vb. ostruire, ostacolare.
obstruction, n. ostruzione f.
obtain, vb. ottenere.
obtrude, vb. intrùdersi.
obtuse, adj. ottuso.
obviate, vb. evitare.
obvious, adj. òvvio.
occasion, 1. n. occasione f. 2. vb. cagionare.
occasional, adj. occasionale.
occasionally, adv. di quando in quando.
Occident, n. occidènte m.
occidental, adj. occidentale.
occlusion, n. occlusione f.
occult, adj. occulto.
occupant, n. occupante m., inquilino m.
occupation, n. occupazione f., professione f.
occupy, vb. occupare.
occur, vb. accadere, succèdere.
occurrence, n. avvenimento m.
ocean, n. ocèano m.
ocean liner, n. transatlàntico m.
o'clock, n. ora f.
octagon, n. ottàgono m.
octave, n. ottava f.
October, n. ottobre m.
octopus, n. ottòpode m., pòlipo m.
ocular, adj. oculare.
oculist, n. oculista m.
odd, adj. (numbers) dìspari; (queer) strano.
oddity, n. stranezza f.
odds, n. probabilità f.
odious, adj. odioso.
odor, n. odore m.
of, prep. di; (from) da.
off, adv. via.

offend, vb. offèndere.
offender, n. responsàbile m.; (accused) imputato m.
offense, n. offesa f.
offensive, 1. n. offensiva f. 2. adj. offensivo.
offer, 1. n. offèrta f. 2. vb. offrire.
offering, n. offèrta f.
offhand, adv. estemporaneamente.
office, n. ufficio m.; (dentist's, doctor's) gabinetto m.; (o. supplies) oggetti di cancelleria m.pl.
officer, n. ufficiale.
official, n. and adj. ufficiale (m.).
officiate, vb. officiare.
officious, adj. inframmettènte.
offshore, adv. vicino alla tèrra.
offspring, n. pròle f.
often, adv. spesso.
oil, 1. n. òlio m. 2. vb. ùngere, lubrificare.
oil-cloth, n. tela cerata f.
oily, adj. oleoso.
ointment, n. unguènto m.
okay, interj. va bene.
old, adj. vècchio.
old-fashioned, adj. passato di mòda.
olfactory, adj. olfattòrio.
oligarchy, n. oligarchìa f.
olive, n. (tree) olivo m.; (fruit) oliva f.
ombudsman, n. mediatore m.
omelet, n. frittata f.
omen, n. presàgio m.
ominous, adj. infàusto.
omission, n. omissione f.
omit, vb. omèttere.
omnibus, n. àutobus m.
omnipotent, adj. onnipotènte.
on, adv. and prep. su, sopra.
once, adv. una vòlta; (formerly) un tèmpo.
one, num. uno.
onerous, adj. oneroso.
oneself, pron. sè stesso (sg.); sè stessi (pl.).
one-sided, adj. unilaterale.
one-way, adj. (fare) di corsa sémplice; (street) a sènso ùnico.
onion, n. cipolla f.
onion-skin, n. carta velina f.
onlooker, n. presente m., testimone m.

only, 1. *adj.* único. 2. *adv.* solamente, soltanto; (but) ma.
onslaught, *n.* attacco *m.*
onset, *n.* attacco *m.*, principio *m.*
onto, *prep.* su, sopra a.
onus, *n.* ònere *m.*
onward, *adv.* avanti.
ooze, 1. *n.* melma *f.* 2. *vb.* trasudare.
opacity, *n.* opacità *f.*
opal, *n.* opale *m.*
opaque, *adj.* opaco.
open, 1. *adj.* apèrto. 2. *vb.* aprire.
opening, *n.* (breach) apertura *f.*; (start) inízio *m.*; inaugurazione *f.*
open-minded, *adj.* imparziale, apèrto.
opera, *n.* òpera *f.*
opera-glasses, *n.* binòcolo da teatro *m.* (*sg.*).
operate, *vb.* operare.
operatic, *adj.* lírico.
operation, *n.* operazione *f.*
operative, *adj.* operativo.
operator, *n.* operatore *m.*
operetta, *n.* operetta *f.*
ophthalmic, *adj.* oftàlmico.
opinion, *n.* opinione *f.*, parere *m.*
opium, *n.* òppio *m.*
opponent, *n.* antagonista *m.*
opportune, *adj.* opportuno.
opportunism, *n.* opportunismo *m.*
opportunity, *n.* occasione *f.*
oppose, *vb.* opporre, *tr.*
opposite, 1. *n. and adj.* oppòsto (*m.*). 2. *adv.* dirimpètto. 3. *prep.* dirimpètto a.
opposition, *n.* opposizione *f.*
oppress, *vb.* opprímere.
oppression, *n.* oppressione *f.*
oppressive, *adj.* oppressivo.
oppressor, *n.* oppressore *m.*
optic, *adj.* òttico.
optician, *n.* òttico *m.*
optics, *n.* òttica *f.*
optimism, *n.* ottimismo *m.*
optimistic, *adj.* ottimístico.
option, *n.* opzione *f.*
optional, *adj.* facoltativo.
optometrist, *n.* optometrista *m.*
optometry, *n.* optometría *f.*
opulence, *n.* opulènza *f.*

opulent, *adj.* opulènto.
or, *conj.* o (before *o*, od); sía, ossía.
oracle, *n.* oràcolo *m.*
oral, *adj.* orale.
orange, *n.* (tree) arància *m.*; (fruit) arància *f.*
orangeade, *n.* aranciata *f.*
oration, *n.* orazione *f.*
orator, *n.* oratore *m.*
oratory, *n.* oratòria *f.*
orbit, *n.* òrbita *f.*
orchard, *n.* òrto *m.*, frutteto *m.*
orchestra, *n.* orchèstra *f.*
orchid, *n.* orchidèa *f.*
ordain, *vb.* ordinare.
ordeal, *n.* ordàlia *f.*; (fig.) pròva *f.*
order, 1. *n.* òrdine *m.* 2. *vb.* ordinare.
orderly, *adj.* ordinato.
ordinance, *n.* ordinanza *f.*
ordinary, *adj.* ordinàrio.
ordination, *n.* ordinazione *f.*
ore, *n.* minerale *m.*
organ, *n.* òrgano *m.*
organdy, *n.* organza *f.*
organic, *adj.* orgànico.
organism, *n.* organismo *m.*
organist, *n.* organista *m.*
organization, *n.* organizzazione *f.*
organize, *vb.* organizzare.
orgy, *n.* òrgia *f.*
orient, *vb.* orientare.
Orient, *n.* Oriènte *m.*
Oriental, *adj.* orientale.
orientation, *n.* orientazione *f.*
origin, *n.* orígine *f.*
original, *adj.* originale; (former) primitivo.
originality, *n.* originalità *f.*
ornament, 1. *n.* ornamento *m.* 2. *vb.* ornare.
ornamental, *adj.* ornamentale.
ornate, *adj.* ornato.
ornithology, *n.* ornitología *f.*
orphan, *n. and adj.* òrfano (*m.*).
orphanage, *n.* orfanotròfio *m.*
orthodox, *adj.* ortodòsso.
orthography, *n.* ortografía *f.*
orthopedic, *adj.* ortopèdico.
oscillate, *vb.* oscillare.
osmosis, *n.* osmòsi *f.*
ostensible, *adj.* ostensibile.

ostentation, *n.* ostentazione *f.*

ostentatious, *adj.* ostentato.

ostracize, *vb.* ostracizzare.

ostrich, *n.* struzzo *m.*

other, *adj.* altro.

otherwise, *adv.* altrimenti.

otter, *n.* lontra *f.*

ouch, *interj.* ahi!

ought, *vb.* use conditional of dovere.

ounce, *n.* óncia *f.*

our, *adj.* nòstro.

ours, *pron.* nòstro.

ourselves, *pron.* noi stessi *m.,* noi stesse *f.*

oust, *vb.* espèllere.

ouster, *n.* espulsione *f.*

out, *adv.* fuòri.

outbid, *vb.* offrire di più

outbreak, *n.* scòppio *m.*

outburst, *n.* scòppio *m.*

outcast, *n.* pària *m.*

outcome, *n.* evènto *m.*

outdoors, *adv.* all'apèrto.

outer, *adj.* esteriore.

outfit, 1. *n.* corredo *m.* 2. *vb.* corredare, fornire.

outgoing, *adj.* espansivo.

outgrow, *vb.* crescere oltre una certa misura.

outgrowth, *n.* risultato *m.*

outing, *n.* escursione *f.,* gita *f.*

outlandish, *adj.* curioso, strano.

outlast, *vb.* sopravvivere a.

outlaw, *n.* bandito *m.*

outlet, *n.* sbocco *m.,* sfògo *m.;* (electrical) presa elèttrica *f.*

outline, *n.* schizzo *m.*

outlive, *vb.* sopravvivere a.

outlook, *n.* propsettiva *f.;* previsioni *f.pl.*

outnumber, *vb.* essere in maggior nùmero.

out of, *prep.* fuòri di; (motion) fuòri da.

out-of-date, *adj.* arretrato.

out-of-print, *adj.* esaurito.

out-of-tune, *adj.* stonato.

out-of-work, *adj.* senza lavoro.

outpost, *n.* avamposto *m.*

output, *n.* produzione *f.;* rendimento *m.*

outrage, *n.* oltràggio *m.*

outrageous, *adj.* oltraggioso.

outrank, *vb.* precédere.

outright, *adv.* completamente.

outrun, *vb.* oltrepassare.

outside, 1. *n. and adj.* estèrno (*m.*). 2. *adv.* fuòri. 3. *prep.* fuòri di; (except) all'infuòri di.

outskirts, *n.* sobborghi *m.pl.,* periferia *f.*

outstanding, *adj.* eccellente; (debt) arretrato.

outward, 1. *adj.* esteriore. 2. *adv.* vèrso l'estèrno.

outwardly, *adv.* esteriormente.

oval, *n. and adj.* ovale (*m.*)

ovary, *n.* ovàia *f.*

ovation, *n.* ovazione *f.*

oven, *n.* forno *m.*

over, *adv. and prep.* sopra; (o. again) di nuòvo; (o. and o.) ripetutamente.

overbearing, *adj.* prepotènte.

overcoat, *n.* sopràbito *m.*

overcome, *vb.* sopraffare, superare.

overdue, *adj.* scaduto.

overflow, *vb.* stripapare, traboccare.

overhaul, *vb.* rimèttere a nuòvo.

overhead, 1. *n.* spese ordinàrie *f.pl.* 2. *adj. and adv.* in alto.

overkill, *n.* esagerazione retòrica *f.;* reazione sproporzionata *f.*

overlook, *vb.* omèttere, trascurare.

overnight, 1. *adj.* notturno. 2. *adv.* durante la nòtte.

overpass, *n.* cavalcavia *m.*

overpower, *vb.* vincere.

overrule, *vb.* decidere contro; (law) cassare.

overrun, *vb.* invàdere.

oversee, *vb.* sorvegliare.

oversight, *n.* negligènza *f.*

overstuffed, *adj.* imbottito.

overt, *adj.* apèrto.

overtake, *vb.* raggiùngere.

overthrow, 1. *n.* sconvolgimento *m.* 2. *vb.* sconvòlgere, sovvertire.

overtime, *n.* straordinàrio.

overture, *n.* sinfonìa *f.*

overturn, *vb.* capovòlgere.

overview, *n.* quadro generale *m.*

overweight, *n.* peso eccessivo *m.*

overwhelm, *vb.* sopraffare.

overwork, 1. *n.* lavoro eccessivo *m.* **2.** *vb.* lavorare troppo.

owe, *vb.* dovere.

owing, *adj.* dovuto; **(o. to)** dovuto a.

owl, *n.* civetta *f.*, gufo *m.*; **(o. service)** servizio notturno *m.*

own, 1. *adj.* pròprio. **2.** *vb.* possedere.

owner, *n.* possessore *m.*

ox, *n.* bue *m.*

oxygen, *n.* ossígeno *m.*

oyster, *n.* òstrica *f.*

P

pa, *n.* babbo *m.*

pace, *n.* passo *m.*

pacific, *adj.* pacífico.

pacifier, *n.* pacificatore *m.*

pacifism, *n.* pacifismo *m.*

pacifist, *n.* pacifista *m.*

pacify, *vb.* pacificare.

pack, 1. *n.* pacco *m.*; **(gang)** banda *m.*; **(cards)** mazzo *m.*; **(dogs)** muta *f.* **2.** *vb.* imballare; **(suitcases)** fare le valígie.

package, *n.* pacco *m.*

packer, *n.* imballatore *m.*

packing, *n.* imballàggio *m.*

pact, *n.* patto *m.*

pad, 1. *n.* cuscinetto *m.* **2.** *vb.* imbottire.

padding, *n.* imbottitura *f.*

paddle, 1. *n.* remo *m.* **2.** *vb.* remare; **(splash)** spruzzare; **(spank)** sculacciare.

paddock, *n.* campo *m.*

padlock, *n.* lucchetto *m.*

Padua, *n.* Pàdova *f.*

Paduan, *adj.* padovano.

pagan, *n. and adj.* pagano *(m.)*.

page, 1. *n.* pàgina *f.*; **(servant)** pàggio *m.* **2.** *vb.* chiamare.

pageant, *n.* cortèo *m.*

pageantry, *n.* pompa *f.*, fasto *m.*

paginate, *vb.* impaginare.

pagoda, *n.* pagòda *f.*

pail, *n.* sécchia *f.*

pain, *n.* dolore *m.*, pena *f.*

painful, *adj.* doloroso.

painkiller, *n.* analgèsico *m.*

painless, *adj.* indolore.

painstaking, *adj.* coscienzoso.

paint, 1. *n.* colore *m.*; **(make-up)** belletto *m.* **2.** *vb.* dipingere.

painter, *n.* pittore *m.*

painting, *n.* pittura *f.*, dipinto *m.*

pair, *n.* paio *m.*

pajamas, *n.* pigiama *m.pl.*

pal, *n.* compagno *m.*, amico *m.*

palace, *n.* palazzo *m.*

palatable, *adj.* gustoso.

palate, *n.* pàlato *m.*

palatial, *adj.* magnífico.

pale, 1. *adj.* pàllido. **2.** *vb.* impallidire.

paleness, *n.* pallore *m.*

palette, *n.* tavolòzza *f.*

pall, *vb.* perder sapore *m.*

pallbearer, *n.* persona che règge i cordoni *f.*

pallid, *adj.* pàllido.

palm, *n.* palma *f.*

palpitate, *vb.* palpitare.

paltry, *adj.* meschino.

pamper, *vb.* viziare.

pamphlet, *n.* opùscolo *m.*

pan, 1. *n.* padèlla *f.* **2.** *vb.* criticare aspramente; **(p. out)** riuscire.

panacea, *n.* panacèa *f.*

pancake, *n.* frittèlla *f.*

pancreas, *n.* pancreas *m.*

pane, *n.* **(p. of glass)** vetro *m.*

panel, *n.* pannèllo *m.*

panelist, *n.* relatore a un convegno *m.*

pang, *n.* spàsimo *m.*

panic, *n.* pànico *m.*

panorama, *n.* panorama *m.*

pant, *vb.* anelare, ansare.

panther, *n.* pantèra *f.*

panties, *n.* mutandine (da dònna) *f.pl.*

pantomime, *n.* pantomima *f.*

pantry, *n.* dispènsa *f.*

pants, *n.* pantaloni *m.pl.*

panty hose, *n.* collant *m.* *(Italy)*; ghette *f.pl. (Switzerland)*

pap, *n.* pappa *f.*

papa, *n.* papà *m.*

papacy, *n.* papato *m.*

papal, adj. papale.
paper, n. carta f.; (newsp.) giornale m.; **(wall-p.)** carta da parati f.
paperback, n. libro in brossura m.
paper-hanger, n. tappezzière in carta m.
paperwork, n. trafila burocràtica f.
paprika, n. pàprica f.
par, n. pari f.
parable, n. paràbola f.
parachute, n. paracadute m.
parade, n. parata f.
paradise, n. paradiso m.
paradox, n. paradòsso m.
paradoxical, adj. paradossale.
paraffin, n. paraffina f.
paragraph, n. paràgrafo m.
parakeet, n. pappagallo m.
parallel, n. and adj. parallèlo (m.).
paralysis, n. paràlisi f.
paralyze, vb. paralizzare.
paramedic, n. paramèdico m.; assistente mèdico m.
parameter, n. paràmetro m.
paramount, adj. suprèmo.
paraphrase, 1. n. paràfrasi f. **2.** vb. parafrasare.
parasite, n. parassita f.
parcel, n. pacco m.
parch, vb. inaridire.
parchment, n. pergamena f.
pardon, 1. n. perdono m. **2.** vb. perdonare.
pare, vb. (nails) tagliare; (fruit) sbucciare.
parent, n. genitore m.
parentage, n. paternità f.
parenthesis, n. parèntesi f.
pariah, n. pària m.
Paris, n. Parigi f.
parish, n. parròcchia f.; **(p. priest)** pàrroco m.
Parisian, adj. parigino.
parity, n. parità f.
park, 1. n. parco m. **2.** vb. parcheggiare.
parking, n. postéggio m. **(p. area)** autoparchéggio m.; **(p. lights)** luci di posizione f.pl.
parkway, n. viale m.; (superhighway) autostrada f.

parley, 1. n. parlamento m. **2.** vb. parlamentare.
parliament, n. parlamento m.
parliamentary, adj. parlamentare.
parlor, n. salòtto m.
Parmesan, adj. parmigiano.
parochial, adj. parrocchiale.
parody, 1. n. parodía f. **2.** vb. parodiare.
parole, n. paròla d'onore f.
paroxysm, n. parossismo m.
parricide, n. patricidio m.
parrot, n. pappagallo m.
parse, vb. analizzare grammaticalmente.
parsimonious, adj. parsimonioso.
parsimony, n. parsimònia f.
parsley, n. prezzémolo m.
parson, n. pàrroco m.
part, 1. n. parte f. **2.** vb. separare, tr.
partake, vb. partecipare.
partial, adj. parziale.
partiality, n. parzialità f.
participant, n. partecipante m.
participate, vb. partecipare.
participation, n. partecipazione f.
participle, n. particípio m.
particle, n. particèlla f.
particular, adj. particolare; (fussy) esigente.
parting, n. separazione f.
partisan, n. and adj. partigiano (m.).
partition, n. partizione f.; (wall) muro divisòrio m.
partly, adv. in parte.
partner, n. compagno m., sòcio m.
partnership, n. associazione f.; società f.
part of speech, n. parte del discorso f.
partridge, n. pernice f.
party, n. (political) partito m.; (social) ricevimento m.; (legal) parte in càusa f.; (person) individuo m.; (group) gruppo m.
pass, 1. n. passo m. **2.** vb. passare; (auto) sorpassare; (exam.) superare; (go beyond) oltrepassare.
passable, adj. (road) praticàbile; (work) passàbile.

passage, n. passàggio m.

passé, adj. fuòri di mòda; (faded) appassito.

passenger, n. passeggèro m.

passer-by, n. passante m.

passing, n. (auto) sorpasso m.

passion, n. passione f.

passionate, adj. appassionato.

passive, n. and adj. passivo (m.).

Passover, n. Pasqua ebràica f.

passport, n. passapòrto m.

past, n. and adj. passato (m.).

paste, 1. n. pasta f., còlla f. 2. vb. incollare.

pastel, n. and adj. pastello (m.).

pasteurize, vb. pasteurizzare.

pastille, n. pastìglia f., pasticca f.

pastime, n. passatèmpo m.

pastor, n. pastore m.

pastry, n. pasticcerìa f.

pastry shop, n. pasticcerìa f.

pasture, n. pàscolo m.

pasty, 1. n. pasticcio m. 2. adj. (color) pàllido.

pat, 1. n. colpetto m.; (butter, etc.) panetto m. 2. vb. bàttere leggieramente.

patch, 1. n. pèzza f. 2. vb. rappezzare, rattoppare.

patchwork, n. raffazzonamento m.

patent, 1. n. brevetto m. 2. vb. brevettare.

patent leather, n. pèlle verniciata f.

paternal, adj. patèrno.

paternity, n. paternità f.

path, n. sentièro m., pista f.

pathetic, adj. patètico.

path finder, n. esploratore m.

pathology, n. patologìa f.

pathos, n. pàtos m.

pathway, n. sentièro m.

patience, n. paziènza f.

patient, adj. paziènte.

patio, n. cortile m.

patriarch, n. patriarca m.

patrician, n. and adj. patrizio m.

patricide, n. patricidio m.

patrimony, n. patrimònio m.

patriot, n. patriòta m.

patriotic, adj. patriòttico.

patriotism, n. patriottismo m.

patrol, n. pattùglia f.

patrolman, n. poliziòtto m.

patron, n. patròno m.

patronage, n. patronato m.

patronize, vb. comprare da.

pattern, n. modéllo m.

pauper, n. pòvero m.

pause, n. pàusa f.

pave, vb. pavimentare.

pavement, n. selciato m.

pavilion, n. padiglione m.

paw, n. zampa f.

pawn, 1. n. pegno m.; (chess) pedina f. 2. impegnare.

pay, 1. n. paga f. 2. vb. pagare; (p. in) versare.

payable, adj. pagàbile.

paycheck, n. assegno-paga m.

payday, n. giorno-paga m.

payment, n. pagamento m., versamento m.

payoff, n. pagamento m.; profitto m.

payroll, n. libro paga m.

pea, n. pisèllo m.

peace, n. pace f.

peaceable, adj. pacìfico.

peaceful, adj. tranquillo.

peach, n. (tree) pèsco m.; (fruit) pèsca f.

peacock, n. pavone m.

peak, n. cima f., picco m.

peak hour, n. ora di punta f.

peal, 1. n. scampanìo m. 2. vb. scampanare.

peanut, n. aràchide f.

peanut butter, n. pasta d'aràchidi f.

pear, n. (tree) pero m.; (fruit) pera f.

pearl, n. pèrla f.

peasant, n. contadino m.

pea soup, n. minestra di piselli f., (fig.) grande nebbia f.

peat, n. torba f.

pebble, n. ciòttolo m.

peck, vb. beccare.

peculiar, adj. (special) peculiare; (queer) strano.

peculiarity, n. peculiarità f.

pecuniary, adj. pecuniàrio.

pedagogue, n. pedagògo m.

pedagogy, n. pedagogìa f.

pedal, 1. n. pedale m. 2. vb. pedalare.

pedant, n. pedante m.

peddle, vb. vèndere al minuto.

peddler, *n.* venditore ambulante *m.*

pedestal, *n.* piedestallo *m.*

pedestrian, 1. *n.* pedone *m.* **2.** *adj.* pedèstre; (pertaining to pedestrians) pedonale.

pediatrician, *n.* pediàtra *m.*

pedigree, *n.* genealogìa *f.*

peek, *vb.* sbirciare.

peel, *vb.* sbucciare. pelare.

peep, 1. *n.* occiata *f.* **2.** *vb.* (look) dare un' occhiata; (appear) spuntare.

peephole, *n.* spioncino *m.*

Peeping Tom, *n.* guardone *m.*

peer, 1. *n.* pari *m.* **2.** *vb.* guardare curiosamente.

peevish, *adj.* stizzoso.

peg, *n.* piolo *m.*

pelt, 1. *n.* (skin) pèlle *f.* **2.** *vb.* assalire.

pelvis, *n.* pèlvi *f.*

pen, 1. *n.* penna *f.;* **(fountain p.)** penna stilogràfica. **2.** *vb.* scrìvere.

penalty, *n.* pena *f.*

penance, *n.* penitènza *f.*

penchant, *n.* inclinazióne *f.*

pencil, *n.* làpis *m.,* matita *f.*

pendant, *n.* pendènte *m.*

pending, 1. *adj.* pendènte. **2.** *prep.* in attesa di.

penetrate, *vb.* penetrare.

penetration, *n.* penetrazióne *f.*

penicillin, *n.* penicillina *f.*

peninsula, *n.* penìsola *f.*

penitence, *n.* penitènza *f.*

penitent, *n. and adj.* penitènte *(m.).*

pen-knife, *n.* temperino *m.*

penniless, *adj.* al verde.

penny, *n.* sòldo *m.*

pension, *n.* pensióne *f.*

pensive, *adj.* pensoso.

pent-up, *adj.* rinchiuso.

penury, *n.* penùria *f.*

people, *n.* (folks) gènte *f.;* (nation) pòpolo *m.*

pepper, *n.* pepe *m.*

per, *prep.* per.

perambulator, *n.* carrozzèlla *f.*

perceive, *vb.* scòrgere.

per cent, *adv.* per cènto.

percentage, *n.* percentuale *f.*

perceptible, *adj.* percettìbile.

perception, *n.* percezióne *f.*

perch, 1. *n.* (fish) pesce pèrsico *m.;* (pole) pèrtica *f.;* (for birds) posatòio *m.* **2.** *vb.* posarsi; (roost) appollaiarsi.

perdition, *n.* perdizióne *f.*

peremptory, *adj.* perentòrio.

perennial, *adj.* perènne.

perfect, 1. *adj.* perfètto. **2.** *vb.* perfezionare.

perfection, *n.* perfezióne *f.*

perforation, *n.* perforazióne *f.*

perform, *vb.* eseguire; (a play) rappresentare; (sing) cantare; (instrumental music) suonare.

performance, *n.* esecuzióne *f.,* rappresentazióne *f.*

perfume, 1. *n.* profumo *m.* **2.** *vb.* profumare.

perfunctory, *adj.* casuale.

perhaps, *adv.* forse; **(p. even)** magari.

peril, *n.* perìcolo *m.*

perilous, *adj.* pericoloso.

perimeter, *n.* perìmetro *m.*

period, *n.* perìodo *m.*

periodic, *adj.* periòdico.

periodical, *n. and adj.* periòdico *(m.).*

periphery, *n.* periferìa *f.*

periscope, *n.* periscòpio *m.*

perish, *vb.* perire.

perishable, *adj.* deperìbile.

perjure oneself, *vb.* spergiurare.

perjury, *n.* spergiuro *m.*

perk, *vb.* alzare; **(p. oneself up)** mettersi in ghinghieri.

permanent, *adj.* permanènte.

permeate, *vb.* permeare.

permissible, *adj.* permissìbile.

permission, *n.* permesso *m.*

permit, 1. *n.* permesso *m.* **2.** *vb.* perméttere.

permute, *vb.* permutare.

pernicious, *adj.* pernicioso.

perpendicular, *n. and adj.* perpendicolare *(m.).*

perpetrate, *vb.* perpetrare.

perpetual, *adj.* perpètuo.

perplex, 1. *adj.* perplèsso. **2.** *vb.* rèndere perplèsso.

perplexity, *n.* perplessità *f.*

per se, *adv.* di per sè.

persecute, *vb.* perseguitare.

persecution, *n.* persecuzióne *f.*

perseverance, *n.* perseveranza *f.*

persevere, vb. perseverare.
Perisan Gulf, n. Golfo Pèrsico m.
persimmon, n. cachi m.pl.
persist, vb. persistere.
persistent, adj. persistènte.
person, n. persona f.
personage, n. personàggio m.
personal, adj. personale.
personality, n. personalità f.
personally, adv. personalmente.
personnel, n. personale m.
perspective, n. prospettiva f.
perspiration, n. sudore m.
perspire, vb. sudare.
persuade, vb. persuadere.
persuasive, adj. persuasivo.
pertain, vb. appartenere.
pertinent, adj. pertinènte.
perturb, vb. perturbare.
peruse, vb. scòrrere.
pervade, vb. pervàdere.
perverse, adj. pervèrso.
perversion, n. perversione f.
pervert, vb. pervertire.
pessimism, n. pessimismo m.
pestilence, n. pestilènza f.
pet, 1. n. and adj. favorito (m.);
  (animal) animale domèstico m. **2.**
  vb. vezzeggiare.
petal, n. pètalo m.
petition, n. petizione f.
petrify, vb. pietrificare.
petrol, n. benzina f.
petroleum, n. petròlio m.
petticoat, n. sottana f.
petty, adj. meschino, piccolo.
petulance, n. petulanza f.
petulant, adj. petulante.
pew, n. banco in chièsa m.
phantom, n. fantasma m.
pharmacist, n. farmacista m.
pharmacy, n. farmacía f.
phase, n. fase f.
pheasant, n. fagiano m.
phenomenal, adj. fenomenale.
phenomenon, n. fenòmeno m.
philanthropy, n. filantropía f.
philately, n. filatèlica f.
philosopher, n. filòsofo m.
philosophical, adj. filosòfico.
philosophy, n. filosofía f.
phlegm, n. flèmma m.
phlegmatic, adj. flemmàtico.
phobia, n. fobía f.
phonetic, adj. fonètico.

phonograph, n. grammòfono m.
phosphorus, n. fòsforo m.
photocopier, n. fotocopiatore m.
photocopy, n. fotocopia f.
photoelectric, adj. fotoelèttrico.
photogenic, adj. fotogènico.
photograph, 1. n. fotografía f. **2.**
  vb. fotografare.
photographer, n. fotògrafo m.
photography, n. fotografía f.
photostat, n. riproduzione ana-
  stàtica f.
phrase, n. frase f.
physical, adj. físico.
physician, n. mèdico m.
physicist, n. fisico m.
physics, n. fisica f.
physiology, n. fisiología f.
physiotherapy, n. fisioterapía f.
physique, n. fisico m.
pianist, n. pianista m.
piano, n. pianofòrte m.
picayune, adj. meschino.
piccolo, n. ottavino m.
pick, 1. n. piccone m. **2.** vb.
  (gather) raccògliere; (select) scégliere.
picket, n. picchetto m.
pickle, n. salamòia f.; (trouble)
  impiccio m.
pickpocket, n. borsaiòlo m.
picnic, n. gita f.
picture, n. quadro m.
picturesque, adj. pittoresco.
pie, n. tòrta f.
piece, n. pèzzo m.
Piedmont, n. Piemonte m.
Piedmontese, adj. piemontese.
pier, n. (dock) banchina f., mòlo
  m.; (pillar) pilone m.
pierce, vb. forare, traforare.
piercing, adj. lancinante, acuto.
piety, n. pietà f.
pig, n. pòrco m.; maiale m.
pigeon, n. piccione m.
pigeonhole, n. casèlla f.
pigment, n. pigmento m.
pigsty, n. porcile m.
pigtail, n. codino m.
pike, n. picca f.; autostrada f.
pile, 1. n. (heap) ammasso m.,
  mucchio m.; (post) palafitta f. **2.**
  vb. ammucchiare.
pilfer, vb. rubacchiare.
pilgrim, n. pellegrino m.

pilgrimage, n. pellegrinàggio m.

pill, n. píllola f.

pillage, 1. n. sacchéggio m. **2.** vb. saccheggiare.

pillar, n. pilastro m., pilone m.

pillow, n. guanciale m.

pillowcase, n. fèdera f.

pilot, n. pilòta m.

pimp, n. ruffiano m.; lenone m.

pimple, n. forùncolo m.

pin, n. spillo m.

pinch, 1. n. pizzicòtto m. **2.** vb. pizzicare.

pine, 1. n. pino m. **2.** vb. languire.

pineapple, n. ananàs m.

pine cone, n. pigna f.

ping-pong, n. tennis da tàvola m.

pink, adj. ròsa.

pinnacle, n. pinnàcolo m.

pint, n. pinta f.

pioneer, n. pionière m.

pious, adj. pío.

pipe, n. tubo m.; (tobacco) pipa f.

piper, n. pìffero m.

piquant, adj. piccante.

pirate, n. pirata m.

pistol, n. pistola f.

piston, n. pistone m., stantuffo m.

pit, n. buca f.

pitch, 1. n. (tar) pece f.; (throw) làncio m.; (music) tòno m. **2.** vb. (hurl) lanciare.

pitchblende, n. pechblenda f., uraninite f.

pitcher, n. bròcca f.; (thrower) lanciatore m.

pitchfork, n. forca f.

pitfall, n. tràppola f.

pitiful, adj. pietoso.

pitiless, adj. spietato.

pity, 1. n. pietà f.; (shame) peccato m.; (what a p.) che peccato!

pivot, n. pèrnio m.

pizza, n. pizza, f.

placard, n. cartèllo m.

placate, vb. placare.

place, 1. n. posto m., luògo m.; (take p.) aver luògo; accadere. **2.** vb. méttere; porre.

placid, adj. plàcido.

plagiarism, n. plàgio m.

plague, n. pèste f.

plain, 1. n. pianura f. **2.** adj. (clear) chiaro; (simple) sémplice, modèsto.

plaintiff, n. attore m.

plan, 1. n. piano m., progètto m., (map) pianta f. **2.** vb. progettare.

plane, 1. n. piano m.; (airplane) aeroplano m.; (carpenter's) pialla f. **2.** vb. piallare.

planet, n. pianeta m.

planetarium, n. planetàrio m.

planetary, adj. planetàrio.

plank, n. asse f., tàvola f.

plant, 1. n. pianta f.; (factory; installation) impianto m. **2.** vb. piantare.

plantation, n. piantagione f.

planter, n. piantatore m.; (plantation owner) proprietàrio di piantagione m.

plasma, n. plasma m.

plaster, 1. n. intònaco m.; (medical) empiastro m. **2.** vb. intonacare.

plastic, 1. n. plàstica f. **2.** adj. plàstico.

plate, n. piatto m.; (photographic) lastra f.; (auto) targa f.

plateau, n. altopiano m.

platform, n. piattaforma f.

platinum, n. plàtino m.

platitude, n. banalità f.

platoon, n. drappèllo m., plotone m.

platter, n. piatto grande m.

plaudit, n. applàuso m.

plausible, adj. plausìbile.

play, 1. n. (game) giòco m.; (joke) schèrzo m.; (theater) dramma m. **2.** vb. giocare; (on stage) recitare; (instrument) suonare.

player, n. (game) giocatore m.; (instrument) suonatore m.

playful, adj. scherzoso.

playground, n. campo per ricreazione m.

playmate, n. compagno di giòchi m.

playwright, n. drammaturgo m.

plea, n. preghièra f.; (excuse) scusa f.

plead, vb. esortare, implorare; (give as excuse) addurre come scusa.

pleasant, adj. piacévole.

please, 1. vb. piacere a. **2.** adv., interj. per favore.

pleasing, adj. piacévole, grato.

pleasure, *n.* piacere *m.*

pleat, *n.* piéga *f.*

plebiscite, *n.* plebiscito *m.*

pledge, 1. *n.* pegno *m.* **2.** *vb.* impegnare.

plentiful, *adj.* abbondante.

plenty, 1. *n.* abbondanza *f.* **2.** *adj.* **(p. of)** molto.

pleurisy, *n.* pleurite *f.*

pliable, pliant, *adj.* pieghévole.

pliers, *n.* pinze *f.pl.*, pinzette *f.pl.*

plight, *n.* situazione *f.*

plot, 1. *n.* (conspiracy) complòtto *m.;* (story) intréccio *m.;* (land) appezzamento *m.;* (plan) pianta *f.*

plow, 1. *n.* aratro *m.* **2.** *vb.* arare.

plowman, *n.* bracciante *m.;* contadino *m.*

pluck, 1. *n.* fégato *m.* **2.** *vb.* cògliere.

plucky, *adj.* coraggioso.

plug, 1. *n.* tappo *m.;* (electric) spina *f.* **2.** *vb.* tappare.

plum, *n.* (tree) susino *m.;* (fruit) susina *f.*, prugna *f.*

plumage, *n.* piumàggio *m.*

plumber, *n.* trombàio *m.*, stagnino *m.;* idráulico *m.*

plumbing, *n.* impianto idráulico *m.*

plume, *n.* penna *f.*

plummet, *vb.* precipitare.

plump, *adj.* grassòccio.

plum tree, *n.* susino *m.*

plunder, 1. *n.* bottino *m.*, prèda *f.* **2.** *vb.* saccheggiare, predare.

plunge, 1. *n.* tuffo *m.* **2.** *vb.* tuffare, *tr.*

plural, *n.* and *adj.* plurale *(m.).*

plus, *prep.* più.

plutocrat, *n.* plutócrate *m.*

plywood, *n.* legno compensato *m.*

pneumatic, *adj.* pneumàtico.

pneumonia, *n.* polmonite *f.*

poach, *vb.* (hunt illegally) andare a càccia di fròdo; (eggs) cuòcere in camícia; (poached eggs) uòva affogate.

poacher, *n.* cacciatore di fròdo *m.*

pocket, 1. *n.* tasca *f.* **2.** *vb.* intascare.

pocket-book, *n.* portafògli *m.*

pocket-size, *adj.* tascàbile.

pod, *n.* bacello *m.*

podiatry, *n.* cura dei pièdi *f.*

poem, *n.* poesía *f.*, pòema *m.*

poet, *n.* poèta *m.*, poetéssa *f.*

poetic, *adj.* poètico.

poetry, *n.* poesía *f.*

poignant, *adj.* doloroso.

point, 1. *n.* punto *m.* **2.** *vb.* puntare; **(p. to)** indicare; **(p. out)** additare.

pointed, *adj.* acuto.

pointless, *adj.* privo di senso.

poise, *n.* equilíbrio *m.*

poison, 1. *n.* veleno *m.* **2.** *vb.* avvelenare.

poisonous, *adj.* velenoso.

poke, *vb.* spíngere; (fire) attizzare.

Poland, *n.* Polònia *f.*

polar, *adj.* polare.

pole, *n.* (post) palo *m.;* (rod) pertica *f.;* (wagon) timone *m.;* (electrical, geographical) pòlo *m.*

police, *n.* polizía *f.*

policeman, *n.* vigile *m.*, poliziòtto *m.*

policy, *n.* política *f.;* (insurance) polizza *f.*

polish, 1. *n.* (material) lùcido *m.;* (gloss) lucidatura *f.* **2.** *vb.* lucidare.

Polish, *adj.* polacco.

polite, *adj.* cortese.

politeness, *n.* cortesía *f.*

politic, political, *adj.* político.

politician, *n.* político *m.*

politics, *n.* política *f.*

poll, 1. *n.* (head) tèsta *f.;* (voting) votazione *f.;* **(p.-tax)** capitazione *f.* **2.** *vb.* (get, in voting) ottenere.

pollen, *n.* pòlline *m.*

pollute, *vb.* contaminare.

polonaise, *n.* polacca *f.*

polygamy, *n.* poligamía *f.*

polygon, *n.* polígono *m.*

pomp, *n.* pompa *f.*, fasto *m.*

pompous, *adj.* pomposo, fastoso.

poncho, *n.* impermeàbile *m.*

pond, *n.* stagno *m.*

ponder, *vb.* ponderare.

ponderous, *adj.* ponderoso.

pontiff, *n.* pontéfice *m.*

pontoon, *n.* pontone *m.*

pony, *n.* cavallino *m.*

pool, *n.* stagno *m.;* (money) fondo comune *m.*

poor, *adj.* pòvero.

pop, 1. n. scòppio m.; (father) babbo m. **2.** vb. scoppiettare.

popcorn, n. pop-corn m.

pope, n. papa m.

popeyed, adj. con gli occhi fuori dalle òrbite.

poppy, n. papavero m.

popular, adj. popolare.

popularity, n. popolarità f.

populate, vb. popolare.

population, n. popolazione f.

porcelain, n. porcellana f.

porch, n. veranda f.; (church) pòrtico m.

pore, n. pòro m.

pork, n. maiale m.

pornography, n. pornografìa f.

porous, adj. poroso.

port, n. pòrto m.

portable, adj. portàtile.

portal, n. portale m.

portend, vb. presagire.

portent, n. presàgio m.

porter, n. facchino m., portabagagli m.; (hotel) portière m.

portfolio, n. cartèlla f., portafòglio m.

porthole, n. oblò m.

portico, n. pòrtico m.

portion, n. porzione f.

portly, adj. corpulènto.

portrait, n. ritratto m.

portray, vb. ritrattare.

Portugal, n. il Portogallo m.

Portuguese, adj. portoghese.

pose, 1. n. pòsa f. **2.** vb. posare; (p. as) atteggiarsi a.

position, n. posizione f.

positive, adj. positivo.

possess, vb. possedere.

possession, n. possèsso m.

possessive, adj. possessivo.

possessor, n. possessore m.

possibility, n. possibilità f.

possible, adj. possìbile.

possibly, adv. possibilmente, forse.

possum, n. opòssum m.

post, 1. n. (pole) pàlo m.; (place) posto m.; (mail) pòsta f. **2.** vb. (put up) affiggere; (mail) impostare.

postage, n. affrancatura f.; (p.-stamp) francobollo m.

postal, adj. postale.

post card, n. cartolina postale f.

poster, n. cartèllo m.

poste restante, adv. fermo pòsta.

posterior, 1. n. culo m. **2.** adj. posteriore.

posterity, n. posterità f., pòsteri m.pl.

postgraduate, adj. di perfezionamento.

postman, n. postino m.

postmark, n. timbro postale, m.

postmortem, 1. adj. postumo. **2.** n. autopsìa f.

post office, n. ufficio postale m.

postpone, vb. posporre, rimandare.

postscript, n. poscritto m.

posture, n. posizione f.

pot, n. pèntola f.; (marijuana) marijuana f.

potassium, n. potàssio m.

potato, n. patata f.

potent, adj. potènte.

potential, n. and adj. potenziale (m.)

pot-hole, n. buca f.

potion, n. pozione f.

pottery, n. stovìglie f.pl.

pouch, n. borsa f.

poultry, n. pollame m.

pound, 1. n. libbra f.; (p. sterling) sterlina f. **2.** vb. pestare.

pour, vb. versare; (p. off) travasare.

poverty, n. povertà f., misèria f.

powder, 1. n. pòlvere m.; (face-p.) cìpria f.; (p.-puff) fiòcco da cìpria f. **2.** vb. polverizzare; (one's face) incipriare, tr.

power, n. potere m., potènza f.

powerful, adj. possènte.

powerless, adj. impotènte.

practicable, adj. praticàbile.

practical, adj. pràtico.

practically, adv. praticamente.

practice, 1. n. pràtica f. **2.** vb. praticare, esercitare, tr.

practiced, adj. espèrto.

practitioner, n. professionista m.

pragmatic, adj. prammàtico.

prairie, n. prateria f.

praise, 1. n. lòde f. **2.** vb. lodare.

prank, n. birichinata f., burla f.

pray, vb. pregare.

prayer, n. preghièra f.

preach, vb. predicare.

preacher, n. predicatore m.
preamble, n. preàmbolo m.
precarious, adj. precàrio.
precaution, n. precauzione f.
precede, vb. precèdere.
precedence, n. precedènza f.
precedent, n. precedènte m.
precept, n. precètto m.
precinct, n. distrètto m., circoscrizione f.
precious, adj. prezioso.
precipice, n. precipízio m.
precipitate, vb. precipitare.
precipitous, adj. precipitoso.
precise, adj. preciso.
precision, n. precisione f.
preclude, vb. preclùdere.
precocious, adj. precòce.
precursor, n. precursore m.
predatory, adj. predatòrio, di prèda.
predecessor, n. predecessore m.
predestination, n. predestinazione f.
predicament, n. impíccio m.
predicate, n. predicato m.
predict, vb. predire.
prediction, n. predizione f.
predilection, n. predilezione f.
predispose, vb. predisporre.
predominant, adj. predominante.
preeminent, adj. preminente.
preempt, vb. preacquisire.
prefabricated, adj. prefabbricato.
preface, n. prefazione f.
prefect, n. prefètto m.
prefer, vb. preferire.
preferable, adj. preferíbile.
preference, n. preferènza f.
prefix, n. prefisso m.
pregnancy, n. gravidanza f.
pregnant, adj. gràvida f., incinta f.; (animals only) prègna f.
prehistoric, adj. preistòrico.
prejudice, 1. n. pregiudízio m. 2. vb. pregiudicare.
prejudiced, adj. pregiudicato.
prelate, n. prelato m.
preliminary, adj. preliminare.
prelude, n. prelúdio m.
premature, adj. prematuro.
premeditate, vb. premeditare.
premier, n. primo ministro m.
premiere, n. prima f.

premise, n. premessa f.
premium, n. prèmio m.
premonition, n. premonizione f.
prenatal, adj. prenatale.
prepaid, adj. saldato in anticipo, prepagato.
preparation, n. preparazione f.
preparatory, adj. preparatòrio.
prepare, vb. preparare.
prepay, vb. pagare in anticipo.
preponderant, adj. preponderante.
preposition, n. preposizione f.
preposterous, adj. assvrdo.
prerecorded, adj. preregistrato.
prerequisite, n. primo requisito m.
prerogative, n. prerogativa f.
presage, 1. n. presagio m. 2. vb. presagire.
prescribe, vb. prescrívere.
prescription, n. prescrizione f.
presence, n. presènza f.
present, 1. n. dono m., regalo m., omàggio m. 2. adj. presènte; (be p.) assistere. 3. vb. presentare; regalare.
presentable, adj. presentàbile.
presentation, n. presentazione f.
presently, adv. fra pòco, immediatamente.
preservation, n. conservazione f.
preservative, adj. conservativo.
preserve, vb. preservare, conservare, serbare.
preside, vb. presièdere.
presidency, n. presidènza f.
president, n. presidènte m.
press, 1. n. prèssa f.; (newspapers) stampa f. 2. vb. prèmere; stríngere; (urge) insistere.
pressing, adj. urgènte.
pressure, n. pressione f.
pressure cooker, n. pèntola a pressione f.
prestige, n. prestígio m.
presume, vb. presùmere.
presumption, n. presunzione f.
presumptuous, adj. presuntuoso.
presumptuousness, n. presuntuosità f.
presuppose, vb. presupporre.
pretend, vb. fíngere, far finta; (claim) pretèndere.
pretense, n. finta f.

pretension, n. pretesa f.
pretentious, adj. pretenzioso.
pretext, n. pretèsto m.
pretty, adj. grazioso, bellino.
prevail, vb. prevalere.
prevalent, adj. prevalènte.
prevent, vb. impedire.
prevention, n. prevenzione f.
preventive, adj. preventivo.
preview, n. anteprima f.
previous, adj. precedènte.
prey, n. prèda f.
price, n. prèzzo m.
priceless, adj. inestimàbile.
prick, vb. pùngere.
pride, n. orgòglio m.
priest, n. prète m.
prim, adj. affettato.
primary, adj. primàrio.
prime, adj. primo, principale.
prime minister, n. primo ministro m.
primitive, adj. primitivo.
prince, n. príncipe m.
princess, n. principessa f.
principal, 1. n. capo m., direttore m. **2.** adj. principale.
principally, adv. principalmente.
principle, n. princípio m.
print, 1. n. stampa f.; (impression) impronta f. **2.** vb. stampare.
printed matter, n. (mail) stampe f.pl.
printer, n. stampante f.
printing, n. stampa f.; (press-run) tiratura f.
printing-press, n. màcchina per stampare f.
printout, n. foglio stampato prodotto da un calcolatore elettrònico f.
prior, 1. adj. anteriore. **2.** adv. prima; **(p. to)** prima di.
priority, n. priorità f.
prism, n. prisma m.
prison, n. prigione f.
prison van, n. cellulare m.
prisoner, n. prigionièro m.
privacy, n. intimità f., solitùdine f.
private, 1. n. soldato sémplice m. **2.** adj. privato.
private eye, n. investigatore privato m.
privation, n. privazione f.
privet, n. ligustro m.

privilege, n. privilègio m.
privy, n. latrina f.
prize, 1. n. prèmio m. **2.** vb. apprezzare.
probability, n. probabilità f.
probable, adj. probàbile.
probate, 1. n. omologazione f. **2.** vb. omologare.
probation, n. pròva f.
probe, vb. sondare.
probity, n. probità f.
problem, n. problèma f.
procedure, n. procedimento m.; (legal) procedura f.
proceed, vb. procèdere.
process, n. procèsso m.
procession, n. processione f.
proclaim, vb. proclamare.
proclamation, n. proclamazione f.
procrastinate, vb. procrastinare.
procure, vb. procurare.
prod, 1. n. pùngolo m.; stimolo m. **2.** vb. stimolare.
prodigal, adj. pròdigo.
prodigy, n. prodígio m.
produce, 1. n. prodotti agricoli m.pl. **2.** vb. produrre.
producer, n. produttore m.; impressario m.
product, n. prodotto m.
production, n. produzione f.
productive, adj. produttivo.
profane, 1. adj. profano. **2.** vb. profanare.
profanity, n. bestémmie f.pl.
profess, vb. professare.
profession, n. professione f.
professional, 1. n. professionista m. **2.** adj. professionale.
professor, n. professore m.
proficient, adj. espèrto.
profile, n. profilo m.
profit, 1. n. guadagno m., profitto m., vantàggio m. **2.** vb. approfittare.
profitable, adj. vantaggioso.
profiteer, n. pescecane m.
profligate, n. and adj. prodigo m., dissoluto m.
profound, adj. profondo.
profoundly, adv. profondamente.
profundity, n. profondità f.
profuse, adj. profuso.
progeny, n. prole f.

prognosis, n. prògnosi f.

program, n. programma m.

progress, 1. n. progrèsso m. 2. vb. progredire.

progressive, adj. progressivo.

prohibit, vb. proibire.

prohibition, n. proibizione f., divièto m.

prohibitive, adj. proibitivo.

project, 1. n. progètto m. 2. vb. (plan) progettare; (stick out) spòrgere.

projectile, n. proièttile m.

projection, n. proiezione f.

projector, n. proiettore m.

proliferation, n. proliferazione f.

prolific, adj. prolífico.

prologue, n. pròlogo m.

prolong, vb. prolungare.

prolongation, n. prolungamento m.

prominent, adj. prominènte.

promiscuous, adj. promìscuo.

promise, 1. n. promessa f. 2. vb. prométtere.

promote, vb. promuòvere.

promotion, n. promozione f.

prompt, adj. pronto.

prompter, n. suggeritore m.

promulgate, vb. promulgare.

pronoun, n. pronome m.

pronounce, vb. pronunciare.

pronunciation, n. pronùncia f.

proof, n. pròva f.; (printing) bòzze f.pl.

proof-read, vb. corrèggere le bòzze di.

prop, 1. n. puntèllo m. 2. vb. puntellare.

propaganda, n. propaganda f.

propagate, vb. propagare.

propel, vb. spíngere innanzi.

propeller, n. èlica f.

propensity, n. propensione f.

proper, adj. pròprio.

property, n. proprietà f.

prophecy, n. profezìa f.

prophesy, vb. profetizzare.

prophet, n. profèta m.

prophetic, adj. profètico.

propitiate, vb. propiziare.

propitious, adj. propízio.

proponent, n. proponènte m.

proportion, n. proporzione f.

proportionate, adj. proporzionato.

proposal, n. propòsta f.

propose, vb. proporre, tr.

proposition, n. propòsta f.

proprietor, n. proprietàrio m.

propriety, n. conveniènza f.

propulsion, n. propulsione f.

prorate, vb. rateizzare.

prosaic, adj. prosàico.

proscribe, vb. proscrívere.

prose, n. pròsa f.

prosecute, vb. intentare giudízio contro.

prosecutor, n. esecutore m.; (law) pùbblico ministero m.

proselyte, n. prosèlite m. and f.

prosody, n. prosodìa f., mètrica f.

prospect, n. prospètto m.

prospective, adj. prospettivo.

prosper, vb. prosperare.

prosperity, n. prosperità f.

prosperous, adj. pròspero.

prostitute, n. prostituta f.

prostrate, 1. adj. prostrato. 2. vb. prostrare.

protagonist, n. protagonista m.

protect, vb. protèggere.

protection, n. protezione f.

protective, adj. protettivo.

protector, n. protettore m.

protégé, n. protètto m.

protein, n. proteína f.

pro tempore, adj. provvisorio, ad interim.

protest, 1. n. protèsta f. 2. vb. protestare.

Protestant, n. and adj. protestante (m.).

Protestantism, n. protestantésimo m.

protocol, n. protocòllo m.

proton, n. protone m.

protoplasma, n. protoplasma m.

protract, vb. protrarre.

protrude, vb. spíngere fuòri, tr.

protuberance, n. protuberanza f.

proud, adj. orgoglioso.

prove, vb. comprovare.

proverb, n. provèrbio m.

proverbial, adj. proverbiale.

provide, vb. provvedere.

provided, conj. purché.

providence, n. provvidènza f.

province, n. provincia f.

provincial, adj. provinciale.
provision, n. provvista f.
provocation, n. provocazione f.
provoke, vb. provocare.
prowess, n. prodezza f.
prowl, vb. vagare intorno.
proximity, n. prossimità f.
proxy, n. (person) procuratore m.; (document) procura f.
prudence, n. prudènza f.
prudent, adj. prudènte.
prune, n. prugna secca f.
pry, vb. ficcare il naso.
psalm, n. salmo m.
pseudonym, n. pseudònimo m.
psychedelic, adj. psichedèlico.
psychiatrist, n. psichiatra m.
psychiatry, n. psichiatria f.
psychoanalysis, n. psicoanàlisi f.
psychological, adj. psicológico.
psychology, n. psicologia f.
psychosis, n. psicòsi f.
ptomaine, n. ptomaína f.
public, n. and adj. pùbblico (m.).
publication, n. pubblicazione f.
publicity, n. pubblicità f.
publish, vb. pubblicare.
publisher, n. editore m.
pudding, n. budino m.
puddle, n. pozzànghera f.
puff, 1. n. sbuffo m.; (powder-p.) fiòcco da cipria m. **2.** vb. sbuffare.
pugnacious, adj. pugnace.
pull, 1. n. tirata f. **2.** vb. tirare.
pulley, n. puléggia f.
pulmonary, adj. polmonare.
pulp, n. polpa f.
pulpit, n. pùlpito m.
pulsar, n. pùlsar m.
pulsate, vb. pulsare.
pulse, n. polso m.
pump, 1. n. pompa f. **2.** vb. pompare.
pumpkin, n. zucca f.
pun, n. freddura f.
punch, 1. n (drink) pònce m.; (blow) pugno m. **2.** vb. (make hole) perforare; (hit) colpire; dar pugni a.
punctual, adj. puntuale.
punctuate, vb. punteggiare.
punctuation, n. punteggiatura f.
puncture, 1. n. puntura f.; (tire) foratura f. **2.** vb. forare.

pungent, adj. pungènte.
punish, vb. punire.
punishment, n. punizione f.
punitive, adj. punitivo.
puny, adj. dèbole.
pupil, n. alunno m., scolaro m.
puppet, n. burattino m.
puppy, n. cùcciolo m.
purchase, 1. n. compra f.; (grasp) presa f. **2.** vb. comprare.
purchasing power, n. potere d'acquisto m.
pure, adj. puro.
purée, n. passato m.
purgative, n. and adj. purgante (m.).
purge, 1. n. purga f. **2.** vb. purgare.
purify, vb. purificare.
puritan, n. and adj. puritano (m.)
puritanical, adj. da puritano.
purity, n. purezza f., purità f.
purple, n. pórpora f.
purport, 1. n. significato m. **2.** vb. use future of verb which in English is dependent on "purport".
purpose, n. fine m., scòpo m., propòsito m.; (on p.) appòsta.
purposely, adv. appòsta.
purr, vb. fare le fusa.
purse, n. borsa f.
pursue, vb. inseguire, perseguire.
pursuit, n. inseguimento m.
pus, n. pus. m.
push, 1. n. spinta f. **2.** vb. spíngere.
pusher, n. spacciatore m.
pushy, adj. aggressivo, insistente.
put, vb. méttere, porre, ficcare; (p. back) riméttere; (p. down, suppress) sopprímere; (p. in) inserire; (p. off) rimandare; (p. on) indossare; (p. out, extinguish) spégnere; (p. up with) soffrire.
putrid, adj. pùtrido.
putsch, n. insurrezione f.
puzzle, n. indovinello m.; (crossword p.) cruivèrba m.
puzzling, adj. di difficile soluzione.
pygmy, n. pigmèo m.
pyramid, n. piràmide f.
pyre, n. pira f.
python, n. pitone m.

Q

quadrangle, *n.* quadràngolo *m.*
quadraphonic, *adj.* quadrofònico.
quadruped, *n.* quadrùpede *m.*
quail, 1. *n.* quàglia *f.* **2.** *vb.* scoraggiarsi.
quaint, *adj.* strano.
quake, 1. *n.* trèmito *m.* **2.** *vb.* tremare.
qualification, *n.* qualificazione *f.*, qualífica *f.*, requisito *m.*
qualified, *adj.* idòneo.
qualify, *vb.* qualificare; (be fit) èssere idòneo.
quality, *n.* qualità *f.*
qualm, *n.* nàusea *f.*; (fig.) scrùpolo *m.*
quandary, *n.* perplessità *f.*
quantity, *n.* quantità *f.*, somma *f.*
quarantine, *n.* quarentena *f.*
quarrel, 1. *n.* lite *f.* **2.** *vb.* litigare.
quarry, *n.* cava *f.*
quarter, *n.* (one fourth) quarto *m.*; (region; mercy) quartière *m.*; (three months) trimèstre *m.*
quarterly, *adj.* trimestrale.
quartet, *n.* quartetto *m.*
quartz, *n.* quarzo *m.*
quasar, *n.* quàsar *m.*
quaver, *vb.* tremolare.
queen, *n.* regina *f.*
queer, *adj.* strano.
quell, *vb.* sopprímere.
quench, *vb.* estínguere; (q. one's thirst) dissetare.

query, 1. *n.* domanda *f.* **2.** *vb.* domandare.
quest, *n.* ricerca *f.*
question, 1. *n.* domanda *f.*, questione *f.* **2.** *vb.* interrogare; (doubt) dubitare di.
questionable, *adj.* dùbbio.
question mark, *n.* punto interrogativo *m.*
questionnaire, *n.* questionàrio *m.*
quick, 1. *adj.* ràpido, pronto, svelto. **2.** *adv.* prèsto.
quicken, *vb.* affrettare, tr.
quicksand, *n.* sàbbie mòbili *f.pl.*
quiet, 1. *n.* quiète *f.* **2.** *adj.* quièto; (be, keep q.) tacere.
quilt, *n.* trapunta *f.*
quinine, *n.* chinino *m.*
quintet, *n.* quintétto *m.*
quip, *n.* motto *m.*
quit, *vb.* (leave) lasciare; (stop) cessare, sméttere; (resign) diméttersi.
quite, *adv.* completamente, pròprio.
quiver, 1. *n.* farètra *f.* **2.** *vb.* tremare; (shiver) rabbrividire.
quixotic, *adj.* donchisciottesco.
quiz, 1. *n.* esame *m.* **2.** *vb.* esaminare.
quorum, *n.* quorum *m.*
quota, *n.* quòta *f.*
quotation, *n.* citazione *f.*
quote, *vb.* citare.

R

rabbi, *n.* rabbino *m.*
rabbit, *n.* conìglio *m.*
rabble, *n.* plebàglia *f.*, volgo *m.*
rabid, *adj.* rabbioso.
rabies, *n.* ràbbia *f.*
raccoon, *n.* procione *m.*
race, 1. *n.* (contest) corsa *f.*; (breed) razza *f.* **2.** *vb.* córrere.
race-track, *n.* ippòdromo *m.*
racial, *adj.* razziale.
racism, *n.* razzismo *m.*
racist, *adj.* razzista.
rack, 1. *n.* (torture) ruòta *f.*; (for

feed) rastrellièra *f.*; (luggage) reticella *f.*; (railroad) cremaglièra *f.* **2.** *vb.* torturare.
racket, *n.* (tennis) racchetta *f.*; (uproar) frastuòno *m.*, baccano *m.*
radar, *n.* (instrument) radiotelèmetro *m.*; (science) radiotelemetría *f.*
radiance, *n.* fulgore *m.*
radiant, *adj.* raggiante.
radiate, *vb.* irradiare, tr.
radiation, *n.* irradiazione *f.*

radiator, n. radiatore m.
radical, n. and adj. radicale (m.).
radio, 1. n. ràdio f. 2. adj. **(pertaining to r.)** radiofònico.
radioactive, adj. radioattivo.
radiology, n. radiología f.
radish, n. ramolàccio m., ravanèllo m.
radium, n. ràdio m.
radius, n. ràggio m.
raffle, n. lottería f.
raft, n. zàttera f.
rafter, n. travicèllo m.
rag, n. céncio m., stràccio m.
ragamuffin, n. straccione m.
rage, 1. n. ràbbia f. 2. vb. infuriare.
ragged, adj. cencioso.
raid, n. incursione f.
rail, n. rotaia f.; (bar) sbarra f.
railcar, n. automotrice f.; **(electric r.)** elettromotrice f.
railing, n. ringhièra f.
railroad, 1. n. ferrovía f. 2. adj. **(pertaining to r.s)** ferroviàrio.
railway, n. ferrovía f.
rain, 1. n. piòggia f. 2. vb. piòvere; **(r. cats and dogs)** diluviare.
rainbow, n. arcobaleno m.
raincoat, n. impermeàbile m.
rainfall, n. precipitazione atmosfèrica f.
rainy, adj. piovoso.
raise, vb. (bring up) allevare; (erect) erígere; (grow) coltivare; (increase) aumentare; (hoist) innalzare; (lift) levare; (collect) raccògliere; (intensify) alzare.
raisin, n. uva secca f.; **(sultana r.)** uva sultanina f.
rake, 1. n. rastrèllo m. 2. vb. rastrellare.
rally, 1. n. (recovery) ricùpero di fòrze m.; (meeting) raduno m. 2. vb. riunire, tr.
ram, 1. n. (animal) montone m.; (post) battipalo m. 2. vb. bàttere; cacciare.
ramble, vb. divagare.
ramify, vb. ramificare.
ramp, n. piano inclinato m.
rampage, n. stato d'eccitazione m.
rampart, n. bastione m.
ranch, n. fattoría f.
rancid, adj. ràncido.
rancor, n. rancore m.

random, n. **(at r.)** a casàccio.
range, 1. n. (distance) portata f.; (mountains) catena f.; (scope) estensione f.; (sphere) sfèra f.; (stove) cucina econòmica f. 2. vb. (arrange) disporre; (vary) variare.
rank, n. (line) fila f.; (position) grado m.
ransack, vb. frugare dappertutto.
ransom, 1. n. riscatto m. 2. vb. riscattare.
rap, 1. n. colpo m., pícchio m. 2. vb. colpire, picchiare.
rapacious, adj. rapace.
rape, vb. violare.
rapid, adj. ràpido.
rapport, n. rappòrto m.
rapture, n. èstasi f.
rare, adj. raro; (underdone) pòco còtto, al sangue.
rarely, adv. raramente.
rascal, n. briccone m.
rash, 1. n. eruzione f. 2. adj. inconsiderato.
raspberry, n. lampone m.; (Bronx cheer) pernàcchia f.
rat, n. ratto m.
rate, 1. n. (price) prèzzo m.; (speed) velocità f. 2. vb. classificare, tr.
rather, adv. piuttosto.
ratify, vb. ratificare.
ratio, n. rappòrto m.
ration, 1. n. razione f.; **(r.-card)** tèssera annonària f. 2. vb. razionare.
rational, adj. razionale.
rattle, n. ràntolo m., rumore secco m.
raucous, adj. ràuco.
ravage, 1. n. devastazione f. 2. vb. devastare.
rave, vb. delirare.
ravel, n. grovíglio m.
raven, n. corvo m. 2. adj. corvino.
ravenous, adj. affamato.
ravine, n. canalone m., burrone m.
ravish, vb. incantare, entusiasmare; rapire.
raw, adj. grezzo, crudo.
raw material, n. materie prime f.pl.
ray, n. ràggio m.
rayon, n. ràion m.

razor, n. rasòio m.

reach, 1. n. portata f. 2. vb. (get to) arrivare a; raggiùngere; (extend) allungare.

react, vb. reagire.

reaction, n. reazione f.

reactionary, adj. reazionàrio m.

reactor, n. reattore m.

read, vb. lèggere.

reader, n. (person) lettore m.; (book) libro di lettura m.

readily, adj. prontamente.

reading, n. lettura f.

ready, adj. pronto; (r.-made) già fatto.

real, adj. reale, vero.

real estate, n. beni immòbili m.pl.

realist, n. realista m.

realtor, n. agente immobiliare m.

reality, n. realtà f.

realization, n. realizzazione f.

realize, vb. (make real) realizzare; (be, become aware of) rendersi conto di.

really, adv. realmente, veramente, davvero.

realm, n. reame m., regno m.

ream, n. risma f.

reap, vb. miètere, reccògliere.

rear, 1. n. (back) parte posteriore f.; (r.-guard) retroguàrdia f. 2. vb. (bring up) allevare; (raise) alzare; (erect) èrgere, tr.; (lift) sollevare; (of horse) impennarsi.

rearmament, n. riarmo m.

rear-view mirror, n. spècchio retrovisore m.

reason, 1. n. ragione f. 2. vb. ragionare.

reasonable, adj. ragionévole.

reassessment, n. rivalutazione f.

reassure, vb. rassicurare.

rebate, n. sconto m.

rebel, 1. n. and adj. ribèlle (m.). 2. vb. ribellarsi.

rebellion, n. ribellione f.

rebellious, adj. ribèlle.

rebirth, n. rinàscita f.

reborn, be, vb. rinàscere.

rebound, 1. n. rimbalzo m. 2. vb. rimbalzare.

rebuff, n. ripulsa f.

rebuild, vb. ricostruire.

rebuke, 1. n. rimpròvero m. 2. vb. rimproverare.

rebuttal, n. confutazione f.

recalcitrant, adj. ricalcitrante.

recall, vb. richiamare.

recant, vb. ritrattare.

recapitulate, vb. ricapitolare.

recede, vb. recèdere.

receipt, n. ricevuta f.; (document) quietanza f.

receive, vb. ricévere.

receiver, n. ricevitore m.

recent, adj. recènte.

recently, adv. recentemente.

receptacle, n. ricettàcolo m., recipiènte m.

reception, n. accoglienza f.; (party) ricevimento m.

receptive, adj. ricettivo.

recess, n. (in wall) rientranza f.; (vacation) vacanze f.

recipe, n. ricètta f.

recipient, n. ricevènte m.

reciprocate, vb. ricambiare.

recitation, n. recitazione f.

recite, vb. recitare.

reckless, adj. avventato.

reckon, vb. (count) contare; (deem) stimare; (think) pensare.

reclaim, vb. redímere; (land) bonificare.

reclamation, n. bonifica f.

recline, vb. reclinare.

recognition, n. riconoscimento m.

recognize, vb. riconóscere.

recoil, vb. indietreggiare.

recollect, vb. ricordare, rammentarsi.

recommend, vb. raccomandare.

recommendation, n. raccomandazione f.

recompense, 1. n. ricompènsa f. 2. vb. ricompensare.

reconcile, vb. riconciliare.

recondition, vb. riparare.

reconsider, vb. riprèndere in esame.

reconstruct, vb. ricostruire.

record, 1. n. memòria f., ricordo m., registro m.; (top achievement) primato m.; (phonograph) disco m.; (r. library) discoteca f.; (r. player) giradischi m. 2. vb. registrare; (phonograph) incidere.

recording, n. incisione f.

recount, vb. (tell) raccontare; (count again) contare di nùovo.

recourse, n. ricorso m.; **(have r.)** ricórrere.
recover, vb. ricuperare.
recovery, n. ricùpero m.; (medical) guarigione f.
recreation, n. ricreazione f.
recruit, 1. n. rècluta f. **2.** vb. reclutare.
rectangle, n. rettàngolo m.
rectifier, n. rettificatrice f.
rectify, vb. rettificare.
rectitude, n. rettitùdine f.
rectum, n. retto m.
recuperate, vb. ricuperare.
recur, vb. ricórrere, ritornare.
recurrent, adj. ricorrente.
recycle, vb. riciclare.
red, adj. rosso.
red cell, n. glòbulo rosso m.
redeem, vb. redímere.
redeemer, n. redentore m.
redemption, n. redenzione f.
red-light district, n. quartiere a luci rosse m.
redress, n. riparazione f.
reduce, vb. ridurre.
reduction, n. riduzione f.
reed, n. canna f.; (for instrument) ància f.
reef, n. scòglio m.
reel, 1. n. (bobbin) naspo m.; (spool) rocchetto m.; (dance) trescone m. **2.** vb. traballare; **(r. off)** dipanare.
refer, vb. riferire, tr.
referee, n. àrbitro m.
reference, n. allusione f., riferimento m.; **(cross-r.)** rimando m.; **(r. room)** sala di consultazione f.
referendum, n. referendum m.
refill, n. riempire di nùovo.
refine, vb. raffinare.
refinement, n. raffinatezza f.
refinery, n. raffineria f.
reflect, vb. riflèttere.
reflection, n. riflessione f., riflèsso m.
reflex, n. riflèsso m.
reflexive, adj. riflessivo.
reform, 1. n. riforma f. **2.** vb. riformare.
reformation, n. riforma f.
refractory, adj. ribèlle.
refrain, vb. trattenere, tr.
refresh, vb. rinfrescare, ristorare.

refreshment, n. ristòro m.
refrigerator, n. frigorífero m.
refuge, n. rifùgio m.; **(take r.)** rifugiarsi.
refugee, n. rifugiato m.
refund, vb. restituire.
refusal, n. rifiuto m.
refuse, 1. n. (waste matter) rifiuti m.pl. **2.** vb. rifiutare.
refutation, n. confutazione f.
refute, vb. confutare.
regain, vb. ritornare a.
regal, adj. regale.
regard, 1. n. riguardo m., rispétto m. **2.** vb. (look at) guardare; (concern) riguardare; (consider) considerare.
regarding, prep. riguardo a.
regardless, adv. ciò nonostante; **(r. of)** malgrado.
regent, n. regènte m.
regime, n. regime m.
regiment, n. reggimento m.
region, n. regione f.
register, 1. n. registro m. **2.** vb. registrare.
registration, n. registrazione f.
regret, 1. n. rimpianto m., rincrescimento m. **2.** vb. rimpiàngere, rincréscere (with English subject in dative).
regular, adj. regolare.
regularity, n. regolarità f.
regulate, vb. regolare.
regulation, n. regolamento m.
regulator, n. regolatore m.
rehabilitate, vb. riabilitare.
rehearsal, n. pròva f.
rehearse, vb. provare.
reign, 1. n. regno m. **2.** vb. regnare.
reimburse, vb. rimborsare.
reins, n. rèdini f.pl.
reincarnation, n. nùova incarnazione f.
reindeer, n. rènna f.
reinforce, vb. rinforzare.
reinforcement, n. rinfòrzo m.
reinstate, vb. riméttere.
reiterate, vb. reiterare.
reject, vb. rigettare, respíngere.
rejoice, vb. rallegrare, tr.
rejoin, vb. (answer) replicare; (join again) ricongiùngersi.
rejoinder, n. rèplica f.
rejuvenate, vb. ringiovanire.

relapse, 1. *n.* ricaduta *f.* **2.** *vb.* ricadere.

relate, *vb.* (tell) narrare; (be connected with) riferirsi a; riguardare; (connect) méttere in relazione. **r. to,** entrare in rapporto con.

related, *adj.* affine, connésso.

relation, *n.* (story) narrazione *f.;* (connection) rappòrto *m.;* relazione *f.;* (person) parènte *m.*

relationship, *n.* rappòrto *m.;* (kinship) parentela *f.*

relative, 1. *n.* parènte *m.* **2.** *adj.* relativo.

relativity, *n.* relatività *f.*

relax, *vb.* allentare, *tr.*

relaxation, *n.* distensione *f.*

relaxing, *adj.* distensivo.

relay, *vb.* ritrasméttere.

release, 1. *n.* liberazione *f.* **2.** *vb.* liberare, sprigionare.

relent, *vb.* aver pietà.

relentless, *adj.* implacàbile.

relevant, *adj.* pertinènte.

reliable, *adj.* affidàbile.

reliant, *adj.* fiducioso.

relic, *n.* avanzo *m.;* (religious) relíquia *f.*

relief, *n.* sollièvo *m.;* (social work) assistènza *f.;* (diversion) diversivo *m.;* (replacement) càmbio *m.;* (help) soccorso *m.*

relieve, *vb.* sollevare; (help) soccórrere; (free) liberare; (alleviate) alleviare.

religion, *n.* religione *f.*

religious, *adj.* religioso.

relinquish, *vb.* abbandonare.

relish, 1. *n.* gusto *m.;* (sauce) condimento *m.* **2.** *vb.* gustare.

reluctance, *n.* riluttanza *f.*

reluctant, *adj.* riluttante.

rely, *vb.* confidare.

remain, *vb.* restare, rimanere.

remainder, *n.* rèsto *m.*

remark, 1. *n.* osservazione *f.* **2.** *vb.* osservare.

remarkable, *adj.* notévole, rimarchévole.

remarry, *vb.* risposarsi *(refl.),* prèndere in seconde nozze.

remedy, 1. *n.* rimèdio *m.* **2.** *vb.* rimediare a.

remember, *vb.* ricordarsi di.

remembrance, *n.* ricòrdo *m.*

remind, *vb.* rammentare.

reminiscence, *n.* reminiscènza *f.*

remiss, *adj.* negligènte.

remit, *vb.* (send) spedire; (forgive) riméttere.

remittance, *n.* spedizione *f.*

remnant, *n.* rèsto *m.,* rimanènte *m.*

remonstrance, *n.* remostranza *f.*

remorse, *n.* rimòrso *m.*

remorseful, *adj.* pentito.

remote, *adj.* remòto.

remote control, *n.* telecomando. *m.*

removable, *adj.* mòbile, rimuovíbile.

removal, *n.* rimozione *f.*

remove, *vb.* tògliere, rimuòvere.

remuneration, *n.* rimunerazion *f.*

renaissance, *n.* rinascimento *m.*

rend, *vb.* strappare.

render, *vb.* rèndere.

rendezvous, *n.* appuntamento *m.*

rendition, *n.* esecuzione *f.*

renege, *vb.* rifiutare.

renew, *vb.* rinnovare.

renewal, *n.* rinnovamento *m.*

renounce, *vb.* rinunciare a.

renovate, *vb.* rimodernare.

renown, *n.* rinomanza *f.*

renowned, *adj.* rinomato.

rent, 1. *n.* affitto *m.,* pigione *f.* **2.** *vb.* affittare, noleggiare.

rental, *n.* nolèggio *m.*

repair, 1. *n.* riparazione *f.* **2.** *vb.* riparare.

reparation, *n.* riparazione *f.*

repatriate, *vb.* rimpatriare.

repay, *vb.* ripagare, rimborsare.

repeal, 1. *n.* abrogazione *f.,* rèvoca *f.* **2.** *vb.* abrogare, revocare.

repeat, 1. *n.* (music) ripresa *f.* **2.** *vb.* ripètere, replicare.

repel, *vb.* respíngere.

repent, *vb.* pentirsi di.

repentance, *n.* pentimento *m.*

repercussion, *n.* ripercussione *f.*

repertoire, *n.* repertòrio *m.*

repetition, *n.* ripetizione *f.;* (theater) rèplica *f.*

replace, *vb.* sostituire, rimpiazzare.

replenish, *vb.* riempire di nuòvo.

reply, 1. *n.* risposta *f.;* (rebuttal) rèplica *f.* 2. *vb.* rispóndere; replicare.

report, 1. *n.* (bang) detonazione *f.;* (news) notízia *f.;* (rumor) voce *f.;* (memoir) rapporto *m.* 2. *vb.* dare notízia di; (complain of) denunciare.

reporter, *n.* cronista *m.,* giornalista *m.*

repose, 1. *n.* ripòso *m.* 2. *vb.* riposare.

reprehend, *vb.* riprèndere.

reprehensible, *adj.* rimproveràbile.

represent, *vb.* rappresentare.

representation, *n.* rappresentazione *f.*

representative, 1. *n.* deputato *m.* 2. *adj.* rappresentativo.

repress, *vb.* reprímere.

repression, *n.* repressione *f.*

reprimand, 1. *n.* rimpròvero *m.* 2. *vb.* rimproverare.

reprisal, *n.* rappresàglia *f.*

reproach, 1. *n.* rimpròvero *m.* 2. *vb.* rimproverare.

reproduce, *vb.* riprodurre, *tr.*

reproduction, *n.* riproduzione *f.*

reproof, *n.* rimpròvero *m.*

reprove, *vb.* rimproverare.

reptile, *n.* rèttile *m.*

republic, *n.* repùbblica *f.*

republican, *adj.* repubblicano.

repudiate, *vb.* ripudiare.

repudiation, *n.* ripùdio *m.*

repulse, 1. *n.* ripulsa *f.* 2. *vb.* respíngere.

repulsive, *adj.* repellènte.

reputation, *n.* reputazione *f.*

repute, *vb.* reputare.

reputedly, *adv.* secondo l'opinione generale.

request, 1. *n.* richièsta *f.,* domanda *f.* 2. *vb.* richièdere, domandare.

require, *vb.* richièdere, esígere.

requirement, *n.* esigènza *f.,* requisito *m.*

requisite, 1. *n.* requisito *m.* 2. *adj.* necessàrio.

requisition, 1. *n.* requisizione *f.* 2. *vb.* requisire.

requite, *n.* contraccambiare.

resale, *n.* rivèndita *f.*

rescind, *vb.* rescíndere.

rescue, 1. *n.* liberazione *f.* 2. *vb.* liberare.

research, *n.* ricerche *f.pl.*

resell, *vb.* rivèndere.

resemblance, *n.* rassomiglianza *f.*

resemble, *vb.* rassomigliare a.

resent, *vb.* offèndersi di.

resentful, *adj.* risentito, offeso.

resentment, *n.* risentimento *m.*

reservation, *n.* risèrva *f.;* (tickets) prenotazione *f.*

reserve, 1. *n.* risèrva *f.* 2. *vb.* riservare; (tickets) prenotare.

reservist, *n.* riservista *m.*

reservoir, *n.* serbatòio *m.*

reset, *vb.* regolare; rimettere nella condizione originale.

reside, *vb.* risièdere, abitare.

residence, *n.* residènza *f.,* abitazione *f.*

resident, 1. *n.* abitante *m.* 2. *adj.* residènte.

residue, *n.* resíduo *m.*

resign, *vb.* diméttersi; (r. oneself, give up hope) rassegnarsi.

resignation, *n.* dimissione *f.;* (loss of hope) rassegnazione *f.*

resist, *vb.* resistere.

resistance, *n.* resistènza *f.*

resolute, *adj.* risoluto.

resolution, *n.* risoluzione *f.*

resolve, 1. *n.* decisione *f.* 2. *vb.* risòlvere, sciògliere; (decide) decídersi.

resonance, *n.* risonanza *f.*

resonant, *adj.* risonante.

resort, 1. *n.* (recourse) ricorso *m.;* (vacation place) stazione *f.;* luògo di soggiorno *m.* 2. *vb.* ricórrere.

resound, *vb.* risonare, risuonare.

resource, *n.* risorsa *f.*

respect, 1. *n.* rispètto *m.* 2. *vb.* rispettare.

respectable, *adj.* rispettàbile.

respectful, *adj.* rispettoso.

respective, *adj.* rispettivo.

respiration, *n.* respirazione *f.*

respite, *n.* trégua *f.*

respond, *vb.* rispóndere.

response, *n.* risposta *f.*

responsibility, *n.* responsabilità *f.*

responsible, *adj.* responsàbile.

responsive, adj. rispondente, sensibile.

rest, 1. n. (remainder) rimanènte m.; (repose) ripòso m. **2.** vb. riposare.

restaurant, n. ristorante m., ristoratore m., trattoria f.; **(r.-keeper)** trattore m.

restful, adj. riposante.

restitution, n. restituzione f.

restless, adj. irrequièto.

restoration, n. restaurazione f.

restore, vb. restaurare.

restrain, vb. trattenere.

restraint, n. contròllo m.

restrict, vb. restríngere.

restriction, n. restrizione f.

result, 1. n. risultato m. **2.** vb. risultare.

resume, vb. riassùmere, ripréndere.

résumé, n. riassunto m.

resurgent, adj. risorgènte.

resurrect, vb. risuscitare.

resurrection, n. resurrezione f.

retail, 1. adv. al minuto, al dettàglio. **2.** vb. véndere al minuto, véndere al dettàglio.

retain, vb. ritenere, conservare.

retake, vb. ripréndere.

retaliate, vb. ricambiare.

retaliation, n. rappresàglia f.

retard, vb. ritardare.

retention, n. ritenzione f.; (remembering ability) memòria f.

reticence, n. reticènza f.

reticent, adj. reticènte.

retina, n. rètina f.

retinue, n. sèguito m.

retire, vb. ritirare, -rsi.

retort, vb. replicare, ribàttere.

retract, vb. (pull back) ritrarre; (withdraw) ritrattare.

retreat, 1. n. ritirata f. **2.** vb. ritirarsi.

retribution, n. retribuzione f.

retributive, adj. retributivo.

retrieve, vb. recuperare.

retriever, n. cane da presa.

retroactive, adj. retroattivo.

retrospect, n. sguardo retrospettivo m.

retrospective, adj. retrospettivo.

retry, vb. ritentare; (law) processare una seconda volta.

return, 1. n. ritorno m.; **(r. ticket)** biglietto d'andata e ritorno m. **2.** vb. tornare; ritornare.

return address, n. mittente m.

reunion, n. riunione f.

reunite, vb. riunire.

revamp, vb. rinnovare.

reveal, vb. rivelare.

revel, 1. n. (noisy good time) baldòria f.; (drunken rout) gozzoviglia f. **2.** vb. far baldòria; gozzovigliare.

revelation, n. rivelazione f.

revelry, n. baldòria f.

revenge, 1. n. vendetta f. **2.** vb. vendicare.

revengeful, adj. vendicativo.

revenue, n. entrata f.

reverberate, vb. riverberare.

revere, vb. riverire.

reverence, n. riverènza f.

reverend, adj. reverèndo.

reverent, adj. reverènte.

reverie, n. fantasticheria f.

reverse, 1. n. rovèscio m., contràrio m.; (auto) màrcia indiètro f. **2.** vb. rovesciare; (direction) invertire.

revert, vb. ritornare.

review, 1. n. rivista f., riesame m.; **(book r.)** recensione f. **2.** vb. passare in rivista; riesaminare; (book) recensire.

revise, vb. rivedere.

revision, n. revisione f.

revival, n. ravvivamento m.; (theater) ripresa f.

revive, vb. ravvivare.

revocation, n. rèvoca f.

revoke, vb. revocare.

revolt, 1. n. rivòlta f. **2.** vb. rivoltare. tr.

revolting, adj. rivoltante.

revolution, n. rivoluzione f.; (turn) giro m.

revolutionary, adj. rivoluzionàrio.

revolve, vb. girare.

revolver, n. rivoltèlla f.

revue, n. rivista f.

reward, 1. n. ricompènsa f. **2.** vb. ricompensare.

rewind, vb. riavvòlgere, ribobinare.

rewinding, *n.* riavvolgimento *m.*, ribobinatura *f.*
rhetoric, *n.* retòrica *f.*
rhetorical, *adj.* retòrico *m.*
rheumatic, *adj.* reumàtico.
rheumatism, *n.* reumatismo *m.*
rhinoceros, *n.* rinoceronte *m.*
rhubarb, *n.* rabàrbaro *m.*
rhyme, 1. *n.* rima *f.* 2. *vb.* rimare.
rhythm, *n.* ritmo *m.*
rhythmical, *adj.* rítmico.
rib, *n.* còstola *f.*
ribbon, *n.* nastro *m.*
rice, *n.* riso *m.*
rich, *adj.* ricco.
riches, *n.* ricchezza *f.*
rid, *vb.* sbarazzare.
riddle, *n.* enigma *m.*, indovinello *m.*
ride, 1. *n.* corsa *f.* 2. *vb.* (on horse) cavalcare; (other transport) andare.
rider, *n.* cavalière *m.*
ridge, *n.* (mountain) cresta *f.*, crinale *m.*; (between furrows) pòrca *f.*
ridicule, 1. *n.* ridicolo *m.* 2. *vb.* deridere.
ridiculous, *adj.* ridicolo.
rifle, *n.* fucile *m.*
rig, 1. *n.* equipàggio *m.*; (ship) atrezzatura *f.* 2. *vb.* equipaggiare; attrezzare.
right, 1. *n.* (side) dèstra *f.*; (justice) giusto *m.* 2. *adj.* (side) dèstro; (straight) diretto; (correct) corrètto; (be r.) aver ragione. 3. *vb.* (set upright) drizzare; (correct) corrèggere.
righteous, *adj.* giusto.
righteousness, *n.* giustízia *f.*
right of way, *n.* precedènza *f.*
rigid, *adj.* rígido.
rigidity, *n.* rigidezza *f.*
rigor, *n.* rigore *m.*
rigorous, *adj.* rigoroso.
rim, *n.* bordo *m.*, orlo *m.*
ring, 1. *n.* (circle) cérchio *m.*; (for finger) anèllo *m.*; (boxing) quadrato *m.*; (on bell) suòno *m.*, scampanellata *f.* 2. *vb.* suonare; (r. out) risuonare; (form a r. around) accerchiare.
rinse, *vb.* risciacquare.

riot, 1. *n.* tumulto *m.* 2. *vb.* creare disordini.
rip, *vb.* strappare.
ripe, *adj.* maturo.
ripen, *vb.* maturare.
ripoff, 1. *n.* furto *m.* 2. *vb.* rubare.
ripple, *n.* increspatura *f.*
rise, 1. *n.* (increase) aumènto *m.*; (origin) origine *f.* 2. *vb.* alzarsi, levarsi, sorgere.
risk, 1. *n.* rischio *m.* 2. *vb.* arrischiare, rischiare.
risky, *adj.* rischiòso.
rite, *n.* rito *m.*
ritual, *n. and adj.* rituale *(m.)*.
rival, 1. *n. and adj.* rivale *f.* 2. *vb.* rivaleggiare con.
rivalry, *n.* rivalità *f.*
river, *n.* fiume *m.*
rivet, 1. *n.* chiòdo ribadito *m.* 2. *vb.* ribadire.
roach, *n.* scarafàggio *m.*
road, 1. *n.* cammino *m.*, strada *f.*, vía *f.* 2. *adj.* (pertaining to roads) stradale.
roam, *vb.* vagare.
roar, 1. *n.* ruggito *m.* 2. *vb.* ruggire.
roast, 1. *n.* arròsto *m.* 2. *vb.* arrostire.
roast beef, *n.* roastbeef, *m.*, rosbif *m.*
roasting, *n.* (of coffee) torrefazione *f.*
rob, *vb.* derubare; (r. completely) svaligiare.
robber, *n.* ladrone *m.*
robbery, *n.* furto *m.*
robe, *n.* vèste *f.*
robin, *n.* pettirosso *m.*
robot, *n.* autòma *m.*
robust, *adj.* robusto.
rock, 1. *n.* ròccia *f.*; (music) (musicaccia) rock *f.*; (fortress) ròcca *f.*; (pertaining to r.) roccioso. 2. *vb.* dondolare.
rocker, *n.* (rocking-chair) sèdia a dòndolo *f.*
rocket, *n.* razzo *m.*
rocking, *adj.* dondolante; (r. chair) sedia a dòndolo *f.*; (r. horse) cavallo a dòndolo *m.*
rocky, *adj.* roccioso.
rod, *n.* verga *f.*
rodent, *n.* roditore *m.*
roe, *n.* cèrva *f.*

rogue, n. briccone m.
roguish, adj. bricconesco.
rôle, n. ruòlo m.
roll, 1. n. ròtolo m.; (bread) panino m.; (list) ruòlo m.; (of ship) rullio m. **2.** vb. rotolare; (ship) rullare.
roll call, n. chiamata f., appello m.
roller, n. rotèlla m., rullo m.
roller-bearing, n. cuscinetto a rotolamento m.
roller coaster, n. ottovolante m., montagne russe f. pl.
roller skate, 1. n. pàttini a rotelle m.pl. **2.** vb. pattinare coi pàttini a rotelle.
Roman, adj. romano.
Roman Catholic Church, n. Chiesa Cattòlica Apostòlica Romana f.
romance, n. romanzo m.
romantic, adj. romàntico.
Rome, n. Roma f.
romp, vb. giocare vigorosamente.
roof, n. tètto m.
roof garden, n. giardino pènsile m.
room, n. (in house) càmera f., stanza f.; (space) posto m., spàzio f.
roommate, n. compagno di stanza m., compagna di stanza f.
rooster, n. gallo m.
root, n. radice f.
rope, n. còrda f., fune f.
rosary, n. rosàrio m.
rose, n. ròsa f.
rosin, n. rèsina f.
rosy, adj. ròseo.
rot, 1. n. putrefazione f. **2.** vb. marcire, imputridire, tr.
rotary, adj. rotatòrio.
rotate, vb. rotare.
rotation, n. rotazione f.
rotten, adj. pùtrido.
rouge, n. rossetto m.
rough, adj. rùvido, rozzo.
round, 1. n. giro m. **2.** adj. rotondo, tondo. **3.** adv. intorno. **4.** prep. intorno a.
rouse, vb. svegliare, risvegliare.
rout, n. rotta f.
route, n. percorso m.
routine, n. routine f., abitùdini f.pl.

rove, vb. errare.
row, 1. n. (fight) lite f.; (uproar) baccano m.; (series) fila f.; (boat ride) remata f. **2.** vb. (raise a row) litigare; (use oars) remare.
rowboat, n. battèllo a remi m.
rowdy, adj. litigioso.
royal, adj. reale, règio.
royalty, n. regalità f.
rub, 1. n. fregata f. **2.** vb. fregare, strofinare.
rubber, n. gomma f.; (overshoe) scarpa di gomma f.
rubbish, n. scarti m.pl.; (nonsense) fandònie f.pl.
ruby, n. rubino m.
rudder, n. timone m.
ruddy, adj. rubicondo.
rude, adj. rude.
rudiment, n. rudimento m.
rue, vb. pentirsi di.
ruffian, n. malfattore m.
ruffle, 1. n. increspatura f. **2.** vb. increspare.
rug, n. (for floor) tappeto m.; (blanket) copèrta f.
rugged, adj. scabroso.
ruin, 1. n. rovina f.; (remain) rùdere m. **2.** vb. rovinare.
ruinous, adj. ravinoso.
rule, 1. n. règola f. **2.** vb. regolare; (reign) regnare.
ruler, n. (lawgiver) sovrano m.; (measuring-stick) righello m.
ruling, 1. n. òrdine m., decreto m. **2.** adj. al governo, governante.
rum, n. rum m.
rumble, 1. n. brontolio m. **2.** vb. brontolare.
ruminate, vb. ruminare.
rummage, vb. frugare, rovistare.
rumor, n. diceria f., voce f.
run, 1. n. (in stocking) cordiglièra f. **2.** vb. córrere; (work) funzionare; (flow) scórrere; (r. across) incontrare; (r. away) fuggire; (r. into) investire.
runaway, n. evaso m., fuggiasco m.
run-down, adj. indebolito, esgusto.
rung, n. piolo m.
runner, n. corridore m.

runner-up, *n.* finalista *m.*
runoff, *n.* ballotaggio *m.*
run-of-the-mill, *adj.* ordinario.
runway, *n.* pista *f.*
rupture, *n.* rottura *f.*
rural, *adj.* rurale.
rush, 1. *n.* afflusso *m.;* (hurry) fretta *f.;*(reed) giunco *m.* **2.** *vb.* affluire; precipitarsi.
rush hour, *n.* ora di punta *f.*
Russia, *n.* Rùssia *f.*

Russian, *adj.* russo.
rust, 1. *n.* rùggine *f.* **2.** *vb.* arrugginire, *tr.*
rustic, *n. and adj.* rùstico *(m.).*
rustle, 1. *n.* fruscìo *m.* **2.** *vb.* frusciare.
rust-proof, *adj.* inossidàbile.
rusty, *adj.* arrugginito, rugginoso.
rut, *n.* solco *m.*
ruthless, *adj.* spietato.
rye, *n.* ségale *f.*

S

Sabbath, *n.* giorno di ripòso *m.*
saber, *n.* sciàbola *f.*
sable, *n.* zibellino *m.*
sabotage, 1. *n.* sabotàggio *m.* **2.** *vb.* sabotare.
saboteur, *n.* sabotatore *m.*
saccharine, 1. *n.* saccarina *f.* **2.** *adj.* saccarino.
sachet, *n.* sacchetto di profumo *m.*
sack, 1. *n.* sacco *m.;* (pillage) sacchèggio *m.* **2.** *vb.* (discharge) licenziare; (plunder) saccheggiare.
sacrament, *n.* sacramento *m.*
sacred, *adj.* sacro.
sacrifice, 1. *n.* sacrificio *m.* **2.** *vb.* sacrificare.
sacrilege, *n.* sacrilègio *m.*
sacrilegious, *adj.* sacrìlego.
sacristan, *n.* sagrestano *m.*
sacristy, *n.* sagrestìa *f.*
sad, *adj.* triste.
sadden, *vb.* rattristare.
saddle, 1. *n.* sèlla *f.* **2.** *vb.* sellare.
sadism, *n.* sadismo *m.*
safe, 1. *n.* cassafòrte *m.* **2.** *adj.* sicuro, salvo; **(s. and sound)** sano e salvo.
safeguard, 1. *n.* salvaguàrdia *f.* **2.** *vb.* salvaguardare.
safety, *n.* sicurezza *f.*
safety island, *n.* isolòtto salvagente *m.*
safety-pin, *n.* spilla di sicurezza *f.*
sage, *n. and adj.* sàggio *(m.).*
sail, 1. *n.* vela *f.* **2.** *vb.* navigare; (depart) salpare.
sailboat, *n.* battèllo a vela *m.*
sailor, *n.* marinaio *m.*
saint, *n.* santo *m.*

sake, *n.* motivo *m.*
salad, *n.* insalata *f.*
salary, *n.* stipèndio *m.*
sale, *n.* véndita *f.,* spàccio *m.*
salesman, *n.* commesso *m.;* **(traveling s.)** commesso viaggiatore *m.*
sales tax, *n.* tassa di scambio *f.*
saliva, *n.* saliva *f.*
salmon, *n.* salmone *m.*
salon, *n.* salone *m.*
salt, 1. *n.* sale *m.* **2.** *vb.* salare.
salty, *adj.* salato.
salutation, *n.* saluto *m.*
salute, 1. *n.* saluto *m.* **2.** *vb.* salutare.
salvage, 1. *n.* salvatàggio *m.* **2.** *vb.* salvare.
salvation, *n.* salvezza *f.*
salve, *n.* unguento *m.*
same, *adj.* stesso.
sample, *n.* campione *m.;* **(s. fair)** fièra campionària *f.*
sanatorium, *n.* sanatòrio *m.*
sanctify, *vb.* santificare.
sanction, 1. *n.* sanzione *f.* **2.** *vb.* sanzionare.
sanctity, *n.* santità *f.*
sanctuary, *n.* santuàrio *m.*
sand, *n.* rena *f.,* sàbbia *f.*
sandal, *n.* sàndalo *m.*
sandwich, *n.* tramezzino *m.*
sandy, *adj.* renoso, sabbioso.
sane, *adj.* sano.
sanguinary, *adj.* sanguinàrio.
sanitary, *adj.* igiènico, sanitàrio; **(s. napkin)** assorbente igiènico *m.*
sanitation, *n.* igiène *f.*
sanity, *n.* sanità *f.*

Santa Claus, n. Befana f. (old woman who brings presents on Twelfth Night).

sap, 1. n. linfa f.; (fool) citrullo m. 2. vb. (weaken) indebolire.

sapling, n. alberello m.

sapling, n. alberello m.

sapphire, n. zaffiro m.

sarcasm, n. sarcasmo m.

sarcastic, adj. sarcàstico.

sardine, n. sardèlla f.

Sardinia, n. Sardegna f.

Sardinian, adj. sardo.

sash, n. cintura f.

sassy, adj. impertinente, vivace.

sassy, adj. impertinente, vivace.

satellite, n. satèllite m.

satin, n. raso m.

satire, n. sàtira f.

satirize, vb. satireggiare.

satisfaction, n. soddisfazione f.

satisfactory, adj. soddisfacènte f.

satisfy, vb. soddisfare.

saturate, vb. saturare.

saturation, n. saturazione f.

Saturday, n. sàbato m.

sauce, n. salsa f.

saucepan, n. casseruola f.

saucer, n. piattino m.

saucy, adj. impertinènte.

sausage, n. salsíccia f.

savage, n. and adj. selvàggio (m.).

save, 1. vb. (preserve) salvare; (economize) risparmiare. 2. prep. salvo.

savings, adj. salvatore; (s. account) conto di risparmio m.

savings, n. risparmio m.; (s.-bank) cassa di risparmio f.

savior, n. salvatore m.

savor, 1. n. sapore m. 2. vb. sapere.

savory, adj. saporito.

saw, 1. n. sega f.; (proverb) provèrbio m. 2. vb. segare.

sawmill, n. segheria f.

saxophone, n. sassòfono m.

say, vb. dire; (s. again) ridire.

saying, n. provèrbio m.

scab, n. crosta f.; (nonstriker) crumiro m.

scabby, adj. crostoso; rognoso.

scaffold, n. patíbolo m.

scaffolding, n. impalcatura f.

scald, 1. n. scottatura f. 2. vb. scottare.

scale, 1. n. scala f.; (balance) bilància f.; (fish, etc.) squama f.; (music) gamma f. 2. vb. scrostare; (climb) arrampicarsi su.

scallop, n. (seafood) conchiglia f., pettine m.; (meat) scaloppina f.

scalp, n. pèlle del crànio f.; scalpo m.

scalper, n. bagarino m.

scan, vb. scrutare; (poetry) scandire.

scandal, n. scàndalo m.; (gossip) maldicènza f.

scandalous, adj. scandaloso.

scant, adj. scarso.

scar, 1. n. cicatrice f. 2. vb. cicatrizzare, tr.

scarce, adj. scarso; (be s.) scarseggiare.

scarcely, adv. appena.

scarcity, n. scarsità f.

scare, 1. n. spavento m. 2. vb. spaventare.

scarecrow, n. spauràcchio m.

scarf, n. sciarpa f.

scarlet, n. and adj. scarlatto (m.).

scarlet fever, n. scarlattina f.

scathing, adj. mordace.

scatter, vb. spàrgere.

scavenger, n. spazzino m.

scenario, n. scenàrio m.

scene, n. scèna f.

scenery, n. paesàggio m.

scent, n. odore m., fiuto m., profumo m.; (track) pista f.

schedule, n. oràrio m.

scheme, n. progètto m.

scholar, n. dòtto m., erudito m.

scholarship, n. borsa di stùdio f.; (knowledge) erudizione f.

school, n. scuòla f.

sciatica, n. sciàtica f.

science, n. sciènza f.

science fiction, n. fantascienza f.

scientific, adj. scientífico.

scientist, n. scienziato m.

scissors, n. fòrbici f.pl.

scoff, vb. schernire, farsi beffe.

scold, vb. sgridare.

scolding, n. ramanzina f.

scoop, 1. n. cucchiàio m., ramaiuòlo m. 2. vb. travasare.

scope, n. (extent) portata f.; (outlet) sfògo m.

scorch, vb. bruciare.

score, 1. n. (points) punti m.pl.; (twenty) ventina f.; (music) partitura f. **2.** vb. segnare.
scorn, 1. n. disprèzzo m., disdegno m. **2.** vb. disprezzare, disdegnare.
scornful, adj. sprezzante, sdegnoso.
Scotch. adj. scozzese.
Scotland, n. Scòzia f.
scoundrel, n. birbante m.; farabutto m.
scour, vb. lavare strofinando.
scourge, 1. n. sferza f. **2.** vb. sferzare.
scout, n. esploratore m.
scowl, vb. aggrottare le ciglia.
scramble, 1. n. parapiglia m. **2.** vb. (climb) arrampicarsi.
scrambled eggs, n. uòva strapazzate f.pl.
scrap, 1. n. pezzetto m.; (fight) tafferùglio m. **2.** vb. scartare; (fight) azzuffarsi.
scrapbook, n. albo di ritagli m.
scrape, 1. n. (trouble) impiccio m. **2.** vb. raschiare.
scraper, n. raschietto m.
scrap paper, n. carta straccia f.
scratch, 1. n. graffiatura f. **2.** vb. graffiare.
scream, 1. n. strillo m. **2.** vb. strillare.
screech, 1. n. stridìo m. **2.** vb. stridere.
screen, 1. n. (furniture) paravènto m.; (sieve) crivèllo m.; (movie) schèrmo m. **2.** vb. (protect) proteggere; (sift) crivellare.
screen test, n. provino m.
screw, 1. n. vite f. **2.** vb. avvitare.
screw-driver, n. cacciavite m.
scribble, vb. scribacchiare.
scribe, n. scriba m.
scriptwriter, n. soggettista m. and f.
scripture, n. scrittura f.
scroll, n. ròtolo m.
scrub, vb. strofinare.
scruple, n. scrùpolo m.
scrupulous, adj. scrupoloso.
scrutinize, vb. scrutare.
skull, n. remo a bratto m.; canotto m.
sculptor, n. scultore m.
sculpture, n. scultura f.

scum, n. schiuma f.; (rabble) feccia f.
scythe, n. falce f.
sea, n. mare m.
seabed, n. letto del mare m.
seafood, n. frutti di mare m.pl.
seal, 1. n. sigillo m.; suggèllo m. (animal) fòca f. **2.** vb. sigillare.
sealing-wax, n. ceralacca f.
seam, n. cucitura f.
seaport, n. pòrto di mare m.
search, 1. n. ricerca f. **2.** vb. ricercare.
seasick, adj. (be s.) soffrire di mal di mare.
seasickness, n. mal di mare m.
season, 1. n. stagione f.; (s. ticket) bigliètto d'abbonamento m. **2.** vb. condire.
seasoning, n. condimento m.
seat, 1. n. (chair) sèdia f.; (place) posto m.; (headquarters) sede f.; (s. belt) cintura di sicurezza f. **2.** vb. far sedere.
second, n. and adj. secondo (m.).
secondary, adj. secondàrio.
secret, n. and adj. segreto (m.).
secretary, n. segretàrio m., -ia f.
sect, n. sètta f.
section, n. sezione f.
sectional, adj. sezionale, secante.
secular, adj. secolare.
secure, adj. sicuro.
security, n. sicurezza f.
sedative, n. and adj. sedativo (m.).
seduce, vb. sedurre.
seductive, adj. seducènte.
see, vb. vedere.
seed, n. seme m.
seek, vb. cercare.
seem, vb. parere, sembrare.
seep, vb. trasudare.
seesaw, n. altalena f.
segment, n. segmento m.
segregate, vb. segregare.
seize, vb. afferrare.
seldom, adv. di rado, raramente.
select, 1. adj. scelto. **2.** vb. scégliere.
selection, n. scelta f., selezione f.
selective, adj. selettivo.
self, pron. stesso; **self-,** di sè stesso.
selfish, adj. egoístico.

selfishness, n. egoismo m.
sell, vb. véndere.
semantic, adj. semàntico.
semantics, n. semàntica f.
semester, n. semèstre m.
semicircle, n. semicérchio m.
semicolon, n. punto e vìrgola, m.
seminary, n. seminàrio m.
senate, n. senato m.
senator, n. senatore m.
send, vb. mandare, spedire, inviare.
senile, adj. senile.
senior, adj. maggiore; (father) padre.
senior citizen, n. persona anziana f.
sensation, n. sensazione f.
sensational, adj. sensazionale.
sense, 1. n. sènso m.; (intelligence) senno m. 2. vb. intuire.
sensible, adj. assennato.
sensitive, adj. sensitivo, sensibile.
sensual, adj. sensuale.
sentence, 1. n. frase f., proposizione f.; (court) condanna f. 2. vb. condannare.
sentiment, n. sentimento m.
sentimental, adj. sentimentale.
separate, 1. adj. separato. 2. vb. separare.
separation, n. separazione f.
September, n. settèmbre m.
septic, adj. infettato, sèttico.
sequence, n. sèrie f.
sequester, vb. isoalre; sequestrare.
serenade, n. serenata f.
serene, adj. sereno.
sergeant, n. sergènte m.
serial, adj. in sèrie, periòdico.
series, n. sèrie f.
serious, adj. sèrio.
seriousness, n. serietà f.
sermon, n. sermone m.
serpent, n. serpènte m.
serum, n. sièro m.
servant, n. domèstico m., sèrvo m.; (s.s, collectively) servitù f.
serve, vb. servire.
service, n. servízio m.
service station, n. stazione di servizio m., benzinàio m.
servile, adj. servile.
servitude, n. servitù f.

sesame, n. sèsamo m.
session, n. sessione f.
set, 1. n. sèrie f.; (clique) cricca f. 2. adj. fisso. 3. vb. (put) méttere; (regulate) regolare; (fix) fissare; (mount) montare.
setback, n. rovèscio m.
setting, n. ambiente m.; (theater) scenario m.; (sun) tramonto m.
settle, vb. (establish) stabilire, tr.; (fix) fissare; (decide) decidere; (arrange) sistemare; (pay) saldare; (s. down to) méttersi a.
settlement, n. (colony) colònia f.; (hamlet) borgo m.; (accounts) regolamento m.; (affairs) sistemazione f.
setup, n. organizzazione f.
settler, n. colòno m.
seven, num. sètte.
seventeen, num. diciassètte.
seventeenth, adj. diciassettésimo.
seventh, adj. sèttimo.
seventieth, adj. settantésimo.
seventy, num. settanta.
sever, vb. staccare, tr.
several, adj. parecchi.
severance, n. interruzione f.; (s. pay) liquidazione f., buonuscita f., indennità di fine contratto f.
severe, adj. sevèro.
severity, n. severità f.
sew, vb. cucire.
sewer, n. fogna f.
sex, n. sèsso m.
sexism, n. sessismo m.
sexist, n. and adj. sessista.
sexton, n. sagrestano m.
sexual, adj. sessuale.
shabby, adj. (worn-out) lògoro; (mean) gretto, meschino.
shack, n. capanna f.
shade, 1. n. ombra f.; (color) tinta f.; (against light) paralume m. 2. vb. ombreggiare; (darken) oscurare.
shadow, n. ombra f.
shady, adj. ombroso.
shaft, n. (mine) pozzo m.; (transmission) àlbero m.; (wagon) stanga f.; (ray) ràggio m.; (arrow) strale m.
shaggy, adj. íspido.
shake, 1. n. scòssa f.; (hand-s.)

stretta di mano f. 2. vb. scuòtere, tr.; (quiver) tremare; (s. hands with) stringere la mano a.

shall, vb. dovere; or use future tense of verb.

shallow, adj. pòco profondo.

shame, 1. n. vergogna f.; (pity) peccato m.; (what a s.) che peccato! 2. vb. gettar vergogna su.

shameful, adj. vergognoso.

shampoo, n. sciampò m.

shape, 1. n. forma f., fòggia f. 2. vb. formare, foggiare.

share, 1. n. parte f.; (stock) azione f. 2. vb. condivídere.

shark, n. pescecane m.

sharp, 1. n. (music) dièsis m. 2. adj. acuto.

sharpen, vb. aguzzare.

sharply, adv. acutamente; (harshly) aspramente.

sharpness, n. acutezza f.

shatter, vb. frantumare.

shave, vb. ràdere, tr., fare la barba a, tr.

shaving cream, n. crema da barba f.

shawl, n. scialle m.

she, pron. ella f., essa f., lèi f.

sheaf, n. fàscio m., covone m.

shear, vb. tosare.

shears, n. cesòie f.pl.

sheath, n. fòdero m., guaína f.

shed, 1. n. tettòia f. 2. vb. versare; (lose) lasciar cadere.

sheep, n. pècora f.

sheet, n. (bed) lenzuòlo m.; (paper) fòglio m.; (metal) lastra f.

shelf, n. scaffale m.

shell, 1. n. (egg) gùscio m.; (pod) baccèllo m.; (conch) conchíglia f.; (explosive) bomba f. 2. vb. bombardare.

shellac, n. gomma lacca f.

shellfish, n. frutto di mare m.

shelter, 1. n. ricòvero m. 2. vb. ricoverare, tr.

shelve, vb. mèttere sullo scaffale; (politics) archiviare, insabbiare.

shepherd, n. pastore m.

sherbet, n. sorbetto m.

sherry, n. vino di Xeres m.

shield, 1. n. scudo m. 2. vb. protèggere.

shift, 1. n. (change) cambiamento m.; (turn) turno m. 2. vb. cambiare.

shin, n. stinco m.

shine, vb. brillare, splèndere; (shoes) lucidare.

shingles, n. erpes f.

shining, adj. brillante, luminoso.

shiny, adj. lùcido.

ship, 1. n. nave f. 2. vb. spedire.

shipment, n. spedizione f.

shipper, n. speditore m.

shipping agent, n. spedizionière m.

shipside, n. molo m.

shipwreck, n. naufràgio m.

shipyard, n. cantiere navale m.

shirk, vb. sottrarsi a.

shirt, n. camícia f.

shiver, 1. n. brívido m. 2. vb. rabbrividire.

shoal, n. secca f., banco sabbioso m.

shock, 1. n. scòssa f., urto m. 2. vb. urtare.

shocking, adj. scioccante, disgustoso.

shock therapy, n. terapìa d'urto m.

shoddy, adj. scadente.

shoe, 1. n. scarpa f. 2. vb. calzare; (horse) ferrare.

shoelace, n. làccio per scarpe m.

shoemaker, n. calzolaio m.

shoot, 1. n. (sprout) germóglio m. 2. vb. (gun) sparare; (a person) fucilare, (s. down) abbàttere.

shop, 1. n. bottega f., negòzio m., spàccio m. 2. vb. far còmpere.

shopping, n. còmpere f.pl., spese f.pl.

shore, n. spiàggia f., sponda f.

short, adj. bréve, corto; (s. circuit) corto circùito m.; (run s.) scarseggiare.

shortage, n. mancanza f.

shorten, vb. abbreviare, tr.

shorthand, n. stenografìa f.

shortly, adv. fra pòco.

shorts, n. calzoncini corti m.pl.

shot, n. colpo m., sparo m.; (bullets) pallini m.pl.; (distance) portata f.

should, vb. use conditional of dovere.

shoulder, n. spalla f.

shout, 1. *n.* grido *m.* 2. *vb.* gridare.

shove, 1. *n.* spinta *f.* 2. *vb.* spíngere.

shovel, *n.* pala *f.*

show, 1. *n.* mostra *f.,* esposizione *f.;* (theater) spettácolo *m.* 2. *vb.* mostrare.

shower, *n.* (rain) acquazzone *m.;* (bath) dóccia *f.*

shrapnel, *n.* shràpnel *m.*

shrewd, *adj.* acuto, furbo.

shriek, 1. *n.* strillo *m.* 2. *vb.* strillare.

shrill, *adj.* strídulo.

shrimp, *n.* gamberetto *m.;* (small person) nano *m.*

shrine, *n.* santuário *m.*

shrink, *vb.* contrarsi; **(s. from)** rifuggire da.

shroud, *n.* sudário *m.*

shrub, *n.* arbusto *m.*

shudder, 1. *n.* brívido *m.* 2. *vb.* rabbrividire.

shun, *vb.* schivare.

shut, *vb.* chiùdere.

shutter, *n.* persiane *f.pl.;* scuri *m.pl.* (camera) otturatore *m.*

shy, *adj.* tímido.

Sicilian, *adj.* siciliano.

Sicily, *n.* Sicília *f.*

sick, *adj.* ammalato, malato.

sickness, *n.* malattía *f.*

side, *n.* lato *m.,* fianco *m.*

side-car, *n.* carrozzino *m.*

side-dish, *n.* contorno *m.*

sidewalk, *n.* marciapiède *m.*

siege, *n.* assèdio *m.*

sieve, *n.* crivèllo *m.,* setàccio *m.,* vàglio *m.*

sift, *vb.* setacciare; crivellare.

sigh, 1. *n.* sospiro *m.* 2. *vb.* sospirare.

sight, *n.* vista *f.*

sightseeing, *n.* turismo *m.*

sign, 1. *n.* segno *m.* 2. *vb.* firmare, sottoscrivere.

signal, 1. *n.* segnale *m.;* **(directional s.)** fréccia *f.* 2. *vb.* segnalare.

signature, *n.* firma *f.*

significance, *n.* significato *m.*

significant, *adj.* significativo.

signify, *vb.* significare.

silence, 1. *n.* silènzio *m.* 2. *vb.* azzittire, far tacere.

silencer, *n.* silenziatore *m.*

silent, *adj.* silenzioso, zitto.

silk, *n.* seta *f.*

silken, silky, *adj.* di seta, setàceo.

silkworm, *n.* baco da seta *m.*

sill, *n.* davanzale *m.*

silly, *adj.* sciòcco.

silo, *n.* silo *m.*

silt, *n.* sedimento *m.*

silver, 1. *n.* argènto *m.* 2. *adj.* argènteo.

silver lining, *n.* spiraglio di speranza *m.*

silverware, *n.* posatería d'argento *m.*

silvery, *adj.* d'argento; argenteo.

similar, *adj.* símile.

similarity, *n.* somiglianza *f.*

similarly, *adv.* similmente.

simmer, *vb.* cuòcere a fuoco lento.

simple, *adj.* sémplice.

simple-minded, *adj.* sciocco.

simplicity, *n.* semplicità *f.*

simplify, *vb.* semplificare.

simply, *adv.* semplicemente.

simulate, *vb.* simulare.

simultaneous, *adj.* simultàneo.

sin, 1. *n.* peccato *m.* 2. *vb.* peccare.

since, 1. *prep.* sino da. 2. *conj.* da quando; (because) giacchè, poichè.

sincere, *adj.* sincèro.

sincerely, *adv.* sinceramente.

sincerity, *n.* sincerità *f.*

sinew, *n.* nèrbo *m.*

sinful, *adj.* peccaminoso.

sing, *vb.* cantare.

singe, *vb.* strinare.

singer, *n.* cantatore *m.,* cantatrice *f.*

single, *adj.* solo, ùnico; (unmarried) cèlibe.

single file, *n.* fila indiana *f.*

single-handedly, *adv.* da solo.

single-phase, *adj.* monofase.

singsong, 1. *adj.* monòtono 2. *n.* cantilena *f.*

singular, *adj.* singolare.

sinister, *adj.* sinistro.

sink, 1. *n.* acquàio *m.,* lavandino *m.* 2. *vb.* affondare; (ground) sprofondarsi.

sinner, *n.* peccatore *m.*

sinuous, *adj.* sinuoso.

sinus, *n.* seno frontale *m.*

sinusitis, n. sinusite f.
sip, 1. n. sorso m. **2.** vb. sorseggiare.
siphon, n. sifone m.
sir, n. signore m.
siren, n. sirèna f.
sirloin, n. lombo m.
sister, n. sorèlla f.
sister-in-law, n. cognata f.
sit, vb. sedere.
site, n. sito m.
sitting, n. seduta f.
situate, vb. situare.
situation, n. situazione f.
six, num. sèi.
sixteen, num. sédici.
sixteenth, adj. sedicésimo, decimosèsto.
sixth, adj. sèsto.
sixtieth, adj. sessantésimo.
sixty, num. sessanta.
size, n. grandezza f.; (apparel) misura f.
sizing, n. incollatura f.
skate, n. **1.** pàttino m. **2.** vb. pattinare.
skateboard, n. asse a rotelle m.
skein, n. matassa f.
skeleton, n. schèletro m.
skeptic, n. scèttico m.
skeptical, adj. scèttico.
sketch, 1. n. abbozzo m., schizzo m. **2.** vb. abbozzare, schizzare.
ski, 1. n. sci m. **2.** vb. sciare.
skid, 1. n. slittamento m. **2.** vb. slittare.
ski-lift, n. seggiovìa f.
skill, n. abilità f., destrezza f.
skillful, adj. àbile, dèstro.
skim, vb. (remove cream) scremare; (go over lightly) sfiorare, rasentare.
skin, 1. n. pèlle f. **2.** vb. pelare; (fruit) sbucciare.
skip, vb. saltare.
skirmish, 1. n. scaramùccia f. **2.** vb. scontrarsi.
skirt, 1. n. gònna f., sottana f. **2.** vb. rasentare.
skull, n. crànio m.
skunk, n. moffetta f., pùzzola f.; (person) puzzone m.
sky, n. cièlo m.
skylight, n. lucernàrio m.
skyscraper, n. grattacièlo m.

slab, n. lastra f.
slack, adj. lento.
slacken, vb. rallentare.
slacks, n. calzoni m.pl.
slam, vb. sbàttere.
slander, 1. n. calùnnia f. **2.** vb. calunniare.
slang, n. gèrgo m.
slant, 1. n. pendìo m. **2.** adj. oblìquo. **3.** vb. inclinarsi.
slap, 1. n. schiaffo m. **2.** vb. schiaffeggiare.
slash, 1. n. squàrcio m. **2.** vb. squarciare.
slat, n. stecca f.
slate, n. ardèsia f., lavagna f.
slaughter, 1. n. massacro m., carneficina f., macèllo m. **2.** vb. massacrare, macellare.
slave, n. schiavo m.
slavery, n. schiavitù f.
slave trade, n. tratta degli schiavi f.
Slavic, adj. slavo.
slay, vb. trucidare.
sled, n. slitta f.
sledge hammer, n. mazza f.
sleek, adj. lìscio.
sleep, 1. n. sonno m. **2.** vb. dormire.
sleeping bag, n. sacco a pelo m.
sleeping car, n. vagone lètti m.
sleeping pill, n. sonnìfero m.
sleepless, adj. insonne.
sleepwalker, n. sonnàmbulo m.
sleepy, adj. sonnolento.
sleet, n. nevìschio m.
sleeve, n. mànica f.
sleigh, n. slitta f.
slender, adj. svelto.
sleuth, n. segùgio m.
slice, 1. n. fetta f. **2.** vb. affettare.
slide, vb. scivolare, sdrucciolare.
slide rule, n. régolo calcolatore m.
sliding door, n. porta scorrèvole f.
sliding scale, n. scala mòbile f.
slight, 1. n. disprèzzo m. **2.** adj. esìguo, insufficiènte; (thin) èsile.
slim, adj. sottile.
slime, n. melma f.
slimy, adj. bavoso; melmoso.
sling, 1. n. fionda f. **2.** vb. lanciare, scagliare.
slink, vb. andare furtivamente.

slip, 1. *n.* scivolone *m.;* (mistake) errore *m.;* (paper) striscia *f.;* (underwear) sottovèste *f.* **2.** *vb.* scivolare, sdrucciolare; (make a mistake) sbagliare.

slipper, *n.* pantòfola *f.*

slippery, *adj.* sdrucciolévole.

slit, *n.* fessura *f.*

slogan, *n.* paròla d'òrdine *f.;* (advertising) motto *m.*

slope, *n.* pendènza *f.,* pendìo *m.*

sloppy, *adj.* trasandato.

slot, *n.* fessura *f.*

slot machine, *n.* distributore automàtico *m.*

slouch, *vb.* stare scomposto.

slovenly, *adj.* trascurato.

slow, *adj.* lento; (behind time) indiètro, in ritardo.

slowly, *adv.* lentamente.

slowness, *n.* lentezza *f.*

sluggish, *adj.* lento.

slum, *n.* bassofondo *m.*

slumber, *n.* sonno *m.*

slur, 1. *n.* calùnnia *f.;* (music) legatura *f.* **2.** *vb.* calunniare.

slush, *n.* fanghìglia *f.*

sly, *adj.* furbo.

smack, 1. *n.* (blow) pacca *f.;* (boat) battèllo *m.* **2.** *vb.* (hit) schiaffeggiare; (taste) sapere.

small, *adj.* piccolo.

smallpox, *n.* vaiòlo *m.*

smart, *adj.* elegante, intelligènte.

smash, *vb.* fracassare, frantumare.

smear, *vb.* spalmare.

smell, 1. *n.* odore *m.;* (stench) puzzo *m.;* (sense) fiuto *m.* **2.** *vb.* fiutare; (stink) puzzare.

smelt, 1. *n.* (fish) eperlano *m.* **2.** *vb.* (melt) fóndere.

smile, 1. *n.* sorriso *m.* **2.** *vb.* sorrìdere.

smite, *vb.* colpire.

smock, *n.* (workman's) camiciòtto *m.;* (hospital) càmice *m.*

smoke, 1. *n.* fumo *m.* **2.** *vb.* fumare.

smokestack, *n.* fumaiòlo *m.*

smolder, *vb.* covare.

smooth, 1. *adj.* levigato, lìscio. **2.** *vb.* levigare, lisciare.

smother, *vb.* asfissiare, soffocare.

smug, *adj.* contento di sè stesso.

smuggler, *n.* contrabbandière *m.*

smuggling, *n.* contrabbando *m.*

snack, *n.* spuntino *m.*

snag, *n.* ostàcolo *m.*

snail, *n.* lumaca *f.*

snake, *n.* sèrpe *m.*

snap, *vb.* schioccare; (break) rómpere.

snapshot, *n.* istantànea *f.*

snare, *n.* tràppola *f.*

snarl, 1. *n.* (growl) rìnghio *m.;* (tangle) groviglio *m.* **2.** *vb.* ringhiare, aggrovigliare, *tr.*

snatch, *vb.* afferrare, ghermire.

sneak, *vb.* andare furtivamente.

sneaker, *n.* scarpa di tela *f.*

sneer, 1. *n.* sogghigno *m.* **2.** *vb.* sogghignare.

sneeze, 1. *n.* starnuto *m.* **2.** *vb.* starnutire.

snicker, *n.* risatina *f.*

snob, *n.* snob *m.*

snore, *vb.* russare.

snow, 1. *n.* neve *f.* **2.** *vb.* nevicare.

snowdrift, *n.* ammasso di neve *m.*

snub, *vb.* non salutare.

snug, *adj.* còmodo.

so, *adv.* così; (so far, in time) finora; (so far, in space) fin qui; (so as to) così da.

soak, *vb.* bagnare, inzuppare.

so-and-so, *n.* tal dei tali *m.*

soap, *n.* sapone *m.*

soap opera, *n.* telenovela *f.*

soapy, *adj.* saponoso.

soar, *vb.* volare in alto.

sob, 1. *n.* singhiozzo *m.* **2.** *vb.* singhiozzare.

sober, *adj.* moderato, non ubriaco; (serious) sòbrio.

sobriety, *n.* sobrietà *f.*

so-called, *adj.* cosidetto.

soccer, *n.* calcio *m.*

sociable, *adj.* sociévole.

social, *adj.* sociale; **(s. work)** assistènza sociale *n.f.*

socialism, *n.* socialismo *m.*

socialist, *n.* and *adj.* socialista.

social worker, *n.* assistente sociale *m.* and *f.*

society, *n.* società *f.*

sociology, *n.* sociologìa *f.*

sock, 1. *n.* calzino *m.;* (blow) pugno *m.* **2.** *vb.* (hit) colpire.

socket, n. òrbita f.; (electric) presa f.
sod, n. piòta f., zòlla f.; (with grass) zòlla erbosa f.
soda, n. sòda f.
sodium, n. sòdio m.
sofa, n. sofà m.
soft, adj. molle, mòrbido.
soft-boiled egg, n. uovo alla coque m.
soft drink, n. bíbita non alcoòlica f.
soften, vb. ammollire.
softener, n. ammorbidente m.
soil, 1. n. suòlo m., terreno m. 2. vb. sporcare.
soiled, adj. spòrco.
sojourn, 1. n. soggiorno m. 2. vb. soggiornare.
solace, 1. n. consolazione f. 2. vb. consolare.
solar, adj. solare.
solder, 1. n. saldatura f. 2. vb. saldare.
soldier, n. soldato m.
sole, 1. n. (of foot, shoe) suòla f.; (fish) sògliola f. 2. adj. ùnico.
solemn, adj. solènne.
solemnity, n. solennità f.
solicit, vb. sollecitare.
solicitous, adj. sollécito.
solid, n. and adj. sòlido (m.).
solidify, vb. solidificare, tr.
solidity, n. solidità f.
solitary, adj. solitàrio.
solitude, n. solitùdine f.
solo, n. assolo m.
soloist, n. solista m. or f.
so long, interj. ciao.
soluble, adj. solùbile.
solution, n. soluzione f.
solve, vb. risòlvere.
solvent, n. and adj. solvènte (m.).
somber, adj. fosco, sòbrio.
some, 1. pron. ne. 2. adj. qualche, alcuni; (a little) un po'.
somebody, pron. qualcuno.
somehow, adv. in qualche mòdo.
someone, pron. qualcuno.
somersault, n. capriòla f., salto mortale m.
something, pron. qualcosa, qualche cosa.
sometime, adj. (former) già.
sometimes, adv. qualche vòlta.

somewhat, adv. un po'.
somewhere, adv. in qualche luògo.
son, n. figlio m.
song, n. canto m., canzone f.
son-in-law, n. gènero m.
soon, adv. prèsto, fra pòco.
soot, n. fuliggine f.
soothe, vb. calmare.
soothingly, adv. dolcemente.
sophisticated, adj. sofisticato.
soprano, n. soprano m.
sorcery, n. stregonería f.
sordid, adj. sòrdido.
sore, 1. n. piaga f. 2. adj. dolènte; (angry) adirato.
sorrow, 1. n. dolore m. 2. vb. addolorarsi.
sorrowful, adj. addolorato.
sorry, adj. spiacente.
sort, 1. n. sòrta f. 2. vb. assortire.
soul, n. ànima f.
sound, 1. n. suòno m. 2. adj. sano, giusto. 3. vb. suonare; (take soundings) sondare.
soup, n. minèstra f., zuppa f.
sour, adj. àcido; (unripe) acèrbo.
source, n. fonte f., sorgènte f.
south, n. sud m., mezzogiorno m.
southeast, n. sud-èst m.
southern, adj. meridionale.
South Pole, n. pòlo sud m.
southwest, n. sud-òvest m.
souvenir, n. ricòrdo m.
sovereign, n. and adj. sovrano (m.).
soviet, 1. n. sovièt m. 2. adj. soviètico.
sow, 1. n. scrofa f., tròia f. 2. vb. seminare.
space, n. spàzio m.
space shuttle, n. spola spaziale f.
spacious, adj. spazioso.
spade, n. vanga f.
spaghetti, n. spaghetti m.pl.
Spain, n. Spagna f.
span, 1. n. (measure) spanna f.; (bridge) ponte m. 2. vb. stèndersi su.
Spaniard, n. spagnolo m.
Spanish, adj. spagnolo.
spank, vb. sculacciare.
spanking, n. sculacciata f.
spar, 1. n. àlbero m. 2. vb. (box) fare il pugilato.

spare, 1. *n.* pèzzo di ricàmbio *m.* **2.** *adj.* (extra) di ricàmbio; (thin) magro; (available) disponìbile. **3.** *vb.* aver disponìbile; (save) risparmiare.

spare parts, *n.* pezzi di ricambio *m.pl.*

spare room, *n.* camera per gli òspiti *f.*

spare tire, *n.* ruota di scorta *f.*

spark, *n.* scintilla *f.*

sparkle, *vb.* scintillare.

sparkling, *adj.* scintillante; **(s. water)** acqua gasata *f.* **(s. wine)** vino frizzante *m.*

spark-plug, *n.* candela d'accensione *f.*

sparrow, *n.* pàssero *m.*

sparse, *adj.* rado.

spasm, *n.* spàsimo *m.*

spasmodic, *adj.* spasmòdico.

spatial, *adj.* spaziale.

spatter, 1. *n.* spruzzo *m.* **2.** *vb.* spruzzare.

spatula, *n.* spatola *f.*

spawn, 1. *n.* prole *f.*, progenie *f.* **2.** *vb.* generare.

speak, *vb.* parlare; **(s. ill)** sparlare.

speaker, *n.* oratore *m.*; (presiding officer) presidente *f.*

spear, 1. *n.* lància *f.* **2.** *vb.* trafiggere.

spearhead, 1. *n.* punta di lancia *f.* **2.** *vb.* condurre.

special, *adj.* speciale.

special delivery, *n.* espresso *m.*

specialist, *n.* specialista *m.*

specially, *adv.* specialmente.

specialty, *n.* specialità *f.*

species, *n.* spècie *f.*

specific, *adj.* specìfico.

specify, *vb.* specificare.

specimen, *n.* sàggio *m.*

spectacle, *n.* spettàcolo *m.*; (pl., eyeglasses) occhiali *m.pl.*

spectacular, *adj.* spettacolare.

spectator, *n.* spettatore *m.*

spectrum, *n.* spèttro *m.*

speculate, *vb.* speculare.

speculation, *n.* speculazione *f.*

speech, *n.* discorso *m.*

speechless, *adj.* interdetto.

speed, 1. *n.* velocità *f.* **2.** *vb.* affrettare, *tr.*; **(s. up)** accelerare, *tr.*

speedometer, *n.* tachìmetro *m.*

speedy, *adj.* veloce.

spell, 1. *n.* incantèsimo *m.* **2.** *vb.* scrìvere.

spelling, *n.* ortografìa *f.*

spend, *vb.* (money) spèndere; (time) passare.

spendthrift, *n.* sciupone *m.*

sphere, *n.* sfèra *f.*

spice, *n.* spèzie *f.pl.*

spider, *n.* ragno *m.*; **(s.-web)** ragnatela *f.*

spike, *n.* chiòdo *m.*

spill, *vb.* rovesciare.

spillway, *n.* scàrico *m.*

spin, 1. *n.* (excursion) giretto *m.* **2.** *vb.* filare; (whirl) girare.

spinach, *n.* spinaci *m.pl.*

spine, *n.* spina dorsale *f.*

spinet, *n.* spinetta *f.*

spinster, *n.* zitèlla *f.*

spiral, *n.* and *adj.* spirale *(m.)*

spire, *n.* gùglia *f.*

spirit, *n.* spìrito *m.*

spiritual, *adj.* spirituale.

spiritualism, *n.* spiritismo *m.*

spit, *vb.* sputare.

spite, 1. *n.* dispètto *m.*; **(in s. of)** malgrado. **2.** *vb.* contrariare.

splash, 1. *n.* tonfo *m.*, spruzzo *m.* **2.** *vb.* spruzzare.

splendid, *adj.* splèndido.

splendor, *n.* splendore.

splice, *vb.* congiùngere.

splint, *n.* stecca *f.*

splinter, 1. *n.* schèggia *f.* **2.** *vb.* scheggiare, *tr.*

split, 1. *n.* (crack) fessura *f.*; (division) scissione *f.* **2.** *vb.* (wood) spaccare; (crack) fèndere, *tr.*; (divide) divìdere, *tr.*, scìndere, *tr.*

splurge, *vb.* spèndere molto denaro.

spoil, *vb.* guastare.

spoke, *n.* ràggio *m.*

spokesman, *n.* portavoce *m.*

sponge, *n.* spugna *f.*

sponsor, *n.* mallevadore *m.*; (backer) sostenitore *m.*

spontaneity, *n.* spontaneità *f.*

spontaneous, *adj.* spontàneo.

spool, *n.* bobina *f.*; (film) rocchetto *m.*

spoon, *n.* (large) cucchiaio *m.*; (small) cucchiaino *m.*

spoonful, *n.* cucchiaiata *f.*

sporadic, adj. sporàdico.
spore, n. spòra f.
sport, 1. n. sport m., dipòrto m. 2. adj. sportivo.
sportsman, n. sportivo m.
spot, 1. n. (place) posto m.; (blot) màcchia f.
spouse, n. sposo m., sposa f.
spout, 1. n. becco m. 2. vb. spruzzare.
sprain, 1. n. stòrta f. 2. vb. stòrcere.
sprawl, vb. sdraiarsi.
spray, vb. sprizzare, nebulizzare.
sprayer, n. nebulizzatore m.
spray paint, n. vernice a spruzzo f.
spread, 1. n. distesa f.; (food) banchetto m. 2. adj. disteso, spiegato. 3. vb. stèndere, tr., spiegare, tr.; (diffuse) diffóndere, tr.
spree, n. baldòria f.
sprig, n. ramoscèllo m.
sprightly, adj. brioso.
spring, 1. n. (season) primavera f.; (source) fonte f., sorgènte f.; (leap) salto m.; (metal) mòlla f. 2. vb. sórgere, saltare; (leap up) scattare.
springboard, n. trampolino m.
springtime, n. primavera f.
sprinkle, vb. cospàrgere.
sprinkling, n. spruzzo m.
sprint, 1. n. corsa veloce. 2. vb. córrere velocemente.
sprinter, n. velocista m.
sprout, 1. n. germóglio m. 2. vb. germogliare.
spry, adj. arzillo.
spur, 1. n. sprone m., sperone m. 2. vb. spronare.
spurious, adj. spùrio.
spurn, vb. disdegnare.
spurt, 1. n. scatto m. 2. vb. scattare; (pour out) spruzzare.
spy, 1. n. spione m. 2. vb. spiare; (perceive) scòrgere.
spyglass, n. canocchiale m.
spying, n. spionaggio m.
squabble, n. battibecco m.
squad, n. squadra f.
squadron, n. squadrone f.
squalid, adj. squàllido.
squall, vb. sbraitare.
squalor, n. squallore m.

squander, vb. scialacquare.
square, 1. n. quadrato m.; (open place) piazza f. 2. adj. quadrato. 3. vb. quadrare.
square root, n. radice quadrata f.
squash, 1. n. (drink) spremuta f.; (vegetable) zucca f. 2. vb. spiaccicare.
squashy, adj. tènero; (fruit) maturo.
squat, 1. adj. tarchiato. 2. vb. accosciarsi.
squeak, 1. n. cigolío m. 2. vb. cigolare.
squeamish, adj. schizzinoso.
squeeze, 1. n. stretta f. 2. vb. strìngere; (juice) sprèmere.
squeezer, n. spremiagrumi m.
squirrel, n. scoiàttolo m.
squirt, vb. schizzare, zampillare.
stab, 1. n. pugnalata f. 2. vb. pugnalare.
stability, n. stabilità f.
stabilize, vb. stabilizzare.
stable, 1. n. stalla f. 2. adj. stàbile.
stack, 1. n. mùcchio m. 2. vb. ammucchiare.
stadium, n. stàdio m.
staff, n. (stick) bastone m.; (personnel) personale m.; (music) rigo m.
stag, n. cèrvo m.
stage, n. (theater) palcoscènico m.; (phase) fase f., stàdio m.
stagflation, n. inflazione in un'economía stagnante f.
stagger, vb. barcollare.
stagnant, adj. stagnante.
stagnate, vb. stagnare.
stain, 1. n. màcchia f.; (color) colore m. 2. vb. colorare; macchiare.
staircase, stairs, n. scala f.
stake, 1. n. (post) palo m.; (sum, bet) posta f. 2. vb. rischiare; (bet) puntare.
stale, adj. rafferno.
stalemate, n. punto mòrto m.
stalk, n. gambo m.
stall, 1. n. stallo m.; (vendor's) banco m. 2. vb. (stop) arrestarsi.
stallion, n. stallone m.
stalwart, adj. robusto.
stamen, n. stame m.
stamina, n. vigore m.

stammer, *vb.* balbettare.

stamp, 1. *n.* (adhesive) bollo *m.*; (embossed, impressed) timbro *m.*; **(postage-s.)** francobollo *m.* **2.** *vb.* bollare, timbrare.

stampede, *n.* fuga precipitosa *f.*

stamp pad, *n.* cuscinetto *m.*

stand, 1. *n.* (position) posizione *f.*; (vendor's) padiglione *m.*; (grandstand) tribuna *f.* **2.** *vb.* stare; (put) méttere; (suffer) soffrire, tollerare; **(s. up)** stare in pièdi.

standard, 1. *n.* nòrma *f.* **2.** *adj.* normale.

standardize, *vb.* standardizzare.

standing, 1. *n.* riputazione *f.* **2.** *adj.* permanènte; **(s. up)** in pièdi.

standpoint, *n.* punto di vista *m.*

staple, *n.* (fiber) fibra *f.*; (comm.) prodotto principale *m.*

star, *n.* stella *f.*

starboard, *n.* tribordo *m.*

starch, 1. *n.* àmido *m.* **2.** *vb.* inamidare.

starchy, *adj.* inamidato.

stare, *vb.* guardare fisso.

starfish, *n.* stella marina *f.*

stark, *adv.* completamente.

starlet, *n.* piccola celebrità *f.*

start, 1. *n.* inízio *m.*; (departure) partènza *f.*; (jump) sussulto *m.* **2.** *vb.* cominciare, iniziare; (depart) partire; (jump) sussultare, trasalire.

starter, *n.* (beginner) iniziatore *m.*; (auto) avviamento *m.*

startle, *vb.* allarmare, far trasalire.

startling, *adj.* allarmante, sorprendente.

star system, *n.* divismo *m.*

starvation, *n.* fame *f.*

starve, *vb.* morire di fame.

state, 1. *n.* stato *m.* **2.** *vb.* affermare.

statement, *n.* affermazione *f.*; (bank) rendiconto *m.*; (legal) deposizione *f.*

stateroom, *n.* cabina *f.*

statesman, *n.* uòmo di stato *m.*; statista *m.*

static, *adj.* stàtico.

station, *n.* stazione *f.*, fattoria *f.*

stationary, *adj.* stazionàrio.

stationer, *n.* cartolaio *m.*

stationery, *n.* oggetti di cancelleria *m.pl.*; **(s. store)** cartoleria *f.*

station wagon, *n.* giardinetta *f.*

statistics, *n.* (science) statistica *f.*; (data) statistiche *f.pl.*

statue, *n.* stàtua *f.*

stature, *n.* statura *f.*

status, *n.* condizione *f.*

statute, *n.* statuto *m.*

statutory, *adj.* legale.

staunch, *adj.* fedele.

stay, 1. *n.* (sojourn) permanènza *f.*; (delay) sospensione *f.* **2.** *vb.* restare; (hold back) fermare.

steadfast, *adj.* saldo.

steady, *adj.* fermo, saldo.

steak, *n.* bistecca *f.*

steal, *vb.* rubare; (go furtively) andare di soppiatto.

stealth, *n.* **(by s.)** furtivamente.

stealthily, *adv.* di soppiatto.

stealthy, *adj.* furtivo.

steam, *n.* vapore *m.*

steamboat, *n.* piròscafo *m.*

steamship, *n.* piròscafo *m.*

steel, 1. *n.* acciàio *m.* **2.** *vb.* indurire.

steel wool, *n.* lana di acciàio *f.*, pàglia di acciàio *f.*

steep, *adj.* èrto, rìpido, scosceso.

steeple, *n.* campanile *m.*

steeplechase, *n.* corsa ad ostàcoli *f.*

steer, *vb.* dirìgere.

steering wheel, *n.* volante *m.*, sterzo *m.*; (boat) timone *m.*

stellar, *adj.* stellare.

stem, *n.* stelo *m.*

stencil, *n.* stampino *m.*

stenographer, *n.* stenògrafa *f.*

stenography, *n.* stenografia *f.*

step, 1. *n.* (pace) passo *m.*; (footprint) orma *f.*; (stair) gradino *m.* **2.** *vb.* camminare.

stepfather, *n.* patrigno *m.*

stepladder, *n.* scalèo *m.*

stepmother, *n.* matrigna *f.*

stereotype, *n.* stereotipía *f.*

stereophonic, *adj.* stereofònico.

sterile, *adj.* stèrile.

sterility, *n.* sterilità *f.*

sterilize, *vb.* sterilizzare.

sterling, *adj.* puro; **(pound s.)** sterlina *f.*

stern, 1. *n.* poppa *f.* **2.** *adj.* severo.

stethoscope, n. stetoscòpio m.

stevedore, n. stivatore m.

stew, 1. n. stufato m. 2. vb. stufare.

steward, n. camerière m.

stewardess, n. (boat) camerièra f.; (plane) assistente di volo f.

stick, 1. n. bastone m. 2. vb. (adhere) aderire; (attach) appiccicare, attaccare; (shove) cacciare, ficcare.

sticker, n. etichetta f.

sticky, adj. attaccatíccio, viscoso.

stiff, adj. rígido.

stiffen, vb. irrigidire, tr.

stiffness, n. rigidezza f.

stifle, vb. soffocare.

stigma, n. stigma m.

stigmata, n. stigmate f.pl.

still, 1. n. alambicco m. 2. adj. calmo. 3. vb. calmare. 4. adv. ancora.

still-born, adj. nato mòrto.

still life, n. natura mòrta f.

stillness, n. quiète f., calma f.

stilted, adj. ampolloso.

stimulant, n. and adj. stimolante (m.)

stimulate, vb. stimolare.

stimulus, n. stímolo m.

sting, 1. n. (body-part) pungiglione m.; (wound) puntura f. 2. vb. pùngere.

stingy, adj. avaro, tírchio.

stipulate, vb. stipulare.

stir, 1. n. agitazione f., commozione f. 2. vb. agitare, tr., muòvere, tr.

stirring, adj. commovente.

stitch, 1. n. punto m. 2. vb. cucire.

stock, 1. n. (supply) provvista f.; (lineage) stirpe f.; (animals) bestiame m.; (of gun) càlcio m.; (financial) azioni f. 2. vb. tenere in magazzino.

stockbroker, n. agènte di càmbio m.

stock exchange, n. borsa f.

stockfish, n. stocafisso m.

stockholder, n. azionista m.

Stockholm, n. Stoccolma f.

stocking, n. calza f.

stockpile, 1. n. riserva f.; scorta f. 2. vb. far scorta.

stockroom, n. magazzino m.; depòsito m.

stockyard, n. mattatòio m.

stodgy, adj. ottuso.

stoic, n. stòico m.

stoical, adj. stòico.

stole, n. stòla f.

stolid, adj. stólido.

stomach, 1. n. stòmaco m. 2. vb. tollerare.

stone, 1. n. piètra f., sasso m. 2. vb. lapidare.

stooge, n. (theater) spalla f.; (crime) còmplice m.

stool, n. sgabèllo m.

stoop, vb. curvarsi; (demean oneself) abbassarsi.

stooped, adj. curvo.

stop, 1. n. fermata f. 2. vb. fermare, tr.; (close) otturare, tappare; (cease) smèttere; (cease moving) sostare.

stopgap, n. temporáneo m.

stop-over, n. fermata intermèdia f.

stopper, n. tappo m.

stopping, n. sosta f.

storage, n. magazzinàggio m.

store, 1. n. negòzio m.; (supply) provvista f. 2. vb. immagazzinare, conservare; (fill) riempire.

storehouse, n. magazzino m.

stork, n. cicogna f.

storm, n. tempèsta f.

storm troops, n. truppe d'assalto f.pl.

stormy, adj. tempestoso.

story, n. racconto m., stòria f.

storyteller, n. narratore m.

stout, adj. grasso; (strong) fòrte.

stove, n. fornèllo m., stufa f.

strafe, 1. n. attacco violento m. 2. vb. attaccare violentemente, bombardare pesantemente.

straight, 1. adj. diritto, rètto. 2. adv. direttamente, diritto.

straight-away, n. rettilíneo m.

straighten, vb. raddrizzare.

straightforward, adj. franco.

strain, 1. n. tensione f. 2. vb. sforzare, tr.; (filter) colare.

strainer, n. colino m.

strait, n. stretto m.

strand, 1. n. riva f. 2. vb. arenarsi.

strange, adj. strano; (foreign) stranièro.

stranger, n. stranièro m.

strangle, vb. strangolare.

strap, n. cínghia f.

stratagem, n. stratagèmma m.

strategic, adj. stratègico.

strategy, n. strategìa f.

stratosphere, n. stratosfèra f.

stratum, n. strato m.

straw, n. pàglia f.; (for drinking) cannùccia di pàglia f.

strawberry, n. frágola f.

stray, 1. adj. smarrito. 2. vb. allontanarsi.

streak, n. ramo m., vena f., venatura f.

stream, n. corrènte f., fiòtto m.

streamlined, adj. aerodinàmico.

street, n. vía f., strada f.

streetcar, n. tram m.

strength, n. fòrza f.

strengthen, vb. rafforzare.

strenuous, adj. strènuo.

streptococcus, n. streptocòcco m.

stress, 1. n. sfòrzo m., tensione f.; (accent) accènto m. 2. vb. accentare.

stretch, 1. n. tratto m. 2. vb. tèndere.

stretcher, n. barèlla f.

strew, vb. cospàrgere.

stricken, adj. colpito.

strict, adj. sevèro.

stride, 1. n. passo lungo m. 2. vb. camminare a passi lunghi.

strident, adj. strídulo.

strife, n. conflitto m.

strike, 1. n. (workers') sciòpero m. 2. vb. scioperare; (hit) colpire.

strike-breaker, n. crumiro m.

string, 1. n. filo m., còrda f. 2. vb. infilare.

string bean, n. fagiòlo m.

stringent, adj. rigoroso.

strip, 1. n. striscia f. 2. vb. spogliare, tr.

stripe, n. lista f., striscia f.

strive, vb. sforzarsi.

stroke, 1. n. colpo m. 2. vb. accarezzare.

stroll, 1. n. passeggiata f. 2. vb. passeggiare.

stroller, n. passeggiatore m.

strong, adj. fòrte.

strongbox, n. cassaforte f.

strong drink, n. bevanda alcòlica f.

stronghold, n. roccafòrte f.

structure, n. struttura f.

struggle, 1. n. lotta f. 2. vb. lottare.

strut, vb. pavoneggiarsi.

stub, n. mozzicone m.; (checkbook) madre f.

stubborn, adj. testardo.

stucco, n. stucco m.

stuck, adj. infisso, attaccato.

student, n. studènte m., studentessa f.

student body, n. scolaresca f.

studio, n. stùdio m.

studious, adj. studioso.

study, 1. n. stùdio m. 2. vb. studiare.

stuff, 1. n. (cloth) stoffa f.; (junk) ròba f. 2. vb. rimpinzare, imbottire; (food) infarcire.

stuffed, adj. ripièno.

stuffing, n. ripièno m.

stuffy, adj. opprimente; (nose) chiuso.

stumble, vb. inciampare.

stump, n. (tree) ceppo m.; (arm, leg) moncone m.

stun, vb. stordire.

stunning, adj. stordente, sbalorditivo.

stunt, n. impresa fuòri del consuèto f.

stunt man, n. controfigura f., stuntman, m.

stupendous, adj. stupèndo.

stupid, adj. stùpido.

stupidity, n. stupidità f.

stupor, n. stupore m.

sturdy, adj. gagliardo.

stutter, vb. tartagliare.

Stuttgart, n. Stoccarda f.

sty, n. porcile m.; (eye) orzaiòlo m.

style, n. stile m.

stylish, adj. di mòda.

suave, adj. blando.

subconscious, adj. subcosciènte.

subdivide, vb. suddividere.

subdue, vb. soggiogare.

subdued, adj. soggiogato; (light) tènue; (voice) sommesso.

subject, 1. n. soggètto m.; (of king) suddito m. 2. adj. soggètto. 3. vb. sottoporre, assoggettare.

subjugate, vb. soggiogare.
subjunctive, n. and adj. congiuntivo (m.)
sublimate, 1. n. and adj. sublimato (m.) **2.** vb. sublimare.
sublime, adj. sublime.
submarine, 1. n. sommergìbile m. **2.** adj. sottomarino.
submerge, vb. sommèrgere.
submersion, n. sommersione f.
submission, n. sottomissione f.
submit, vb. sottomèttere, tr.
subnormal, adj. subnormale.
subordinate, n. and adj. subordinato (m.)
subscribe, vb. (write name) sottoscrìvere; (take regularly) abbonarsi; (agree with) aderire.
subscription, n. abbonamento m.
subsequent, adj. successivo.
subservient, adj. servile.
subside, vb. diminuire; (building) sprofondarsi; (earth) cèdere; (water) abbassarsi.
subsidy, n. sussidio m.
substance, n. sostanza f.
substantial, adj. sostanziale.
substitute, 1. n. sostituto m. **2.** vb. sostituire.
substitution, n. sostituzione f.
subterfuge, n. sotterfùgio m.
subtle, adj. sottile.
subtract, vb. sottrarre.
suburb, n. sobborgo m.
subvention, n. sovvenzione f.
subversive, adj. sovversivo.
subvert, vb. sovvertire.
subway, n. metropolitana f.
succeed, vb. (come after) succèdere a; (be successful) riuscire.
success, n. successo m., riuscita f.
successful, adj. riuscito.
succession, n. successione f., sèrie f.
successive, adj. successivo.
successor, n. successore m.
succor, 1. n. soccorso m. **2.** vb. soccórrere.
succumb, vb. soccómbere.
such, adj. tale.
suck, vb. succhiare.
suction, n. aspirazione f.
sudden, adj. improvviso.
suds, n. schiuma f.
sue, vb. citare in giudízio.

suffer, vb. soffrire.
suffice, vb. bastare.
sufficient, adj. sufficiènte.
suffocate, vb. soffocare.
sugar, n. zùcchero m.
suggest, vb. suggerire.
suggestion, n. suggerimento m.
suicide, n. suicídio m.; (commit s.) suicidarsi.
suit, 1. n. (clothes) àbito m.; (cards) colore m.; (request) domanda f.; (law) càusa f. **2.** vb. convenire a, andar bène a.
suitable, adj. conveniènte.
suitcase, n. valìgia f.
suite, n. sèrie f.; (followers) sèguito m.; (music) suite f.
suitcase, n. valìgia f.
suitor, n. corteggiatore m.; (law) querelante m.
sulky, adj. imbronciato.
sullen, adj. cupo.
sultana raisin, n. uva sultanina f.
sultry, adj. soffocante, afoso.
sum, 1. n. somma f. **2.** vb. sommare; (s. up) riassùmere.
summarize, vb. riassùmere.
summary, n. and adj. sommàrio (m.)
summer, 1. n. estate f. **2.** adj. estivo.
summit, n. sommità f., cima f.
summon, vb. chiamare, citare.
summons, n. chiamata f.; (court) citazione f.
sumptuous, adj. sontuoso.
sun, n. sole m.
sunbathe, vb. prendere la tintarella.
sunburn, n. abbronzatura f.
sunburned, adj. abbronzato.
Sunday, n. doménica f.
Sunday school, n. sciola di catechismo f.
sunflower, n. girasole m.
sunglasses, n. occhiale da sole m.pl.
sunken, adj. infossato.
sunny, adj. assolato.
sunset, n. tramonto m.
sunshine, n. sole m.
sunstroke, n. insolazione f.
suntan cream, n. crema solare f.
superb, adj. supèrbo.

superficial, adj. superficiale.
superfluous, adj. superfluo.
super-highway, n. autostrada f.
superhuman, adj. sovrumano.
superintendent, n. sovrintendènte m.
superior, adj. superiore.
superiority, n. superiorità f.
superlative, n. and adj. superlativo (m.)
superman, n. superuòmo m.
supernatural, adj. sopranaturale.
supersede, vb. soppiantare.
superstar, n. superstar m.
superstition, n. superstizione f.
superstitious, adj. superstizioso.
supervise, vb. sorvegliare.
supper, n. cena f.
supplant, vb. soppiantare.
supplement, n. supplemento m.
supply, 1. n. fornitura f., provvista f. 2. vb. fornire, provvedere.
support, 1. n. sostegno m. 2. vb. appoggiare, sostenere.
suppose, vb. supporre.
suppress, vb. supprimere.
suppression, n. soppressione f.
supreme, adj. suprèmo.
sure, adj. sicuro.
surely, adv. sicuramente.
surety, n. sicurezza f.
surf, n. frangènti m.pl.
surface, n. superficie f.
surge, vb. ondare.
surgeon, n. chirurgo m.
surgery, n. chirurgía f.
surmise, 1. n. congettura f. 2. vb. congetturare.
surmount, vb. sormontare.
surname, n. cognome m.
surpass, vb. sorpassare.
surplus, n. avanzo m.
surprise, 1. n. sorpresa f. 2. vb. sorprèndere.
surrender, vb. (hand over) cédere; (yield) arrèndersi.
surround, vb. circondare.
surroundings, n. dintorni m.pl.
surveillance, n. sorveglianza f.
survey, 1. n. esame m.; (geographical) rilevamento m. 2. vb. esaminare.
surveyor, n. agrimensore m.
survival, n. sopravvivènza f.

survive, vb. sopravvivere.
susceptible, adj. suscettibile.
suspect, 1. adj. sospètto. 2. vb. sospettare.
suspend, vb. sospèndere.
suspense, n. incertezza f.
suspension, n. sospensione f.
suspension bridge, n. ponte sospeso m.
suspicion, n. sospètto m.
suspicious, adj. sospettoso; (questionable) sospètto.
sustain, vb. sostenere.
swallow, 1. n. (bird) róndine f.; (food) beccone m.; (drink) sorso m. 2. vb. inghiottire.
swamp, 1. n. palude f. 2. vb. inondare.
swan, n. cigno m.
swap, 1. n. baratto m. 2. vb. barattare.
swarm, 1. n. sciame m. 2. vb. sciamare; (be crowded) formicolare.
sway, vb. oscillare; (influence) dominare.
swear, vb. giurare; (curse) bestemmiare; (s.-word) bestémmia f.
sweat, 1. n. sudore m. 2. vb. sudare.
sweater, n. golf m.
Swede, n. svedese m.
Sweden, n. Svèzia f.
Swedish, adj. svedese.
sweep, vb. spazzare.
sweeper, n. spazzino m.
sweeping, adj. travolgente, completo.
sweepstakes, n. lotteria f.
sweet, adj. dolce.
sweeten, vb. addolcire; zuccherare.
sweetheart, n. innamorato m., innamorata f.
sweetness, n. dolcezza f.
sweet tooth, n. dèbole per i dolciumi m.
swell, 1. adj. magnifico. 2. vb. gonfiare, tr.
swelter, vb. sudare.
swift, adj. veloce.
swim, vb. nuotare.
swimming, n. nuoto m.
swimsuit, n. costume da bagno m.
swindle, vb. truffare.

swindler, *n.* truffatore *m.*
swine, *n.* pòrco *m.*
swing, 1. *n.* (children's) altalena *f.*
2. *vb.* dondolare, penzolare.
swirl, *vb.* turbinare.
swirling, *adj.* vorticoso.
Swiss, *adj.* svizzero.
switch, 1. *n.* (rod) verga *f.;* (railway) scàmbio *m.;* (electric) interruttore *m.* 2. *vb.* (whip) sferzare;
(s. on) accèndere; **(s. off)** spègnere.
switchboard, *n.* centralino *m.*
Switzerland, *vb.* Svízzera *f.*
swivel, *n.* perno *m.*
sword, *n.* spada *f.*
sword-fish, *n.* pesce spada *m.*
syllable, *n.* sillaba *f.*
symbol, *n.* símbolo *m.*
symbolic, *adj.* simbòlico.
sympathetic, *adj.* sensíbile.

sympathize, *vb.* simpatizzare.
sympathy, *n.* simpatía *f.*
symphonic, *adj.* sinfònico.
symphony, *n.* sinfonía *f.;* **(s. orchestra)** orchèstra sinfònica *f.*
symptom, *n.* síntomo *m.*
symptomatic, *adj.* sintomàtico.
synchronous, *adj.* síncrono.
synchronize, *vb.* sincronizzare.
syndicate, *n.* consòrzio *m.*
syndrome, *n.* síndrome *f.*
synonym, *n.* sinònimo *m.*
synonymous, *adj.* sinònimo.
synthesis, *n.* síntesi *f.*
synthetic, *adj.* sintètico.
syphilis, *n.* sifílide *f.*
syphilitic, *adj.* sifilítico.
syringe, *n.* siringa *f.*
syrup, *n.* sciròppo *m.*
system, *n.* sistèma *m.*
systematic, *adj.* sistemàtico.

T

tabernacle, *n.* tabernàcolo *m.*
table, *n.* tàvola *f.*
tablecloth, *n.* tovàglia *f.*
tablespoon, *n.* cucchiaio *m.*
tablespoonful, *n.* cucchiaiata *f.*
tablet, *n.* tavoletta *f.;* (pastille) pastiglia *f.,* pastícca *f.*
tack, 1. *n.* bulletta *f.* 2. *vb.* attaccare; (turn) virare.
tact, *n.* tatto *m.*
tag, *n.* etichetta *f.*
tail, *n.* coda *f.*
tailor, *n.* sarto *m.*
take, *vb.* préndere; (carry) portare; (lead) condurre.
tale, *n.* racconto *m.*
talent, *n.* talènto *m.*
talk, 1. *n.* discorso *m.* 2. *vb.* parlare.
talkative, *adj.* loquace.
tall, *adj.* alto.
tallow, *n.* sego *m.*
tame, 1. *adj.* addomesticato, mansuèto. 2. *vb.* addomesticare, domare.
tamper, *vb.* immischiarsi.
tan, 1. *n.* (sun) abbronzatura *f.* 2. *adj.* castagno. 3. *vb.* abbronzare; (leather) conciare.
tangible, *adj.* tangíbile.

tangle, 1. *n.* garbùglio *m.* 2. *vb.* ingarbugliare.
tank, *n.* serbatòio *m.;* (armored vehicle) carro armato *m.*
tap, 1. *n.* (blow) colpetto *m.;* (faucet) rubinetto *m.* 2. *vb.* percuòtere.
tape, *n.* nastro *m.*
tape recorder, *n.* magnetòfono *m.,* registratore magnètico *m.*
tapestry, *n.* tappezzería *f.*
tar, 1. *n.* catrame *m.* 2. *vb.* incatramare.
target, *n.* bersàglio *m.*
tariff, *n.* tariffa *f.*
tarnish, 1. *n.* appannatura *f.* 2. *vb.* appannare, *tr.*
tart, 1. *n.* tòrta *f.;* (harlot) puttana *f.* 2. *adj.* acre.
task, *n.* cómpito *m.,* incàrico *m.*
taste, 1. *n.* gusto *m.* 2. *vb.* gustare.
tasty, *adj.* gustoso, saporito.
taunt, *vb.* schernire.
taut, *adj.* teso.
tavern, *n.* osteria *f.,* tavèrna *f.*
tax, *n.* imposta *f.,* tassa *f.*
taxi, *n.* taxi *m.,* tassì *m.;* **(t. driver)** tassista *m.*
taxpayer, *n.* contribuènte *m.*
tax rate, *n.* aliquota *f.*
tea, *n.* thè (tè) *m.*

teach, vb. insegnare.

teacher, n. insegnante m. or f., maestro m., maestra f.

teaching aids, n. sussidi didàttici m.pl.

team, n. squadra f.

teamwork, n. lavoro di squadra m.

tea-pot, n. teièra f.

tear, 1. n. làcrima f. **2.** vb. strappare.

tease, vb. tormentare.

teaspoon, n. cucchiaino da thè m.

technical, adj. tècnico.

technique, n. tècnica f.

teddy bear, n. orsachiotto m.

tedious, adj. tedioso.

tedium, n. tèdio m.

telegram, n. telegramma m.

telegraph, 1. n. telègrafo m. **2.** vb. telegrafare.

telephone, 1. n. telèfono m.; (t.-call) telefonata f. **2.** vb. telefonare.

telescope, n. telescòpio m.

teletype, n. telescrivènte f.

televise, vb. trasméttere per televisione.

television, n. televisione f.; (t. screen) teleschermo m.; (t. set) televisore m.

tell, vb. raccontare.

teller, n. cassière m.

temper, 1. n. (anger) còllera f. **2.** vb. temperare.

temperament, n. temperamento m.

temperamental, adj. capriccioso.

temperance, n. temperanza f.

temperate, adj. temperato.

temperature, n. temperatura f.

tempest, n. tempèsta f.

tempestuous, adj. tempestoso.

temple, n. tèmpio m.; (forehead) tèmpia f.

temporary, adj. provvisòrio.

tempt, vb. tentare.

temptation, n. tentazione f.

tempting, adj. tentatore, tentatrice.

ten, num. dièci.

tenable, adj. difendìbile.

tenacious, adj. tenace.

tenant, n. inquilino m.

tend, vb. tèndere; (care for) curare.

tendency, n. tendènza f.

tender, 1. n. carro di scòrta m. **2.** adj. tènero. **3.** vb. offrire.

tenderly, adv. teneramente.

tenderness, n. tenerezza f.

tendon, n. tèndine m.

tenet, n. principio m.; dogma m.

tennis, n. tènnis m.

tenor, n. tenore m.

tense, adj. teso.

tension, n. tensione f.

tent, n. tènda f.

tentacle, n. tentàcolo m.

tentative, 1. n. tentativo m. **2.** adj. sperimentale, tentativo.

tenth, adj. dècimo.

term, n. periodo m.; (school) trimèstre m.

terminal, adj. terminale.

terminate, vb. terminare.

terminus, n. capolìnea m., tèrmine m.

terrace, n. terrazza f.

terrible, adj. terrìbile.

terribly, adv. terribilmente.

terrify, vb. atterrire.

territory, n. territòrio m.

terror, n. terrore m.

test, 1. n. pròva f. **2.** vb. provare, collaudare.

testament, n. testamento m.

testify, vb. testimoniare.

testimony, n. testimonianza f.

text, n. tèsto m.

textile, 1. n. tessuto m. **2.** adj. tèssile.

texture, n. tessitura f.

than, prep. (before nouns, pronouns) di; (elsewhere) che.

thank, vb. ringraziare.

thankful, adj. grato.

that, 1. adj. quel, quello, quella. **2.** pron. quello, quella. **3.** conj. che.

the, def. art. il, lo, la, l'; i, gli, gl', le.

theater, n. teatro m.

thee, pron. te, ti.

theft, n. furto m.

their, adj. loro.

theirs, pron. loro.

them, pron. li, le; loro.

theme, n. tèma m.

themselves, *pron.* si, sè; essi, stessi.

then, *adv.* (at that time) allora; (therefore) dunque; (afterward) pòi.

thence, *adv.* di là.

theologian, *n.* teòlogo *m.*

theology, *n.* teología *f.*

theoretical, *adj.* teòrico.

theory, *n.* teoría *f.*

therapy, *n.* terapía *f.*

there, *adv.* lí, là; ci, vi.

therefore, *adv.* perciò.

thermometer, *n.* termòmetro *m.*

these, *adj. and pron.* questi *m.pl.;* queste *f.pl.*

thesis, *n.* tesi *m.*

they, *pron.* loro; essi *m.pl.;* esse *f.pl.*

thick, *adj.* spesso, folto, dènso, fitto.

thicken, *vb.* infoltire, condensare.

thickness, *n.* spessore *m.*

thief, *n.* ladro *m.*

thieve, *vb.* rubare.

thigh, *n.* còscia *f.*

thimble, *n.* ditale *m.*

thin, *adj.* sottile; (meager) magro.

thing, *n.* còsa *f.*

thingumajig, *n.* còso *m.*

think, *vb.* pensare.

thinkable, *vb.* pensàbile.

thinker, *n.* pensatore *m.*

third, *adj.* tèrzo.

Third World, *n.* Tèrzo Mondo *m.*

thirst, *n.* sete *f.*

thirsty, *adj.* (be t.) aver sete.

thirteen, *num.* trédici.

thirteenth, *adj.* tredicésimo, decimotèrzo.

thirtieth, *adj.* trentésimo.

thirty, *num.* trenta.

this, *adj. and pron.* questo *m.sg.*, questa *f.sg.;* **(t. man)** questi *pron.m.sg.*

thorax, *n.* torace *m.*

thorn, *n.* spina *f.*

thorny, *adj.* spinoso.

thorough, *adj.* complèto.

those, **1.** *adj.* quei, quegli *m.pl.;* quelle *f.pl.* **2.** *pron.* quelli *m.pl.;* quelle *f.pl.*

thou, *pron.* tu.

though, **1.** *adv.* però. **2.** *conj.* sebbène.

thought, *n.* pensièro *m.*

thoughtful, *adj.* pensoso; (careful) attènto.

thoughtless, *adj.* incurante.

thousand, *num.* mille.

thread, **1.** *n.* filo *m.* **2.** *vb.* infilare.

threat, *n.* minàccia *f.*

threaten, *vb.* minacciare.

three, *num.* tre.

threshold, *n.* sòglia *f.*

thrift, *n.* economía *f.*

thrill, *n.* frèmito *m.*

thrilling, *adj.* emozionante; eccitante.

thrive, *vb.* prosperare.

throat, *n.* gola *f.*

throne, *n.* tròno *m.*

through, **1.** *adj.* (direct) dirètto. **2.** *prep.* per, attravèrso; **(go t., pass t.)** attraversare.

throughout, *adv.* dappertutto, completamente.

throw, *vb.* gettare, lanciare, buttare.

thrust, **1.** *n.* spinta *f.* **2.** *vb.* spíngere.

thumb, *n.* pòllice *m.*

thunder, **1.** *n.* tuòno *m.* **2.** *vb.* tuonare.

Thursday, *n.* giovedí *m.*

thus, *adv.* cosí.

thwart, *vb.* frustrare.

thy, *adj.* tuo.

ticket, *n.* biglietto *m.*

tickle, *vb.* solleticare.

ticklish, *adj.* delicato.

tide, *n.* marèa *f.*

tidy, **1.** *adj.* ordinato. **2.** *vb.* ordinare.

tie, **1.** *n.* (bond) legame *m.;* (necktie) cravatta *f.* **2.** *vb.* legare; (make equal score) èssere pari con.

tier, *n.* fila *f.*

tiger, *n.* tigre *m.*

tight, *adj.* stretto, teso.

tighten, *vb.* stríngere.

tile, *n.* tégola *f.*

till, **1.** *n.* cassetto *m.* **2.** *vb.* coltivare. **3.** *prep.* fino a; sino a. **4.** *conj.* finchè.

tilt, **1.** *n.* inclinazione *f.* **2.** *vb.* inclinare.

timber, *n.* legname *m.*

time, *n.* tèmpo *m.;* (o'clock) ora *f.;* (occasion) vòlta *f.*

timetable, *n.* oràrio *m.*
timid, *adj.* tímido.
timidity, *n.* timidezza *f.*
timidly, *adv.* timidamente.
tin, *n.* stagno *m.;* (metal can) latta *f.*
tint, *n.* tinta *f.*
tiny, *adj.* minùscolo.
tip, 1. *n.* (end) punta *f.;* (reward) mància *f.* **2.** *vb.* (tilt) inclinare; (give money to) dare una mància a.
tire, 1. *n.* pneumàtico *m.* **2.** *vb.* stancare.
tired, *adj.* stanco.
tissue, *n.* tessuto *m.;* (facial) fazzoletti detergenti *m.pl.;* scottex *m.;* carta assorbente *f.*
title, *n.* tìtolo *m.*
to, *prep.* a, ad (before a and, optionally, before other vowels).
toast, 1. *n.* pane abbrustolito *m.;* (health) toast *m.,* bríndisi *m.* **2.** *vb.* abbrustolire; (drink health) brindare.
tobacco, *n.* tabacco *m.;* **(t. shop)** tabaccheria *f.*
today, *n. and adv.* òggi *(m.)*
toe, *n.* dito del piède *m.;* **(big t.)** pòllice *m.*
together, *adv.* insième.
toil, 1. *n.* fatica *f.* **2.** *vb.* faticare.
toilet, *n.* latrina *f.,* gabinetto *m.;* **(t. paper)** carta igienica *f.*
token, *n.* segno *m.;* (metal) gettone *m.*
tolerance, *n.* tolleranza *f.*
tolerant, *adj.* tollerante.
tolerate, *vb.* tollerare.
toll, *n.* pedaggio *m.*
tomato, *n.* pomodoro *m.*
tomb, *n.* tomba *f.*
tombstone, *n.* làpide *f.*
tomorrow, *n. and adv.* domani *(m.)*
ton, *n.* tonnellata *f.*
tone, *n.* tòno *m.*
tongue, *n.* lingua *f.*
tongue twister, *n.* scioglilingua *m.*
tonic, *n. and adj.* tònico *(m.)*
tonight, *adv.* stasera.
tonnage, *n.* stazza *f.*
tonsil, *n.* tonsilla *f.*
too, *adv.* (also) anche; (excessively) troppo.

tool, *n.* utensile *m.*
too many, too much, *adj.* troppo.
tooth, *n.* dènte *m.*
toothache, *n.* mal di denti *m.*
toothbrush, *n.* spazzolino per i denti *m.*
toothless, *adj.* sdentato.
tooth paste, *n.* dentifricio *m.*
toothpick, *n.* stuzzicadenti *m.*
top, 1. *n.* sommità *f.* **2.** *vb.* superare.
topcoat, *n.* sopràbito *m.*
topic, *n.* argomento *m.*
topical, *adj.* d'attualità.
topless, *adj.* topless.
top-secret, *adj.* top secret, segretissimo.
topsy-turvy, *adv.* sottosopra.
torch, *n.* fiàccola *f.*
torment, 1. *n.* tormento *m.* **2.** *vb.* tormentare.
tornado, *n.* tornado *m.,* tromba d'aria *f.*
torrent, *n.* torrènte *m.*
torture, 1. *n.* tortura *f.* **2.** *vb.* torturare.
toss, *vb.* buttare, agitare, *tr.*
total, *n. and adj.* totale *m.*
totalitarian, *adj.* totalitàrio.
totter, *vb.* barcollare.
touch, 1. *n.* tocco *m.* **2.** *vb.* toccare.
tough, *adj.* (meat) tiglioso; (hard) difficile.
tour, 1. *n.* viàggio *m.* **2.** *vb.* viaggiare.
touring, tourism, *n.* turismo *m.*
tourist, 1. *n.* turista *m. or f.* **2.** *adj.* turístico.
tournament, *n.* concorso *m.*
tow, *vb.* rimorchiare.
toward, *prep.* vèrso.
towel, *n.* asciugatòio *m.;* **(hand-t.)** asciugamani *m.*
tower, *n.* torre *f.*
town, *n.* città *f.;* **(small t.)** cittadina *f.*
toy, 1. *n.* giocàttolo *m.,* trastullo *m.* **2.** *vb.* trastullarsi.
trace, 1. *n.* tràccia *f.* **2.** *vb.* rintracciare.
track, *n.* binàrio *m.;* (for running) pista *f.*
tract, *n.* tratto *m.*

tractor, n. trattore m.
trade, 1. n. commèrcio m. **2.** vb. commerciare.
trader, n. commerciante m.
tradition, n. tradizione f.
traditional, adj. tradizionale.
traffic, n. tràffico m.
traffic light, n. semàforo m.
tragedy, n. tragèdia f.
tragic, adj. tràgico.
trail, n. sentièro m.
trailer, n. rimòrchio m.; **(house-t.)** carovana f.; **(t. truck)** autotreno m.
train, 1. n. treno m. **2.** vb. allenare.
traitor, n. traditore m.
tram, n. tram m.
tramway, n. tranvía f.
tramp, n. vagabondo m.
tranquil, adj. tranquillo.
tranquilizer, n. calmante m.
tranquillity, n. tranquillità f.
transaction, n. operazione f.
transfer, 1. n. trasferimento m. **2.** vb. trasferire.
transfix, vb. trafiggere.
transform, vb. trasformare.
transfusion, n. trasfusione f.
transition, n. transizione f.
translate, vb. tradurre.
translation, n. traduzione f.
transmit, vb. trasméttere.
transparent, adj. trasparènte.
transport, 1. n. traspòrto m. **2.** vb. trasportare.
transportation, n. traspòrto m.
transsexual, n. trans-sessuale m.
transvestite, n. travestito m.
trap, n. tràppola f.
trash, n. cianfrusàglia f.
travel, 1. n. viàggio m.; **(t. agency)** agenzía viaggi f. **2.** vb. viaggiare.
traveler, n. viaggiatore m.
traveler's check, n. assegno (per) viaggiatori m.
travesty, n. parodìa f.
tray, n. vassòio m.
treacherous, adj. a tradimento, proditòrio; **(deceptive)** ingannévole.
treachery, n. tradimento m.
tread, 1. n. passo m. **2.** vb. calpestare.
treason, n. tradimento m.

treasure, n. tesòro m.
treasurer, n. tesorière m.
treasury, n. tesòro m.
treat, vb. trattare.
treatise, n. trattato m.
treatment, n. trattamento m.
treaty, n. trattato m.
tree, n. àlbero m.
treetop, n. cima dell'àlbero f.
tremble, vb. tremare.
tremendous, adj. tremèndo.
tremor, n. trèmito m.
trench, n. trincèa f.
trend, n. tendènza f.
trespass, n. violazione di confine f.
triage, n. scelta f.
trial, n. pròva f.; **(law)** procèsso m.
triangle, n. triàngolo m.
tribe, n. tribù f.
tribulation, n. tribolazione f.
tributary, n. and adj. tributàrio (m.); **(river)** affluènte (m.)
tribute, n. tributo m.
trick, 1. n. tiro m.; trucco m. **2.** vb. ingannare.
trickle, 1. n. gocciolìo m. **2.** vb. gocciolare.
tricky, adj. ingannévole.
trifle, n. bazzècola f.
trigger, n. grilletto m.
trim, 1. adj. ordinato. **2.** vb. **(clip)** cimare; **(make neat)** ordinare.
trimming, n. guarnizione f.
trinket, n. ninnolo m.
trip, 1. n. viàggio m. **2.** vb. incespicare.
tripe, n. trippa f.
triple, 1. adj. tríplice. **2.** vb. triplicare, tr.
tripod, n. treppiede m.
trite, adj. trito.
triumph, 1. n. trionfo m. **2.** vb. trionfare.
triumphal, adj. trionfale.
triumphant, adj. trionfante.
trivial, adj. meschino.
trolley-bus, n. filobus m.; **(t.-b. line)** filovìa f.
trolley-car, n. tram m.
troop, n. truppa f.
trophy, n. trofèo m.
tropic, n. tròpico m.
tropical, adj. tròpico.
trot, 1. n. tròtto m. **2.** vb. trottare.

trouble, 1. *n.* guaio *m.*; (jam) impíccio *m.*; (bother) disturbo *m.*; fastídio *m.* 2. *vb.* disturbare, infastidire.

troublesome, *adj.* fastidioso.

trough, *n.* trògolo *m.*

trousers, *n.* calzoni *m.pl.*

trousseau, *n.* corredo nuziale *m.*

trout, *n.* tròta *f.*

truce, *n.* trégua *f.*

truck, *n.* càmion *m.*, autocarro *m.*

true, *adj.* vero; (loyal) fedele.

truly, *adv.* veramente; **(yours t.)** Vostro devmo.

trumpet, *n.* tromba *f.*

trumpeter, *n.* trombettière *f.*

trunk, *n.* (tree) tronco *m.*; (luggage) baùle *m.*

trust, *n.* fidùcia *f.*; (comm.) consòrzio *m.*

trustworthy, *adj.* affidàbile.

truth, *n.* verità *f.*

truthful, *adj.* verídico; fedele.

try, *vb.* provare, tentare.

tryst, *n.* appuntamento *m.*

T-shirt, *n.* maglietta *f.*

tub, *n.* vasca *f.*

tube, *n.* tubo *m.*; (radio) vàlvola *f.*

tuberculosis, *n.* tuberculòsi *f.*

tuck, 1. *n.* piéga *f.* 2. *vb.* rimboccare.

Tuesday, *n.* martedí *m.*

tuft, *n.* ciuffo *m.*

tug, *vb.* tirare.

tug-boat, *n.* rimorchiatore *m.*

tuition, *n.* (fee) tassa scolàstica *f.*

tulip, *n.* tulipano *m.*

tumble, 1. *n.* capitómbolo *m.* 2. *vb.* capitombolare.

tumor, *n.* tumore *m.*

tumult, *n.* tumulto *m.*

tuna, *n.* tonno *m.*

tune, 1. *n.* melódia *f.* 2. *vb.* accordare; **(t. in)** sintonizzare.

tuneful, *adj.* melodioso.

tunnel, 1. *n.* galleria *f.*, traforo *m.* 2. *vb.* traforare.

turban, *n.* turbante *m.*

turbine, *n.* turbina *f.*

turbo-jet, *n.* turboreattore *m.*

turbo-prop, *n.* turbo-èlica *f.*

turf, *n.* zolla erbosa *f.*; pàscolo *m.*

Turin, *n.* Torino *m.*

Turinese, *adj.* torinese.

Turk, *n.* Turco *m.*

turkey, *n.* tacchino *m.*

Turkey, *n.* Turchía *f.*

Turkish, *adj.* turco.

turmoil, *n.* confusione *f.*

turn, 1. *n.* giro *m.*; (vehicle) svòlta *f.*; (time around) turno *m.* 2. *vb.* girare.

turncoat, *n.* voltagabbana *m.*

turning point, *n.* svolta cruciale *f.*

turnip, *n.* rapa *f.*

turnout, *n.* (gathering) folla *f.*

turnover, *n.* rovesciamento *m.*; (comm.) giro *m.*

turnpike, *n.* autostrada a pedaggio *f.*

turn signal, *n.* fréccia *f.*

turret, *n.* torretta *f.*

turtle, *n.* tartaruga *f.*

Tuscan, *adj.* toscano.

Tuscany, *n.* Toscana *f.*

tutor, *n.* insegnante privato *m.*

tuxedo, *n.* smoking *m.*

twelfth, *adj.* dodicèsimo.

twelve, *num.* dódici.

twentieth, *adj.* ventèsimo.

twenty, *num.* venti.

twice, *adv.* due vòlte.

twig, *n.* ramoscèllo *m.*

twilight, *n.* crepùscolo *m.*

twin, *n.* gemèllo *m.*

twine, *n.* spago *m.*

twinkle, *vb.* luccicare.

twist, *vb.* tòrcere, *tr.*

two, *num.* due.

tycoon, *n.* magnate *m.*

type, 1. *n.* tipo *m.* 2. *vb.* dattilografare.

typewriter, *n.* màcchina da scrívere *f.*

typhoid fever, *n.* febbre tifoidèa *f.*

typhoon, *n.* tifone *m.*

typhus, *n.* tifo *m.*

typical, *adj.* típico.

typist, *n.* dattilògrafa *f.*

tyranny, *n.* tirannía *f.*

tyrant, *n.* tiranno *m.*

English-Italian

U

udder, *n.* mammèlla *f.*
ugliness, *n.* bruttezza *f.*
ugly, *adj.* brutto.
ulcer, *n.* úlcera *f.*
ulterior, *adj.* ulteriore.
ultimate, *adj.* último.
umbrella, *n.* ombrèllo *m.*
Umbrian, *adj.* umbro.
umpire, *n.* àrbitro *m.*
un-, 1. *with adjectives,* non, in-, a-, s-. **2.** *with verbs,* s-, dis-.
unable, *adj.* incapace.
unanimous, *adj.* unànime.
unbecoming, *adj.* sconveniènte.
unbounded, *adj.* sconfinato.
uncertain, *adj.* incèrto.
uncertainty, *n.* incertezza *f.*
uncle, *n.* zio *m.*
unconscious, *adj.* incònscio.
uncork, *vb.* sturare.
uncouth, *adj.* gòffo.
uncover, *vb.* scoprire, *tr.*
under, 1. *adj.* inferiore. **2.** *adv. and prep.* sotto.
underestimate, *vb.* sottovalutare.
undergo, *vb.* subire.
underground, *adj.* sotterràneo.
underline, *vb.* sottolineare.
underneath, *adv. and prep.* sotto.
underpass, *n.* sottopassàggio *m.*
undershirt, *n.* camiciòla *f.*; canuttièra *f.*
undersigned, *adj.* sottoscritto.
understand, *vb.* capire.
understanding, *n.* comprensione *f.*
undertake, *vb.* intraprèndere.
undertaker, *n.* imprenditore di pompe fùnebri *m.*
underwear, *n.* biancheria íntima *f.*
underworld, *n.* malavita *f.*
undo, *vb.* disfare.
undress, *vb.* svestire, *tr.*
undulate, *vb.* ondeggiare.
unearth, *vb.* dissotterrare.
uneasy, *adj.* inquièto.
unemployed, *adj.* disoccupato.
unequal, *adj.* ineguale.
uneven, *adj.* disuguale.
unexpected, *adj.* inaspettato.

unexpectedly, *adv.* inaspettatamente.
unfair, *adj.* ingiusto.
unfamiliar, *adj.* pòco nòto.
unfavorable, *adj.* sfavorévole.
unfit, *adj.* inàbile, disadatto.
unfold, *vb.* spiegare, *tr.*
unforgettable, *adj.* indimenticàbile.
unfortunate, *adj.* disgraziato, sfortunato.
unfurl, *vb.* spiegare.
unhappy, *adj.* infelice.
uniform, 1. *n.* divisa *f.*, unifòrme *m.* **2.** *adj.* unifòrme.
unify, *vb.* unificare.
unilateral, *adj.* unilaterale.
union, *n.* unione *f.*
unique, *adj.* único.
unisex, *adj.* ùnisex.
unit, *n.* unità *f.*
unite, *vb.* unire.
United Nations, *n.* Nazioni Unite *f.pl.*
United States, *n.* Stati Uniti *m.pl.*
unity, *n.* unità *f.*
universal, *adj.* universale.
universe, *n.* univèrso *m.*
university, *n.* università *f.*
unjust, *adj.* ingiusto.
unjustified, *adj.* ingiustificato.
unknowingly, *adv.* inconsapevolmente.
unknown, *adj.* ignòto, sconosciuto.
unleaded, *adj.* senza piombo.
unleash, *vb.* sguinzagliare; scatenare.
unless, *conj.* a meno che . . . non.
unlike, *adj.* dissímile.
unlikely, *adj.* improbàbile.
unload, *vb.* scaricare.
unlock, *vb.* aprire.
unlucky, *adj.* disgraziato, infelice.
unmarried, *adj.* cèlibe.
unmask, *vb.* smascherare.
unmistakable, *adj.* inconfondìbile.
unofficial, *adj.* ufficioso.
unorthodox, *adj.* non ortodosso.
unpack, *vb.* disimballare.

unpleasant, *adj.* spiacévole.
unqualified, *adj.* (unfit) incompetènte; (unreserved) incondizionato.
unravel, *vb.* districare, *tr.*
unrecognizable, *adj.* irriconoscíbile.
unrighteous, *adj.* iniquo.
unsafe, *adj.* pericoloso.
unsavory, *adj.* insipido; disgustoso.
unscathed, *adj.* incolume.
unseemly, *adj.* sconveniènte.
unsettle, *vb.* sconvòlgere.
unsteady, *adj.* instàbile.
unsuccessful, *adj.* infruttuoso.
untie, *vb.* sciògliere.
until, 1. *prep.* fino a, sino a. **2.** *conj.* finché . . . non.
untruth, *n.* menzogna *f.*
untruthful, *adj.* menzognèro.
unusable, *adj.* inservíbile.
unusual, *adj.* insòlito.
unwarranted, *adj.* ingiustificato.
unwell, *adj.* indisposto.
unwind, *vb.* dipanare.
unworthiness, *n.* indegnità *f.*
unworthy, *adj.* indegno.
up, 1. *adv.* su. **2.** *prep.* su per.
upbraid, *vb.* rimproverare.
upbringing, *n.* educazione *f.*
uphill, 1. *adj.* (hard) àrduo. **2.** *adv.* all'insù.
uphold, *vb.* sostenere.
upholder, *n.* sostenitore *m.*
upholster, *vb.* tappezzare.
upholsterer, *n.* tappezzière *m.*
upon, *prep.* sopra, su.
upper, *adj.* superiore.
upright, *adj.* and *adv.* diritto.
uprising, *n.* sollevazione *f.*

uproar, *n.* baccano *m.*
uproot, *vb.* sradicare.
upset, 1. *n.* sconvolgimento *m.* **2.** *vb.* sconvòlgere. **3.** *adj.* sconvolto.
upside down, *adv.* sottosopra.
upstairs, *adv.* su dalle scale.
uptight, *adj.* teso.
upward, *adv.* in alto.
urban, *adj.* urbano.
urchin, *n.* monèllo *m.*
urge, *vb.* spíngere, sollecitare.
urgency, *n.* urgènza *f.*
urgent, *adj.* urgènte.
urinal, *n.* urinale *m.;* (public) vespasiano *m.*
urinate, *vb.* urinare.
urine, *n.* urina *f.*
urn, *n.* urna *f.*
us, *pron.* noi, ci.
usage, *n.* usanza *f.*
use, 1. *n.* uso *m.* **2.** *vb.* usare, adoperare, servirsi di.
useful, *adj.* ùtile.
useless, *adj.* inùtile.
user, *n.* utènte *m.*
usher, *n.* màschera *f.*
usual, *adj.* sòlito, usuale; **(as u.)** come di sòlito.
usurp, *vb.* usurpare.
usury, *n.* usura *f.*
utensil, *n.* utensile *m.*
uterus, *n.* ùtero *m.*
utility, *n.* utilità *f.;* (light truck) camioncino *m.*
utilize, *vb.* utilizzare.
utmost, *adj.* estrèmo.
utter, 1. *adj.* complèto. **2.** *vb.* proferire, eméttere.
utterance, *n.* espressione *f.*
utterly, *adv.* completamente.
uvula, *n.* ùgola *f.*

V

vacancy, *n.* posto vacante *m.;* (hotel) stanza líbera *f.*
vacant, *adj.* vacante, vuòto.
vacate, *vb.* abbondanare, lasciar líbero.
vacation, *n.* vacanze *f.pl.;* (rest) ripòso *m.*
vaccinate, *vb.* vaccinare.
vaccination, *n.* vaccinazione *f.*
vaccine, *n.* vaccino *m.*

vacillate, *vb.* vacillare.
vacuous, *adj.* vàcuo.
vacuum, *n.* vuòto *m.*
vacuum cleaner, *n.* aspirapolvere *m.*
vagrant, *n.* and *adj.* vagabondo (*m.*).
vague, *adj.* vago.
vain, *adj.* vano; **(in v.)** invano.
valet, *n.* camerière *m.*

valiant, adj. valoroso.
valid, adj. vàlido.
valise, n. valigia f.
valley, n. valle f.
valor, n. valore m.
valuable, adj. prezioso; (expensive) costoso.
value, 1. n. valore m. 2. vb. stimare, valutare.
value-added tax, n. imposta sul valore aggiunto f.
valueless, adj. privo di valore.
valve, n. vàlvola f.
vampire, n. vampiro m.
van, n. (vehicle) carro m.; furgone m.; (front) avanguàrdia f.; (moving v.) furgone per traslòchi m.
vandal, n. vàndalo m.
vanguard, n. avanguàrdia f.
vanilla, n. vaníglia f.
vanish, vb. svanire.
vanity, n. vanità f.
vanquish, vb. víncere.
vapid, adj. insipido.
vapor, n. vapore m.
variance, n. disaccòrdo m.
variation, n. variazione f.
varied, adj. svariato.
variety, n. varietà f.
various, adj. vàrio.
varnish, n. vernice f.
vary, vb. variare.
vase, n. vaso m.
vasectomy, n. vasectomía f.
vassal, n. vassallo m.
vast, adj. vasto.
vat, n. tino m.
Vatican City, n. Città del Vaticano f.
vaudeville, n. spettàcolo di varietà m.
vault, 1. n. (of roof) vòlta f.; (jump) salto m. 2. vb. saltare.
veal, n. vitèllo m.
vegetable, 1. n. legume m.; (v.s) verdura f. 2. adj. vegetale.
vehemence, n. veemènza f.
vehement, adj. veemènte.
vehicle, n. veícolo m.
veil, n. velo m.
vein, n. vena f.; (geology) filone m.
velocity, n. velocità f.
velvet, 1. n. velluto m. 2. adj. di velluto.

veneer, 1. n. piallàccio m. 2. vb. impiallacciare.
venereal, adj. venèreo.
Venetian, adj. veneziano.
vengeance, n. vendetta f.
vengeful, adj. vendicativo.
Venice, n. Venèzia f.
venom, n. veleno m.
venomous, adj. velenoso.
vent, 1. n. foro m.; (expression) sfogo m. 2. vb. sfogare.
ventilate, vb. ventilare.
ventilation, n. ventilazione f.
ventriloquist, n. ventriloquo m.
venture, 1. n. ventura f.; (risk) rischio m. 2. vb. rischiare; (dare) osare.
venturesome, adj. avventuroso.
veracity, n. veridicità f.
verb, n. vèrbo m.
verbal, adj. verbale.
verbose, adj. verboso.
verdict, n. verdetto m.
verge, 1. n. orlo m. 2. vb. (v. on) confinare con.
verify, vb. verificare.
vermilion, adj. vermíglio.
vermin, n. insetti m.pl.
vernacular, n. and adj. vernàcolo (m.), volgare (m.).
versatile, adj. versàtile.
verse, n. vèrso m.
versify, vb. versificare.
version, n. versione f.
versus, prep. contro.
vertebrate, n. and adj. vertebrato (m.)
vertical, adj. verticale.
vertigo, n. vertígine f.
verve, n. brío m.
very, 1. adj. vero; (selfsame) stesso. 2. adv. molto; or add suffix -íssimo.
vespers, n. vèspri m.pl.
vessel, n. (container) recipiènte m.; (boat) nave f.
vest, n. gilè m., panciòtto m.
vestige, n. vestigia f.pl.
vestry, n. sagrestia f.
Vesuvius, n. Vesùvio m.
veteran, n. veterano m.
veterinary, n. and adj. veterinàrio (m.)
veto, 1. n. vèto m. 2. vb. vietare.
vex, vb. irritare.

vexing, *adj.* noioso.
via, *prep.* vía.
viaduct, *n.* viadotto *m.*
vibrate, *vb.* vibrare.
vibration, *n.* vibrazione *f.*
vicar, *n.* vicàrio *m.*
vice, *n.* vízio *m.*
vice versa, *adv.* viceversa.
vicinity, *n.* vicinanza *f.*
vicious, *adj.* vizioso.
victim, *n.* vìttima *f.*
victorious, *adj.* vittorioso.
victory, *n.* vittòria *f.*
victuals, *n.* vettovàglie *f.pl.;* vitto *m.*
videodisc, *n.* videodisco *m.*
videotape, *n.* videocassetta *f.*
view, *n.* vista *f.,* veduta *f.*
vigil, *n.* véglia *f.,* vigília *f.*
vigilant, *adj.* vigilante.
vigor, *n.* vigore *m.*
vigorous, *adj.* vigoroso.
vile, *adj.* vile.
vilify, *vb.* vilificare.
villa, *n.* villa *f.*
village, *n.* villàggio *m.*
villain, *n.* furfante *m.; (in play)* antagonista *m.*
vim, *n.* brio *m.*
vindicate, *vb.* rivendicare.
vine, *n.* vite *f.*
vinegar, *n.* aceto *m.*
vineyard, *n.* vigna *f.*
vintage, *n.* vendémmia *f.*
viol, viola, *n.* viòla *f.*
violate, *vb.* violare.
violation, *n.* violazione *f.,* contravvenzione *f.*
violator, *n.* violatore *m.,* contravventore *m.*
violence, *n.* violènza *f.*
violent, *adj.* violénto.
violet, *n.* viòla *f.*
violin, *n.* violino *m.*
violinist, *n.* violinista *m.*
viper, *n.* vípera *f.*
virgin, *n.* vérgine *f.*
virginity, *n.* verginità *f.*

virile, *adj.* virile.
virility, *n.* virilità *f.*
virtual, *adj.* virtuale.
virtue, *n.* virtù *f.*
virtuous, *adj.* virtuoso.
virulence, *n.* virolenza *f.*
virus, *n.* virus *m.*
visa, 1. *n.* visto *m.* 2. *vb.* vistare.
viscous, *adj.* viscoso.
vise, *n.* mòrsa *f.*
visible, *adj.* visíbile.
vision, *n.* visione *f.; (of v.)* visivo.
visit, 1. *n.* vísita *f.* 2. *vb.* visitare.
visiting card, *n.* biglietto da vísita *m.*
visitor, *n.* òspite *m. or f.*
vista, *n.* vista *f.;* panorama *m.*
visual, *adj.* visuale.
vital, *adj.* vitale.
vitality, *n.* vitalità *f.*
vitamin, *n.* vitamina *f.*
vitiate, *vb.* viziare.
vivacious, *adj.* vivace.
vivid, *adj.* vívido.
vocabulary, *n.* vocabolàrio *m.*
vocal, *adj.* vocale.
vociferate, *vb.* vociare.
vogue, *n.* voga *f.*
voice, *n.* voce *f.*
void, *adj.* nullo; *(devoid)* privo.
volcano, *n.* vulcano *m.*
voltage, *n.* voltàggio *m.*
volume, *n.* volume *m.*
voluntary, *adj.* volontàrio.
volunteer, *n.* volontàrio *m.*
vomit, 1. *n.* vòmito *m.* 2. *vb.* vomitare.
vote, 1. *n.* voto *m.* 2. *vb.* votare.
voter, *n.* votante *m.*
voting, *n.* votazione *f.*
vouch for, *vb.* attestare.
vow, *n.* voto *m.*
vowel, *n.* vocale *f.*
voyage, 1. *n.* viàggio *f.* 2. *vb.* viaggiare.
vulgar, *adj.* volgare.
vulgarity, *n.* volgarità *f.*
vulnerable, *adj.* vulneràbile.

W

wad, *n.* batùffolo *m.; (roll)* ròtolo *m.*
wadding, *n.* ovatta *f.*

wade, *vb.* attraversare a guado.
wag, 1. *n.* buonumore *m.* 2. *vb.* dimenare, scuòtere.

wage, *vb.* (war) fare.
wager, 1. *n.* scommessa *f.* **2.** *vb.* scomméttere.
wages, *n.* salário *m.*
wagon, *n.* carro *m.*
wail, *vb.* lamentarsi.
waist, *n.* cintura *f.*, vita *f.*
waistcoat, *n.* gilè *m.*, panciòtto *m.*
wait, *vb.* aspettare.
waiter, *n.* camerière *m.*
waitress, *n.* camerièra *f.*
waive, *vb.* rinunciare a.
waiver, *n.* rinùncia *f.*
wake, 1. *n.* (vigil) vèglia *f.;* (of boat) scía *f.* **2.** *vb.* svegliare; (be awake) vegliare.
walk, 1. *n.* passeggiata *f.* **2.** *vb.* camminare, passeggiare.
wall, *n.* muro *m.*
wallcovering, *n.* tapezzería *f.*
wallet, *n.* portafògli *m.*
wallpaper, *n.* carta da parati *f.*
walnut, *n.* noce *f.*
walrus, *n.* trichèco *m.*
waltz, *n.* vàlzer *m.*
wan, *adj.* smunto, smorto.
wand, *n.* bacchetta *f.*
wander, *vb.* vagare.
wane, 1. *n.* decadenza *f.* **2.** *vb.* declinare.
want, 1. *n.* bisogno *m.;* (poverty) misèria *f.* **2.** *vb.* desiderare.
war, *n.* guèrra *f.*
ward, *n.* pupillo *m.;* (city) rione *m.*
wardrobe, *n.* guardaroba *m.*
ware, *n.* mèrce *f.*
warehouse, *n.* depòsito *m.,* magazzino *m.*
warlike, *adj.* guerresco.
warlord, *n.* capofazione *m.,* signore della guerra *m.*
warm, *adj.* caldo, caloroso.
warmonger, *n.* guerrafondàio *m.*
warmth, *n.* calore *m.*
warn, *vb.* ammonire, avvertire.
warning, *n.* avviso *m.,* ammonimento *m.*
warp, *vb.* curvare *tr.,* viziare.
warrant, *n.* mandato *f.*
warranty, *n.* garanzia *f.*
warrior, *n.* guerrièro *m.*
warship, *n.* nave da guerra *f.*
wash, 1. *n.* (laundry) biancheria *f.* **2.** *vb.* lavare.
wash-basin, *n.* lavabo *m.*

washing machine, *n.* lavabianchería *m.*
washroom, *n.* lavatòio *m.*
wasp, *n.* vèspa *f.*
waste, 1. *n.* sprèco *m.* **2.** *vb.* sprecare.
wastebasket, *n.* cestino rifiùti *m.*
watch, 1. *n.* (timepiece) orológio *m.;* (guard) guàrdia *f.* **2.** *vb.* guardare.
watchful, *adj.* vigilante.
watchmaker, *n.* orologiaio *m.*
watchman, *n.* guardiano *m.*
water, 1. *n.* acqua *f.* **2.** *vb.* innaffiare.
waterbed, *n.* letto ad acqua *m.*
water-color, *n.* acquarèllo *m.*
waterfall, *n.* cascata *f.*
waterproof, *adj.* impermeàbile.
wave, 1. *n.* onda *f.* **2.** *vb.* sventolare.
waver, *vb.* esitare, vacillare.
wax, 1. *n.* cera *f.* **2.** *vb.* incerare.
way, *n.* via *f.;* (manner) manièra *f.*
we, *pron.* noi.
weak, *adj.* débole.
weaken, *vb.* indebolire.
weakly, *adv.* debolmente.
weakness, *n.* debolezza *f.*
wealth, *n.* ricchezza *f.*
wealthy, *adj.* ricco.
weapon, *n.* arma *f.*
wear, 1. *n.* consumo *m.* **2.** *vb.* portare; (w. out) consumare; logorare.
weary, *adj.* stanco.
weasel, *n.* dònnola *f.*
weather, *n.* tèmpo *m.;* (w. report) bollettino metereologico *m.*
weave, *vb.* tèssere.
weaver, *n.* tessitore *m.*
weaving, *n.* tessitura *f.*
web, *n.* tela *f.*
wedding, *n.* nòzze *f.pl.*
wedge, 1. *n.* bietta *f.,* cùneo *m.* **2.** *vb.* incuneare.
Wednesday, *n.* mercoledí *m.*
weed, *n.* erbàccia *f.*
week, *n.* settimana *f.*
weekday, *n.* giorno feriale *m.*
week end, *n.* fine di settimana *f.*
weekly, *n.; adj.* settimanale (*m.*)
weep, *vb.* piàngere.
weigh, *vb.* pesare.
weight, *n.* peso *m.*

weird, *adj.* strano.

welcome, *adj.* benvenuto.

welfare, *n.* benèssere *m.*

well, 1. *n.* pozzo *m.* 2. *vb.* sgorgare. 3. *adv., interj.* bène.

well-known, *adj.* nòto.

west, *n.* òvest *m.*

western, *adj.* occidentale.

westward, *adv.* vèrso òvest.

wet, 1. *adj.* ùmido. 2. *vb.* inumidire.

whale, *n.* balena *f.*

what, *pron.* che?, che còsa?

whatever, 1. *adj.* qualunque. 2. *pron.* qualunque còsa.

wheat, *n.* frumento *m.*

wheel, *n.* ruòta *f.;* **(w. chair)** sèdia a rotelle *f.*

when, *adv.* quando.

whence, *adv.* donde.

whenever, *adv.* ogniqualvòlta.

where, *adv.* dove.

wherever, *adv.* dovunque.

whether, *conj.* se.

which, 1. *interrog. pron., adj.* quale. 2. *rel. pron.* che, il quale; (after prep.) cùi; **(to w.)** cùi.

whichever, *adj.;* *pron.* qualunque.

while, *conj.* mentre.

whim, *n.* capriccio *m.*

whip, 1. *n.* frusta *f.* 2. *vb.* frustare.

whirl, *vb.* girare.

whirlpool, *n.* vòrtice *m.*

whirlwind, *n.* tùrbine *m.*

whisk broom, *n.* scopetta *f.*

whisker, *n.* basetta *f.*

whiskey, *n.* whiskey *m.*

whisper, 1. *n.* bisbiglio *m.* 2. *vb.* bisbigliare.

whistle, 1. *n.* fischio *m.* 2. *vb.* fischiare.

white, *adj.* bianco.

whiten, *vb.* imbiancare.

white plague, *n.* tubercolosi *f.*

white slavery, *n.* la tratta delle bianche *f.*

who, whom, *pron.* 1. *interrog.* chi. 2. *rel.* che, il quale; (after prep.) cùi.

whoever, whomever, *pron.* chiunque.

whole, *adj.* intèro, tutto.

wholehearted, *adj.* di gran cuore, sincero.

wholesale, *adj., adv.* all'ingròsso.

wholesome, *adj.* sano.

wholly, *adv.* completamente.

whom, see **who.**

whore, *n.* puttana *f.*

whose, *pron.* 1. *interrog.* di chi?. 2. *rel.* cùi.

why, *adv.* perchè.

wicked, *adj.* malvàgio.

wickedness, *n.* malvagità *f.*

wide, *adj.* largo.

wide-angle, *adj.* grandangolare.

widen, *vb.* allargare, *tr.*

widespread, *adj.* diffuso.

widow, *n.* védova *f.*

widower, *n.* védovo *m.*

width, *n.* larghezza *f.*

wield, *vb.* règgere.

wife, *n.* móglie *f.*

wig, *n.* parrucca *f.*

wild, *adj.* selvàggio; (plants) selvàtico; (mad) furioso.

wilderness, *n.* desèrto *m.*

wildlife, *n.* fàuna selvàtica *f.*

will, 1. *n.* volontà *f.;* (testament) testamento *m.* 2. *vb.* (leave) lasciare; (future) use future tense.

willful, *adj.* capàrbio, ostinato.

willing, *adj.* pronto.

willow, *n.* sàlice *m.*

wilt, *vb.* appassire.

win, *vb.* vincere.

wind, 1. *n.* vènto *m.* 2. *vb.* avvòlgere; (watch) caricare.

windmill, *n.* mulino a vento *m.*

window, *n.* finèstra *f.*

window dressing, *n.* vetrinística *f.;* facciata *f.*

windshield, *n.* parabrezza *m.;* paraventi *m.;* **(w.-wiper)** tergicristallo *m.*

windy, *adj.* ventoso.

wine, *n.* vino *m.*

wing, *n.* ala *f.*

wink, *vb.* ammiccare.

winner, *n.* vincitore *m.*

winter, 1. *n.* invèrno *m.* 2. *adj.* **(of w.)** invernale.

wintry, *adj.* invernale.

wipe, *vb.* asciugare.

wire, 1. *n.* filo *m.;* (telegram) telegramma *m.* 2. *vb.* telegrafare.

wireless, 1. *n.* (radio) ràdio *f.* 2. *adj.* sènza fili.

wire recorder, *n.* registratore a filo *m.*

wiretap, *vb.* intercettare.
wisdom, *n.* saggezza *f.*
wise, *adj.* sàggio.
wish, 1. *n.* desidèrio *m.* 2. *vb.* desiderare.
wit, *n.* intelligènza *f.;* (humor) spírito *m.* (wag) buonumore *m.*
witch, *n.* strega *f.*
witch hunt, *n.* caccia alle streghe *f.*
with, *prep.* con.
withdraw, *vb.* ritirare, *tr.*
wither, *vb.* avvizzire.
withhold, *vb.* trattenere.
within, 1. *adv.* dentro. 2. *prep.* entro.
without, *prep.* sènza.
witness, *n.* testimone *m.*
witty, *adj.* spiritoso.
wizard, *n.* stregone *m.*
woe, *n.* calamità *f.,* guaio *m.*
wolf, *n.* lupo *m.,* lupa *f.*
woman, *n.* dònna *f.*
womb, *n.* ùtero *m.*
wonder, 1. *n.* meravíglia *f.* 2. *vb.* meravigliarsi, domandarsi.
wonderful, *adj.* meraviglioso.
woo, *vb.* corteggiare.
wood, *n.* legno *m.;* (forest) bosco *m.,* forèsta *f.*
wooded, *adj.* boscoso.
wooden, *adj.* di legno.
wool, *n.* lana *f.*
woolen, *adj.* di lana.
word, *n.* paròla *f.*
wordy, *adj.* verboso.
work, 1. *n.* lavoro *m.,* òpera *f.* 2. *vb.* lavorare; (function) funzionare.
worker, *n.* lavoratore *m.*
workman, *n.* operaio *m.*
world, *n.* mondo *m.*
worldly, *adj.* mondano.
world-wide, *adj.* mondiale.
worm, *n.* vèrme *m.*

worn-out, *adj.* lògoro.
worry, 1. *n.* preoccupazione *f.* 2. *vb.* preoccupare, *tr.*
worse, 1. *adj.* peggiore. 2. *adv.* pèggio.
worship, 1. *n.* adorazione *f.,* culto *m.* 2. *vb.* adorare.
worst, 1. *adj.* il peggiore. 2. *adv.* il pèggio.
worth, 1. *n.* valore *m.* 2. *adj.* (be w.) valere.
worthless, *adj.* sènza valore.
worthy, *adj.* degno.
would, *vb.* use conditional tense.
would-be, *adj.* millantato, preteso.
wound, 1. *n.* ferita *f.* 2. *vb.* ferire.
wrap, 1. *n.* mantèllo *m.* 2. *vb.* avvòlgere.
wrapping, *n.* involucro *m.*
wrath, *n.* ira *f.*
wreath, *n.* ghirlanda *f.*
wreck, 1. *n.* (ship) naufràgio *m.;* (ruin) rovina *f.* 2. *vb.* naufragare, rovinare.
wrench, 1. *n.* (tool) chiave inglese *f.* 2. *vb.* strappare.
wrestle, *vb.* lottare.
wrestling, *n.* lotta *f.*
wretched, *adj.* mísero.
wring, *vb.* tòrcere.
wrinkle, 1. *n.* ruga *f.* 2. *vb.* corrugare.
wrist, *n.* polso *m.*
wrist-watch, *n.* orològio da polso *m.*
write, *vb.* scrívere.
writer, *n.* scrittore *m.*
writhe, *vb.* contòrcersi.
writing, *n.* scrittura *f.,* scritto *m.*
wrong, 1. *n.* tòrto *m.* 2. *adj.* errato; (be w.) aver tòrto.
wrongdoing, *n.* malefatta *f.,* trasgressione *f.*
wry, *adj.* storto, sbieco.

X, Y, Z

x-rays, *n.* raggi x (pron. ics) *m. pl.*
xylophone, *n.* xilòfono *m.*

yacht, *n.* pànfilo *m.*
yard, *n.* cortile *m.;* (railroad) scalo di smistamento *m.;* (measure) jarda *f.*
yarn, *n.* filato *m.;* (tale) stòria *f.*
yawn, 1. *n.* sbadíglio *m.* 2. *vb.* sbadigliare.
year, *n.* anno *m.*

yearbook, n. annuàrio m.
yearly, 1. adj. annuale. 2. adv. ogni anno.
yearn, vb. bramare.
yell, 1. n. urlo m. 2. vb. urlare.
yellow, adj. giallo.
yelp, vb. guaire.
yes, interj. sì.
yes-man, n. leccapiedi m.
yesterday, n. and adv. ièri (m.)
yet, 1. adv. ancora. 2. conj. tuttavia.
yield, 1. n. produzione f. 2. vb. cèdere; (produce) produrre.
yoke, n. giogo m.
yolk, n. tuòrlo m.
you, pron. tu, te, ti; voi, vi, Lei; La, Lo, Loro.
young, adj. gióvane.
your, adj. tuo; vòstro; Suo; Loro.
yours, pron. tuo; vòstro; Suo; Loro.
yourself, pron. tu stesso; te stesso; voi stessi, Lei stesso; Loro stessi.

youth, n. giovinezza f.
youthful, adj. giovanile.
yowl, 1. n. urlo m. 2. vb. urlare.
Yugoslav, adj. jugoslavo.
Yugoslavia, n. Jugoslàvia f.

zap, vb. colpire repentinamente e inaspettatamente.
zeal, n. zèlo m.
zealous, aj. zelante.
zebra, n. zèbra f.
zephyr, n. zèffiro m., zaffiro m.
zero, n. zèro m.
zest, n. entusiasmo m.
zinc, n. zinco m.
zip code, n. còdice di avviamento postale m.
zipper, n. chiusura lampo f.
zodiac, n. zodiaco m.
zone, n. zòna f.
zoo, n. giardino zoològico m.
zoological, adj. zoològico.
zoology, n. zoologia f.
Zurich, n. Zurigo m.

Useful Words and Phrases

Good day.	Buòn giorno.
Good afternoon.	Buòna sera.
Good evening.	Buòna sera.
Good night.	Buòna nòtte.
Good-bye.	Arrivederci.
How are you?	Come sta?
Fine, thank you.	Bène, gràzie.
Glad to meet you.	Piacere.
Thank you very much.	Molte gràzie.
You're welcome.	Prègo.
Please.	Per favore.
Pardon me.	Mi scusi.
Good luck.	Buòna fortuna.
To your health.	Salute.
As soon as possible.	Quanto prima.
Look out!	Attenzione!
Who is it?	Chi è?
Just a minute!	Un momento.
Please help me.	M'aiuti, per favore.
Do you understand?	Capisce?
I don't understand.	Non capisco.
Speak slowly, please.	Parli adàgio, per favore.
Please repeat.	Ripeta, per favore.
I don't speak Italian.	Non parlo italiano.
Do you speak English?	Parla inglese?
Does anyone here speak English?	C'è qualcuno che parla inglese?
How do you say . . . in Italian?	Come si dice . . . in italiano?
What do you call this?	Come si chiama questo?
What is your name?	Come si chiama?
My name is . . .	Mi chiamo . . .
I am an American.	Sono americano.
May I introduce . . . ?	Vorrèi presentare. . . .
How is the weather?	Che tèmpo fa?
What time is it?	Che ora è?
What is it?	Che còsa è?
Please help me with my luggage.	Per favore, mi aiuti con i miei bagagli.
Is there any mail for me?	C'è posta per me?
May I have the bill, please?	Potrei avere il conto, pèr favore?
Where can I get a taxi?	Dove posso trovare un tassì?
What is the fare to . . . ?	Qual'è il prezzo della corsa fino a . . . ?

Please take me to this address.	Per favore, mi porti a questo indirizzo.
Please let me off at . . .	Per favore, mi faccia scéndere a . . .
How much does this cost?	Quanto còsta questo?
It is too expensive.	È troppo caro.
May I see something cheaper?	Potrei vedere qualcosa di più econòmico?
May I see something better?	Potrei vedere qualcosa di migliore?
It is not exactly what I want.	Non è esattamente quel che vorrèi.
I want to buy . . .	Vorrèi comprare . . .
I want to eat.	Vorrèi mangiare.
I would like . . .	Vorrèi . . .
Can you recommend a restaurant?	Può raccomandare un ristorante?
I am hungry.	Ho fame.
I am thirsty.	Ho sete.
I have a reservation.	Ho una prenotazione.
May I see the menu?	Potrei vedere il menù?
Please give me . . .	Per favore, mi dia . . .
Please bring me . . .	Per favore, mi porti . . .
Is service included in the bill?	Il servizio è compreso nel conto?
Check, please.	Il conto, per favore.
Do you accept traveler's checks?	Si accettano assegni per viaggiatori?
Is there a hotel here?	C'è un albèrgo qui?
Where is the men's (women's) room?	Dov'è il gabinetto per signori (signore)?
Please call the police.	Per favore, chiami la polizia.
Where is the nearest drugstore?	Dov'è la farmacìa più vicina?
Where can I mail this letter?	Dove posso impostare questa léttera?
I am lost.	Mi sono smarrito (m.); mi sono smarrita (f.).
Where is . . . ?	Dov'è . . . ?
What is the way to . . . ?	Qual'è la strada per . . . ?
Take me to . . .	Mi conduca a . . .
I need . . .	Ho bisogno di . . .
I am ill.	Sono malato (m.); sono malata (f.).
Please call a doctor.	Chiami un mèdico, per favore.

I want to send a telegram.	Vorrèi spedire un telegramma.
Where is the nearest bank?	Dov'è la banca più vicina?
Where can I change money?	Dove posso far cambiare del denaro?
Will you accept checks?	Accètta assegni?
What is the postage?	Quanto còsta l'affrancatura?
Right away.	Sùbito.
Help!	Aiuto!
Come in.	Avanti.
Hello (on telephone).	Pronto.
Stop.	Si fermi.
Hurry.	Fàccia prèsto.
Go on.	Avanti.
Right.	A dèstra.
Left.	A sinistra.
Straight ahead.	Sèmpre diritto.

Signs

Attenzione	Caution	Sènso ùnico	One way (street)
Pericolo	Danger		
Uscita	Exit	È vietato fumare	No smokin
Entrata	Entrance	È vietato entrare	No admitta
Alt, Alto	Stop	Signore	Women
Chiuso	Closed	Signori, Uòmini	Men
Apèrto	Open	Gabinetto (di decènza), Cèsso	Toilet
Rallentate, Rallentare	Slow down		

Weights and Measures

The Italians use the *Metric System* of weights and measures, which is a decimal system in which multiples are shown by the prefixes: deci- (one tenth); centi- (one hundredth); milli- (one thousandth); deca- (ten); etto- (hundred); chilo- (abbreviated *k.*) (thousand).

1 centimetro =	.3937 inches
1 mètro =	39.37 inches
1 chilòmetro (abbr. *km.*) =	.621 mile
1 centigramma =	.1543 grain
1 gramma =	15.432 grains
1 ettogramma (abbr. *etto*) =	3.527 ounces
1 chilogramma (abbr. *kg.*) =	2.2046 pounds
1 tonnellata =	2,204 pounds
1 centilitro =	.338 ounces
1 litro =	1.0567 quart (liquid); .908 quart (dry)
1 chilolitro =	264.18 gallons

344